Preface

Two essentially divergent views affect the concept of what constitutes a nation. The rational approach to the question leads to the conclusion that a nation is largely the product of historical development and that it is formed by the sum total of a people's experiences in a given region. The romantic and more mystic approach, on the other hand, evokes the view that a nation is an ethnic entity imbued with a "folksoul," or that it is the spiritual embodiment of a people's will and destiny. Both concepts have influenced Germany's quest for unity, particularly during the last two centuries; both remain influential today. If, for example, Germany is a historical entity, the present division into two Germanies can well be accepted as a new historical reality. The two states can each tread their separate paths and pursue their own development. If, however, Germany is an organic realization of the German folksoul, then unification or reunification —as in past centuries—is a matter of inevitable destiny.

The quest for unity was a significant element in Germany's development already during certain periods of medieval and early modern times. The desire for closer cohesian or, conversely, the very absence of unity affected politics and culture alike. Then, with the general nationalistic awakening in Europe during the Napoleonic era, this quest for unity became a more or less dominant theme in German history. This book, therefore, is particularly concerned with the question of German unity, from the unsuccessful unification movement during the revolution of 1848 to the current problem of the feasibility of German reunification.

The present text is based in part on my earlier *Germany: A History* (Holt, Rinehart, and Winston, 1964) which dealt with Germany from the Early Middle Ages to the postwar revival under Adenauer and Ulbricht. A brief introductory chapter presents the background knowledge required for an understanding of events in 1848 and beyond. A new concluding chapter treats the period from

Adenauer to Brandt, and an entirely new bibliography has been appended. Political and social trends and institutions occupy a place of primary emphasis, with the necessary inclusion of economic changes. Intellectual and artistic developments have been included only peripherally as part of German life, to give the reader a better appreciation of the German scene as a whole.

Despite Leopold von Ranke's injunction to the historian to depict the past "as it actually happened," we should frankly admit that a history such as this text is colored primarily by four factors that result in inevitable distortion. For one, it requires selective coverage to deal with a hundred and twenty-two years in the life of a large and influential nation within the limitations of a single volume. Such pruning and selecting itself distorts the past. Secondly, evaluation of the importance of events requires perspective. Just as a chromatograph separates elements for a chemist and determines their relative weight, so time and subsequent events help the historian decide what possible role a given occurrence may have played in the development of a historical movement. Therefore, when writing about the recent past or about almost contemporary events, the historian may easily be guilty of over- or underestimation. How important, for example, will the *Spiegel* affair turn out to be in the picture of postwar Germany? Or, will the shift in the chancellorship of the Federal Republic from the Christian Democrats to the Social Democrats in 1969 really mark a turning point in German political history? No historian, writing in 1970, should pretend that his assessment of these events is "historically accurate."

A third factor leading to distortion, particularly when dealing with the recent past, is the non-availability of certain source materials. Governments follow varying policies in regard to the time (usually amounting to several decades) that must elapse before archival material is released for use by historians. Similarly, many memoirs and personal papers are not made available to the public while their publication might embarrass living public figures. Thus, even in 1970, the historian cannot know whether he has at his disposal all the important facts involved in the Berlin blockade and airlift of 1948; and certainly it will be a long time before all relevant details and ramifications of the Brandt-Stoph talks of 1970 will be open for historical analysis.

Finally, a fourth factor that affects all writing of history involves the biases and preconceptions which guide the writer in the process of selection, evaluation, and discernment of historical trends. In this connection, I confess unashamedly that I have been brought up in the tradition of political and religious freedom. I have little sympathy with totalitarian ideals—under whatever form or color —that invariably stifle human freedom for the sake of dubious advantage. Admittedly then, when looking at German history, I tend to regard with apprehension whatever coercive features it embodies, whether found in Luther's doctrine, in the Prussian monarchical tradition, in Treitschke's or Hegel's historical philosophy, or in a host of similar developments. Aware of this bias on the part of the writer, which guided his selection and emphasis—I hope without falsifying "historical truth"—the reader is free to form his own opinions of the relative importance of the various threads that form the web of Germany's past.

The writing of any book is expedited when the author receives the encourage-

ment of friends and the help of conscientious assistants, and when he can work in a congenial atmosphere. Hence, my particular gratitude to Miss Ann Sado for her help with the manuscript, and to Miss Anne Sumner for placing at my disposal her lovely beach house at Laguna.

J. E. R.

Altadena, California

Contents

Maps and Charts

MAPS

CHARTS

I

The German Experience

before 1848

Like the French and English, the German people can trace and study their history back to the early Middle Ages. Unlike most European peoples, however, the Germans found it difficult to achieve political unity and to establish more or less stable boundaries. To be sure, they shared cultural affinity during the medieval and early modern periods and were loosely tied together under the feudal aegis of the German Kingdom and the Holy Roman Empire. Yet, it was only in 1871 that most German-speaking people came to be gathered in a single, even though federated, political unit. The history of "Germany" as such thus started only a century ago.

The efforts to create unity among the Germans began in medieval times when some of the rulers of the Holy Roman Empire, like their contemporaries in England, France, and Spain, sought to fashion less feudalized, more centralized states. Thereafter, various further attempts were made to give greater cohesion to the body politic of the Germans, particularly during the Renaissance and Reformation (fifteenth and early sixteenth centuries), during the Thirty Years' War (seventeenth century), and during the post-Napoleonic period (early nineteenth century). Yet, whereas the French, English, and others succeeded in forming nation states, the Germans remained splintered politically. The last unsuccessful attempt at unification was made during the revolutions of 1848–1849.

The unitary movement of 1848 failed as did most of the efforts at liberal and social reforms. Yet 1848 marked a turning point. Whether correctly interpreted or not, the lessons of the 1848 revolutions seemed to portend that Germany could only be unified on a conservative basis. Possibly they also influenced the character of German political life for the ensuing century. It thus seems proper to start the history of modern Germany in 1848, even though a united German state emerged only in 1871.

Yet, to understand the tortuous path

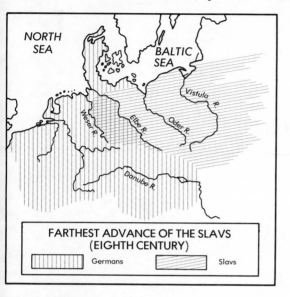

FARTHEST ADVANCE OF THE SLAVS
(EIGHTH CENTURY)

Germans   Slavs

MAP 1

of German history after 1848, undulating between pinnacles of power and disasters of defeat, one must comprehend some of the problems that marked the German experience prior to 1848—problems that lead many later Germans to look upon theirs as a tragic or fateful history. Hence, a brief review of German history before the middle of the nineteenth century is appropriate, if not essential.

THE PROBLEM OF GERMANY'S BOUNDARIES

One of the problems that have plagued the Germans for over a thousand years concerns the determination of Germany's boundaries as well as the related question of what peoples properly belong within the German state. Or, to reduce the question to its simplest terms: Where is Germany?

Shifting Boundaries

Some fortunate nations are endowed with boundaries easily defined by geographic landmarks, linguistic homogeneity, or long historical tradition. However, a glance through any historical atlas readily reveals that Germany's boundaries during the past one thousand years have changed several times in almost every century. The vast plain that stretches for some two thousand miles across northern Europe from the Ural Mountains in Russia to the English Channel is unbroken except for several rivers and offers no neat line of demarcation between Slavic, German, and French speaking peoples. Nor do the mountain ranges in the Southeast, the South, and the Southwest coincide with ethnic differences. Hence, Germany's boundaries depended little on geographic or ethnic considerations, but were primarily the result of wars and power politics. Even today, its eastern frontier is once again in a state of uncertainty, with the Oder-Neisse line (see Map 15) neither recognized by international agreement nor fully accepted by many Germans.

THE EASTERN FRONTIER   When the Germanic tribes, the ancestors of the Germans, moved west into Central and Western Europe between the fourth and seventh centuries and gradually established permanent settlements, the line separating the likewise westbound Slavs from Germans ran somewhere between the rivers Weser and Elbe (see Map 1). Thereafter, this westward movement of Germans and Slavs ceased and the trend was reversed. With Emperor Charlemagne in the late eighth century began the Germans' *Drang nach Osten* (drive to the East).

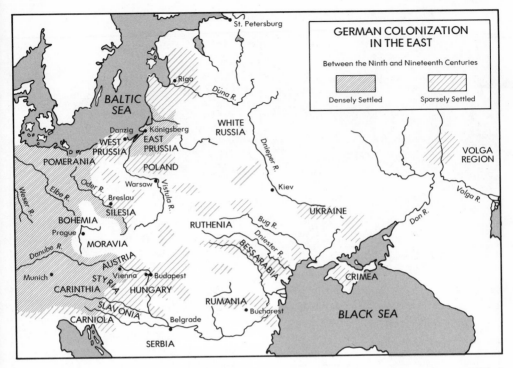

GERMAN COLONIZATION IN THE EAST

Between the Ninth and Nineteenth Centuries

Densely Settled

Sparsely Settled

St. Petersburg

Riga

Düna R.

BALTIC SEA

WHITE RUSSIA

Danzig

Königsberg

WEST PRUSSIA

EAST PRUSSIA

POMERANIA

POLAND

Dnieper R.

VOLGA REGION

Weser R.

Elbe R.

Oder R.

Warsaw

Vistula R.

Breslau

Kiev

Volga R.

SILESIA

UKRAINE

Don R.

BOHEMIA

RUTHENIA

Bug R.

Prague

MORAVIA

Dniester R.

BESSARABIA

Danube R.

AUSTRIA

STYRIA

Vienna

Budapest

CRIMEA

Munich

CARINTHIA

HUNGARY

SLAVONIA

RUMANIA

BLACK SEA

CARNIOLA

Belgrade

Bucharest

SERBIA

MAP 2

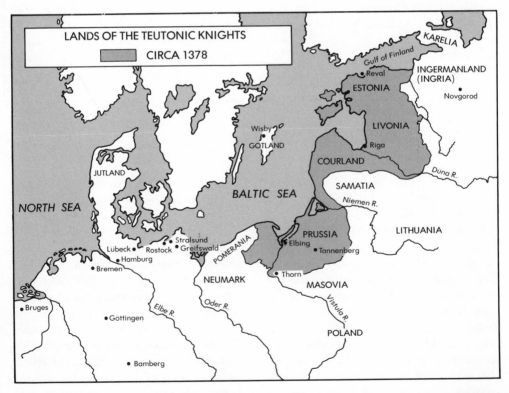

LANDS OF THE TEUTONIC KNIGHTS

CIRCA 1378

KARELIA

Gulf of Finland

INGERMANLAND (INGRIA)

Reval

ESTONIA

Novgorod

Wisby

LIVONIA

GOTLAND

Riga

COURLAND

Düna R.

JUTLAND

SAMATIA

Niemen R.

BALTIC SEA

LITHUANIA

NORTH SEA

PRUSSIA

Stralsund

Elbing

Lübeck

Rostock

Greifswald

Tannenberg

Hamburg

POMERANIA

Thorn

Bremen

NEUMARK

MASOVIA

Bruges

Oder R.

Vistula R.

Elbe R.

Göttingen

POLAND

Bamberg

MAP 3

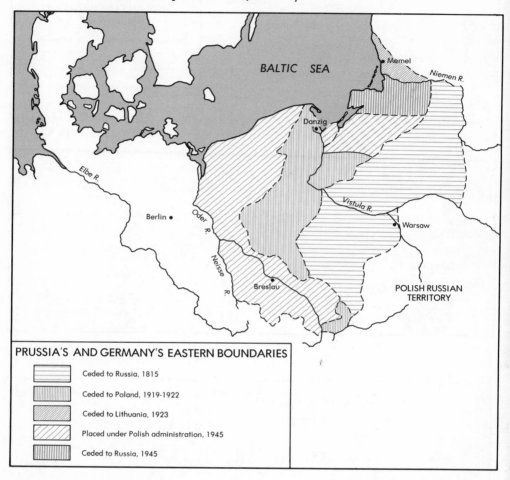

PRUSSIA'S AND GERMANY'S EASTERN BOUNDARIES

Ceded to Russia, 1815

Ceded to Poland, 1919-1922

Ceded to Lithuania, 1923

Placed under Polish administration, 1945

Ceded to Russia, 1945

MAP 4

Over the next centuries, enterprising German princes, ambitious nobles, and zealous bishops gradually conquered and colonized eastward. New duchies and counties were carved out, cities founded, and bishoprics and monasteries established. Successful knights acquired large landed estates and gradually formed a class of so-called Junkers, groups of landholding aristocrats who later, in the nineteenth and twentieth century, exerted much influence on German politics. In the wake of these territorial conquests and the Christian-izing efforts of bishops and monks came German merchants, extending German commercial and cultural influence.

The main thrusts of this eastward expansion went along three avenues: northeast along the shores of the Baltic, east up the valleys of the Oder and Elbe, and southeast down the Danubian plains (see Map 2). As time passed, the local Slavic population was either driven east, converted into soil-tilling serfs, or bypassed and left as independent pockets of Slavdom. During the thirteenth century, an organized reli-

gious crusading order, the Teutonic Knights, gained possession of Prussia and temporarily extended its power north to the Gulf of Finland (see Map 3). At the same time, the Hanseatic League of German merchant towns expanded its commercial dominance as far east as Novgorod, deep inside present-day Russia.

With the partitioning of Poland among Russia, Austria, and Prussia in the eighteenth century, Germany's (or more accurately speaking Prussia's) eastern political border reached its furthest extent (see Map 4). And beyond the political boundaries of the Prussian and Austrian states lay countless pockets of German settlers.

These conquered lands east of the river Elbe—often referred to as "new Germany"—obviously complicate the answer to our question: Where is Germany? How much, if any, of this territory is to be considered "legitimately" German? Moreover, this German eastward expansion over the centuries deeply affected the fates of Poland, Russia, and the peoples of the northern Balkans, a phenomenon still evident in our own day.

During the Napoleonic period at the beginning of the nineteenth century, however, Germany's eastward expansion ebbed (see Map 4). Starting in 1815, Russians and Poles pushed the political boundary back step by step to the Oder-Neisse line of 1945. After World War II, a concerted attempt was also made to eradicate German influence in Eastern Europe by expelling millions of ethnic Germans. Thus, Germany's eastern border is today where it was about a thousand years ago. Yet, despite the desire for permanence on the part of many, no historian can safely predict that Germany has at last found a stable eastern border.

THE WESTERN FRONTIER Germany's western boundary presents a similar problem, though one at present not so acute. The clouded state of the western boundary goes back to the ninth century when the Frankish Empire of Charlemagne was divided into what later became France and Germany. In this division, the Germans obtained all lands east of the rivers Rhone and Meuse, including much territory in which Early French was spoken.

Starting in the late twelfth century, however, the growing French monarchy began to expand eastward toward the Rhine and the Alps, and northward into the Lowlands. In the course of countless wars during the ensuing six centuries, the French succeeded in wresting much territory from the Germans, until by 1766 France had obtained more or less the same boundaries that it holds today.

Germany's border in the west—and south—contracted as a result not only of French conquests but also of the establishment of the new states of Holland, Belgium, Luxemburg, and Switzerland, which gradually seceded from the German Kingdom. Since large parts of these areas are inhabited by people speaking a type of German or closely related language, there is little coincidence between linguistic and political boundaries. Moreover, the repeated conquest and reconquest by France and Germany of the Saar, Alsace, and parts of Lorraine during the past one hundred years point to the continued fluidity of this border.

The German Volk

In line with defining boundaries, the Germans have found it particularly difficult to agree on what peoples are

members of the German *Volk* (ethnic Germans) and should be included in the German state. Racial chauvinists in the nineteenth and twentieth century invented the myth of a superior Aryan or Nordic race, recognizable by their courage, energy, and the purity of their blood, all of whom should form part of the German *Volk*. Even without such shibboleths, however, the determination as to who is a German has been difficult. Linguistic considerations do not help as much as one might expect.

Most of the peoples living between the Alps, the Baltic, and the North Sea speak languages that derived from West Germanic, the language presumably spoken by the tribes who settled in these areas. Such a list would include Austrian, Swiss German, Alsatian, Dutch, Frisian, and even English, before Anglo-Saxon became enmeshed with Norman French. Over the centuries, these languages changed and developed away from the original West Germanic. The further south the tribes settled the more their language shifted away from this origin, with Anglo-Saxon, Dutch, and Low German—spoken along the shores of the North Sea—considerably closer to West Germanic than Bavarian and Austrian. Thus, adjacent languages, such as Dutch, Flemish, Frisian, and Low German gradually shade one into the other, since all are essentially a type of Low West Germanic. On the other hand, there is a considerable difference between Austrian and Low German.

This gradual linguistic transition from the Alps to the Channel would make the drawing of boundaries on the basis of language an impossibility. Unless we were to conclude that all those speaking derivatives of West Germanic should be included in the same state, we would have to fashion some absurd definition of how far a language might shift and develop before its speakers no longer belong to the same linguistic family.

Linguistic criteria for determining boundaries would also have the drawback of disregarding the feelings of the people involved. A good example is Switzerland. On the basis of language affinity, the northern Swiss would have to be incorporated into Germany. Their political sentiments, however, clearly indicate that they do not wish to form a part of the German state, from which they seceded in the fourteenth century.

THE SEARCH FOR UNITY

A second problem afflicting the Germans has been their inability to achieve political unity. Even when an apparently united Germany existed from 1871 to 1945, the exclusion of Austria raised the question of whether the Germans were truly united, since, particularly during the 1920s, many Austrians would have preferred to have their country form a part of the more prosperous German state.

From the early Middle Ages, the Germans felt a more or less pronounced cultural unity, notwithstanding vast differences in local dialects and customs. They also came to share in legends and folktales and acquired common heroes —Siegfried of the *Niebelungenlied,* the popular and powerful medieval Emperor Frederick Barbarossa, the dashing Renaissance Emperor Maximilian I, and the philosopher-king and military genius, Frederick II, the Great, of Prussia. But, as with the ancient Greeks, cultural affinity and common heroes did not suffice to produce political unification.

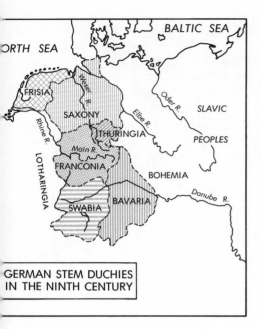

GERMAN STEM DUCHIES
IN THE NINTH CENTURY

MAP 5

Among the many factors that hampered the establishment of political unity were German particularism, the ambivalent status of the Holy Roman Empire, the complexity of Church-State relations, foreign interference, and the question of leadership of a united Germany.

German Particularism

From the time of their settlement in Central Europe, the Germans displayed strong allegiance to local leaders and local customs. Some of the stem or tribal duchies, for example, such as Swabia, Franconia, and Saxony (see Map 5), retained the sentimental attachment of some people long after their political significance had vanished in the Middle Ages. When these original duchies based on ethnic cohesion dis-

integrated, new political units were created, some miniscule in size and power, others substantial, resembling miniature states. Ambitious nobles founded duchies, counties, or other entities, based on feudal, dynastic, or simply territorial considerations. Some bishops made their sees politically independent, and wealthy burghers acquired rights of complete self-government for many of the more important towns.

The development of these numerous political units, each fiercely jealous of its independence, made it impossible to establish a strong monarchy as was being done in England and France during the later Middle Ages. Loyalty to king or emperor, it seems, always took second place behind allegiance to the local prince or the interests of the local community. This absence of allegiance to a central unit—an allegiance that in most other nations developed rather naturally over hundreds of years—may account for the somewhat frantic and artificial attempt to instill nationalism in the Germans during the last century.

As the power of the emperor diminished even further during early modern times, the secular states, bishoprics, and free towns acquired more independence, with many of them retaining their own armies, establishing their own laws, collecting their own tolls and taxes, and coining their own money. By 1648, this splintering of Germany received legal recognition in the Treaty of Westphalia that ended the Thirty Years' War (see Map 6). Several hundred "states" within the Holy Roman Empire were granted more or less absolute sovereignty, while over a thousand so-called imperial knights, each commanding a few squares of land, became semi-independent. German par-

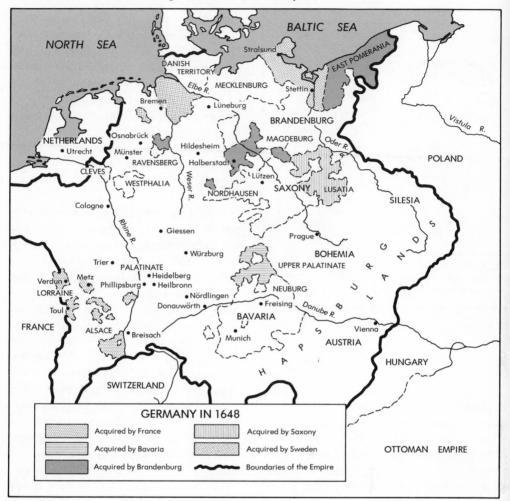

MAP 6

ticularism had atomized the German Empire at a time when France was completing its development of a highly centralized absolute monarchy.

The Holy Roman Empire

Conceivably, the framework of the empire could have given unity to Germany. Indeed, at certain times, particularly in moments of crisis, such as threatened invasions by the Magyars or Turks, the imperial institutions provided an instrument for joint action. On the whole, however, the very existence of the empire proved detrimental to the development of Germany into a centralized nation state.

The German Empire, usually referred to as the Holy Roman Empire, was a vague successor to the Frankish Empire of Charlemagne and the Roman Empire of ancient times. From 962

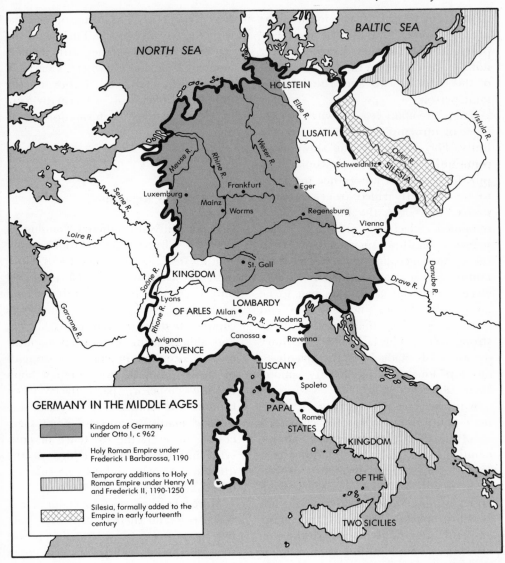

GERMANY IN THE MIDDLE AGES

 Kingdom of Germany
under Otto I, c 962

Holy Roman Empire under
Frederick I Barbarossa, 1190

Temporary additions to Holy
Roman Empire under Henry VI
and Frederick II, 1190-1250

Silesia, formally added to the
Empire in early fourteenth
century

MAP 7

to 1806, most of the kings of Germany also bore the title "Emperor of the Holy Roman Empire." As kings of Germany, they claimed suzerainty over certain lands, most of them lying north of the Alps; as emperors, they claimed universal sovereignty over all Christendom as well as specific political control of territories situated both north and south of the Alps—in other words, more land than was manifestly German (see Map 7). The empire therefore included lands where the German language was not spoken; whereas, on the other hand, as Germans colonized eastward, there came to be lands in which German was

spoken but which did not form a part of the empire. Thus the German Empire and the German Kingdom were not the same, despite the fact that most of the time the two were ruled by the same person.

There are many reasons why the existence of this empire hampered German unity. For one, given the slowness of communications, the Holy Roman Empire for centuries was rather too large to be efficiently ruled from a central source. Moreover, the imperial crown remained elective, although some princely families, such as the Hapsburgs, managed to retain it in their family for several centuries. To get elected, imperial candidates had to be lavish with bribes and promises and thus undermine their potential as strong rulers. The lack of a hereditary dynasty also made it more difficult to develop long-standing loyalty among their subjects.

A further factor interfering with German political unity was the emperor's involvement in non-German affairs. Control over Italy and southeastern France, for example, brought the Germans wealth, but also sapped their energies in numerous wars that could not possibly benefit Germany. And many emperors were so involved with the governance and exploitation of other lands that they paid scant attention to the needs of Germany. There was, for instance, the Hohenstaufen Emperor Frederick II (1215–1250) who was also King of Sicily and King of Jerusalem and so embroiled in Italian affairs that he let the German bishops and princes shift for themselves under the nominal supervision of his son. Or, again, there was the Hapsburg Emperor Charles V (1519–1556) who, as King of Spain, was preoccupied with the conquest of the New World and, as ruler of Austria, with the advance of the Turks into the upper Balkans. Together with involvement in Italy and elsewhere, Charles V found little time to devote to the urgent problems of a Germany convulsed by Luther's reformation movement.

Church-State Relations

German unity also suffered from highly complex Church-state relations, more complicated than in other states. Since most of Germany was Christianized only beginning in the eighth century, at a time when political power was completely decentralized, many bishops and abbots acquired unusual amounts of influence. The independent strength of these bishoprics was often a boon to the emperor, particularly when bishops and emperors contended side by side against a powerful pope. Generally, however, the existence of powerful bishoprics merely added to the diffusion of power and the emasculation of the emperorship.

Moreover, the emperors' claim to universal rule and their control over Italy led to a series of spectacular power struggles between emperors and popes from the eleventh to the fourteenth centuries. During the eleventh century, for example, Emperor Henry IV and Pope Gregory VII engaged in the so-called investiture controversy, which in essence involved the question whether emperor or pope controlled the bishops within the empire. Other struggles between popes and emperors concerned the control of Italy, matters of taxation, and such nebulous points as overall imperial or papal supremacy. To be sure,

many other medieval monarchs, particularly the French kings, fought with the popes, but no other rulers were so often sidetracked from their own tasks by anti-papal campaigns as were the German emperors.

Finally, the Reformation added immensely to the splintering of Germany. During the sixteenth century, some states, as for instance Sweden, became completely Protestant; others, like Spain, remained completely Catholic; Germany, however, became divided into Lutheran, Catholic, and Calvinist states, with each ruler eventually allowed to determine the religion of his subjects. This religious splintering, underscored by religious wars, not only further divided the Germans among themselves, but also gave greater power to the territorial princes and hence weakened the role of the emperor. For, those princes who turned Lutheran gained wealth and influence by confiscating the property of the Catholic Church and by assuming control over the new religious establishment; whereas, princes who remained Catholic could bargain with the pope for greater autonomy within the Catholic Church, lest they, too, might turn Protestant.

Foreign Influence

Germany's location in Central Europe made it naturally vulnerable from many sides and turned its soil repeatedly into a battleground for other nations. Its geographic position also made it easy for neighboring states to gain influence over its affairs, while at the same time it permitted German princes easily to get involved in the affairs of neighboring states.

In medieval times, when European peoples lived presumably in a Christian universe, "foreign" influence was hard to measure. By the sixteenth century, however, it became evident that the increasingly centralized French monarchy could benefit greatly from German disunity. Hence French rulers and diplomats recognized the advantage of supporting individual German princes, whether Protestant or Catholic, against any attempts by the German emperors to strive toward greater centralization of power. From the sixteenth to the end of the eighteenth century, France followed this policy by extending foreign aid to many of the German states, provided they would side with France in her anti-Hapsburg stand. German disunity was thus enhanced by French gold and diplomacy.

By the seventeenth century, foreign influence on Germany became paramount. The end of the Thirty Years' War saw other powers—Sweden, Denmark, and Holland—control all the outlets of German rivers, so that Germany was effectively cut off from overseas trade (see Map 6). The Treaty of Westphalia had made France and Sweden the guarantors of Germany's constitutional framework. And French culture began to swamp Germany. By the early eighteenth century, German polite society spoke French, thought French, acted French, and entertained mistresses in the French style. It was to take a veritable cultural revolution to eradicate this French influence.

At the same time, German princes became increasingly enmeshed in non-German affairs. The duke of Saxony was elected to the kingship of Poland at the end of the seventeenth century; the duke of Hanover became king of England in the early eighteenth century; the Austrian Hapsburgs acquired dominion over vast stretches of the upper

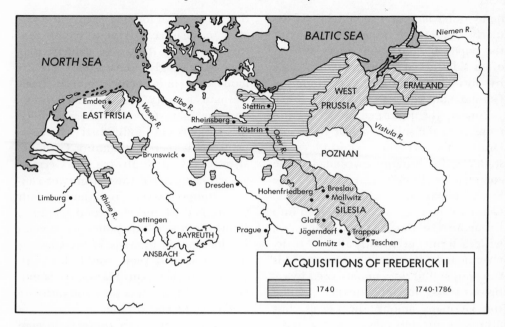

MAP 8

Balkans. These, and many other similar instances, further detracted from the possibility of turning the German states into a united German state.

The Question of Leadership

Unity requires leadership. In France, from the tenth century on, Paris and the Capetian dynasty developed gradually into the metropolis and rulers of the new kingdom. Although the provinces at times were to challenge such centralization of government, Paris and the Capetians continued to rule France. Similarly, from the time of William the Conqueror (eleventh century), London was destined to become the heart and center of the rising English monarchy.

Developments in Germany, however, differed. Various powerful duchies and dynastic families vied for preeminence.

Until the fifteenth century, the center of gravity of the empire shifted with each change in imperial dynasty, so that no single center developed around which the future state might grow. Then, starting in the fifteenth century, a solution to the question of leadership seemed to be found when the Hapsburg dynasty began to consolidate its holdings in Austria and tried to impose a more centralized rule on the entire German Empire. The religious split of the Reformation, however, which occurred more or less at the same time, put a rapid end to this hope.

When the imperial framework lost all political meaning in the seventeenth century, several of the larger states within the empire—Bavaria, Saxony, Prussia, and Austria—appeared as likely candidates for possible leadership of the German states. Yet, by the eighteenth century, with the reign of the

Prussian King Frederick II (1740–1786), who considerably expanded Prussian territory (see Map 8), rivalry for leadership had been reduced to a duel between Prussia and Austria. This conflict, the outcome of which was to decide which of the two states would put its stamp on the whole of Germany, began in 1740 and ended, as we shall see, with Prussia's victory in 1871.

THE AWAKENING OF GERMANY

A German folk legend, revived by nationalists in the nineteenth century, told of Emperor Frederick Barbarossa asleep inside a mountain. One day he would awake and found a new thousand-year *Reich* (empire). Except for the implied chauvinism, the metaphor is apt. After the vitality displayed during the era of the Renaissance and Reformation, Germany had been somnolent. Then, almost abruptly, in the late eighteenth century, Germany awoke, first culturally, then politically and economically.

After over a century of cultural domination by France, German writers and intellectuals in the 1770s began to rebel against foreign models and pseudoclassical rules for writing. The German language was resuscitated as a fit mode of expression. Germany's own history and folk tales served again as literary inspiration. The Germans were rediscovering their own *Volksseele* (folk soul). Soon German culture, particularly in literature, music, and philosophy, was blossoming with vitality during the Romantic period, turning Germany into the proverbial land of "poets and thinkers."

The Impact of the French Revolution and Napoleon I

The French Revolution of 1789 and the subsequent Napoleonic era profoundly affected Germany. The ideals of liberty, equality, and fraternity were echoed across the Rhine among the intelligentsia and segments of the middle classes, while fear of radicalism and of the demands for constitutional limits on arbitrary government frightened many of the little princes out of their bewigged lethargy. Knowledgeable Germans might admire the French revolutionary experiment or be repelled by the bloody excesses of revolutionary terror, but they could not remain indifferent.

When in the course of the long wars that lasted from 1792 to 1815 French armies overran most of Germany and sought to spread their new sociopolitical concepts under the auspices of military occupation, many Germans abandoned their cosmopolitan views and became increasingly nationalistic. Napoleon's continuous recharting of Germany's political configuration further added to this national feeling. The French conqueror liquidated many of the smaller states, regrouped lands into larger political units, and, in 1806, abolished the Holy Roman Empire, since the remaining German states were to live henceforth under the protectorship of France. This reorganization of the German states at once helped and hindered ultimate German unification. The amalgamation of people into fewer political units brought them closer together. At the same time, the enlargement and strengthening of Napoleon's favorite client states, such as Bavaria and Württemberg, enabled their rulers to place greater obstacles into the path

of Prussia's drive to absorb all of Germany.

Prussia's complete defeat by Napoleon's armies in the battle of Jena (1806) and its subsequent military occupation by the French further changed German history. To lift the state out of the mire into which it had fallen, even the hesitant King Frederick William III (1797–1840) now authorized a thoroughgoing reform of the sociopolitical framework. The army, the tax system, municipal government, education, and other facets of Prussian life were reorganized, serfdom was abolished, and class mobility encouraged through the removal of property restrictions. The king even promised the issuance of a constitution. The Prussian government, as it were, attempted to strengthen the state through a revolution from above. These reforms were accompanied by a veritable outburst of nationalism, typified by Ernst Moritz Arndt's (1769–1860) patriotic hymns and battle songs, composed to glorify the German fatherland.

Finally, during the Wars of Liberation (1813–1815), when Napoleon's armies were gradually expelled from Germany, and when the fate of the surviving German states hung in the balance, nationalistic enthusiasm evoked hopes for some type of immediate unification of Germany. Once again, however, Austro-Prussian rivalry vitiated all expectations. Under the skillful diplomatic guidance of Prince Metternich (1773–1859), Austria succeeded in foiling Prussia's attempt to rally the German states under its own aegis. Instead, Metternich helped devise a political framework for the German states which for the time being insured continued German disunity while preserving Austria's paramount influence.

The German Confederation of 1815

While Napoleon I was meeting his final doom at Waterloo, the European powers completed their work at the Congress of Vienna to decide on the political restoration of the Continent after the chaos of the Napoleonic wars. The Vienna settlements of 1815 created a German Confederation (see Map 9) of thirty-nine sovereign states, nominally guided by a federal diet meeting at Frankfurt under the presidency of Austria. The Confederation was to be a "perpetual" union aimed at maintaining "the external and internal security of Germany and the independence and inviolability of the individual German states." Although the articles of confederation stipulated that each state would grant a constitution to its people, the most important states, Prussia and Austria, refused to comply with these liberal stipulations. The decades after 1815, often called the Metternich era since Prince Metternich exerted so much influence on the German states, were in fact years of stringent conservatism, during which frequent attempts were made to extirpate the ideas of the French Revolution.

Prussia emerged from the Vienna settlements considerably strengthened and enlarged in territory, including the Saar and Ruhr regions, so rich in coal and industrial potential. Within a few decades, the Prussian state was to enter the industrial revolution in full force and achieve industrial preeminence within the German Confederation. To further its economic expansion and to counteract British merchandise which poured into Germany through British-held Hanover, Prussia devised the *Zollverein* (Customs Union), which proved to be a profitable way for extending its

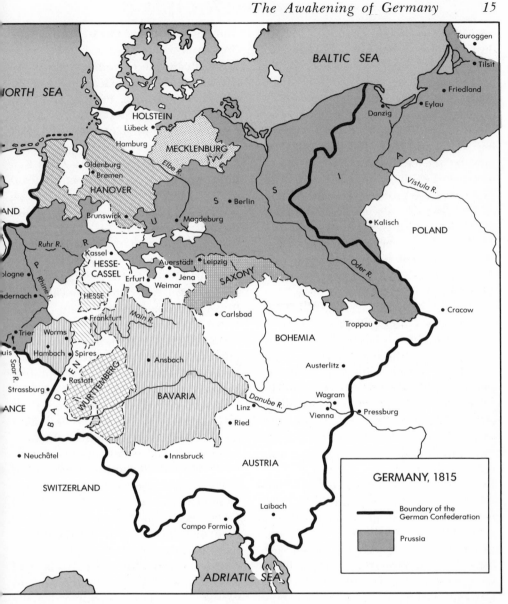

MAP 9

economic influence. Austria, meanwhile, less aggressive in industrial and commercial ventures, and plagued by the problem of controlling numerous alien nationalities in an age of rising nationalism, became weaker in potential power, although outwardly it retained its political sway.

The conservative tendencies of Metternich and most German rulers were poorly suited to cope with the needs of a society that was rapidly being trans-

formed by economic changes. The industrial revolution was beginning to draw people from agriculture to the burgeoning cities and create an urban proletariat. New means of transportation and communication, railroads and the electric telegraph, as well as growing economic interdependence were binding the German states ever closer together. Yet those in power did little to assuage the growing demands of the middle class for a share in political power and for new attempts at German unification. Hence, tension between liberals and conservatives increased and erupted in occasional unrest, as in a series of minor revolutions in 1830.

The advent of King Frederick William IV (1840–1858) in Prussia temporarily raised the hopes of liberals and those seeking unification. The new king launched his reign with lavish hints at reforms in Prussia and in Germany. He granted more powers to local provincial estates, decreed an amnesty for political prisoners, and relaxed political censorship. But he resisted until 1847 the convocation of a united all-Prussian diet. In essence, the king was extremely conservative and hardly understood the needs and demands of his people. Thus, as the decade of the 1840s proceeded, social unrest increased and clamors for constitutional limitations on the Prussian monarchy as well as for a closer German union reached near-revolutionary proportions.

The task of unifying Germany raised countless questions. Three possible solutions concerning the size of the union were advanced: *Grossdeutschland,* including all the lesser German states, together with Austria, Prussia, and their dependent alien populations; *Kleindeutschland,* embracing the lesser states and Prussia with its Polish possessions, but excluding the entire Austrian Empire; or an ethnically homogeneous state, including only German-speaking peoples—a solution that would require the dismemberment of Austria and Prussia by forcing them to relinquish their non-German territories. Moreover, there remained the question of leadership: Austrian Hapsburgs or Prussian Hohenzollerns might assume control; a secondary state, such as Bavaria, might act as mediator in a triumvirate; or a directorate of the five kings and the emperor, with rotating chairmanship, might be established. Furthermore, there was the problem of finding a balance between Protestant and Catholic states. Finally, questions of political and social reforms inextricably affected all other considerations: liberals and conservatives, constitutional monarchists and republicans, social reformers and moderates—all produced their own programs. When the revolution erupted in 1848, the drawing boards of journalists and politicians, of activists and idealists, were replete with vaguely formulated programs for the unification of Germany and the reform of its body politic.

Years of Decision, 1848–1858

THE REVOLUTIONARY YEARS, 1848–1849

During the first four months of 1848, revolutions spread like an epidemic over large areas of Europe. The Italian states, France, Austria, the German states, Hungary, Poland, and Rumania were scenes of major revolts; pressure and demonstrations in Belgium, Denmark, Holland, and Switzerland forced the governments to grant concessions or new constitutions. Only Russia, England, Spain, and a handful of smaller nations escaped the revolutionary disorders.

Social injustices and occasional economic crises added to the ferment. The plight of the agricultural laborers, who constituted a large segment of the rural population, grew worse. Natural disasters, such as failure of the potato crop in 1846–1847, brought them near starvation and made them tinder for revolutionary fires. The semirural population, such as the Silesian weavers who depended on the textile cottage industry, suffered from the introduction of machinery. In Silesia the open rebellion in 1844 was bloodily repressed by the Prussian army. Saxony, Hanover, Württemberg, and most of the other states experienced periodic disorders and minor uprisings frequently caused by economic failures and unemployment. The years 1846 and 1847, particularly, were filled with swelling agitation: a Polish revolt in Cracow in 1846, ruthlessly suppressed by Austria, scattered across Germany Polish refugees eager to propagate their revolutionary invectives against authoritarian Austria, Russia, and Prussia. At the same time, a plague swept across Germany, leaving death and misery in its wake. A world-wide trade and financial crisis shook the security of the middle class. Coupled with crop failures, it brought food shortages to the cities.

The various revolutions were essentially interrelated. The initial sparks of revolt jumped from capital to capital like signals of a semaphore, and some revolutionaries collaborated on an international scale. Most of the revolutions produced radical shifts in foreign policy that in turn affected the revolutionary movements in neighboring states.

An Over-all View
of the German Revolutions

Within Germany, revolutions occurred in almost all the states—some involving armed clashes and bloodshed, others consisting of peaceful demonstrations and petitions, followed by more or less gracious concessions on the part of the rulers. Taken as a whole, these revolutionary outbreaks were complex and confusing, for they lacked unity of purpose. On the one hand, there were over thirty separate revolts in the various states; on the other, there was one all-German revolution aimed at uniting the states into a single political entity. Different classes—serfs and peasants, workers and small artisans, middle and upper bourgeois—participated in the revolts, each fighting for its own aims, which usually were different from, if not antagonistic to, those of the other classes. Class war appeared in 1848 as it rarely had before in Germany and complicated the revolutionary struggle.

At least three major aims can be crystallized: one was the nationalistic goal of unifying Germany, which served to some degree as a coalescing factor for the revolts. A second goal was political. The revolutionaries everywhere demanded basic civil rights and a measure of popular sovereignty, although they differed on the degree of desirable changes. Finally, a third set of aims was social and economic. Those still in serfdom wanted freedom; the agricultural proletariat desired emancipation from the dominance of the landlord; city workers demanded shorter hours, higher wages, and a guarantee of employment; merchants called for freedom from economic restrictions; and the ultraradicals preached socioeconomic egalitarianism.

The three aims—one might call them three types of revolution—national, political, and social, interacted and were frequently at cross-purposes. Germany actually was not ready for a social revolution, and it is doubtful that the aims of the socialist extremists could ever have been implemented in 1848. But the same judgment does not apply to the national and political revolutions. Conceivably either one of them alone might have succeeded, but the intertwining of the three confused the issues. The middle class was ultimately forced to choose between unification and liberalism. They chose unification and doomed both. Similarly, fear of the egalitarian aims of the lower classes drove the middle class into reliance on the conservative forces of order and stability—thereby aborting the social revolution and undermining their own liberal aspirations.

Despite the complexity of the years of insurrections, they can be divided into distinct periods. The months from late February to May 1848 constituted the phase of initial revolutionary outbreaks, marked by liberal and national revolts with an occasional social rebellion. A new period began in June 1848, initiating the first phase of reaction. The fall of the insurgent city of Prague to the forces of the Austrian general, Prince Alfred Windisch-Graetz (1787–1862), proved that the Austrian army was still an effective bulwark of conservatism. Reaction began to reassert itself in Germany and the Austrian Empire, causing the failure of most of the liberal movements. The period ended in April 1849, when Frederick William's refusal of an all-German crown seemingly dashed hopes for the national unitary movement (see

pages 38–39). Finally, there was a brief third phase: a new wave of revolutions swept over most of the states between April and August of 1849. Liberals and nationalists rose, hoping to salvage at least a portion of their initial gains. The lower classes in the south and the west rebelled when they realized that their initial sacrifices on the barricades had brought them no social or economic benefits. This second wave of revolutions was in the end mercilessly crushed by the armies of Prussia, Austria, and Württemberg, and prepared the way for a decade of conservative reaction in the 1850s.

German Reaction
to the French Revolution of 1848

It is commonly stated that when news of the overthrow of King Louis Philippe in Paris crossed the Rhine in February 1848, it immediately unleashed revolts in its wake. Although this assertion is generally correct, German reaction was considerably more complicated.

REVERBERATIONS AMONG THE MIDDLE CLASS Among the middle class there was joy at the Paris revolution. Establishment of the Second French Republic bolstered the liberal aspirations of the Germans and seemed to augur well for their future. Groups of citizens in the western German states sent professions of friendship and admiration to the provisional government of France. Initially the main worry of the German liberals was that Austria, Prussia, and others might launch a monarchical crusade to deny the French those liberties that the Germans sought for themselves. Such a war would benefit only the conservative forces, particularly reactionary Russia. This feeling was reflected in a petition handed on March 4 to King Louis I (1825–1848) of Bavaria by a group of Munich students: "If a Franco-Russian war is inevitable and Germany is involved, German liberals will fight with France against Russia."

On the other hand, the French Revolution of 1848 reminded Germans of 1792 and Napoleon. Rumors of imminent French invasion stalked the countryside of southwest Germany and made the people wary of the blessings of imported liberty. This fear of invasion strengthened their desire for unity. "Unite to be strong" became a common slogan in the press, accompanied by demands for common defense measures by the federal diet or for the creation of a stronger federation capable of defending German soil against expected French aggression. Thus from the very beginning, nationalism was being appreciably strengthened while the banner of liberalism was being raised.

The panic-like fear of French aggression lessened somewhat after the revolutions had gained ground in the various German states, and after Alphonse de Lamartine, France's provisional head of government, had proclaimed his peaceful intentions. In fact, popular fear shifted from west to east. Friendship between French and German liberals seemed assured, but Russia's attitude remained an enigma. Gradually the fear of a Russian war to re-establish autocracy outweighed all misgivings about France. In late May, the revolutionary National Assembly (see pages 32 ff.) at Frankfurt even agreed enthusiastically to conclude a "fraternal pact" with the

French National Assembly, although the French were warned not to entertain designs on the Rhineland.

THE ATTITUDE OF THE GOVERNMENTS The attitude of the German governments and the ruling circles was, of course, vastly different. As early as 1847, Frederick William IV of Prussia had predicted a French upheaval, and had unsuccessfully tried to persuade Victoria and Albert of England to join a coalition to prevent a revolution in France When the news of the revolt in Paris reached Berlin, the Prussian king felt bewildered. Secretly he was delighted at the overthrow of King Louis Philippe, the usurper who owed his throne not to legitimacy and divine right but to the popular revolution of 1830. On the other hand, he was filled with fear. He felt certain the French would invade Belgium, the Rhineland, and Italy, and propagate their revolutionary doctrine by the sword. To Victoria, Metternich, and Nicholas I, he proposed re-establishing the anti-French coalition of 1814 to safeguard the settlement of 1815. The four powers were to restrict the subversive disease to France, and to prepare for a counteroffensive in case the new French Republic should launch a revolutionary war. England assured Berlin that it would fight if France violated Belgium or the Rhineland, but refused to join an a priori coalition that might needlessly antagonize Paris. The tsar offered troops if needed to defend Germany, and Metternich discussed common defensive measures with Frederick William's friend and advisor, Joseph von Radowitz (1797–1853). However, neither the other courts nor Frederick William's own cabinet welcomed the proposal for a coalition.

Among the governments of the lesser German states the news from Paris evoked varying degrees of panic. Initially, the princes feared the spread of the radical ideas more than an invasion by French armies, but they did not dare call for a crusade against Paris lest such a war unleash revolts among their own subjects. Many requested the federal diet to take defensive measures for safeguarding the Rhine frontier. But even in these critical days, they displayed their usual particularism and distrust of one another. Bavaria made an offer of friendship to Paris, and at the same time called for a German conference on defense against the French. Baden objected to letting Prussian troops cross its territory to man the federal fortress of Rastatt.

But after the revolts had struck the German states and liberal cabinets had been installed, the princes became more fearful of invasion. Lamartine's famous Manifesto of March 4, in which he proclaimed that the policy of the French Republic would be based on peace and friendship, assuaged but did not still this fear across the Rhine. Most German rulers hardly considered the moderate Lamartine strong enough to maintain his course against the radicals in Paris. Moreover, there were ambiguous phrases in the manifesto likely to create conflicts. France, Lamartine proclaimed, no longer recognized the treaties of 1815 and desired to regain the influence and position it deserved. And his promise of aid to all oppressed nations, especially Poland, sounded ominously like a similar offer in 1792 that had preceded the revolutionary wars. If the Poles rose against Russia and Prussia, French armies might stream across Germany to come to their assistance, or revolutionary

groups within Germany might demand French aid to overthrow their local rulers.

Although Lamartine vaunted his love of peace to all ambassadors, events in Paris, the activities of German and Polish exiles in France, and the bellicose speeches and articles of the French radicals hardly reassured the German princes. "France would be happy," cried the revolutionary *La Réforme,* "to fight once more for the salvation of the world and to implant her sword in the breast of the last king." And in a public speech, the republican leader Alexandre Ledru-Rollin urged all Germans to shake off their "odious yoke" and prophesied that "soon the breath of the people will blow away the dust of the throne where idle kings used to slumber."

ACTIVITIES OF THE EXILES These foreign complications loomed in the background of the revolutionary events in the German states. The possibility of a revolutionary war launched by France clouded the western horizon until June 1848: meanwhile the chance of a Russian war in favor of monarchical reaction lurked in the east.

A particular problem was presented by the German refugees in Paris who had organized the German Democratic Club and were exerting increasing pressures on the weak French provisional government. Together with *émigré* Poles and exiles of other suppressed nationalities, they sought aid in order to establish liberal regimes in their homelands. The intimidated provisional government allowed them to deliver before the French Assembly rousing speeches in which they demanded money, arms, munitions, and clothes for launching their own campaigns of liberation. Lamartine, hard pressed by sympathetic French radicals, and eager to rid Paris of these revolutionary mobs, finally had the government vote the Germans a grant of 60,000 francs. With Lamartine's tacit approval, the nationalistic poet Georg Herwegh (1817–1875) then organized the refugees into a German legion, numbering between fifteen and eighteen thousand men. To preserve amicable international relations, Lamartine notified the German governments that he was "repatriating foreigners." Baden, by then led by a liberal ministry, replied that it would gladly welcome the returnees, provided they came "in small groups and unarmed." But Lamartine had to confess his impotence, and admitted that the German legion had already left Paris. Thereupon the German federal diet issued a call for mobilization and sent Baden, Hessian, and Württemberg troops to protect the Rhine frontier. Even liberal Germans denounced this foreign meddling in German affairs and expressed fear that the so-called "German" legion might be a disguised prelude to a full-fledged French invasion.

Although emotions ran high, the episode did not lead to war with France. Encouraged by the news of new revolutionary outbreaks in Baden, the German legion crossed the Rhine on April 24. But insufficiently armed and poorly led by the idealistic Herwegh, the motley legion was rapidly defeated by the armies of Württemberg and the whole "liberation" movement collapsed.

The Revolutions outside Prussia and Austria

After news of the Paris revolution reached the German states, demonstrations occurred almost everywhere. In

Munich, where tension had run high for some time—partly because the infatuated King Louis I insisted on awarding a title of nobility to his low-born Irish mistress, the dancer Lola Montez—popular pressure forced the abdication of the king and the flight of the courtesan. Lola departed to seek gold in California, and Maximilian II (1848–1864) ascended the Bavarian throne, supported by a moderately liberal ministry.

Few other rulers were forced to abdicate. In most states, as in Württemberg and Hesse, the uprisings merely brought about installation of a more liberal cabinet and satisfaction of some of the people's demands. The most common petitions called for the basic freedoms, for trial by jury, and for an extension of the people's rights under the constitution. In some regions, especially those close to revolutionary France, the uprisings were more violent and the demands more radical.

The Grand Duchy of Baden, for instance, deeply influenced by neighboring Switzerland and France, experienced early sporadic uprisings of a more radical nature. Peasants rose against their noble landlords, and members of the middle class protested against paying taxes without a voice in the government. On February 27, Gustav Struve (1805–1870) initiated a revolt in Mannheim and proclaimed his intention of establishing a republic. Two days later, demonstrations in Heidelberg and Karlsruhe forced the grand duke to accede to certain popular demands. He permitted freedom of the press and trial by jury, and allowed the middle class to form an armed militia, which they demanded both as a counterweight to the ducal army and as a protection against social revolution from below. The duke agreed to set up a liberal and constitutional ministry and to press for the convocation of an all-German parliament.

Up to this point, the revolution in Baden paralleled those of many other states. The moderate revolutionaries had seemingly gained their aims by early March. But fear of the radical left made the new ministry overly legalistic and slow in its reforms—a phenomenon common to upper-middle-class revolutions. Hence the lower classes and the radicals took matters into their own hands. New bloody peasant risings occurred, manor houses were burned and proprietors massacred. On April 12, 1848, Struve boldly proclaimed the establishment of a Baden republic near Constance, hoping to obtain assistance from Herwegh and his German legion on their way from Paris. This republican experiment was short-lived. Its supporters were routed in clashes with the army even before Herwegh's legion crossed the Rhine to meet a similar fate. The grand duchy as a whole then settled down to a quiet, benevolent liberalism. But the indomitable Struve attempted a third republican revolt on September 21; once again his cause was suppressed by the army.

The strength of radicalism and republicanism in Baden was perhaps not typical, but two important phenomena of this revolution were paralleled in most German states. Almost everywhere the incumbent governments softened the revolutionary *élan* of the upper-middle class by granting immediate moderate concessions. Although these concessions deprived the governments of few, if any, essential elements of power, they pleased the middle classes

and turned them into defenders of the regime against the more far-reaching demands of the lower class. Second, in all states the army generally remained loyal to the governments. Despite the creation of national militias, the armed forces retained a monopoly on military power and remained an instrument with which the rulers could crush those rebellions that threatened to undermine their real power or the privileges of their class. Failure to subvert the armies ultimately doomed the chances of the revolutionaries.

Revolution in Austria

The revolutions in the Austrian Empire differed from those in Germany. The social and political aspects were, of course, similar, but whereas the national revolution in Germany was centripetal, aimed at uniting the German states, in Austria it was centrifugal, aimed at securing autonomy for the component nationalities (see Map 10).

REBELLIONS AND DISINTEGRATION The February revolts in Sicily, rapidly reverberating up the Italian peninsula, soon created unrest in Austria's possessions south of the Alps. Tension in Lombardy and Venetia, in turn, unleashed currents of revolt among other subject populations and in Vienna itself. Prepared by revolutionary propaganda and encouraged by the news of other revolts, Viennese students and bourgeois staged a demonstration on March 12 that led to clashes with imperial troops. Despite the mildness of the uprising, Emperor Ferdinand (1835–1848) agreed to yield, since not only his own Viennese but also most of his other subject populations were in re-

bellion. Metternich was forced to resign, and control of Vienna was turned over to a national guard. The repressive Metternich laws were revoked and the convocation of a constituent assembly was promised.

Meanwhile, the Hungarians adopted their own constitution, the March Laws, and obtained from the vacillating emperor recognition of autonomous status. The Croatians rose to demand self-rule, the Milanese forced the withdrawal of Austrian troops, the Venetians set up an independent republic, and the Czechs clamored for autonomy. By early April, Moravia and even the outlying districts of Galicia, Transylvania, and Dalmatia rebelled against the central authority of Vienna. In addition, the Kingdom of Piedmont-Sardinia declared war on Austria in defense of its Italian compatriots in Lombardy.

The Hapsburg emperor gave way on all sides. He promised autonomous rights to Croatia, Bohemia, and Hungary, and issued a fairly liberal constitution for Austria itself—acting hastily before the Austrian Constituent Assembly might propose a more radical political frame. Although it permitted creation of a responsible ministry, Ferdinand's constitution did not mollify the Viennese liberals. The emperor's attempt to disband the national guard and dissolve the radical student committees in the middle of May, together with disappointment with the imperial constitution, provoked a second wave of uprisings in the Austrian capital. Even the emperor's permission for the re-forming of the student committees and his promise to revise the constitution failed to soften the revolutionary mood. To escape the pressure of the agitators, Ferdinand finally fled

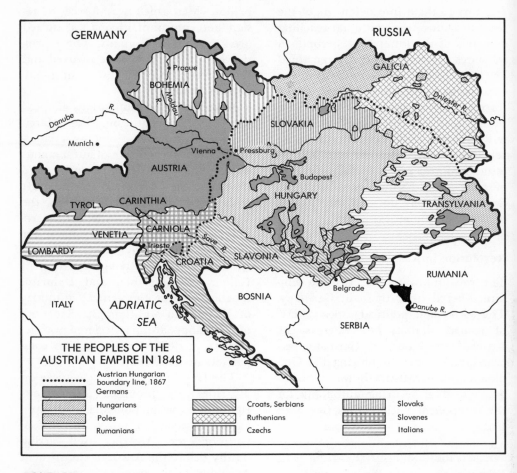

GERMANY   RUSSIA

Prague
BOHEMIA   GALICIA

Danube R.   Dniester R.

Munich   SLOVAKIA

Vienna   Pressburg

AUSTRIA   Budapest

TYROL   CARINTHIA   HUNGARY   TRANSYLVANIA

VENETIA   CARNIOLA
LOMBARDY   Trieste   Save R.   SLAVONIA
                  CROATIA   RUMANIA

ITALY   ADRIATIC   BOSNIA   Belgrade   Danube R.

SEA   SERBIA

THE PEOPLES OF THE
AUSTRIAN EMPIRE IN 1848

- Austrian Hungarian boundary line, 1867
- Germans
- Hungarians
- Poles
- Rumanians
- Croats, Serbians
- Ruthenians
- Czechs
- Slovaks
- Slovenes
- Italians

MAP 10

from Vienna to Innsbruck, and the
Austrian capital fell under the complete control of a revolutionary committee of public safety.

Thus, by the end of May, the Austrian Empire seemed on the verge of
disintegration. The revolution had
been temporarily successful in Vienna,
while Czechs, Magyars, and other subject peoples were apparently gaining
independence or at least autonomy.
The war against Piedmont was going
badly, and the emperor, urged by England and discouraged by the initial
success of Piedmontese troops, was

ready to grant independence to Lombardy. Obviously, during the spring of
1848 Austria was in no position to
exert much influence on German
affairs.

THE FIRST PERIOD OF REACTION   But
in the end the commanders in the field
proved more resilient than the imperial court. In the middle of June,
Prince Windisch-Graetz, commander of
the Austrian troops in Bohemia, put
an end to the autonomous movement
among the Czechs by bombarding
Prague into submission and placing all

of Bohemia under tight military dictatorship. Six weeks later, General Joseph Radetzky (1766–1858) defeated the Piedmontese in the decisive battle of Custozza, signed a temporary armistice with Piedmont, and re-established Austrian control over all of Lombardy. Thus the energetic action of two Austrian generals and their armies reinstituted imperial control over portions of the empire during the early summer months of 1848, initiating the first period of reaction. Only Vienna itself and Hungary remained in the hands of disaffected forces.

In late July, the Constituent Assembly that Emperor Ferdinand had promised in March finally opened its meetings in Vienna. Its liberal members rejected Ferdinand's constitution as inadequate and started to frame their own more democratic instrument. The new assembly also attempted to assume control over the revolutionary forces in Vienna, trying to act as a provisional executive and legislative body. It passed some liberal measures of which only a few—such as the final and complete eradication of serfdom—survived the revolution.

In early September, the imperial government tried to reassert its authority over Hungary and Vienna itself. To use one subject people against another seemed the most convenient expedient. The Croatians, under Baron Joseph Jellachich (1801–1859), were urged to invade Hungary to help repress the rebellion in Budapest, but this first attempt failed. The Hungarians not only repelled the Croatian invasion but advanced to the gates of Vienna to give encouragement to the revolutionaries in the Austrian capital. Ferdinand, who had meanwhile returned to his capital, fled once again, and a new

revolt occurred in Vienna. The constituent assembly itself split into two factions. Its moderate members withdrew to the provincial town of Kremsier, where they hoped to work undisturbed, while the more radical delegates remained in Vienna to support the revolution. By the middle of October, Vienna was again in the hands of the insurgents, while the armies of Windisch-Graetz and Jellachich were advancing to invade the city. After a thunderous bombardment on the last day of October, Vienna was forced to open its gates to the imperial and Croatian armies. The fall of the Austrian capital signaled the triumph of reaction. Those revolutionary leaders who were unable to flee were promptly executed. Except in Hungary, the revolution collapsed. In Austria, Bohemia, and Lombardy, imperial power reasserted itself.

In late November, the highly skilled Prince Felix von Schwarzenberg (1800–1852) assumed the post of chief minister, determined to maintain the integrity of the Austrian dominions. One of his first acts was to persuade the weak emperor, who had become compromised through political pledges, to resign in favor of his eighteen-year-old grandson, Francis Joseph I (1848–1916). The inexperienced new emperor left the tasks of government almost completely in the hands of his capable, conservative minister. Thus Austria and the Hapsburg Empire came to be ruled—and restored—during the next four years by the diplomatic skill of this "new Metternich."

SCHWARZENBERG'S REGIME Schwarzenberg's tasks were clear: he had to eradicate the remaining pockets of rebellion among the subject peoples

and quickly strengthen Austria's international position, so that Vienna could resume its dominant role in Germany before the German states fell completely under the yoke of Prussia.

The most important preliminary step was to subdue Hungary. In January 1849, Prince Windisch-Graetz seized Budapest but even this military success did not settle the Hungarian problem. The Magyars desired not merely autonomous rights but also a share with the German-speaking Austrians in controlling the other subject populations of the empire. Schwarzenberg's constitutional ideas of centralizing all power in Vienna clearly went counter to such Hungarian hopes. As a result, the Magyars rose again in April, expelled Windisch-Graetz' army of occupation, and proclaimed an independent Hungarian Republic under the leadership of the radical Louis Kossuth (1802–1894). Since many Austrian troops were then again in Italy campaigning against Sardinia, Schwarzenberg gladly accepted Russia's offer of help against the Hungarians. Emperor Nicholas I, ever the guardian of conservatism, had become frightened at the progress of republicanism in neighboring Hungary. Proclaiming that the rebellion "endangers the tranquillity of the two Empires" and that "it was but natural that the two Cabinets should understand one another on this point of common interest," Nicholas dispatched troops into Hungary. Crushed between Russian and Austrian forces, the Hungarian rebels were finally forced to lay down their arms in August. Kossuth's republic was dissolved, Austrian power firmly re-established, and a new bond of friendship created between the two conservative emperors, Nicholas and young Francis Joseph.

Meanwhile Schwarzenberg had also met the threat in Italy successfully. When Sardinia-Piedmont reopened the war in March 1849, Radetzky quickly defeated the invading armies at Novara. The armistice this time was followed by a peace treaty that reconfirmed all of Austria's rights over Lombardy. In the summer, Austrian troops then laid siege to Venice and bombarded and starved the Venetians into surrender. With the fall of the Venetian Republic in August, Vienna re-established its authority over all its subject peoples. The Hapsburg Empire had been saved; the movements for autonomy and liberalism had been crushed everywhere.

Schwarzenberg had also broached the problem of a new political framework. On March 1, 1849, the moderate rump of the constitutional convention, sitting at Kremsier, produced its constitution. As expected, it was a mildly liberal document that took account of the aspirations of the subject peoples by prescribing decentralization for the empire. However, Schwarzenberg, true to his principles, dissolved the constitutional convention and disregarded its work. He could neither condone the notions of popular sovereignty implied in the document nor accept its federal character. Instead, he issued his own constitution with a highly centralized administrative system. The local diets of the subject peoples were to have little authority, all essential power emanating from Vienna. His one concession to liberalism, at least on paper, was the provision for a central diet representative of all subjects, and for a ministry responsible to this diet. The centralized character of Schwarzenberg's system had a profound effect on developments in Ger-

many. By binding the various ethnic groups of the Austrian Empire into a tighter union, it complicated the prospect of creating a state embracing only German-speaking peoples. For Austria itself, however, Schwarzenberg's constitution had a merely symbolic value, for the minister and his young emperor continued to base their government on military autocracy, with the explanation that unsettled conditions did not yet permit implementation of the new constitution.

Revolution in Prussia

Even more important to the future of Germany than the uprisings in Austria was the fate of the revolution in Prussia. Ever since the dismissal of the United Diet in 1847, tension and speculation had run high among Frederick William's subjects. When the news of the fall of King Louis-Philippe was received in Berlin on February 26, tension gave way to bewilderment and consternation. Every successive dispatch telling of revolts in southern Germany and bringing more details from Italy and France reminded the liberals that it was time to act in behalf of their ideals. The streets of Berlin rapidly abounded with rumors of impending plots. Yet the "loyal Berliners"—as the king later called his people—seemingly made docile by centuries of indoctrination in obedience, were slow to react to the challenge. It is noteworthy that Berlin was the last major city to enter the revolutionary fray.

Disorders within Prussia first broke out in the Rhineland, in Silesia, and in East Prussia. On March 3, crowds entered the city hall of Cologne to place six demands before the startled city fathers. Besides the usual call for suffrage, civil rights, and a popular militia, the petitioners requested protection for labor, a guaranteed minimum standard of living, as well as state education for all.

THE MARCH DAYS IN BERLIN A week later, unrest in Berlin produced the first overt action. Middle-class groups organized political meetings to request a reconvening of the United Diet and a free press. At the same time, the lower class made itself heard. Among Berlin's factory workers, numbering about 40,000 (not counting families and apprentices), poverty was again on the increase. The price of potatoes was still high, a typhus epidemic was spreading through the city, and a recession had produced layoffs at the big Borsig factory and other enterprises. Radical leaflets appeared and socialist leaders urged the workers to organize for action. On March 11, a group of workers sent a petition to the king, begging him to "speedily do away with the present distress among laborers and make their future secure," and suggesting establishment of a labor office composed of wage earners and employers, elected by their respective groups, to help improve labor conditions.

Despite the moderation of these petitions, Frederick William IV displayed the hesitancy and vacillation characteristic of his actions during the next crucial month. On March 13, the first incidents occurred between crowds, police, and army. A single barricade was put up and promptly destroyed by the army without bloodshed.

During the next four days, Berlin was in a continual emotional seesaw. Ever-larger crowds gathered daily to

demand royal concessions, haphazard barricades were erected and quickly destroyed by roving cavalry, occasional stones were thrown at the palace of the King's brother, the conservative Prince William, but except in two cases, bloodshed was avoided. The king, for his part, continued his ambivalent stand. He made vague promises of reforms while calling for additional troops and police to keep the petitioners in check.

The news of Metternich's fall convinced even the timid Berliners that the "impossible" was possible. Late on March 17, crowds signed a petition to the king calling for withdrawal of the hated troops from the capital. The following morning the same crowds gathered before the royal palace to present their petition. To their surprise, several deputations were admitted to the palace and the king agreed to discuss their grievances.

During the preceding night, Frederick William had once again changed his course. Perhaps frightened by the fall of the once-mighty Austrian minister, the king now made concessions. He formed a new cabinet under the liberal Ludolf Camphausen (1803–1890), and prepared two proclamations to his people. In these, he reconvened the United Diet for April, presumably to write a constitution for Prussia, lifted most censorship restrictions, and promised to work for changes in the German Confederation. On the other hand, he dismissed the moderate commander of the 15,000-man Berlin garrison and replaced him by the more conservative and reliable General Max von Prittwitz—a step of long-range significance, since assured assistance of the army proved infinitely more important for the course of the revolution than all the royal proclamations and promises.

When the two proclamations appeared on the billboards of Berlin in the early afternoon of the eighteenth, the crowds in front of the palace swelled to threatening proportions. The people had presumably gathered to thank their monarch for his liberal concessions, but the sight of the masses frightened the king. General von Prittwitz was ordered to clear the square in front of the palace. As the grenadiers advanced, two musket shots were discharged. Although no one had been injured, the people felt betrayed; the crowd turned into an angry mob. Fighting ensued, barricades were erected in many quarters of Berlin, and all through the night there was street fighting between the army and the population.

The court immediately admitted that the shots had been fired by two soldiers (later brought before a court-martial that acquitted them), but it was asserted that the shots were accidental and that the troops had not received orders to fire on the crowd. Although this explanation may be correct, it is equally conceivable that the two grenadiers acted on secret orders of General von Prittwitz in order to frighten the king into determined opposition to the mob. If so, the scheme failed, for Frederick William was horrified and frightened by the bloodshed. No military man, he craved love and obedience from his people. During the night of fighting, he oscillated between pity for his subjects and indignation at their defiance of his authority.

In the early morning hours he ordered his troops to cease fighting, and had a white flag raised over the royal palace. Royal couriers then roamed through the city, posting the

king's tender letter "To my dear Berliners" (*"An meine lieben Berliner"*). "By reasons of my proclamation of this day, convening the Diet," he wrote, "you received proof of the loyal sentiments of your King toward you and our common German Fatherland." He indicated that the happy occasion had been marred by "a band of rowdies," and that royal troops had been asked to clear the square merely to avoid "insults to my brave and faithful soldiers." The two shots had been accidental and had hurt no one, but "a band of rascals, mostly foreigners . . . a week in hiding here," had misused the incidents to put "thoughts of vengeance into the heated heads of many of my loyal and beloved Berliners." He swore that the troops had acted merely in self-defense, and concluded with pathos: "Your loving Queen, prostrate with suffering, joins her heartfelt and tearful prayers to mine."

On the same Sunday morning, March 19, Frederick William took the next step in concessions. After the truce became effective, he attended church and then negotiated with envoys from the barricades. He agreed to withdraw his troops from Berlin if the people in turn would tear down the barricades. As a result, the royal garrison immediately began to evacuate the city, even before the insurgents started to dismantle their strongposts. By oversight—or again by design of General von Prittwitz—not even a small protective detachment was left to guard the royal palace.

Frederick William had placed himself completely at the mercy of his people. The prisoners taken by the army during the night were released, the mob controlled the streets, and a motley band of students and merchants made themselves voluntary guards of the royal palace and its frightened occupants. On the same afternoon, the king and queen had to submit to their first open humiliation. The insurgents carried their dead into the courtyard of the palace, and the royal family had to participate from the balcony in a ceremony honoring the fallen rebels. It seemed that revolution in Prussia had triumphed.

The power of the crowds also frightened the middle classes, which feared the workers might make social demands and endanger property and business. Bourgeois groups volunteered as a militia to maintain law and order and safeguard their interests. But the period of humiliation for Frederick William had not yet ended. On March 20, crowds gathered again, demanding the release of all political prisoners and demonstrating against the conservative Prince William. The king not only had the prison doors opened, but also sent his brother William, the future emperor of Germany, to England. On the following day, he even seemed to enjoy himself in a fraternal honeymoon with his subjects. He rode through the streets of Berlin wearing the revolutionary colors, black-red-gold, the symbols of German unity and of the Wars of Liberation, but not the colors of the Hohenzollerns or of Prussia. He made flattering speeches to the insurgents and praised their worthy sentiments. "To my people and to the German nation" he made his famous ambiguous remarks: *"Preussen geht fortan in Deutschland auf,"* which could mean either that "Prussia will henceforth be dissolved in Germany," presumably through the creation of a union of coequal states, or that "Prussia will henceforth prosper in Ger-

many," that is, that Prussia would gain even more power by uniting with the other states. This and similar pronouncements by Frederick William, at a time when he had seemingly accepted liberalism, brought him into the limelight of the movement for German unification, which was gaining ground during this same month.

GRADUAL REASSERTION OF ROYAL POWER But the honeymoon between the king and his Berliners did not last much longer. The king's attendance at the burial of the revolutionary dead, on March 22, was the last major act in the drama of revolutionary cooperation. During the month of April, the citizen guards experienced increasing difficulty in maintaining order in Berlin. Radical elements grew in strength, and many a bourgeois longed for a return of royal troops as a safeguard against a possible social revolution.

When the United Diet met, it acted in the legalistic fashion that characterized other German revolutions of 1848. Instead of assuming additional powers, it arranged for the election of a constituent assembly for Prussia and then disbanded. The elections for this constituent assembly, based on universal but indirect male suffrage, were held in early May and resulted in a strongly liberal, almost radical assembly that opened its meetings in Berlin on May 22. With Berlin in the hands of liberals, and a constituent assembly gathered to write a constitution for all of Prussia, the cause of liberalism seemed assured.

Yet the apparent victory was a deception. The constituent assembly engaged in interminable debates throughout the summer, whereas prompt action on a constitution was required. Frederick William left Berlin in May for Potsdam, where he felt more secure under the protection of his army. There he forgot the days of the liberal honeymoon and came again under the influence of reactionary advisers. Although the insurgents in Berlin did not realize it, the revolution was, in fact, lost. The liberal Camphausen ministry meanwhile drifted along, awaiting the outcome of the constitutional convention. Although well intentioned, this government provided little succor to the liberal cause in Prussia, and devoted its main attention to foreign affairs and the national unification movement.

Camphausen's minister of foreign affairs (Heinrich Freiherr von Arnim-Heinrichsdorff) championed a mixed course of liberalism and German nationalism. He hoped to unify Germany under Prussia while guaranteeing a modicum of liberal safeguards. Unlike most Prussians—and for that matter, most Germans—he advocated at least a partial restoration of Polish autonomy. Because he realized that championing autonomy for Poland would arouse the displeasure of Russia, he sought an anti-Russian alliance with France. The reactions to this proposal throw an interesting light on conditions in 1848. Paris showed interest in the plan, since French liberals had always had an affection for Poland. They favored friendship with a liberal Prussia, but feared an anti-Russian alliance, which they thought might lead to war. German liberals, on the other hand, favored the anti-Russian aspect of the scheme but looked with suspicion on its pro-Polish features. But the future of the plan depended on the attitude of Frederick William. The Prussian king had always been

pro-Russian. While he might be persuaded to extend a diplomatic smile to the Second French Republic, he would never consent to an open break with the tsar. The bulk of the Prussian officers shared the king's feelings. German liberals might flirt with Paris and flaunt St. Petersburg, but the Prussian officers held the French republicans in contempt, whereas they had an affinity for conservative Russia.

Under these circumstances, no anti-Russian alliance was made. It became clear that the king and his military advisers still determined policy, although Prussia was officially governed by a liberal cabinet. This was particularly evident in the Danish, Polish, and all-German questions, in which Prussia sided with the conservative forces (see pages 34–37).

On November 2, three days after Vienna was retaken by the reactionary forces, Prussia, too, embarked on an official change of policy. The liberal Camphausen ministry was dismissed and replaced by a new government under the conservative Count of Brandenburg, a natural son of the king's grandfather and an outspoken advocate of monarchical supremacy. Baron Otto von Manteuffel (1805–1882) returned to the Ministry of Interior. The king disregarded the assembly's protest against the change in ministry. In fact, a week later he exiled the constituent assembly to the city of Brandenburg, even though it had not yet completed a constitution for Prussia. A month later, Frederick William reasserted his authority even further. He re-entered Berlin with troops, dissolved the civic guard and the assembly, and issued his own constitution. The royal document, prepared by Manteuffel, embodied some features elaborated by the delegates, but was clearly a monarchist constitution reserving full powers for the king. Elections on the basis of the new constitution took place in January 1849, and the newly elected delegates convened in February. But even then new quarrels erupted between the king and his subjects.

As occurred in many parts of Germany, a second wave of uprisings shook Prussia in the spring of 1849. The Rhineland, in particular, was the scene of democratic and socialistic risings. Following the mood of the people, the diet attempted to revise Frederick William's constitution to make it more democratic. Annoyed, the king thereupon dissolved the new assembly and changed the electoral procedure in the hope of excluding the liberal and democratic elements. Thus by the summer of 1849, Prussia had returned firmly to the conservative camp. Despite astonishing early successes, the revolution had failed in its over-all aims and had produced few permanent gains.

The Unitary Movement

While rebellions were sapping the strength of the state governments, determined groups were working for German unification. On March 5, 1848, fifty-three liberals met at Heidelberg to discuss a closer union of all German states. The conferees, mostly from southwestern and central Germany, generally echoed Heinrich von Gagern's (1799–1880) view that a union could best be achieved under a constitutional monarchy. Some, however, convinced that Germany could never be unified so long as the particularistic princes retained power, saw Germany's salvation only in the establishment of a

united republic. In the end all agreed to work for unity by legal means, and called on present and past members of German state legislatures to convene at Frankfurt at the end of March to discuss plans of action. A committee of seven was to arrange the convening of this Frankfurt preparliament, or preliminary parliament.

On March 31, some 600 voluntary delegates appeared at Frankfurt. Attendance reflected the varying degrees of liberalism of the states: 124 came from all of Prussia, while tiny Hesse-Darmstadt furnished 84, and Baden 72. The five-day meeting evoked violent debates between the small republican minority, led by Struve and others, and the large majority of moderate monarchists. In the end the moderates carried the day, although they did agree to have the all-German constituent assembly elected by universal male suffrage. They asked the federal diet in Frankfurt to order the election of 1 delegate for every 50,000 Germans for the purpose of attending a national assembly and framing a constitution for all of Germany. Before disbanding on April 4, the preparliament elected an organizational and preparatory committee of fifty to remain at Frankfurt.

THE NATIONAL ASSEMBLY AT FRANK-FURT   Elections of delegates were soon held all over Germany. Although suspicious of a popular body created by universal suffrage, no prince dared prevent the elections in his state. In the absence of strong support from Austria—itself in the grip of revolution—and under pressure from his liberal cabinet and excited subjects, even Frederick William consented to the elections. At best the princes could hope that moderate delegates would be elected and that the Frankfurt assembly would be an advisory rather than a constituent or legislative body. They hoped that the federal diet and the individual governments would retain power to discuss, reject, or ratify whatever constitution the delegates might produce at Frankfurt.

The National Assembly—often called the Frankfurt Parliament—opened its first session in St. Paul's Church in Frankfurt on the Main on May 18, 1848. Although 830 delegates had been elected, usually only about 500 attended the sessions. The delegates represented almost the entire political spectrum, but the majority stood for middle-class forces of order and moderation. The extreme right-wing conservatives generally boycotted the sessions, and few really left-wing radicals had been elected. The membership was largely composed of the professional classes—lawyers, university professors, businessmen, doctors—and members of the clergy, the officer corps, and local diets. The lower classes were omitted, and even regional representation was very uneven. Austria with its 18 million subjects should have sent 360 delegates, but sent only a handful, since the non-German groups boycotted the elections. Prussia, too, was notably underrepresented; the smaller liberal states shared the bulk of the membership. Yet despite irregularities in the haphazard electoral proceedings, and even though it lacked political skill, the Frankfurt Parliament represented an astounding array of talent and intellect.

When the sessions began, there were, of course, no political parties to facilitate parliamentary maneuvers. But soon like-minded people began to congregate in local restaurants to discuss

possible programs of action and thus fashioned a modicum of party life. The many factions can be divided into four groups. On the Right were the Prussian conservatives, representing the aspirations of Frederick William IV and certain groups of Prussian nobles and intellectuals (led by Radowitz and Baron Georg von Vincke). They sought a German constitutional, military monarchy or empire in which Prussia would dominate. Such a government should be founded on monarchical and not popular sovereignty, and rest on the consent of the princes of Germany, who would continue to play an important role in the new state. To the left of this group were the non-Prussian conservatives, representing the interests of the kings and princes who were wary of Prussian leadership. These monarchists, while wishing to reserve considerable power to the ruling princes, were willing to accept certain liberal, constitutional measures. One such plan called for the addition of a popular assembly representing all Germans to be added as a lower house to the existing federal diet in Frankfurt.

The third and largest group may be labeled constitutionalists or democratic monarchists. It contained some of the most brilliant minds of the assembly, including Heinrich von Gagern, the poet Arndt, the historian Dahlmann, the journalist Georg Gervinus, and the writer Jacob Grimm. Essentially, they represented the majority view of the Heidelberg meeting that had launched the whole program for unification. They were divided on such details as whether or not to include Austria, whether to have a hereditary or an elective ruler, and whether to make him an emperor or not. But they essentially sought to establish as liberal a regime as compatible with their concept of monarchy. Finally, on the left stood a fourth small but vociferous group of republicans, led by the enthusiastic orator Robert Blum (1807–1848). The republicans came mostly from southwest Germany, and some espoused socialistic ideals. The group gained little power at Frankfurt, and ultimately hoped to impose its ideas through popular uprisings outside the framework of the Frankfurt Assembly.

The opening of the meetings at St. Paul's Church was greeted with mixed feelings by the old federal diet. It was not clear whether the new assembly had any legal right to supersede the diet or whether its function was merely that of a constituent body. In the absence of clear instructions from their home governments, most delegates wavered in their attitude. The congratulatory message of the diet to the new assembly reflected this confusion. It spoke of "the force of extraordinary events" and the "ardent desire of our whole fatherland" that had produced an "assembly such as had never before been seen in all our history"; and ended with the noncommittal phrase: "The German governments and their common organ, the Diet, . . . gladly yielding to the spirit of the time, extend a hand of welcome to the representatives of the nation."

On May 19, the assembly elected as its president Heinrich von Gagern, whose skilled parliamentarianism was to guide the stormy debates during the coming months. In his opening speech, Gagern proclaimed: "We must frame a constitution for Germany, and we derive our authority for this purpose from the sovereignty of the nation." It appeared as though Gagern was to launch the assembly onto a truly revo-

lutionary path. During the succeeding weeks, he made it clear that the assembly's task was not merely to write a constitution, but also to act as a central legislative and executive government for all of Germany. For this purpose, he had the federal diet suspended, a move the princes at the time did not dare oppose. The assembly was thus free to create its own executive. On June 28, the delegates in St. Paul's finally chose Archduke John of Austria (1782–1859) as imperial regent, and authorized him to appoint his own cabinet and form a provisional central government. The choice of the Hapsburg duke, who was known for his mild liberalism, showed Gagern's acumen. The installation of a legitimate prince as provisional ruler was bound to give comfort to the moderates, and might secure for the central government the respect of the princes of Germany. Archduke John immediately set up a provisional ministry, including the Austrian Anton von Schmerling (1805–1893) as minister for foreign and internal affairs, a Prussian (Peucker) as minister of war, and a Hamburg lawyer (Heckscher) as minister of justice.

From its inception, the new provisional government enjoyed a strangely ambiguous status. It was officially recognized by the German states, but not obeyed on vital issues. Foreign democratic nations, such as France and the United States, sent accredited ambassadors, but other states ignored its existence. Above all, Archduke John's government carried an empty mandate, for it lacked diplomatic and military resources with which to enforce its decisions in Germany.

While the executive in Frankfurt acted as an all-German shadow government, study committees of the assembly worked on the proposed constitution. In sublime oratory and with remarkable intellectual acuity, the delegates lost themselves in the intricacy of seemingly insolvable problems. The questions of a *Gross* versus a *Kleindeutschland*; of republic, empire, or monarchy; of imperial versus states rights; of fundamental civil rights; of the rights of ethnically non-German groups; and a thousand others occupied the delegates for the remainder of the year 1848. Failing to comprehend that revolutions must be accomplished rapidly, the delegates debated interminably while the forces of reaction in Austria and Germany were regaining ground.

THE FRANKFURT ASSEMBLY AND GERMAN NATIONALISM Almost all the questions studied at Frankfurt involved the nationalistic feelings of the delegates. As the French envoy to Frankfurt remarked: "A dizzy feeling seemed to seize the Parliament of Frankfurt every time a question of conquest presented itself to them or when they could foresee the possibility of enlarging their territory under pretext of protecting the German nationality." Even most liberals displayed surprisingly intense Pan-German feelings in regard to Schleswig-Holstein or to the subject populations of Austria and Prussia. Hegel's mythical entity, the "state," seemed to outweigh considerations of humanity and liberty. Pointing with pride to Generals Radetzky, Windisch-Graetz, and Jellachich, who were crushing the rebellions of the subject peoples, a deputy declared: "Let us first found real power, and then establish freedom, which is impotent without power." The moderate

Gagern sounded equally chauvinistic. We must "embrace as satellites in our planetary system," he declared, "those peoples in the Danubian basin who have no talent for and no claim to independence." Nor did the delegates show any qualms about their inconsistency. With equal relish they invoked the principle of nationality to secure Schleswig-Holstein from Denmark, and appealed to authoritarianism to deny this same ideal to the Poles.

Three events in the summer of 1848 exemplify this nationalistic attitude of the Frankfurt parliamentarians. By playing into the hands of the reactionaries, they ultimately undermined both liberalism and the chances for unification. One such event concerned the Czechs of Bohemia. They had been invited to send delegates to the Frankfurt Assembly on the assumption that they would form a part of the future united Germany. The Czechs, however, preferred a political future apart from Germany, and called their own Pan-Slav Congress in Prague—an action that provoked the delegates at Frankfurt into lengthy tirades against the Czech secessionists. In a manifesto of June 12, the Czechs complained: "The Germans threaten many Slavic peoples with violence if they will not agree to assist in the building up of the political greatness of Germany." The manifesto continued: "We Slavs utterly decry such pretensions, and reject them the more emphatically the more they are wrongfully disguised in the garb of freedom," and ended with a plea to the Saxons and Prussians to "abandon at long last the systematic denationalization of the Slavs . . . in East and West Prussia." But the shortsighted representatives at Frankfurt under-

stood only German nationalism. When five days later, General Windisch-Graetz bombarded Prague into submission and destroyed the hopes of Czech secessionists, the Frankfurt Assembly applauded this "victory of German weapons." Few stopped to think that it spelled a triumph for reaction.

A second test of the nationalistic feelings of the Frankfurt parliamentarians concerned Poland. During the honeymoon period with his "dear Berliners," Frederick William of Prussia had granted an amnesty to the Poles and hinted that his Polish subjects would be given the right to stay outside the proposed new German state. As a result, the Poles immediately established a National Polish Committee in Poznan, and sent a deputation to Berlin to request re-establishment of a Polish kingdom, and to offer the crown to a Prussian prince. Although Prussia's foreign minister (Arnim) showed sympathy toward such a project, Frederick William could not allow the establishment of an independent Polish kingdom through which he would lose Prussia's eastern lands and probably provoke war with Russia. But he granted temporary concessions. On March 24, he issued a decree allowing the establishment of a Polish national guard, the development of local autonomy for the Poles, and the creation of regiments in Poznan.

This decree provoked consternation in St. Petersburg, but it was wildly acclaimed by the Poles as well as by German and French liberals. In early April, however, radicals gained the upper hand in Poland, and refused to accept Frederick William's concessions as sufficient, insisting instead on complete independence. Anti-Prussian uprisings followed, and soon turned into

outright revolt. The Prussian government consequently reversed its stand and decided on repression. By mid-April, there was open warfare between the Polish rebels and the Prussian army. When in May, the French provisional government decided against assistance to the Poles, Prussian troops could complete their crushing of the rebels without fear of international involvement.

By the time the Frankfurt Assembly opened, the Prussian armies were getting the upper hand over the insurrection. The parliamentarians immediately showed much interest in the Polish question, and a few voiced sympathy for Polish aspirations. But a three-day debate on the issue, begun on July 24, revealed that the mood of most delegates had changed. The Polish insurrection offended their idea of German grandeur, and its radicalism frightened even the moderates. Finally, in the style of a debating society, the assembly put to a vote the question whether the "partition of Poland had been a shameful wrong." Only a hundred delegates cast an affirmative vote. The accompanying debate showed that the majority of conservative and moderate delegates, and even some liberals, felt that Prussia had the right, if not the duty, to subdue the Poles for the sake of expanding German culture.

The third event involving nationalism concerned the two duchies of Schleswig and Holstein (see Map 11). Schleswig, containing a slight majority of Danes, did not belong to the German Confederation. Holstein to the south, overwhelmingly German in population, had become a member in 1815. Both duchies were tied together politically and loosely joined to Denmark in personal bond to the Danish crown.

In 1846, the Danish king, (Christian VIII) had asserted his intention of eventually integrating both duchies into Denmark, and his pronouncement had provoked indignation in the duchies as well as in Germany. The question became acute in January 1848 upon the accession of a new king, Frederick VII, who issued a constitutional draft that clearly threatened the political independence of the two duchies. The affected populations agitated in favor of their autonomous rights, and refused to grant allegiance to the new king. They chose, instead, to recognize as ruler Duke Christian of Augustenburg, from a side line of the royal house of Denmark. When the Danish king sent troops to enforce his decision, the duchies rose in revolt under the leadership of Augustenburg. On March 24, 1848, they seceded from Denmark, established a provisional government in Kiel, and appealed to the federal diet in Frankfurt for support.

Thus Germany was forced to take a stand on the matter. Without hesitation, the diet championed the rights of the duchies, and requested Prussia to send military aid in the name of the German Confederation. Even the moderates then preparing for the Frankfurt assembly applauded this decision. Since Frederick William of Prussia was not averse to championing German expansion, he dispatched Prussian troops to the duchies. By May, they were fighting against Danish troops and invading southern Jutland.

But matters changed in June. Prussian troops made little headway, and, without a navy, Prussia could expect a long campaign. Moreover, Britain and Russia, both interested in maintaining an independent Denmark as

guardian of the entrance to the Baltic, exerted pressure on the belligerents to accept mediation. Most important, however, was the change at Frankfurt. When the federal diet abdicated its powers to the new National Assembly, Frederick William suddenly saw himself no longer fighting for the confederation of princes, but in the name of a revolutionary body with doubtful credentials. Consequently, on August 26, he signed the armistice of Malmö, providing for the evacuation of Danish and Prussian troops from both duchies, and their administration by a joint Danish-German commission.

Since Frederick William had never acknowledged that he had been fighting in the name of the National Assembly, he concluded this armistice without consulting the delegates at Frankfurt. News of the armistice provoked tumult and indignation there. The delegates had faithfully applauded every minor victory of Prussian arms, and had even collected money to purchase a navy for the war against Denmark. They considered their nationalistic aims betrayed by Prussia's abandonment of the inhabitants of Schleswig-Holstein. Heated debates followed. A majority wished to reject the armistice and continue the war, until the realization that the assembly lacked all military power made them recognize the futility of this course. Therefore, on September 16, Parliament voted by a small majority to accept the armistice. The vote provoked a symptomatic rebellion in the city of Frankfurt. The nationalists proclaimed that the assembly itself had betrayed the German cause, and called for its overthrow. Radicals roamed the streets, murdered some delegates, and disrupted proceed-

ings in St. Paul's Church. The assembly finally had to call on nearby Prussian and Austrian troops stationed in the fortress of Mainz to protect the delegates and crush the rebellion.

Thus the Danish problem not merely underlined the nationalistic fervor of the parliamentarians, but also ended ominously, with the assembly pitifully dependent on the soldiers of reactionary Prussia and Austria.

THE FRANKFURT CONSTITUTION After September 1848, the majority of the Frankfurt delegates grew increasingly conservative. The radical uprisings in Frankfurt, Struve's renewed attempt to establish a republic in Baden, and occasional flickers of social revolt made the delegates wary of liberalism. The Frankfurt riots also made them recognize their reliance on the armies of the princes, and realize that Germany could probably never be unified "by the people" against the will of the princes.

Between spurts of pretending to act as the government of all Germany, the delegates worked diligently in committee to hammer out the proposed constitution. It is typical of their lack of practical vision that they devoted their first major effort to the formulation of abstract ideals. In January 1849, the assembly accepted a declaration of fundamental rights, an eloquent tribute to the idealism of the majority of the delegates.

The more urgent question of a new political framework was infinitely more difficult to solve. Possibilities changed every month, as various princes regained power lost in the spring of 1848. In October a first and tentative compromise was reached regarding the size of the union. The assembly voted

to include only German lands that had no organic ties with non-German territory. But the delegates did not agree on what was to be considered German land. Strictly interpreted, this stipulation would have required Prussia and Austria to divest themselves of territories with non-German-speaking populations, or to transform the organic links to these lands into a personal union under the crown. The first solution was unlikely to be acceptable to Berlin and Vienna, whereas the second seemed impractical in an age of rising nationalities. Austria, at any rate, could hardly follow such a policy and hope to survive as a major European power. In fact, Prince Schwarzenberg was to pursue a diametrically opposite course by forcing increased centralization on the Austrian patchwork of nationalities. And it soon appeared that the Prussian delegates looked upon Prussia's Polish lands as inherently German territory, but considered Lombardy, Venetia, Hungary, and some of the other subject states of the Austrian Empire clearly non-German territories. Hence they voted for this resolution, because they favored a *Kleindeutsch* framework, and hoped to use this maneuver to exclude Austria from the proposed new union.

On March 27, 1849, the completed constitution was finally accepted by the National Assembly. It created a federal state in which the central government was to be endowed with considerably more authority than the old federal diet, including control over a federal army, foreign policy, and economic affairs. The government was to be headed by a hereditary emperor empowered with merely a suspensive veto over legislation. The national legislature was to consist of two houses: a *Staatenhaus,* half chosen by the state

governments and half elected by the lower houses of the state legislatures; and a lower house, the *Volkshaus,* elected by universal, direct, male suffrage on the basis of secret and equal ballots. The federal ministry was to be responsible to the national parliament.

The strongly democratic character of the constitution was largely the result of a last-minute political stratagem of Austrian and other delegates who did not want the king of Prussia to obtain the leadership of a unified Germany. They voted with the democrats and liberals for universal manhood suffrage and only a suspensive veto in hope of prejudicing Frederick William against the constitution. This seemed the only way to prevent Prussian absorption of Germany, since Austria had obviously forfeited its chances of leading the new state. Schwarzenberg's centralizing policies and his constitution of March 4, with its insistence on the unity of all Hapsburg lands, had torpedoed the last hopes for a *Grossdeutschland* solution. The reconquest of Budapest in January and the victory of Novara over the Piedmontese on March 23 showed that Schwarzenberg's intentions were not a hollow boast. At the same time, Austria's resurgence made it probable that it would not let events in Germany go unchallenged.

FREDERICK WILLIAM'S REFUSAL OF THE CROWN On March 28, the National Assembly elected Frederick William IV as "Emperor of the Germans," and sent a delegation to Berlin to offer the crown to the Prussian ruler. Actually, the stratagems of the Austrians to make the crown distasteful to the Hohenzollern prince had not been necessary. Frederick William's "March liberalism" had never been more than a brief infatuation, and his proclamations on

German unification had always been mere window dressing for his desire to extend Prussian power. In August 1848, in a public speech in Cologne, Frederick William had already addressed a friendly warning to the Frankfurt assembly: "Gentlemen, do not forget that there are still princes in Germany, and that I am one of them." But the assembly had largely ignored the warning. The king's actions in Schleswig-Holstein should, of course, have shown how little he respected the Frankfurt assembly, but the delegates could not know how thoroughly he actually despised it. By December 1848, he had decided never to accept a crown "created by an Assembly born of revolutionary seed, even if offered with princely approval." Just as the Prussian diet had infuriated him in November by attempting to strike from the royal title the phrase "by the Grace of God," so he felt that only the Almighty and the princes could resuscitate the "thousand year old crown of the German nation." Whatever Frankfurt could produce would "stink of the revolution."

When the delegation of parliamentarians offered him the crown, Frederick William made a conditional refusal. He would accept provided all princes and states of Germany gave their approval, and provided the Frankfurt Constitution served merely as a proposal that all the German governments could then discuss and modify. The latter proviso amounted to a complete repudiation of the work of the parliamentarians. The news of these conditions dismayed the monarchists in Frankfurt. Having battled republicans and radicals for a year in an effort to preserve the throne of Germany, they now felt betrayed by the Prussian ruler, who did not seem

to understand that their constitutional framework was the best possible compromise. For their part, the princes and state governments immediately acted on Frederick William's challenge. The bulk of the small states, and even the kings of Saxony and Hanover, expressed approval. But under Austrian pressure Bavaria, Baden, and Württemberg hesitated. Austria, whose delegates had been officially withdrawn from Frankfurt on April 5, of course, had no intention of concurring. Hence on April 21, Frederick William felt justified in announcing his outright refusal of the German crown.

When the hapless delegation returned to Frankfurt, the hope of unification had evaporated. Some governments had recalled their delegations; other members had left of their own accord. Only a small group of liberals remained, still hoping to find some way to unify Germany. In May, this rump of the old assembly was forced to leave Frankfurt, and adjourned to Stuttgart to continue for a short time its ephemeral existence. These liberal delegates felt temporarily encouraged by new waves of revolts in many parts of Germany.

THE LAST REVOLTS Once again, the radicals in Baden led the way. This time even the bulk of the army defected to the liberal forces, the grand duke fled, and a republic was proclaimed in Baden. Soon democratic uprisings—evoked by the failure of the Frankfurt experiment and by apprehension that the revolution had been lost—occurred in Saxony, Bavaria, and the Rhineland. Spurred on by socialists —including Karl Marx (1818–1883), whose newspaper *Neue Rheinische Zeitung* appeared regularly in Cologne until it was closed by the government

on May 19—workers and peasants also rose to turn these rebellions into social revolutions. The workers could justly feel that their barricades had brought them no gains.

This time Prussia showed no hesitation in applying military suppression. After putting down the revolts in the Rhineland, Prussian armies turned south. On June 18, they helped the troops of Württemberg disperse the rump assembly in Stuttgart. By July, the rebellion in Baden was crushed and the grand duchy placed under Prussian military occupation. The last rebels either fled or fell before firing squads. In Saxony, Bavaria, and the other states, the rulers firmly re-established their power.

On May 15, while this final rebellion was at its height, Frederick William once again issued a famous proclamation "to my people," in which he explained his views and justified his conduct. "Taking as a pretense the interests of Germany, the enemies of the fatherland have raised the standard of revolt to overturn the order of things established by both divine and human sanction." He explained that he had refused the emperorship because "the assembly has no right to bestow the crown without the consent of the German governments." He asserted that he had tried to reach an understanding with the assembly, but that most members had departed, and the rump was dominated by terrorists who used German unity as a pretense for "fighting the battle of godlessness, perjury, and robbery—a war against monarchy." Showing his true concept of government, he continued: "But if monarchy were overthrown, the blessings of law, liberty, and property would be doomed." Finally, he concluded that he had by no means given up hope of

unifying Germany—on his own terms —and that his government had "taken up with the more important German states the work on the German constitution begun by the Frankfurt Assembly."

The Failure of the Revolutions

All these events indicate why the revolutions failed. An excess of nationalism, of intellectual idealism, and of reliance on moderate, legal means among the Frankfurt parliamentarians; middle-class fear of social revolution, which forced the bourgeois to look to autocracy for the protection of property and social privileges; political inexperience; diffusion of aims; innate strength of the autocratic regimes—these and other explanations help interpret the failure of the unification movement and of the separate revolts in the states. Carl Schurz's observation may be correct: "The Parliament would have been sure of success in creating a constitutional German Empire, if it had performed that task quickly and elected and put into office its *Kaiser* while the revolutionary prestige of the people was still unbroken." That would have been within the first few months after the March revolutions. But, as Schurz continued, by searching for a perfect solution, these "noble, learned, conscientious, and patriotic men" of the Frankfurt assembly became bogged down in minutiae of little consequence. They lacked the "genius that promptly discerns opportunity," and were not "mindful of the fact that in times of great commotion, the history of the world does not wait for the theoretical thinker."

Moreover, the unification movement was hampered by distrust among the various states and jealousy among the

princes. During the republican revolts in the Black Forest, for instance, the army and the bourgeois of Baden, although unable to quell the revolt by themselves, did not want the aid of Württemberg troops. Above all, there was the dislike of most southerners for Prussia. When Frederick William's proclamation of March 21, regarding the possible merging of Prussia and the rest of Germany became known in the south, anti-Prussian demonstrations flared up in many states. In Stuttgart, the Prussian ruler was publicly burnt in effigy. In Munich, rioters in front of the Prussian embassy warned that "the people of Germany and the princes will rise united to repulse the dictatorship of one man." In addition, there was the continued Austro-Prussian rivalry, lessened only by Frederick William's attachment to the Hapsburgs that made him refuse to take advantage of Austria's preoccupation with its subject peoples during the greater part of 1848.

Although they describe conditions in Germany in the mid-nineteenth century, such explanations should not be interpreted as throwing light on the "German mind" or on the "nature of the German people"—an attempt lately undertaken by many historians. Instead of stressing the uniqueness of the German revolutions and attributing their failure to "German characteristics," one should recall that the revolutions in Italy, Austria, and other states failed as spectacularly, and that even the Second French Republic was abortive and led to the dictatorship of Louis Napoleon.

Despite failure, the revolutions left important legacies. All German states emerged at last with constitutions, giving the German middle class, if not actual power, at least a sense of participation. At the same time, the acrimony of socialist agitation and the violence of some uprisings had brought class hatreds into a new focus. The workers felt bitter and frustrated, while among the propertied classes, fear of the "red specter" became permanent.

It is often asserted that the legacy of the revolution included a loss of faith among the liberals that permanently colored German history. In isolated cases, this no doubt occurred. The re-establishment of conservatism after 1849 may account for the wave of pessimism and lack of self-reliance that afflicted certain groups in the succeeding two decades. But it must be remembered that the princes failed as much as the liberals. Only much later, after unification was achieved by their opponents, did many liberals feel frustration and hopelessness.

Among the legacies of 1848 were the lessons of what not to do—although one may wonder how often statesmen learn from the past. Prince William later observed that "whoever wants to rule Germany must conquer her. À la Gagern [that is, by words] it does not work." Bismarck was to reiterate this idea in his famous speech of 1862: "The great questions of the day will not be settled by speeches or by majority votes—that was the mistake of 1848 and 1849—but by blood and iron!" Thereafter it became popular to assume that the primary lesson of 1848 was that Germany could be unified only by force. In reality, such a statement foreshadows a justification for the use of force rather than a deduction from the lessons of 1848. The failures of 1848 could legitimately provide future statesmen with many guiding caveats: not to underestimate the power of the princes; to create a favorable climate among foreign pow-

ers, particularly Russia; to construct the new state with the support of the mass of the people. But it is a perversion of historical interpretation to read into these lessons a mandate for the use of force.

Prussia's Last-Minute Attempt at Unification

As Frederick William IV had proclaimed on May 15, 1849, he still hoped to unify Germany on his own terms. Radowitz elaborated a plan to unite the states into a close federation, with the king of Prussia as president of a college of princes. This proposed state, sometimes called the "Prussian Union," was to enter into a close economic and political alliance with the Austrian Empire.

At the end of May, delegates from the states met at Berlin to discuss the new scheme. Austria and Bavaria withdrew after a few days, but Saxony, Hanover, and Prussia worked out a draft constitution for the new union. Twenty-eight minor states eventually agreed to join, and arrangements were made for the convocation of a federal parliament to discuss a final constitution. Briefly it appeared as if Prussia might succeed where Frankfurt had failed.

But when elections for the federal parliament were held in January 1850, the likelihood of failure became apparent. From the beginning, Saxony and Hanover had asserted that they would enter the union only if all other German states would join. Bavaria's and Württemberg's failure even to hold elections now prompted Saxony and Hanover to boycott the scheme. Hence the federal parliament at Erfurt, opening on March 20, 1850, was attended only by delegates from Prussia and the small states. The four kingdoms—Saxony, Bavaria, Württemberg, and Hanover—and Austria remained on the side lines. The hopelessness of the scheme was further stressed by the alienation of the moderates. Prussia had meanwhile returned to thorough conservatism. The revised Prussian Constitution of January 1850 amply demonstrated the king's reawakened authoritarianism. Consequently, the Prussian delegates at Erfurt had been instructed to insist on conservative modifications of Radowitz' draft constitution. Although formally accepting the revised draft, the moderates now lost their remaining faith in the Prussian ruler. Boycotted by the four kings and distrusted by the moderates, the Prussian Union was doomed.

Prince Schwarzenberg sensed Austria's opportunity to seize the initiative from Prussia. On May 16, he recalled to Frankfurt the old Diet of the German Confederation, insisting that it had never legally ceased to exist, but had merely suspended its functions during the turbulent days of 1848. Some of the small states promptly seceded from the Prussian Union, and rejoined the old diet under Austrian leadership. But Frederick William was not ready to concede defeat. He claimed that the diet of 1815 no longer existed, and called some of the small states of his union to a meeting in Berlin. Prussia and Austria stood in clear opposition, and some believed that only war could settle the issue. In such a contest, Austria clearly held the trumps. It enjoyed the backing of Russia and the unmatched diplomatic skill of Schwarzenberg. Its armies were well prepared and strengthened by recent victories in Italy and Hungary, whereas the Prussian forces were in a poor state of training. Tension be-

tween the two states approached the breaking point over an insignificant incident in Hesse-Cassel that was skillfully exploited by Schwarzenberg. With Austrian encouragement, the autocratic duke had dismissed his liberal ministry and had begun collecting taxes without consent of the estates. When his subjects protested and even his army officers joined the opposition, the discomfited duke appealed for help to the federal diet at Frankfurt. In September, the diet, now consisting of Austria, the four kingdoms, and a few minor states, voted to uphold monarchical sovereignty, and promised the duke help against his unruly subjects. The Hessian people, however, appealed to Frederick William, and since Hesse-Cassel was in the Prussian union, the king considered its affairs within his sphere of influence.

Frederick William was baffled by the problem. Intervention in Hesse-Cassel might lead to war with Austria, and would also align Prussia on the side of rebellious subjects. Nonintervention, on the other hand, would place Prussia on the side of monarchical solidarity, but at the price of abandoning to Austria attempted leadership in Germany. Crown Prince William urged action, and Radowitz advocated boldness. Prussian troops were dispatched to Hesse. Schwarzenberg immediately prepared for war, and the frightened Frederick William sought the mediation of the tsar. A meeting in Warsaw at the end of October was attended by Nicholas, Francis Joseph, and Prince Charles of Prussia. Despite the close family ties that united Berlin and St. Petersburg, Nicholas backed Austria. Russia, dismayed by Frederick William's vacillation during the revolutionary days, by his flirtations with the liberals, and by his attempt to

weaken Denmark, awarded Austria carte blanche in Germany.

With this guarantee from Russia, Schwarzenberg acted at once. Bavarian troops were sent to Hesse in the name of the federal diet to aid the duke. If Prussian troops engaged them on the field, an Austro-Prussian war would result. On November 2, Frederick William decided to capitulate. He dismissed the aggressive Radowitz, who had been minister of foreign affairs for only a few months, and called for the resignation of Count von Brandenburg. In his stead, Otto von Manteuffel, a reactionary thoroughly opposed to war with Austria, was appointed chief minister. Schwarzenberg understood the new mood in Berlin and pressed his advantage. He demanded the dissolution of the Prussian Union as well as the evacuation of Prussian troops from Hesse. To stress his determination, he sent Austrian troops toward Hesse.

Prussia offered to negotiate, and Manteuffel and Schwarzenberg finally met at Olmütz in Bohemia on November 29. Prussia made so many concessions that this meeting is frequently called the "Humiliation of Olmütz." Prussia agreed to withdraw its troops from Hesse (with the exception of a single face-saving battalion), to recognize the re-establishment of the old federal diet under Austria's leadership, and to disband the Prussian Union. To soften Prussia's humiliation, Austria agreed to hold a conference in Dresden to discuss a possible revision of the federal statutes. But this conference, which lasted four months, proved fruitless. The diet was reconstituted in its old form, as if no revolution had occurred. In May 1851, Austria and Prussia even concluded a three year antirevolutionary alliance, whereby Prussia

promised to help Austria in case of rebellions in Italy, although Austria extended no similar guarantee regarding Prussia's subject Poles. Germany returned to a modicum of the stability that preceded the events of 1848. Clearly Prussia had lost the first round in the struggle for pre-eminence in the unification movement.

THE 1850s

The enthusiasm and idealism of the revolutionary interlude were followed by years of sober realism. Stodgy conservatism based on princely power and a duteous bureaucracy again became dominant in politics. Realism in literature turned from political interests to the life of the commercial middle classes or to bourgeois tragedies. Fear of socialism, of the revolutionary proletariat, and of radical liberalism was so pronounced that the diet annulled the Declaration of Rights of 1848 passed by the National Assembly.

But this new conservative period was not an age of reaction like that inaugurated in 1815. Industrial, commercial, and social changes and the revolutionary years had ushered in the "age of the masses." Even petty autocrats felt compelled to pay lip service to popular demands. In France, Napoleon III veiled his dictatorship with plebiscites and social paternalism. In Germany, constitutions, no matter how imperfect and restricted, endowed the governments with a semblance of popular support.

In international affairs, too, the Metternich system had disappeared. The 1815 settlement had become shaky, and the Concert of Europe had disintegrated. During the following decades, wars became the order of the day for settling international questions.

The Prussian Constitution

The year 1850 opened with Frederick William's promulgation of the final version of the Prussian Constitution, which he had revised several times during the previous year, each time making it more conservative. According to its terms, the king appointed all ministers, who would be responsible only to him. The ministers, composing the Ministry of State (*Staatsministerium*), did not form a cabinet in the British sense, but simply represented the responsible heads of the nine administrative departments of the government. The king, furthermore, had power to propose or veto legislation, and his proclamations had the force of law. At his side was a Council of State (*Staatsrat*), appointed by him and endowed with largely ornamental functions. The task of debating bills submitted by the crown and of approving all financial appropriations was entrusted to the bicameral diet (*Landtag*). The upper chamber (*Herrenhaus*) of 365 delegates was to consist of 115 hereditary lords—including former sovereigns of territories absorbed by Prussia—200 civil servants and clergymen, and 50 members appointed by the king for life, mostly city patricians, university professors, and members of professions.

The 433 delegates to the lower chamber (*Abgeordnetenhaus*) were to be elected in open ballots by indirect suffrage based on a three-class voting system. The first step occurred in the primary electoral districts, in which one elector was to be chosen for every 250 inhabitants. Here all qualified male voters over the age of twenty-four were

divided into three groups on the basis of direct tax payments. Those paying one third of the taxes were assigned to the first voting category, those paying the second third to the second category, and all others—including those paying no taxes—to the third category. Each of the three categories voted for the same number of electors. Under this system, the category with the highest tax assessment in a given district often was composed of only one or two individuals, while the group with the lowest tax assessment normally included the bulk of the population. The upper two categories together controlled two thirds of the votes in the primary districts, but represented only an estimated 17 percent of the electorate. The remaining 83 percent of the population possessed only one third of the votes. In the second step of the voting procedure, the elected representatives of the three groups in turn voted by absolute majority for one delegate to be sent to the lower house of the parliament—a device that further tended to underfranchise the lower-income groups.

This intricate system, which remained in effect until World War I, was, of course, designed to exclude the liberals from the parliament. During most of the 1850s, when many liberals sulked under the dull repression of Frederick William's regime and boycotted the elections, the three-class scheme produced the desired effect: conservative majorities dominated the parliament. But when the liberals again took hope in 1858 after the retirement of the king, the sociological miscalculations inherent in the system became apparent. Liberalism, it turned out, was concentrated in the well-to-do middle class, which was comfortably represented under the three-class vote.

The conservative peasantry, numerous but not wealthy, had been largely disenfranchised, on the other hand. Hence even this system produced liberal majorities in the years after 1858, even though it always underfranchised the proletariat.

The Last Years of Frederick William's Reign

The conservative tenor of the 1850 constitution reinforced the Manteuffel regime. While the king became more estranged from his people, Manteuffel developed a system based on tyrannical pettiness and degradation. Eavesdropping and police surveillance, arbitrary arrest of liberals, censorship of the press, and political favoritism for the nobility marked his administration. The Junkers again enjoyed unlimited esteem, and were even given back some feudal powers over the peasants on their estates. In 1854, the constitution was again altered toward greater conservatism. Public meetings were prohibited and political clubs dissolved. A new school regulation instructed teachers that the main aim of education was to impart to students Christianity, patriotism, and love of their king.

The stultifying atmosphere of the Manteuffel regime evoked disgust rather than rebellion. Because of the numerous restrictions, political parties as such could not be formed, but likeminded groups built a basis for future party life by forming around certain influential newspapers. The ultraconservatives gathered around the *Kreuzzeitung*, of which Bismarck had been a founder in 1848. The more moderate monarchists, including Prince William, the heir to the throne, assembled under the banner of the *Preussische Wochenblatt*. The harassed liberals for the

moment had no such standard-bearer.

Despite political oppression, Prussia made phenomenal strides in its economic expansion. Growing industrialization, banking, and communications made it more prosperous and economically sound. This was also reflected in Prussia's foreign trade. The *Zollverein* not only survived the troublesome revolutionary years but emerged more successful than ever. By 1853, most of the recalcitrant states had joined. Only Austria and five others stayed out. Because of Prussia's low tariffs, Vienna could neither afford to join the customs union nor succeed in breaking it up by luring the southern states out of their profitable arrangement. Hence the Zollverein assumed importance as a unifying factor on the basis of *Kleindeutschland.*

Conservatism also marked Prussia's foreign policy during the 1850s. The decade opened with a temporary settlement of the Danish problem. In March 1849, Denmark had broken the armistice of Malmö. Three months of inconclusive fighting by the Prussian army and Schleswig-Holstein volunteers against Danish forces had finally led to a second armistice in July 1849, followed by a peace treaty with Denmark, which Prussia concluded in the name of all Germany. But the rebels continued to defy Copenhagen, and Austria, once again a champion of monarchical authority, insisted on quelling the disorders. At Olmütz Prussia was forced to concur with Schwarzenberg's scheme. The federal diet in Frankfurt was authorized to restore order in Schleswig-Holstein, and Austro-Prussian troops and commissioners were sent to the duchies to help Denmark subdue the rebels. Against such formidable opposition, the rebellion collapsed, and in 1852 the great powers gathered in London to settle the international aspect of the problem (see page 58). The conclusion of the Danish episode demonstrated the change in Prussian policy. In 1848–1849, Prussia had fought on the side of the duchies for the sake of German nationalism. After Olmütz, it threw its weight into the opposite camp to uphold monarchical sovereignty and suppress the rebellious subjects.

Frederick William's next problem in foreign affairs stemmed from the Crimean War (1854–1856). His mind was already clouded by approaching insanity and his policy was unsure. Despite Russia's unfriendly attitude in 1850, Frederick William could not conceal his admiration for Nicholas I, whom he called "one of the noblest of men, . . . one of the truest hearts, and . . . one of the greatest rulers." Consequently he was disturbed when England and France sided with Turkey to make war on Russia. He was also horrified on religious grounds at the "help which England in unchristian folly gives to Islam against Christians."

But, afraid that Napoleon III might violate the Rhineland borders, Frederick William did not dare aid Russia. Although both England and Russia wooed him, he remained on the side lines. At one point he was ready to help England if it guaranteed the Rhineland against French attack. At another, he became anti-British when he heard rumors that England and France might stir up revolutions in Austria if the latter did not join the war against Russia. When free shipping on the Danube was threatened by Russia's occupation of the Danubian Principalities, he agreed to a defensive alliance with Austria, but at the same time made sure that this action would not antagonize Russia.

In the end, Prussia's neutrality had advantages as well as disadvantages. The inactivity entailed a serious loss of prestige, so that Berlin hardly figured at the peace conference in Paris in 1856. On the other hand, benevolent neutrality gained Prussia the gratitude of Alexander II, who ascended the throne of Russia in 1855. It marked the beginning of a switch in Russian policy from a pro-Austrian stand to renewed friendship with Prussia, a shift that was to be of vital importance in the decade of the 1860s.

Incipient Decline of Austria

Austria made an astonishing recovery from the revolutions that had almost destroyed it. Outwardly the nation appeared as powerful in 1850 as it had in the days of Metternich; internally its system was rotting. After Prince Schwarzenberg's death in 1852, Alexander von Bach (1813–1893) assumed the work of governmental centralization, as minister of the interior. The Constitution of 1849 was revoked, and the Viennese bureaucracy ruled the sprawling empire, with the support of army and police. The subject peoples, especially the unruly Hungarians, were everywhere suppressed and the German minority was entrusted with ruling power. The emperor and his ministers openly catered to the nobility, the army, and the clergy, who had all helped overcome the revolution. A new concordat concluded with the papacy in 1855 awarded wide powers over education and financial support to the Church.

But this Bach system, as it was called, produced neither administrative efficiency nor financial solvency. The subject populations were momentarily quiescent but unreconciled to their fate. And unlike Prussia, Austria failed to make decisive economic strides.

In foreign relations, Austria was also unsuccessful. In 1849 and 1850, after the collapse of the rebellions, it joined Russia in demanding from Turkey extradition of Kossuth and other Hungarian rebels given asylum in the Ottoman Empire. When Britain and France threatened war unless the Austro-Russians withdrew their demand, the latter complied. Their vindictive request thus brought them nothing but the scorn of the western powers.

The disputes over Russian influence in Turkey, which led to the Crimean War, placed Austria in a difficult position. Nicholas at first expected that Austria would side with him in gratitude for his help in subduing the Hungarian rebellion. But Schwarzenberg supposedly remarked in 1849, "We will astonish the world by our ingratitude," and Emperor Francis Joseph fulfilled this prediction. Austria tried to protect its Danube interests by leaning toward England and France and making a defensive alliance with Prussia, but to the western allies these maneuvers smacked of duplicity. Repeatedly Austria mobilized its forces to threaten Russia's flank, but in the end remained neutral.

The Crimean War brought Austria no benefits; instead, it hastened Austrian decline. Austrian finances had been strained through mobilization and the country had become isolated among the European powers. Its diplomatic equivocation made it suspect to England and France, and its anti-Russian attitude made it permanently lose the friendship of the tsar. Estrangement from Russia and political isolation from the West became of paramount importance during the subsequent decade, when Austria was toppled from its pinnacle by France and Prussia.

The Unification Period, 1858–1871

BEGINNING OF A NEW ERA

The years 1858–1859 opened a new era in German history, which impelled the gradual disintegration of the Austrian Empire, and pointed toward the ultimate triumph of Prussia. These years were marked by the end of ultraconservatism in Prussia, the first of a series of military defeats for Austria, and the revitalization of German nationalism. The period began with a change of leadership in Prussia. /

The Accession of William I

The health of King Frederick William IV had been failing for some time. Attacks of insanity finally forced him to appoint his brother William as regent. Although the mentally deranged Frederick William lived another three years, William in fact assumed complete control of the government in 1858 and ultimately became king in 1861, as William I.

Born in 1797, William had partici-

pated in the final battles of the Wars of Liberation as a lad of seventeen, and thereafter spent a lifetime in service to his beloved army. After becoming a general in 1825, he trained troops, served on army commissions, and became better versed in military affairs than any other Hohenzollern ruler since Frederick the Great. During the Revolution of 1848, the conservative prince had been temporarily exiled to England, but he had returned in time to participate in the counterrevolution of 1849 by commanding the Prussian troops sent to quell revolts in Baden. After 1850, he obtained some administrative experience by acting as governor of the Rhineland and Westphalian provinces.

William believed in monarchical untouchability, but he lacked the romantic and reactionary tendencies of his brother. His conservatism had become more moderate, and more appropriate to the times. He accepted the existence of a parliament and constitutionalism as unalterable, albeit unpleasant, facts

of his reign, and was willing to work with them, provided they did not impinge on the honor of the Hohenzollern dynasty and the Prussian army. In political matters, foreign as well as internal, he trusted bold action more than had his vacillating predecessor, and he usually followed a course with perseverance and determination. Vital decisions in German history during the succeeding several decades are usually credited to Bismarck. Although this view is largely true, even a Bismarck could have achieved little without the support of a determined ruler. In view of Bismarck's aim of unifying Germany, William's main failing was that throughout his life he remained more Prussian than German.

A sigh of relief throughout Prussia greeted William's assumption of power in 1858. The sixty-one-year-old prince, a shrewd judge of character, immediately dismissed the reactionary Otto von Manteuffel. He refused to appoint the vehement Otto von Bismarck, who was ambitiously hoping to become chief minister, and instead chose the moderate Prince Anthony of Hohenzollern-Sigmaringen (1811–1885), the head of the Catholic branch of the dynasty. All political groups, except the ultraconservatives, were pleased by this appointment. The parliamentary elections of 1859 showed the result. With the reestablishment of civil liberties, the liberals ceased their boycott of elections, and voting resulted in a majority for the moderately liberal representatives. Only one action by the new ruler warned the liberals of impending conflicts. William knew from experience the relatively poor state of training and organization of the Prussian army. He promptly appointed as minister of war the conservative Count Albert von

Roon (1803–1879), a close friend and adviser of Bismarck's. Roon in turn made General Helmuth von Moltke (1800–1891) chief of the Prussian General Staff. Together with Roon and Moltke, William soon embarked on army reforms that enabled Prussia to win the wars of the 1860s, but engendered the most vehement conflict in its constitutional history.

The Italian War of 1859

A second event that ushered in the new era was the Italian War of 1859. Largely for reasons of prestige, Napoleon III had agreed to help Sardinia dislodge Austria from northern Italy, provided the Viennese government could be made to look like the aggressor. Despite British and Russian efforts at mediation, Austria actually blundered into declaring war on Sardinia, and the French emperor fulfilled his promise of aid. The campaigns against the Franco-Sardinian forces, fought in Lombardy, went badly for Austria. It evacuated the province, although its armies were not destroyed in the field. Clearly Austria lacked the leadership and determination shown in 1848 and 1849, and after a campaign of barely three months, Austria and France agreed on an armistice.

It is interesting that both Napoleon and Francis Joseph desired a rapid termination of hostilities because of the attitude of Prussia. The war had evoked much sympathy for Austria among southern Germans, and had rekindled the fear that Napoleon III might violate the Rhineland border in a repetition of the campaigns of his uncle, Napoleon I. Prussia had taken advantage of this anti-French mood and begun to mobilize its troops. William

had offered military aid to Austria on the condition that Prussia be allowed to command all the troops of the German Confederation in the war against France. Vienna, however, feared that consent to such a stipulation would represent abandonment of its own preeminent position in Germany. Hence it refused and hastened to make peace with France. As Moltke later remarked, "Austria would rather give up Lombardy than see Prussia at the head of Germany." Austria and France concluded a peace whereby Lombardy was ceded to Sardinia and the way opened for Italian unification. The dismemberment of Austria had begun, and in accordance with previous agreements between Napoleon and Cavour of Sardinia, France was enlarged by the addition of Nice and Savoy.

The effects of this war on Germany were manifold. The dismemberment of the Austrian Empire in Italy raised hopes among Austria's other subject populations and weakened its international prestige. At the same time, Austro-Prussian rivalry, dormant since the days of Olmütz, was revived. French successes also gave a boost to German nationalism, which had been fairly quiescent during the 1850s.

Above all, the victory of little Sardinia and the initial steps toward uniting Italy acted like an electric shock on the German unification movement. State governments resumed discussion of possible schemes for union. Groups of former members of the Frankfurt Assembly met to devise new plans. In 1859, the Hanoverian Rudolf von Bennigsen (1824–1902) founded the *Nationalverein* (National Association), which was to play a vital role in the creation of a united Germany. Everywhere, it seemed, liberals revived their

hopes. Extreme conservatism was weakened by the loss of Frederick William IV and by the failure of the Austrian experiment with centralization. Even southern liberals, although still pro-Austrian and suspicious of Prussia, began to conclude that unification under Prussia's new ruler might be the only feasible, if not the best, solution. And applying the lessons of Italy to the problem of German unity, the radicals proclaimed that "Austria must be crushed, dismembered, destroyed, . . . its ashes . . . strewn to the four winds!" They reasoned that "the executioners of Italy are also our oppressors, and our freedom requires separation from Austria."

The Prussian Army Reform and the Constitutional Struggle

The feverish revival of the unification movement and of liberal aspirations formed the background for Prussia's constitutional struggle that led to the appointment of Bismarck as head of the Prussian ministry. This struggle arose over William's and Roon's determination to reorganize the Prussian army. [1]

For many reasons the army was in need of reform. It was still organized on principles developed during the Napoleonic campaigns, even though Prussia's population had nearly doubled and its military requirements had vastly altered since 1815. The mobilization of 1859 had shown the army's inefficiency and there were many besides William, in both Prussia and other states, who agreed that the renewed French menace and the impending task of unifying Germany demanded an effective military force.

Roon proposed to increase the

peacetime strength of the army from 150,000 to 213,000 men, and to enforce the legal three-year period of compulsory service for recruits, which had not been applied because of lack of funds. He wanted to reduce total liability for service from nineteen to sixteen years, placing men three years on active duty with the line forces, then four years in the stand-by reserve, followed by nine years in the *Landwehr*—an emergency reserve force. Above all, the *Landwehr,* more democratic in composition and rules of conduct, was to be placed under stricter supervision by the regular army. Finally, the minister of war wished to supply the forces with up-to-date equipment, in particular the breech-loading needle gun, which could be loaded and fired in the prone position and thus revolutionize infantry fighting.

When these proposals were submitted to the lower chamber in the spring of 1860, they were voted down by the liberals and moderates, who commanded a majority. The Progressives—as the new moderate liberal party was called—admitted the need for an efficient and enlarged military establishment but opposed the Prussian style of militarism. At heart, they wanted a "parliamentary army," which could become a pillar of a more liberal and popular regime. Moreover, they were not averse to using the reform issue as a lever for extracting constitutional concessions from the king, in particular a decrease in the power of the upper chamber. Consequently, they refused to approve the proposed enforcement of three years of service for recruits and the contemplated tighter control over the *Landwehr*.

Although the diet possessed legislative powers, the king could have legally circumvented the legislature's rejection of the army bill by issuing a royal proclamation. But the projected reforms required additional funds, and the lower chamber had the power of granting or withholding taxes. William was in a quandary. He regarded the army as being solely under the jurisdiction of the crown, and thought the parliament's duty was to vote the required funds without attaching strings. The revolutionary days had shown that without control of a reliable army, the entire monarchical structure would be in jeopardy. And William was convinced that a semi-independent bourgeois-oriented *Landwehr* might be easily subverted, and that a three-year period of service was needed to indoctrinate recruits in proper allegiance to the crown.

Rebuffed by the diet, the government withdrew the reform bill and simply requested additional appropriations in the general budget. When these were granted, Roon commenced his reforms. The same maneuver was repeated in 1861, although this time the parliamentarians were aware that the government was circumventing their powers, and approved the larger budget only by a scant majority. New elections in the winter produced an even greater majority for the liberal forces, and when the crown tried in early 1862 to outwit the diet by the same scheme, it met defeat. The lower chamber refused to approve the budget without a detailed breakdown. William rejected this demand, which would have implied parliamentary control not merely over the army but over the entire executive. He dissolved the lower chamber and called for new elections.

When the elections of 1862 increased

liberal representation, the constitutional struggle reached an impasse. William, now king in his own right, contemplated abdication rather than submission to the will of the parliament. "I will not reign," he is supposed to have stated, "if I cannot do it in such a fashion as I can be answerable for to God, my conscience, and my subjects." But Roon advised him instead to request Bismarck to lead the struggle against the parliament. Bismarck was quickly recalled from his post as ambassador to France, and when he promised to advocate reorganization of the army "in opposition to the majority in parliament," William agreed "to continue the battle and . . . not to abdicate." Bismarck was thereupon appointed chief minister. The so-called era of incipient liberalism was ended and Prussia fell under the shadow of a new spirit.

BISMARCK'S INITIAL WORK

Early Career

Otto Eduard Leopold von Bismarck-Schönhausen (1815–1898) was a tall, robust Junker from Brandenburg, the son of a middle-class mother and an estate owner of petty though ancient nobility. He had received a good education at the universities of Göttingen and Berlin, and had acquired an astonishing fluency in French and English that facilitated his later diplomatic career. At the age of twenty-one he entered the Prussian civil service, but his arrogant love of independence and hatred of city life with its "stink of civilization," as he called it, soon filled him with disgust and contempt for the career of a bureaucrat. He withdrew to his estate to indulge in boisterous drinking and to try his hand

in rural management. He loved the country life of a gentleman farmer, and was proud of being "no democrat," but of being "born and raised as an aristocrat."

In 1845 he represented his district and his class in the provincial diet and two years later became involved in general Prussian politics, as a member of the United Diet. On this brief occasion, he emerged on the national political scene as a staunch defender of monarchical conservatism and a loyal supporter of the king, whom he later called "'the central point of all my thinking and all my actions." His speeches on behalf of royal absolutism were precise in thought and distinguished in language, but suffered from poor delivery and an excessive amount of sarcasm.

From that time he remained in public service and in politics, although he frequently spoke of his desire to retire to his estate. In 1848 he served in the Prussian assembly, and the following year became a member of the lower chamber in the Prussian diet. Frederick William, though grateful for such loyal support, was somewhat fearful of the vehemence of the "terrible Junker," and hesitated to offer him a major post. However, in 1850 Bismarck was sent to the Erfurt Parliament, and from 1851 to 1859 served as Prussian envoy to the federal diet at Frankfurt. While at Frankfurt, Bismarck kept up his political connections in Prussia, continuing as a member of the lower chamber in the Prussian diet until 1852, when the king appointed him to the upper chamber. Finally, in 1859, the new regent of Prussia made Bismarck ambassador to Russia, and in 1862 transferred him to the court of Napoleon III.

Hence when in September 1862 Bis-

marck was made minister-president and minister of foreign affairs, he was well prepared for his new post. Through his various positions, his frequent travels, and his correspondence, he had become well acquainted with conditions in Prussia, in the German Confederation, and at key capitals of the world. Through his years at Frankfurt, he knew most of the influential officials in the other German states. The Prussian king had sent him on special missions to Vienna and other capitals. And although only an ambassador, Bismarck had frequently tried to influence Prussia's foreign policy through memoranda and advice, which he freely dispatched to his home government. His training and experiences had thus made him ready to become what Carl Schurz called "a veritable Atlas carrying upon his shoulders the destinies of a great nation."

As borne out in his later actions when in control in Prussia and Germany, his experiences provided him with a keener interest in foreign than in domestic affairs. His work in the various Prussian parliaments had instilled in him not only a deep hatred of parliamentarianism, but also the conviction that foreign affairs were generally more important than domestic matters. His letters, dispatches, and conversations of the 1850s show the keen grasp of foreign relations that helped him become one of the most skilled manipulators of diplomatic crises in his time.

Ideas on Government and Unification

The ideas he expressed before 1862 on Prussia's foreign relations are of interest since they foreshadow his later actions. His work at Frankfurt made him fully aware of the unsatisfactory functioning of the federal diet. In the end, he looked upon the German Confederation as then organized as "an oppressive and sometimes perilous tie" for Prussia. He repeatedly advocated that either the federal framework be altered, or Prussia's relations to the diet changed before it had to be transformed *"ferro et igni"*—a favorite expression of Bismarck's, meaning "by iron and fire."

His experiences at the diet also changed his earlier admiration for the Hapsburgs to distrust of Austria. He gradually came to suspect the sincerity of every Austrian proposal and finally became convinced of the inevitability of "a death struggle" between Prussia and Austria. For an eventual war with Austria, Prussia needed allies, and Bismarck scanned the international horizon. Repeatedly he seized on Russia as a logical candidate. He considered a pact with Russia "the cheapest among all continental alliances," since Prussia could obtain it without sacrificing vital interests. During the Crimean War, he warned against siding with Britain and France, and thereafter he continued to insist on friendly relations with the tsar.

On relations with France, his views were more ambivalent. Always a pragmatist in politics, he derided his colleagues who objected to cooperation with France because of Napoleon's revolutionary background. He pointed out that many European thrones were not truly "legitimate," and that many other nations were imperialistic. In international politics he felt that "standards of morality and justice" could hardly serve as criteria for action. Bismarck did not fear France, nor did he trust Napoleon. But he perceived advantages in smiling at France with-

out committing Prussia to a full-fledged alliance. During the Austro-French War over Italy, he was pleased to see France weaken Austria. When the regent mobilized Prussian troops against France, Bismarck dispatched memoranda to Berlin objecting to support for Austria and even suggesting military aid to France in order to crush Vienna once and for all.

Bismarck's lukewarm preference for France was also conditioned by his knowledge of the prevailing mood in southern Germany. This area had always looked for outside support to either Vienna or Paris. In a Prussian struggle against Austria, the southern states might be more at ease if Prussia and France were at least tacit friends.

Most significant among Bismarck's early suggestions to the foreign office was his insistence on flexibility in international commitments. Diplomatic planning should always open onto two possible courses. The opponent could be permitted to guess both plans as long as he could not ascertain which would ultimately be followed. He objected to the dull rigidity with which foreign affairs had been conducted under Frederick William IV, and suggested a pragmatic and flexible approach, which under his own direction later sometimes bordered on sheer opportunism.

Although a Prussian Junker to his marrow, Bismarck had extended his horizon through his political apprenticeship in Frankfurt and at foreign courts. He did not lose his "Prussian national consciousness," as he called it, yet unlike many of his fellow Junkers, he recognized the contributions that other German states and German national feeling as a whole could furnish to a united Germany. But apart

from his conviction that Austria should be expelled from Germany and that this would probably require force, prior to 1862 he produced few specific ideas on the subject of unification. That Prussia would have to assume leadership in Germany Bismarck did not doubt, but how this could be accomplished was not yet clear.

Many historians, relying excessively on Bismarck's own memoirs written in the 1890s, ascribe to the Prussian minister an almost Mephistophelean adroitness in manipulating the diplomatic chessboard to obtain his ends. They infer that, from the outset, Bismarck planned the myriad steps required for the unification of Germany, including each of the three wars that Prussia was to fight in the 1860s. Everything, according to these writers, fits into a neat pattern the chancellor had worked out in advance. Actually this is part of the legend that Bismarck delighted in bequeathing to posterity. Bismarck was a masterful diplomat, a sagacious judge of men and situations, but his success derived not from adherence to a rigid pattern—a political behavior he rejected as unsound—but from brilliant improvisations. With more speed and perspicacity than most of his opponents possessed, Bismarck could assess a new situation and decide on a successful course of action. Herein lay Bismarck's success.

Bismarck's Solution to the Constitutional Struggle in Prussia

In his first speech to the budget committee of the Prussian diet after his appointment as minister-president, Bismarck said prophetically: "The eyes of Germany are not fixed upon Prussia's liberalism, but upon her armed

might." In another speech, he remarked: "Our strength cannot spring from cabinet or newspaper politics, but only from the actions of a great armed power." He thus announced his determination to support the king and Roon in the proposed army reforms at the price of destroying liberalism and constitutional government. He authorized collection of taxes without a budget and without parliamentary approval, thereby enabling the army to continue its reorganization.

To the Prussian diet he showed no willingness to compromise. He scornfully asked the parliamentarians: "Are we to be ruled monarchically like a great power, or, as conceivable for a mere small state, by professors, judges, and small town politicians?" When informed by the delegates that they represented the will of the people, he advised them that true statesmen mold public opinion rather than being influenced by it. When the diet persisted in its refusal to grant funds, he dismissed the lower chamber, to the applause of the conservative minority. There was much agitation throughout Prussia, and most of the press vituperated against Bismarck's highhanded actions. Even King William feared a revolution. But Bismarck felt secure and pursued his chosen course.

When the diet reconvened in January 1863, it reiterated its refusal to approve the budget. Once again Bismarck lectured the delegates in a famous speech. He contended that the constitution of 1850 provided no solution in case of conflict between the crown and parliament. "Necessity alone is the determining factor," and Bismarck reasoned that since the state must continue to exist and requires funds for its existence, the state also has the right to collect taxes, regardless of the attitude of parliament. When the parliamentarians protested and criticism grew louder, Bismarck resorted to sterner measures. In June he again dismissed the diet and called for new elections. Strict censorship was reimposed, liberals were imprisoned, and the civil service was purged of those who showed open sympathy with the representatives. The repressive atmosphere of the 1850s returned. A few advocated refusal to pay taxes. Accused of sedition, they were thrown into jail. The moderate forces, including Crown Prince Frederick, publicly complained about the return of unlimited authoritarianism, but the civil service and the army supported the king, and William in turn stood behind his chancellor. The old Prussian combination of power had been revived, taxes continued to be paid, and there was no open rebellion.

The divergence between public opinion and the government can be seen in the results of the new elections of October 1863. The country sent to Berlin an even more liberal representation, which proved as frustrated and powerless as its predecessor in the face of the crown's determination. The deadlock was to continue for another three years, but starting in 1864, Bismarck and Prussia became increasingly involved in foreign affairs; and because of his success in the foreign arena, his arrogant treatment of the Prussian diet was less and less criticized.

First Successes in Foreign Affairs

RELATIONS WITH RUSSIA A few months after assuming power, Bismarck had an opportunity for implementing his pro-Russian policy. In

1862, Emperor Alexander II had whetted the appetite of the freedom-minded Poles by granting them increased political rights. Not satisfied by the tsar's offers, Polish radicals demanded complete independence and began an insurrection in January 1863. Rather than grant more concessions, Alexander sent his army to beat down the rebellion. Polish uprisings in the nineteenth century, especially after the revolutions of 1830 and 1848, always attracted the sentimental interest of Europe. It was not surprising, therefore, that England, France, and Austria sent protests to the tsar concerning the repressions in Poland. These protests, of course, were not serious, since France was then occupied in Mexico, England showed no interest in active intervention, and Austria was unlikely to desire a free Poland that could become a rallying point for its own Polish subject populations. Yet the tsar resented the interference in what he considered his own affairs.

Bismarck, however, refused to join the European powers. Instead he dispatched Count Constantin von Alvensleben to St. Petersburg to offer Prussian aid against the rebels. In February 1863, by the Convention of Alvensleben, Prussia agreed to mobilize troops along its Polish border to prevent the spread of the revolution and, if called upon, to assist Alexander in his territory. By May Russia had crushed the revolt without Prussian military aid, but the tsar was grateful to Bismarck, and Russia's friendship was to be of value to Prussia during the ensuing decade.

Bismarck's action had not been designed merely to gain Russia's friendship. As early as 1848 he had remarked that an "independent Poland would

be the irreconcilable enemy of Prussia." And a successful rebellion in Russian Poland might all too easily provoke a smilar rising of Poles in Prussia's eastern territories. The Prussian conservatives and Junkers, for their part, were delighted with Bismarck's action, whereas the liberals deplored Prussia's realignment on the side of autocratic Russia.

AUSTRO-PRUSSIAN RIVALRY IN THE EARLY 1860s After the war with France in 1859 and the loss of Lombardy, the Austrian Empire once again seemed at the brink of collapse. Its financial resources were depleted and its subject populations quivered with unrest. It was symptomatic that the Hungarians had sent volunteers to help the Italians against Austria. Moreover, Austria's prestige in Germany had suffered through the Italian debacle.

To strengthen Austria's internal structure, Emperor Francis Joseph experimented with a slight relaxation of centralized authoritarianism. He took as his minister Anton Schmerling, the comparatively liberal lawyer who had served as minister of foreign affairs in the Frankfurt provisional government of 1848. In October of 1860, Schmerling issued the "Diploma," which instituted a measure of decentralization by granting local rule to the former diets. Since these diets were not based on national divisions but on feudal arrangements, the Diploma satisfied none of the aspirations of the subject peoples and proved unworkable. In 1861, the emperor produced a different plan, the "February Patent," providing for a central parliament of the empire based on an electoral system in which classes rather than regions were to be represented. It was a renewal of the old

Hapsburg hope of governing the multifarious empire with the support of the upper classes of the various peoples.

The central parliament worked fairly smoothly, although the Hungarian deputies were ominously absent. Hungary had been promised re-establishment of its own parliament with supreme powers over the Magyar lands. Since the emperor was unwilling to implement this concession, the Hungarians continued their passive opposition, which vitiated the whole new system. Hence in the long run, the February Patent too, proved a failure, and Vienna resorted to its tried methods of absolutist repression of the local nationalities.

Despite internal instability, Austria attempted to enter the German scene more actively. In 1861, Prussia had proposed revisions of the federal constitution to entrust more power to the federal diet. The attempt was thwarted, but continued submission of similar proposals finally goaded Vienna into action. In August 1863, Francis Joseph summoned to Frankfurt a congress of all German princes to discuss a reform of the diet. Since King William and Bismarck were at the time occupied with the Prussian constitutional struggle, the emperor thought his proposals would encounter little opposition. The king of Saxony in person delivered the invitation to William, who considered it unwise and impolite to refuse. Bismarck, however, thought otherwise: attendance by the king of Prussia at such a conference would enhance the prestige of Austria and possibly spoil the chances of German unification under Prussian auspices. Bismarck's reasoning finally prevailed over the king.

When the conference opened, it was attended by all German states except Prussia. Vienna proposed the establishment of a tighter union, governed by a directory of five princes under the presidency of Austria. A parliament of deputies was to be established, with members drawn from the diets of the various states. Always more suspicious of Prussian than of Austrian intentions, the princes accepted the proposal in principle. But the absence of Prussia killed all chances of success, and the plan remained a dead letter.

Immediately thereafter Bismarck made a countermove that evoked astonishment and even cynical derision. He proposed that the German parliament of deputies should not be drawn from the state diets, but should represent all of Germany on the basis of universal suffrage. Since Bismarck was at the time locked in battle with Prussia's diet—which was not elected by equal suffrage, but based on the three-class vote—his proposal was considered insincere by many Germans and ridiculed by the Prussian liberals. But as he proved in 1867, when establishing the Reichstag of the North German Confederation on the basis of universal male suffrage, Bismarck was not in principle opposed to such a representative body for Germany. In fact, he considered such a body the only sound basis for uniting German public opinion, provided it had no real power over the executive. Moreover, his proposal was an example of masterful diplomacy. It was bound to let Prussia take the initiative from Austria, which on principle and in practice could not allow universal suffrage. And it was likely to mitigate some of the distrust felt by German liberals for Prussian authoritarianism. His proposal was, of course, rejected, but it helped

put Austria once again on the sidelines.

THE DANISH PROBLEM After the Prusso-Danish War of 1848–1849, the Danish problem had in theory been settled by the London Protocol of 1852, subscribed to by England, France, Russia, Prussia, Austria, Denmark, and Sweden, but not by the German federal diet (see pages 36, 46, and Map 11). Since King Frederick VII had no heirs, the protocol vested succession to the Danish crown as well as to the duchies of Schleswig and Holstein in Christian of Glücksburg, a relative of the king through the female line. It also guaranteed the integrity of the existing Danish boundaries, and stipulated that Holstein would remain in the German Confederation and at the same time enjoy autonomy within the Danish Kingdom. The Augustenburg claimant was indemnified for his lost expectancy of the duchies by a monetary payment. For the moment all participants seemed content, except for the heirs of the Augustenburg line and the nationalists at the Frankfurt diet, both of whom withheld their consent to the protocol.

But the problem was far from settled. During the 1850s, King Frederick VII and the Danish nationalists repeatedly tried to integrate the duchies into the Danish monarchy. A revised, more centralizing constitution for Denmark was to be applied also to Schleswig and Holstein. These attempts invariably resulted in unrest in the duchies and in appeals to the German Confederation, which forced the Danish king to postpone his plans under threat of war. The Frankfurt diet also warned Frederick against separating the two duchies, although legally only Holstein could claim some form of German protection. But despite English and French admonitions to exercise caution, the Danish king submitted to his parliament in March 1863 a bill stipulating that the new Danish constitution would apply to Schleswig, and that Holstein, although remaining semiautonomous, would have to pay national taxes to the Danish state. When he rejected German demands to withdraw these proposals, the diet at Frankfurt voted for federal execution against Denmark and called on Hanover and Saxony for military action.

Six weeks later, King Frederick VII suddenly died. In accordance with the London Protocol, he was succeeded by Christian IX of Glücksburg. The new ruler was as nationalistic as his predecessor, and with the support of parliament, he proceeded to incorporate Schleswig into his kingdom. An outburst of indignation shook the duchies and large segments of German nationalists. At the same time, Duke Frederick of Augustenburg disclaimed his father's renunciation and styled himself the rightful ruler of Schleswig-Holstein. Prussia and Austria hesitated, but the German diet, not being a signatory to the London Protocol, dispatched Hanoverian and Saxon troops into Holstein and Lauenburg, which were both federal territories. With the support of the German diet, the Holsteiners then proclaimed Frederick of Augustenburg their ruler on the theory that the Salic Law did not recognize succession through the female line and thereby voided King Christian's legal title to the duchy. They also talked of complete secession from Denmark. To avoid conflict with the German forces, Danish troops were temporarily withdrawn from Holstein.

The course of the crisis depended largely on the attitude of Austria and Prussia. Austria actually had no direct interest in the northern duchies, but its desire not to let Prussia derive any advantage from the situation drew it irretrievably into the crisis. As an initial step, Bismarck decided to uphold the London Protocol and persuaded the court of Vienna that the duke of Augustenburg, whom the federal diet had recognized, represented a revolutionary element. Jointly Vienna and Berlin then recognized King Christian IX, an action that complied with the stipulations of the London Protocol. Throughout Germany, Bismarck's recognition of King Christian was decried as a betrayal of German national interests. The federal diet had hoped to bring about the secession of both Schleswig and Holstein from Denmark and their consolidation into a new federal German state under the duke of Augustenburg. But Bismarck had different ideas. The creation of a new small state that might side with the other petty principalities in opposing Prussian leadership could hardly appeal to him. Moreover, he wanted Prussia to be free to act independently and not become a mere executor for the will of the Frankfurt diet, as had happened in 1848. Ultimately he hoped to find some way whereby both duchies, or at least Holstein with Lauenburg, could be annexed to Prussia. Their acquisition would furnish Prussia an outlet to the North Sea, the important Baltic port of Kiel, control of the mouth of the vital Elbe River, and greater commercial pressure on Hanover. In exaggerated respect for Bismarck's political machinations, many historians falsely look upon his intervention in the Danish affair as merely a means to destroy the

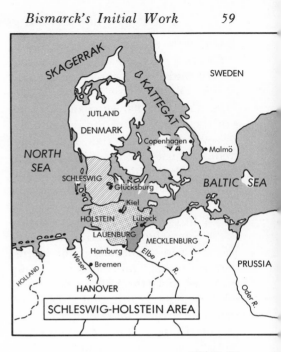

MAP 11

German Confederation, expel Austria from Germany, and bring about German unification under Prussian leadership. To be sure, the Danish crisis weakened the federal diet and eventually embarrassed Austria; but Bismarck's main aim in 1864 was the aggrandizement of Prussia.

Acting as a champion of international treaties, Bismarck made an alliance with Austria providing for joint action and the exclusion of the Frankfurt diet from further negotiations with Denmark. In January 1864, Austria and Prussia demanded that King Christian abide by the London Protocol and safeguard the semiautonomous status of the two duchies. The Frankfurt diet opposed this action because it implied a reversion to the *status quo ante*; naturally the Danish king rejected the request because it contravened the aspirations of his nationalistic supporters.

THE WAR AGAINST DENMARK   Upon Denmark's rejection of their demand, Austria and Prussia agreed on military action. On February 1, 1864, 37,000 Prussian and 23,000 Austrian troops began their invasion of the duchies. Bypassing the Hanoverian and Saxon troops, which still occupied Holstein, they invaded Schleswig and then Jutland. By April, the superior power of the Austro-Prussians had forced the Danes to evacuate their troops to the islands, and the mainland of Denmark had fallen to the invaders. The federal diet in Frankfurt, of course, was deeply disturbed, since this military action was conducted by Prussia and Austria on their own account and not in the name of the German Confederation. The powers, on the other hand, stood by while Denmark was being defeated. Napoleon was busy in Mexico; Russia was friendly to Prussia; and Britain, although worried about Denmark's independence, could hardly interfere against military action by Austria and Prussia ostensibly designed to uphold the London Protocol: it could only urge another conference.

With defeat of Denmark in sight, an armistice was made on May 12 and a conference was held in London to debate the fate of the duchies. Various suggestions were made: one was to partition Schleswig, but the intransigence of the Danes and of the German federal diet prevented agreement, much to the delight of Bismarck, who preferred a total defeat of Denmark so that he could dictate his own terms.

Fighting resumed in late June. Prussia ferried troops to the islands and was successful in several minor engagements. Realizing the hopelessness of his position, King Christian agreed to a final armistice on July 20. Bismarck now asserted that the London Protocol had lost validity and that peace was to be made solely by the three belligerents—Denmark, Austria, and Prussia. After lengthy negotiations, Denmark signed the Peace of Vienna in October 1864, whereby Schleswig, Holstein, and Lauenburg were completely detached from Denmark and ceded not to the German diet but to Austria and Prussia for their joint disposal.

Prussia had succeeded in its first maneuver: the duchies had been separated from Denmark but not combined into a new state under the duke of Augustenburg. Many unsolved problems remained, involving agreement with the federal diet and with Austria. The diet still insisted on turning the duchies into a new, independent German state. Since it could hardly expect to annex the duchies itself and it was opposed to Prussian aggrandizement, Austria, too, now favored this solution. Or else it could insist on territorial compensation, letting Prussia absorb the duchies in return for the cession of Prussian territory—perhaps in Silesia—to Austria. But Bismarck would not sanction the loss of a square foot of Prussian land. He was willing to accept the diet's proposal only on condition that the military forces of the new state would be incorporated into those of Prussia, and that its railroads and communications would be run under Prussian direction—in short, the duke of Augustenburg would be a puppet of Berlin.

Prussian determination and Austrian vacillation decided the issue on a temporary basis. Hanover withdrew its troops from Holstein, as did Saxony under threat of war from Berlin. The Austrians were then persuaded to accept the compromise Agreement of

Gastein (August 1865). Prussia was allowed to annex the tiny Duchy of Lauenburg, in return for paying 2.5 million Danish thalers to Austria. Joint sovereignty over the two large duchies was retained by Austria and Prussia, with Schleswig under temporary administration by Prussia, and Holstein under Austria. For the purpose of communications with Schleswig, Prussia was awarded two military roads through Holstein. The important harbor of Kiel, in Holstein territory, became a joint port but was put under Prussian administration. The Agreement of Gastein represented no permanent solution. Joint sovereignty over the duchies by the two rival powers was a legal fiction not likely to endure for long. Essentially the agreement favored Prussia, for Austria had abandoned its support of the duke of Augustenburg, and Prussia had attained military and economic power over the duchies. But again the Machiavellian character of the agreement is frequently exaggerated. It is said that Bismarck devised the arrangement because he knew it would embarrass Austria and make an Austro-Prussian war inevitable. Although aware that German unification under Prussia was unlikely without a military defeat of Austria, in 1865 he was primarily concerned with obtaining the duchies for Prussia, and the Gastein Agreement embodied a step in this direction.

The Beginning of Unification

The temporary settlement of the Danish problem brought Bismarck little popularity at home. Most Prussian liberals had favored the Danish War, but the victories had not been spectacular enough to convert their distrust of Bis-

marck into admiration. Hence they continued to oppose Bismarck on the issue of the army budget, even though the reorganization of the army had proved of some value in the Danish War.

Bismarck, however, paid little heed to the internal discontent. His attention was devoted to convincing King William of the inevitability of war with Austria and to making the necessary preparations for such a conflict. In the end, it proved more difficult to persuade the king than to arrange for a favorable international alignment.

FOREIGN PREPARATIONS In October 1865, Bismarck vacationed at Biarritz, and seized the opportunity to discuss German problems with Napoleon III. He hinted at the possibility of an Austro-Prussian war and tried to find out whether France would maintain benevolent neutrality. Napoleon, never the shrewdest of diplomats, was no longer at the height of his political power. The failure of the Mexican adventure, the miscarriage of his Italian plans, loss of popularity at home, together with his own failing health, seemed to make him desperate for cheap success that might restore him to glory. As a champion of the ideals of nationalism, he was not averse to the establishment of a unified German state. On the other hand, he believed in a European equilibrium that required French aggrandizement if a large German state were created beyond the Rhine. During the preceding years, Napoleon had repeatedly sent secret negotiators to Bismarck to suggest that France would not oppose Prussia's attempt to reorganize Germany, provided France obtained commensurate compensations in the Rhine-

land. At Biarritz Bismarck referred to these offers, and without committing himself, made Napoleon feel that such an arrangement could be worked out. The French emperor presumably expected any Austro-Prussian war to be long and exhausting for both sides, so that France could seize the desired Rhineland possessions while Austria and Prussia were busy fighting in the east.

Convinced of his diplomatic skill, Napoleon then offered Bismarck his mediation to bring about a Prusso-Italian alliance. From such a combination, Italy might gain Venetia, which Napoleon had failed to obtain for the Italians in the 1859 war. On the other hand, Napoleon hardly expected Prussia to derive much military support from such an alliance.

With Prussia's right flank reasonably secure, Bismarck concentrated on the Italian alliance. Negotiations between Turin and Berlin were protracted, for the Italians distrusted Bismarck, and King William was loathe to make an alliance with a foreign power against Austria, which he still considered a German state. In the end, William contented himself with striking from the draft treaty a clause that would have required Italy to declare war also on the south German states should they side with Austria in the impending conflict. The offensive and defensive alliance between Prussia and Italy was signed in April 1866. Italy promised to declare war on Austria and not sign a separate peace, provided war between Prussia and Austria broke out within three months of the signing of the treaty. In return, Italy was to obtain Venetia.

Thus by the spring of 1866, Bismarck had completed his preparations.

Roon's army stood ready, Russia's friendship had been assured, and French neutrality more or less certain. He had even found in Italy a welcome ally for keeping a number of Austrian divisions engaged south of the Alps.

APPROACH OF THE AUSTRO-PRUSSIAN DUEL   It would be incorrect to conclude that Bismarck alone was preparing for the war he considered inevitable. Nor was he the only statesman who during the spring of 1866 was searching for pretexts that would unleash such a war. The Austrians, too, had concluded that the economic, political, and military progress of Prussia was such that Austria would permanently lose its position in Germany unless Prussia could be brought down. A mere political humiliation, such as that of Olmütz, seemed no longer sufficient. A military defeat was required, and Austria expected the bulk of the German states to help it crush Prussia. Hence, Austria also prepared for the war and was busy stirring up pretexts.

During 1865, Austria had gained some internal stability through the emperor's decision to conciliate the Hungarians. Four years of unsuccessful attempts to implement the "February Patent" had convinced Francis Joseph that Hungarian cooperation was essential for the survival of his monarchy. The moderate Hungarian liberal Ferencz Deák (1803–1876), who in the Revolution of 1848 had been pushed aside by the radical republicans, offered to work out a compromise to satisfy the autonomous aspirations of the Magyars while safeguarding the unity of the empire. A committee under Deák began to elaborate a draft proposal that eventually led to the establishment of the Dual Monarchy. When

in the same year Italy had offered to settle its differences with Austria by purchasing Venetia for a sizable sum, Austria had declined unconditionally. It felt strong enough to hold its own against Italian demands, and at the same time to stand up to Prussia in the Danish duchies and at the federal diet.

In May 1866, the Viennese government found out about the Prusso-Italian alliance. To avoid a two-front war, the emperor offered Italy outright possession of Venetia, provided it would break its alliance with Prussia. But Italy felt bound by its commitment to Berlin, and rejected the offer. Vienna then made overtures to Paris, which on June 12 ended in the conclusion of a secret Austro-French treaty. In return for French neutrality, Austria agreed to cede Venetia to Napoleon, who in turn would present it to Italy. This clause, which was to obviate Italy's entry into the expected war on the side of Prussia, showed again that Austria considered its position in Germany more important than its possessions in Italy. In another clause, Napoleon awarded Austria a free hand to change the German federation, provided France received adequate territorial adjustments. In two separate agreements, Napoleon thus promised neutrality in return for territorial compensations, bestowing French blessing for a reorganization of Germany in one case to Prussia, and in the other to Austria.

Meanwhile, friction between Austria and Prussia increased from week to week in the Danish duchies as well as in the federal diet. Realizing the tenuousness of his hold on Holstein, the emperor gave encouragement to the supporters of Augustenburg. The es-tablishment of an independent state of Schleswig-Holstein within the German confederation seemed the only way to keep the duchies from falling into the hands of Prussia. Bismarck promptly accused Vienna of contravening the Convention of Gastein. He then reintroduced his proposal to reform the federal diet by the addition of a lower house based on universal suffrage. To bring matters to a head, he suggested that Austria be excluded from the confederation, since it opposed establishment of a democratic federal parliament. Austria countered not merely by rejecting Bismarck's plan, but by proposing that the federal diet be empowered to decide the fate of Schleswig and Holstein, a suggestion that clearly violated the Gastein Agreement.

By mid-April 1866, Prussia and Austria both began to mobilize. King William became gradually convinced that Austria would not abide by the Gastein Agreement and could not be trusted. Incidents in the duchies, where Prussian troops had to pass through Austrian-held territory, began to multiply. Sensing the imminence of war, Russia, Britain, and France on May 28 proposed a European congress to settle the fate of the duchies and mediate among Italy, Austria, and Prussia. Turin and Berlin promptly accepted the invitation, but Austria's reply stipulated that none of the three powers should be permitted territorial gains as a result of the conference. Since both Italy and Prussia sought territorial aggrandizement, whereas Austria was on the defensive, such a stipulation was understandable, but the powers interpreted it as unwillingness to negotiate. As a result, no congress was held and Austria remained diplomatically

isolated during the ensuing critical months.

A week later, on June 6, Austria provided Bismarck with the desired excuse for action. The Austrian governor of Holstein called a session of the members of the Holstein diet to discuss their own wishes for the future of their duchy. Bismarck notified Vienna that this action nullified the Convention of Gastein, and that henceforth the Treaty of Vienna would again be in force, according to which both duchies were entrusted to the joint administration of Prussia and Austria. Accordingly he dispatched Prussian troops to occupy Holstein. Austria promptly withdrew its own outnumbered troops from Holstein to adjacent Hanover, and asked the diet at Frankfurt to order federal execution against Prussia for having violated the federal territory of Holstein.

A paroxysm of emotion and anti-Prussian feelings ran through the German states at the news of Prussia's occupation of Holstein. Bavaria, Saxony, Hanover, and most other states sided with Austria and voted in favor of war against Prussia to keep it from swallowing the Danish duchies. War was declared on June 14. Only Weimar, Mecklenburg, and a few other small states in northern Germany sided with Prussia. The Prussian envoy promptly left Frankfurt, declaring that Prussia henceforth considered the federal diet dissolved, and hostilities commenced.

THE SEVEN WEEKS' WAR   William I felt uncomfortable as a protagonist in a civil war among Germans. He saw the war more as a defensive action than as a possible step toward the unification of Germany. On June 18, he issued an address to the Prussian people, stressing that only recently he had cooperated with Austria "to free a German land from foreign domination." But, he complained, Austria was jealous of the "more youthful Prussia," and had incited the German states against Berlin. "Throughout Germany we are surrounded by enemies," he proclaimed, who falsely thought Prussia "paralyzed by internal discord." Stressing his love of peace and readiness to negotiate, he concluded by warning his enemies of the preparedness of his army, and reminding his subjects that they were fighting for the very existence of Prussia.

The ensuing military operations proved the value of the army reforms undertaken by William, Roon, and Moltke. They also revolutionized concepts of warfare. In less than a week, Prussian armies were fully assembled and on the move. By June 29, two weeks after the outbreak of war, Hanover had capitulated, and the Prussian central armies turned to threaten the states south of the Main. Meanwhile on June 22, three Prussian armies had poured into Bohemia from three different points. One of them had passed through Saxony unhindered. By the judicious use of railroads and the telegraph, Moltke coordinated and directed the movements of his armies from headquarters in Berlin in such a way that they converged with frightening speed and precision on the bulk of the Austrian forces gathered northeast of Prague.

As early as July 1, the Austrian High Command sensed the impending catastrophe. After a few minor skirmishes, they urged the emperor to request an armistice. Two days later, the debacle occurred. At the Battle of Sadowa (or Königgrätz) the Austrians were routed, and Bohemia lay open to the Prussian forces. The breech-loading needle gun,

which the Prussians lying prone fired at the standing Austrians, had proved its value. And King William, who during the battle had exposed himself to cannon fire, had shown that despite his age he was a "soldier king" of the old type, worthy of the respect of his subjects.

Meanwhile the Italians had honored their commitment and had entered the war on June 20. Four days later they were soundly defeated by the Austrians at the second battle of Custozza, and in the following month, the Italian fleet was beaten by the Austrian navy. Despite their victory, the Austrians were eager to conclude hostilities in the south to have a freer hand against Prussia. On the day of Sadowa, July 3, they kept their secret bargain with France and ceded Venetia to France, to be transferred to Italy. This gesture came, of course, too late, for after Sadowa, Austria was in no position to continue the fight against Prussia, even if it could have rapidly transferred all its troops north of the Alps.

After Sadowa, Prussian armies started to move south through Bohemia toward Austria and Hungary. Napoleon III now offered his mediation. Not anticipating Prussia's lightning warfare, he had not readied his own forces. Yet he wished to prevent the complete collapse of Austria, which would have fundamentally disturbed the balance of power in central Europe. Bismarck and Francis Joseph accepted the offer of French mediation, although Bismarck insisted that his terms be accepted by Austria before conclusion of an armistice. King William and the army, however, favored continuation of the war to achieve the final prostration of Austria.

The king, the royal council, and Bismarck argued fiercely about termination of the war and conditions for peace. William assumed a pseudomoral posture, insisting on the need for punishing Austria for its breach of agreements and demanding sizable territorial cessions. Similarly, he claimed annexations from every German state that had opposed Prussia in the war. The excellence of his military machine and the taste of victory at Sadowa had apparently changed his views about the defensive character of the war.

Bismarck stanchly resisted William, and apparently under threat of resignation, finally carried his view. He opposed continuation of the fighting on military and diplomatic grounds. He pointed out that the defeat of Italy gave Austria renewed resilience north of the Alps, that Hungary was intact and in its present mood would firmly oppose a German invasion. Moreover, cholera and dysentery were sapping the Prussian army, and fighting in the hot Danubian plains might easily lead to a military fiasco. Above all, he suggested that a prolonged war would give France the time needed to prepare its forces and throw its weight into the balance. He was against "wounding Austria too severely," and according to his memoirs, derided William's ideas of "punishing the opponent." In international rivalries, he claimed, both parties are guilty, and it was not Prussia's task to mete out punishment, but to "found German unity." He reasoned that destruction of Austria would result in the rise of numerous Magyar and Slavic states and that such fracturing of southeastern Europe would create permanent instability. The annexation of Bohemia or other Austrian lands would drive Austria into the arms of France or Russia. Primarily he warned against creating "needless bitterness or desire for re-

venge" among the Austrians or the other German states, so as not to jeopardize future alliances.

Having overcome his sovereign's resistance, Bismarck concluded an armistice with Vienna. The Preliminary Peace of Nikolsburg, signed on July 26, seven weeks after the beginning of the war, contained all decisions ultimately incorporated into the Treaty of Prague signed a month later. Prussia demanded no territory from Austria and only a small monetary indemnity. On the other hand, the old German Confederation was legally declared dissolved and Austria in effect deprived of its position among the German states. Prussia was awarded Schleswig and Holstein and agreed to hold a plebiscite in Schleswig to determine which of the Danish-speaking areas wished to be retroceded to Denmark— a plebiscite held only after Germany's defeat in World War I. Moreover, Prussia was allowed to annex the states of Hanover, Nassau, Electoral Hesse, and Frankfurt, and was given freedom to organize a new federation among the states north of the Main. The southern states, Bavaria, Württemberg and the others, were allowed to retain their independence, and to be free to organize their own southern confederation or to join an alliance with Prussia.

An armistice with the southern states was signed only on August 2. Not certain that Bismarck would persist in his policy of lenient treatment of the vanquished, Bavaria and the others appealed to Napoleon to assist them in obtaining the best possible peace terms from Prussia. But Bismarck held a political trump. On August 5, Napoleon's ambassador to Berlin, Count Vincente Benedetti (1817–1900) presented to Bismarck an official demand for compensations in the Rhineland. This was no longer a secret request presented by private agents of the emperor, but a public demand for the cession of all or parts of the Bavarian Palatinate and the west Rhenish possessions of Hesse-Darmstadt, including the city of Mainz. Bismarck rejected the request on the pretext that it was distasteful to German nationalism, and sent copies of the French demand to the southern states, at the same time offering them peace terms of extreme leniency. Except for minor border rectifications, he stipulated no territorial cessions and only an insignificant war indemnity. Perturbed by the revival of Napoleonic designs on the Rhineland and impressed by Bismarck's apparent selflessness, the southern states not only signed the offered peace treaties but also entered into secret defensive and offensive alliances with Prussia, whereby they agreed to place their armies under Prussian command in case of war with France.

REPERCUSSIONS OF THE WAR IN AUSTRIA AND PRUSSIA   Austria's lightning defeat sealed its exclusion from Italy and Germany, and the battle of Sadowa sounded the death knell for hopes for a *Grossdeutschland,* until they were revived by Hitler under vastly different auspices. Despite its defeat, Austria remained a foremost European power, but its eyes were thenceforth cast down the Danube Valley, and its center of gravity was shifting from Vienna toward Budapest.

The war gave greater urgency to the task of achieving a compromise with the Hungarians. The plans of Deák's committee were more or less completed, but a major decision was still to be made: whether to adopt a

federal or a dual system. The former Saxon prime minister, Count Friedrich von Beust (1809–1886), who was now the chief minister in Vienna, was a stanch champion of German superiority. A federation in which all nationalities shared equal power would have submerged the German-speaking minority. Hence Beust favored a dual system, in which the Magyars and Germans together would hold the reins over the remaining nationalities. Together with the Hungarian statesman Count Gyula Andrássy (1823–1890), Beust and Deák finally agreed on terms for the "Compromise" enacted in 1867, creating the Dual Monarchy of Austria-Hungary under the personal rule of Emperor Francis Joseph. Only foreign and military affairs and over-all finances were to be regulated by joint Austro-Hungarian ministries. In other matters, each state was governed by its own parliament, and controlled its own subject populations. Yearly meetings of sixty delegates from each parliament were to be organized for the discussion of joint problems. The new constitutional framework afforded relative stability to the Austro-Hungarian monarchy, but the increased power of the Hungarians made it impossible for the emperor to resume any significant role in German affairs.

The defeat of Austria and the resulting aggrandizement of Prussia also had profound repercussions within Prussia. As a liberal from the Rhineland noted, countless thousands "acclaimed the god of the moment, success!" The king and his army, the conservative Junkers, and, above all, Bismarck, with his authoritarian methods, stood vindicated. The unconstitutional acts of the government had led to a glorious victory. The question arose whether liberals thenceforth could conscientiously claim that the people's representatives deserved a voice in the affairs of government.

A realignment of political thought and allegiances became immediately evident. Elections to the Prussian lower house, held in July, 1866, almost quadrupled the ranks of the conservatives. The country was in a mood of compromise and forgiveness. Only certain Catholics, Socialists, and die-hard Progressives stood steadfast in their opposition to Bismarck and refused, as Wilhelm Liebknecht (1826–1900) put it, to let his halo of fame wash away the stain of his violation of the constitution. King William was ready for conciliation, and admitted that the tax collections of the preceding years had been illegal. Even Bismarck agreed to make the gesture of a concession. He submitted to the diet a Bill of Indemnity that retroactively sanctioned the budgets of 1862 and subsequent years and legalized the illegal collection of taxes. The bill also stipulated the total allowable expenditures for the current year, for which the government promised to submit a budget in 1867. This bill was accepted by a 3 to 1 majority in September of 1866. Subsequently the diet gave Bismarck a resounding vote of confidence, and requested the king to reward the successful minister. William made him Count von Bismarck.

True liberals looked upon the Bill of Indemnity as a dark omen for the future. To be sure, by even requesting such a bill, the government seemed to confirm the right of the diet to vote on the budget. But by retroactively legalizing the government's unconstitutional acts, the diet had undermined its position. In the future, the crown could always point to the precedent

of the 1860s when the diet *ex post facto* conceded its shortsightedness and accorded apparent infallibility to the executive. Many liberals considered it a worse defeat than the one in 1848, since in 1866 the people had not succumbed to military suppression but had been dazzled by military glory.

The Bill of Indemnity caused a significant split in the Progressive party. The old-style Progressives stuck to their constitutional principles and voted against it. The majority, however, veered to the right and joined the members of the *Nationalverein* to found the National Liberal party. This group voted for the bill. Their liberalism was directed more toward economic aims and the maintenance of free trade than toward doctrinaire constitutionalism. The National Liberals found adherents in other North German states that Prussia was about to annex or incorporate into the North German Confederation. Their commercial interests made them particularly faithful supporters of Bismarck's attempt to unify Germany. The National Liberals thus became one of the first parties to extend its program and membership beyond the confines of Prussia.

At the same time, the Conservatives split over Bismarck's reorganization of northern Germany. The old-style Conservatives mistrusted Bismarck's National Liberal supporters and his proposals for unifying northern Germany on the basis of universal suffrage. They began to suspect that Bismarck had abandoned his Junker principles and saw no reason for the Bill of Indemnity. They thought that after the victory on the battlefield, the army should have destroyed the diet. Instead, the crown had lowered itself by asking forgiveness from the representatives of the people. Moreover, the Conservatives objected to the deposition of the princely dynasties in the annexed territories as a violation of the monarchical principle. Certain Conservatives, however, abandoned their party and sided with Bismarck. Coming more from industrial and financial than agricultural circles, these upper-middle-class representatives, who ultimately formed the Free Conservative party, applauded Bismarck's success in the effort to unify Germany. This group, like the National Liberals, quickly found adherents outside the confines of Prussia.

It is perhaps ironic that the year that witnessed the weakening of liberalism also became the year in which Prussian and German party life sprang into full bloom. Within a few years, these parties, with their numerous splinters, became a formidable echo of German public opinion, although under Bismarck's system they were never to enjoy political power. It is also interesting that the pragmatic Bismarck thenceforth found support among those groups, whether liberal or conservative, that adopted an equally pragmatic attitude. The doctrinaires—liberal, socialist, conservative, or Catholic—remained in the powerless opposition.

THE NORTH GERMAN CONFEDERATION
By the Treaty of Prague, Prussia was allowed to annex Hanover, Nassau, Electoral Hesse, and the city of Frankfurt, and had the option of reorganizing the states north of the Main into a new federation. When the Prussian lower chamber protested against the annexations, Bismarck replied: "Our right is the right of the German nation to exist, to breathe, to unite." But

actually these annexations were undertaken not to unite Germany, but to unite Prussia. The work begun by Frederick William, the Great Elector, in the seventeenth century was finally consummated by Bismarck. Until then, no continuous link had existed between Prussia's possessions in the Rhineland and those in north-central Germany. Absorption of Hanover and Electoral Hesse made Prussian lands contiguous from Königsberg to the French border. Annexation of Frankfurt can perhaps be explained on ideological grounds, since it was the former symbolic capital of Germany. The fate of Nassau appears less subject to justification. According to Bismarck, its dukes were dangerously devoted to the Hapsburgs; moreover, King William harbored a traditional Hohenzollern dislike for its dynasty.

Yet Bismarck was firmly opposed to Prussian absorption of all the northern states. The resulting accretion in Prussia's power would have antagonized too many Germans and alarmed the foreign powers. A federal system, however, was more likely to assuage the powers, and would also make it easy for the southern states eventually to join the north without abandoning their independence. Federalism would also respect the rights and privileges of the various ruling houses, and the upper chamber representing the state governments would act as a welcome conservative influence.

The North German Confederation was essentially Bismarck's own creation, tailored to suit his purposes. In August 1866, Prussia concluded treaties with the twenty-one remaining states north of the Main, guaranteeing the territorial integrity of all parties and stipulating their agreement to enter into a common federation. Meanwhile the armies of all states were placed under the control of the Prussian crown. Plenipotentiaries from all states were called to Berlin to discuss Bismarck's constitutional draft, which was later submitted to a popularly elected constituent assembly. The Prussian minister was evidently in a conciliatory mood. His democratic respect for the rights of the small states and the demands of public opinion astonished his contemporaries. On certain points, he even permitted the assembly to modify his draft—substituting the secret ballot for his proposed open vote. In essentials, of course, the North German Constitution as finally promulgated in July 1867 contained all Bismarck's requirements (see Map 12).

The king of Prussia was made the hereditary president of the confederation and its permanent chief executive. He was given full control over foreign and military affairs, supervision over the federal civil service, and power to declare war and peace. As commander in chief, he controlled all federal forces. Prussian military law, uniforms, organization, and recruitment were extended to the confederate armies so that the confederate forces were in fact an extension of the Prussian army. No similar arrangement was made for the navy, since Prussia as yet had no navy to speak of. A new federal naval ministry was therefore created.

The rulers were permitted to retain a semblance of sovereignty. With their own diets, they could dispose of local affairs and collect provincial taxes. Recognizing the vanity of the petty princes, Bismarck even allowed them to maintain their own representation abroad, a meaningless gesture since all

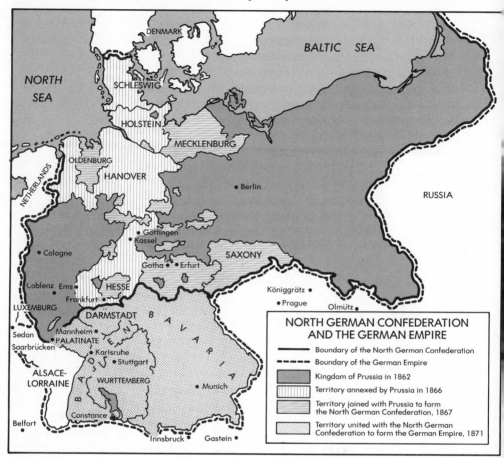

MAP 12

foreign affairs were handled from Berlin. Yet some of the princes—the king of Saxony was one—actually continued to send ambassadors to the major courts of Europe.

The legislature of the confederation comprised two houses. The upper house or *Bundesrat* consisted of delegates who represented the state governments and hence resembled the former federal diet, except for its increased powers over federal legislation. The delegates voted en bloc, as instructed by their governments, casting a total of 43 votes, of which 17 were assigned to Prussia. Since 14 votes

sufficed to veto any constitutional amendments, Prussia could prevent any change in the constitution. The lower house or *Reichstag* was elected on the basis of universal male suffrage from the entire territory of the confederation. It shared in the legislative process with the upper house, but the Bundesrat possessed more legislative power than the Reichstag.

All essential power rested in the executive—the king of Prussia and his federal chancellor. Bismarck was immediately appointed to this all-important post, while at the same time, as minister-president of Prussia and first

minister of the King of Prussia, he became the presiding officer of the Bundesrat. Since Bismarck also acted as foreign minister and ran various governmental departments in Prussia, he now held so many posts that to keep his files straight he sometimes corresponded with himself in his various capacities. In true Bismarckian spirit, he refused to establish parliamentary responsibility. To make the federal government responsible to the Reichstag would undermine the authority of the states and give power to political parties and popular representatives, whom Bismarck at heart despised. He thought it essential that the states—primarily, of course, the Prussian state—retain their supremacy. Consequently, his constitution made the federal government responsible only to the chief executive, the king of Prussia. Since Bismarck always preferred to work alone and bully others, he did not permit the organization of a ministerial cabinet. Cooperation with colleagues of more or less equal rank was to him an impossibility. He insisted that governmental "responsibility existed only when there is a single man who can be held accountable for any mistakes."

The North German Constitution, which with some modifications later became the constitution of the German Empire, was a skillful mixture of constitutionalism and authoritarianism. It functioned with amazing smoothness under Bismarck's direction, but after his dismissal, it became quickly evident how personal a creation it was. The historian Heinrich von Sybel (1817–1845), a member of the constituent assembly in 1867, lauded the constitution as a product of pragmatic analysis of political conditions rather than the issue of academic imagination, as had been true of the Frankfurt constitution of 1849. He thought that the three main "political facts" of 1867 were well represented in the framework. The presidency embodied the power, prestige, and military might of Prussia. The Bundesrat represented the "vitality" of the smaller states and their princes, supported by "historic tradition and local sentiment," and the Reichstag embodied public opinion. Since Sybel was a supporter of Bismarck's he failed to add to this astute analysis that public opinion was given only a sounding board in the Reichstag, and was left without true political power.

THE FINAL ROAD TO UNIFICATION

The annexations of 1866 and the creation of the North German Confederation made Prussia the undisputed master of northern Germany. The process of unification had begun. It remained to be seen whether it could be completed without another war.

The Question of War

According to most evidence, Bismarck apparently convinced himself that a war against France would rekindle the patriotic all-German fervor of 1813 needed to draw the south German states into a unified Germany. "A common national war against our aggressive neighbor," he wrote in his memoirs "would serve better than anything else to bridge the historical gulf which dynastic and ethnic feelings and modes of life had created between the south and the north of our fatherland." Once unification had been achieved, he re-

marked, "our feeling of nationality . . . was conserved and strengthened mainly through war. . . . It is regrettable that it could not have been done peacefully—but it is grounded the more firmly for all that." But Bismarck did not concede that such a war was the *sine qua non* of unification.

Unquestionably there were many obstacles to bringing the southern states into a union with Prussia. Most southern Germans distrusted the militarism and authoritarianism of the Prussian government and harbored a residual, rather sentimental love for the Austrian Hapsburgs. Many Prussians, for their part, remained suspicious of southern ultramontanism. Moreover, the traditional particularistic jealousies among the southern states themselves were still alive. It is characteristic that the Baden envoy, when negotiating the peace treaty with Prussia in 1866, suggested that since Bavaria's size might be a hindrance to a closer bond among the German states, it should be reduced in size—the Rhenish Palatinate transferred to Baden and northern border strips ceded to Prussia. Bismarck reports a similar enlightening incident. When hearing rumors of Hesse being compensated for territorial losses north of the Main by the addition of sections of northwestern Bavaria, the populations of the affected areas voiced complaints. As Catholics, they objected to being transferred to Protestant Hesse, and as subjects of a king, they resented becoming citizens of a mere duchy.

But these problems were not insurmountable. Hanoverians felt an equally deep-seated antagonism toward Prussians, and after its annexation by Prussia in 1866, Hanover was a center of friction. Yet this animosity was gradually overcome and, as Bismarck had to admit, even Hanoverians became loyal Germans. The federal ties of the North German Confederation were loose enough so that the southern states could have been persuaded to enter in 1866. But Bismarck's excessive caution at the time made him forfeit the opportunity, and later, when France was better prepared for war, it was too late.

Perhaps because Bismarck was a Junker, he tended to overlook the fact that industry, science, engineering, banking, and trade were unifying the German states at an ever-increasing pace, just as the Common Market in our day is drawing the western European countries together, irrespective of the lag in common political institutions. In the 1860s, banks and joint-stock companies, chemical and electrical industries, and, above all, coal and steel consortia were spreading over the German lands, regardless of state boundaries. Almost all regional tolls were abolished on river transport to allow faster and cheaper shipping. Roads, railroads, telegraph, and improved postal services, conventions on monetary units and credit arrangements— all helped to draw the states together. As Lord Keynes later remarked, "The German Empire was built more truly on coal and iron than on blood and iron."

Then, too, the Zollverein was expanding in the 1860s. Until 1863, Austria had made repeated, though unsuccessful attempts to break up the customs union. But the tariff arrangements were so favorable for the various states that during the Austro-Prussian War tariffs throughout Germany were collected as usual, the funds transmitted to Berlin, and from there distributed

to the member states of the Zollverein —even though the outbreak of hostilities had legally invalidated the treaties, and the German states were at war with Prussia.

The creation of the North German Confederation also brought about changes in the Zollverein. The old tariff congress, in which each member state had a veto, was transformed into a bicameral customs parliament. In the upper house, the states were represented, and questions were decided by majority vote. The lower house, inaugurated in 1868, was based on popular elections throughout Germany. This parliament, with its representation from the southern states, debated common economic and political problems. Although it accomplished little in its first two years, it was another medium for closer cooperation.

But the German states did not exist in a vacuum. Unification in 1866 would have been feasible, since France had anticipated a long Austro-Prussian war and an Austrian victory, and was ill prepared for intervention. Once this opportunity for unification had been missed, the attitude of France became of vital importance. Repeatedly in the period 1866 to 1870, Bismarck expressed his conviction that France would seek to gain by force those compensations out of which it had been cheated by the lightning victory of Sadowa. Moreover, he fully realized that Napoleon needed to restore his prestige, and might choose to find the opportunity in a Franco-Prussian war. Time and again Bismarck predicted a war with France, while stressing his own love of peace. "I shall never consent to a war that is avoidable, much less seek it. But this war with France will surely come. It will be clearly forced upon us by the French Emperor."

One may, of course, contend that if Bismarck wanted such a war in order to unify Germany, he merely used clever tactics by repeatedly predicting it and pushing the blame in advance, onto Napoleon. But there is sufficient evidence that large segments of the French ruling classes desired such a war as much as Bismarck did. Internal political problems of the imperial regime, the traditional fear of a strong Germany, and perplexity over the lightning victory of Sadowa, among other reasons, made the French government yearn for a spectacular diplomatic, if not a military, victory. Napoleon's championing of the rights of nationalities had made him sympathetic in principle to German aspirations for unity. But the French fiasco in Mexico, caused largely by Mexican nationalism, and his ambivalent involvement in the Italian unification movement—in which he favored Italian nationalism but felt compelled to give the pope in Rome military protection against the Italian nationalists—had cooled the emperor's idealistic ardor. "If Bismarck draws the southern German states into the North German Confederation," he remarked in 1868, "our guns will go off by themselves."

The Approaching Conflict with France

During the years 1866–1870, Napoleon fostered many diplomatic intrigues for territorial compensations. Each French step was parried by Bismarck, eager to seize every opportunity to coalesce German public opinion against France. From these critical years, Napoleon emerges as bungling and impatient,

Bismarck as a resourceful superb improviser. But again the exaggeration of the popular picture of Bismarck pulling all the strings to set up the Franco-Prussian War in Prussia's favor should be noted. In fact, the initiative for the most part lay with the French, but Bismarck's countermeasures usually were effective in stimulating German nationalism and in improving the chances for unification.

After the rejection of his demand for territorial cessions in the Rhineland in early August 1866, Napoleon looked elsewhere for compensations. In late August, the French Ambassador Benedetti discussed with Bismarck the possibility that France might seize Belgium and Luxemburg, in return for allowing the unification of all of Germany. The French later insisted that the proposal originated with Bismarck. Actually the suggestion evolved from Napoleon's desire to shift French eyes away from Mexico, where he was about to abandon Maximilian, and Bismarck seized the occasion for his own purpose. He urged Benedetti to submit the scheme in writing—thereby acquiring a useful document that, at the needed moment, could be shown to prove French expansionism.

During the winter of 1866–1867, while French troops were being withdrawn from Mexico, France negotiated with the king of Holland, the sovereign of Luxemburg, for the cession of this strategic district. Luxemburg had been an official part of the old German Confederation and was still occupied by Prussian troops. After the demise of the old German Confederation in 1866, Luxemburg's legal status lacked clarity, and the French asserted that Prussia had lost the right to man its fortresses. In private conversations with the French ambassador, Bismarck pretended to concede that France should be allowed to acquire the duchy, but he cautioned that German public opinion might oppose the loss of territory that had belonged to the German Empire for a thousand years.

By the spring of 1867, the king of Holland had given his agreement to the intended transfer. Napoleon seemed on the verge of obtaining at least a part of his desired compensation. But in April, Bismarck was interpellated on the matter in the Reichstag of the North German Confederation. There is good reason to believe that Bismarck had arranged the questioning himself to bring the matter to public attention, while he assumed the role of mediator between German national feelings and French demands. The German press immediately echoed with anti-French proclamations, while demands were voiced in Paris for the forceful ouster of Prussian troops from Luxemburg. The frightened king of Holland withdrew his assent to the transfer of his duchy.

A Franco-Prussian war appeared imminent. It was avoided because neither side felt prepared for it. Strikes and political unrest were debilitating the French state; the army was not effectively prepared; and the emperor was loath to spoil the impending grand opening of the International Exposition at Paris, through which he hoped to bolster his prestige and repair his reputation as a man of peace. Nor was Prussia ready for a general war. Even the General Staff was not certain that the army was prepared to engage the French forces, which still enjoyed a formidable reputation. King William feared risking the recent gains, and, contrary to legend, even Bismarck was

not yet convinced that a war with France was the only path to unification. Consequently the chancellor pursued an ambivalent course. To frighten Napoleon, he published the secret defensive and offensive alliances Prussia had concluded with the southern states in the previous year, while at the same time he cautioned the Reichstag "to take into account the understandable apprehensions of France." He believed the crisis would enhance German national feeling, and hoped a display of German unity might make Napoleon acquiesce in German unification.

In the end, both Paris and Berlin felt relieved when the matter was taken out of their hands by the European powers, which, at the urging of Russia, called an international conference to deal with the problem of Luxemburg. The London Conference (May 1867), attended by France, Prussia, Austria, Russia, England, and Holland, produced a compromise embodying a setback for Prussia and a rebuff for France. Luxemburg was officially separated from the defunct German Confederation and declared a sovereign grand duchy, united in family bonds to the dynasty of Holland. All Prussian troops were to be evacuated, Luxemburg's fortresses were to be dismantled, and her perpetual neutrality was to be guaranteed by the signatory powers.

Conclusion of the Luxemburg crisis dispelled the overt clouds of war. In the following month, the Prussian royal couple, accompanied by Bismarck and Moltke, attended the Paris International Exhibition and were warmly entertained by Napoleon. These signs of Franco-Prussian friendship, however, could not conceal the fact that the outcome of the Luxemburg crisis had fundamentally altered Napoleon's views

on Germany. He blamed Prussia for foiling his designs on Luxemburg, and concluded that war with Prussia might, after all, be inevitable. Hence he decided to strengthen his military resources, and cast about for allies.

A law of January 1868 provided for a sizable increase in the French army. At the same time new weapons were introduced to bring the forces up to Prussian standards of modernization. Above all, the French General Staff pinned much hope on the development of its secret weapon, a machine gun based on a Belgian invention and considerably more powerful than the American Gatling gun invented in the early 1860s.

Finding allies proved difficult for Napoleon. In August 1867, he visited Francis Joseph in Salzburg, and a few months later, the Austrian emperor went to Paris. Discussions of a possible alliance continued for two years, and produced a tentative draft treaty in 1869. But no firm anti-Prussian alliance was ever concluded, although Napoleon continued to delude himself that Austria would aid him in a war against Prussia. The Austrian minister Beust, a bitter enemy of Bismarck's, actually favored such a pact, but the Hungarian Andrássy saw no reason to help Vienna regain influence in Germany. Since Budapest carried much weight in the newly created Dual Monarchy, Austria in the end maintained neutrality.

Napoleon was equally unsuccessful in gaining an alliance with Italy, whose aid in a war with Prussia would actually have been of little benefit to the French. In 1867, when Napoleon had felt obliged to dispatch another expeditionary force to Rome to protect the pope from attacks by Italian

nationalists, he had revived Italian animosity against France. As long as French troops occupied Rome, no firm alliance between Italy and France was conceivable. Thus France found itself alone in the crucial year 1870.

Bismarck had also learned from the Luxemburg crisis. The rallying of an all-German national enthusiasm after the civil war of 1866 seemed the only positive result. Besides entailing the loss of Luxemburg, the maneuver had merely antagonized France to the point that war with France seemed to be likely as soon as the French felt ready. Although King William was stanchly opposed to such a war, Roon and Moltke speeded plans for the training of the enlarged army of the North German Confederation and for a joint offensive with the armies of the southern German states. By 1870, the Prussian General Staff felt ready, and hoped for a speedy outbreak of the war before the French would catch up with their own training and equipment.

The Hohenzollern Candidacy and the Outbreak of War

In September 1868, a liberal revolution in Spain had overthrown the corrupt regime of Queen Isabella II and resulted in her flight and deposition. Throughout 1869, the Spanish provisional government had searched for a new ruler among the dynasties of Europe. The Spanish crown had been offered to Italian, Portuguese, and German princes, all of whom had declined. By the spring of 1870, only Prince Leopold of Hohenzollern-Sigmaringen (1835–1905) was still under serious consideration, having neither accepted nor rejected the proffered crown. Prince Leopold was the son of Charles An-

thony of Hohenzollern-Sigmaringen, who had been prime minister of Prussia under Frederick William IV. As a Catholic and a brother-in-law of the king of Portugal, he seemed well suited to lead the Spanish nation. He was a distant relative of both King William of Prussia and Emperor Napoleon of France. Moreover, in 1866, both France and Prussia had secretly helped his brother Charles assume the newly created throne of Rumania as Carol I. It appeared, therefore, that Leopold might be equally acceptable to Spain, France, and Prussia.

Leopold's candidacy, however, became the immediate cause of the outbreak of the Franco-Prussian War. The French government objected vehemently to the elevation of a Hohenzollern prince to the throne of Spain. It feared such action would revive the empire of Charles V and imperil the honor of France as well as the equilibrium of Europe. Napoleon felt that Prussia had gained enough power in 1866 and should not extend its influence over the Iberian peninsula. The French did not look upon Leopold of Hohenzollern-Sigmaringen as just any German prince. His father, Charles Anthony, was a friend of Bismarck's, and had shown his subservience to Prussian interests by voluntarily ceding the Sigmaringen lands to Prussia. Moreover, the war party in Paris, encouraged by certain cabinet officers and Empress Eugenia, sensed in the issue an opportunity for restoring Napoleon's prestige by humbling Prussia diplomatically or militarily.

Contrary to the impression left by Bismarck in his memoirs, which discreetly omit all references to his own activities during the spring of 1870, the Prussian chancellor was involved

in the question of the candidacy from the very beginning. Officially Bismarck considered the matter as a family affair of the Hohenzollerns. Whether Leopold accepted the throne or not, he claimed, was no concern of the Prussian government. Behind the scenes, however, he worked assiduously to promote Leopold's cause. By 1870 the prospect of war was no longer unwelcome to him, since the Prussian General Staff had assured him of the readiness of the army. But to assert that his sole aim was to goad France into declaring war on Germany so that the Germans could unite in defense of their fatherland is another oversimplification of the Bismarck legend. The chancellor saw other advantages in the Spanish candidacy besides a possible war. A Hohenzollern in Madrid, even though he might not remain completely subservient to Prussian interests, could always exert pressure on France when Prussian diplomacy required it. A friendly Spain would also open new markets to Prussia. Finally, the issue seemed such that even without war Napoleon was bound to lose further prestige, provided Bismarck could arrange it that the Prussian government did not seem directly involved. It was important that the members of the Spanish Cortes should elect their own ruler. If Napoleon then forced the Spaniards to rescind the election, European opinion would accuse him of gross interference in Spanish internal affairs and France would add to its isolation resulting from the Mexican fiasco. Or if the Spaniards refused his demands, Napoleon's prestige would be further dimmed and he might even be toppled from power.

Hence Bismarck negotiated secretly with envoys from Spain and with representatives of the Hohenzollern family. Leopold showed little eagerness to accept the crown, but declared himself ready to obey his father's command. Charles Anthony, in turn, placed his son at the disposal of King William. But it was difficult for Bismarck to persuade William to approve the candidacy. The Prussian king feared a war with France and saw little value in the venturesome scheme. Negotiations within the Hohenzollern family council, which Bismarck secretly attended, dragged on throughout the spring. The chancellor sent agents to Madrid to ascertain the mood of the Cortes. For his plans it was important that the Spaniards elect Prince Leopold with a resounding vote, so that there could be no accusation that Prussia had imposed its candidate on the Spanish people. When assured of the cooperation of the Cortes, William finally acquiesced, and on June 19, Leopold privately communicated his acceptance to the Spanish envoys. It had been agreed that Leopold's acceptance was to be kept secret until the Cortes had officially elected him, so that Napoleon would be confronted with a *fait accompli*. To give further credence to the fiction that the affair had been wholly a family matter, the members of the Prussian government dispersed to their respective summer resorts. The king went to Ems, Bismarck retired to his estate, and even Roon and Moltke left the capital.

But the Spaniards bungled the arrangements. The Cortes disbanded before electing Prince Leopold. Instead, on July 2, Madrid simply announced that he had accepted the crown. The French now had proof of what they had suspected for some time. The Parisian press immediately clamored for

war against Prussia. Violently anti-Prussian speeches were launched in the French assembly, and the duke of Gramont, Napoleon's foreign minister, warned that unless Leopold's candidacy were forthwith withdrawn, "Frenchmen would know how to do their duty without hesitation and without weakness." Gramont then instructed Ambassador Benedetti to demand immediate satisfaction from the Prussian king.

On July 9 and again two days later, Benedetti spoke to King William at Bad Ems. In essence, he demanded that the Prussian ruler order Prince Leopold to renounce the Spanish crown. The interviews were friendly. William was concerned about the prospect of war and disturbed by the bellicose mood of Paris, but he felt his royal honor would suffer if he accepted the French order. Hence, he officially rejected it, while secretly urging Prince Leopold to withdraw his name for the sake of peace.

On July 12, Charles Anthony of Hohenzollern-Sigmaringen officially announced his son's withdrawal from the Spanish candidacy. Those who had feared war were delighted by the announcement. The friction between France and the Hohenzollerns appeared dissolved without loss of prestige to either party. But those who wanted war felt frustrated. When hearing of Leopold's renunciation, Bismarck felt dumfounded. He even considered resigning, fearing that Germany had been humiliated and his own plans undermined. In his memoirs he noted:

I felt very dejected, for short of picking an artificial excuse for a quarrel, I saw no means of repairing the corrosive damage which a timorous attitude was about to inflict on our national position. In those days I already looked upon the war as a necessity, realizing it could no longer be avoided without loss of honor.

The war party in Paris felt equally disturbed. The Hohenzollern candidacy had been thwarted, but in such a way that France could not honestly claim a diplomatic victory. Furthermore, there was the possibility that Prince Leopold might again change his mind, since as a private citizen he was not bound by any official government promises. The duke of Gramont decided to push for a diplomatic triumph over Prussia, even at the risk of war. He telegraphed Ambassador Benedetti to demand a third audience with King William and extract from him a written promise that no Hohenzollern would ever again be a candidate for the Spanish throne. On July 13, the French ambassador complied with this crucial demand of his government. Rather than wait for an official audience in the afternoon, Benedetti approached the king during his morning promenade at Ems. This informal violation of traditional protocol in itself led to misinterpretations. William naturally refused the requested guarantees and promises. Quite possibly Benedetti's somewhat emotional importuning embarrassed and irritated William, who had never felt comfortable with Bismarck's intrigues and longed for an end to the disagreeable cabal of the candidacy. Despite the tension, however, the interview was cordial. When during the same afternoon, Leopold's official renunciation of the candidacy reached Ems, William sent Benedetti a copy of the statement, with a note that the matter now seemed closed and that he saw no need for Benedetti to come to the afternoon audience. When

the king left Ems that evening by train, Benedetti was at the station to pay his respects, and William extended to him the customary compliments. It is clear, therefore, that the events at Ems, although personally disagreeable to William, represented no affront to either France or Prussia.

Yet they were turned into a *casus belli* by Bismarck's now famous version of the Ems Telegram. Before leaving Ems, the king had authorized a dispatch to Bismarck, who had returned to Berlin, informing him of the events of the day, with permission at his discretion to relay this information to the press and to Prussian embassies abroad. With the tacit approval of Moltke and Roon, who assured him that the army was ready for immediate action and that a "speedy outbreak of war was more favorable than delay," Bismarck edited the dispatch from Ems before sending it to the press and the foreign office. By deletions and change of tone, Bismarck's version of the Ems dispatch implied that the Prussian king had been insulted by the French ambassador, who in turn had been rebuffed by the king. Bismarck was confident that his telegram would "act like a red cloth in front of the Gallic bull" and that he had found a way to safeguard German honor. Moltke is said to have called it "a clarion-call to arms."

The telegram appeared in the press and on embassy bulletins on the following day, and produced the desired effect on both sides of the Rhine. Parisians clamored for revenge against Prussia for the insult to their ambassador. Mobs shouting "To Berlin!" roamed the streets of Paris, and, despite warnings by the opposition, the French cabinet demanded war credits and mobilization. In Berlin and even outside Prussia, crowds gave vent to their hatred of France by singing "The Watch on the Rhine" and demanding satisfaction for the insult to King William. Only William himself, who knew what really happened at Ems, still opposed war when he arrived at Berlin on July 15. On the same day, however, news arrived that France had declared general mobilization. The war fever in Paris had triumphed. William promptly authorized Bismarck to proceed with Prussia's own mobilization. Four days later, on July 19, France issued a declaration of war. The magic telegram had worked its miracle: Bismarck had his war with France at a time of his own choosing and in a manner that made France look like the aggressor.

The Franco-Prussian War

Napoleon III had hoped that Austria, and possibly Italy, would side with France, and that the South German states would retain a benevolent neutrality despite their treaties with Berlin. The strategic plans of the French High Command had envisioned assembling forces in southern Germany for a push into Central Prussia by way of Saxony, where they could receive the assistance of Austrian armies from Bohemia. Such hopes proved to be vain. Austria, Italy, England, and Russia maintained strict neutrality, and the south German states honored their treaty obligations and mobilized alongside Prussia.

Württemberg, Baden, and Hesse immediately placed their troops at Prussia's disposal. Among Bavarians there was a brief hesitation between their dislike for Prussia and their hatred of

the "French aggressor" before they, too, decided "to show their German heart" and join the war against Napoleon. For the first time since 1814, the German states were united in a common effort. As had occurred during the Wars of Liberation, enthusiasm for the war was fanned by poets, journalists, and pamphleteers. Gruesome tales of French behavior in the first military skirmishes made the Germans self-righteous in their anti-French pronouncements. "May God punish the sinful French and destroy the new Babylon," became a war slogan.

The military campaigns once again proved the efficiency of Prussia's preparations. Within ten days the North German army was raised from 300,000 to 900,000 men; even the forces of the southern states assembled speedily. Skillful use of railroads allowed massing the bulk of the German forces in the Palatinate and completion of total mobilization within eighteen days. Thus France was invaded in early August, before the French army had completed its own preparations. During August, three German armies maneuvered in Alsace and Lorraine, encountering the French in numerous minor engagements. To gain time, they bypassed or invested fortresses instead of stopping to capture them. Moltke's primary goal was to envelop the main part of the French army before attempting to push inland toward Paris. Losses on both sides were heavy, but the French had to give ground almost continually. Emperor Napoleon, in the field and pretending to command the armies, proved no match for the skillful Moltke.

By the end of August, most of the land east of the Meuse River had fallen to the Germans, except for sev-

eral important fortified towns, such as Metz and Strassburg, in which strong French garrisons had been encircled by the invader. The discouraging news from the front toppled the cabinet that had helped push France into the war. Empress Eugenia, acting as regent, was barely able to retain control of the government.

Disaster struck the French on September 1. A sizable French army, with Napoleon himself in its midst, was encircled by superior German forces at Sedan, near the Belgian frontier. Massive German artillery fire foiled all French attempts to break out of the encirclement. With 13,000 men killed and 30,000 captured, the pathetic emperor, who had always dreaded the carnage of battle, decided to surrender. "Not having been able to die in the midst of my troops," he wrote to King William, "it only remains for me to surrender my sword to the hands of your Majesty." The capitulation of Sedan was negotiated, and on September 2, Napoleon, together with some 40 generals and 83,000 men, accepted imprisonment by the Germans. The confrontation between the shattered emperor of the French and the robust and gleeful Bismarck, who had donned a Prussian uniform for the occasion, has frequently been depicted in print and on canvas. Emotionally, it was a memorable event, but politically it lacked significance, for Napoleon no longer spoke for France. The following day, the emperor departed for his residential prison, the castle of Wilhelmshöhe near Kassel.

The victory of Sedan opened northern France to the invaders, although the fortresses of Metz and Strassburg continued to resist capture and held down sizable units of the German

army. Nonetheless, a German army reached the outskirts of Paris on September 19 and began investing the city.

Meanwhile the news of Napoleon's surrender had caused a revolution in Paris. On September 4, Parisian mobs had forced the empress to flee, had proclaimed a republic, and had installed a provisional government pledged to repel the invader and "not abandon a foot of French soil." Mindful of the prodigious success of the French republican armies in 1792, the French liberals vowed that the unleashed forces of the Third Republic would sweep the aggressor from the land. They expected that the German forces would be pinned down in the sieges of Strassburg, Metz, and Paris while new French armies were being raised in the provinces.

The overthrow of Napoleon and establishment of a republic intensified the question whether the Germans were fighting against Napoleon or against the French, and whether their aim was to unify Germany or to gain territory. The historian Heinrich von Treitschke (1834–1896) proclaimed in an article entitled "What We Demand from France": "The nation [France] is our enemy, not this Bonaparte, who rather obeyed than led it." A desire for belated revenge against injustices suffered by earlier generations fanned the emotions of many Germans. When asked, "Against whom is Germany fighting now that Napoleon III, who declared the war, is vanquished and imprisoned?" the historian Ranke (1795–1886) replied: "Against Louis XIV!" Not all sounded as vindictive as the composer Richard Wagner, who urged Bismarck to obliterate Paris from the earth. But to justify their nationalis-

tic and expansionist desires, many Germans assumed a moralistic tone that sounded arrogant and insincere in an age of *Realpolitik*. Treitschke wrote of the "idealistic and moral forces [of the Germans] which can only be released through a just war." He intoned against "the sins of France," and insisted that "the sense of justice to Germany demands the lessening of France." He pointed to Alsace and Lorraine, which he called "the beautiful homelands of the German stock where the old *Reich* once suffered its deepest humiliation," and insisted that "these territories are ours by the right of the sword, and [that] we shall dispose of them in virtue of a higher right—the right of the German nation." Questions of self-determination did not perturb the Prussian historian. "We Germans," he wrote, "know better than these unfortunate ones what is good for the people of Alsace."

For strategic reasons, the Prussian generals demanded cession of all of Alsace and Lorraine, including the fortresses and fortified towns west of the Vosges mountains, so that German outposts would henceforth stand at the edge of the plains of northern France. Bismarck himself showed similar arrogance toward the French, though his demands were more moderate. During the Sedan negotiations, he complained of the pride and jealousy of the French, whom he accused of having attacked Germany some thirty times in two centuries. When the question of immediate peace negotiations was raised, he replied to the French: "If we make peace now, as soon as you could, in five or ten years, you would reopen the war." He insisted on the need of a buffer between France and Germany. "We need land, fortresses, and

borders which in future will protect us from all French attacks." His territorial demands, however, were not so far-reaching as those of the Prussian generals.

Since the French refused to negotiate peace on the basis of territorial cessions, the war was continued. The long siege of Paris (132 days) was started, engendering the radical revolution of the Paris Commune against the forces of moderation. The city of Strassburg fell on September 28, and a month later, Metz surrendered with a garrison of 173,000. Despite the civil war inside Paris and the increasing futility of their cause, the French hoped for a reversal of fate, based on the slender success of their provincial armies, fighting primarily in the Loire Valley. By the end of 1870, most of France north of the Loire, except Paris and Brittany, was under German control, and food and supplies in the capital were running low. Finally, on January 28, Paris capitulated. Even then, savage fighting continued in the area of Belfort and Dijon near the Swiss border, where Garibaldi with a volunteer army attempted to help the French republicans in a last-minute effort. But in early February, the fortress of Belfort also surrendered, and the French armies in Burgundy were dispersed or escaped into neutral Switzerland to avoid capture. The Germans had won the war, and France was ready to submit to its fate.

Meanwhile French elections had been held, and a new government established provisionally at Bordeaux under the leadership of Louis Thiers. Peace negotiations with Bismarck were undertaken. The harshness of the German terms and Bismarck's inflexibility mortified the French negotiators, but

France was in no position to reject the terms and resume fighting. Protracted pleading saved only Belfort for the French. On March 1, 1871, the French National Assembly accepted the preliminaries that were then incorporated into the Treaty of Frankfurt of May 10. According to its provisions, France ceded eastern Lorraine and all of Alsace, except for Belfort, and was to pay an indemnity of five billion francs. German troops were to occupy northern France until full payment had been made.

Creation of the Second German Empire

In early August 1870, after the initial German victories near the frontier in which troops of the southern states participated effectively, Crown Prince Frederick of Prussia (1831–1888), the heir to the throne, developed his own plans for creating a united Germany. But his liberal tendencies and his predilection for the British style of parliamentarianism made him suspect in the eyes of Bismarck, who in any case disliked interference in what he considered his own domain.

Disregarding the crown prince's views, Bismarck opened official negotiations with the southern states in September. They were asked to join the North German Confederation on the basis of mutual treaty arrangements. Bavaria at first refused to commit itself and presented counterdemands that Bismarck found unacceptable. For the moment, Bismarck decided to proceed without Bavaria. Delegates from the four southern states were invited to sign the treaties of accession at Versailles, which had become William's field headquarters. Baden and Hesse

acceded at once and without reservations. At the urging of Bavaria, however, Württemberg delayed its commitment. Bismarck then tried to entice the two recalcitrant southern rulers by a mixture of threats and promises. He threatened to exclude them from the customs union, but at the same time offered them special concessions to sweeten their loss of sovereignty. Württemberg was easily persuaded, but Bavaria resisted until November before finally signing the treaty. The *Sonderrechte* (special rights) granted to the two kingdoms included the right to control their own armies in time of peace, administer their own postal and telegraph services, and run their own railways. Bavaria obtained additional concessions: a permanent seat on a number of committees of the Bundesrat, the federal upper house; freedom to determine its own laws on marriage and citizenship; and—a vital point to Bavarians—the right to establish their own taxes on beer.

The signing of the treaties between the North German Confederation and the four southern states did not touch on the question of the official framework for a unified Germany. The southern states could simply have adhered to an expanded North German Confederation without changing its leadership from a president to an emperor and without adding all the other imperial paraphernalia. In fact, William I himself, most Prussian Junkers, and many others in and outside Prussia objected to the creation of an "imperial" superstructure. To William, no honor could be higher than the revered title of King of Prussia, borne by his illustrious Hohenzollern ancestors. But Bismarck looked upon the imperial title as "a political necessity." He be-

lieved that the ideal of *Kaiser* and *Reich* retained a romantic aura, particularly for non-Prussians. German nationalists saw in the establishment of a Reich not the re-creation of the pitiful Holy Roman Empire of more recent centuries, but a revival of the glorious days of the Hohenstaufens. For decades, historians, journalists, novelists, and poets had been rekindling admiration for Germany's medieval past. The patriots now saw the day when their wishes could be fulfilled. Conceivably, also, Bismarck found a symbolic meaning in the imperial title. For centuries it had been held by the Germans until wrested from them by the first Napoleon. The Germans had now vanquished Napoleon III and recaptured the title, together with Lorraine, the ancient homeland of imperial dignity.

It is impossible to generalize on the symbolic and emotional values attached to the concepts of *Kaiser* and *Reich*. In medieval times, they had signified in a vague way power and universal dominion, but after 1300 they had gradually become hollow dignities. With Napoleon I, they had acquired new significance, denoting imperialism and expansionism. Louis Napoleon, before becoming emperor in 1852, had tried to convince France and the world to disregard the slogan "Empire means war," insisting that his "conquests" would be solely for "religion, morality, and comfortable living." Yet his regime had been a long series of colonial and European wars. Bismarck also asserted that the Reich would be peaceful and not bent on expansion. But the wars of the 1860s and, to no small extent, the assumption of the now hexed imperial title gave Germany the reputation of an aggressor nation.

After persuading William to accept the dignity, Bismarck still had to determine the precise title. The southern kings would not brook the name "Emperor of Germany," which would make the Hohenzollern ruler of all the states and hence superior to ordinary kings. "Emperor of the Germans—in the style of Napoleon's "Emperor of the French" —was rejected by William as sounding too democratic. "Emperor in Germany" was considered but pleased no one. The final proclamation made William "German Emperor." It was a designation all could accept; in popular language it soon became simply *Der Kaiser.*

Finally, the question remained of how the new crown should be offered to the Prussian king. Recalling the fiasco of 1849, Bismarck threatened that if the princes did not offer the crown to William, he would have the ceremony performed by the North German Parliament. After long pressure and possibly some financial bribing, he finally persuaded the mad king of Bavaria, Louis II, to face the inevitable and to enhance his own personal dignity by taking the initial step. Louis then invited his princely colleagues to join him in offering the crown to William. After obtaining their consent, he sent a letter—dictated by Bismarck himself—to the Prussian king, requesting him to accept the crown.

At last the empire was ready to be proclaimed (see Map 12). The North German Parliament had voted its approval, but the coronation had to be postponed until the Bavarian Parliament consented. On January 18, 1871, the imperial coronation took place in the Hall of Mirrors in Versailles. The ceremony, as well as William's Proclamation of the Empire, bore a characteristic Hohenzollern imprint and foreshadowed a German Empire that was to be no more democratic than the Kingdom of Prussia had been. The official accounts in the gazettes described the splendor of the coronation, with King William "surrounded by sovereigns, generals, and soldiers." "Owing to the necessities of the times," the reports indicated, "the German people were represented at the ceremony only by the German army." Actually a delegation from the North German Parliament had reached Versailles but was not admitted until after the imperial coronation. It is not known who first devised the plan to hold the coronation at Versailles, a decision most insulting to France. But it is interesting that the humiliation of France seemed to outweigh any need to have the new emperor crowned on German soil. There was no reason why William and Bismarck had to be near the battle front, for by January 18 the war was almost over, and their presence was not necessary for completing the campaign.

William's proclamation stressed that he owed his imperial crown not to the German people, but, if to anyone, to the army and the princes. "The German princes and the free cities," he said, "have unanimously called upon us to renew and to assume the German imperial office." Throughout his speech, William referred solely to the princes and to the governments of the free cities—which, no doubt to his regret, were not run by noble lords. No mention was made of the German people; no role was assigned to them in the creation of the Empire and, as the constitution was to show, no rights were to be reserved for them under the new framework.

The Imperial Constitution

The constitution of the Second Reich, adopted by the new Reichstag in April 1871, was essentially an extension of the constitution of the North German Confederation, now enlarged to include twenty-five states and Alsace-Lorraine. The latter was organized as a *Reichsland* under an imperial governor, and not given the status of a federal state. Unlike the draft of 1849, the instrument of 1871 contained no bill of rights, and all attempts to append a list of fundamental rights were defeated. On the other hand, the document contained numerous articles dealing with fiscal matters, customs, railroads, commerce, the postal service—particulars not normally included in constitutions. Article 54 even stipulated that "every German . . . should serve in the standing army for seven years," a specification usually left to statutes or other legislation.

The Prussian king was made hereditary German emperor and commander in chief of the army and navy, and awarded power over foreign affairs and all imperial appointments, including the selection of the chancellor and his cabinet ministers. He could even "enter into alliances and treaties with foreign states" without consulting anyone. With the consent of the Bundesrat, he could declare war, dissolve the Reichstag, and enact federal execution against a recalcitrant member state—except Bavaria, which had been granted special immunity from this clause.

The bicameral legislature paralleled that of the North German Confederation. The Reichstag, whose members were elected for five years on secret district ballot by direct suffrage of all males over twenty-five years of age,

had relatively little power. Together with the upper house, it could legislate on all matters under the jurisdiction of the federal government —army, navy, customs and taxes, industry, trade and communications, currency and banking, patents, weights and measures, censorship, criminal and civil law, and others—but actually the Bundesrat dominated legislation, since no laws could be promulgated without its consent. Except for its powers over the budget—a doubtful privilege in view of the constant threat of dissolution and the outcome of the constitutional struggle in Prussia in the early 1860s—the Reichstag acted more as a steam valve for popular opinion than as a real parliament. It could exercise no control over the executive. There was no parliamentary responsibility for the cabinet, and no vote of confidence. Moreover, until 1906, its members received no pay and its system of representation became quickly grossly outdated. Elections were based on geographic districts rather than on population, and no reapportionment of districts was undertaken during the empire's forty-seven years of existence. Hence the agricultural districts continued to exert strong influence in the Reichstag despite the progress of urbanization.

The Bundesrat retained the preeminent position it had enjoyed under the North German Confederation. Its members were appointed like ambassadors by the rulers of the twenty-five states and were forced to vote en bloc. The number of seats was raised to 58, and Prussia retained its 17—later increased to 20 by treaties with small states that relinquished their vote to Prussia. But since the veto of 14 votes for all constitutional amendments was

kept, Prussia retained its power to prevent constitutional changes.

The constitution turned Germany into an odd mixture of federalism and centralism under the aegis of Prussia. "Imperial legislation" was to "take precedence over state legislation," but its enforcement was often left to the states. Moreover, the states retained control over their own judiciary, police, taxation, and educational and other policies. And through the Bundesrat, each state could potentially exercise important powers. On the other hand, the federal superstructure was a powerful extension of the authority of the Prussian king, and had the effect of merging the German states in Prussia. The king of Prussia was automatically "the presiding officer of the Federation." It is interesting to note, for example, that no arrangements were made for an imperial salary or an imperial castle. Even as emperor of Germany the king of Prussia derived his income solely from Prussia and resided in Berlin's "royal Prussian castle." As a state, Prussia dominated the federation through its size, population, wealth, and army. It represented three fifths of the territory of the empire and sent to the Reichstag 235 out of a total of 397 delegates. In terms of political power, the Prussian king and the chancellor, who was appointed by and was responsible to the Prussian ruler, dominated the Bundesrat and the Reichstag and were in fact the fountainhead of all power within the Reich. Prussia's predominance was symbolically evident in the new flag adopted by the empire: it was not the black, red, and gold of 1813 and 1848, but black, white and red—the colors of the Hohenzollerns mixed with those of the commercial Hanseatic cities.

The New Reich, 1871–1890

BISMARCKIAN GERMANY

The Germany that arose from the battlefields of the Franco-Prussian War of 1870 might well be called Bismarck's Germany—not merely because Bismarck laid its foundations, but also because he virtually controlled its destiny during the next twenty years.

Bismarck had guided Prussia successfully through three wars, and had procured the imperial crown for his king. Yet in 1871, he evidently had no intention of withdrawing from the political scene. No doubt he was motivated partly by personal ambition and love of power, but more important was his realization that the process of unifying Germany had not been completed. He was habitually distrustful of others, and hesitated to leave this task to less experienced men. Moreover, William I apparently considered governing without him an impossibility, and Bismarck remained in office partly because of the wishes of his sovereign.

The Temper of the Gründerzeit

The decades after the formation of the empire, called *Gründerzeit* (period of the founders) by the Germans, were characterized by nationalism and materialism. The Germans were proud of their achievements on the battlefield, and a tremendous industrial and commercial expansion made them self-confident and prosperous. Nationhood also seemed to unleash latent energies in the fields of letters, arts, and sciences. Press and theater, concert halls and opera houses, universities, libraries, and laboratories—all were vibrant with activity.

Sentimental patriotism was encouraged more than ever in the so-called *Heimatkunst,* short stories, dramas, and novels depicting the life of country folk living in close communion with the beautiful though mysterious German countryside. Local patriotism was fostered by numerous historical societies, which collected source materials in the various regions of Germany. In Prussia particularly education was designed "to sow the seeds of patriotic, religious, and moral sentiment in the children." The Prussian school of historians asserted that the historian's task was to educate the public in nationalism and to guide the statesmen by revealing the glories of the nation's past. Treitschke, Sybel, and Johann Gustav Droysen (1808–1884), the foremost members of this school, interpreted

German history in the light of the "destiny" of the Hohenzollern dynasty; they praised German nationalism and waged relentless attacks on France, Austria, and the Catholic Church.

Perhaps because the Germans had waited so long to achieve nationhood, they now reveled in it. Hence in some circles, nationalism, formerly directed toward the clearly defined goal of achieving unity, now became a noisy creed mixed with elements of Pan-Germanism and anti-Semitism. An excellent example is furnished by the composer Richard Wagner (1813–1883). A romantic rebel in his youth, he had been occasionally embroiled in politics, although he had devoted his main attention to composing and conducting. Because of his involvement in the revolution of 1848–1849, he had fled to Switzerland, where his writings and compositions had become increasingly nationalistic. He returned to Germany only after proclamation of a political amnesty in 1861. Three years later, King Louis II of Bavaria became Wagner's patron. The opera house at Bayreuth that the king had constructed for Wagner soon became a mecca for lovers of grandiose opera and for German superpatriots. During Wagner's Bayreuth period (1872–1881), he composed the gigantic *Ring des Niebelungen,* a perfect embodiment of mystic nationalism. But besides writing operas, Wagner wrote eight volumes of prose works, among them articles on "Judaism in Music," "What Is German?" and "German Art and German Policy." In these and other writings, he stressed the superiority of the German *Volk* and his belief that a "Barbarossa-Siegfried will some day return to save the German people in time of deepest need." The Jews, whom he thought incapable of speaking the German language or producing German music, he regarded "with repugnance" as the "demons of the decline of mankind." To Wagner, democracy was alien and disgusting, an invention of Jews and Frenchmen. Above all, he revered the mystic primeval force of the German folk soul (*Volksseele*), which he tried to capture in his music dramas. Richard Wagner societies sprang up all over Germany to venerate their master's German music as "the ideal bond" for cementing the unity of the German fatherland.

The materialism of the *Gründerzeit* found newly invigorated expression in both philosophy and literature. Realism, which had first appeared in the novel and the drama in the mid-nineteenth century, continued to dominate literature. The novelist and essayist Theodor Fontane (1819–1898), who for a while had edited the *Kreuzzeitung,* remained the idol of the conservatives with his realistic novels of contemporary life. Fondness for prosperity and for solid middle-class standards was echoed in the novels of Gustav Freytag (1816–1895), a champion of commercial life. Soon the literature of the period began to reflect the increased misery that industrialization and urbanization had brought to the lower classes. In the late 1880s, German naturalism burst into bloom with the dramas of Gerhart Hauptmann (1862–1946). His early plays *Before Sunrise* and *The Weavers* pointed up the poverty of the lower classes, and gave great impetus to the literature of social concern.

Whereas most Germans basked in the comforts brought by unification and nationhood, not all could joyfully accept Bismarck's creation. Some re-

gretted that unification had not been achieved on the basis of *Grossdeutschland*. Others opposed the chancellor's autocratic tendencies. Certain ethnic, religious, and political groups—Poles, Alsatians, ultramontanes, and socialists in particular—were leery of the new Reich. In addition a few perspicacious observers, such as Friedrich Nietzsche (1844–1900), objected to the superficiality and chauvinism of the new German spirit. In his *Unzeitgemässe Betrachtungen* (*Untimely Observations*), he warned that the victory over the French did not necessarily herald a victory for German civilization. And he complained that "today everything is determined by the coarsest and most evil forces, by the egotism of an acquisitive society and by military potentates."

Industrial and Commercial Expansion

Political unification by itself, of course, was not likely to eradicate entrenched particularism. Of more importance for uniting the Germans was the rapid industrialization transforming the Reich. It drew the Germans together economically, and produced an unprecedented prosperity that made many of them forget the past.

Between 1871 and 1890, Germany's population rose from 41 million to over 49 million (56 million by 1900, and 64 million by 1910), despite the emigration of well over 2 million Germans to the New World. Parenthetically, it might be pointed out that the population of France during this period increased only from 36 million to 38 million. The demographic balance was shifting in Germany's favor.

Prior to 1850, Germany had been essentially an agricultural area. Between then and 1870, industrial and financial progress had been considerable, especially in the construction of railroads and the promotion of banking. But the really spectacular expansion started with the founding of the empire, as seen by the shift of the population from country to city. Whereas there were only eight towns with more than 100,000 inhabitants in 1871, there were twenty-six by the time the chancellor retired in 1890. The number of those gaining their livelihood in agriculture fell from 60 percent of the population in 1871 to about 40 percent in 1890. The greatest economic stimulus occurred during the first five years of the empire. The new central government encouraged industrialization, and the 5 billion francs of war indemnity provided easy credit, which, incidentally, led to considerable speculation in financial circles.

The Germans emphasized heavy industry. In iron and steel production, they soon surpassed England, as can be seen from the table.

STEEL OUTPUT IN METRIC TONS		
Year	*Germany*	*England*
1870	169,000	286,000
1890	2,161,000	3,637,000
1900	6,645,000	5,130,000
1910	13,698,000	6,374,000

German industry also specialized in chemicals and electrical equipment. Transportation, too, was stressed. The merchant marine soon became the second largest in the world, lagging behind only that of England. The expansion of the railroads and the development of inland water transport aided both industry and agriculture.

This rapid development that transformed the German economy within a few decades into one of the most industrialized in the world is frequently called the "German miracle." Similar superficial assertions are often made today concerning Germany's astounding recovery after World War II. To be sure, the Germans worked with efficiency and assiduity, devoting much time and energy to the development of science and its application to industry. But hard work and perseverance alone did not bring about this expansion. Starting almost from scratch, Germany was not handicapped by outmoded models and methods. Consequently its industrial plant was up-to-date and the Germans could rationalize and streamline industrial processes. Moreover, the German government played an important role in this economic development. Despite the ideals of certain liberals, classical economists had relatively little influence in Germany. German industry never experienced a long period of *laissez faire*. The government assumed ownership of the railroads, regulated industry, encouraged large-scale amalgamations for the sake of greater efficiency, and provided subsidies, tax privileges, and tariff protection. Big industry and government therefore cooperated closely in the aim of making Germany powerful, both politically and economically. In the tradition of German paternalism, the government exercised supervision over the economy. In turn, economic interest groups exerted pressure on the government so that it would operate in their favor. Thus industry grew more and more powerful. The trend favored the establishment of huge cartels that covered entire industries, such as steel, coal, and chemicals, and dominated whole segments of German life. This concentration of industry and the close relationship between government and industry were of considerable importance in later years, and were probably not auspicious for the development of democracy in Germany.

Expansion of industry was accompanied by the growth of German financial institutions. A number of important credit banks had been founded in the 1850s and 1860s, but as occurred in industry, the real period of growth started after the founding of the empire. German banks, especially the Reichsbank and the famous "D" banks (so called because their names all started with a "D"—the *Diskonto, Dresdner, Darmstädter,* and *Deutsche* banks), specialized in industrial production credit and frequently acted as holding companies for large industrial concerns. This amalgamation of financial and industrial interests produced a greater concentration of economic power in the hands of small groups of individuals than occurred in most other Western countries.

BISMARCK'S INTERNAL WORK

Perhaps the best explanation for Bismarck's remaining in office after 1871 was that he felt his task was not yet completed. With the promulgation of the constitution of 1871, Germany was outwardly united, but a thousand years of localism and particularism were not eliminated by a mere political proclamation. Hence, besides administering internal and foreign affairs, Bismarck had to weld the various states into a unified empire.

As soon as possible after the victory

over France, the new central government proceeded with the task of unifying the new Reich economically. A common currency was created, the postal and telegraph systems of the various states were united—except those of Bavaria and Württemberg—and the metric system of weights and measures was adopted everywhere. Construction of an extended railroad network was pushed with speed in order to link all parts of the country. Coordination of the different legal systems took more time, but the main step in this direction was taken in 1876 with the establishment of the Common Court of Appeals in Leipzig. This was followed by the issuance of a common code of criminal law and finally—though only in 1896—by a common civil code.

Political Life

Bismarck's Germany may be characterized as "absolutism in democratic forms." Although Germans enjoyed universal male suffrage and representative government of a sort, in the imperial constitution there were few of the checks and balances that Americans take for granted. Control emanated almost exclusively from above (see pages 85–86). As minister-president of Prussia and chancellor of the Reich, Bismarck was vested with tremendous power. Legally, he was not responsible to the Reichstag, although he did try to gain its support to further his legislative program and to receive a measure of popular backing. Bismarck's cabinet had no power of its own, but rather resembled a managerial staff. The chancellor hired and fired ministers—with the automatic consent of the emperor—much as an industrialist replaces divisional or departmental heads. The ministers were responsible to Bismarck for the conduct of their particular department but were not consulted on over-all policy.

Ultimately, Bismarck was dependent solely on the goodwill and confidence of his emperor. While William I was alive Bismarck's position was impregnable. After his old friend and protector died (1888), Bismarck was unable to maintain himself and fell from power two years later.

However, Bismarck's power should not be overestimated. One is easily misled by the epithet the "Iron Chancellor," and by the usual photographs showing him as a stern Prussian Junker. To be sure, Bismarck was powerful, but he was no dictator, and his power was limited. Particularism persisted, and Bismarck knew that the princes of the larger German states—particularly Bavaria and Württemberg—would not easily be reconciled to a secondary role in the new Germany. Opposing these princes might push them straight into the arms of Austria or France and thus open the possibility of renewed international conflict, something Bismarck chose to avoid at all cost. He was therefore cautious in his dealings with the Bundesrat and proceeded warily in all matters affecting the rights of the states.

It is also significant that Bismarck, who had done so much for the aggrandizement of the Prussian army, was unable to control it. William I looked upon himself as a soldier, and while he was content to let Bismarck run the government, he jealously regarded the army as his private domain. Nor did the commanding generals, such as Moltke, brook any interference in military affairs.

The relationship between the civilian

authorities and the army in Germany deserves further consideration, for it presented problems that have remained acute in Germany. The inability to achieve civilian control over the armed forces was to plague the Weimar Republic; relations with the army were a problem even in the Hitler era, and the question is still being debated today in connection with Germany's present-day rearmament policies. In America, the armed forces are supervised by a civilian secretary of defense who, although appointed by the President, is ultimately responsible to the people through their electoral power. In Germany, however, the Prussian army had been created by the kings as their own instrument of power—one might almost say as their own property. There had been no revolution in Germany comparable to those in France and America; no "nation in arms," no minutemen, no national guard—except for brief periods during the Wars of Liberation and the Revolution of 1848—that might have evolved into a people's army truly independent of the ruler and subject to the people's direction. The army had stayed strictly apart during the nineteenth century, when a certain amount of democratization had been allowed to take place in government. It was not democratized internally, nor placed under civilian control. And the creation of a *German* army concomitant with the establishment of the Reich was in fact a mere expansion of the *Prussian* army. Prussian army laws and regulations were extended to all component units, and all soldiers and officers swore allegiance to the king of Prussia. Only Bavaria, Württemberg, and Saxony were permitted to retain their own semiautonomous regiments,

within the framework of an all-German army under Prussian direction and leadership.

Since Germany had the forms of a democracy, Bismarck also had to contend with the various political parties that grew more numerous and active after 1871. Reichstag elections were held every three, later five, years, unless required sooner because of dissolution by the Bundesrat and the imperial chancellor. Since parliamentarianism in the British sense did not exist, Bismarck himself could afford to belong to no particular party. Yet because he required a base of operation within the Reichstag to assure passage of legislation and approval of the budget, he aligned himself with this or that group as the occasion demanded, and felt free to switch his allegiance when such support no longer suited his purposes. In this kind of political maneuvering he proved a master.

In 1871 there were six major and over a dozen minor parties with national status, as well as countless parties operating only on the local level (see Chart 1). From the beginning, German parties tended to splinter with frightening rapidity. Germany was to be plagued as much as any other European country by the atomization of its political life. The usual political individualism and tenacious adherence to abstract principles, which may account for splintering in other European countries, only partly explains the problem in Germany. Regional differences, local interests, as well as past traditions of the various states, frequently made it impossible for people from different parts of the Reich to collaborate in a common party, even though they might be in agreement on most major issues. Ethnic

Chart 1   ELECTION RESULTS, 1871–1912

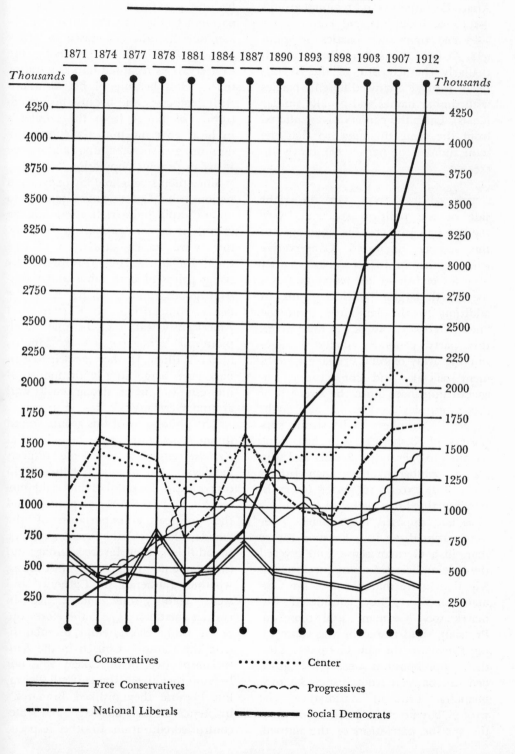

minorities—such as Danes, Poles, and Alsace-Lorrainers—and regional groups —such as Bavarians and Hanoverians —formed their own parties or splinters. At first, this subdividing was particularly characteristic of the liberals (who formed many different parties with similar names and usually similar ideals). Later the conservatives suffered from the same dilemma, so that the total number of parties constantly increased.

THE CONSERVATIVES On the right side of the political spectrum were the Prussian Junkers. They belonged to the loosely organized Conservative party, which in 1871 received slightly over an eighth of the votes and was the fourth largest political group. In addition to the landlords from the "new" Germany east of the Elbe River, this party generally included high-ranking army officers, Prussian government officials, and conservative Lutheran ministers. Since the strength of this group lay in Prussia, one might expect its members to be strong supporters of Bismarck, who had done so much to aggrandize Prussia and who was a member of their own Junker class. But, except for brief intervals, they remained distrustful of Bismarck's aims and opposed his policies. They were nationalistic in a Prussian rather than in a German sense, and revered the title and traditions of the Prussian Kingdom more than those of the German Empire. They considered Bismarck too "German" and too "unPrussian," and feared he was submerging Prussia in the new Germany. That their apprehensions were partly justified can be seen from Bismarck's own memoirs. Prussian nationalism, he wrote, "has no more justification than the specific patriotism of the individual German states. . . . As soon as I became convinced that the Prussian national feeling was the anvil to hammer out the others, I ceased to follow lopsided Prussian aims." Moreover, the Conservatives regarded him as a traitor to his class because of his flirtations with democracy and because his sequestration of power from the landlords in local governmental affairs was undermining their remaining hold on the Prussian peasant population.

Since their stronghold lay in agrarian regions, the Conservatives tended to oppose rapid industrialization and the growth of modern capitalism. Initially, they were stanch supporters of free trade. But in the late 1870s, pressed by rising prices of both labor and industrial goods, and suffering from the heavy competition of Russian and American wheat, they became champions of protective tariffs. Finally, under William II, they participated in backstage bargaining with industrial interests to put a strong tariff wall around Germany.

The philosophy of this group, voiced in one of its newspapers, the influential *Kreuzzeitung,* was in some respects medieval. Its members believed in corporatism, in quasi-divine right monarchy, and in the social prestige and the political all-importance of the "modern knights," the Prussian officers. In addition, they favored strong and independent religious institutions, whether Lutheran or Catholic, and were against state interference in church matters. They therefore opposed Bismarck's attempt to subordinate the Catholic Church in the *Kulturkampf* (see below, page 98), not because they liked Roman Catholicism, but because they disliked Bismarck's insistence on civil marriages and state-controlled education. In other respects,

this group echoed ideals of the romantic period. In a pseudo-Hegelian spirit, they revered the state—primarily the Prussian state—as a living organism to which the individual is subordinate.

In Bismarckian Germany, the Conservative party was not very powerful. But at that period Bismarck's manipulations kept all parties from acquiring true power. Nevertheless, its influence was frequently felt, and until World War II the party represented one of the fundamental aspects of German sociopolitical opinion.

THE FREE CONSERVATIVES Whereas the Conservatives usually opposed Bismarck, the Free Conservatives, Germany's third largest party in 1871, more frequently supported him. The philosophy of this party to a great extent resembled that of the Conservatives, from which it had split in 1866, but its stronghold lay primarily in the "old" Germany and therefore largely outside Prussia. Strongly pro-German in their nationalistic feelings, its members felt grateful to Bismarck for having achieved unification. In fact, in 1871 they adopted as alternate party label the name *Reichspartei,* presumably to show their enthusiasm for the new Reich. Besides landholders, this group also included some of the powerful industrialists and capitalists from the Ruhr, who quickly recognized the economic possibilities provided by an enlarged Germany. Many of the more influential members of this party became government officials in the 1870s.

THE NATIONAL LIBERALS More toward the center of political opinion were the many groups that at one time or another had split off from the Progressive party. During the first decade of empire under Bismarck, the most

influential of these were the National Liberals, who had split off from the Progressives over the issue of the Bill of Indemnity (see page 68). The National Liberals, the strongest party in Germany, had polled over a quarter of the votes cast in the elections of 1871. To be sure, they had retained part of their liberal ideals, but as in 1866, whenever there was a conflict of interests between liberalism and national unity or furtherance of the Reich, they threw their support to the latter.

Most of the National Liberals came from the upper levels of the middle class. They were an urban group, not at all Prussian in outlook. Like the Free Conservatives, many had economic interests in industry or commerce. They consequently looked with favor upon Bismarck's efforts to unify Germany economically and financially and credited him with the increased prosperity resulting from Germany's expanded markets. One can easily see why Bismarck, in turn, relied on them heavily in the early years after 1871. They had helped him in the three difficult years preceding the Franco-Prussian War, and they now supported his fight against the Catholic Church, against the agrarian Conservatives, and against remaining particularism. Toward the end of Bismarck's first decade as chancellor, however, they became increasingly disenchanted with his administration. They disliked his compromise with the Catholic Church and his veering toward the Conservatives. On the other hand, they were pleased with some of his new policies and particularly welcomed Germany's entry into the colonial arena in 1883.

In due course, these National Liberals lost most of their liberal ideas. Like the Conservatives, many of them

abandoned advocacy of free trade in favor of protectionism. As their liberalism declined, they became increasingly nationalistic. In party politics, they gradually lost importance. But just as the Conservatives were less significant as a party than they were as representatives of German thought, so the National Liberals represented views that are worth recalling. One of their premises remained important in German life: the idea that strengthening Germany is more vital than principles of freedom, democratization, or individual liberty.

THE PROGRESSIVES   To the left of the National Liberal party were the old-style Progressives. They, too, were subject to constant splits, realignments, and changes of name. In 1866, this party had remained true to its principles of constitutional government, and had refused to vote for Bismarck's Bill of Indemnity. In 1871, it polled less than 10 percent of the vote and was the fifth party in size. Although pleased with the democratic measures embodied in the constitution of 1871, the Progressives were opposed to Bismarck's autocratic administration. They adhered to their belief in free trade, and disapproved of the tariffs of 1879 and later. They wanted to develop Germany rather than diffuse their energies through imperialistic adventures. They distrusted the Junker class and the army, and strove without success to subject the military to civilian control. And they would have preferred a constitutional monarch to their anachronistic "divine right" ruler.

In the course of the 1880s and 1890s, the Progressives modified their principles considerably. They changed from typical late eighteenth- and nineteenth-century liberalism, which called the "least" government the "best" government, to the modern approach that assigns to government certain protective functions. Although disagreeing with the socialists on methods as well as aims, the Progressives gradually called for state help in social work and labor relations. They came to approve of limited tariffs and government-run education, and called for a balanced consideration of the rights of the state as a whole versus those of individual citizens.

Their influence under the Bismarckian system was not very great, but they represented an important bridge between the spirit of '48 and the liberal democratic tendencies that were to assert themselves once again after World War I.

THE CENTER PARTY   Although the parties discussed so far were largely Protestant in membership, religion did not form their primary base of cohesion. Rather, they were based on political, economic, or class ideals. The Center party, however, was of a different nature. Its basis was largely religious. It was founded in 1870 primarily as a political organ of German Catholicism, and immediately became very powerful. At the polls in 1871, it gained more votes than any other party except the National Liberals, and it continued to exert much influence in German political life for decades. Though largely a middle-class party, its support came from all walks of life, and class interests played a relatively minor role in its policies.

The religious division of Germany continued to have repercussions in German politics. Since the days of Frederick the Great, the rivalry between

Protestant Prussia and Catholic Austria had maintained a precarious balance between the two major religions of the Germans, but with the establishment of Bismarck's Reich and the exclusion of Austria, there could no longer be a balance. Prussia was in the saddle, and Germany seemingly was to become a Protestant nation. Hence it is understandable that the Center party in its early years was distinctly wary of the Reich and usually anti-Bismarckian in its policies. Its leader, Ludwig Windthorst (1812–1891), not merely supported the interests of the Catholic Church, but also encouraged the aspirations of various groups at odds with the new Germany —the Poles in West Prussia and Poznan, the newly conquered Alsatians and Lorrainers, the Bavarians who bewailed their lost independence, and certain Hanoverians who regretted their destroyed kingdom. The anti-Bismarckian stance of the Center party lasted for nearly the first decade of the new Reich, and provided the background for the famous *Kulturkampf*.

THE SOCIALISTS Finally, on the left side of the political scale were various socialist and workers' groups. In 1870, organized socialism was fairly new and relatively weak. Only 2 (out of 397) socialist representatives were elected to the Reichstag of 1871. The first German socialist organization of any importance, the General Association of German Workers, had been founded by Ferdinand Lassalle (1825–1864) in Leipzig in 1863. Lassalle had rejected most of the utopian solutions of earlier decades, but had refused to embrace the new theories of Karl Marx in their entirety. Thoroughly democratic in outlook, he had advocated universal suffrage to enable workers to influence legislation. His workers' organization was to use political weapons rather than violence to gain social and economic aims. In addition, Lassalle had hoped to eliminate the "exploitation by capitalists" decried by Marx—not through state ownership of the means of production but through establishment of industrial cooperatives owned by the workers.

Lassalle's premature death in a duel in 1864 left the German workers divided for almost a decade. Some continued to advocate his policies, but were willing to compromise with Bismarck. These followers of Lassalle were somewhat nationalistic and did not object to the existence of a strong state. Many of them supported Bismarck's Bill of Indemnity. Other groups of workers rapidly fell under the influence of Wilhelm Liebknecht, who had spent thirteen years of exile in London in the company of Karl Marx. When Marx founded the First International in 1864, Liebknecht tried to bring German workers into the new international movement. With August Bebel (1840–1913), he developed an anti-Lassallean and anti-Bismarckian program. His group vehemently opposed the Bill of Indemnity, Prussia's militarism and expansionism, and the impending war with France. In 1869, Liebknecht and Bebel formally organized their followers into the Social Democratic Workingman's party.

German socialism gained some strength during the early years of the Reich. The Lassalleans quickly grew wary of Bismarck's policies, and at a large congress held in Gotha in 1875, they agreed to merge with Liebknecht's followers. The result of the merger produced the Socialist Workingman's

party, more frequently called the Social Democratic party (SPD). Although Liebknecht, the international Marxist, became the leader of the new party, the program adopted at Gotha was largely based on the ideas of Lassalle, so much so that Marx himself bitterly denounced it. The new combined party greatly increased its representation in the Reichstag, so that Bismarck soon considered it a danger to his system and devoted his energy to eradicating German socialism.

The Kulturkampf

Soon after the founding of the empire, the spectacular attempt to subordinate the Roman Catholic Church to the new imperial government split Germany into opposing camps. Although this attempt was essentially a fight for power between the government and the Catholic Church, some contemporary journalists called it a struggle between two ways of life or two civilizations, and hence gave it the inappropriate name *Kulturkampf* (battle of cultures).

There can be no doubt that the entire struggle was more political in nature than religious. Still religion had its share in the temporary reawakening of the rivalry between Catholics and Protestants. Protestants at the time looked with apprehension on the efforts of Pope Pius IX to reassert the power of the Catholic Church, while German Catholics regarded with suspicion the political victories of Protestant Prussia.

Historical forces were also involved. The last great fight between popes and emperors had ended in the fourteenth century. After that, with a few exceptions, such as Napoleon I, the emperors had been too weak to challenge the popes. As a result, there had been few quarrels between Empire and papacy for some six centuries. Significantly, the fight was reopened when the German Empire was re-established on a strengthened basis in 1871. The fact that the new emperor was also a Protestant, the first Protestant emperor in history, only heightened the mutual suspicion. Although Bismarck insisted that the Germany of 1871 was a satisfied nation and harbored no imperialistic ambitions, the very fact that the old Reich had been resurrected seemed to recall the long papal-imperial rivalry of the Middle Ages and set the stage for a new struggle. Bismarck himself must have been conscious of this, since he referred so frequently during this struggle to the days of the medieval Emperor Henry IV. But although much has been written about the *Kulturkampf,* it is even now impossible to ascertain the true motives behind the chancellor's actions. To justify his attempted curtailment of its power, Bismarck simply characterized the Catholic Church as *reichsfeindlich*—an enemy of the Reich.

Bismarck desired a thoroughly unified Reich. A strong independent Catholic Church that he could not control would have been as distasteful to him as it had been to all autocratic rulers of previous centuries. He therefore set out to weaken the Catholic Church in Germany and place it under the supervision of the state. Between 1871 and 1875, numerous laws and ordinances were passed for this purpose. In 1872, the Society of Jesus and its affiliates were banished from German territory. The so-called May Laws of 1873 transferred to the government the right to sanction church appointments, gave the state control over all clerical educa-

tion, and restricted the jurisdiction of ecclesiastical courts. Two years later civil marriage was made compulsory, and pressure was brought on disobedient clergy by withholding government-collected church taxes. The Catholic press was censored and the publication of papal letters of remonstrance prohibited. Finally, all Catholic religious orders—except those devoted to tending the sick—were abolished and some recalcitrant priests fined and imprisoned.

For several years this new "investiture controversy" raged in bitter acrimony. Bismarck was aided by a split in the ranks of the Catholics themselves. Not all Catholics had readily accepted the strong stand taken by Pope Pius IX in his Syllabus of Errors of 1864 and in the subsequent dogma of Papal Infallibility. The so-called Liberal or Old Catholics had refused to follow the pope, and had split off from the Church. They sided with Bismarck, not because they wanted the Church's independence destroyed, but because they hoped to see the papal drive for centralization weakened. Their stand recalled the attitude of certain German bishops who sided with Henry IV in his struggle against Gregory VII. Besides this help from the Old Catholics, Bismarck also received support from the National Liberals, from many Protestant groups, and from nationalistic conservatives, who were instinctively opposed to "foreign" influence in Germany.

On the other hand, the Catholic Center party was not alone in opposing Bismarck in the *Kulturkampf*. All elements in the Reich that disliked Bismarck's policy of centralization sided with the Center party, particularly the Poles, Bavarians, and Alsace-Lorrainers. Many Protestants also favored the forces opposing Bismarck because they disapproved in principle of the subjection of church to state.

The *Kulturkampf* finally ebbed in the late 1870s. It can hardly be said that Bismarck called off the struggle because he felt he had accomplished his aim. On the contrary, as a result of the attack, the Center party had more than doubled in strength, and by 1878 almost equaled the National Liberals in the Reichstag. Rather, Bismarck came to realize that little could be achieved by continuing the struggle. Instead of helping to unify the Reich, the *Kulturkampf* crystallized the opposition of particularistic elements. Moreover, political alignments in Germany were changing, and Bismarck was losing some of his traditional supporters.

The chancellor therefore prepared to come to terms with the Center party. Good fortune helped his plans. After the death of Pope Pius IX in 1878, the papacy was led by the more conciliatory Leo XIII. Negotiations with the papacy were started at once, although neither side was officially willing to cede many points. Bismarck refused to abrogate the anti-Catholic laws immediately, and the pope would not negotiate on any other basis. But since Bismarck was eager to make peace with the papacy and gain the support of the Center party for his new policies, especially for the tariff legislation, he simply ceased to enforce the laws. Some of the anti-Catholic laws were later amended and some were abrogated entirely; only a few, such as the law on compulsory civil marriage, remained. The papacy was placated by these measures, and the *Kulturkampf* ended gradually after 1878. It was followed

by a large-scale realignment of the forces that supported Bismarck.

The Tariff of 1879 and Political Realignments

In the elections of 1878, the Conservatives and the Free Conservatives each increased their Reichstag representation by 19 seats, while the National Liberals lost 29. These electoral results, coupled with the debate on impending tariff legislation, demonstrated to Bismarck the need for reshuffling his political support. The gains made by the two conservative parties and by the Center made it advisable for the chancellor to come to terms with them. At the same time, he realized that he could no longer rely so heavily on the National Liberals in his parliamentary maneuvers, since they were declining in strength and since some of them opposed him on the tariff question.

The chancellor had come to favor protective tariffs for German industry and agriculture to strengthen them against foreign competition and to increase the revenue of the Reich, which depended to a great extent on customs receipts. He also hoped to encourage German production in order to make the Reich as self-sufficient as possible. To procure adoption in the Reichstag of his tariff of 1879, he therefore relied on a combination of Conservatives, Free Conservatives, Centrists, and a few National Liberals, who voted for the bill in opposition to the remaining National Liberals, the Progressives, and the Social Democrats. The Conservatives, representing the agricultural interests, had been severely threatened by American and Russian imports, and offered general political support to the chancellor in return for tariff protection on their produce. Moreover, some of the National Liberals, especially those in industry who had suffered from the two minor depressions of 1873 and 1877, were also ready to abandon their doctrinaire stand on free trade and accept the tariff. A large part of the Center party was equally willing to vote for the tariff, provided their other contentions with Bismarck could be resolved.

The Anti-Socialist Struggle

Besides the tariff question there was another issue conducive to this political realignment: the rising strength of the Social Democrats. In the early 1860s, Bismarck had momentarily contemplated collaborating with Ferdinand Lassalle to gain the workers' support for his efforts to unite Germany. The two men admired each other's political sagacity and found common ground in their preference for a strong, centralized government. But during the 1870s, Bismarck had come to distrust the motives of the Socialists. Although their Gotha program of 1875 was fairly Lassallean and evolutionary, the Socialists were internationalists, pacifists, antimilitarists, and thus suspect to Bismarck. In the 1877 elections, they polled half a million votes—more than the Free Conservatives and almost as many as the Conservatives. Moreover, their leaders in the Reichstag, Bebel and Liebknecht, had led an incessant campaign against Bismarck's programs. And the conservative landowners and large industrialists who now sided with Bismarck gladly supported the chancellor in his efforts to nip in the bud the "red" danger to their way of life.

The purported justification for the suppression of German socialism were two attempts on the life of Emperor William. Although neither of the would-be assassins was connected with the Socialists, Bismarck at once called for strong measures against all socialist organizations. His bills failed to pass in the Reichstag, and he dissolved it. As was seen, the new elections of July 1878 gave him the support of the Conservatives that he needed to obtain a majority for his proposals. In October of that year, the chancellor's anti-Socialist legislation passed in the Reichstag. These laws were a curious attempt to reconcile discriminatory measures against a particular group with the democratic principles of free elections. On the one hand, Socialists were forbidden to organize into groups. They could hold occasional meetings, but only under strict police supervision. Their aims were decried as "subversive" to the public order and hostile to the interests of the state, and most of their publications were outlawed. Financial contributions to "subversive" groups were declared illegal. On the other hand, the new legislation permitted Socialists to be elected to public offices, for during the parliamentary debates, a majority in the Reichstag had refused to undermine the principle of free representation by disenfranchising the Socialists. Thus the anomaly existed that while officially the Socialists (and their publications) were forced to go underground and some of them were jailed on charges of subversion, they still could become members of the Reichstag and hold free debate therein.

Besides enforcing the anti-Socialist laws, which were periodically renewed until 1890, Bismarck tried to prevent the growth of German socialism also by adopting some of its goals for improving the lot of the German workers. In 1881 he launched a program of social legislation that was so comprehensive and farsighted that it immediately placed Germany far ahead of other nations in this field of national policy. Bismarck's aim was, of course, not solely to take steam away from the Socialists. In internal policies, the chancellor had never favored the extreme *laissez-faire* ideas of the nineteenth-century liberals. On the contrary, in the style of the old Prussian paternalism, he proclaimed that it was the obligation of the state to protect the weak. As a sincere Christian, he felt it the duty of everyone, especially of the government, to help alleviate the suffering of the sick, the old, and the infirm. Finally, as a statesman he realized that the state as a whole would be strengthened if none of its members was so weak as to endanger the rest of the body politic. One must remember that he always saw social reform from the viewpoint of the state and not from that of the worker who demanded help as an inherent right. Bismarck "passed social laws because they were necessary; social reform was never to him a passion, but always a policy."

After some parliamentary delays, the first legislation was adopted in 1883. A Health Insurance Law provided for financial and medical aid to workers laid off because of sickness. One third of the cost of this insurance was to be borne by the employer and two thirds by the worker. The following year saw the passage of the Accident Insurance Law, under which disabled workers were to be compensated and widows of workers killed on their jobs

were to receive pensions. Premiums for this system were to be paid entirely by the employers. Finally, in 1889, an Old Age and Invalidism Insurance Law made provisions for all retired workers over the age of seventy and for those permanently disabled at an earlier age. The cost of this program was to be borne by employers, workers, and the state itself. After Bismarck's dismissal from office in 1890, additional social legislation was passed to improve the lot of the lower classes. But Bismarck's system of social security alone considerably improved the material well-being of the German workers.

It is commonly asserted that Bismarck failed in his anti-Socialist struggle, since neither the anti-Socialist laws nor the social security legislation curbed the growth of German Socialism. In fact, between 1878 and 1890, the Social Democrats increased their representation in the Reichstag from 9 to 35 seats, and by 1912 became the largest party in Germany, obtaining 20 percent of all votes cast. But the increase in the party's numerical strength does not mean that Bismarck failed to steal some of the Socialists' thunder; in fact he may have contributed measurably to the incipient emasculation of Socialism in Germany. By helping the workers in some of their social problems and by heightening their sense of security, he softened their revolutionary ideals and strengthened the evolutionary, more middle-class-oriented wing of the party. He acted in the Prussian tradition dating back to the days of Napoleon I that revolution or change must come from above. By bestowing benefits from above instead of giving in to pressure from below, Bismarck weakened the

political strength as well as the virulence of the Socialist movement.

In the long run, this development proved detrimental to German socialism and perhaps equally so to German democratization. The workers could claim no credit for their improved status, since they had not really fought for the benefits they received. On the contrary, many of them came to believe that their own political action was of little importance, since the state seemed ready to take care of them. There appeared to be less need for workers' associations, workers' parties and democratic or revolutionary political action, since the state was cognizant of their needs. Consequently German trade-unionism and socialism, although growing numerically, did not develop the same sense of fruitful achievement and political responsibility as did similar movements in England and France, where they were forced to a much greater extent to fight for their cause.

The Problem of Ethnic Minorities

Cementing German internal unity required more than fighting Catholic particularism and Socialist internationalism. Within Germany there were millions of Poles, Danes, Alsatians, and Lorrainers who spoke no German and had few reasons to be loyal to the new Reich. Revived Polish patriotism, Catholic solidarity—for with the exception of the Danes, these ethnic minorities were mostly Catholic—as well as French sympathy and tacit support for their cause, turned the treatment of these peoples into a constant problem for the German government. Since the central administration hoped gradually to eradicate exaggerated pro-

vincial patriotism, particularly in southern Germany, it considered it all the more essential to assimilate these alien elements into Germany's social and political body. Consequently, the federal and Prussian governments inaugurated a policy of forced Germanization. Prussia dealt with the Danes and the Poles, since they lived on territory under Prussian jurisdiction. Alsace and Lorraine, on the other hand, which were not given statehood until 1911, were governed as an imperial territory by the federal government directly from Berlin. In all these regions with ethnic minorities, the speaking of German was made compulsory in school and at public functions. Land was transferred, sometimes forcibly, from local owners to German colonists. Manifestations of non-German sentiments were suppressed, and Germans were induced to migrate to the critical regions in order to alter the ethnic composition of the population.

Yet this drive to Germanize the minorities, which reflected the nascent Pan-German movement, was on the whole unsuccessful, no matter how methodically conducted. The Poles tenaciously held onto their land and customs, and the resistance of the Alsace-Lorrainers was so persistent that the imperial government ultimately had to concede them a certain amount of local autonomy.

THE FOREIGN POLICY OF BISMARCK

The German Reich of 1871 was the product of three wars. In the process of its creation, Bismarck had repeatedly proclaimed that only force

could unify Germany. This bellicose attitude alone aroused the apprehensions of the European powers. These fears were further nourished by certain extreme nationalists in Germany, who announced that its military might made Germany a world power destined to dominate the Continent. In addition, the emergence of a strong and united Germany with a burgeoning economy had radically altered the international balance in Europe. Russia was bound to be upset over the presence of a powerful neighbor on its western frontier. For over a century Russia had tried to prevent such an occurrence, since it would discourage Russia's possible future expansion toward the heart of Europe. Austria's status was fundamentally changed. Expelled from Germany, Austria turned its full attention toward expanding into the Balkans, an area in which it was fated to clash with Russian designs. Finally, France, defeated and deprived of Alsace-Lorraine through the Peace of Frankfurt, appeared unwilling to reconcile itself to being inferior to Germany. The chimera of a war of revenge hovered over Paris.

Thus Bismarck's role in foreign affairs after 1871 was not easy. He called Germany a satiated nation harboring no further territorial aims. This was not simply a deceitful diplomatic maneuver. His reiteration of Germany's peaceful intentions—in fact, all his assiduous attempts to maintain the peace of Europe—were based on shrewd political considerations. In connection with the war scare of 1875, he noted in his diary:

Such a war [with France] would . . . probably have provoked an alliance among Russia, Austria, and England and possibly have brought about active intervention on

their part against the new and not yet consolidated *Reich*. This would have put Germany onto the same path which led the first and second French Empires to their downfall through a policy of continued war. Europe would have looked upon our action as a misuse of our acquired strength, and everyone, including the centrifugal forces in the *Reich* themselves, would have constantly been on guard, or at war with Germany. After the surprising proof we gave of our military strength, it was the peaceful attitude of German policy which contributed to conciliating the foreign powers and internal opponents sooner than we had expected. . . .

There were, of course, more than a few Germans who insisted that Germany was not "satiated," that the "gathering-in" of Germans on the Continent had not been completed, or that overseas expansion was the next essential step. But as early as the Revolution of 1848, Bismarck had opted in favor of a *Kleindeutschland* solution because he considered it the most feasible. He saw no reason to change his mind in 1871. To go beyond—to risk war—would be to run the chance of destroying his entire work. Any major European war that might upset the *status quo* of 1871 presented inherent dangers to Germany. Consequently, the Iron Chancellor proclaimed himself a guardian of peace during his entire remaining tenure of office and his foreign policy rested on these considerations.

Relations with France

In 1871, France was a weak nation. Its armies had been defeated and the empire of Napoleon III had collapsed. The civil war in Paris, the loss of territory, the payment of the war indemnity to Germany, as well as internal political dissension, were all sapping France's strength. The Treaty of Frankfurt of 1871 had specified that German troops were to occupy certain northern departments of France until the full indemnity of five billion francs had been paid. As long as France lay prostrate and partially occupied by German army units, Bismarck could feel relatively safe from a French war of revenge.

But French recovery was surprisingly rapid. Barely two years after its defeat, and one year ahead of schedule, France paid off its indemnity to Germany, forcing an early withdrawal of the German occupation contingents. Moreover, in 1873, the conservative royalists came to political power in Paris. Their program was fervently nationalistic and bellicose. They favored strengthening the army, spoke of supporting the pope against the new Italian monarchy, and hinted at a war of reprisal against Germany.

France's resurgence rekindled the distrust between the two countries and lay at the heart of several war scares (in 1875 and 1887–1888). Berlin and Paris made an occasional effort at establishing friendly relations, but the wound of Alsace-Lorraine would not heal, and no sincere reconciliation was effected. Persisting mutual suspicion produced an armament race that grew in intensity over the next decades. To keep French eyes averted from the Rhine, and to dim French hopes of recovering the lost provinces, Bismarck openly encouraged the French government to acquire more African colonies.

Bismarck was determined to keep France isolated at all cost. Germany, he felt, could always repeat the victory of 1870 over France alone, but if

France were to acquire a major ally, such as England, Austria, or Russia, any ensuing general conflagration would entail dire consequences for Germany. This decision to isolate France became one of the pivots of his foreign policy. To make a *rapprochement* between France and Italy more difficult, he encouraged both to covet Tunisia. Similarly, he tried to fan the distrust between France and England by pretending to support each in their competing claims in Egypt and Morocco. As long as these nations sought similar spheres of influence in Africa, Germany was relatively safe from the possible threat of an anti-German coalition. But it was even more important for Bismarck to keep Austria and Russia from befriending France: such an alliance would threaten Germany with a two-front war. In this case, Bismarck could not reach his aim by fanning conflicts between the nations. He had to rely on a complicated system of alliances. Critics have often asserted that the web of alliances he fashioned for this purpose was too complicated to be durable and that it ultimately led Europe closer to war—but it did accomplish Bismarck's primary aim. As long as he was in charge of Germany's foreign relations, France remained isolated.

Relations with Austria

Fundamental to the security system with which Bismarck tried to undergird the Reich was his alliance with Austria. A friendly Austria would at least guarantee a peaceful southern border. Above all, internal considerations made it important for Berlin to be on friendly terms with Vienna. If antagonized, Austria might easily reassume its old role—that of a rallying point for all discontented anti-Prussian, and especially Catholic, elements in Germany—and thereby endanger the internal unity of the Reich.

The new era of Austro-German *rapprochement* was opened when Emperors William I and Francis Joseph met in 1871 and again in 1872 to discuss relations between their countries. But in befriending Austria, Bismarck did not wish to alienate Russia. This was to prove difficult, for Russia and Austria clashed continually over spheres of influence in the Balkans, and it demanded more diplomatic dexterity than even Bismarck could muster to support at the same time two countries at loggerheads with each other. Russia was acting as protector of the Serbs against Turkey and Austria. Moreover, it hoped to extend its border into Rumania, and to acquire a protectorate over the central Balkans. Austria, on the other hand, hoped to inherit from Turkey at least the land along the Adriatic coast and to subjugate the Serbs, who were acting as a rallying force for a strong anti-Austrian Pan-Slav movement.

During the Near Eastern crisis of 1875–1878, Bismarck was repeatedly called upon to declare himself either for Russia or for Austria. The 1875 insurrection against Turkey in Bosnia-Herzegovina, followed in 1876 by the Bulgarian revolt and the Serbo-Turkish War, and in 1877 by the Russo-Turkish War, threatened to produce a general European war. Britain dispatched its fleet to the Straits at Constantinople, and tension between Austria and Russia nearly reached a breaking point. After much secret bargaining among the powers, an International Congress finally met in Berlin in 1878 to settle

the Near Eastern question. England's Disraeli generally supported Austria's Andrássy because both wished to keep Russia from gaining paramount influence over the Balkans. Italy and France played distinctly minor roles, while Bismarck tried to act, as he put it, "the honest broker" among Austria, Russia, and Turkey. In the final settlement, Serbia, Rumania, and Montenegro were recognized as independent states. Turkey was reduced in territory but not completely destroyed, Austria was allowed to occupy Bosnia-Herzegovina, and Britain to take Cyprus. France, Italy, and Germany received no territorial awards. Russia, on the other hand, was permitted to keep some of its conquests from the Russo-Turkish War, but less than it had hoped. At the same time, Russia's role as protector of the Balkan Slavs lost some of its halo because of its inability to assert its demands.

During the Congress of Berlin, Bismarck managed to walk a tightrope between Russia and Austria for a surprisingly long period. Yet in the end his "brokership" was interpreted by Russia as unfriendly to its interests, and unleashed strong Russian recriminations against Germany. This crisis and the resulting clamor induced the chancellor to tie Germany more closely to Austria. He had not abandoned hope of retaining Russia's friendship if possible, and Emperor William I steadfastly favored close relations with his cousin Alexander II. But for the moment Bismarck decided to lean more on Austria than on Russia, because the former seemed the more reliable nation. Austria had gained much internal stability after its reorganization of 1867, and had proved its for-

eign prestige in the Near Eastern crisis. Russia, on the other hand, was in the throes of internal disorders that led to the assassination of Emperor Alexander II a few years later.

The result of Bismarck's decision was the Dual Alliance of 1879 between Germany and Austria-Hungary, a defensive alliance stipulating that both nations would fight together if either were attacked by Russia, and that either would observe benevolent neutrality if the other were attacked by a power other than Russia. In order not to antagonize Russia, Bismarck kept the treaty secret until he defiantly published it during the war scare of 1888, at a time when Russo-German relations had cooled off considerably. The Dual Alliance was renewed periodically until the outbreak of World War I. The nucleus of Bismarck's security system, it was the most stable of all the alliances in the European diplomatic network. Bismarck considered it advantageous because it kept Germany from being completely isolated. However, it undermined Russo-German relations and involved Germany in the tangled affairs of the Balkans by strengthening Austria's hand vis-à-vis Russia and by tacitly promising Germany's support in Austria's Balkan ventures.

Relations with Italy

During the 1870s and 1880s, conditions were auspicious for drawing Italy and Germany into friendship and possible alliance. Both were new nations, essentially isolated and in need of finding a place in the European state system. Their histories provided so many common bonds and so much similarity

that the two countries might feel instinctively drawn together. Prussia and Italy had been allied in 1866, and Prussia's victory over Austria had sealed Italy's acquisition of Venetia. Four years later, the Franco-Prussian war had provided Italy the opportunity to seize Rome when Napoleon had to recall his troops. Finally, both nations could profit from such an alliance. To keep France isolated, Bismarck found it advantageous to support Italy in its struggle with France over trade relations, colonial expansion, and spheres of influence in the Mediterranean. Italy, for its part, gladly accepted German backing for its designs on Tunisia and for insurance against renewed French intervention in Italy on behalf of the pope.

Friendly relations between the two countries were cemented in 1873 when the king of Italy visited Berlin. However, no alliance was made until Italy had been completely rebuffed by France and alienated by French seizure of Tunisia in 1881. In 1882, Italy joined Germany and Austria in the Triple Alliance. This secret treaty, renewed periodically until World War I, was a defensive alliance guaranteeing mutual aid if one of the partners was "attacked [by] and engaged in a war with *two* or more great powers." If one of the three allies found itself at war with only *one* other power, the treaty stipulated that the other two were to observe benevolent neutrality. The Triple Alliance was thus useful to Bismarck for obtaining Austro-Italian assistance in a possible two-front war against Russia and France. So that this alliance would not contradict the secret Dual Alliance between Berlin

and Vienna, a special clause provided that each of the three allies had the right to aid one of the partners "if it should see fit," even when the treaty obligations called only for benevolent neutrality. Thus, if Russia attacked Austria or Germany, Berlin and Vienna could still present a common front against St. Petersburg.

Each partner in this alliance hoped to gain security for recent territorial acquisitions—Germany for Alsace-Lorraine, Austria for Bosnia-Herzegovina, and Italy for Rome. Article 2 specified that both partners would aid Italy in case that country "should be attacked by France, without direct provocation on her part." The Italians, in turn, were treaty-bound to help the Germans if Germany were attacked by France. No similar special clauses were inserted for Austria, which felt sufficiently protected by the guarantee of Italian neutrality and the assurance of German aid (stipulated in the Dual Alliance) in any war with Russia.

Although this alliance strengthened Germany and became another cornerstone in Bismarck's system, it was punctuated by many question marks. Italian irredentist demands on Austrian territory—particularly the Trentino and Trieste—and Italian hopes of acquiring lands and influence in the western Balkans caused constant tension between the two southern partners in the Triple Alliance. Moreover, Italy stipulated in a specially appended declaration that it would not fight against Great Britain; hence the alliance did not strengthen Germany in the Anglo-German colonial duel about to open. Finally, Italy expected the alliance to act primarily as a support against France. After its differences

with France over trade and colonies were settled—as happened by 1902—Italy cooled measurably toward its Austro-German friends and proved the weakest link in the alliance.

Relations with Russia

During his entire tenure of office, Bismarck tried to maintain friendly relations with Russia. This attitude was the continuation of long-standing Prussian policy. Frederick the Great, in the eighteenth century, had been the last to experience a two-front war against Russia and France, and later statesmen continued to recall Frederick's advice that friendship with Russia was a prerequisite if Prussia hoped to undertake anything in central Europe that might antagonize the French. This lesson had been underscored in the two decades preceding unification. Russia's anti-Prussian and pro-Austrian attitude during the revolutionary period 1848–1850 had been important in preventing Prussia from unifying Germany and had contributed measurably to its humiliation at Olmütz (see page 43). Consequently, Bismarck had decided to cultivate good relations with Russia in the preparatory years of German unification. During the Crimean War, when he was Prussian envoy to the diet at Frankfurt, he had argued successfully against German intervention on the side of England. At the time of the Polish rebellion of 1863, he had earned the gratitude of Alexander II by aligning Prussia solidly on the side of Russian repression of the insurgents. Finally, Bismarck and William I were exceedingly grateful to Russia for maintaining benevolent neutrality during the critical years when Prussia crushed Austria and France in the process of unifying Germany.

As early as 1872, William I, Francis Joseph, and Alexander II met in Berlin. Their meeting recalled the days of the "Holy Alliance," when it was thought that solidarity among the three eastern powers would bring stability to Europe. They discussed outstanding issues and tried to devise solutions for the troubled Balkan area. The Austrians and Germans asked the tsar to curb the nascent Pan-Slav movement inside Russia, since they feared it might endanger their possession of Slavic lands. No formal treaties were signed, but the talks foreshadowed the Three Emperors' League concluded in the following decade. Bismarck hoped to create such a league in order to maintain peace in eastern Europe and "undergird," as he wrote in his memoirs, "the solidarity of the monarchical system of order as represented by the three Emperors . . . in the face of the disorderly tendencies of a social republic such as France." It is interesting to recall here that Bismarck had secretly tried to enhance the power of the republican elements in France during the founding of the Third Republic, when it was as yet undecided whether France would adopt republican or monarchical institutions. He did this largely to ensure that France and Russia would find it harder to come to terms, for he thought it unlikely that autocratic Russia would put much trust in a republican France, despite Alexander II's mild liberalism.

Then came the rapid French resurgence in 1873 and the ensuing war crisis with France. Bismarck was forced to lean even more heavily on Russia. The two emperors, William and his

nephew Alexander, exchanged several more visits, and a Russo-German military convention was concluded that would help Germany in any trouble with France.

However, during the Near Eastern crisis of 1875–1878, as was seen, Bismarck thought it impossible to support all of Russia's demands. He found himself more and more in disagreement with the Russian foreign minister, Prince Gorchakov. Bismarck's decisions at the Congress of Berlin in 1878 earned him the friendship of England and the gratitude of Austria, but at the same time antagonized Russia. Despite William I's determination to side with Russia, Bismarck's view of Germany's over-all position between Russia and Austria had led him to tie Germany more closely to Austria by signing the Dual Alliance. Russo-German relations had reached a momentary low.

But Alexander II did not want to see Russia isolated in the face of an Austro-German alliance. Negotiators were sent to Berlin and Vienna to discuss new agreements among the three powers. The tsar was particularly disquieted by renewed war dangers in the Balkans, caused this time by disputes among Turkey, Montenegro, and Greece. Bismarck was equally interested in improving relations with St. Petersburg. Only Austria showed momentary hesitation. Hence the actual Three Emperors' League was not concluded until the summer of 1881, after the assassination of Alexander II and the accession of his son, Alexander III. This treaty obligated the other two partners to observe benevolent neutrality if one of them became involved in war with a fourth power. In any conflict with Turkey, the three agreed to hold mutual consultation in regard to territorial adjustments. The treaty gave Russia and Germany some reassurance in any conflict with England or France, respectively, but its primary aim was to prevent conflict between Austria and Russia. For this reason the treaty and appended protocol made specific disposition for the future of areas of outstanding Austro-Russian friction in the Balkans. The pact was to have a duration of three years and was kept secret.

For the moment Bismarck felt that Germany's position had once again been secured, yet he feared that this new alliance would disintegrate in the face of the frequent crises in the Balkans. Consequently, in the following year he concluded the Triple Alliance with Austria and Italy to gain added security against a possible two-front war. In 1883 he adhered to an alliance previously concluded between Austria and Rumania. Since Rumania lay in the path of Russia's advance into the Balkans, this Austro-Rumanian-German alliance was patently directed against Russian expansion toward the south, and once again showed that Bismarck preferred Austria over Russia.

Imperfect and fragile as the alliance of the three emperors was, it served Bismarck's purpose of keeping Russia friendly and discouraging it from forming an alliance with France. Consequently, despite recurring Austro-Russian friction, he managed to get the alliance renewed in 1884 for a second three-year term. Shortly thereafter, however, a new Near Eastern crisis flared up. War broke out between Serbia and Bulgaria, and Bulgaria itself was shaken by revolution.

The crisis lasted from 1885 to 1888, and involved Austria, Russia, Turkey, and England. In addition, there was renewed tension between Germany and France. Europe once again seemed dangerously close to war. The result of these crises was the breakdown of the Three Emperors' League, which Russia refused to renew in 1887. To protect Germany, Bismarck increased German armaments, and renewed the Triple Alliance with Austria and Italy. However, he still felt obliged to take special steps to keep Russia from aligning itself with France in order to avoid the encirclement of Germany. He therefore concluded with Russia the so-called Reinsurance Treaty of 1887, which was to replace the link lost through the demise of the Three Emperors' League.

Like that league, this Russo-German alliance was no military agreement. It did not call for either partner to aid the other militarily. It merely stipulated benevolent neutrality in case either power was involved in war, unless Russia should attack Austria or unless Germany should declare war on France. With this treaty in effect, Bismarck could face the war scare with greater assurance. Yet for added protection, he published the hitherto secret Dual Alliance to dampen Russian imperialistic ardor in the Balkans by convincing Russia of Austro-German solidarity. At the same time, he saw to it that France was informed of the terms of the secret Triple Alliance in order to dam the French clamor for a war of revenge.

The terms of the Reinsurance Treaty, which was kept secret until 1890, reveal Bismarck as rather unscrupulous. In order to please Russia, he encouraged its aspirations to dominate Bulgaria and the Turkish Straits, both areas in which he knew it would be steadfastly opposed by Great Britain and by his ally, Austria. Thus, the Treaty of Reinsurance was in effect contrary to the Dual Alliance, in spirit if not in actual terms. Yet despite these conflicting commitments, the treaty served its purpose for Bismarck. The failure to renew it in 1890—which was one of the issues leading to Bismarck's resignation—signaled the first step in the destruction of his security system and the beginning of the encirclement of Germany that was to be so disastrous for the nation in World War I.

Relations with England

During the two decades of Bismarck's chancellorship, Great Britain was concerned primarily with colonial expansion, while at home much of its energy was consumed by the Gladstone-Disraeli struggle, by questions of internal reform, and by the Irish problem. Hence, Britain remained aloof from Continental developments unless they directly affected its interests. Whenever Danish independence was threatened, England intervened on the diplomatic scene, for Denmark controlled the entrance to the Baltic Sea, an important waterway for British trade. Likewise it was British policy to safeguard the Low Countries, since Britain desired no major power to dominate the southern coast of the Channel. Finally, it entered the international fray whenever the fluid Balkan situation suggested that Russia might subjugate Turkey and gain possession of the Straits, since this would affect vital British interests in the eastern Mediterranean. However, Britain was reluctant to become involved in the

numerous international squabbles of the Continent over areas where its own interests were not involved. Despite frequent wooing by the larger powers, Britain refused to enter alliances that would limit its freedom of action.

Britain generally favored a balance among the major Continental powers. It had not been frightened by the unification of Germany, but had rather welcomed the new country as a counterweight to French power. During the war scare of 1875, however, Britain tried to restrain possible German bellicose intentions, for it feared the new equilibrium between the two countries would be upset if Germany were to crush France a second time.

On the whole, it was therefore easy for Bismarck to chart his course in regard to Great Britain. He strove to cultivate friendly relations—although he never succeeded in drawing it into an alliance. During the 1870s, when Germany was not yet a protagonist in the colonial field, bonds between the two countries were strong. Bismarck did his best to encourage Britain in its colonial designs in areas where it might clash with French or Russian interests. Such a policy he thought would help prevent any possible Anglo-French or Anglo-Russian entente and might ensure the continuation of Britain's aloofness from the European scene.

But when Germany entered the colonial field in 1883, friction arose between the two countries. Bismarck found himself forced to effect a brief *rapprochement* with France in order to convince England of the dangers of opposing all German attempts to establish colonies. He urged France to show a united front with Germany,

since both countries found their central African ventures threatened through British opposition. In 1884, Bismarck arranged for a joint Franco-German invitation to all powers interested in Africa to attend a colonial conference in Berlin. During the meeting, Britain and Portugal found themselves opposed by France, Belgium, and Germany and agreed to accept compromise solutions. Hereafter, disagreements between Germany and England again subsided. As Britain clashed more and more with France and Russia in the colonial world, it agreed to work out agreements with Germany and, as it were, to admit Germany gracefully into the colonial club. Thus relations between the two countries resumed their friendly tone after 1885, and remained so until Bismarck's dismissal in 1890, when William II embarked on his new imperialistic policy, which had little regard for assuaging the growing apprehension of Great Britain.

Creation of a Colonial Empire

Bismarck's policy was centered in Europe. He was not interested in *Weltpolitik*—world politics—as William II was to be later on. As late as 1881, he stated:

> While I am imperial Chancellor, we shall not engage in any colonial policy. We have a navy which is not seaworthy and do not need any vulnerable spots in other parts of the world which would fall as booty to the French as soon as war breaks out.

He appeared convinced that Germany should concentrate its energy on the Continent and not become entangled in international complications through a race for colonies.

On the other hand, manifold pressures were exerted on the government

to push Germany into the colonial field. German traders and missionaries had begun to penetrate Africa as early as the 1840s; by the 1870s their increased importance made it more difficult for the government to refuse to recognize and support them. Merchants, industrialists, and shipbuilders favored the acquisition of colonies, insisting that Germany's rapid industrialization and growth of population made it essential to obtain new sources of food, markets for manufactured goods, and outlets for surplus population. Some proclaimed that Germany ought to collect colonies in order to gain the prestige of a first-rate power, while others reasoned that colonies could be used for deportees. Finally, there were those who believed that Germany's excessive vitality, which could no longer be expressed on the Continent without danger of provoking a major war, should best be diverted to overseas adventures. In the early 1880s Bismarck decided to give in. Some historians advance the theory that Bismarck was not really pressured into abandoning his anticolonial stand, but rather welcomed the opportunity to antagonize England and create inside Germany a national feeling that served his political purposes. Thus, A. J. P. Taylor writes in *The Course of German History*:

> Colonial disputes with England gave Bismarck an easy popularity with national feeling in the *Reichstag* and in Germany. ... In colonial affairs what mattered to him was the dispute, not the reward; and he was both astonished and annoyed at British acquiescence in his demands, which at once deprived him of his quarrel and saddled him with unwanted colonies.

But one should seek the cause of Bismarck's change of position not in Anglophobia, but rather in his desire to obtain added support from certain political groups in the Reich—the industrial and commercial interests and the ultranationalists.

In 1878, the German Africa Society had started to set up posts in East Africa. The *Kolonialverein* (German Colonial Society) had been founded in Frankfurt in 1882, and in 1883 German merchants claimed the territory around Angra Pequena, which was to become the southern portion of German Southwest Africa. Bismarck agreed to extend the protection of the German flag over these new ventures and defended the new colonial ambitions in the face of British opposition. The period from 1883 to 1885 became years of feverish colonial expansion. By 1885, Germany had asserted its sovereignty over all Southwest Africa, German East Africa, and the Cameroons, Togoland, and parts of Zanzibar in Africa, as well as northeast New Guinea, the Bismarck Archipelago, and the Marshall and Solomon islands in the Pacific. In fact, except for a few later acquisitions in the Pacific—such as Samoa, the Marianas, and Tsingtao on the Chinese mainland—Germany acquired all its colonial empire in the brief span of two and a half years. By 1913, this empire was organized into ten colonies, covering 1,231,000 square miles, with thirteen million people (see Map 13). In area it was the third largest agglomeration of colonies, after those of England and France. Although Bismarck henceforth defended and supported German colonial affairs, it was not the government but rather private merchants and trading companies who acquired these lands. Only after private interests had secured the land did the German gov-

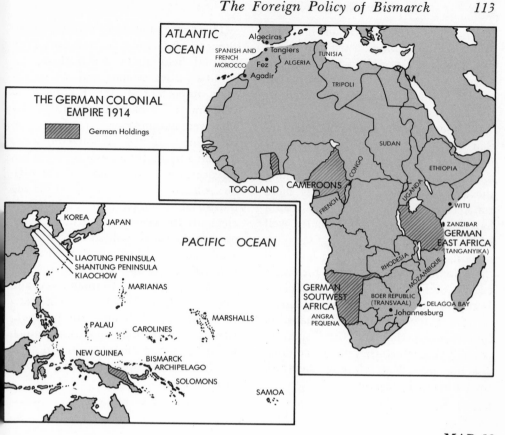

THE GERMAN COLONIAL
EMPIRE 1914
German Holdings

ATLANTIC
OCEAN

Algeciras
Tangiers
SPANISH AND
FRENCH
MOROCCO   Fez   ALGERIA
TUNISIA
Agadir
TRIPOLI
SUDAN
ETHIOPIA
CONGO
TOGOLAND   CAMEROONS
FRENCH
UGANDA
WITU
ZANZIBAR
GERMAN
EAST AFRICA
(TANGANYIKA)
RHODESIA
MOZAMBIQUE
GERMAN
SOUTHWEST
AFRICA
BOER REPUBLIC
(TRANSVAAL)   DELAGOA BAY
ANGRA
PEQUENA   Johannesburg

KOREA   JAPAN
PACIFIC   OCEAN
LIAOTUNG PENINSULA
SHANTUNG PENINSULA
KIAOCHOW
MARIANAS
PALAU   CAROLINES
MARSHALLS
NEW GUINEA
BISMARCK
ARCHIPELAGO
SOLOMONS
SAMOA

MAP 13

ernment step in to protect German interests, and it was not until after Bismarck's dismissal from office that a full-fledged Colonial Office was established in Berlin.

The main reasons traditionally advanced for Germany's entry into the colonial arena were these: (1) to obtain raw materials for its industry, acquire new outlets for manufactured goods, improve trade, and stimulate shipbuilding—in short, for economic profit; (2) to acquire land for its surplus population; (3) to achieve the prestige of a first-class power; (4) to find an escape valve for excess energy; and finally (5) to bring the benefits of European civilization to native peoples.

There is no consensus whether any

of these aims were accomplished. To be sure, Germany soon imported considerable quantities of basic materials from its colonies—such as copper, cocoa, diamonds, rubber, and hemp. But no agreement exists among economists whether these imports warranted the large investments and corollary expenses. Perhaps greater profits could have been reaped from ordinary trade with other countries. When Germany lost its colonial empire in 1919, many observers suggested that it should be happy to be freed from this financial and economic liability. The second possible purpose—the acquisition of colonies for settling excess population —is unanimously regarded as a failure. By the outbreak of World War I,

fewer than 30,000 Germans had migrated to the colonies, a truly insignificant number, especially when one considers that during the same period several million Germans migrated to the Americas.

This leaves three intangible purposes that are hardly susceptible to a clear definition. Unquestionably the German Empire after 1871 ranked among the first-class powers. But it is mere conjecture whether Germany could have held that position equally well had it eschewed colonization. One must remain as hesitant in judging how well the colonies served as outlets for excess energy, or how deeply and beneficially European civilization was implanted on the colonies. Many Germans, of course, stress that the brief span of years during which they owned colonies did not permit developing them for their intended purpose.

There are, however, certain consequences of Germany's entry into the colonial field about which there can be little disagreement and which became important during the reign of William II. Colonial expansion by whatever nation sooner or later provoked international friction. Germany's sudden imperialism was no exception. Advocates of colonialism and the various colonial associations joined the big industrial interests and nationalistic elements to become powerful lobbyists on the German political front. The acquisition of a colonial empire provided these groups with a motive for building a powerful German navy, and offered William II a world-wide arena for exercising his flamboyant *Weltpolitik*—two factors that contributed much toward clouding the international scene in the two decades preceding World War I.

The Empire of William II:

The First Decade, 1890–1900

THE PERIOD
OF TRANSITION

Bismarck's tenure of office lasted until 1890, but the last two years of his long "reign" were essentially years of transition to the "Wilhelmian Reich." The death in 1888 of the ninety-one-year-old William I, with whom Bismarck had built the empire, foreshadowed the end of an era. It jeopardized both Bismarck's power and the whole governmental and constitutional system that the chancellor had fashioned to suit his own requirements.

The Ninety-nine Days
of Emperor Frederick

The new ruler, the fifty-seven-year-old Frederick III,[1] was mortally ill with cancer of the throat. An operation performed a month before his accession had temporarily prolonged his life, but

[1] As German emperor, he should have borne the title Frederick I, but he is known by his Prussian designation, Frederick III.

he was not expected to survive more than a few months. Despite the gloomy atmosphere at the court, the change of rulers was greeted with enthusiasm by German liberals. The new emperor and his English wife, Victoria, were known to be more liberal and democratic than the usual Hohenzollerns. They shared a warm admiration for British parliamentary institutions and had many friends among members of the Progressive party and the liberal intelligentsia. But the frequent assertion that Frederick III could have turned Germany into a truly democratic empire is mere conjecture. It is quite possible that historians have overrated the strength of his liberal convictions.

Before their accession, Frederick and Victoria had often quarreled with Bismarck. The crown prince had openly objected to the authoritarianism of the regime, and the chancellor had not tried to conceal his contempt for the idealistic tendencies of the royal heir. But because Frederick knew how brief his

reign would be, his first act as emperor was to request "his father's faithful and courageous counsellor" to remain at the helm of the state. The new ruler—who had by this time lost the use of his vocal chords—and the wily old chancellor tacitly agreed to hide all signs of friction and disagreement. Even so, Frederick's three months' reign revealed so many points of difference between emperor and chancellor that it is fairly obvious that Bismarck would not have continued in office had the new emperor's health permitted a longer reign.

Bismarck did his best to isolate the royal pair. He feared the influence of the progressives on the sick emperor, as well as foreign interference through the empress, who, he complained, "never ceased to look upon England as her fatherland." Most of Frederick's proposed measures were opposed by Bismarck. The chancellor refused to let Frederick include the imprisoned Social Democrats in the traditional amnesty proclaimed by the new ruler. Nor would he permit the emperor to bestow special honors on his liberal friends. Frederick was not even allowed to dismiss the demagogic, anti-Semitic court pastor, Adolf Stöcker (1835–1909), the leader of the Christian Social party—not because Bismarck particularly liked Stöcker, but because he feared such a dismissal might be interpreted as a concession to the Progressives. Finally, Bismarck successfully interfered in a project dear to the empress's heart: to have her daughter marry Prince Alexander of Battenberg (1857–1893), who in 1886 had relinquished the throne of Bulgaria. The young prince had incurred the wrath of Emperor Alexander III, and Bismarck believed his marriage to a

Hohenzollern princess might endanger Russo-German relations. Bismarck stirred up a violent press campaign against the proposed marriage, and finally won his point—together with the irreconcilable hatred of the empress.

Bismarck permitted only one imperial measure to pass unchallenged. In early June 1888, Frederick dismissed the Prussian minister of the interior, Robert von Puttkamer (1828–1900), a hated authoritarian who had delighted in persecuting the Social Democrats in Prussia and had used his police powers to influence elections. Puttkamer's dismissal gave the liberals added reason for loving the dying emperor.

But Frederick's reign was short. Ninety-nine days after his accession, he died, leaving the crown to the twenty-nine-year-old William II.

The Character of William II

William II, whom many Americans call simply "the Kaiser," was not prepared for the task he inherited in 1888. Two years before, his father had urged Bismarck to give the young prince some training in internal policy, so that he would acquire at least a minimum of administrative knowledge; and he had warned the chancellor not to let William dabble in foreign affairs because of his "immaturity," his "inexperience," and his "predilection for exaggeration." In accordance with his parents' wishes, the prince's education had been simple. The first Prussian prince to attend an ordinary public gymnasium—at Kassel—he had then studied at the University of Bonn, and finally served as an officer at Potsdam and Berlin. But, although a quick learner who dabbled in many fields, he showed

no interest in learning the art of politics, and once even boasted that he had never read the constitution he was supposed to uphold.

His lifelong immaturity was marked by an almost childish love of drama and bombast. His temperament lacked a sense of moderation. His decisions were often impulsive, and his craving to be admired and to occupy a place in the forefront of the political stage knew few bounds. Addicted to assuming military poses, he owned about a thousand different uniforms, and on one typical occasion, decked himself out in an admiral's uniform to attend a public performance of Wagner's *The Flying Dutchman*. King Edward VII of England, his uncle, once remarked: "My nephew William must always strut about like a peacock; if he cannot do that, he feels inferior and unhappy."

Some psychologists attribute his conceit to unconscious compensation for a congenital defect that resulted in his left arm being shortened and crippled. Through Spartan self-discipline, he learned to ride a horse and to eat properly with a special fork. Yet it is felt that the incongruity of a "cripple" on the military throne of the Hohenzollerns led him to seek glory and admiration in other ways. Sadly susceptible to flattery, he liked being surrounded by obsequious courtiers who shielded him from criticism, so that he often was ignorant of the disastrous effect of some of his actions. Confident of his own capabilities and believing in the divine mission of the Hohenzollerns—as evinced in the biography he wrote about his dynasty, *My Ancestors*—he bragged that he ran the Reich almost singlehandedly and hence was often, and at times unjustly, blamed for all mishaps. "I chart the course correctly and it shall be followed!" he announced in the naval terms so dear to him. Ignorant of the constitution, he thought he had the power to command the princes of the Reich and even to levy taxes without consent of the Reichstag. "That is the trouble," he once said, "my subjects should simply do what I tell them; but they always want to think for themselves and all the difficulties arise from that." In reality, though, he was not interested in running the government, nor was he able to do so; he could not even dominate his own ministers nor surmount the fog of court intrigues. He loved to make speeches, but he hated work that required concentration. He displayed much interest in the army and the navy, where his activities were less circumscribed by the Reichstag, but primarily he liked to enjoy himself and was fond of hunting, fishing, and traveling. It has been estimated that he spent about one fifth of his entire reign on the pleasure yacht "Hohenzollern." Since he usually traveled for over half the year, when he was largely out of touch with political affairs, his claim of personal government was indeed a fiction.

Many of William's ideas were strangely contradictory. He believed in "divine right" monarchy and was undisguisedly partial to the nobility. His anachronistic views hardly fitted the new industrial society. On the other hand, he loved all things modern, and was vitally interested in industry and engineering. Industrialists and entrepreneurs, such as Friedrich Alfred Krupp (1854–1902) and the shipping magnate Albert Ballin (1857–1918), were among his frequent companions. He also professed deep interest in the social problems of his subjects; yet his

first proclamations after his accession were directed to the army, and only after three days did he address the people, significantly without reference to the constitution. He was essentially kind and friendly, a man of peace; yet he loved taking a bellicose stance and rattling the sabers of his soldiers.

Much has been written about William and the source material on him is prodigious. Many unwarranted accusations have been flung at him, such as a French indictment of his entire reign as "a permanent conspiracy against world peace." He cannot be blamed for all the problems of the era that bears his name; greater onus must fall on the system of government that allowed the continuation of the Bismarckian framework without a Bismarck.

Bismarck's Dismissal

Soon after William II's accession, it became apparent that differences between the impulsive and vainglorious emperor and the experienced Bismarck would not permit long-term cooperation between them. The fault lay not merely in their respective infatuation with power, but also in the system. Under the constitution, all power was vested in the emperor. But William I had delegated most authority to his chancellor, and Frederick III had not lived long enough to alter the arrangement. The ambitious young William II, however, was bent on exercising the power he considered his prerogative. As the grand duke of Baden remarked so aptly: "The real question was whether the Bismarckian or the Hohenzollern dynasty should reign."

Besides this underlying struggle for power, there were many specific points on which emperor and chancellor disagreed. In foreign and domestic affairs, Bismarck was conservative and Continental in his outlook, content to remain in the tried and chosen path. He saw no reason for changing legislation or alliances or tampering with the system and showed little appreciation of the new demands of expanding industry, world markets, and an increased proletariat. William, however, was consciously fostering the image of a new era. Without definite aims or adequate preparation, he was impatient to embark on new paths and expected immediate results. As Bismarck complained, William wanted to have a birthday every day.

An early clash occurred in the spring of 1889, on the occasion of a miners' strike in the Ruhr. The emperor was eager to gain the love of his subjects by ostentatious concessions and, without consulting Bismarck, invited the strikers to send envoys to Berlin to discuss their grievances. Convinced of the justice of the strikers' demands, he publicly threatened withdrawal of all troops from the Ruhr so as to leave the industrialists at the mercy of the strikers, unless the mine owners immediately raised wages. Bismarck was shocked that the emperor would make such rash threats before hearing both sides in the conflict. But he could not dissuade William from making his impetuous pronouncement.

Bismarck spent the winter of 1889–1890 on his estate. During his absence from Berlin, various intrigues were engendered in the entourage of William II by those who hoped to profit from the chancellor's dismissal. When Bismarck returned to attend the Crown Council of January 24, the first public clash occurred between the emperor

and his chancellor. William had decided that Bismarck's system of social security was insufficient. Partly under the influence of Pastor Stöcker and his Christian Socialism, the emperor had devised a new set of labor laws. He wished not merely to extend the insurance coverage, but also to regulate working conditions—abolish Sunday work, limit child and female labor, ensure fair treatment of workers, and safeguard their health and morals. An official body was to be set up to represent workers before employers and government. And finally he called for an international conference on labor problems, so that similar legislation might be adopted by all countries in order to avoid unfair competition. William had discussed these proposals with friends, but had not submitted them to Bismarck or any ministers. When the Crown Council convened, the draft was introduced as a surprise. Bismarck was annoyed that the bill was presented without his prior approval. He also objected to the implied excessive governmental interference in industry and the lack of forethought in not providing for compensation to the workers for the loss of Sunday wages. Despite Bismarck's objections, the emperor published the proposed social reforms in the official imperial gazette, without the customary countersignature of his chancellor. The rift between the two was thus communicated to the public at large.

Soon new disagreements arose. The anti-Socialist laws of 1878 came up for renewal. Bismarck insisted on new and harsher measures, which were opposed by the emperor and a majority of the Reichstag. In the end, Bismarck's refusal to accept less stringent legislation caused the lapse of all anti-Socialist legislation. At the same time, Bismarck's support in the Reichstag was undermined by new elections (see Chart 1). In 1890, the Free Conservatives, or *Reichspartei,* and the National Liberals each lost over half their seats —decreasing from a combined total of 140 to a mere 62—while Bismarck's opponents, the Progressives and the Social Democrats, increased from a total of 43 to 111. This electoral upset, so rarely mentioned by historians when discussing the fall of Bismarck, must have influenced his position and his outlook for the future. Constitutionally he was, of course, not dependent on a vote of confidence from the Reichstag. But the loss of support in that body at a time when he was also losing the confidence of his emperor unquestionably undermined his position. At a minimum, he was faced with seeking a realignment of supporting parties, without which a proper legislative program was impossible. According to some, Bismarck even contemplated forcing a constitutional reform that would do away with the anomalous pseudo parliamentarianism he himself had instituted.

At the same time, Bismarck and William disagreed on matters of foreign policy. William's watchword—"The course remains the same, full steam ahead!"—shows how little he understood Bismarck's more subtle policy, which never operated at full throttle. When in the early months of 1890, Russia inquired about renewing the Treaty of Reinsurance, the Kaiser hesitated. He wished to remain faithful to the alliance with Vienna, and felt that the treaty with Russia presented inherent dangers to Germany in any Austro-Russian war, even though it did not require German neutrality if Rus-

sia attacked Austria. Moreover, the Foreign Office, inspired by Baron Fritz von Holstein (1835–1909), opposed the alliance. Bismarck, however, always considered the Russian treaty a fundamental part of his international system and had lost some of his faith in the reliability of an Austria in which the Slavs and Magyars had increased their power at the expense of the Germans. Hence the question of renewing the treaty, while in no way a cause of Bismarck's dismissal, contributed to the tension between the emperor and his minister. William was openly jealous and suspected that the tsar had sent his ambassador (Shuvalov) to negotiate a renewal of the treaty solely with Bismarck and that Alexander III was maintaining a private correspondence with the chancellor. William had heard that in one of these letters to Bismarck, Alexander referred to him as an "ill-bred youngster." The emperor finally decided against renewal of the important Treaty of Reinsurance.

A question of administrative protocol brought about the final break. A royal decree of 1852 stipulated that all executive affairs had to pass through the hands of the chief minister before submission to the king of Prussia, and that only the chief minister and the minister of war could confer directly with the king. All other royal audiences needed the presence or the consent of the first minister. This rule had admirably fitted Bismarck's administrative requirements, and he insisted that its retention was requisite for administrative coordination. In fact, by allowing him to supervise all governmental activities, this regulation gave Bismarck his day-to-day basis of power. William, however, felt imprisoned by it. He complained that Bismarck could talk and negotiate with whomever he liked, whereas the emperor did not enjoy this privilege without the chancellor's permission. Moreover, he insisted that Bismarck's frequent absences from Berlin made the decree untenable. In March 1890, he finally ordered Bismarck to rescind the decree and made Bismarck's refusal a cause for dismissal.

Bismarck's "resignation" engendered bitter recriminations between the two protagonists, as seen in their private letters and posthumous memoirs. The emperor bestowed on the retiring chancellor the meaningless dignity of duke of Lauenburg—meaningless since William I had already made Bismarck a prince—and sent him his life-sized portrait as a "sign of never ending gratitude." In shortsighted vindictiveness he ordered the new chancellor, Caprivi (see below), not to consult his predecessor about current conditions. The Prussian government even requested the refunding of eleven days of salary by the chancellor, who retired on March 20, a few days before the end of the first quarter of 1890. The embittered ex-chancellor withdrew to his estate for the eight remaining years of his life, and launched an interminable barrage of criticism against his successors and their "new course" in foreign and domestic affairs.

The news of Bismarck's "deposition" provoked considerable consternation abroad. Bonds declined on the Paris market. Foreigners had generally come to look upon the German chancellor as a guarantor of the peace. Substitution of the impetuous young emperor seemed to forebode instability. But inside Germany there was surprisingly little excitement. Only two ministers considered handing in their own resig-

nations, and on the whole, politicians and the people at large accepted the event passively. Some newspapers and Reichstag delegates even sighed with relief. Bismarck's most spectacular successes during the period of unification were almost a generation in the past. His rigidity and aloof, domineering manner had not endeared him to the new generation and had even begun to mark him as a man of the past. Buoyant with optimism and confident in their own ability to handle the future, those in government showed little regret at his disappearance.

THE FIRST DECADE

The four chancellors who succeeded Bismarck in the "Wilhelmian Reich" did not possess the abilities of their illustrious predecessor. The Prussian officer and bureaucrat General Count Georg Leo von Caprivi de Caprera de Montecuccoli (1831–1899) held the office from 1890 to 1894, and was followed by the Bavarian Prince Chlodwig Karl Viktor zu Hohenlohe-Schillingsfürst (1819–1901) from 1894 to 1900. The suave and talented Prince Bernhard von Bülow (1849–1929) was chancellor from 1900 to 1909, and finally the hapless Theobald von Bethmann-Hollweg (1856–1921) served from 1909 until the total collapse of the Bismarckian system in 1917. The relatively mediocre performance of these chancellors and their cabinets is frequently blamed on Bismarck, who had failed to train political successors, and whose authoritarian system had not allowed others to gain political experience. While it is true that the prevailing system was not auspicious for the development of political experi-

ence, it would be wrong to assert that no talented candidates existed for the important posts. Rather, they were not given a chance by William II, who had no desire to efface himself behind a new Bismarck.

Conciliation under Caprivi

Caprivi, the first of the four, was made chancellor of the Reich, federal foreign minister, and minister-president of Prussia—and thus in theory was vested with Bismarck's powers. He had had some forty years of military experience, as officer in the field, as administrator in the War Ministry, and as chief of the Admiralty, but in politics and diplomacy he was a novice. He felt duty-bound to the emperor, and worked faithfully on everyday problems and daily dispatches, but he failed to develop over-all views and a broad policy. He lacked the self-assertion as well as the vision necessary to dissuade the emperor from his grandiose ventures. Nor could he block the backdoor maneuvers of such intriguers as Baron von Holstein, the determined privy councilor in the Foreign Office, or Count Alfred von Waldersee (1832–1904), chief of the General Staff, confidant of the emperor, and husband of William's ex-mistress.

In his "new course," William was eager to placate all parties and inaugurate an era of harmony. Caprivi's gentle, conciliatory attitude fitted this mood. Compared with Bismarck, he was liberal in economic, social, and foreign matters. As a military man, he was free from all party affiliations, but contrary to political wisdom, he never tried to align reliable support in the Reichstag.

Many issues faced by Caprivi in-

volved bringing government policies abreast of rapidly changing economic and social conditions. During the 1890s the population of Germany increased almost 15 percent—from 49.4 million in 1890 to 56.4 million in 1900—not because of an increase in the birth rate but because of a sharp reduction in the death rate and in emigration. Employment in industry, trade, and commerce rose quickly, while the percentage of those remaining in agriculture declined steadily. By 1895 only 36 percent earned their living from agriculture, almost 40 percent were engaged in industry, and 12 percent were in trade and communication; the remainder were in government, domestic, and other services. The larger cities doubled and tripled their populations without adequate provision for a corresponding increase in housing. By 1910, over 21 percent of the population were to live in cities with more than 100,000 inhabitants. Rents soared exorbitantly, and people were forced to sublet portions of rooms. In Berlin around 1900, for example, an average of 3.69 people shared each heatable room, and 10 percent of the one-room apartments were occupied by six or more people, many of whom were boarders. Production and trade indices were skyrocketing, and there was opportunity for many in the lower middle class to move from poverty toward prosperity. But wages remained low, and most of the proletariat rose no more than from want to bare subsistence wages. The cleavage between rich and poor remained exceptionally severe.

LABOR LEGISLATION AND TARIFFS   One of Caprivi's early measures stemmed from William's continued desire to conciliate the workers by enacting the labor protection program that Bismarck had opposed. Although Bismarck had placed Germany in the vanguard of the social insurance system, it was backward in the field of labor legislation. In the summer of 1890, a law established labor courts. These industrial courts, consisting of an impartial presiding officer and elected associates representing both labor and management, were to mediate disputes between employers and employees. A year later, a law on labor protection made Sunday a legal holiday, limited child and female labor, prohibited payment of wages in kind, set up a protective code against harmful occupations, limited the power of employers to levy fines, and even suggested the establishment of workers' councils or factory committees to help determine employment policies. The powers of previously authorized government factory inspectors were increased to enforce these new regulations. Unquestionably much of this legislation was wholesome, despite the spottiness of its enforcement. But it neither conciliated the workers nor softened the opposition of the militant Socialists, who in this same year in their Erfurt Program, took a more doctrinaire, Marxist stand on the class struggle.

To secure outlets for Germany's growing industry, Chancellor Caprivi sought to create a sort of "common market" in central and eastern Europe. Bismarck's protective tariff of 1879 had helped German industry grow, but had not opened up new markets abroad. He had negotiated most-favored-nation clauses with a number of countries, but no reciprocal trade treaties, which might have forced him to lower tariffs on imports into Germany. Between

1891 and 1894, Caprivi concluded with eight European nations a series of trade treaties in which duties were reduced and fixed for a period of twelve years, thereby permitting German industry to plan a long-term price and production program. Actually, the government had not wished to lower agricultural tariffs for fear of undermining Germany's own food production and rendering it vulnerable to blockade in time of war. On the other hand, reduction of agricultural tariffs would result in lower food prices, which in turn would permit industry to pay lower wages and hence produce cheaper and more competitive goods. Furthermore, most of the countries desiring to import German industrial goods could pay for them only in agricultural produce. Hence, as a price for concluding the trade treaties, Germany had to agree to reduce import tariffs on grain.

The treaties were accepted in the Reichstag, since the industrialists stood to profit by them and the liberals favored the principle of free trade. Although the agricultural interests did not favor this tariff policy, they were not adequately organized to oppose the measures. Also, because droughts had pushed up the world grain price they did not feel immediately threatened by imports of grain. Nonetheless, Caprivi's tariff policies suddenly provoked a realignment of political forces. Argentinian exports and an unexpected abundance in the Russian harvest in 1892–1893 lowered grain prices and hurt the landlords east of the Elbe. Since the new treaties prevented raising the tariffs, the agriculturalists blamed their plight on Caprivi's administration. To fight for their economic interests, the Prussian estate

owners organized the League of Landlords (*Bund der Landwirte*) in 1893. This league quickly became one of the most powerful pressure groups in Germany, more important than most political parties with their official representation in the Reichstag. The league, largely composed of Prussian conservatives from the "new Germany," also attracted estate owners from other regions, who had formerly belonged to the Center and National Liberal parties. To secure wider support, especially among the smaller peasant proprietors of the south and southwest, it made a tacit alliance with the League of German Peasants (*Deutsche Bauernbund*) and backed their demands for high tariffs on all agricultural products, not merely on grain. The League of Landlords gave a powerful boost to the conservative forces. In fact, agricultural interests quickly assumed dominance within the Conservative party—despite the fact that industry surpassed agriculture in importance on the national economic scene—and were partially responsible for Caprivi's fall from power in 1894.

William II's initial policy of conciliation extended in many other directions. To please the liberal majority in the Prussian legislature—and increase revenue—he authorized a bill for the levying of a progressive income tax in Prussia. To eradicate remaining resentment from the *Kulturkampf,* he ordered repayment to the Catholic Church of all funds withheld in the 1870s, and he even supported, although unsuccessfully, an education bill in 1892 that would have transferred more supervisory power over primary education to the Catholic Church. The emperor also insisted on fairer treatment for the people of Alsace-Lorraine,

and attempted to reconcile the Polish minority to Prussian rule by suspending Bismarck's policy of forcible Germanization of the eastern lands, which had been inaugurated in 1886.

THE ARMY BILL AND THE ELECTIONS OF 1893 Despite these attempts to placate so many groups, William encountered difficulties with the Reichstag in regard to his military program. In 1890, the Reichstag agreed to add 18,000 men to the standing army, and to allocate additional funds for an expansion of the artillery services. But neither William nor Caprivi was satisfied with these increases. French rearmament programs and growing cooperation between France and Russia —facilitated and encouraged by William's failure to renew the Treaty of Reinsurance with Russia—gave Caprivi nightmares of a possible two-front war. Hence in 1893, the government presented a new army law calling for an increase of 84,000 men and high expenditures for new weapons. To gain the support of the liberals, Caprivi offered a reduction of the period of obligatory military service from three to two years and quinquennial in lieu of septennial approval of the army budget—a step that would increase the Reichstag's supervision over the army. This proposed reduction of military service is often regarded as evidence of Caprivi's democratic idealism, yet one should recall that he also asked for increased draft quotas. The same number of soldiers formerly drafted in three years would now be recruited in two. The proposal would thus quickly strengthen the available number of trained reservists and make Germany better prepared for a possible war.

Despite the enticements held out to the liberals and despite Caprivi's warnings about the Franco-Russian threat, the requested army law was defeated in the Reichstag. Determined to increase the military establishment, the emperor authorized Caprivi to dissolve parliament and call for new elections. The ensuing electoral campaign of 1893 was fought largely on the issues of the recently defeated education and army bills as well as the trade treaties. The election results favored the extremist parties, with a corresponding loss in the center of the political spectrum (see Chart 1). On the Right, the fairly new Anti-Semitic party increased its votes fivefold over the 1890 election, and gained 16 instead of their previous 5 seats. The right wing as a whole —which, besides Conservatives, Free Conservatives, and Anti-Semites, now included the National Liberals—increased its representation from a combined 140 to a total of 169 representatives. The Social Democrats, for their part, gained 9 seats. But most important for the fate of the army program was a new split among the Progressives. After the various liberal elements had united in 1884 and joined a left-wing splinter of the National Liberals to reform the *Freisinnige Partei* (literally, Freethinking party, though usually translated as Progressive party), they now again divided more or less into their original components. The left wing, the Progressive People's party (*Freisinnige Volkspartei*), under the guidance of Eugen Richter (1838–1906), remained doctrinaire in its opposition to militarism and continued to oppose the army bill. The more compromising Progressive Union (*Freisinnige Vereinigung*) voted for the army bill to gain a reduction in the period of military service. Caprivi's military proposals

were finally adopted by the new Reichstag, although by a scant majority.

But four years of the "new course" left Emperor William thoroughly disappointed: his longing for adulation was not satisfied; no one seemed conciliated; the Conservatives complained about the new tariffs; the Socialists opposed his regime, despite his social legislation and his refusal to renew Bismarck's anti-Socialist laws; even the minority groups whom he had tried to placate did not appreciate him. In 1894, he complained loudly about ingratitude, expressing his disappointment particularly about the opposition of the nobility. He finally decided to abandon the "new course," relinquished thoughts of conciliation, and determined to return to Bismarck's sterner policies, particularly the fight against all "subversive elements." Count Caprivi, hardly the proper instrument for such a policy, was dismissed.

The Chancellorship of Hohenlohe

As new chancellor, William appointed the seventy-five-year-old Prince Chlodwig zu Hohenlohe-Schillingsfürst, who had considerable experience for the position. Among many other political activities, he had been minister-president of Bavaria, had worked effectively for the unification of Germany, and served as an influential, somewhat liberal, and stanchly antiultramontane member of the Reichstag. From 1874 to 1878 he had been ambassador to Paris, then worked as German foreign secretary under Bismarck, and finally occupied the post of governor of Alsace-Lorraine. But by 1894, Hohenlohe had become a tired old man, polite and ineffectual. The emperor could easily dominate him, and William's personal rule henceforth assumed greater importance, subject to fitful interference by intriguing subordinates.

In some respects it was not difficult to arouse national emotions for a fight against what Bismarck had called the *Umsturzparteien* (revolutionary parties). The nation at large entertained an almost neurotic fear of the ever-increasing Social Democrats. Not only the conservatives and the solid middle classes inveighed against the red specter, but also many liberals and even status-conscious domestic servants hated the workers and were terrified by Socialist talk of class warfare and revolution. Any imputation of crimes to the Socialists was readily accepted by the general public, and Socialists were frequently beaten up in the streets, while the police—as occurred later in the Weimar Republic—closed an eye or even arrested the victims as violators of the peace. Even in normally liberal Saxony, fear of socialism resulted in a change of the electoral system. Universal suffrage was replaced by an indirect three-class electoral system similar to Prussia's, with the result that the Socialists lost 15 of their 16 seats in the lower legislature.

At the same time, the conservatives were becoming more vociferous and dogmatic. Conciliation and harmonious cooperation figured no more in their views than in those of the militant Socialists. Stöcker and his Christian Socialists vigorously pushed their demagogic agitation against Jews, Progressives, and Social Democrats, under the banner of vague "Christian and Germanic" principles. In their party program of 1892, the Conservatives had demanded an unconditional fight against the Social Democrats as enemies of the

state, as well as "local self-administration based not on universal suffrage but on the natural and organic subdivisions of the people," which in essence meant a return to medieval corporatism.

Yet William and Hohenlohe were unable to get the Reichstag to pass new anti-Socialist legislation. The proposed bill "for the suppression of agitation" did not specifically mention the Social Democratic party, and most parties therefore feared that the measure might be used to restrict their own freedom. Even inside Prussia, the government's efforts to suppress the SPD failed when the bill was declared unconstitutional by the Prussian Supreme Court. A final attempt in 1897 to introduce in the Reichstag a law making it illegal to incite a strike or to join an association that might hinder work or put pressure on employers was also defeated. The Progressives and the Center party saw no reason to weaken the SPD, which was frequently a useful ally in parliamentary maneuvers against the government.

Thus William's "aggressive course" (*Kampfpolitik*) fizzled out as had his "new course." The campaign for anti-Socialist legislation had shown that, despite the rising strength of the conservatives, the parties favoring constitutionalism were determined to defend the principle of equal political rights for all. Beyond this, it had accomplished nothing except to embitter the two million Socialist voters and their sympathizers. The government had talked a lot but had never applied much pressure to ensure passage of its program. Hohenlohe had hardly exerted himself, and William, more interested in foreign affairs, had done little to help his chancellor.

In domestic legislation, the era of Hohenlohe was unspectacular. In 1896, the Common Civil Code for the Empire, compilation of which had been started under Bismarck, was finally enacted. In 1899, the provisions of the laws on old age and invalidism were extended and a new Association Law was promulgated to allow greater freedom for the formation of clubs and associations. Of greater consequence than these purely internal matters was the enactment of the first German Naval Law of 1898, which will be examined below in conjunction with foreign affairs. The old chancellor himself was not much involved in its passage nor in the intrigues surrounding it. He retired from office in 1900, and died shortly thereafter.

The Beginning of Weltpolitik

As in internal affairs, the young emperor was eager to launch Germany's foreign policy on a "new course." In a speech in 1896, he proclaimed that "the German Reich has become a *Weltreich*," and he justified his view on the grounds that "everywhere in distant lands live thousands of our compatriots." Bismarck's outlook had been Continental. Once Germany had been unified in 1871, he had not wished to become involved in colonial ventures or imperialistic expansion. He thought additional frontiers would merely bring added dangers. But, in the long run, as was seen, his reluctance had been overcome by economic expansion. From the very first, however, William II showed no hesitation about removing the Continental limits from Germany's political horizon. His was to be a *Weltpolitik* and Germany not just a European but a world power.

William's deliberate and much-publicized shift from the Continent to the world arena is often regarded as a prime cause of World War I. Yet it should be examined within the context of the late nineteenth century, a period of rampant imperialism, through which ran a strong strain of social Darwinism [2] on the international scene. Economic expansion of the great powers—in shipping and banking, in the search for raw materials and markets, in the creation of large trusts and interlocking cartels—furnished the dynamics of much of their foreign policies. Similarly, Germany's own economic life continually expanded beyond its borders, and drew it, willy-nilly, into the maelstrom of world politics. The politically minded Bismarck conceivably never grasped the full significance of this development, which began during his chancellorship; William, however, was delighted to take full advantage of all its implications.

Most of the great powers—except Italy, which was defeated in 1896 in its attempt to seize Ethiopia—were gathering in imperialistic conquests during the 1890s: Britain and France primarily in Africa, Russia in Manchuria, Japan in Formosa and on the Chinese mainland, and the United States in Puerto Rico, Hawaii, Guam, and the Philippines. Naturally Germany was intent on garnering its share. Bülow, who became foreign minister in 1897, insisted that its *Weltpolitik*

[2] Social Darwinism, the attempt to apply Darwin's theories of natural selection and survival of the fittest to the realm of politics. The stress was put on the sword as the symbol of authority rather than on the rule of law, and it was asserted that the strongest individuals and nations, not necessarily those abiding by law and morality, were destined to survive the struggle among men and states. See also pp. 137 and 168.

did not imply that Germany desired to dominate the world. But, he asserted, since others conquered, it deserved "equal rights," an open door to the world, "a place in the sun," as he put it.

Germany, Japan, the United States, and to some extent Italy, became world powers in the 1890s. As late-comers among the great powers, they were regarded by the other nations as upstarts and intruders on the world scene who threatened the established equilibrium. Yet there was an essential difference between rising powers such as Japan and the United States, and Germany. The imperialistic aims of the former appeared clear, well defined, and limited, with the possible exception of American acquisition of the Philippines. The emperor's *Weltpolitik,* on the other hand, was nebulous and noisy. Bolstered by unscrupulous advisers and supported by boisterous pressure groups at home, William played the role of a tactless and pretentious *parvenu.* Germany's yearning for influence seemed to know no limits; its actions betrayed no recognizable direction. In Bismarck's time, the powers could sense the extent of German aspirations. Under William, no one knew the bounds of German aims, perhaps least of all the emperor himself. From the shores of China and the Pacific Isles to the coasts of Africa and the rivers of the Near East, Germany interfered everywhere. As William announced in 1900: "On the seas and in distant lands, no great decisions should be made without Germany and without the German Emperor." Railroads in Turkey, the British fight with the Boer Republic, the Boxer rebellion in China, the actions of the United States in the Philippines—everything

presented William with an excuse for intervention.

William's craving for adulation and power was evident also in the manner in which he conducted foreign affairs. He constantly interfered personally in diplomatic matters normally handled by ministers and ambassadors, made impromptu speeches on foreign policy, and in 1905 even negotiated a treaty with Russia on the spur of the moment. His staff felt obliged to remind him that "solidarity between Your Majesty and the Foreign Office is an urgent necessity," and that it might well happen that "Your Majesty's personal intervention destroyed the functioning of the machine." But worried about Germany's insecure position and eager to find acclaim, the emperor smiled in all directions to gain friends, rather than pursuing the less spectacular but more steady course of a firm alliance system such as Bismarck's. His zigzag course earned him distrust rather than friendship, for when he failed to get instantaneous professions of friendship, he usually turned his back and smiled at others. This fitful behavior particularly characterized his relations with England and Russia. His methods were aptly described by an undersecretary in the Foreign Office, speaking of the famous Baghdad Railroad: "By now bowing before the British Lion and then curtsying to the Russian Bear, we will wiggle our railroad through to Kuwait."

Thus the expanding Germany, guided by the moody young emperor with his bombastic speeches, abandoned the cautious framework of Bismarck's Continental system and jumped into the wide arena of world politics. From his retreat, the aging Bismarck noted in his memoirs: "In the future, as in the past, we need not merely armaments but also a sane political course to guide the German ship of state through the coalitions to which we are exposed because of our history and our geographic situation." But William II and his advisers insisted on moving ahead unchecked, and even Bülow and Bethmann-Hollweg, the chancellors after 1900, in the last analysis relied more on armaments and bluff than on tact and politics.

PRESSURES BEHIND THE THRONE Officially, the government of the Reich was a one-man affair, with all power concentrated in William II. But in reality, various individuals in his public and private entourage exercised a strong influence on German policy. Since much of this power was exerted indirectly and secretly, it is difficult even now to evaluate its real importance in certain cases.

In William's confidence were his friend Count Philipp zu Eulenburg (1847–1921) and Pastor Stöcker, both of whom encouraged the young emperor's supernationalistic fervor. There were the skillful Albert Ballin and Alfred von Tirpitz (1849–1930), one of the strongest personalities in the Wilhelmian Reich. Both sought to direct William's eyes ever more to the high seas and to naval expansion of all types. Besides these, Count Alfred von Waldersee, who succeeded Moltke as chief of staff in 1888, acquired considerable power through intrigues and well-timed flattery. Waldersee harbored a fierce hatred of Bismarck as well as of Russia, and helped turn William against both. In fact, from his intrigues in 1889–1890, it is difficult to judge whether he wished to topple Bismarck in order to destroy the Russo-German

alliance, or to undermine relations with St. Petersburg in order to dislodge the chancellor. He looked forward to plunging Germany, on the side of Austria, into a war with Russia, and even entertained hopes of some day assuming the chancellorship himself, even though he noted in his private diary: "I have the conscious realization that I am not up to such tasks."

Most powerful, though least known at the time, was Fritz von Holstein, privy councilor in the Foreign Office, "the evil spirit in German politics," as one historian has called him. A misanthropic, lonely man, filled with bitter suspicions (he always carried a pistol), he had served in the diplomatic service in St. Petersburg, Washington, and Paris. In 1876, Bismarck had appointed him to the Foreign Office in Berlin. The chancellor had known how to dominate him and use his particular skills at diplomatic intriguing. He employed Holstein frequently for secret missions and backstage maneuvers, and noted of him: "To be used in the basement only!" After 1886, Holstein began to intrigue with Bismarck's opponents to gain in power through removal of the mighty chancellor. Blithely insisting that a Franco-Russian alliance was inconceivable, he worked against renewal of the Treaty of Reinsurance, and helped persuade William to remove the "Bismarck dynasty." During the 1890s, his influence on the new chancellors and on Germany's foreign policy increased steadily (see pages 149 ff.). Recently discovered sources reveal that in many instances, until his removal from office in 1906, he had the decisive voice in foreign affairs. Yet he always remained in the background, and few at the time recognized his pervasive influence.

Apart from these individual intriguers, various pressure groups affected the course of German foreign policy, sometimes more by embarrassing the government than by exerting direct influence on its actions. The League of Landlords and the Naval League were two such groups that, for reasons of economic gains, lobbied for measures with far-reaching repercussions in foreign affairs (the tariffs of 1902 and the construction of a powerful high-seas fleet). Perhaps the noisiest among these groups was the All-German League, founded in 1890 as a protest against the Heligoland Treaty, through which William attempted a *rapprochement* with England by compromising on competing colonial claims. The All-German League, which published its own *All-Deutsche Blätter* (*All-German Pamphlets*), preached a policy of might and expansionism. Although it always remained small in membership—never more than about 22,000—it became representative of vociferous Pan-Germanism. Its pamphlets appealed to "German honor" and engendered distrust of other nations by denouncing the activities of their "clandestine and evil" agents. Considering themselves "Germans first of all," these Pan-Germans always looked upon coexistence and compromise in foreign affairs as treasonous, stressed their readiness to fight at William's call, and stanchly demanded their "share of the world as a conquering nation." Their policies and aims foreshadowed the later annexationist demands of certain groups in World War I.

THE "NEW COURSE" IN FOREIGN AFFAIRS   William's "new course" in 1890 consisted of loosening the existing bonds between Germany and Russia,

placing more confidence in the Triple Alliance, and attempting to establish closer relations with England. The changed attitude toward Russia was of fundamental importance for all other foreign relations. William harbored no liking for Emperor Alexander III, and considered the Treaty of Reinsurance too binding in view of the Dual Alliance with Vienna. But unlike some of his advisers, he had no intention of bringing about a real split between Berlin and St. Petersburg, much less of provoking a war. In fact, there were frequent periods in the 1890s and 1900s when William entertained very cordial relations with the Russian court, especially after his young cousin Nicholas II became tsar in 1894. At times Germany and Russia even cooperated actively, as, for example, in 1895 and subsequent years when they fashioned a common front against Japan. But the lapse of the Treaty of Reinsurance marked the end of any formal alliance between the two nations in the period before World War I. It opened the door to the gradual splitting of Europe into two camps and to the eventual "encirclement" of Germany—two developments Bismarck had tried so assiduously to avoid.

Russia was in no mood to remain isolated. Faced with German refusal to renew the treaty, Alexander III showed more interest in the overtures of France, despite the traditional tsarist hatred of French republicanism. Reciprocal visits by high officials and by their respective fleets resulted in negotiations for a Franco-Russian military convention. Alexander's initial hesitations to commit himself to a firm alliance were gradually overcome as William II's stanch pro-Austrian attitude, German *rapprochement* with England, and Caprivi's new army law drove him

more and more into the arms of France. In 1894, the two countries ratified the first of a series of military conventions. Russia was to aid France if the latter were attacked by Germany, or by Italy supported by Germany. Similarly, France would assist Russia if she were attacked by Germany or by Austria with German help. This pact, periodically reaffirmed and widened in its stipulations, was thus patently directed against the Triple Alliance. Its formation marked the beginning of the entente system that was to divide Europe into two hostile camps.

Rather than depend on Russia, William chose to rely on the Triple Alliance, which was renewed and tightened in 1891. Few in the Foreign Office seemed to question the value of this alliance. Yet it should have been clear that Austria's reliability and usefulness as an ally were becoming more doubtful. The Slavs and Magyars of the Austrian Empire were constantly gaining in power at the expense of the Germans and embroiling Vienna in Balkan affairs that were not necessarily of vital interest to Germany. At the same time, Italy did not develop into a strong ally. It showed an ever-growing interest in acquiring African colonies, and demanded German backing for these ventures as a price for the alliance. Above all, one should recall that Bismarck had created the Triple Alliance in the days when Germany's aspirations were limited to the Continent. Since all three nations were then land powers, with insignificant navies, such an alliance had been well designed to assure the peace in Europe. But William's *Weltpolitik* needed a different framework, and Austria and Italy could not serve as adequate supports for the new German foreign policy.

Perhaps a subconscious recognition

of the insufficiency of the Triple Alliance led William to seek a *rapprochement* with England. The story of the repeated attempts to bring about closer Anglo-German relations is a tortuous one. Time and again during the pre-war period, the two nations seemed about to bury their disagreements and establish mutual trust and friendship, if not an alliance, but each time such steps were frustrated—usually, though by no means exclusively, through some thoughtless act of William's, who at heart despised the English. The Heligoland Treaty of 1890 was the first step. Bismarck had favored settling all colonial disputes with England, and Chancellor Caprivi, who thought that Germany had already acquired more colonies than it could use, was glad to complete the negotiations. Certain business circles and the Pan-Germans, of course, favored colonial expansion rather than retrenchment. But Caprivi and others in the government wondered whether the money and sacrifices expended were justified in view of the meager benefits attained. Also, the German government was becoming increasingly involved in suppressing native rebellions, especially in Tanganyika, where the East African Trading Company was unable to handle the insurrections. Consequently, Caprivi gladly subscribed to a withdrawal of certain German claims. According to the Treaty of Heligoland, Germany relinquished its protectorate over Witu and its claims to Uganda and Zanzibar. The German rights to the coast of East Africa were confirmed, and the frontier between German and British East Africa was defined. In return, England ceded to Germany the tiny island of Heligoland, some hundred miles off the mouth of the Elbe. This treaty, considered treasonous by the Pan-Ger-mans, was followed by a state visit of William to London. The Anglo-German *rapprochement* was seemingly successfully started, yet this appearance was deceptive. England was basically cool to the German advances, and William's unsteady course could not furnish a basis for a real Anglo-German alliance.

THE ZIGZAG OF THE MID-1890s   Within a few years after Bismarck's dismissal, Germany's foreign policy began to waver between contradictory courses. On the one hand, William made occasional attempts to pursue the Anglo-German *rapprochement*. On the other, he frequently turned his back on the Channel, smiled at England's rival, France, and tried to regain the friendship of Russia.

Anglo-German relations were complicated by many areas of friction, one of which was economic. The rising German industrial output of the 1880s had engendered a sharp trade rivalry. Rather than impose protective tariffs England hoped to dam the flood of German goods by appealing to British patriotism. It forced the Germans to stamp their wares "Made in Germany," but the label soon became a mark of quality workmanship rather than a deterrent to British buyers. At the same time, the rapid growth of the German merchant marine enabled Germany to carry most of its exports in its own ships and thus deprive Britain of this lucrative trade. English newspapers in the 1890s frequently spoke of a "commercial war" between the two nations; Germans even called the rivalry a "matter of life and death."

Another irritant was the beginning of German penetration into the Near East. In 1888, a railroad from Hungary to Constantinople had been opened,

completing the line from Berlin to the Turkish capital. The sultan then invited German companies to build the next link, from the south shore of the Bosporus to Ankara in central Turkey. A German consortium headed by the *Deutsche Bank* created the Anatolian Railroad Company and launched the first leg of what was to become the Berlin-to-Baghdad railroad. German industrialists and financiers viewed the project as a welcome expansion in a new direction, but Bismarck had perceived its political implications and warned that the Reich would not lend its official support to the venture. William II's attitude was naturally different. A German-built and German-controlled railway into the heart of the Near East fitted his dreams of *Weltpolitik*. He had visions of possible German settlements in Turkey, of extending German political influence over the entire Near East, and of becoming, as he later announced in an official speech in Palestine, the "friendly protector of the 300 million Muslims in the world." Consequently, the railroad scheme received his full backing after 1890. When the link to Ankara was completed in 1892, negotiations with the Turks were at once undertaken concerning further concessions for extensions to the south. England promptly submitted bids of its own, out of commercial as well as political considerations. But the Germans successfully thwarted the British efforts, and received the contract for the link to Konia, which was completed by 1896. The German victory of 1893 thus added to Anglo-German friction.

Africa also remained a source of Anglo-German disagreements, despite the compromises of the Treaty of Heligoland. In 1893, the two nations clashed again over a disputed border in northern Tanganyika. Moreover, Holstein, together with Baron Adolf Marschall von Bieberstein (1842–1912), who directed the Foreign Office, elaborated the curious theory that England's friendship and alliance could best be gained by antagonizing it wherever possible: London would learn from experience that it was preferable to have Germany as a friend than as an enemy. This theory gradually found credence among many influential German policy makers and partly accounts for Germany's stand against England in the Sino-Japanese War of 1895 and in the Transvaal conflict.

The quasi independence of the Boer Republic had been recognized by Gladstone in 1884, but discovery of new gold and diamond deposits had caused British imperialists to have second thoughts about abandoning this territory. Unofficial plans were made, largely with the connivance of Cecil Rhodes, for British recovery of the Transvaal. The Boers, under the leadership of Paul Kruger, in turn pinned some hopes on German support against England. William II encouraged the illusion and in 1894 dispatched two warships to Delagoa Bay, in an ostentatious gesture to bolster the Boer Republic against possible British attack. The insufficiency of the German fleet in the face of the British Navy and the fact that Portuguese territory blocked all passage from Delagoa Bay to the Transvaal made such a demonstration militarily meaningless. Yet it was a typical Wilhelmian irritant.

Late in the following year, Dr. Leander Jameson, from the South Africa Company in Rhodesia, invaded the Transvaal with a few hundred men in the hope of unleashing a pro-

British revolution in Johannesburg. The German government deliberated immediately on possible steps to help the Boer president against Jameson's raiders. Portugal was asked to grant German troops free passage through Mozambique, but refused. Even Kruger rejected the proffered aid. In fact, within barely a week, the Boers captured Jameson and his troops and suppressed all seeds of rebellion in Johannesburg. Hence Germany was given no occasion for active intervention.

World opinion strongly condemned Jameson's raid, but the powers maintained a discreet silence, since England not only disavowed all complicity but even tried and condemned Dr. Jameson. William and some of his advisers, however, refused to adopt such a tactful path. They were intoxicated by bold ideas, such as offering the Transvaal protection against future English aggression. When news of the Boer victory reached Berlin, William dispatched a telegram to Kruger, congratulating him for having successfully repelled the "disturbers of the peace" without foreign help, and for having "safeguarded the independence of the country from outside attacks." The telegram raised a storm of protest in England, which resented German interference in its colonial problems. The incident also shocked most of the other powers, who were not accustomed to this style of diplomacy.

While attempting to antagonize Britain into friendship, William also sought to improve relations with Russia. The "new course" toward the Polish minorities in Germany had frightened Alexander III, who feared it might raise similar hopes among the Poles under Russian control. Moreover, a tariff war between the two

nations had caused considerable tension. These irritants were now assuaged. In 1893, Caprivi negotiated a new tariff treaty with St. Petersburg, and in the following year, Prussia's conciliatory policy toward its Polish subjects was terminated. The accession of Nicholas II in late 1894 further improved the chance for better Russo-German relations. William at once set out to woo his young cousin, the tsar, in order to regain Russian friendship, but showed no willingness to enter a new alliance. William and Nicholas remained firm friends over the next decades, corresponding constantly and advising each other on vital issues; frequently they exchanged visits or joined in common vacations. Down to the very day Germany declared war on Russia in 1914, the two rulers consulted on how to safeguard the friendship between their two nations. Yet they never seriously attempted to re-form Bismarck's alliance and, of course, proved incapable of delaying the outbreak of war.

In 1895, Russia's eyes were turned to Asia. Japan had emerged victorious from the Sino-Japanese War, and by its annexations on the mainland was threatening tsarist designs on Manchuria and Korea. During the war, England had tacitly favored Japan, but Germany, France, and Russia intervened jointly in behalf of China and actually forced Japan to retrocede a part of its conquest (the Liaotung Peninsula). Since Russia and France at the time were joined in an anti-German military pact, the cooperation of Germany with these two neighbors seems indeed strange. Actually, Germany found it useful to cooperate now and then with France in colonial matters, particularly when the action was designed to frustrate British plans. And

cooperation with Russia fitted William's mood of the mid–1890s.

But German intervention on behalf of China was not motivated solely by a desire to gain the favor of Nicholas. It marked the beginning of German penetration in the Far East—another phase of William's *Weltpolitik*. Germany's commercial interests in the area and William's longing for added prestige turned Germany suddenly into a strong contender for a sphere of influence in China. From this intervention, the Germans in 1897 secured Tsingtao and a dominant economic hold on the Shantung Peninsula.

THE GERMAN NAVY   Before the accession of William II, Germany had almost no navy. The futile attempt of the National Assembly at Frankfurt in 1848 to acquire naval forces had discouraged the Germans from repeating a similar experiment. During the 1850s and 1860s, Prussia had acquired a few coastal vessels; but even after unification, the navy assumed no important role. Bismarck had finally allotted negligible funds for the construction of a small naval force, enough to lend perfunctory support in colonial problems, but not sufficient to constitute a fighting navy. When Caprivi took over the Admiralty, he stressed construction of coastal defenses and torpedo carriers, but showed no interest in developing a high-seas fleet.

The accession of William II brought about a fundamental change in the German navy. The young emperor, himself an avid yachtsman, took great interest in all naval matters. An expanded naval program clearly seemed to go hand in hand with the new world-wide arena of German activities. He proclaimed succinctly: "Imperial

might means sea power." Starting in 1890, he placed technical experts at the head of the navy, and separated the Admiralty from army control. New ships were launched, although not according to any over-all planning and with relatively limited funds. In 1895, the important Kiel or Kaiser Wilhelm Canal was completed, linking the North Sea to the Baltic. German ships could now pass from one sea to the other without fear of a Danish blockade, and the fleet gained greater flexibility. But despite this progress, the German navy remained a negligible weapon. When the lack of naval strength became apparent in the Boer and China crises, William determined to construct a high-seas fleet commensurate with his ambitions.

In 1897, he placed Admiral Tirpitz in charge of the Imperial Naval Office (*Reichsmarineamt*). Tirpitz, the ennobled son of a civil servant, was a ruthlessly determined and skillful advocate of German naval expansion. Quite possibly he tried at first to avoid politics and develop his naval plans along purely technical and strategic lines, but before long, he was deeply involved in the internal political squabbles surrounding the naval program, as well as in the shaping of German foreign affairs. Tirpitz was a forceful advocate of a so-called German risk fleet, a navy so big that England would not risk a war with Germany for fear of sustaining such damage that its naval supremacy would be endangered. He was motivated by an intense hatred of England, and by the naïve belief, shared by William, that England could be frightened into friendship. In a famous memorandum of 1907, he was to write: "This constant danger of war with England . . .

will cease and even change into England's desire to befriend us only when our fleet is further strengthened." This theory, which required a constant increase in naval construction, was one of the causes of the naval armaments race between Germany and England in the prewar decade.

In 1898, Tirpitz proposed the first of a series of naval laws. He sought to build up the fleet and naval personnel through a program based on long-term budgets resembling those of the army. His first proposal stipulated a total of 17 ships of the line, 8 coastal vessels, 35 cruisers, and reserve ships. Seven ships of the line and 9 cruisers were to be built within seven years. The proposal was accepted by the Reichstag, although doctrinaire liberals disliked relinquishing financial control over naval expenditures by fixing the budget for seven years. But almost immediately Tirpitz and his supporters found the size of the contemplated navy inadequate. The Spanish-American War, in which Germany intervened perfunctorily, and the acquisition in 1899 of new possessions in the Pacific—the Mariana, Caroline, Palau, and Marshall islands—prompted Tirpitz to request a doubling of the naval strength in a new seventeen-year construction program proposed in 1899.

This second naval bill encountered more opposition. Many Centrists, most Progressives, and all Socialists fought the proposal. But Tirpitz was a master propagandist. The Navy League, which he had helped organize in 1898, became a formidable pressure group rallying public opinion behind the idea that a world power should also be a naval power. And William II echoed this thought with his call: "Our future lies on the seas!" The Pan-Germans,

at any rate, desired a navy to protect the colonial empire and to endow Germany with the prestige and power of a first-rate nation. The industrial interests also favored construction of a large fleet, since it would increase production. Moreover, more than a few liberals favored the navy for purely domestic, political reasons. Not only would a large fleet be good for trade and industry; it would also act as a liberal influence on internal politics. The army had traditionally been the province of the nobility. An enlarged navy, without the aristocratic taint of the army officer corps, would increase prospects for bourgeois power. The navy would be run largely by middle-class technicians and could hardly be used for the repression of internal rebellions. In the eyes of the liberals, therefore, increasing the navy represented a step toward democratization. The revolution of 1918 was to prove that these considerations were not so farfetched as they seem.

A crucial question was whether the Conservatives could be induced to vote for the bill. In Prussia especially, they continued to be dominated by the League of Landlords, which opposed the idea of a large fleet but still sought the reintroduction of high agricultural tariffs. The industrialists, on the other hand, wanted their fleet but opposed higher tariffs on food. A compromise was finally effected between the two groups, with the aid of government intervention and pressure from Tirpitz's Naval League. The industrialists promised to vote for higher agricultural tariffs when the current treaties expired in 1902; in return, the agrarians supported the naval program. This anomalous alliance between industry and agriculture remained important in

the domestic politics of the next decade.

After this political realignment, the second Naval Law was passed in the Reichstag in 1900. Germany was launched on the naval race with England. The government had wanted to finance this naval program largely on the basis of loans, but the Reichstag insisted on raising taxes. A new stamp tax on shares, lotteries, and commercial sea transports, and higher taxes on champagne, liquors, and beer were to help pay for the scheme that would turn Germany into the second greatest naval power in the world.

The Cultural Milieu

The lightning transformation of Germany through industrial and material progress continued unabated under William II. Cities burgeoned; production indices skyrocketed; self-assurance and optimism were comfortably bolstered by prosperity. New inventions enhanced the growing faith in science, and encouraged the application of scientific methods in nonscientific fields. In the popular mind, capitalists, industrialists, entrepreneurs, and scientists were ranked with army officers and civil servants as the heroes who had created the nation and were responsible for its amazing progress.

But while Germany experienced constant change, its social structure remained conservative, its class divisions entrenched. The numerous members of the upper aristocracy, although largely deprived of their governmental powers, still lived in a world apart. Even the lower nobility, many of whose members still dominated the officer corps and the higher echelons of the civil service, claimed and maintained a social status strangely discordant with an age of universal suffrage. As in earlier times, ambitious bourgeois aspired to be admitted to the sacrosanct milieu of the noble class.

Below the nobility and the officer corps, but still at a vastly elevated level, were those with titles or academic degrees. Everyone in the civil service of the federal and state governments, down to almost the lowest clerk, assumed a title, of which the German vocabulary contains a plethora. Each had its untranslatable distinctions. In the postal service, for instance, were *Postrat, Postdirektor, Postmeister, Posthalter, Postschreiber, Postsekretär, Postverwalter, Postwärter,* and a host of others. A title, even if it designated him only as a third clerk in a city post office, gained the bearer the humble respect of the nontitled burghers. University titles and degrees became a similar mark of distinction. The middle and lower bourgeois emulated the practice in order to maintain a respectful level above the proletariat and peasantry. Even technicians, merchants, artisans, and craftsmen who achieved some status adopted for themselves and their wives titles that they bore proudly and that they had inscribed on their tombstones. Thus the wife of a chimney sweeper who had passed his trade examination and had paid his admission dues to a master craft guild styled herself *Frau Schornsteinfegermeister* (wife of a master chimney sweeper). This mania for titles and craving for social distinction had a divisive and unhealthful influence on the development of the nation.

The comforts of prosperity and the pride in new nationhood persisted in buoying up materialism and militant nationalism. Among some groups this

led to a boisterous social Darwinism in which racialism, nihilism, and "action for action's sake" combined into a powerful ethos. Nietzsche's *Thus Spake Zarathustra* and *Beyond Good and Evil,* both published in the 1880s, were misappropriated by these circles. The philosopher's devastating blows at militarism, socialism, chauvinism, factionalism, egalitarianism, and Christianity were turned into aimless nihilism. His self-reliant, rational superman was twisted into a muscular superbeast. These ideas also found currency among the youth. As in the early nineteenth century, youth groups (such as the *Wandervögel*) organized hiking excursions or military games, sang war songs, and dreamed of heroic actions in which they could display valor and strength. But unlike earlier student groups, which advocated definable aims such as German unification, their twentieth-century counterparts were nihilistic in their disdain for society and sought action largely for the sake of action.

A strong dichotomy marked the life at universities and the course of education as a whole. Humanistic and practical learning vied for predominance. Scholarship still brought surprising results and opened new fields. Historiography, for example, was infused with new vitality through crossbreeding with other sciences. Wilhelm Dilthey (1833–1911) applied philosophy to historical analysis, while Max Weber (1864–1920) and others fruitfully combined history and sociology. But much of this was accomplished almost in spite of the prevailing atmosphere at universities, at which learning degenerated into pedantry in research and veneration of "omniscient professors." At the same time, unlike in the revolutionary year 1848, most intellec-

tuals disdainfully disassociated themselves from the stream of political life. Even students showed more interest in dueling and drinking bouts and in emphasizing their social superiority to the nonacademic world than in preparing to participate in the political life of their nation—a development that augured the unfortunate fate of the Weimar Republic after World War I.

Among writers and journalists there were many who could not wholeheartedly embrace the empire of William II. Despite occasional censorship and libel suits by the government, a steady stream of criticism was launched by numerous periodicals against the antiquated governmental framework, the pretensions of the aristocracy, the bombast of the military clique, and the extravagance of capitalists and industrialists.

Naturalistic drama thrived with new plays by Hauptmann and the works of the prolific Hermann Sudermann (1857–1928). A nostalgic regret at the decay of the peaceful though dull atmosphere of early nineteenth-century merchant life characterized *Buddenbrooks* (1901), the first major novel of the young Thomas Mann (1875–1955). But many of the writers shielded themselves from the crass reality of Wilhelmian materialism, and took refuge in belated romanticism or in the new movement of symbolism. Munich and Vienna became centers of neoromanticism in literature and music, as well as painting. Most famous among the symbolists were Stefan George (1868–1933) and his numerous disciples, who cultivated an extreme form of art for art's sake, remained aloof from the world about them, and sought spiritual satisfaction in the esthetic forms of their poetry.

6

The Empire of William II:
The Bülow Era, 1900–1909

In October, 1900, Prince Bernhard von Bülow became chancellor after having served as minister of foreign affairs for three years. Bülow showed some skill in devising an over-all policy in domestic affairs, and at first seemed able to make Emperor William more tractable. Compared to his two predecessors, he was an able chancellor. But he never acquired the strength or determination to steer Germany's internal policy on a constant course in the face of the demands of the various pressure groups. In foreign affairs his diplomacy was superficial, and oblivious of the danger of Germany's growing isolation. Historians have traditionally blamed Bülow for the baneful turn of Germany's foreign relations during the first decade of this century. In his posthumous memoirs, Bülow placed the blame on William, Holstein, and others. The truth, no doubt, lies between these two indictments. A stronger chancellor could perhaps have saved Germany from the stigma of international distrust; but it is doubt-

ful whether any minister could have overcome a system that permitted the nation's ruler, miscellaneous intriguers, and assorted pressure groups constantly to intervene in the administrative course.

CONSERVATISM UNDER BÜLOW

Guide lines for the Bülow era at home were based on a realignment of forces and a new policy. After the failure of conciliation (1890–1894) and *Kampfpolitik* (1894–1898), the administration chose to maintain the *status quo* wherever possible by uniting all conservative forces—especially agrarians and industrialists—into a common front against the growing proletariat. This program accentuated the internal divisions in the nation and enhanced the bitterness of the class antagonism preached by the left-wing Socialists. Moreover, it proved an inadequate policy for a society changing as fast as prewar Germany.

Yet Bülow and Emperor William II chose to treat all matters—tariff questions, colonial administration, the naval laws, the treatment of minorities, constitutional reform in Prussia, and the Reich—under the aegis of conservatism.

The tariff laws of 1902 provide a typical example of the government's new policy. Agricultural producers, particularly on the large estates of the northeast, had suffered an economic squeeze during the 1890s. The industrial boom had pushed up wages, the cost of production, and interest rates; while the relatively low tariffs of 1893 had depressed the price of grain because of foreign competition. Consequently, many estates were mortgaged and encumbered with debts. Despite increasing pressure from the League of Landlords and the government's recognition of the problem, only minor palliative measures were taken in the 1890s to aid the agrarians, for the tariffs were set by treaties that could not be altered before their expiration. The government reduced the land tax, lowered the import quota for live cattle, and made easier credit available to landowners. These minor remedies did not satisfy the agrarians, who were adamant about reintroducing high protective tariffs. All other government suggestions were rejected. The landlords refused to accept such proposals as government price fixing for all grain, domestic as well as foreign, the adoption of diversified instead of one-crop farming, or government aid for settling small peasant owners on the large estates, a sort of disguised land reform.

After 1897, the government showed more and more inclination to mollify the agrarians. The political maneuvers preceding the passage of the second Naval Law showed the value of using the agrarians as a counterweight to the industrialists and of combining both into a conservative coalition. There were other political reasons for favoring the agrarians. The rural areas furnished the bulk of the soldiers and noble officers for the army. Also, the steady increase in the number of Socialist deputies in the Reichstag and the obstructionism displayed by most Progressives and Centrists against William's foreign policy forced the government into greater reliance on the conservative parties.

In 1901, Bülow announced his willingness to raise minimum grain tariffs more or less to their pre-1891 level when the current treaties expired. The announcement produced a storm of opposition and months of debate in committees and on the floor of the Reichstag, ending with a six-week filibuster by the Social Democratic deputies. The extremist agrarians considered the proposed tariffs too low; all advocates of free trade continued to oppose tariffs on principle; and the Socialists campaigned against the "bread-usury" that would raise the cost of the laborer's food without other compensations. Bülow tried to mediate among the conflicting interests, but in the end sided largely with the Conservatives. In December 1902, the Reichstag, with the votes of the Conservatives, the National Liberals, and some Centrists, passed a bill authorizing negotiations with other governments on new tariffs. The treaties, finally completed by 1905, were effective for twelve years. Caught between agrarians and the industrialists, the government not only raised agricultural tariffs but also included additional protective barriers for German industry.

The tariff episode of 1902 cemented the alliance between the government and the Conservatives, and produced a deepened split between producers and consumers. In the electoral campaign of 1903, the Socialists campaigned largely on this issue, and as a result, increased their representation in the Reichstag to 81 seats, and obtained some 3 million votes, or about 30 percent of the total cast—thereby becoming the second largest party in the parliament and by far the largest in popular vote (see Chart 1).

ECONOMIC AND SOCIAL CHANGES

Agriculture and Industry

Conditions in agriculture improved measurably in the years after 1902, aided by the new tariffs, by a general rise in world grain prices, and by greater productivity resulting from the use of better fertilizer. To compete with the large estates, the smaller farmers resorted to cooperatives. From 1900 to 1912, the number of such agricultural cooperatives doubled from 13,600 to 26,000. At the same time, speculation in land continued to boost the value of the highly mortgaged estates. But while the improved status of the landlords created better markets for industrial consumer goods, higher agricultural prices also raised the cost of living, adding to the tension between rich and poor, producers and consumers. Furthermore, the economic status of the simple agricultural laborers was hardly altered. Little social legislation protected them, and the 1891 colonization law, by which the government was to have financed the opening of small farms, had produced

few results. In two decades, only about 22,000 new peasant farms were created under this program. To keep wages at a minimum, many landlords east of the Elbe imported cheap Polish agricultural workers. Hence the farm laborers failed to profit from the improved conditions in agriculture, and tended to share the bitterness of the city proletariat.

Increased home production was not enough to make the country self-sufficient in food. Meat and grains continued to be imported in large quantities to feed the bulging population —which increased from 56.4 million in 1900 to 64.9 million in 1910. Thus Germany, like England, remained vulnerable to blockade in time of war.

The continued large-scale industrial expansion, which pushed Germany past England in the production of many basic items, such as iron and steel, also accentuated politico-economic problems. Big industry grew bigger and politically more powerful, while small industry declined. In the two decades of industrial boom before World War I, the number of independent entrepreneurs and small enterprises decreased, whereas the total labor force increased sharply. Capital and industrial ownership became concentrated in fewer and fewer hands. The formation of cartels and syndicates, frequently owned or controlled by the large banks, was encouraged by the government to assure better utilization of scarce resources. The government was also engaged in commerce and industry, for it owned most of the railroads and many coal mines as well as other enterprises. Yet certain cartels became so powerful that the government occasionally found it impossible to resist their pressure; for example, in 1904, when the Prussian

state tried to purchase more coal mines, it was prevented by the coal trust.

Besides increasing the political and economic power of big industry, industrial concentration also forged a widening gap between the growing mass of workers and the dwindling number of entrepreneurs. On the whole, the workers benefited from the rising standard of living; but higher food prices, importation of cheap foreign labor, lack of job security, and social envy fanned their dissatisfaction with the economic and political regime. Some additional social legislation raising the minimum age for child labor and regulating working hours was passed under Bülow, and the social insurance system was enlarged. But these measures did not touch the deeper social problems, for no attempt was made to incorporate the laborers into the fabric of society. The workers continued in their social limbo, feared and resented by the middle and upper classes.

The Labor Movement

During this period, the labor movement was determined to gain recognition for its unions. The Association Law of 1899 made it legal for unions to organize, and they rapidly grew in membership. The largest, the Social Democratic unions, increased from 680,000 members in 1900 to 2,500,000 in 1912. But the entrepreneurs formed associations in order to present a united front against the unions' demands, and steadfastly refused to recognize the workers' bargaining rights. On this point, the industrialists were supported particularly by the Prussian government. Hence the workers became distrustful of the government because

they resented its apparent partiality toward big business. The strike of some 220,000 Ruhr miners in 1905 illustrates these conditions. When the miners' union presented its grievances—concerning layoffs, unhealthful work conditions, money fines, and increased travel time into deeper pits without added wages—the mine administrators refused to recognize the rights of the union to bargain for the workers. The government contemplated arbitration, but the workers had no faith in governmental mediation and began a strike. After a few days, the strike had to be called off because the workers lacked the requisite reserve funds. To show its good intentions, the Prussian government then attempted to pass a law making layoffs without provisions for the dismissed miners more difficult, but the law was rejected by the conservative upper house. Bülow, in the end, barely managed to get a law passed that permitted miners' unions to present grievances even though it did not accord them a legal title to collective bargaining. It was a pale measure, which hardly earned the chancellor the gratitude of the labor population.

The Workers and Socialism

In confronting business and government, the workers found few mediators. Stöcker's Christian Social party was unsuccessful in its efforts to absorb the labor movement on the basis of a demagogic reconciliation of the classes. Nor did Friedrich Naumann's (1860–1919) virulent and visionary National Socialist party succeed in bringing about social mediation. Naumann, a former disciple of Stöcker's, had conceived a mass movement to unite workers and bourgeois in a nationalistic

fervor overriding all domestic issues. Since world commerce required the support of the workers, he favored mock democratization at home as a buttress for an aggressive foreign policy. Like Hitler's later movement of similar designation, Naumann's was at heart not interested in socialism but rather in nationalism. Sensing this incompatibility, the workers shunned his movement, and the National Socialist party was dissolved after its electoral defeat of 1903.

Hence the various workers' associations—the large socialist unions as well as the small Catholic and the even smaller liberal unions—and above all the Social Democratic party remained the only spokesmen for the workers. But the SPD itself was not united in its aims and aspirations. Officially the party continued to adhere to its Erfurt Program of 1891, which had demanded nationalization of all land, mines, natural resources, factories, tools, and means of transportation; the extension of suffrage to all men and women aged twenty-one or over; popular control over decisions on war and peace; popular election of government officials rather than appointment from above; free legal and medical aid; and abolition of all indirect taxes and customs. In fact, however, few Socialists deluded themselves into believing that such large-scale aims were about to be realized. The bulk of the workers pressed for more tangible, immediate gains— improved working conditions or fewer hours of work—while the intelligentsia of the SPD fought over the question of how the ultimate aims were to be achieved.

The radicals, led in the prewar period by Rosa Luxemburg (1870–1919), Franz Mehring (1846–1919),

Karl Kautsky (1854–1938), and Karl Liebknecht (1871–1919), continued to preach Marxian principles. They insisted that reliance on electoral campaigns for the Reichstag and the prevailing wait-and-see attitude of the Socialists would never topple the conservative Prussian government nor overthrow the capitalistic regime. Instead, they advocated intensification of the class war and a revolutionary struggle employing strikes and violence where necessary, in order to plunge the entire monarchical and capitalistic system into chaos and ultimately annihilate it.

Opposed to the radicals were the revisionists, strongly influenced by Eduard Bernstein (1850–1932), whose *Evolutionary Socialism* had appeared in 1899. Bernstein decried the theory of the class struggle, since it prevented possible alliance of the proletariat with the liberal segments of the middle class. He saw no evidence of an impending collapse of bourgeois society, and disputed Marx's prediction of an inevitable acceleration in the concentration of wealth. He noted, on the contrary, that the propertied classes were becoming numerically larger rather than smaller, and that the progress of democracy and industry was slowly changing their character. Influenced by the Fabians in England, where he lived in exile, he urged workers to struggle for democracy rather than for social upheaval, and to achieve their aims gradually, in alliance with the lower middle class.

The revisionist program was heatedly debated at the Dresden Congress of the Social Democratic party in 1903 and finally rejected by majority vote, on the grounds that it tended to obscure class differences and muddle the dis-

tinction between the socialist proletariat and the "bourgeois reactionaries." But this reaffirmation of orthodox Marxism—echoed two months later in London when the Russian Social Democratic party held its meeting of exiles and accorded Lenin and the extremists (Bolsheviks) a majority vote over the moderates (Mensheviks) led by Georgi Plekhanov—failed to unite the Socialists on a common basis. In Prussia, where Socialist representation was small because of the three-class vote and urban underenfranchisement, and where hatred of the aristocratic government was particularly pronounced, Socialists continued to be revolutionary. In the Reich at large, where Socialists had better representation and state governments were somewhat more liberal, the more evolutionary or revisionist tendencies prevailed—despite the Dresden pronouncement. But everywhere, the Socialists persisted in a rather negative attitude toward the state, which made it difficult for bourgeois friends of labor to effect any mediation.

TREATMENT OF MINORITIES

Besides the workers and the agricultural proletariat, there were many other groups who remained essentially unreconciled to the Wilhelmian Reich. Segments of the Catholic Center party, and such particularistic groups as the so-called Guelphs of the former state of Hanover retained their negative attitude toward the imperial government, despite William's occasional conciliatory gestures. Antagonism was even more pronounced among certain ethnic minorities, such as the Poles and the Alsace-Lorrainers.

German Poland

After William's unsuccessful attempt at conciliating the Poles, he had returned to Bismarck's policy of colonizing Prussia's eastern provinces so as to increase the German element at the expense of the Poles. The Prussian government protected and favored German merchants, and attempted to speed up German cultural infiltration at all levels. A German academy was established at Poznan, a technical institute was set up in Danzig, and German schools were multiplied throughout all Polish-speaking districts. But the government encountered problems when it tried to transfer Polish land to German ownership. The Prussian Land Commission, charged with this task, could not settle many Germans, since the Poles, peasants as well as nobles, steadfastly refused to sell their landholdings. Between 1891 and 1900, the Germans in the province of Poznan managed to increase by 3.75 percent; but this change hardly "Germanized" the region, since the Polish population increased by 10.5 percent during the same period. In 1898, the Prussian government appropriated millions for a "colonization fund" to help German settlers buy up Polish properties. Actually, over the succeeding ten years, few Polish estates were purchased by Germans, for most of the funds were required to help the Germans retain their own land. Many Poles worked in the Ruhr mines or elsewhere in the booming German factories and saved money with which, after their return to Poznan, they bid for land owned by Germans. Their financial offers were so attractive that the German landowners found them hard to resist. Consequently, the Prussian government

found itself forced to loan money to German peasants to enable them to outbid or reject the Polish offers.

Realizing that it was fighting a losing battle, the Prussian government proposed sterner measures in 1907. Legislation was introduced to empower the Prussian Land Commission to expropriate Polish lands. But the diet rejected the bill. The Center party sympathized with the Catholic Poles, the Progressives objected on principle, and even the Conservatives feared possible later violation of their own property rights. Moreover, the government produced no adequate plans concerning resettlement of the Poles whose lands would be expropriated. A watered-down compromise law was finally adopted in 1908, giving the Land Commission power to expropriate a limited amount of land (about 173,000 acres), but under the new chancellor after 1909, Bethmann-Hollweg, the commission seldom availed itself of its expropriatory powers. Consequently, the new law merely further antagonized the Poles without achieving its purpose of Germanizing the eastern lands. In all their years under German domination, the Poles never became reconciled to their German overlords and continued to be a separate and distinct entity.

Alsace-Lorraine

A similar treatment was accorded Alsace-Lorraine. Organized as a *Reichsland* in 1871, the two provinces were placed under control of an imperial governor and a local committee, operating under the Bundesrat. During the first two decades after the Franco-Prussian War, while French demands for revenge were frequently heard, the Alsace-Lorrainers looked with suspicion upon their German masters. Their status seemed temporary and uncertain. The imperial governors favored the clergy and the upper middle class, but failed to reconcile the lower classes to the German regime.

In the 1890s, French talk of revenge receded, and German economic prosperity made itself felt in the two annexed provinces. The dictatorial regime of the governors was relaxed, and in 1902 their special police powers were rescinded. But the population now voiced new demands, in view of the likelihood that the provinces were to remain German indefinitely. They objected to the inferior status they held within the empire. Various political parties began to agitate for full autonomy for their provinces, and for the same semisovereign rights enjoyed by the German federal states. The Berlin government, however, refused to honor these demands, since it feared the Alsace-Lorrainers might use their greater freedom to cement better relations with France.

German suspicions concerning the reliability of their Alsace-Lorraine subjects were fanned anew by the increased Franco-German friction in the years after 1904. The population of these provinces continued to be an oppositional minority pressuring the government to concede autonomy. In 1910, under Bethmann-Hollweg, the government finally tried to conciliate the provinces. A bill was introduced in the Reichstag to eliminate the Bundesrat's control over Alsace-Lorraine and to grant to the provinces a constitution establishing a two-chamber system—a lower elected house, and an upper chamber composed of members of the professions and imperial appointees. The Reichstag added a further pro-

vision granting the provinces three seats in the Bundesrat. But government and Reichstag refused to attach the rights of sovereignty and equal status with other states (*Länder*) to this constitution, which was finally promulgated in 1911. Emperor William continued to remain direct overlord of the provinces, and the governor, still appointed by him and supported by German army contingents, retained his supreme powers. The Alsace-Lorrainers were also deprived of any power to amend this constitution, a power expressly reserved to the Reichstag.

The new constitution pleased the moderates in the provinces and lessened friction with the Reich at large. But the more nationalistic Alsatians and Lorrainers were not mollified by the hollow favors bestowed upon them by the German Reichstag. Encouraged by the growing international tension between France and Germany, they used every blunder of the German military and civilian officials to stir up unrest. The famous Zabern affair in November 1913, in which German officers in the Alsatian town of Zabern acted rashly, injuring a civilian and illegally arresting others in reprisal for anti-German demonstrations, was such a case. The excitement it produced in the two provinces showed the deep-seated antagonism felt by most of the population. It appeared evident that after forty-three years of German rule, Germany had failed to absorb Alsace-Lorraine. At the same time in the empire at large, the Zabern affair afforded the opposition groups—Social Democrats, Center, minorities, and even certain liberals—a welcome opportunity for publicly venting their pent-up displeasure with the government's militaristic regime.

FINANCES AND PARTY POLITICS

Imperial Finances

Despite the increasing prosperity, the imperial government was constantly in debt, and neither Bülow nor the autocratic Emperor William was strong enough to redress this situation. The existing system of financial decentralization allowed the individual states to pocket most of the tax receipts. The Reich, dependent largely on income from customs duties and monopolies and on annual levies (called "matriculation fees") from the states, had no way of forcing the latter to increase their contributions. And when new taxes were proposed to augment the imperial revenue, the Reichstag usually voted them down.

Thus the debts of the Reich rose to 1400 million marks in the decade before 1892, whereas the various German states accumulated financial surpluses. Caprivi's proposed tax reforms were rejected, and the increased army expenditures were paid for from current revenues and loans. Increased prosperity rather than fiscal skill account for the fact that the national debt rose only another 200 million marks between 1895 and 1900. Furthermore, the Reichstag, in a rare mood of fiscal responsibility, insisted on financing the new navy through new and higher indirect taxes. Yet these measures hardly sufficed to balance the budget. After 1901, even ordinary expenses had to be covered partially by loans, and the imperial debt continued to spiral upward.

In his four last years as chancellor, Bülow repeatedly attempted to bring solvency to the empire. In 1905 and 1906, he tried to raise revenue by introducing a variety of new direct and

indirect taxes—on beer, tobacco, receipts, bills of freight, railroad tickets, and automobiles—as well as a direct inheritance tax. But he was forced to compromise with the Reichstag opposition and settle for less than half the requested revenue, raised exclusively from indirect levies.

The naval construction law of 1906 and other increased expenses produced a new deficit in 1907 and a forecast for an even greater imbalance for 1908. The government therefore submitted new tax proposals, requesting a wider distribution of levies among the population in order to mollify all groups. It proposed abolishment of certain "nuisance" taxes—on sugar and railroad tickets, for example; it requested 400 million marks in new indirect taxes —on brandy, beer, tobacco, and other consumer items—a tax preferred by the Conservatives since it largely burdened the poorer classes; and it again demanded a progressive inheritance tax on land, favored by the Socialists because it placed the burden on the wealthier landowners.

These government proposals produced stormy debates in the Reichstag throughout the winter of 1908. The Progressives and Socialists opposed indirect taxes, but were willing to vote with the government, since the inheritance tax would strongly affect the rich and distribute the burden of taxation somewhat more fairly. The Conservatives, however, vehemently objected to an inheritance tax, adopted parliamentary obstructionism, and resorted to such dubious slogans as "spare the widows, tax the living." They had always disliked paying federal taxes, since these would indirectly increase the power of the Reichstag, which was suspect to them because of its popular base. They preferred paying taxes, if at all, to the Prussian government, which they controlled.

Bülow warned prophetically: "The Conservative Party is digging its own grave by misreading the signs of the time and refusing to recognize legitimate demands." He finally demanded a vote on his entire tax program, as if to make the matter a vote of confidence in parliamentary fashion. He emphasized the "all-or-nothing" aspect of his demands. The Conservatives, however, refused to approve the proposals unless the inheritance tax were omitted, and the Center joined them in an effort to split Bülow's party support and topple him from power. The inheritance tax clause was defeated in the end by 194 (Conservatives, Center, and Anti-Semites) to 186 (Free Conservatives, National Liberals, Progressives, and Socialists), and the emasculated tax bill was adopted by 226 to 127. Bülow, already at odds with Emperor William over questions of foreign policy, saw in the defeat of his tax legislation a rebuff to his administration, and handed in his resignation.

Party Politics Under Bülow

According to the constitution, there was no reciprocal connection between the executive and the legislative branches of the German government. William and his ministers were not accountable to the Reichstag, and the representatives shared no responsibility for the government's actions. Yet Bülow's resignation in 1909 seemed to demonstrate that Germany was drifting into a kind of parliamentarianism made necessary by political requirements that were rendering the government increasingly dependent on the

support of the Reichstag. Unquestionably, over the decades, the search for a cooperative majority among the representatives had become a major task for all chancellors, for without the backing of enough votes, the government could not enact a legislative program. Bismarck himself had faced this problem, but to a large extent he had led the parties and dominated the Reichstag. In the 1890s, however, and even more in the 1900s, during Bülow's regime, the task had become more complicated. Legislative and financial requirements of the government were constantly increasing while its power over the Reichstag was decreasing. Party leaders and economic pressure groups were pulling first one way and then another, so that the government was frequently dragged helplessly along.

But despite the growing importance of the Reichstag, the imperial entourage retained its deprecatory view of this parliamentary body. Emperor William and his advisers seemed to share Treitschke's view, expressed in 1886: "An irresponsible parliament, produced by changing elections, split into small parties—an assembly that lacks all the traditions of a ruling estate—possesses neither the power nor the unity nor the moral stature to dominate the Reich." And, of course, they thoroughly agreed with Treitschke's prediction that "the great decisions of our history will be taken by the crown of the Hohenzollerns." Even among the population at large, the Reichstag enjoyed relatively little confidence. Fraudulent voting and failure to reapportion electoral districts undermined its representative nature, despite the heralded universal male suffrage. The constant splintering of the

parties over minor doctrinal or economic issues prevented many voters from establishing deep ties with political groups and their representatives in the Reichstag.

The delegates themselves rarely showed any consideration of all-German problems. Since the system made it impossible for a party to "come to power," political leaders could indulge in unlimited bargaining or obstructionism without the sobering influence of exercising statesmanship. For the most, each delegate represented a class or a region, an economic interest or political doctrine, and bargained accordingly. The Prussian Conservatives, for example, refused to vote the money for a canal connecting the Weser and the Elbe—a vital link in Germany's inland water system—and insisted that the funds be spent instead on extending railroads in eastern Prussia, a measure that would benefit almost solely their own grain production. Similarly, the Center party in the Reichstag agreed to approve an increase in the number of noncommissioned officers only if in return the other parties would agree to alter the anti-Jesuit laws so as to permit individual Jesuits to reside in Germany. For their part, Socialists, Progressives, National Liberals, Poles, and Alsatians fought their own battles, pulling the Reichstag in myriad directions. And neither the absentee emperor nor his chancellor had the strength to set Germany on a definitive course.

A government crisis in 1906 gave Chancellor Bülow the opportunity to establish a new working relationship with the Reichstag and to set up a pseudo-parliamentary government based on cooperation between the executive and the legislative branches. Emperor Wil-

liam had become disillusioned with Bülow. Court intrigues fanned by the ubiquitous Eulenburg, the ill-fated Algeciras Conference of 1906 (see page 157), and Bülow's failure to obtain from the Reichstag sufficient funds for colonial administration had turned the emperor against his chancellor. Bülow, for his part, was unhappy with William's international *faux pas* and tired of the behavior of the Reichstag, which had refused his requested taxes and obstructed his colonial policy. Moreover, Bülow found that the Center party voted more and more frequently with the Socialists to block government action, so that he felt the need for a new alignment. To find a new *modus vivendi* with the parties and perhaps to prove his prowess to William, Bülow dissolved the Reichstag in the fall of 1906 and called for new elections.

The election campaign of January 1907 was fought in an aura of militancy and chauvinism. The government desired to allocate more funds to the construction of railroads, ports, and military installations in the colonies, particularly in Southwest Africa, where a rebellion had been seething for some time. But the Socialists and most bourgeois delegates had vetoed such funds, partly on principle and partly because they envisaged more profitable investments elsewhere. The colonial issue was therefore made a major campaign item. Government speakers and conservative candidates appealed to the emotions of the populace, and proclaimed that Germany's honor was at stake in the colonies.

Bülow added a second issue to the election campaign. He desired a new working majority in the Reichstag and thought it expedient to try to unite all bourgeois parties against the Socialists, ostensibly to strengthen the Reich against internal enemies, but actually to form a progovernment bloc and revive Bismarck's anti-Socialist *Kampfpolitik*.

Bülow's campaign was successful. The elections (see Chart 1) in which almost two million more voters cast ballots than in 1903, brought electoral gains to all parties except the Socialists, Guelphs, and Alsatians. In fact, the Socialists, although gaining a quarter of a million votes over 1903, lost half their seats—a measure of the inequity of the Reich's electoral districting. Bülow's new "bloc," consisting of Conservatives, *Reichspartei* (Free Conservatives), National Liberals, Progressives, and Anti-Semites gave him a working majority of 203—of a total of 397 votes—and made him independent of the Center and the minority parties. The chancellor could thus hope for a better chance to push his programs through the Reichstag.

As a result, Germany assumed an air of parliamentarianism in 1907 and 1908. Supported by his bloc, Bülow was able to enact parts of his program which he termed "conservative with some liberal reforms." New social legislation was passed, the Association Laws were amended, the criminal code was revised, the stock exchange was regulated, and the stringent proceedings against lese majesty curtailed. On most national questions and foreign matters the bloc parties could cooperate and defeat the Socialist and Center parties which now clearly formed the opposition.

But at heart, the bloc was a fragile construction. The Progressives cooperated only reluctantly with the right wing parties and frequently demanded concessions. The Conservatives for their part feared the spread of liberalism. In the end, the tax debates of

1908 split the bloc and ended Bülow's hope for cooperation between government and a majority of the Reichstag. Because he had been weakened in prestige by the famous *Daily Telegraph* affair (see pages 158 ff.) of 1908 and thwarted in his tax program, Bülow's resignation in 1909 appeared like the result of a vote of no confidence. With Bülow's departure his bloc disintegrated. Economic pressure groups, political splinters, and doctrinaire interests once again assumed dominance in the Reichstag and made it impossible for the new chancellor, Bethmann-Hollweg, to rule with the parties. The landed interests controlled the Right, and the Socialists—who had regained their electoral strength to become the largest single party by 1912—dominated the Left. In the middle, the bourgeois banded together in the *Hansa-Bund,* an economic association founded in 1909 in imitation of the League of Landlords. It advocated "equal opportunity for all trades, commerce, and industry," and aimed at "breaking the pernicious influence of the one-sided agrarian demagogues." The various progressive parties joined in 1910 to form the Progressive People's party, in a vain attempt to shore up the middle-of-the-road parties. In reality, Germany had lost its opportunity to establish a parliamentary system— short of altering the entire electoral and political structure of the Reich.

FOREIGN AFFAIRS UNDER BÜLOW

When Bülow assumed responsibility for the Foreign Office in 1897—three years before assuming the chancellorship—the international scene seemed auspicious for Germany, and the optimistic Bülow, anticipating easy success, glanced lightly at possible dangers. England was occupied with Egypt and the Boers; Russia and England were clashing in the East; France and England were in conflict over the Sudan; even Spain and far-off America were about to be embroiled in war. Germany, alone among the major powers, was free from entanglements and in a position to gain from the discomforts of the others.

In some respects, Germany skillfully used the occasion to enhance its power and prestige. It obtained the Carolinas and a major part of the Samoan Islands. Backed by French financiers, it received the concession for the Turkish railway to Baghdad, and in 1899 began construction of this vital link of the Berlin-to-Baghdad railroad—much to the dismay of Russia and Britain. In conjunction with Anglo-Franco-Russian contingents, Germany interfered in the Boxer Rebellion in China, and managed to reaffirm its newly acquired position in the Far East.

On the other hand, the optimistic Bülow and the obstinate Holstein did nothing to keep William from turning these years of opportunity into a field day for his bombastic *Weltpolitik,* which antagonized the powers without bringing concrete benefits to the Reich. In 1898, William visited Turkish Palestine and publicly promised to protect Turkish integrity—at a time when Britain and Russia were secretly suggesting to Germany that Turkey be partitioned into spheres of influence. In the same year, he ordered his nascent fleet to steam to the Philippines to run unwarrantable interference between the Spanish and United States navies. And in 1900, when German troops invaded China together with those of other powers, William again

antagonized the world with his pretentious claims of vengeance for the murder of the German envoy to Peking.

Failure to Conclude an Alliance with England

Most damaging for Germany's future was its failure to achieve an alliance with England during this period. Great Britain, at odds with France and Russia, was seeking support on the Continent. Its overtures to Russia in January 1898 having been rebuffed, England turned to Germany. Joseph Chamberlain, Britain's powerful colonial secretary, and Prime Minister Salisbury made repeated offers to William to work out a fundamental Anglo-German understanding, if not an alliance. They assumed that Germany would welcome such overtures to help extricate it from the squeeze of the Franco-Russian alliance. Bülow and Holstein, it is clear, enjoyed this sudden wooing by England, but saw no reason for making these advances any easier. William himself was hesitant, for he liked his freedom from commitments, which permitted him almost unlimited international philandering. Yet he had qualms of conscience. At the end of May 1898, he wrote to the tsar, his "dearest Nicky," to tell him that "quite unexpectedly" he found himself "faced with a decision of vital importance" for his country. He informed Nicholas of the thrice-repeated offer of an English alliance, and begged his advice as a "friend and confidant." In typical Wilhelmian terms, he admitted that he had refused the previous overtures offhand, but that the last proposal seemed so good that "I deem it my duty toward Germany, to ponder thoroughly before answering." He

finally begged the tsar to tell him what Russia could offer if Germany rejected the British alliance, and terminated his letter: "May God help you find the right solution and decision," as if asking Nicholas to decide what was best for Germany and for his "devoted friend Willy."

Nicholas II replied that three months earlier England had offered to iron out all differences with Russia by dividing Asia into respective spheres of influence, and that the proposal had filled him with suspicion: "Never before had England made such an offer to Russia." Hence, Nicholas confessed, he had refused it "without thinking twice," and implicitly urged William to do likewise.

William rejected the British overtures of 1898, and continued his aloofness in the succeeding years. Chamberlain tried to reopen the matter a few more times, but Bülow instructed his ambassador in London "to listen politely" but to agree to nothing. And Holstein, convinced that the threat of an English *rapprochement* with France and Russia was a hoax, gloated over Chamberlain's "feverish attacks of friendship," and insisted that "time is on our side."

Actually, the failure to bring about an Anglo-German alliance in the period 1898–1901 opened the doors to Germany's prewar encirclement. The fault, of course, lay not solely with Germany. Nor had the nascent German navy as yet become an insurmountable hindrance to an Anglo-German *rapprochement*. England, it must be remembered, was still a colonial power. Although it sought a Continental support for its clashes overseas with France and Russia, England was reluctant to tie itself to the Continent by a tight

alliance that might interfere with its colonial objectives.

The Germans, for their part, did not reach for England's tentatively proffered hand. The Pan-Germans, the Navy League, and other fervent nationalists feared that friendship with England might curtail Germany's colonial opportunities and obviate the need for a large navy. Holstein and the Foreign Office, confident that an Anglo-French or an Anglo-Russian entente was impossible, expected high profits from Germany's waiting game. The emperor himself may have recognized the danger of Germany's continued isolation, but he hardly worked hard enough to provide a determined direction to German foreign policy.

By 1902, the chances for an Anglo-German *rapprochement* had passed. The accession of the Francophile King Edward VII, who flouted his German imperial nephew, dampened relations between London and Berlin. In 1902, England found in Japan the desired anti-Russian ally and hence no longer sought Germany's friendship so eagerly. Germany had missed the opportunity to emerge from its Continental isolation, and now entered the era of encirclement.

The Beginning of Encirclement

The problem of Germany's gradual encirclement and increasing isolation resulted from two different trends: on the one hand, the Triple Alliance with Austria and Italy was weakening, even disintegrating; on the other, England, Japan, France, and Russia were slowly drawing closer together. In the first decade of the twentieth century, this problem was barely recognized by the German Foreign Office. Holstein re-

mained blissful and confident until dismissed in 1906, and Bülow showed little apprehension. Perhaps the government's fitful reactions to international developments showed its inner insecurity. But Bülow failed to identify the danger of encirclement in a positive sense by adopting a new course that would bring an end to Germany's growing isolation.

"Encirclement" actually involved more than international relations; it constituted the unconscious beginning of a German national psychosis of anxiety. Notably after World War I, this fear of encirclement (*Einkreisungsangst*) was to become quasi-paranoiac. But well before the war, many Germans, particularly conservatives, reacted with intense emotions to the chimera of a ubiquitous enemy, and attributed all national calamities to the hostile ring girdling the nation or to "the enemy within," whom they suspected of collaborating with foreigners. They tended to project their own xenophobia onto the world at large, and ascribed hostile feelings to all other nations. This anxiety made them appear quarrelsome and antagonistic to the foreign powers. A vicious circle developed. German swagger provoked among the powers anti-German alliances, which in turn heightened Germany's paranoiac reactions.

Germany thus became an outcast among the nations. The British and French press gleefully denounced every awkward step of German diplomacy, and labeled Germany the troublemaker of the world. Even before the advent of World War I, Germany acquired the reputation imputed to France, Spain, and other "aggressor" nations in previous centuries. This ill repute—stemming partly from the powers' jeal-

ousy of Germany's meteoric rise and largely from irritation with William's clumsy *Weltpolitik*—colored international relations in the prewar decade and, one might say, produced the theory of German "war guilt" well in advance of the war. In turn, it nourished Germany's brooding feeling of injustice and heightened its irritability and distrustfulness.

Much of the powers' suspicions of German intentions can be attributed to the incredibly undiplomatic behavior of the German Foreign Office and its spokesmen. At the first Peace Conference at The Hague in 1899, for instance, the German delegates acted like boorish novices. The majority of the twenty-six nations attending the conference distrusted the Russian proposals for disarmament, but tactfully circumvented the problem by directing the discussion to international arbitration and the need for limiting the horrors of war. The German envoys, however, supported by a press that decried pacifism as befitting only weak or rich nations but not growing states like Germany, talked squarely against disarmament. They proclaimed that Germany was not overarmed and that they saw no reason that it should stop arming. All the other major powers at the conference undoubtedly felt as Germany did but had the tact not to make the admission publicly. German frankness produced nothing but increased international suspicions.

A similar spectacle was presented at the second Peace Conference in 1907. Great Britain desired to safeguard its naval supremacy by an international agreement limiting future naval construction. Again none of the major powers cherished such a proposal, but Germany again aroused the suspicion of the nations by acting as a blunt spokesman for naval expansion.

WEAKENING OF THE TRIPLE ALLIANCE
The alliance among Germany, Austria, and Italy was renewed for a six-year period in 1902—as it was to be in 1908 and again in 1912. But its value to Germany had become doubtful. Even if the alliance had remained firm, the Continental character of Germany's two allies and the smallness of their navies made them poor support for Germany's global commitments. But the alliance did not even remain firm. Italy was becoming a dubious partner, and the Italians made it clear that inadequacy of their navy would discourage them from fighting France or England.

Above all, Italy had been drawing closer to France. The trade war between the two ended in 1898 with the signing of a Franco-Italian commercial treaty. In the following years, the two countries agreed on mutually respecting each other's spheres of interests in Africa, with France tacitly relinquishing Tripoli to Italy, and Italy abandoning all claims to Tunisia. The Italians felt that Germany would be of little aid in helping them conquer the African empire of their dreams, but that the acquiescence of Britain and France was essential, since their navies could frustrate Italian designs overseas. In 1902, Italy and France even concluded an agreement—the exact terms of which were not revealed to the German government—in which Italy more or less agreed to remain neutral in a Franco-German war. The Italian king emphasized the new amity by visiting Paris in the following year.

Perspicacious observers recognized that Italy's defection rendered the

Triple Alliance worthless to Germany. But Bülow shrugged it off as merely an "extra dance" with another partner that would not endanger the "Italo-German honeymoon." Actually, Italy's *rapprochement* with France also threatened to undermine its peaceful relations with Austria. Austro-Italian friction over the Trentino and Trieste regions had lain dormant after 1882. But French backing now permitted the Italians to resume anti-Austrian irredentist agitation.

Austria, too, was a weak link in the alliance. Apart from its entanglement in the Balkans, which sapped its usefulness to Berlin in the event of a Franco-German war, it was disintegrating internally. After 1897, antagonism among its minorities threw the tottering empire into continual parliamentary crises. There was also discord between Austrians and Hungarians over control of the military, with the result that no substantial increase of the army was undertaken between 1889 and 1912.

FORMATION OF THE ENTENTES While Germany's alliance system was losing strength, the other powers were drawing closer together. In 1902, Great Britain abandoned its long-standing "splendid isolation," and concluded a firm alliance with Japan. Two years later, France and England settled their many colonial differences, particularly in Africa, and signed the Entente Cordiale, despite the complication that their respective allies, Russia and Japan, were at the time engaged in the Russo-Japanese War. The German government at first saw few serious implications in this Anglo-French agreement, which was merely a *rapprochement* and not a full-fledged alliance.

The Entente was to retain this appearance of informality until the outbreak of World War I. In fact, however, tighter bonds soon developed between Paris and London, especially after Sir Edward Grey became British foreign secretary and arranged for unofficial talks between military advisers of the two states to draw up plans for possible wartime cooperation. The German government had only vague suspicions of these arrangements.

Finally, England and Russia also examined areas of colonial friction and reached compromises that permitted the formation of an Anglo-Russian Entente in 1907. Informal and tenuous as these two Ententes were, they represented the beginning of the Anglo-Russo-French front that eventually surrounded Germany in 1914.

To counter this development, the German government had two choices: the positive step of befriending one of the great powers and thereby breaking Germany's own isolation, or the negative approach of attempting to split their nascent alliances. William, Bülow, and Holstein attempted both on various occasions, but failed in all their efforts.

THE ATTEMPT TO BEFRIEND RUSSIA The year 1904 offered the opportunity for a German *rapprochement* with St. Petersburg. Russia was engaged in a losing war with Japan. Its French ally stood on the side lines, and even concluded the Entente with England, which at the time was an ally of Japan. Great Britain was frankly anti-Russian and refused to let the Russian fleet pass through the Suez Canal on its way to the Far East. When Russian men-of-war mistakenly sank a British fishing vessel in the North Sea, open hostilities al-

most erupted between the two nations. Hence Russia stood seemingly alone, and William seized the occasion to attempt a *rapprochement*.

Despite British protests, Germany supplied coal to the Russian fleet on its long journey to the Pacific. William visited St. Petersburg to encourage his tsarist cousin, who was losing battle after battle against the Japanese and was facing an increasingly restless populace inside Russia. But William's reception was cool. Nicholas lacked confidence in the German ruler and was unwilling to jeopardize his alliance with France. For although France was not obliged to help Russia in the war against Japan, it reassured St. Petersburg to have a partner in Europe while Russia was engaged in the Far East.

In October, William tried to overcome the tsar's scruples in regard to France by proposing to unite the Triple Alliance of Germany, Austria, and Italy, with the Franco-Russian Dual Alliance. He wrote to Nicholas that he realized that France was obligated "to share Nicholas' bed," but suggested that France should also feel obliged occasionally to "caress Germany or give her a kiss," rather than go "crawling into the bedroom of that ever-intriguing grab-all on the island [England]." But France preferred to abide by its agreement with England, and Nicholas would do nothing without French participation.

In the summer of 1905, on the occasion of a yachting vacation with Nicholas, William tried more of his personal diplomacy. There was no longer any possibility of drawing France into a pact with Germany and Russia: Berlin and Paris stood on the verge of war in the first Moroccan Crisis. But by then Russia had lost the war against Japan, and numerous insurrections, strikes, and mutinies had shaken the tsarist regime in a prelude to the October Revolution of 1905. William simply wrote up a draft treaty, presented it to the tsar on the Russian yacht, and in a scene engendered more by emotion than by rational negotiations, persuaded Nicholas to sign it.

This so-called Treaty of Björkö, drafted, as William informed Bülow, "with the aid of God," was specifically limited to mutual Russo-German protection on the Continent. It could therefore be of no value to Germany in a conflict with Great Britain. Moreover, it lacked the safeguards of Bismarck's Reinsurance Treaty in regard to the Austro-German alliance. William's draft did not specify German neutrality if Austria attacked Russia. On the contrary, its terms would have forced Germany to fight on Russia's side. And since Russia was still firmly allied with France, the Treaty of Björkö could not have helped Germany in a Franco-German War. One wonders, therefore, what William possibly hoped to accomplish.

When notified ex post facto of the proposed treaty in a letter from the exuberant emperor, Bülow promptly asked to be relieved of his post. He was horrified at William's personal diplomacy and his thoughtless action in risking the alliance with Vienna without achieving at least equivalent gains. Softened by an ignominious defeat in the Far East and weakened by internal insurrections, Russia hardly appeared a worthwhile ally to Bülow.

It was typical of William that, when thus reprimanded by Bülow, he did not attempt to justify his impetuous behavior aboard the tsar's yacht, but

appealed to his minister, "his best and most intimate friend," not to abandon him simply "because the situation seems critical." In a tearful, almost hysterical letter, he reminded Bülow of the heroic suffering he had endured at his minister's behest—chiefly in connection with his visit to Tangier in the course of the first Moroccan Crisis —and begged him to stay in office. "Jointly, we shall work together for the greater glory of Germany," he wrote. Although insisting that Bülow's resignation would embarrass him "eternally," he added paradoxically: "The day after your request for dismissal would not find the Emperor alive! Think of my poor wife and children!"

Bülow stayed and the Björkö draft was shelved. The Russian Foreign Office, anyhow, had refused to ratify the treaty proposal. Germany abandoned its attempt to befriend Russia, and turned with greater energy to Holstein's scheme for splitting the Anglo-French Entente by proper exploitation of the Moroccan Crisis.

The First Moroccan Crisis

Morocco, rich in natural resources, remained one of the few African regions still available for colonization. An international convention in 1880 had stipulated respect for Morocco's independence and guaranteed equal commercial rights for all nations. But by the turn of the century, Moroccan local government had become anarchical and European penetration had begun. Britain and France both had designs on the sultanate. Each offered Germany a share in the spoils in the hope of getting support against its rival, but Germany rejected all advances. Al-though Holstein could not conceive of the possibility of a Franco-British *rapprochement*, he preferred to leave Morocco as a point of friction between the two. Meanwhile all the powers continued their commercial penetration, and the French even began territorial encroachment across the borders from neighboring Algeria.

By early 1905, France had completed its preparations for openly proclaiming a protectorship over the sultanate. Italian acquiescence had been obtained in return for a free hand in Tripoli. Agreement with Spain was reached when northern Morocco was reserved for Spanish penetration. And the Entente Cordiale, although officially guaranteeing the *status quo* of both Egypt and Morocco, had in fact placed the latter at the disposal of France. Thus only Germany had not indicated advance approval when France openly negotiated with the sultan for political control over his state.

At this point Holstein decided to use Morocco as a wedge for breaking the Anglo-French "ring" and convinced Bülow of the merits of his plan. William was to give official endorsement to Morocco's independence and demand continuation of the open-door policy established by the Convention of 1880. Bülow and Holstein were sure that England and the United States would endorse such a step, which was not pro-German but favored all nations, and that consequently England would have to renege on its promise of support to France. To make it more dramatic, they insisted that William make such a pronouncement on Moroccan soil. William disliked the plan, its diplomatic implications as well as his assigned role, but he reluctantly agreed to play his part.

On the last day of March 1905, he landed at Tangier and rode through the streets of the city, "mounted on a strange horse despite his limited riding ability," as he later described it, "acclaimed by crowds which included bribed anarchists." He was received by the sultan's uncle, to whom he expressed public assurance that Germany stood behind Morocco's independence. A week later, Germany and the sultan called for an international conference to discuss the Moroccan problem.

One of the first in a series of international crises that blackened Germany's reputation developed immediately. Europe was astonished by Germany's audacity and baffled by its intentions. Maurice Rouvier, the French premier, feared a possible war with Germany at a time when France was not prepared and when its Russian ally could not be expected to furnish much assistance. He therefore offered to meet the Germans in a bilateral conference to discuss compensations for Germany—possibly an Atlantic port in Morocco or parts of the French Congo—in return for German agreement to French occupation of Morocco.

But Bülow and Holstein were not interested in compensations or in a bilateral conference that would recognize France's special rights over the sultanate. They wanted to humiliate France at an international conference that would uphold the Convention of 1880, and hoped to split the newly formed Entente Cordiale. England had promised France diplomatic support for the conquest of Morocco, but because by tradition England favored a policy of free trade, the Germans expected that Great Britain would refuse to back French desires for exclusive control over Morocco, and thereby antagonize the French. As to France, Bülow felt confident that it would not risk war, although Holstein was not averse to an armed conflict. The German government actually was not in agreement about the results to be expected from the crisis it had created. Count Alfred von Schlieffen (1833–1913), the German chief of staff, favored a preventive war against France at a moment when its Russian ally still had the remnants of its defeated forces on the Pacific front. But William was adamant about guarding the peace. He still hoped to bring France—and Russia—into alignment with the Triple Alliance, and thought, as he had about England in the 1890s, that Paris could be frightened into a *rapprochement* with Germany.

The French foreign minister, Théophile Delcassé, the architect of the Anglo-French Entente, meanwhile consulted with London and drew the erroneous conclusion that Britain was ready to join France in a war against Germany if necessary. Although England agreed to support French aspirations to Morocco, it was hardly prepared to conclude a firm military alliance with France. Certain of British help, Delcassé urged a firm anti-German stance. But the French government as a whole was not convinced of British support. Anxious to avoid war, it forced Delcassé to resign.

The fall of Delcassé was a victory for Germany, and William promptly rewarded Bülow by making him a prince. France had been humiliated. But Holstein had not yet achieved his purpose of splitting the Anglo-French Entente, and he persisted in his demand for an international conference.

The powers were horrified at Germany's intransigence but finally agreed to a meeting.

When the nations convened at Algeciras from January to April 1906, Germany found itself isolated. England, Spain, Russia, and even Italy supported France. Austria alone sided with Germany, but made it clear that Austria would not fight for Morocco. Germany maintained its legalistic stand that it merely wished to uphold equal treaty rights for all, and continued to reject all French offers for a bilateral settlement. Legally, the German position was irreproachable, but the powers regarded it as further evidence of German pugnacity.

At several points, the deadlocked conference looked like a prelude to war. But William did not want war and ordered the withdrawal of one German demand after another. The obstructionist Holstein was finally dismissed from his post. The final acts of the conference upheld the fiction of the sultan's sovereignty and of free and equal trading rights for all nations, while awarding France and Spain special police powers and economic privileges that paved the way for eventual annexation.

As a result of this first Moroccan Crisis, Germany again gained nothing but ill repute. After grandiose promises, it had let down the sultan of Morocco and had rejected the chance for special economic rights or compensations in a bilateral deal with France. Its position had been legally sound but diplomatically foolish. It had not succeeded in splitting the Entente Cordiale; on the contrary, it had publicly revealed its own isolation. At the same time, Germany fanned the fires of French nationalism, which brought to power Georges Clemenceau, an inveterate foe of Germany.

Relations with England

Until 1906, Germany's growing navy had been primarily the kind of "risk fleet" advocated by Tirpitz. But when England launched the Dreadnought, a new type of battleship with heavy armor plate and 12-inch guns, Germany promptly passed a new naval law to increase its own fleet and to provide for the construction of similar ships. Since the armament and fire power of these new superbattleships rendered the older types obsolete, Germany could acquire parity with England if it could build dreadnoughts at the same speed as Great Britain. Thus began the second phase of the Anglo-German naval rivalry, which gradually drove England more firmly into the anti-German camp.

In the summer of 1906, King Edward visited William, and requested that Germany scale down its naval program in the interest of Anglo-German friendship. Bülow and his cabinet, made cautious by the Moroccan Crisis, urged William to make concessions. But he looked upon the German navy with personal pride. Acting on Tirpitz' advice, he rejected Edward's request, and Germany pursued its naval program.

In the following year, England attempted unsuccessfully to dam German naval expansion through the second Peace Conference at The Hague, and then concluded its *rapprochement* with Russia. Thus the naval race not only prevented improvement in Anglo-German relations, but also produced inter-

national friction and increased Germany's isolation. Even Tirpitz noted in a memorandum that England might attack Germany, as it had previous naval challengers, such as Spain, Holland, and France, in an effort to safeguard its supremacy on the seas. He concluded that Germany should speed up its naval program. However, the German ambassador in London, who questioned the wisdom of Germany's naval policy, reported that England would never attack Germany despite the provocative nature of its naval program.

Early during the Bosnian Crisis, in the summer of 1908, Edward once again visited Germany to discuss the naval question with his imperial nephew. William insisted that a large fleet was required to protect Germany's growing trade. When asked by Edward's undersecretary for foreign affairs (Sir Charles Hardinge), how the fleet could protect world-wide trade when it usually remained close to the home ports, William admitted: "Because our London embassy advised that the less the British see our fleet, the better." Edward and his secretary again urged a slowing down of naval construction, but William remained adamant and threatened: "Then we would have to fight, for it is a question of national honor and dignity." According to a report William sent to Bülow after this interview, he stressed his determination by looking the undersecretary "sharp in the eye" and "baring his teeth—which made a deep effect. One must always deal with the English in this manner."

Once again Bülow was embarrassed by his ruler's personal diplomacy. He wrote to William: "I know that the creation of a German fleet is the task

which history has placed before Your Majesty." But he urged caution and warned that the English might be goaded into war if they "take it for certain that our naval armaments will be continued like this *ad infinitum.*" He intimated that England's greater resources would at any rate always permit it to construct ships faster than Germany. To soften his tone, he pledged his eagerness to help William "achieve his life work," but insisted that England's offers to come to terms should not always be rejected categorically.

It soon became evident how little William understood the seriousness of the situation. On October 28, 1908, two months after the meeting of Edward and William, the *Daily Telegraph* in London published an interview with William, together with a tongue-in-cheek commentary by the anonymous English interviewer. In the interview, William repeatedly boasted of his love of peace and called the English as "mad, mad, mad as March hares" for always distorting German actions and insinuating that Germany "holds a dagger" behind its back. In bragging terms, he claimed that he had really favored England in the Boer War, that the German General Staff had worked out the military plans for England to defeat the Boers, and that he alone had resisted Franco-Russian pressure to embarrass England by joint intervention on the side of the Boers. Further, he insisted that he had wished only to safeguard private German interests in Morocco and that the German newspapers that had taken a bellicose stand on Morocco were run by "mischief makers." According to William, the German navy presented no threat to England, since its duty was to protect

trade, "especially in the Far East." But he warned that only he and "a minority of the best elements in Germany" felt friendship for England. "Large sections of the middle and lower classes of my own people are not friendly to England." Yet, he assured his interviewer, he commanded the Germans, and he promised continued friendship toward Britain, provided his services were appreciated by the English.

William had made many previous *faux pas* in interviews and speeches, and in his fitful attempts at personal diplomacy. But never before had he managed to antagonize almost everyone at home and abroad in a single communication: He had revealed Russian and French diplomatic secrets in regard to anti-British intervention in the Boer War; the Japanese resented the statement that the German fleet was to protect trade "especially in the Far East"; and the whole content and tone of the interview naturally aroused the ire of the English—not least the insinuation that the bulk of the Germans hated England and that German military plans had helped England win the Boer War.

Inside Germany, the *Daily Telegraph* affair created an even greater storm. The liberal press vituperated against the insinuation that "the best elements" in Germany were those not belonging "to the middle or lower classes," and objected to the implication that William could command German feelings. Even the conservatives were aghast at his indiscretion. During a tempestuous three-day debate, the Reichstag demanded a curb on the emperor's personal diplomacy; but no united action resulted and the delegates failed to take advantage of the occasion by pressing for parliamentary

responsibility. William simply laughed at the furor and went on a vacation. Bülow, officially responsible for the publication of the interview, tried to enhance his own prestige by acting as spokesman for the Reichstag and the nation at large vis-à-vis William. He claimed he had not approved the text of the press release before its publication, but had passed it on to a subaltern. In view of the unclear lines of responsibility that permeated the government, it is impossible to know whether Bülow had read the text and passed it on to embarrass his monarch and thus use the resulting scandal to put an end to William's personal diplomacy; or whether, indeed, some subaltern approved it, since both Bülow and the foreign minister were away from Berlin at the time.

In the end, Bülow had an official audience with Emperor William and announced the latter's promise to be more cautious in his private utterances. But nothing was done to change the governmental system that permitted such impulsive diplomacy. For a while, William was more careful in his speeches, but he probably never grasped the import of his indiscretion, which had further undermined Germany's international reputation.

The Bosnian Crisis

In most aspects, the complex Bosnian Crisis of 1908–1909 appears like a rehearsal for 1914, and brought Europe perilously close to war. Partly to put a halt to Austro-German penetration through the Balkans, Russia and England pressed for political reforms in Turkish Macedonia. At the same time, the Young Turk Revolution restored a constitutional regime to Turkey in

an effort to strengthen Turkish national unity. This revolution not only frustrated Russia's hopes of gaining greater influence over Turkey and free passage through the Straits for its warships, but also undermined the position of Germany, which had acted as a friend of the reactionary sultan. Finally, Austria-Hungary used the Turkish upheaval as an excuse for annexing the provinces of Bosnia and Herzegovina, which it had administered since 1878, while Bulgaria on the same day broke away from Turkey and declared its complete independence. Serbia and Montenegro, which had nourished hopes of acquiring portions of Bosnia-Herzegovina, protested against Austria's actions and started military preparations against Austria. Russia threw its support to Serbia, and the Anglo-French Entente stood behind Russia.

The varied and complex aspects of this crisis, which involved every Balkan state and implicated all the major European powers, are not germane to this analysis. But Germany's reaction is significant. Instead of resuming Bismarck's arbitrative role of 1878 and 1886–1887, in which he had placed himself between Austria and Russia, in order not to lose its last dependable ally, Germany sided unequivocally with Austria. While sending reassuring messages to London and Paris, Germany flexed its muscles toward the east and rather peremptorily pressured Russia into abandoning Serbia. Thus the crisis passed. Austria retained its gains, but neither Russia, Serbia, nor Turkey received compensations.

The relatively easy victory of Austria-Hungary and Germany gave Berlin an illusory self-confidence. Bülow concluded that the Triple Entente was, after all, not to be feared in times of crisis. Unquestioning support of Austria had proved to be correct policy. In reality, however, the course of the crisis inspired Berlin with unwarranted optimism. Russia had backed down not because it feared the strength of the German army, but because it had not yet recovered from its defeat by Japan. Thereafter Russia was to recover the self-confidence it had lost in the Russo-Japanese War and thereby change the balance, whereas Germany was to adopt the same stand in 1914.

The First Storm, 1909–1918

THE LAST YEARS OF PEACE

Theobald von Bethmann-Hollweg, who came from a family of bankers and politicians, assumed the chancellorship in the summer of 1909. He was to be the last chancellor under the Bismarckian framework of politics. Within less than a decade after his appointment, |the external might of Bismarck's Reich crumbled under the impact of World War I, and his internal system disintegrated under the stress of tensions and revolutions.| The five remaining years of peace were characterized by frequent international crises and by internal frictions that inexorably led to the flare-up of war and revolt. To be sure, the Bethmann-Hollweg government made some accommodations to alleviate international tension. And, perhaps encouraged by the greater flexibility shown by the Socialists and the Liberals, the chancellor displayed occasional willingness to conciliate the internal opposition by progressive policies. But the right wing showed little inclination to make concessions. The system remained inflexible, and despite his good inten-

tions, Bethmann-Hollweg lacked the force and foresight to impose radical changes.

Failure to Reform Prussia

One of Bethmann-Hollweg's first steps was an attempt at reforming Prussia's antiquated electoral system, a measure that had been vaguely promised by Bülow in January 1908. The representative character of the Prussian diet continued to be warped by the three-class system (see pages 44 ff.), which divided the electorate into classes on the basis of districts and tax assessments and which operated by use of indirect elections and open ballots. Only one minor change in the electoral law had been made since its promulgation in 1850, and all but the few who profited from its inequity had been demanding reform for decades. The public ballot permitted fraud and intimidation of voters. Assignment to electoral groups on the basis of tax payments grossly underfranchised the proletariat. And failure to redraw electoral districts despite the cityward movement of seventy years gave a vast

advantage to the landlords of the east over the industrial entrepreneurs and the city proletariat of the west. This inequity is best seen in a comparison of electoral results in Prussia with those in Germany at large. In 1908, the Socialists succeeded for the first time in obtaining representation in the Prussian diet with the election of 7 deputies in a total of 443, at a time when they polled about 30 percent of all the votes cast in a Reichstag election. Conversely, the right-wing parties—Conservatives and Free Conservatives—dominated the Prussian diet of 1913 with 45.6 percent of the seats, even though they made up only 14.3 percent of the delegates in the Reichstag of 1912. Considering in addition the power of the upper house (consisting largely of the landlords from the area east of the Elbe) over the Prussian legislature, and the dominant position that Prussia itself held within the Reich, one can understand the clamor of the Liberals and the Socialists for electoral reforms in Prussia.

As chancellor of the Reich and minister-president of Prussia, Bethmann-Hollweg wanted to please the opposition parties in the Reichstag without unduly antagonizing the conservatives of Prussia. Hence in February 1910, he hesitantly submitted modest reform proposals to the Prussian legislature, together with the obviously contradictory implication that the existing electoral law actually allowed a fairly equitable representation of public opinion. He suggested abolition of the public ballot and of the indirect voting arrangement. Secret voting would be welcomed by peasants and workers; direct elections would eliminate the rotten borough system and please the urban population. But his proposals

retained the three-class division under a highly complicated formula weighing each vote according to the financial status of the voter. One vote from the first class, those paying the most taxes, was to equal 4 votes from the second class and 5.3 votes from the lowest class. Since under the existing system a few very rich had dominated the first class, it was proposed that tax assessments over 5000 marks be disregarded when voters were assigned to electoral classes. And to mollify the middle class, intellectuals and professionals were to be raised into the next higher voting class than indicated by their tax payments.

But even these moderate proposals were defeated. The left wing demanded universal, equal, and direct suffrage. The Conservatives, and even the Center, looked upon the measure as a dangerous opening to the left wing. Bethmann-Hollweg, never a fighter, withdrew his proposals, and the anachronistic electoral system remained a cancer in the body politic of Prussia.

Bethmann-Hollweg and the Reichstag

In other less crucial legislative areas, Bethmann-Hollweg was more successful, although he was unable to establish a working arrangement with parties for support in the Reichstag. After the failure of Bülow's bloc, parties and pressure groups again split into mutually antagonistic sections, and parliamentary alignments resumed their chaotic course. The only major change occurred on the Left. The political leadership of the Social Democratic party, as well as that of the growing socialist trade unions, adopted an increasingly moderate and evolutionary

path. After their electoral defeat of 1907, the Socialists rebounded in 1912 to gain 4.25 million votes—about 35 percent of all votes cast—and 110 seats, making them by far the strongest party in the Reichstag. Once again renouncing the doctrine of the class struggle, they agreed to collaborate with the recently united Progressives, who remained the fourth largest party in electoral votes. Jointly these two commanded 152 delegates out of the total of 397 in the Reichstag, and presented a vital power in the legislature.

Maneuvering among the parties, Bethmann-Hollweg succeeded in passing a capital gains tax that pleased the Socialists. He also managed to balance the budget for three consecutive years. A constitution was passed for Alsace-Lorraine, and the Imperial Insurance Code was enacted in 1911. The latter brought uniformity to all existing schemes for old-age pensions, accident insurance, sickness benefits, and provisions for invalidism. It also extended coverage to orphans, widows, domestic employees, and agricultural laborers, and increased some benefits, although many of the Socialists' demands for increases were refused because of financial considerations.

The chancellor also faced the question of the army budget when the regular five-year appropriations ended in 1911. The last major increase in the German army had been effected in 1893. After 1898, most of the funds had been allocated to the navy, the darling of the emperor, of the Reichstag, and of public opinion. The War Department itself had not particularly pushed for an increase in troop strength. In fact, General Karl von Einem (1853–1934) the minister of war, had favored improvement of the army's training

and equipment rather than an increase in its size. "The German army," he wrote, "has now reached a size which clearly is beyond the limits of a healthful development and which constitutes serious dangers." Not the least of these "dangers" to the conservative minister was the threat of excessive democratization of the officer corps. On the other hand, the famous Schlieffen plan, evolved in 1905 as strategy in a possible two-front war, called for a considerable increase in troop strength. But its author, Count Alfred von Schlieffen, chief of staff from 1891 to 1905, had done nothing to convince the ministry of this need. Even in 1906, after the first Moroccan Crisis, the War Ministry had kept its demands moderate, although Bülow favored an increase in the strength of the army. In view of the financial problem of increasing the military budget, Bülow in the end had not pushed the matter in the quinquennial appropriations of 1906.

But a new trend opened in 1911, intensifying the armaments race with France. General Josias von Heeringen (1850–1926), the minister of war, complained that Germany devoted only 15.5 percent of its budget to the army as against 34 percent by France, and pressed for a considerable increase in troops and expenditures. Bethmann-Hollweg at the time was not yet worried about the international situation, and requested an increase of only 10,000 men, mostly technicians, to bring the peacetime army to a strength of 515,000. Shortly after passage of the army bill of 1911, international tension rose sharply with the second Moroccan Crisis. The chancellor and the War Ministry prepared to ask for an additional 30,000 men in 1912. Public

opinion seemed to favor the proposed increases, for in the general elections of January 1912, the main issues were not foreign policy, defense budgets, nor armaments, but rather economic and tax questions. Despite the electoral triumph of the Social Democratic party, which opposed an increase in the army, the new Reichstag approved the requested military increase in 1912. This second increase, kept relatively moderate to avoid the need for new taxes, required an additional 56 million marks, most of it obtained through deficit financing.

By the summer of 1913, the need for a more vigorous armaments program seemed evident to Bethmann-Hollweg. The wars in Tripolitania and the Balkans, increases in Russian armaments, and the breakdown of Anglo-German naval discussions moved the new chief of staff, Helmuth von Moltke (1848–1916) to demand three new army corps. The government at once proposed a bill calling for the immediate addition of some 120,000 men and 20,000 regular and noncommissioned officers, at a cost of about 200 million marks, as well as an added 900 million marks for the strengthening of fortresses and armaments. In addition, the bill projected a further increase of the army by an additional 190,000 men. Only the Socialists, Poles, and Alsatians opposed these demands in the Reichstag, and the big army increases were quickly approved. However, financing the measures presented problems. All proposals for new indirect or direct taxes were rejected. In the end, by getting approval for a special one-time capital levy, the so-called defense contribution, Bethmann-Hollweg succeeded in raising a portion of the funds required. Although they continued their opposition to the increase in the army's strength, the Socialists voted for the tax levy because it would fall on the well-to-do classes.

The Prewar Crises

The conduct of Germany's foreign affairs did not change radically with Bethmann-Hollweg's appointment. The new chancellor was less optimistic than Bülow, and made several perfunctory attempts to break the "ring" around Germany. But he was unwilling to loosen the bonds with Vienna in order to improve relations with Russia, or to reduce the size of the fleet in order to achieve an understanding with Great Britain. He was not a forceful leader, and he received little support from Emperor William, who now remained more in the background of the political scene. Much power, on the other hand, was exercised by Alfred von Kiderlen-Wächter (1852–1912), a favorite of the emperor. He was secretary of foreign affairs from 1910 to 1912, and enjoyed a heyday of bluff and intrigue during the second Moroccan Crisis.

In 1910, there was a brief improvement in relations between Russia and Germany. The Balkans were momentarily quiescent, and Nicholas II visited William II at Potsdam. No fundamental agreement on the future of the Balkans appeared possible, but Russia finally withdrew its opposition to Germany's further extension of the Baghdad Railway system. Berlin, in turn, agreed not to interfere in Russia's penetration of northern Persia.

At the same time, Germany maneuvered skillfully among the various revolutionary and counterrevolutionary factions in Turkey and succeeded in cementing Turkish-German relations.

This *rapprochement* ultimately led to a full-fledged wartime alliance. Although militarily weak and politically unstable, Turkey could act as a minor wedge against Germany's total encirclement, provided the intervening Balkan area could be made safe for Austro-German contact with Turkey.

But the war between Turkey and Italy over Tripoli, which erupted in September 1911, presented Germany with a dilemma, since it was allied with Italy and friendly with Turkey. The war threatened Germany's economic interests in the Turkish Empire, and frightened Austria by endangering the *status quo* in the Balkans. The war lasted a year, and the Turks were finally forced to recognize Italy's seizure of Tripolitania. During the hostilities, Germany succeeded in maintaining a benevolently neutral attitude toward both antagonists. Abandoned by all the major powers, which had secretly promised Italy a free hand in Tripolitania, and nearly stabbed in the back by its Balkan neighbors, Turkey was glad to have the moral support of Germany—and to some extent of Austria—even though it received no military help. Italy, on the other hand, was appreciative of the tacit backing of the Triple Alliance, since military operations in the eastern Mediterranean proved difficult, and it could expect no Anglo-French support. The course and outcome of the war over Tripoli both strengthened and weakened the Triple Alliance. In recognition of its usefulness, the three partners renewed the alliance for another six-year term in December 1912 and added new agreements concerning naval cooperation, although the validity of the current treaty extended to 1914. On the other hand, Italy's acquisition of Tripolitania

made it even more dependent on the good will of Britain and France, whose navies dominated the Mediterranean, and rendered it less willing to assume a firm anti-French or anti-British stand.

THE SECOND MOROCCAN CRISIS   While fairly successful in guiding Germany's relations with Turkey and its conduct during the war over Tripoli, Kiderlen-Wächter meanwhile rekindled the suspicions of the powers during the second Moroccan Crisis. After 1905, France had pursued its penetration of Morocco. In 1909, it had finally made a bilateral arrangement with Germany, promising an open door to German economic interests in return for German recognition of France's political interests in Morocco. Hereafter the French moved ahead boldly, and in 1911 dispatched troops to the capital of Fez on the pretext of quelling disorders. After having rejected all proposals for compensation in 1905 and in the intervening years, Germany suddenly demanded indemnification. Believing France to be unwilling to offer compensations unless threatened, Kiderlen-Wächter sent the German gunboat *Panther* to Agadir in Morocco, ostensibly to protect German merchants and their property against raids by local tribes. Kiderlen-Wächter notified the powers that Germany's intentions were peaceful, while at the same time he accused France of unilaterally violating the Algeciras Convention. The German foreign minister evidently was resurrecting the old game of trying to frighten France, but at the same time he wished to press for maximum concessions.

The appearance of the *Panther* in Moroccan waters caused consternation in France and England, but was hailed

with exuberance by the nationalists in Germany. France hesitated between picking up the gauntlet and offering timely concessions. England, pressed by David Lloyd George, then chancellor of the exchequer, warned Germany not to go too far, and made preliminary preparations to ready its fleet and to arrange for military cooperation with France. Emperor William and his foreign minister worked at cross-purposes. William wanted no war and so notified the French, but Kiderlen-Wächter assumed a harsher stand in order to obtain maximum concessions. Franco-German negotiations continued through July and August, but the crisis reached critical proportions when France, backed by England, decided to use intimidation itself and threatened to send warships to Agadir. This action in turn. piqued the German ruler.

With war in sight, Kiderlen-Wächter finally agreed to negotiate seriously, and requested cession of the entire French Congo in exchange for Germany's abandoning all claims to Morocco. But his hand was weakened, since his mistress, the wife of a Russian diplomat, was in the pay of the French government and had revealed that Kiderlen-Wächter's secret correspondence showed that Germany was not ready for war. France therefore retained the upper hand in the negotiations, and succeeded in scaling down German demands. In a final convention between the two countries, France received a free hand in Morocco and in compensation turned over to Germany 106,000 square miles of Congo backland, infested with sleeping sickness and economically as yet worthless. Thus war was averted. Germany had obtained compensations of doubtful value, after having rejected a possibly better settlement in 1905. The crisis had once again given Germany an unsavory reputation and had cemented the Anglo-French Entente.

In early 1912, England made a last effort to come to terms with Berlin on the naval question. It offered to help Germany in Africa in return for German agreement to limit its naval expansion. But Tirpitz and Emperor William refused to agree to naval limitations and, on the contrary, called for increased construction of warships. This British offer, if indeed it was advanced seriously, probably represented Germany's last chance to loosen the Entente. Thereafter Berlin and London continued to cooperate on occasions, and even succeeded in ironing out colonial problems, as occurred in the summer of 1914 when they finally settled their rivalry in the Near East, and Germany agreed not to continue the Berlin-to-Baghdad Railroad to the Persian Gulf. But their relations always lay under the shadow of the naval race and could hardly lead to a permanent understanding.

THE BALKAN WARS   The Balkan Crises of 1912 and 1913 were true overtures to the outbreak of World War I. In the First Balkan War of 1912–1913, Bulgaria, Serbia, Greece, and Montenegro fought against Turkey for territorial expansion, particularly in Thrace, Macedonia, and Albania. The Second Balkan War, in 1913, pitted Serbia, Greece, Turkey, and Rumania against Bulgaria in a fight over the spoils of the preceding war. All the European powers became deeply involved in both wars. Austria and Italy were intent on making Albania an independent state in order to keep it

out of the hands of the Greeks, Serbs, and Montenegrins, who all coveted portions of this mountainous land. Austria, in particular, was adamantly against Serbian aggrandizement, especially Serbian acquisition of any part of the land along the Adriatic coast. Russia and France championed the cause of Serbia. Russia at first also supported Bulgaria, but gradually abandoned it when Bulgarian troops advanced into Turkey and threatened the Straits. Russia's abandonment of Bulgaria and its resulting defeat in the Second Balkan War eventually made Bulgaria turn toward Austria and Germany, on whose side it finally entered World War I in 1915. Germany, for its part, was sympathetic to Turkey and Austria during most of the crisis.

By the winter of 1912, the outbreak of a general war seemed likely. Russia and Austria prepared for mobilization, and it seemed unavoidable that their respective allies would be drawn into the conflict. England exerted pressure on the Balkan countries as well as on the major powers, and succeeded in getting up a conference of ambassadors in London to discuss the crisis. England hoped to enlist German help in mediation between Serbia and Austria. William and Bethmann-Hollweg felt somewhat perplexed. They showed little sympathy for Austria's harsh Balkan policy; yet they understood its interest in containing Serbia, since Serbian nationalism and expansionism created unrest in Austria's own Slavic territory. Hence they advocated conciliation, and at the same time assured Vienna of their support, since they did not wish to jeopardize the alliance.

In the end, the crisis once again passed when Russia, unprepared for war as it was, backed down and abandoned Serbia. Thus Austria was given a free hand to force Serbia and Montenegro to evacuate Albania. For the moment, it had achieved its aim. Again, the Triple Alliance and the Triple Entente had withstood a crisis. It was to be the last of the rehearsals.

The Outbreak of World War I

After a relatively calm spring, Europe was only slightly aroused by news of the assassination of Austria's heir to the throne at Sarajevo, on June 28, 1914. Murdering rulers or political opponents was not rare in the Balkans. The ruling princes of Montenegro and Serbia had been assassinated in 1860 and 1868, respectively. A similar fate had befallen the king of Serbia in 1903 and the grand vizier of Turkey in 1913. Yet three weeks after Sarajevo, friction between Austria-Hungary and Serbia approached the breaking point when the former issued its stern ultimatum demanding satisfaction for the murder, as well as concessions that the latter found degrading.

Fairly confident of Russian support, the Serbs rejected some of Austria's demands and readied their armies. Austria, in turn, ordered partial mobilization, and on July 28 declared war on Serbia. The next few days were filled with frantic diplomatic maneuvers by the powers to save the peace or achieve stronger positions in the event of war. Russia decided to aid the Serbs, and hesitated merely between a general mobilization and a partial mobilization directed against Austria only. At the same time, it negotiated with Vienna for a settlement that would satisfy Austria without destroying Serbia. Nicholas also appealed to William to restrain his Austrian ally. France for

its part assured Russia of support, and England called for an international conference, but did nothing to restrain Russia. When on July 30 Russia opted in favor of a general mobilization, Germany on the following day sent an ultimatum to St. Petersburg asking for an immediate rescinding of the order. Berlin also inquired in Paris whether France would side with Russia in case of a German-Russian conflict. Meanwhile the German government tried to restrain as well as reassure the Austrians, who declared a general mobilization on the same afternoon.

On August 1, the die was cast. Russia refused to heed Germany's ultimatum—despite the tsar's tearful promises of friendship to William—and France mobilized. In accordance with strategy outlined in the Schlieffen plan, Germany then seized the initiative. It immediately declared war on Russia, two days later on France, and on August 4 also on Belgium. On August 4, after German armies had invaded Belgium, England declared war on Germany. The stage was set for World War I.

UNDERLYING CAUSES   It would be impossible in a study of this type to analyze in detail the causes of the war or the problem of war guilt. The many analyses that have been published are familiar to most readers. The accusation that Germany and its allies alone caused the war—as stipulated in Article 231 of the Versailles Treaty—is today rejected by scholars. Popular among the Allied nations in the early years after World War I, it was revived during the height of Hitler's aggressions. But stripped of its emotional content, it cannot stand the test of historical scrutiny. Innumerable factors mingled to unleash the war.

Many underlying causes are often cited by historians: militant nationalism, the armaments race, competitive imperialism, the alliance system, commercial rivalry, among others. It is often customary to blame the war on German militarism. To be sure, a martial spirit had colored Prussian history for several centuries, the army and the officer corps had occupied a preferred position on the German scene, and social Darwinism had found widespread acceptance in the Reich of Bismarck and William II. Germany had produced more than its share of jingoists, and made more of a fetish of war and sheer power than had most other nations. Friedrich von Bernhardi (1849–1930), one of the prophets of this cult, had written in 1911: "War is a biological necessity . . . . without it an unhealthful development follows which excludes all advancement of the race, and hence all true civilization." And a great number of young people had embraced this creed with almost religious fervor. But again it must be recalled that jingoism was popular in many lands, and that force and violence had become acceptable to the generation nurtured on the glorious tales of colonial victories. In England the political thinker Walter Bagehot proclaimed as a "fundamental law" that "those nations which are strongest tend to prevail over the others; and in certain marked peculiarities the strongest are the best." In France, syndicalists, among others Georges Sorel, preached violence as the means to social salvation; even in the United States, Theodore Roosevelt had advocated a policy of force.

IMMEDIATE CAUSES Moreover, no single nation and no single statesman can be held responsible for the crucial act that lit the fuse.

Austria's demands on Serbia were unreasonably harsh, but the cocky nationalism and intrigues of tiny Serbia were unquestionably provocative and likely to goad any major power into action. Russia's clumsy eagerness to mobilize, the intrigues of its powerful ambassador to Paris, Alexander Izvolski, who had somehow concluded that Russia could gain the Straits only in the course of a general war, and Russia's determination not to abandon the Serbs again as it had done in 1912–1913 were hardly counterbalanced by Nicholas II's pathetic attempts to maintain the peace through personal appeals to William II. England's failure to take a clear and public stand during the crucial week before Germany's invasion of Belgium, as well as Sir Edward Grey's almost blind faith in the magic power of international conferences, gave London a nebulous role at the height of the crisis. France and Germany stood all too uncritically behind their respective allies, Russia and Austria, in an issue that, seen objectively, was not of vital national interest to either. Yet Emperor William's famous "blank check" to Emperor Francis Joseph, so often misrepresented in discussions of the war, was in fact nothing more than a report by Bethmann-Hollweg to the German ambassador in Vienna of a conference between the emperor and the Austrian ambassador to Germany. After discussing the Serbian crisis and its relation to Rumania and Bulgaria, William sent his assurances to Vienna that he would "faithfully stand by Austria-Hungary, as re-

quired by the obligations of his alliance and of his ancient friendship." This "blank check" can hardly be labeled as proof of guilt by making Germany an accomplice in Austria's declaration of war on Serbia. Poincaré, the French president, extended similar encouragement to his ally in St. Petersburg. Moreover, Berlin sent subsequent dispatches to Vienna urging caution in Austria's dealings with the Serbs.

THE QUESTION OF GERMAN WAR GUILT

But its clumsy diplomatic behavior in the prewar decades had made Germany suspect in the eyes of world opinion long before 1914. And its invasion of neutral Belgium at the beginning of the war clinched the German reputation of being an aggressor.

Most Germans, long burdened by the chimera of encirclement, genuinely believed that the war was purely defensive. William II, probably in all sincerity, stated publicly that the war had been forced on Germany, and in his proclamation to the army and navy urged the armed forces to "protect the fatherland against the infamous surprise attack." Bethmann-Hollweg, in his Reichstag speech of August 4, insisted that Germany was fighting a defensive war, but admitted that the possibility of a French attack on the German flank had made it essential for Germany to violate Belgian neutrality. "We were forced to overlook the *justified* protest of the governments of Luxemburg and Belgium. We shall try to make up for this injustice—I speak openly—this injustice we are committing, once our military aims have been accomplished." Officially, the Germans also claimed that French officers had first violated Belgian neutral-

ity by moving into Belgian fortresses before the outbreak of war, and that French flyers had dropped bombs on German territory a day before Germany declared war on France. But all these feelings and proclamations did not prevent the Allies from pointing to the invasion of Belgium as proof that Germany was the sole aggressor and responsible for the war.

The invasion of Belgium was undertaken on purely military considerations. The politicians were not consulted, and it was hoped that Belgium would not offer resistance and would agree to let the German army pass unmolested. German strategy was based on the Schlieffen plan, which assumed that Russia would take longer for its mobilization and movement of troops to the frontier than would France, and that it would be advisable to crush France first before turning to the east. Believing that the French would probably concentrate their troops in the west for a drive into Alsace-Lorraine and southern Germany, Schlieffen had proposed guarding the southern flank with only minor contingents, while throwing the bulk of the German armies through Belgium in a giant wheeling motion to envelop Paris from the west and then to sweep eastward to attack the main body of the French forces from the rear. The Schlieffen plan provided that after this lightning defeat of France, the German troops would be transferred to the eastern front to face the Russian armies. The success of this strategy depended in part on the speed of its execution. German troops had to pass through Belgium and invade northern France before the French had time to mobilize fully. This military requirement of speed, laid down by the General Staff,

outweighed all political considerations. Once Russia had mobilized and a Russo-German war seemed inevitable, the Schlieffen plan assumed that France would automatically enter the war on Russia's side. The politicians were given no time for hesitation or accommodation. Strategy required that the German armies be hurled against the west within specified hours after the outbreak of war in the east. Hence Germany invaded Luxemburg less than twenty-four hours after declaring war on Russia, declared war on France on the following day, and then commenced the invasion of Belgium, thereby adding to its reputation of being the aggressor.

THE COURSE OF THE WAR

Upon the outbreak of hostilities the Triple Alliance disintegrated at once when Italy refused to support Austria's offensive against Serbia and announced its neutrality, which it exchanged a year later for active intervention on the side of the Allies. In November 1914, the Central powers were joined by Turkey, and in late 1915 by Bulgaria. The Serbo-Russo-Franco-Belgo-British Alliance, for its part, gradually grew to include eighteen other nations, adding Montenegro, Japan, Italy, Portugal, Rumania, the United States, Greece, China, and a host of Latin-American states. Ultimately, the four Central powers found themselves at war with twenty-three nations.

The Theaters of Operation

The war was fought in eight distinct theaters of operation: the western front

in northern France and southern Belgium; the eastern front against Russia, from the Baltic to the Black Sea; the Balkan front against Serbia, Montenegro, and later Rumania and Greece; the Italian front in northeastern Italy; the various Turkish fronts on all the confines of Turkey's large territory, from the Dardanelles to Armenia and from Persia to Palestine. In addition, there were colonial campaigns in Africa, Asia, and the Pacific islands; an air war over England, Germany, and France; and naval fighting on and below the seas.

THE WAR IN THE WEST The German forces were mobilized swiftly in accordance with the timetable set up by the General Staff, and rolled across Belgium with surprising speed, despite more stubborn local resistance than anticipated. But the chief of staff, Moltke, did not execute the Schlieffen plan in all its bold aspects. It is therefore impossible to ascertain whether the failure of the German armies to achieve their goal resulted from defects in the plan itself or from Moltke's deviations from it. Fearing a French invasion of southern Germany, Moltke detached more units from the northern army to protect Alsace-Lorraine than called for by Schlieffen. Moreover, he prematurely transferred several divisions from the French front to the east because he felt overconfident of victory over France, and was frightened by Russia's rapid concentration of forces. Thus weakened, the northern German armies were not quite capable of achieving their mission. After wheeling across Belgium, they came within about twenty miles of Paris; but in early September, during the gigantic Battle of the Marne, they were hurled back

and lost their initiative. Schlieffen's plan had failed, and according to many military analysts, Germany forfeited its chances for ultimate victory during these early months of the conflict. After consolidating their lines along the river Aisne, the Germans abandoned Schlieffen's strategy and attempted to push their northern flank toward the English Channel. They succeeded in gaining the ports of northern Belgium, but stubborn resistance by English, Belgian, and French forces prevented them from breaking through to the Channel and thereby shortening the front by about 100 miles.

Thereafter the western front hardened along hundreds of miles of muddy trenches and twisted barbed wire. Although there was fighting on many other fronts, both sides clung to the belief that the ultimate decision of the war would be achieved by a breakthrough or by attrition of the enemy on the front in France. Commanders were frequently changed, and every year masses of new recruits were assembled on each side and slaughtered in month-long battles that never altered the front by more than a few miles. In the late spring of 1915, for example, the French gained a strip of three miles in a battle that lasted six weeks and cost them some 400,000 casualties. In 1916, the Germans tried for five months to pound their way into Verdun and failed at the cost of about 300,000 men. During the same summer, the British lost 60,000 men in a single day in an unsuccessful offensive. Even the sudden employment of new weapons could not alter the stalemate. In the long run, the German resort to poison gas in 1915 helped no more than the British introduction of tanks in 1916. Even in 1917, the fighting in the

west remained indecisive, despite its horrendous cost in lives and matériel. Germany was beginning to feel shortages caused by the blockade and by attrition of its resources. But success on the Balkan fronts against Serbia and Rumania, as well as the internal collapse of Russia, gave the German High Command confidence that the war on the western front could be won in 1918, before the arrival of large American reinforcements.

THE EASTERN FRONT In the east, along the extended front from the Baltic to Rumania, Russian forces concentrated more quickly and assumed the initiative more rapidly than expected by the Central Powers. They advanced successfully against the Austrians in southeastern Poland and Bucovina, and at the same time invaded East Prussia, which the startled Germans prepared to evacuate. A timely change of command among the Germans repaired the situation. The local commander was dismissed. In his place, old General Paul von Beneckendorff und von Hindenburg (1847–1934) was called from retirement and given the task of saving East Prussia.

Within three weeks after this change of command, the Russians were expelled from East Prussia in the course of two big battles that cost them enormous casualties and over 200,000 prisoners. Actually, Hindenburg was an undistinguished careerist more famed for his knowledge of East Prussian geography than for his military skill; a subordinate commander in the field had made all tactical dispositions to prepare for this victory before Hindenburg arrived on the scene. But the Battle of Tannenberg—which German patriots celebrated as symbolic revenge

for the defeat of the Teutonic Knights on the same spot in 1410—made Hindenburg the hero of the nation. He was raised to the rank of field marshal, given command over the entire eastern front, and later, in 1916, over all German field armies. In fact, however, Hindenburg worked throughout the war in close collaboration with his highly skilled and ambitious chief staff officer, General Erich Ludendorff (1865–1937), who made most of the strategic and political decisions officially credited to Hindenburg. Yet popular adulation was accorded to Hindenburg, who during these years built his undeserved reputation that served him as an eventual stepping stone to the presidency of the Weimar Republic.

During the winter of 1914–1915, combined Austro-German drives into Russian Poland failed to make much headway, but several offensives in the spring and summer of 1915 yielded far-reaching results. Memel, Lithuania, and the bulk of Poland fell into German hands, and the Russians lost their initial gains in the Carpathian region. The loss of about a million men and severe shortages in war matériel, aggravated by governmental inefficiency and breakdowns, were beginning to weaken the Russian war effort. Despite this impairment, Russia launched two counteroffensives in 1916, partly in response to Allied requests to draw German-Austrian pressure away from the western and Italian fronts. Russia's offensive persuaded Rumania to enter the war against Austria and Germany. In answer, Austrian, Bulgarian, and German forces rapidly seized most of Rumania and extended the eastern front to the Black Sea. But after some initial success, in the course of which

Austria suffered enormous losses, the Russians were again repelled by the Central Powers. Within Russia, these failures led to despair and demoralization and ultimately to revolution.

At first the revolution of March 1917 in Russia did not greatly alter the status of the eastern front. Despite disorder at home, the Provisional Government in Russia pressed for continuation of the war against the Central powers, and launched another great offensive in Galicia in the summer. Once again, initial success gave way to defeat. By September, the Russian armies, punctured by revolutionary and counterrevolutionary confusion, were beginning to dissolve in the field. While the Germans occupied Latvia in the north and straightened their lines on the rest of the front, Russian contingents and individual soldiers were tramping homeward to participate in the revolutionary upheaval. After the Bolsheviks assumed power in the November Revolution, one of Lenin's first acts was to negotiate for an armistice, which came into effect on December 15, 1917. No longer faced by an organized enemy in the east, the Germans now began to shift the bulk of their contingents to the western front.

But some troops were still needed in the east. The remaining Rumanian armies were finally defeated in the spring of 1918, and Rumania signed the peace treaty of Bucharest in May. The Russians at first rejected the harsh terms demanded by the Germans, whereupon the Germans resumed their advance until March 3, when the Bolsheviks agreed to the terms of the Treaty of Brest Litovsk. By it, Russia renounced sovereignty over Finland, Lithuania, Latvia. Estonia, Poland, the Ukraine, and the regions beyond the Caucasus, with Germany and Austria given the right to determine the future status of these areas. In addition, Germany was promised regular delivery of crude oil and other vital materials. The German armies now helped organize the newly independent states, sent troops to occupy Finland and the Ukraine, and soon found themselves involved in the Russian civil war.

THE SOUTHERN FRONTS The western and eastern fronts occupied the main attention of the German war machine, since France and Russia were direct neighbors of Germany. But German armed forces also had to assist the other Central powers in their battles against the Allies. In 1914, Austria twice failed in attempts to invade tiny Serbia. During the following year, when the Allies showed their intention of launching a campaign through the Balkans—which was finally initiated when the French and British landed some troops at Saloniki—Germany decided to assume a greater role in the Balkans. Bulgaria was persuaded to join the Central powers, and German troops were dispatched to support a new Austrian offensive against Serbia. In the fall of 1915, Serbia rapidly collapsed under the joint impact of an Austro-German offensive from the north and a Bulgarian push from the east. Although the Italians halted the Austrian advance in the mountains of Albania and the Allies helped evacuate Serbian troops, the Allied armies at Saloniki were unable to impede the drive of the Central powers. Much of the Balkan area was thus opened to Austrian and German occupation, and the Central powers gained direct contact with their ally Turkey.

During 1916, the Balkan front remained relatively stable from the Adriatic to the Aegean Sea. German, Austrian, and Bulgarian troops fought French, British, Serbian, and Italian units in Albania and Macedonia. In the following year, the Allies finally succeeded in forcing Greece into the war on their side, and they began to pour more men and matériel into the Saloniki front. But the lines of the Central powers held throughout the summer of 1918. Only by September 1918 had the Allies concentrated sufficient forces to launch a giant offensive. In rapid order, the Bulgarian, German, and Austrian lines were broken and Bulgaria was forced to seek an armistice, which it signed on September 30. During October the Italians seized Albania, the Serbs reconquered their own lands, while the Allies crossed Bulgaria to attack Turkey from the north and to liberate Rumania. The Balkan front, in fact, ceased to exist before the war ended in the west.

Germany also found itself ultimately embroiled in the Italian campaigns. During the first eight months of the war, Italy's status had been unclear. It had refused to join the Central powers on the pretext that Austria's attack on Serbia had not been defensive and that Germany had declared war on Russia and France without the justification of "sufficient provocation" stipulated in the Triple Alliance. Nevertheless, Italy had continued to negotiate with Vienna and Berlin in the hope of satisfying its irredentist demands in the Tyrol, Venezia Giulia, and along the Adriatic coast. By 1915, Germany had actually persuaded Vienna to make these territorial sacrifices, but the Allies had meanwhile offered Italy even greater concessions, at the expense of Austrian territory, and Italy decided to join them.

Italy declared war on Austria-Hungary in May 1915, but no official state of war existed between Italy and Germany until the following summer. For two years, the Italians attempted to breach the Austrian defenses north of Trieste. But in eleven separate battles they gained no more than a few miles. Their advances in fierce mountain fighting in the southern Alps were equally negligible. The Austrians, for their part, tried to break through from Trent toward the Adriatic in the spring of 1916, but were equally unsuccessful. Finally, in late 1917, the German High Command decided to intervene on the Italian front. Six divisions were dispatched to aid the Austrians in a fall offensive. Within a few weeks, the Italians were routed and thrown back to the river Piave, abandoning all of northeastern Italy. The Italians appeared demoralized and on the verge of collapse.

In 1918, the Allies furnished greater support to Italy. Austria-Hungary, on the other hand, began to disintegrate. Incited by Polish, Czech, and Yugoslav national councils in exile, local nationalities within the empire provoked disorders and weakened its fighting strength. Throughout the summer, the Austrian lines in Italy held firm, despite growing desertion of its soldiers. But when the Italians finally rallied for an offensive in late October 1918, the Austrian army simply collapsed. The Italians were able to advance rapidly and to force the Austrians to sign an armistice on November 3.

German forces became involved also in the Near East. Turkey concluded a

military alliance with Germany on August 1, 1914, directed primarily against Russia. But before Bulgaria's entrance into the war and the defeat of Serbia, it was almost impossible for Germany to send effective aid to the Turks. The Germans merely dispatched two large cruisers to Constantinople in order to bind Turkey more firmly to the Central Powers. On October 29, 1914, a combined Turko-German naval force bombarded Russian Black Sea ports, whereupon the Allies declared war on Turkey. For the next two years, Turkey had to fight its campaigns alone, aided only by German military advisers and by clandestine attacks by German submarines in the Aegean Sea. Turkey fought the Russians in the Caucasus and along the borders of Persia, the British in the Sinai Peninsula and lower Mesopotamia, and the combined Allies on the Gallipoli Peninsula at the entrance to the Straits. In 1917, the Germans finally dispatched a small army to aid the Turks in Palestine, but logistical considerations kept this support fairly small. In the end, Turkey was overwhelmed by foreign invasions and local Arab uprisings, and signed an armistice on October 30, 1918.

THE LOSS OF THE GERMAN COLONIES At the outbreak of the war, Germany did not have sufficient local troops to defend its far-flung colonial empire. Within a few months, most of its colonies were seized by the British, Australians, New Zealanders, South Africans, Indians, French, and Japanese. The German Cameroons and German Southwest Africa held out a bit longer against foreign incursions, but only German East Africa was able to offer effective resistance, so that parts of

it remained in German hands until the end of the war.

AIR WARFARE In the course of the war, England, France, and Germany, and later the United States, made considerable use of airplanes. Air mastery over the front lines in the west shifted back and forth between England and Germany, depending on experimentation with new types of planes and their relative rates of production. Airplanes were used most spectacularly for aerial duels between aces, but their true military value lay in general reconnaissance, artillery observation, and occasional support of ground troop movements. As the war progressed, planes of both sides were used in larger formations to carry out bombing raids on London, Paris, and the Rhineland cities of Germany. Property damage ran relatively high, but such raids always had more psychological than strategic value. Starting in 1915, the Germans plagued England with bombing raids by dirigibles, sometimes employing as many as seven at a time, until the English improved their defenses against such attacks.

THE WAR AT SEA During the first year of the war, roving German cruisers preyed on Allied shipping in the various oceans of the world, and made surprise raids on Allied outposts. By early 1915, these raiders had all been caught by the British fleet and had been sunk or had scuttled themselves. The British, meanwhile, had started their blockade of the North Sea, in order to strangle Germany's economy and at the same time bottle up the German fleet in home waters. Nonetheless, individual light cruisers re-

peatedly slipped through the blockade to lay mines around the entrances to British ports, bombard English coastal towns, or raid Atlantic shipping.

However, Germany's powerful high-seas fleet as such was never really used in the war. Despite repeated urging by Tirpitz that the massed fleet should steam forth and boldly challenge the British Grand Fleet, in order to break the British blockade and then blockade England not merely with submarines but also with surface ships, William II refused to sanction such plans. Like an earlier Prussian ruler, who feared to lose a single beloved grenadier, William II acted as though his fleet had been built to be admired but not to be risked in battles. After Tirpitz resigned in 1916, a portion of the fleet was finally permitted to challenge the British in the only major naval engagement of the war (May 31, 1916). Both sides claimed victory, and this naval battle, fought off northern Jutland, remains to this day a controversial subject among naval historians. After Jutland, most of the German fleet again remained in home waters until the end of the war.

Germany's primary efforts at sea were devoted to submarine campaigns. At first, submarines were employed almost exclusively against enemy warships. But in February 1915, the Germans decided to counter the British blockade of Germany by launching a submarine blockade of England. In this first phase of unrestricted underseas warfare, which lasted from February to September 1915, German subs attacked merchant shipping regardless of nationality, and sank, among countless others, the British liner *Lusitania,* which had many American passengers,

thereby bringing Germany and the United States to the brink of war. During the next year and a half, German policy changed repeatedly. In order not to antagonize the United States, the Germans for a time concentrated their underseas attacks largely on British shipping; a brief second period of unrestricted warfare followed from March to May 1916.

Finally in January 1917, the German High Command decided on an all-out effort to starve Britain into submission. A total submarine blockade was proclaimed, even at the risk of driving the United States into the war, for it was expected that Britain would have to surrender before the United States could render effective military aid to the Allies. The resultant submarine campaign reached its height between March and October 1917. It not only brought the United States into the war, but also inflicted almost paralyzing damage on Allied shipping and the British economy. But in the end the Germans lost their gamble. The British perfected the convoy system and new methods for detecting and destroying submarines. The Allied shipbuilding program was also stepped up, so that soon more tonnage was built every month than the Germans could sink. By the winter of 1917, it was evident that Germany could not win the war by torpedoing Britain into submission. The German High Command then placed its last hopes on the spring offensive in France.

At the war's end, the remaining German fleet was surrendered to the Allies according to the terms of the armistice, and then interned at Scapa Flow in northern Scotland, where the German crews scuttled it in June 1919.

The German Home Front

MORALE On the whole, the Germans welcomed the outbreak of war with enthusiastic ardor. Volunteers from all walks of life rushed to enlist in such numbers that the army at first could not absorb them all. "To be honest," a recruit noted in his diary, "we were fed up with this lazy peace." A typical reserve officer described the spiritual fervor that filled the hearts of his comrades as they moved into the initial battles. "It was one of the most beautiful hours of my life," he wrote, "and I am proud to have experienced it." An observer in the capital depicted the departure of the jubilant troops who were leaving "to face a life of vigorous action, the highest type of existence." Everywhere the soldiers dedicated their lives to their emperor, "to the last drop of blood." A Socialist Reichstag deputy who had volunteered for service wrote from the front: "to shed one's blood for the fatherland is not difficult; it is enveloped in romantic heroism."

This initial enthusiasm soon dwindled. Mounting casualties, misery in the trenches, and shortages of food and supplies at home were stripping the "holy campaign" of its aura. By 1916, the Allied blockade, shortages of manpower and of fertilizer on the farms, as well as political and economic mismanagement, brought hunger to the cities and disillusionment to the civilian population. Thereafter, as food rations dwindled, disenchantment with war continued to grow. By the summer of 1918, famine, epidemics, and strikes had reduced civilian morale to the point where few, if any, were still ready to praise the glory of war.

However, it was a long time before this disenchantment altered the optimism of the nation. The German press monotonously reiterated that the Allies were patently failing to win the war, and that each onslaught against the German lines was being repelled. The German armies were deep inside Russian and French territories, and the population readily believed the frequent prophecies that the next major German offensive would crumble the Allied lines and overwhelm the enemy. By 1917, this extreme optimism began to wane, especially in those few political leaders who were better informed on the true status of the German war effort. Loss of faith in final victory led to greater internal tensions, which gradually forced the government to grant political concessions. But it is noteworthy that Ludendorff and Hindenburg, who assumed an almost complete dictatorship over political as well as military affairs in 1917, succeeded through censorship and propaganda in keeping the nation at large uninformed about the true military situation. Almost down to the day the front collapsed in the west, the average German clung to the belief that his armies were invincible. The sudden reversal from hope and confidence to the realization of total collapse and unmitigated defeat came to most Germans as a disillusioning shock, which in part explains the stunned pessimism of the early days of the Weimar Republic.

MOBILIZATION OF THE TOTAL ECONOMY No previous war had required so complete a use of the total resources of the participants as the Great War of 1914–1918. Like other nations, Germany had to devise new means to

achieve total mobilization of the economy. Such measures tended inevitably to strengthen the powers of the central government. They also revealed the continued bitter cleavage between producers and consumers, industrialists and unions, conservatives and liberals, despite the much-heralded closing of ranks for the sake of prosecuting the war.

Fearing a British blockade and a consequent lack of raw materials, the Germans immediately set up a War Raw Materials Board in the Ministry of War. Its organizer and initial director was Walther Rathenau (1867–1922), the Jewish president of AEG, Germany's huge general electric corporation. Rathenau promptly appropriated vital raw materials, whether in industry, commerce, or private possession, and then created separate divisions for every type of material—chemicals, wool, jute, rubber, leather, and so forth. These divisions, approximately sixty in number, soon resembled distinct companies—many of them based on a mixture of private and state ownership—and were placed under the direction of the War Department. By supervising all industrial planning, including the production of chemical substitutes, the War Raw Materials Board acquired great power over the entire economy, not merely over raw materials. It assumed the authority to close small, inefficient plants and set maximum prices, and it tried to equalize profits. Rathenau's work proved successful, but he became the target of bitter attacks and denunciations. A number of big industrialists complained of Rathenau's "state socialism" and launched an anti-Semitic campaign against him. The press accused him of causing food shortages, although

his office had nothing to do with food. In March 1915, Rathenau bowed before the storm and resigned, but the board he had organized continued to grow in power and importance.

Meanwhile the government also attacked the problem of food. About a thousand price-control and rationing offices, similar to the American OPA in World War II, were set up to establish maximum prices and attempt rationing. Various governmental agencies were created to centralize buying and the distribution of all food and animal fodder, but none of them proved very effective. Harvests and livestock constantly decreased, prices rose, and a black market flourished. Fertilizer, draft animals, seeds, and agricultural manpower were all in short supply. In addition, the situation was aggravated by a running feud between the agricultural producers and the state. General Wilhelm Groener (1867–1939) and others who directed the policy of the War Food Office frankly advocated protection of the consumer as opposed to the producers. The conservative landlords and many of the smaller peasants, however, objected to price fixing and governmental control of production. Like the industrialists, they decried the new state socialism, and refused to grow food to be sold at low prices. They insisted that the government should content itself with providing fertilizer, but leave the market free so that peasants had an incentive to produce. In retaliation against the government, and despite the famine in the cities, some let their lands lie fallow and others grew merely enough to feed themselves.

By late 1916, shortages in all resources, human and material, became so acute that the government adopted

a new concept of total mobilization. While dictatorial powers over all political matters were gradually taken over by the army, every aspect of the economy was placed under control of a newly created War Office supervised by General Groener. All existing agencies, such as the War Raw Materials Board, the War Food Office, and the Munitions Board, were put under the over-all supervision of the War Office, which thus assumed control over the procurement and feeding of labor, weapons, munitions, raw materials, synthetics, transport, imports, and exports—in short, over every aspect of the nation's finances, economics, and labor.

One of Groener's first tasks was to help draft a compulsory labor law that gave the state power to assign work to all males between the ages of seventeen and sixty. Here again a struggle ensued. The industrialists in the Reichstag produced a draft law without consulting the unions or including protective clauses against the abuse of workers. Groener, supported by the Socialists and the trade unions, insisted on inserting into the law guarantees of workers' rights in regard to wages, working conditions, and related matters. Once again, despite the urgency of the situation, the bitter antagonism between labor and producers came to the fore. Most of the safeguards were included in the final law, and the industrialists again denounced what they regarded as growing state socialism.

THE POLITICAL TRUCE As late as December 1913, Emperor William had written privately to the retired Bülow: "First let us shoot down the Socialists, or behead them, or somehow make them harmless, then we can face an external war." Yet on August 1, 1914, he told the populace: "In time of war, all parties cease and we are all brothers." His conciliatory attitude produced an unofficial truce among political parties (*Burgfrieden*) and a temporary cessation of criticism of the government. Most Germans welcomed this closing of ranks behind the common war effort. But a few left-wing Socialists suggested that the government be first compelled to institute important internal reforms before support be granted to the war effort, and some extreme conservatives feared that the political truce gave the internal enemies of the Reich the opportunity to destroy Germany from within. As one conservative deputy put it: "For heaven's sake, this means we shall lose the war politically on the home front."

According to the constitution, the emperor needed only the approval of the Bundesrat to decide on war or peace. Hence the Reichstag was not consulted on the question of declaring war, but its consent was needed to finance the war effort. On August 4, 1914, the Reichstag unanimously approved an initial war credit of 5 billion marks. By voting this financial support, the parties in effect placed their stamp of approval on the war. The deputies of the Social Democratic party voted in caucus 96 to 14 in favor of war credits, and in accordance with customary party discipline, all 110 delegates accepted the decision of the majority. In view of the Socialists' heralded pacifism and the subsequent split in their ranks over the conduct of the war, it is worthwhile to examine the speech of their leader before the vote on the war budget.

Hugo Haase (1863–1919) declared

that the war was caused by imperialistic policies for which his party took no responsibility, since it had always opposed them. He indicated that the Socialists, together with their French brethren, had labored until the final moment to try to prevent the war. But, he said, now that war had come, there was danger of invasion. "It is not up to us today to decide for or against peace, but to grant the required means for the defense of our country." Above all, it was urgent, he proclaimed, to prevent a victory of Russian despotism. "In agreement with the Socialist International, we recognize the right of every people to national independence and self-defense, just as much as we condemn every war of conquest." And he ended by expressing hope for a quick peace and friendship among neighboring peoples.

The political truce not only put an end to disputes among the parties, it also brought about an abdication of power by the members of the Reichstag. Never having exercised much political power, they now disbanded after voting the war credits, and left the conduct of the war effort in the unsupervised hands of the executive and the military. Not even an attempt was made to deputize a standing committee of delegates to work with the government on the task of prosecuting the war. During the next two years, the Reichstag was only rarely convened. Not until 1917 did it again become an active forum for discussion in conjunction with the question of war aims.

THE QUESTION OF WAR AIMS William II had proclaimed that Germany was not motivated by lust of conquest, and Bethmann-Hollweg had clearly indi-

cated that proper amends would be made for the violation of Belgium. On August 14, the SPD had issued a set of war aims designed to safeguard Germany's independence and integrity —including the retention of Alsace-Lorraine. The proclamation proposed that all colonial empires be opened to traders and immigrants from all nations. It demanded freedom of the seas, and opposed dismemberment of Austria-Hungary and Turkey. At the same time, it opposed German conquest of foreign soil, which would only "weaken the inner unity and strength of the German national state" and violate the principle of self-determination.

But as hope for a short war began to fade, divergent opinions on war aims came to the foreground and threatened to shatter the harmonious political truce. Certain ultraconservatives, in particular, distrusted Bethmann-Hollweg, and looked for ways to overthrow his regime in order to ensure their own war aims. In late August 1914, the All-German League, irritated by the news that the chancellor desired an early, quick, and lenient peace with France and England, started deliberations on this matter. They voiced the fear that the SPD, the Jews, certain weak officers, financiers, and other "traitors" might gain power over the government and introduce universal suffrage in Prussia. The chairman of the All-German League organized numerous meetings with leading industrialists and conservatives, such as Alfred Hugenberg (1865–1951), Gustav von Bohlen und Halbach (1870–1950), Hugo Stinnes (1870–1924), Emil Kirdorf (1847–1938), and others—many of whom later supported the rise of Hitler —and with representatives of the

League of Landlords, the League of German Peasants, the Union of German Industrialists, and other conservative pressure groups. From these meetings originated the first comprehensive set of war aims of the conservatives, which were circulated in a memo addressed to some two thousand influential citizens in the Reich.

The government attempted to stop this agitation by the All-German League. In January 1915, it ordered a search of the homes of several conservatives, confiscated the memoranda on war aims, and placed certain members of the All-German League under surveillance. Bethmann-Hollweg feared that publication of the annexationist demands of the conservatives would spoil the political truce by antagonizing the SPD and would make Germany look more than ever like an aggressor in the eyes of the world.

Despite this prohibition, the program of the All-German League received the adherence of numerous groups, including some Centrists, National Liberals, and university professors. The complete outline of war aims was finally sent to the chancellor in May 1915, under the guise of a petition, and was subsequently published in the press.

The petition stated that it would be folly to conclude a premature peace while Germany's position was militarily favorable, unless the peace brought better security for its western and eastern frontiers, an extension of its sea power, the "possibility of unchecked economic development," and a "stronger position in the world." Specifically, it demanded enormous territorial acquisitions: a large section of northern France, including the coastal districts to the Somme, to secure Germany access to the Channel; areas containing iron ore to make Germany more self-sufficient; and as much other territory as required by "military and strategic considerations." The petition also called for a protectorate over Belgium and vast expansion in the east to award Germany space for colonization, military security against Russia, and more agricultural lands. The populations of the ceded territories should be removed if possible so that Germans could be settled in these lands and that no new foreign elements would be introduced into the Reich. For similar reasons, the eastern borders should be sealed to prevent further influx of Jews. The petition also demanded a colonial empire "to satisfy Germany's manifold economic interests," and a weakening of England's domination of the seas. Finally, in view of the later treaties of Brest Litovsk and Versailles, it is noteworthy that these conservative war aims demanded a war indemnity "suitable to our requirements," and expressed the belief that Germany's future safety lay in a "serious economic and military weakening of our enemies."

Bethmann-Hollweg was not in sympathy with such extreme demands, but he was not a forceful leader and usually found it easier to straddle the fence. He reiterated his prohibition of public discussion of war aims, but in a speech in December of 1915, he expressed vague demands for "guarantees of security" against future threats to Germany and for German economic gains. By April 1916, he declared publicly that the prewar status could not be re-established, thus giving encouragement to the annexationists, who continued to push their demands clandestinely.

By the end of 1916, the debate on war aims could no longer be repressed. The government lifted its restrictions and permitted more or less free discussion. It at once appeared how deeply the nation was divided between those who insisted on peace without annexations and those who urged that the sacrifices borne by the nation required adequate compensation in the form of conquests. Slogans were devised to label opposing viewpoints. The conservatives derided the notion of a "peace of hunger"; the liberals opposed a "Hindenburg peace." In July 1917 the *Kreuzzeitung* editorialized: "Victory or peace of renunciation, this seems to be the big question of the moment," completely omitting the possibility of defeat.

Questions of war aims, of internal reform, and of peace proposals now became intertwined to shatter the political truce and to split the nation— seemingly as a prelude to the revolution of 1918. Between December 1916 and the summer of 1917, various attempts were made to bring about an armistice, through direct negotiations among the belligerents and through mediation by President Wilson and Pope Benedict XV (1914–1922). In principle, the German government agreed to proposals for future disarmament and international arbitration; but under pressure from Hindenburg, Ludendorff, and the conservatives, it avoided commitments about the evacuation of conquered territories and the rehabilitation of the devastated foreign lands. Actually, it appears that a peace of understanding could have been achieved in the summer of 1917. The German population was weary of the war; Russia was in the grips of revolution; French morale was low; the Italians were woefully unsuccessful; England was exhausted; and the United States was as yet ill prepared for the war it had just joined. But the conservatives and the military in Germany rejected the thought of a peace without victory and without gains, and successfully thwarted all attempts at mediation.

The more liberal groups and the lower classes, for their part, also demanded compensation for their sacrifices. But they sought such requital largely on the home front. They wanted political concessions from the government, as well as social and economic improvements. Bethmann-Hollweg and William II, who had been pushed increasingly into the background by the military, thus found themselves pressed from both sides. The conservatives insisted on a firm stand against political reform as well as on a vigorous war effort. The liberals pressed for internal reforms and a peace of understanding.

In his Easter Message of April 1917, Emperor William gave the first public indication that he recognized the demands of the liberals. He promised a revision of the Prussian electoral system after the war, although he did not pledge support for the introduction of universal suffrage. This was to be the beginning of a hapless attempt at revolution from above. In July 1917, William took a further step. In an imperial decree, he promised equal universal suffrage for Prussia in the next reform program.

Ironically, the first victim of these proposals was the imperial chancellor. The liberals had never been attached to him and did not consider him the proper man for negotiating a peace of understanding. The conservatives

and the military now withdrew the little support they had given him. They feared that Bethmann-Hollweg lacked determination to resist the pressure for political reform and to push their war aims with sufficient vigor. Hindenburg and Ludendorff hurried to Berlin, and on the following day Bethmann-Hollweg was dismissed. The new chancellor, Georg Michaelis (1857–1936), was a colorless bureaucrat, an appointee of Ludendorff's. He carried neither prestige nor power, and his subservience to the High Command made it easier for Ludendorff to cement his military dictatorship.

Bethmann-Hollweg's dismissal and the ascendancy of Ludendorff acted as a coalescent on the opposition. The Social Democrats, the Progressives, and the Centrists now united, at least on the floor of the Reichstag—a union that foreshadowed the typical coalitions of the later Weimar period. The leader of the Center party, Matthias Erzberger (1875–1921), initially a proponent of a strong peace, had come to the conclusion that total victory was impossible. Even during the war he had frequently traveled abroad, and had realized that "Austria was at the end of her strength" and that the munitions ratio was constantly increasing in favor of the Allies. Moreover, he was convinced that the submarine campaign would not succeed in forcing England to its knees before the United States entered the war in full strength. Certain that "a peace à la Ludendorff" was unobtainable, he also believed democratization at home to be a *sine qua non* for a peace of understanding, since the entrenched military and conservative elements would never consent to such a peace so long as they retained a monopoly of political power. Erzberger

communicated his convictions to his fellow delegates in various Reichstag speeches, and finally presented to them a Peace Resolution. This measure was adopted by the Reichstag on July 19, 1917. It was carried by a favorable vote of 212 Centrists, SPD, and Progressives against 126 negative votes, with 17 abstentions. It urged the government to seek a peace of reconciliation, and voiced its opposition to territorial conquests as well as to "political, economic, and financial oppression" of other peoples. At the same time, it demanded constitutional reforms that would democratize Prussia and impose parliamentary checks on the federal government.

As an attempt at opening the road to peace, the resolution of 1917 was a failure. Chancellor Michaelis pretended to heed the mandate of the majority parties, while at the same time remaining an obedient tool of the military dictators. He boasted privately that "one can, in fact, make any peace one likes, and still be in accord with the Resolution." Erzberger also failed to exploit the opportunity for using the resolution as a wedge for gaining greater political power for the Reichstag. As military dictator, Ludendorff had little difficulty in outmaneuvering the opposition and keeping the Reichstag powerless.

Despite these failures, the Peace Resolution had important repercussions. Besides paving the way for a coalition of the liberal and leftist parties, it also produced a frenzied reaction among the rightists and deepened the political cleavage of the nation. In September 1917, Admiral Tirpitz and the Prussian government official Wolfgang Kapp (1858–1922), together with other conservatives from various politi-

cal parties, formed the German Fatherland party for the purpose of opposing Erzberger's "peace of hunger" and promoting a victorious or "Hindenburg peace." This group also launched a campaign of defamation against the advocates of a soft peace, labeling as defeatists and traitors those who signed the resolution. Thus was created the theory of the "stab in the back," the legend that was to grow into a gangrenous sore in the body politic of the Weimar Republic.

DISUNITY AMONG THE SOCIALISTS
While the High Command dominated the political scene—although, as Ludendorff complained, not always adequately supported by the emperor—and the liberals stood in passive dismay at the impending disaster, groups of workers, trade-unionists, and Socialists grew increasingly adamant in their opposition to the government. Socialist unity had long ceased to exist. The left-wing radicals in the Reichstag had submitted to the party's majority decisions at the outbreak of the war, but many of the rank and file had resented the apparent capitulation of their leaders to the capitalists and their war. As early as December 1914, when new war credits were requested, Karl Liebknecht—the son of Wilhelm Liebknecht, the founder of the Marxist wing of the SPD—opposed his more accommodating Socialist colleagues and voted against the budget. He then began to agitate openly against the war. To silence him, the government drafted Liebknecht into the army, and finally jailed him when he continued his demonstrations. Leadership of the left-wing dissidents then passed into the hands of Rosa Luxemburg until Lieb-

knecht's release from prison. Encouraged by the success of the Bolshevik Revolution in Russia, this group rapidly gained additional adherents among war-weary workers, but it remained outside the Reichstag and in a status of semilegality. During the winter of 1917–1918, it helped foment a few strikes in war plants and circulated propaganda on the futility of the war effort among soldiers and, more particularly, sailors. Under the name of Spartacus League, organized in 1917, it became the forerunner of the German Communist party.

A larger and more influential splinter of the Socialists, with representation in the Reichstag and a broad following among the rank and file, was the USPD or Independent German Social Democratic party, formally organized in 1917. Its leaders, such as Hugo Haase, Karl Kautsky, and Eduard Bernstein, represented various Socialist views, revolutionary as well as revisionist. Starting in December 1915, the Reichstag members of this amorphous group had voted against further war credits, and because of their refusal to acquiesce in the more compromising stand of the central committee of the SPD—at this time usually called the Majority Socialists to distinguish them from the two splinter groups—they had finally been expelled from the party and formed their own organization. They insisted that the political truce was a capitalistic hoax to undermine the class struggle. They hated the middle and upper classes and the annexationist war aims. Particularly after the overthrow of the tsarist rule in Russia, they saw no reason for continuing the war, and became adamant in their demands for

peace. Once formed, the USPD grew rapidly in membership, although differences among its leaders did not permit it to coalesce into a homogeneous party. It engaged in denunciations of the annexationists and at times co-operated with the Spartacists, but generally remained within the bounds of legality until the outbreak of revolution in the fall of 1918.

THE END OF THE WAR

The Last Months of Confidence

For almost a year after the Peace Resolution, the annexationists felt triumphantly sure that they had been wise in rejecting a peace of reconciliation. As Ludendorff noted in his memoirs, the High Command stood by its convictions in regard to war aims until "July/August 1918, as long, that is, as it hoped to safeguard the requisites of life for the German people." The Treaties of Brest Litovsk and of Bucharest (see page 173), providing for German territorial, political, and economic aggrandizement, were drawn up in harmony with the views of the annexationists. They were negotiated by the military, in conjunction with their new puppet chancellor, Count Georg von Hertling (1843–1919), who had replaced Michaelis in the fall of 1917. The Reichstag had not been consulted. Some of the liberals had already lost self-assurance in the face of Ludendorff's military victories. The pleas of others for an end to the mad dream of self-delusion were now rejected even more decisively. In such a mood, the German High Command merely smiled at the British war aims publicly announced by Lloyd George on Jan-

uary 5, 1918, and shrugged off as trans-atlantic reveries the Fourteen Points Wilson presented to the United States Congress three days later.

The rout of the Italian armies, Russia's withdrawal from the war after the Soviet Revolution, the defeat of Rumania, the anticipated success of the spring offensive in the west, all made Ludendorff confident that he could win a military decision over the Allies. The termination of hostilities on the eastern front allowed Ludendorff to transfer to the west large reserves with which he hoped to break through the Anglo-French lines. From March until June 1918, the Germans launched their last series of gigantic offensives. Although creating minor breaches and once again crossing the Marne toward Paris, the Germans failed. With the help of newly arrived troops from the United States, the Allies stemmed the German offensive. By July, a counterattack was launched, initiating the gradual rollback of the German armies that ultimately forced the Germans to request an armistice.

Request for an Armistice and Belated Democratization

As soon as the terms of the Armistice of November 1918 became known, the conservatives—the so-called National Opposition—intensified their complaints about a stab in the back. Briefly stated, this accusation amounted to an exculpation of the High Command and the annexationist forces by alleging that the German army had not been defeated in the field of battle but had been stabbed in the back by revolutionary elements at home, namely by Communists, Socialists, and other

"un-German" factions. Since this theory became an essential steppingstone in the revitalization of conservatism after the revolution and in the ultimate rise of Hitler, the circumstances of the armistice and the events preceding the November Revolution warrant particular analysis.

In July 1918, the German offensive in the west gradually gave way to the Allies' counteroffensive. By early August, the Allied advance gained speed and the German position became increasingly hopeless. August 8, according to Ludendorff, was the "Black Day" on which the German lines began to crumble and on which the High Command was forced to weigh the need for peace. A week later, the government began to investigate possible avenues for arranging peace with the Allies. But nothing was done for a few weeks, although the armies in the field were gradually rolled back by the attacking French, British, and American forces. During September, the situation became desperate. The Balkan front collapsed, Bulgaria withdrew from the war, the Dual Monarchy was on the verge of disintegration, and the retreat in the west continued.

On September 28, Ludendorff noted that the collapse of the Balkan front might render Germany's position untenable "even if the western front could possibly hold out." On the following day, Hindenburg suddenly warned the government to seek an immediate armistice, which he and Ludendorff hoped could be concluded while German armies still occupied a strip of northern France. "As yet the German forces are holding out," Hindenburg notified Berlin, "but the situation deteriorates daily!" In view of the stab in the back theory, it is interesting to note that Hindenburg made no reference to the demoralization of his troops by Communist agitators, an accusation that later became popular.

The unexpected admission by the High Command of imminent disaster on the western front had far-reaching repercussions on the home front. Those who had remained blissfully optimistic were rudely plunged into realization of the catastrophe at hand. Count Hertling resigned at once, and Emperor William issued an edict promising a new government that would represent the will of the people. On October 4, Prince Maximilian of Baden (1867–1929), the liberal heir to the throne of the Duchy of Baden, was installed as chancellor. Belatedly, Germany was given quasi-parliamentary government, for Maximilian promised to govern with the consent of the majority in the Reichstag—those parties, in fact, that had supported the Peace Resolution of 1917. Erzberger joined the new government as minister without portfolio, and even the conservatives agreed to cooperate with Maximilian in order to gain an "honorable end to the war." The High Command's sudden relinquishing of power to the civilian government and acquiescence in the establishment of parliamentary government was a part of Ludendorff's calculated withdrawal from the political scene, so that the army could be exonerated from the blame of defeat.

Prince Maximilian, in conjunction with the Austrians, at once notified President Wilson that the Central Powers were ready to discuss peace terms on the basis of the Fourteen Points. While waiting for a reply, Ludendorff expressed hope that peace could be

obtained soon, while his armies were still more or less intact, and could if necessary exert pressure during the negotiations. But the Allies unexpectedly injected a new problem. Woodrow Wilson made it plain that so long as Germany was ruled by military and monarchical authority, it could not expect a negotiated peace, but would have to surrender unconditionally.

Until this time, there had been relatively little "republicanism" in Germany. Discontent with William II and with his political system had seldom touched the imperial framework as such, perhaps because the notion of a Reich appealed to the romantic emotions of even the most discontented opposition. But now the question of the continuation of the monarchy seemed linked with the survival of Germany as a state. The SPD, joined by many liberals, promptly called for Emperor William's abdication.

Unrest, strikes, and minor outbreaks of rebellion marked the last days of October, while the field armies continued their slow retreat before Allied pressure. On October 26, General Ludendorff resigned his command, presumably to keep his hands untarnished by defeat, although Hindenburg remained as commander in chief. General Groener assumed Ludendorff's place and inherited the thankless task of supervising the army during the final two weeks of the war. General Groener and Maximilian now vainly attempted to persuade William to abdicate. According to an unverified story, Groener even urged William to go to the front, presumably in the hope that he would be hit by a bullet and thus gloriously leave the German political scene.

With Germany poised on the brink of disaster, militarily unable to prosecute the war and equally unable to conclude a peace so long as William II remained at the helm of the collapsing Reich, outright revolutions broke out in various sections of the country. The sailors at the Kiel naval base mutinied on October 29 and refused to set out to sea on a last-minute raid against England. By November 3, red flags were waving from the German fleet at Kiel, and the mutinous sailors, supported by USPD shock troops, were battling police and special army units in the streets of the city. The rebellion rapidly spread along the coast to Hamburg, Bremen, and Lübeck. On November 7, revolution erupted in Munich, resulting in the overthrow of the Bavarian monarchy. In all corners of Germany, Spartacists and Independent Socialists agitated against the regime, while the moderate Socialists warned against "Russianizing Germany." Still William II rejected all pleas for his abdication.

If the army had been able to maintain its position in the field, these revolutionary outbreaks at home could perhaps have been considered a stab in the back. But the front lines had given way long before the outbreaks occurred, and the revolts produced only two indirect results. Certain conservatives wished to speed up the return of the army so that it could effectively crush the rebellion at home. And Wilson hastened to inform the Germans that the Allies agreed to an armistice and to discussion of peace terms on the basis of the Fourteen Points, with the exception of certain British reservations regarding freedom of the seas, and of Allied demands for Ger-

man payment for the rehabilitation of occupied lands.

The day after receiving Wilson's communication, Prince Maximilian sent Erzberger with an armistice commission to France to negotiate with the Allies. Hindenburg sent a personal message to Erzberger before the latter's departure for Compiègne: "Above all, the army needs a rest. Godspeed and try to salvage the best for our fatherland." Erzberger was accompanied by a general to advise him on military matters, but it is symptomatic that the High Command attempted to disassociate itself from the humiliating task of seeking an armistice. General Groener noted in his memoirs: "I was glad to see the army and the High Command remain as unsullied as possible in these unfortunate negotiations." The military thus tried to avoid responsibility for Germany's collapse; in fact, Matthias Erzberger later had to carry the brunt of the hatred of those who asserted that Germany had needlessly surrendered.

The Armistice demands presented to Erzberger at Compiègne on November 8 were harsh and amounted to almost unconditional surrender. The Allies wished to make sure that Germany would be in no position to resume the war. Erzberger tried in vain to obtain alterations of the terms, and finally wired to ask Hindenburg's advice. The latter advised Erzberger to seek certain changes, but urged him "to conclude negotiations in any case, even if the modifications cannot be achieved." The military situation was desperate and conclusion of peace essential. The army thus sanctioned the Armistice and it can hardly be asserted that surrender was the work of revolu-

tionaries. After Erzberger received Hindenburg's advice on November 10, he signed the Armistice terms, which became effective on November 11.

Meanwhile Maximilian of Baden and General Groener had continued to press William to abdicate. No amount of persuasion seemingly could convince him to abandon the throne of the Hohenzollerns. When revolutionary unrest erupted in Berlin, the chancellor finally decided to force the issue. On November 9, he announced William's abdication without having received any authorization. The Socialists thereupon proclaimed the establishment of a republic, while William II, at his wartime headquarters, was still hesitant as to his course of action. Only after Hindenburg and Groener finally convinced him that even the army might no longer be loyal to him, did he take the course of prudence and flee to Holland during the night of November 9–10.

The Armistice Terms

The Armistice was originally to last thirty days, but its eighteen clauses reduced Germany's military strength to such a point that there could be no serious thought of a resumption of the war. The German armies were to withdraw immediately from all lands west of the Rhine and even evacuate a special neutral zone east of the Rhine. In the east, "all troops were to withdraw behind the boundaries of August 1, 1914," although no fixed time limit was given for this withdrawal, presumably because of the uncertainties of the Russian civil war. Rumania, Austria-Hungary, and Turkey were to be evacuated. The Treaties of Brest

Litovsk and Bucharest were declared voided. Large quantities of military and industrial matériel were to be turned over to the Allies: cannons, machine guns, mortars, airplanes, locomotives, railway cars, trucks, as well as the bulk of the battle fleet and parts of the merchant marine. The blockade of Germany was to remain in effect—a decision bitterly resented by the Germans—and Allied armies were to occupy the left bank of the Rhine, with the cost of occupation to be borne by the Germans.

Under the terms of the Armistice the German forces at once began their retreat and released all Allied prison-ers. Where possible, the field armies were transported home in orderly fashion. But morale at the front was at its lowest point, transport was lacking, and discipline not always enforceable. Strikes and revolutionary outbreaks hampered orderly operations, and many field units simply dissolved, with individual soldiers making their way home as best they could.

The Allies followed on the heel of the retreating and disintegrating German forces. By early December, they had invaded the Rhineland and had begun to occupy the cities of Cologne, Coblenz, and Mainz, as well as surrounding districts.

Germany's First Republic, 1918–1929

THE BASIS OF THE WEIMAR REPUBLIC

The German Republic of 1919 to 1933, popularly called the Weimar Republic, was Germany's first experiment with a republican form of government and with the parliamentary system.[1] From its inception, the new regime was burdened by many serious handicaps. The aftermath of war and defeat, the harsh Treaty of Versailles, inflation, and disorder poisoned the soil on which the young republic was to grow. Moreover, the upheaval of November 1918 that brought forth the Weimar Republic was not a true revolution marking a clear break with the past. On the contrary, few fundamental changes were effected in Germany's social, economic, and even political structure when the empire of William II suddenly gave way to the fragile, democratic Weimar Republic. This semiabortive character of the revolution of 1918 was to be vitally important for the fate of the republic.

The Character of the November Revolution

The revolution in Berlin, as was seen in the last chapter, was preceded by upheavals in other parts of Germany. The mutiny of the sailors in Kiel and its spread had led to the formation of soviets (councils) of workers and soldiers in many regions. It seemed at first as if Germany were following the example of the Bolshevik Revolution. But in most cases, these soviets did not fall under the control of radicals; their members showed more interest in mild social reform than in outright revolution.[1]

Not the establishment of the soviets but the overthrow of the monarchy in Bavaria gave the impetus to further changes. In the hope of ending the war and the "imperial fraud," and of goading his fellow Socialists into action, the Independent Socialist Kurt Eisner (1867–1919) proclaimed a Bavarian Republic on November 7, 1918. If necessary, he was willing to press

190

for Bavarian independence. The abdication of the Wittelsbach monarchy acted as a green light all over Germany. Princes everywhere felt forced to lay down their scepters, and local government either remained in the hands of civil servants or was seized by soviets or other emergency bodies.

Only Emperor William II hesitated to abdicate, until Maximilian of Baden made a revolutionary decision and forced the issue. On November 9, without William's consent, the chancellor simply announced that "the Emperor and King has decided to relinquish the throne." Although constitutionally he had no right to appoint a successor, Maximilian then turned the chancellorship over to Friedrich Ebert (1871–1925), the leader of the Majority Social Democrats. Its illegality notwithstanding, this act was hardly very revolutionary, since the Majority Socialists, as the largest party, had earned the right to rule on the basis of the democratic procedures that had been tacitly accepted by William during the last year of his reign. Transference of the chancellorship to the leader of the Socialists did not even imply an automatic end to monarchy in Germany. Maximilian as well as Ebert initially thought of a regency. The unrevolutionary character of this transfer of power was highlighted by the cordial meeting between Prince Maximilian and his successor. The two met in a friendly conference to discuss the change of government, and Maximilian "entrusted the fatherland" to the care of Ebert, in whom he had considerable confidence. It was as if the retiring chancellor wanted to relinquish a bankrupt enterprise, hoping that new management might pull it out of the doldrums. And rather than grab power by force, the Socialists accepted it almost reluctantly, as if by default.

The second revolutionary step occurred on the same day when Philipp Scheidemann (1865–1939), an impetuous member of the executive committee of the SPD proclaimed the German Republic from the steps of the Reichstag—possibly to head off action by the more revolutionary left-wing radicals. Scheidemann had not consulted his colleagues. It was characteristic of the new regime that Ebert, who was convinced that only a legally elected Constituent Assembly had the right to decide for or against a republic, screamed at Scheidemann after the proclamation: "You have no right to proclaim the Republic!"

These two measures—the forced abdication of Emperor William and the proclamation of the German Republic—were the only truly revolutionary aspects of the change of regime. Beyond this, the disorders of November 1918 hardly constituted a *bona fide* revolution. No significant change occurred in the alignment of political power. The bureaucracy and the army, which had been so important since the days of the Great Elector, retained their prominent social position and political influence. The judiciary remained unchanged. Even social and economic changes were minimal. Although the kings, dukes, and princelings were deposed, the aristocracy preserved its social prerogatives. Despite a democratic constitution and universal suffrage, the ancient spirit of respect for titles—whether noble, academic, or bureaucratic—continued to foster wide class distinctions and warp the ideals of equality and fraternity that the Socialists and Progressives had preached. Moreover, no attempt was made to

diminish the overwhelming power of the Prussian government by decentralizing Prussia or splitting it into a number of smaller states. The Prussian agrarians, the Rhineland industrialists, the aristocratic officer corps retained their conservative influence. It is interesting that the traditional term "Reich" was retained to designate the German state, even though Germany was no longer an empire. As the poet Rainer Maria Rilke (1875–1926) noted disappointedly, there had been "no change of heart."

The failure to effect a clear break with the past and to attempt a fundamental transformation that might have given Germany a vital and viable democratic structure was partly due to the circumstances of the period, as will be seen in subsequent sections. But in part, it can also be attributed to the idealistic and unrevolutionary character of the bulk of the Socialists. Like most of his colleagues, Ebert, in his own words, "hated social revolution like sin." Imbued with a deep respect for legality, most of the Socialists actually aspired to acquire traditional middle-class status rather than to transform German society. Many of them, including Ebert, who ultimately became the first president of the young republic, were not even antimonarchist at heart.

A comparison with the two Russian revolutions of 1917 is instructive. The Socialists and the Constitutional Democrats who overthrew the tsarist regime in March 1917 refused to sanction any critical reforms while the revolutionary temper was still hot. Consequently, they failed to extend their basis of power, and their revolutionary *élan* lost its appeal. In the November Revolution of 1917 however, Lenin's Bolsheviks acted quite differently. Intent on seizing complete power and gaining immediate popular support for their movement, the Bolsheviks directed their first revolutionary decrees to the nationalization of all land and industry. In Germany, Ebert and his friends acted like the Socialists and Constitutional Democrats in Russia, insisting that only the legally elected representatives of the people could decree reforms. Afraid that truly revolutionary social changes would play into the hands of the radical Left, they seemed more intent on safeguarding the purity of their evolutionary ideals than on consolidating their power. Unlike Lenin's first decrees, their initial proclamation of November 10 dealt with questions of moderate social and political reform, specifically the institution of the eight-hour day and of universal equal suffrage, and the guaranteeing of civil as well as property rights. Even more typical in its bourgeois and liberal preoccupation was the proclamation of November 12. It set as the task of the new government the "realization of the Socialist program." But the nine points of the proclamation did not touch on such fundamental Socialist principles as land reform, social security, nationalization of basic industry, or an extension of free public education. Instead, they were devoted to liberal demands such as guarantees of free assembly, free speech, free exercise of religion, an amnesty for political prisoners, and "the lifting of censorship of the theater."

The Provisional Government

On November 10, Ebert set up a provisional government to direct German affairs until nation-wide elections

would establish a constituent assembly.[1] The provisional government included three members of the Majority Socialists and three Independent Socialists. Since it lacked any other basis of authority, Ebert's cabinet called itself a committee of people's commissars, ruling in the name of the Central Committee of the moderate soviets of workers and soldiers. In reality, the soviets quickly lost the little importance they had enjoyed, and the provisional government acted more or less as an autonomous body. Among its most prominent members were Ebert, Scheidemann, and Hugo Haase, the leader of the Independent Socialists.

[1] **THE TASKS CONFRONTING EBERT** The provisional government was at once beset by numerous problems whose solutions were to affect the outcome of Germany's republican experiment. For one, there was profound disagreement and distrust among the various factions of Socialists. The Spartacists, who were not represented on the governing body, favored a complete social revolution in the style of the Bolsheviks in Russia. The USPD, with its mixture of revolutionary and revisionist adherents, wanted government by the soviets of workers and soldiers, although not necessarily a radical overturn of the social spectrum. The Majority Socialists preferred the calling of a legally elected national constituent assembly that would decide on the future framework for Germany. These differences, particularly those between the Majority Socialists and the radical Spartacists, led Ebert at once to the fateful decision that he had to align himself with the forces of order and semiconservatism in order to crush the ultraradicals. In addition, the pro-visional government had to arrange for and supervise the execution of the Armistice, undertake the demobilization of the armed forces, deal with famine and economic chaos, keep law and order in the face of attacks from the radical Left as well as the conservative Right, and govern Germany until a constitution had been framed and a permanent government formed.

Most important of the problems faced by Ebert was the question of keeping order and maintaining the integrity of Germany. Mindful of the experiences of the Mensheviks during the Bolshevik Revolution, the provisional government did not want to become a tool of the soviets of workers and soldiers. Nor could they count on local police forces as sufficient protection against the more radical elements of the Spartacists. The Independent Socialists were urging the immediate creation of a citizens' militia, composed of Socialist and republican elements, which would defend the new regime, but Ebert feared that such shock troops might become vanguards of Bolshevism. Instead, he immediately made an arrangement with General Groener (Ludendorff's replacement) that was to have dire consequences for the Weimar Republic. Ebert and Groener agreed to cooperate against the extreme radicals. Groener indicated that he would persuade Hindenburg to remain for the time being as commander in chief —Hindenburg actually stayed at his post until Germany accepted the Treaty of Versailles in June 1919— and to have the army recognize and cooperate with the new revolutionary government. The army was to help keep order and to crush the extreme left wing. Support by the military would enhance the prestige of the pro-

visional government. In return, Ebert agreed to let the old officers remain in charge of the military units. He promised not to destroy the army and not to create a people's militia or a "red army" in the manner of Lenin. No doubt, a German civil war was thus avoided. But this arrangement between the army and the government, reaffirmed a year later between Ebert and General Hans von Seeckt (1866–1936), the new chief of the *Truppenamt*—the Weimar euphemism for the former General Staff, which was outlawed by the Treaty of Versailles—threatened the future of German democracy. It entrusted the survival of Weimar into the hands of the conservative military, who at heart remained monarchists and imperialists. General Groener aptly remarked in his memoirs: "I and my colleagues saw to it to keep our daggers unsheathed and to safeguard the High Command unsullied for the future."

Order was threatened not only by the Spartacists but also by returning veterans. Countless demobilized soldiers, returning with their weapons to their starving families, found nothing but bitterness and disillusionment. There was no program for rehabilitation to civilian life. Many youngsters had left school to volunteer for the front, and now returned with no trade or training other than fighting. Few jobs were available. Consequently a dangerous number of them joined the Free Corps, bands of semiorganized fighting units grouped around a leader at whose direction they engaged in street fighting or open warfare, wherever chance might take them. The formation of Free Corps units was at first actively encouraged by Hindenburg and other officers. Some of these marauding Free Corps fought in the Baltic area in the Russian civil war and the Russo-Polish War; others made themselves available for suppressing uprisings or executing political murders within the Reich. A few of these units joined the radical Left, but the bulk turned to the extreme Right. Nurtured on the stab-in-the-back theory, they blamed the Socialists for the defeat and for their resulting plight, and were always available for attempts at overthrowing the "traitors of the fatherland." The Free Corps thus posed a serious threat to the provisional government. Yet the Majority Socialists lacked the power to disband them; in fact they were forced to accept them as a temporary ally against further subversion from the radical Left. Hence Ebert and his Socialist minister of war after December 1918, Gustav Noske (1868–1946), found themselves relying on the Free Corps and the army for repressing left-wing uprisings.

The provisional government was mainly intent on keeping the revolution from turning further to the Left. Ebert begged the old civil servants to stay at their posts to help maintain order. He resisted all suggestions for land reform lest they disrupt the production of food and worsen the famine caused by the war and the continued Allied blockade. And he refused to nationalize the basic means of production, not only because he awaited the verdict of a properly elected assembly but also because he was afraid of disrupting the already teetering economy. Above all, he feared that overly violent social and economic changes might open the door to a Communist revolution.

Ebert's moderate and antirevolutionary stand was, of course, not due solely to his bourgeois and evolutionary beliefs. One must recall that the German

army had not disintegrated as had the Russian army and that it represented a power factor in German politics. Ebert was thus forced to pursue a middle course that might satisfy a majority of his SPD followers without provoking interference by the military. Moreover, Ebert had to take account of the international situation. The Allies were at the time supporting the anti-Communist forces in Russia and were gradually getting actively involved in the Russian civil war. It seemed obvious that the western powers, particularly the French, would not have tolerated the establishment of a radical regime in Germany and that the Allied armies would very likely have marched into unoccupied Germany to prevent its Bolshevization.

THE SPARTACIST UPRISINGS The Spartacists, who disapproved of Ebert's seeming conservatism, opposed the proposal for calling a national assembly, and favored immediate sovietization of Germany. They began to receive financial aid and advice from Lenin and the Russian communist party, assumed the name of German Communist party (KPD), and made a bid for power in an uprising in December 1918. Ebert and his provisional government did not hesitate to call on the army to crush the Communists. The insurrection was successfully quelled by army and Free Corps units, but not without profound repercussions. Although the unions and most workers had not lent their support to the Spartacists, it was nevertheless difficult for them to understand why a Socialist government, supposedly representing the proletariat, should use the conservative army and the reactionary Free Corps to fire on the workers. Some of the Independent Socialists

had sided with the Spartacists. In protest over the government's action, the USPD quit the provisional government. Haase and his Independent colleagues insisted that the "blood bath of December 24" proved that Ebert had given his minister of war unlimited power to use the army against the workers. The USPD wanted no "responsibility for the fact that a representative of the old system of tyranny [General von Lequis, in charge of the troops that repressed the Spartacists] has been given discretionary power over the lives of the people." Haase insisted that one should negotiate with the Communists, not shoot them down.

A few weeks later, the Communists made a second attempt at insurrection in Berlin. They called for a strike, which was poorly supported by the workers, and tried to wrest control of the government from the Majority Socialists. A number of USPD members again sided with them. But once again, Ebert called for military help, and the army and the Free Corps crushed the rebellion. The Spartacist leaders, Rosa Luxemburg and Karl Liebknecht, were taken prisoner and shot on their way to jail, much to the consternation of the liberal elements in Germany. For the second time, the provisional government had suppressed the advocates of social revolution and given encouragement to the conservative forces. Further revolts during February and March were similarly subdued by Noske's armed forces.

THE REVIVAL OF THE BOURGEOIS PARTIES While the SPD turned more conservative and the extreme Left was being robbed of its *élan,* the bourgeois parties regained their composure, and the antirevolutionaries took heart. The

January 1919 election for the National Constituent Assembly, which was boycotted by the Communists, gave the SPD and the USPD 165 and 22 delegates respectively, while giving a total of 260 seats to the various middle-of-the-road and conservative parties. In Bavaria, a brief counterrevolution took place in February. Kurt Eisner was assassinated—the first of many prominent liberals to meet this fate—and an attempt was made to re-establish the monarchy. In reprisal, the Communists succeeded in gaining control of the government in April and in establishing a Bavarian soviet republic. But this radical experiment was crushed in the beginning of May by the combined efforts of the federal army and various Free Corps units. Hereafter radicalism was eradicated from Bavaria, and Munich became a stronghold of conservatism.

After the National Constituent Assembly convened at Weimar in early February, it chose a new interim government to serve until a republican constitution would come into effect. Friedrich Ebert was elected as first President of the German Republic, and Scheidemann was made Prime Minister. The cabinet consisted of seven Majority Social Democrats, five Democrats (see page 203), and three Centrists. The all-Socialist character of the government had expired with the revival of the bourgeois parties.

While the delegates to the National Constituent Assembly labored in the provincial town of Weimar, far removed from the revolutionary turbulence of the industrialized cities, the new provisional government faced not only continued internal disorder but also the problem of concluding peace with the Allies.

The Treaty of Versailles

In January 1919, representatives of the victorious nations convened in Paris and debated throughout the spring on the terms to be imposed on Germany. After much bickering and dissension (which is not directly of concern in a discussion of German history), the Allies submitted a draft to the German provisional government with the obvious implication that the stipulated terms had to be accepted. The German delegation protested vigorously against the terms of the treaty, asserting that it violated Wilson's Fourteen Points and represented not a negotiated agreement but a "dictated peace." Scheidemann refused to sign it and resigned from the government, proclaiming that the hand that "imposes such chains upon us [by signing the document] must wither." Groener advised that resumption of hostilities would be hopeless, but Hindenburg declared that although "the outcome of further military operations was highly doubtful," as a soldier he preferred "an honorable fall to an ignominious peace." Finally, the National Assembly appointed a new cabinet willing to accept the treaty, albeit under protest. The Assembly then voted 237 to 138 in favor of submitting to the Allied demands, and Hindenburg resigned from his post of commander in chief.

In many respects, the Treaty of Versailles, with its over 400 clauses and numerous appendices, was in agreement with Wilson's Fourteen Points. But in a few specific items and, above all, in its spirit, the treaty violated Wilson's idealism. It was no peace of reconciliation designed to undo injustice, but a document based on hate and vengeance.

TERRITORIAL AND DISARMAMENT CLAUSES 'Germany was to return Alsace-Lorraine to France and cede three small border districts to Belgium, after the holding of a plebiscite to determine the wishes of the population.'A plebiscite was also to be held in Schleswig, as a result of which a large northern strip was transferred to Denmark in 1920, while a smaller southern area remained with Germany. In addition, the coal-rich Saar district was to be internationalized and governed by the League of Nations. At the end of fifteen years, a plebiscite was to decide whether the Saar should be returned to Germany or joined with France. Meanwhile, "as compensation for the destruction of the coal mines in the north of France and as part payment towards the total reparations due from Germany," all the coal mines of the Saar were to be handed to France "in full and absolute possession."

In the east, the territorial losses were even more extensive. To re-create an independent Poland with free access to the Baltic, the provinces of Poznan and West Prussia, which Prussia had acquired in the eighteenth century, were to be turned over to Poland. Danzig was to become a free city, under the protection of the League of Nations, with special port privileges reserved for Poland. East Prussia was thus physically separated from the rest of Germany, even though Poland guaranteed free passage to persons and goods over its territory. This Polish Corridor, as it came to be called, was to become an international irritant in the interwar period, much like the East German strip between West Berlin and the Federal Republic of Germany after World War II. Furthermore, Germany had to cede the Memel district, which the League of Nations eventually awarded to Lithuania, and had to submit to plebiscites in large sections of East Prussia, which, however, resulted in no territorial losses. Finally, plebiscites were to decide the disposition of Upper Silesia, which was meanwhile occupied by French troops. When the voting in 1921 favored Germany, the Polish minority, tacitly encouraged by the French occupation forces, rose in rebellion. The League of Nations eventually made a decision that was greatly resented in Germany. The bulk of the land and population of Upper Silesia was awarded to Germany, but Poland was given most of the mines and industrial complexes (see Map 14).

Despite Wilson's Fifth Point, urging "a free, open-minded, and absolutely impartial adjustment of all colonial claims . . . ," the Treaty of Versailles deprived Germany of all its overseas possessions, which were turned into mandates of the League of Nations, occupied and governed by various Allied powers. The total loss of their colonial empire created severe resentment among many Germans, even though the colonies had been more of a drain on the imperial budget than a boon to the economy. Deprivation of the empire was largely a blow to the German ego, a toppling from among the ranks of world powers.

As a preliminary step toward implementing Wilson's Fourth Point, reducing national armaments "to the lowest point consistent with domestic safety," the Treaty of Versailles sought to destroy the German war machine. The German armed forces were to be reduced to 100,000 men, including a maximum of 4000 officers, by March 31, 1920 at the latest. There was to be no

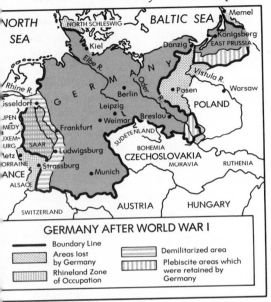

MAP 14

conscription. Enlisted men were to serve a minimum of twelve years, officers at least twenty-five; thus the Germans could not secretly train a large reserve by arranging for a rapid turnover of personnel. The German General Staff was to be abolished. Germany was to have no military planes, tanks, or poisonous gases; the number and size of guns was to be limited; the size of the navy was to be restricted; and no submarines were to be allowed. To safeguard France and Belgium, a strip of thirty miles east of the Rhine was to remain forever demilitarized, without fortifications and without military installations of any type. Finally, to ensure that Germany abided by these limitations, an Inter-Allied Commission of Control was to be established in Berlin, entitled to inspect German military matters at its discretion.

ECONOMIC AND PUNITIVE CLAUSES Besides the territorial and military clauses, the treaty contained many sections

dealing with economics, most of them connected with the matter of reparations. "To enable the Allied and Associated Powers to proceed at once to the restoration of their industrial and economic life," 'Germany was to pay five billion dollars in the first two years. Meanwhile the Reparations Commission would assess by May 1921 the total payments required from Germany to compensate "for all damage done to the civilian population of the Allied and Associated Powers and to their property." The Germans were thus forced to sign, as it were, a blank check for an unspecified amount. They were also to deliver specific raw materials, such as coal and lumber, and surrender to the Allies their foreign assets as well as the bulk of their merchant marine. In addition, they were to build ships for the Allies, and permit Allied vessels to navigate freely on all German rivers.

The variety of punitive and special provisions inflamed the German temper as much as, if not more than, the material losses. "As a guarantee for the execution of the present Treaty by Germany," Belgian, British, American, and French troops were to occupy the western portion of the Rhineland, together with bridgeheads on the right bank of the river, for a period of fifteen years. Also, Germany was required to recognize the independence of Austria, Czechoslovakia, and Poland. While such recognition appears self-evident in line with international law, it was aimed at preventing Germany and Austria from merging, even if the two German-speaking states should desire it, unless special consent were given by the Council of the League of Nations.

To justify the demand for repara-

tions and to mark Germany in the eyes of world opinion, the Allies inserted Article 231 into the treaty—the so-called guilt clause. It placed on Germany and its allies the responsibility for causing "all the loss and damage," and stated that the war had been imposed on the Allied powers "by the aggression of Germany and her allies." The Allies indicted Emperor William "for a supreme offense against international morality and the sanctity of treaties," in view of the violation of Belgian neutrality, and demanded the trial of persons "accused of having committed acts in violation of the laws and customs of war." On the basis of these clauses, England's prime minister, Lloyd George, tried to negotiate William's extradition from Holland so that he could be tried before a special tribunal of five judges, one each from Great Britain, France, Italy, United States, and Japan. Probably to the secret relief of the Allies, who were thus spared possible embarrassment, Queen Wilhelmina declined to extradite the former emperor. Since the German government also refused to surrender to the Allies any of the Germans whom the victors sought to arraign before military tribunals, a compromise was eventually arranged whereby the German Supreme Court at Leipzig was to try the accused. Of the 900 who appeared on the Allied list, the Germans eventually prosecuted 12 and pronounced 6 guilty.

Finally the treaty contained various petty stipulations regarding restoration of war booty from previous wars. "The trophies, archives, historical souvenirs or works of art" carried off during the Franco-Prussian War of 1870 were to be restored to France within six months. Also the "skull of the Sultan Mkwawa," which the Germans had taken from their former East African colony, was to be handed over to the British government.

Apart from the obvious economic consequences, the Treaty of Versailles produced far-reaching repercussions in Germany. Only the realization of their military impotence and the fear of civil war drove the more coolheaded legislators to advise acceptance of the treaty rather than risk reopening the war, as Hindenburg was willing to do. But those Socialists and Centrists who in the end accepted the treaty, albeit as an inescapable disaster, became saddled with the onus of having "betrayed Germany." Throughout the period of the Weimar Republic, denunciation of the so-called *Diktat* (dictated peace) of Versailles became the emotional shibboleth of the conservative parties. The "November criminals" who had perpetrated the stab in the back were now linked with the "red and black traitors" (Socialists and Catholics) who had signed the shameful peace. There is no question among historians that the Treaty of Versailles was not a wise peace. But its wisdom or folly is less important than what the Germans chose to make of it. From its inception the Weimar Republic suffered under the burden of the treaty, and Hitler rode to power on the promise of undoing it.

The Weimar Constitution

A month after the signing of the Treaty of Versailles, the Constituent Assembly enacted its republican constitution. It was an impeccably democratic document, with long sections devoted to guarantees of civil rights. It created a lower house, still called the *Reichs-*

tag, the delegates to which "were to represent the entire people."[1] They were to be elected by universal, equal, direct, and secret ballot, at least once every four years, on a basis of proportional representation. The voters were to select their representatives by party lists, a system that made the party organizations more important than the political merits of the individual candidates. The system of proportional representation, practiced in many other European democracies, entailed the advantage of providing a voice for all political views, but it also encouraged the formation of countless splinter parties that were to become a scourge for the Weimar Republic and one of the causes of its political instability.

The upper house, or *Reichsrat,* was composed of delegates from the German states (*Länder*), which had been reduced from 25 to 18 by the amalgamation of 8 small central states into the single state of Thuringia. The separate states were allowed considerably fewer powers than they had enjoyed under the Bismarckian system. As a result the new Reichsrat could exercise little substantive authority. The Weimar constitution, although retaining the federal system, entrusted far more power —executive, legislative, judicial, as well as financial—to the central government than had the Constitution of 1871.

The president of the Reich was chosen for a term of seven years in direct elections "by the entire German people." Only in Friedrich Ebert's case was an exception made; the Constituent Assembly simply confirmed his provisional title of President without resorting to a formal national election. The president's powers were considerably less than those previously held by the emperor. For every action, he needed the countersignature of the Reich chancellor or of the cabinet officer concerned. He could be removed by a two-thirds vote of the Reichstag in conjunction with a popular referendum. Yet the president's influence over the affairs of the Reich remained considerable. It was his duty to appoint the chancellor, who, together with the cabinet, acted as the real executive. As is true of any parliamentary system, the chancellor and his ministers had to "enjoy the confidence of the Reichstag during their tenure of office." But in spite of this requirement of a vote of confidence, his power to choose the chancellor made the president quite important, particularly when it is recalled that Germany suffered twenty changes of cabinets in the period from 1919 to 1933.

Probably the most famous article of the constitution was Article 48, which dealt with the president's emergency powers. It empowered the president to compel a state government, if necessary with the help of the armed forces, "to fulfill the duties incumbent upon it." Similarly, if "public safety and order are seriously disturbed or imperiled," the president could employ the armed forces to restore order and could "temporarily suspend" the fundamental civil rights guaranteed by the constitution. Countless commentaries have been written about this Article 48, which has been denounced as containing the fatal seed that would later destroy the republic. Since it was employed over 200 times and ultimately abused to such a degree that it helped pave the way for Hitler's dictatorship, the article itself has been blamed as the lethal flaw in the constitution. Significantly, the present Bonn consti-

tution contains no similar clause. Yet Article 48 was hedged with numerous safeguards giving the Reichstag power to repeal the emergency measures of the president. It is not the fault of the constitution that during most of the Weimar period, the Reichstag lacked the required working majorities essential to make the safeguards effective. Moreover, one must recall that the constitution was framed at a time of extreme instability. Attacks from the Right and the Left were threatening the existence of the republic. Just as French President Charles de Gaulle included a similar emergency clause in his 1958 constitution for the Fifth French Republic to deal with the threats to the republic, so the framers of the Weimar Constitution felt the need for such provisions.

The Weimar Parties

In many respects, the political parties of the Weimar period resembled those that had developed during the empire, with two exceptions: more parties existed, and their number kept on increasing as new groups splintered off from existing organizations; and the more extremist parties tended to gain in strength at the expense of those with more moderate programs (see Chart 2). On the extreme Left was the Communist party (KPD), the former Spartacist League. It openly followed instructions from the Third International and advocated Communist policies as laid down in Moscow. The Communists boycotted the elections to the Constituent Assembly, but thereafter presented themselves at the polls, although they never participated in a coalition cabinet. Between 1924 and 1930, their voting strength hovered at around 10 percent, until it rose somewhat after 1930, in the dying years of the republic.

The Independent Socialist party (USPD), which as we saw had been formally organized in 1917, enjoyed a brief but important existence. After helping to run the provisional government immediately after the November Revolution, the USPD members refused to serve in further cabinets, in view of their opposition to the Majority Socialists' flirtation with the conservative forces. But they polled 2 million votes in 1919 and 5 million in 1920, briefly emerging as the second strongest party in the Reich. They supported the government in the crucial days of 1919 and 1920 when it was attacked from the Right and the Left, and helped push through the Reichstag acceptance of the colossal reparations bill presented by the Reparations Commission in 1921. Yet the meteoric rise of the USPD was reversed as suddenly as it had started. After 1922, most of the Independents rejoined the Majority Socialists, while a few of the more doctrinaire went over to the Communists. The USPD ceased to exist after 1924, when it polled a mere 98,000 votes.

The Majority Socialists (SPD), despite the loss of members to the KPD and the USPD, remained the largest party in the Reich until 1932, when it was suddenly surpassed by Hitler's National Socialists. But it is significant that the SPD was the largest party only in the sense that it polled a few more votes than any other single group. It obtained by no means a majority of the votes. From a high of 38 percent of the votes cast in 1919, it quickly dropped to 21 percent in 1920 and remained around this percentage ex-

Chart 2 THE POLITICAL BAROMETER OF THE WEIMAR REPUBLIC

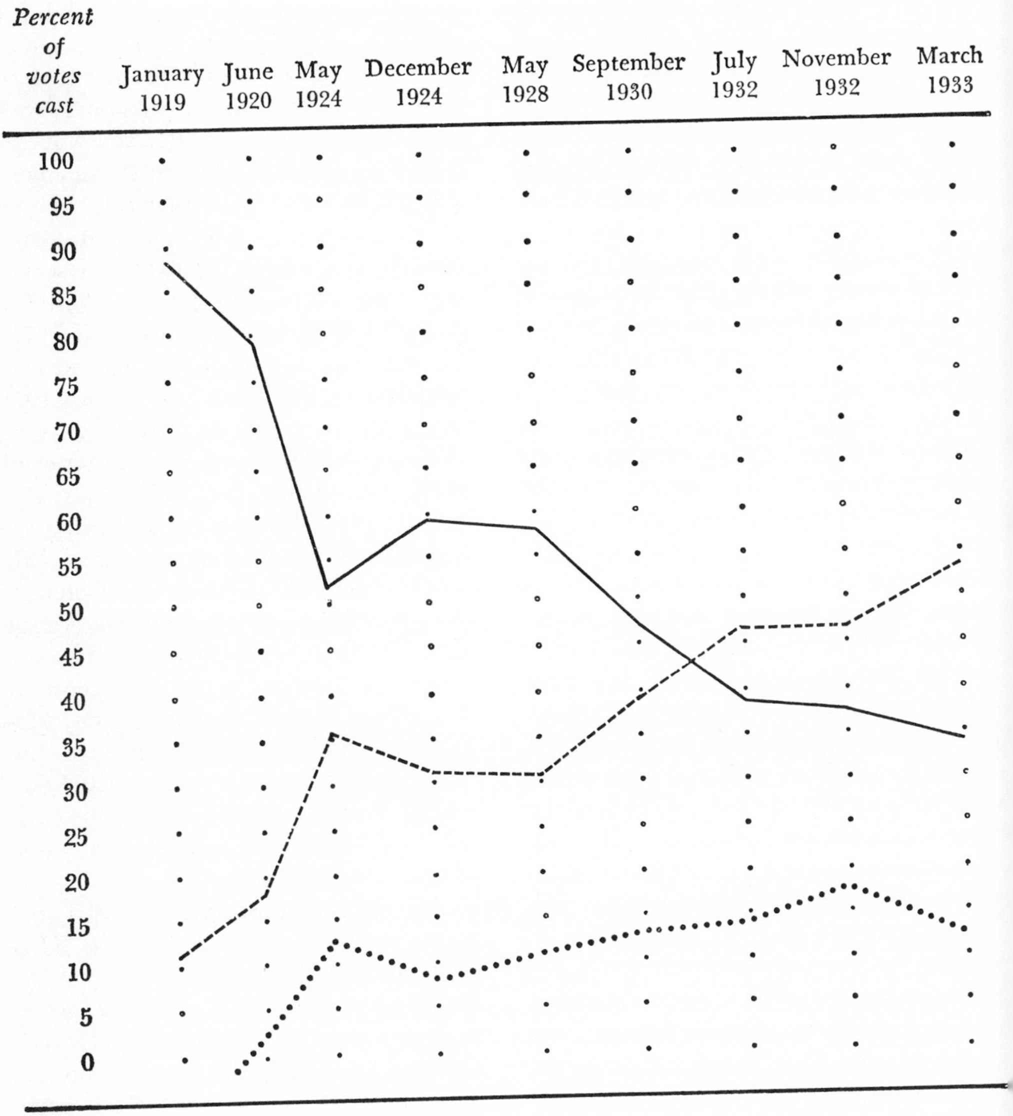
Percent of votes cast
January 1919
June 1920
May 1924
December 1924
May 1928
September 1930
July 1932
November 1932
March 1933
100
95
90
85
80
75
70
65
60
55
50
45
40
35
30
25
20
15
10
5
0

•••••••••••••••• The extreme left (Communist party)

———————— The moderate parties, supporting Weimar (Socialists, Centrists, Bavarian People's party, Democrats, German People's party)

---------------- The anti-Weimar parties of the right (German National People's party, National Socialists, Economic party, and other conservative splinter groups)

cept for a mild rise in the later 1920s. The failure of the Socialists to obtain a majority can be attributed not only to the existence of too many parties and the system of proportional representation, but also to the idealistic policies of the Socialist leaders. In a way, Ebert and Scheidemann were the founders of the republic, but although they were Socialists, they created no Socialist republic. By refusing to institute a program of nationalization, even though it was demanded by many of the rank and file in their party, by aligning themselves with the conservative forces of law and order, and by permitting the army to fire on the workers, the SPD lost much of its appeal among the proletariat, as evinced in the election results of 1920. Another explanation for this loss of popularity lies in the social structure of Germany and in the temper of the times. Unlike its counterpart in Soviet Russia, the German middle class represented the dominant element and was in no mood for further revolutionary experiments. The shock of the Treaty of Versailles, for which the Socialists were unjustly blamed, disillusioned the electorate. As the electoral results of the 1920s clearly show, either the middle class longed for a return to normalcy and voted for middle-of-the-road parties, or it was filled with nationalistic indignation and voted for the rapidly rising conservative parties. At any rate, the SPD lost control of the chancellorship in June 1920 and, with the exception of the period 1928–1930, was never again to recapture it. Until 1923, the SPD served in most cabinets, but thereafter, again except for 1928–1930, it was not even represented in the government.

Rather than the Socialists, the real "Weimar party" was the Center, which showed remarkable electoral stability, was represented in every coalition government until 1932 and headed 9 of the 21 cabinets that ran the Weimar Republic. In 1920, the Bavarian People's party split off from the Center, to pursue a slightly more conservative course and ride its hobbyhorse of Bavarian particularism. But on most national issues it continued to cooperate with its parent body. Taken together, the Center and the Bavarian People's party consistently polled between 15 and 20 percent of the votes cast. As was true during the empire, the Center remained a polygenetic party, held together loosely by the Catholicism of its members. Its political orientation is difficult to define. It supported the Weimar Republic and the latter's democratic ideals, but its basic philosophy, initially somewhat left of center, veered to the right in the mid-twenties and gradually turned increasingly conservative.

Another "Weimar party" was the German Democratic party (DDP), formed in November 1918 by remnants of the former Progressives and the more liberal segments of the National Liberal party. It included doctrinaire liberals as well as idealists and humanitarians. During the political crisis provoked by the necessity of signing the Treaty of Versailles, the DDP withdrew from the government, but thereafter was represented in every cabinet between 1919 and 1931. Since this party helped constitute the backbone of the democratic institutions of the Weimar Republic, the history of its attraction to the voters is of interest. The DDP polled 5.5 million votes, 18.6 percent of those cast, in the 1919 elections to the National Assembly. As early as

1920, it dropped to 2.3 million votes or only 8.3 percent. Thereafter it gradually dwindled to less than 4 percent by 1930. To stress its increasingly nationalistic attitude, it changed its name to German State party, but even this did not help its survival. By 1932, it reached a low of only 1 percent of the votes cast, permitting it merely two delegates in the Reichstag.

Considerably to the right in the political spectrum was the new German People's party (DVP), with its leader Gustav Stresemann (1878–1929). This party represented business and industry, and embraced the bulk of the conservative wing of the former National Liberal party. Its orientation was at heart monarchist, but once the republic seemed more or less firmly established, Stresemann and his party supported it to the best of their ability. The DVP became the fourth largest party in 1920, gaining almost 14 percent of the votes cast, and it had representatives in every cabinet from 1920 to 1931. But it is symptomatic of the fate of the Weimar Republic that this party, too, lost its popularity with the voters. By 1930, it was down to 4.5 percent and continued to decline thereafter.

Among the truly conservative parties was the important German National People's party (DNVP), monarchist and ultraconservative in aspirations, representing big industry and the Prussian landlords. It opposed the very existence of the Weimar Republic and freely supported all oppositional ventures from the extreme Right, particularly the Free Corps and other nationalist and racialist groups. The DNVP grew rapidly during the early years of the republic. In 1924, it obtained over 6 million votes, and became the second largest party, the backbone of all opposition to democratic government, to compliance with the terms of Versailles, and to cooperation with the Allies. In the ensuing years of relative political and economic stability, it lost considerable strength. Although it rebounded somewhat in the dying years of the republic, it lost many adherents to Hitler's National Socialists, a group that was far more fanatic, far more conservative, and far more tightly organized than the DNVP.

The National Socialist party (NSDAP), which ultimately toppled the republic, will be dealt with in detail in the subsequent chapter. It is enough to note here that when the NSDAP first presented itself at the polls in 1924, it drew just under 2 million votes. In 1930, it suddenly emerged as the second largest party, and by July 1932, it received almost twice as many votes as the Socialists and became by far the largest party in Germany, with its 37.4 percent of the vote.

In addition to these nine major parties, the Weimar Republic was plagued by countless splinter groups, many of which attracted enough voters to qualify for representation in the Reichstag: the Economic party, the Christian-Social People's Service, the League of Landlords, the Christian National Peasants' and Agriculturalists' Popular party, the German Hanoverian party, the German Social party, the German Peasant party, the Christian People's party, and numerous others, some of which operated only at the state (*Land*) level. These parties represented social and economic interests, and most of them were at the far Right of the political arena. Their mere existence helped to proliferate political allegiances and imperil governmental stability.

The existence of these multifarious

parties necessitated the formation of coalitions to obtain parliamentary majorities in the Reichstag. The result was a merry-go-round of cabinets, similar to that experienced by the French Republic in the years after World War II. Of the twenty-one cabinets between 1919 and 1932, the most stable stayed in office twenty-one months, in the period of relative quietude of 1928 and 1929. Most cabinets survived barely a few months.

The Burdens of the Young Republic

The preceding analysis of the basis of the Weimar Republic highlights the burdens imposed upon it, and in part explains its ultimate failure. The Weimar Republic was born without much planning or preparation, almost as if by accident, and was largely the consequence of the military collapse at the end of the war. It was greeted with indifference by large segments of the German population and soon lost the support of many of the workers and most of the lower middle classes. After the disillusionment of the Treaty of Versailles, it faced the onslaught of oppositional forces that, fortified by the legend of the stab in the back, saw in the republic little more than a symbol of shame and national disgrace. The relative lack of experience with truly democratic forms, the failure to break significantly with the past, the disappearance—largely through assassination—of many of its more forceful and imaginative leaders, and the economic and financial disasters of the early 1920s turned the republican framework into a thin veneer hiding the cancer of discontent and disillusionment. In addition, the victorious powers of World War I, particularly France, showed little understanding of

or sympathy for the sensibilities of Germany's new democracy, and thereby contributed considerably to the ultimate victory of the antidemocratic forces within the Reich.

THE YEARS OF UNREST, 1919–1924

Political Instability

The first five years of the republic revealed an alarming instability in the new regime. Governmental coalitions were patched together at frequent intervals, but none proved viable. Of the twelve cabinets between 1919 and 1924, only two lasted about a year; seven others survived less than six months. Only one of these cabinet changes resulted from normal political causes: the realignment of parties after the election of 1920, requiring the formation of a new cabinet. All other changes arose from resignations caused by internal attacks from right- or left-wing extremists or from repercussions of the Treaty of Versailles—the loss of Upper Silesia, the announcement of reparations schedules, French occupation of the Ruhr, and other national calamities provoked largely by French interpretation of that treaty.

"The shameful dictate of Versailles" —coupled with the legend of the stab in the back, with fear of communism, and with the disillusionment of demobilized veterans—produced, as we have noted, a strong resurgence of extreme conservatism and nationalism. This was evident in the electoral results of the period 1920–1924 as well as in the formation of numerous small groups of extreme nationalists, dedicated to anti-Semitism, anti-Bolshevism, the annihilation of democracy, and the abrogation of the Treaty of Versailles.

One such group, founded in 1919, was the German Worker's party, which later became the National Socialist German Workers' party (NSDAP) and which Hitler turned into his instrument for power. This antidemocratic mood provided the background for a series of attempts to overthrow the young republic from the Right and replace it by some type of dictatorial regime.

THE KAPP PUTSCH Among the more spectacular of these attempts was the Kapp *Putsch* of March 1920. A small group of army and naval officers, led by General Walther von Lüttwitz (1859–1942) and encouraged by Ludendorff, and groups of old-line conservatives brought together by the same Wolfgang Kapp who had sponsored the German Fatherland party in 1917 (see page 183) decided to overthrow the national government. As their shock troops, they enlisted the aid of a disaffected army brigade, which (under the command of its captain, Hermann Erhardt) acted more like a Free Corps than a unit of the regular army. Its members had fought as a Free Corps against the Communists in Poland during 1919, and were now threatened with unemployment, since the brigade was marked for disbandment in accordance with the disarmament clauses of the peace treaty. Hence they were readily persuaded to try to topple the government. The prospect of such an insurrection was welcomed by many conservatives, who, however, cautiously withheld overt support until its outcome could be foreseen.

When the insurrectionists marched on Berlin, the government requested the commanders of the regular army to organize the defense of the capital. Their reply was ominous for the future of the republic. Although willing to fight against Communist mutinies, they rejected the suggestion of dispatching the *Reichswehr* (regular army units) against fellow soldiers, albeit rebellious ones. The flaw in the Ebert-Groener bargain of 1918 (see page 193) at once became apparent. The army had agreed to support the government against the extreme Left, but had expressed no similar willingness in the case of attacks from the Right.

Left without armed support, President Ebert and the Socialist chancellor Gustav Bauer (1870–1944) appealed to the workers and to members of the SPD to "paralyze the economic life" of the nation by a general and complete strike and to "strangle the reactionary clique and fight with all available means against the return of William II." The members of the government then fled from the capital in order to escape possible imprisonment. Unhindered by police and regular army, the insurrectionists seized Berlin and announced the formation of a new government under the dictatorship of Kapp. But the workers rose to the defense of the Weimar Republic. Socialist, Catholic, and Independent unions called a general strike, which was also supported by the liberal and left-wing parties. Only the Communists withheld cooperation: chaos and revolution were favored by Lenin as means of achieving Communist ends. The general strike was extremely successful. Life in the capital came to a halt, and communications stood still. Kapp proved incapable of imposing his dictatorship on a passive population. After a few days he fled and was eventually jailed. Ebert and the cabinet returned to Berlin and persuaded the workers to return to their jobs. The Kapp *Putsch* had failed.

But the rapid collapse of the in-

surrection hardly concealed the sickness of the regime. It is symptomatic that the government did not profit from the experience. To be sure, a new chancellor, Hermann Müller (1876–1931), was installed, and Noske, who had shown his incapability of controlling the armed forces, was dismissed as minister of war. But the SPD leadership, still in command of a majority of the electorate, failed to placate the workers, who had stood fast against the "Baltic lansquenets" and the "military dictatorship." Labor demanded action on a program of nationalizing heavy industry, democratizing the civil service, and substituting a popular militia for the Free Corps and the *Reichswehr*. The government made promises, but in the end met none of the demands. It appeared that even the Kapp *Putsch* did not modify Ebert's overriding fear of sovietization. Of course, it should again be pointed out that Ebert's choice of action was limited. He could hardly have launched a determined fight against the Right so long as he required the army's support to remain in power. The Kapp *Putsch* had shown that the military could not be trusted to act forcefully against conservatism. On the other hand, army and Free Corps could always be relied on to crush risings of the radical Left. When violent Communist uprisings in the Ruhr followed on the heels of the Kapp *Putsch* in the spring of 1920, Ebert found no hesitation among the military when he dispatched them to subdue the rebellion.

Yet Ebert might conceivably have shown more foresight by at least attempting to bring the army into stricter obedience to the government. Instead, in March 1920, he transferred the command of the *Reichswehr* to the highly controversial General von Seeckt, who had been chief of the *Truppenamt* since November 1919. An excellent organizer and administrator, Seeckt was a stanch conservative and an admirer of power politics (see page 214) who believed that "the flourishing of the nation is inseparably tied to the *Reichswehr*," and decried as stupid the slogan "Never again war!" Above all, he hoped to build up the army. Since his plans contravened the Treaty of Versailles, he had to proceed secretly. Hence he hoped the military would, for the time being, stay apart from the political convulsions of the country and he ordered his officers to keep out of politics under threat of expulsion from the army.

The Communist uprisings in the Ruhr were widely supported by non-Communist workers. They were crushed mercilessly by the army and the Free Corps, an event that further disillusioned the proletariat about their government. The hapless republic, fighting against both extremes, was thus faced with a constantly shrinking base of power. And the French gleefully added to its troubles. Although the French government would hardly have welcomed the establishment of communism in the Rhineland, it insisted that the Germans had violated the Treaty of Versailles by sending troops into the demilitarized zone. In reprisal, French troops occupied Frankfurt on the Main and some towns in the Ruhr for a period of six weeks. The effect on Germany was a further weakening of the government's prestige and an increase of power for the vociferous nationalists.

Armed attacks on the republic from Left and Right continued during the next years at a subdued pace, until they flared up with greater violence

in the troubled year 1923. The friction with France over reparations and the Franco-Belgian occupation of the Ruhr, coupled with runaway inflation, brought the Weimar Republic to the brink of dissolution by the autumn of that year. Supported by French and Belgian troops, a new wave of separatism, similar to the movement that had failed in 1919, swept over the Rhineland. Pro-French elements established a Rhineland Republic, claiming independence from Prussia. The movement ultimately collapsed in January 1924. Meanwhile Saxony went temporarily Communist, and a monarchical restoration was plotted in Bavaria. The famous Beer Hall *Putsch* of November 1923, in which Hitler and his National Socialists, supported by Ludendorff (who seemed to be present any time there was a chance to overthrow the republic from the Right), attempted unsuccessfully to gain control of the Bavarian government, was but one more in a series of attacks on the Weimar Republic. And the government's actions in each case were similar. The attacks from the left were crushed ruthlessly, while Hitler, for example, was jailed for less than a year.

POLITICAL MURDER   Political instability also manifested itself in the inability of the government to ferret out subversive elements and maintain law and order. In the summer of 1920, the government was finally able to comply with Allied demands that the Free Corps be outlawed. This was possible because General Seeckt, as a strict disciplinarian, disapproved of the Free Corps with their relish for personal allegiance rather than for military obedience. The army therefore withdrew its tacit support from the Free Corps. But even after they were officially disbanded, many of them continued to flourish under various disguises, such as gymnastic clubs, trucking firms, or other cover organizations. They could thus retain their weapons and their *esprit de corps,* and be ready to engage in street fighting when it seemed opportune. Frustrated in gaining their immediate objective of overthrowing the republic, some of these organizations specialized in political murders. In secret meetings, they condemned to death leaders who, because of leftist leanings or willingness to fulfill the obligations imposed upon Germany by the Treaty of Versailles, had become "traitors to the fatherland." As Rosa Luxemburg and Karl Liebknecht had been shot in 1919, and Hugo Haase, the leader of the USPD, murdered shortly thereafter, so the roll call of death continued in the early 1920s. Matthias Erzberger, the former leader of the Center, who had accepted the armistice terms, was shot in 1921, and even his widow continued to be persecuted by the nationalist fanatics with written threats to desecrate the tomb of her husband. These same elements tried to intimidate government ministers with letters threatening to execute all "traitors" who accepted the imposed reparations and complied with Versailles. Walter Rathenau, who had helped organize the German war effort in 1914 and served as foreign minister in 1922, was assassinated in the heart of Berlin. Similarly, the leader of the separatist Rhineland Republic was murdered in January 1924. Besides these party leaders, innumerable lesser known liberals fell victims to political assassination.

The government seemed incapable

of stemming the activities of these fanatic exterminators, the forerunners, as it were, of Hitler's Gestapo. The Centrist chancellor Joseph Wirth (1879–1956) might complain in 1922 to the Reichstag that the ultraconservatives were "plunging Germany into an atmosphere of murder," and the "political morality of the jungle"; he might exclaim: "There is the enemy, . . . dropping his poison into the wounds of the nation . . . and there can be no doubt, the enemy is on the right." But in the final analysis, nothing was done to stop the erosion. The conservative judiciary, with its allegiance still halfway in the empire of William II, constantly meted out lenient sentences to those trying to assassinate the republic from the Right, while proceeding severely against similar offenses by left-wing elements.

Financial Instability and the Question of Reparations

Economically and financially, Germany emerged exhausted from World War I. The labor force was undernourished and reduced, the soil lay depleted, and raw materials were in short supply. Deficit financing during the war and the sharp decline in production of consumer goods had inflated prices and depreciated the German mark. The losses in territory, population, productive capacity, and raw materials resulting from the Treaty of Versailles, as well as from social unrest of the immediate postwar period, further aggravated the dislocation of the national economy.

THE DILEMMA OF REPARATIONS Besides suffering from the consequences of war and defeat and from short-

sighted imperial financial policies, the economy wobbled under the indeterminate reparations claims of the Allies. Versailles had, in fact, presented Germany with a blank bill. Neither methods of payment nor a total and final amount had been stipulated. Hence neither the German government nor the business community could—if they had wished to—devise meaningful plans for settling their obligations. Initially, the Germans simply surrendered to the Allies the small gold reserves they had left, together with foreign assets, manufactured goods, and quantities of remaining raw materials. Meanwhile the Reparations Commission held interminable conferences to bring order to the Allied demands. At various meetings during 1920 and 1921 —at Spa, Paris, and London—the Allies agreed on a division of the spoils. France was to receive 52 percent of the total, the British Empire 22 percent, with the remaining 26 percent to be divided among Italy, Belgium, and other nations. The United States demanded no share. The Allies tacitly accepted the French proposal of sanctions against Germany if it should default on the imposed payments, and finally arrived at a total bill of 33 billion dollars, in gold marks as well as reparations in kind, to be paid over a period of thirty years.

This staggering demand produced an immediate government crisis in Berlin. The semiconservative German People's party resigned, forcing the formation of a new cabinet in which, significantly, a major role was again played by the Social Democrats, one of the few parties willing to accept the onerous obligations of defeat. The Allies threatened to invade the Ruhr unless Germany accepted the repara-

tions bill. Hence the new cabinet signed the schedule of payments and promptly borrowed 250 million gold dollars in London in order to pay the first installment under the new arrangement.

Borrowing from the Allies in order to pay reparations or floating bonds in Allied capitals for similar purposes became one of the customary ways in which Germany paid some of the reparation demands. Similarly, foreign speculators, especially Americans, invested heavily in Germany, buying up German industrial shares, real estate, and paper marks. Between 1919 and 1922, about 1 billion dollars flowed into German hands, which the government turned over to the Allies as reparations. Considering in addition the complicated picture of inter-Allied loans contracted during the war, in which the United States and Great Britain alone had each loaned out some 7 billion dollars, one can get some idea of the intricacies of international finance during this period.

But Germany did not pay reparations merely out of Allied investments and loans. It transferred to the Allies railroads, real estate, buildings, equipment, ships, and raw materials in the ceded territories, and it also made annual deliveries of coal, chemicals, timber, ships, rolling stock, machinery, and vast quantities of other supplies demanded by the Allies for the reconstruction of their industries. These payments in kind produced further economic problems inside Germany, and led to sharp discord with the Allies, since no agreement could be reached on their exact value. Germany's inflation was continuing and the mark was further depreciating. Whereas before the war, the ratio of the mark

to the dollar had been 4 to 1, and 8 to 1 by early 1919, it stood near 250 to 1 by late 1921. Under these conditions, the assessed value of deliveries in kind varied considerably between Allies and Germans. For the first three postwar years, the Germans calculated the value of total payments in kind at 10 billion, whereas the Reparations Commission set their book value at only 2 billion dollars.

Accepting the lower assessment of the Reparations Commission, France constantly accused the Germans of being in arrears with deliveries. In March 1921, the French seized Düsseldorf and surrounding towns in reprisal against Germany's defaulting on its deliveries, a charge heatedly denied by the Germans. During 1922, Franco-German friction over reparations became more acute. The German mark began to collapse. By August it stood at almost 2000 to the dollar, and the Reparations Commission agreed to grant a temporary moratorium on payments and deliveries. Great Britain, growing gradually more sympathetic to Germany, offered to cancel all war debts and withdraw all reparations demands, provided the Allies, in particular the United States, would do the same. The response of the United States to this proposal is well summarized through President Coolidge's succinct remark "They hired the money, didn't they?" Since the United States refused to cancel any debts—agreeing only to lower interest rates and lengthened periods of repayment—the Allies continued to press for reparations from Germany. England and France had already lost heavily when Lenin had repudiated all Russian debts, and France, in particular, was in no mood to accommodate the Germans. Prime

Minister Poincaré's whole policy of reconstruction was based on expectation of German payments. Despite British pleas for reasonableness and Italian proposals for a compromise, Poincaré was willing to grant a moratorium on reparations payments only in return for French acquisition of German factories and mines. On this basis he thought France could satisfy some of its demands for deliveries in kind and prevent Germany from completely defaulting on reparations.

OCCUPATION OF THE RUHR AND RUNAWAY INFLATION   England and France began to differ sharply on the issue of reparations. The Entente Cordiale was crumbling, giving some Germans the hope of ending the years of "encirclement" and regaining a place among the western powers. But Poincaré remained adamant. In December 1922, he declared Germany in default in deliveries of coal and timber, and in January 1923, he sent French and Belgian troops to occupy the Ruhr and operate the German mines and factories for the benefit of France. England refused to participate in these measures and, in fact, criticized the French action.

The Franco-Belgian occupation of the Ruhr became the high point in the reparations drama, and led to the final collapse of the German economy and the German mark. Moreover, it dangerously undermined the weak underpinning of the Weimar Republic by rousing German nationalism to a feverish pitch and indirectly leading to the ruination of the middle class.

Unable to resist the invasion militarily, the German government ordered passive resistance. Once again the workers showed their loyalty to the Berlin government by heeding this call for a general strike. They refused to work for their new French masters, sabotaged the factories, and occasionally even attacked French occupation units. Only a few Rhinelanders cooperated with the occupiers and aided the abortive attempt to establish a separate Rhineland Republic. On the whole, the French reaped little but trouble. Unable to count on the local labor force, they had to use troops to operate the mines and factories, and in the end acquired few worthwhile economic benefits. Perhaps the only boon was the lesson that such peremptory treatment of Germany paid no dividends, a lesson that paved the way for the more cooperative spirit marking the subsequent years.

Passive resistance entailed for the Germans not only unemployment and famine but also runaway inflation. To meet its obligations and support the unemployed in the Ruhr, the government printed money without regard to its backing. Once this started on a grand scale, prices soared and the inflation ran amuck. By summer, prices were rising ten- or a hundredfold in a single day. Incapable of printing new money with sufficient speed, government presses overprinted old denominations by adding zeros in red. A 100-mark bill of one day became a million-mark bill of the next. Finally, city governments issued their own emergency money (*Notgeld*), printed on silk, leather, linen, or whatever was at hand, and permission to overprint was granted to reputable private concerns throughout the country, as money lost value so rapidly that it might be worthless by the time it was shipped from Berlin to other areas of the nation. It was the time when housewives had

to shop many times a day, since a pound of butter costing 100,000 marks in the morning might cost 500,000 in the afternoon. These were also the days of the warm beer, when customers ordered two steins at a time, since the price might go up while they drank their first one. By November, a week's subscription to a Berlin newspaper cost 500 billion marks. In the end, paper money lost all value, except as a souvenir of frightening times. When the inflation ended and money again was stabilized, the rate of exchange was to be 1 trillion of the old marks for a single new one.

Much has been written about this inflation, and many false accusations have been made. To say that the German government inflated its currency to pay off reparations at a cheaper rate is an economic fallacy. The inflation. had started long before the occupation of the Ruhr. The latter merely sent it on a gallop toward collapse. The transfer of payments as reparations could not be made in German marks, anyway, whether inflated or normal, unless these marks were backed by gold or productive capacity. The Allies could hardly have been expected to welcome the receipt of billions of paper marks unless these could be used for purchasing German goods. Hence it was German productive capacity and not German paper money that alone could pay off the reparations debt. Inflation helped the government solely by reducing its internal debt and by allowing it to pay less for the labor and other production costs of the goods delivered to the Allies as reparations in kind.

Part of the cause of the inflation was the government's inherited reluctance to raise taxes. Reconstruction, social services, welfare schemes, municipal improvements—including the ubiquitous public swimming pools for the lower classes—were financed largely through deficit spending. New demands were met through an increase in paper money rather than by an increase in taxes. At the same time, the growing supply of money was not balanced by an enlarged reservoir of production. On the contrary, deliveries in kind decreased the availability of these goods on the home market, thereby further cheapening money and again driving up the cost of living. The unstable cabinets between 1919 and 1922 lacked the strength to put a drastic end to this vicious circle by increasing taxes and decreasing the amount of paper money in circulation. The Franco-Belgian occupation of the Ruhr added to the financial deterioration. Sequestration of the Ruhr industries further lowered Germany's productive capacity and the amount of goods available, while, on the other hand, the printing presses produced more and more paper money to finance the added relief burdens assumed by the government. One cannot know with certainty whether in the end the galloping inflation completely escaped the control of the wobbly Berlin cabinet, or whether, as some have asserted, the final printing spree was a deliberate attempt on the part of Berlin to destroy the German financial structure in order to torpedo France's exploitation of the Ruhr and demonstrate to the Allies the impossibility of abiding by the reparations schedule.

Germany's International Position

The defeated nation, quite naturally faced a hostile and unsympathetic world. The attitude of the powers at Versailles had clearly shown that the

past was not to be forgotten. The pariah was not admitted to the newly created League of Nations nor allowed to participate in the early disarmament conferences. Germany remained isolated and despised, and Berlin could justly complain of constant interference by France, which did its best to antagonize Germany and, as it were, rub salt into the wounds of the defeated "Boche." By 1921, the specter of a new encirclement haunted the Foreign Office in Berlin. France signed a treaty of mutual assistance with Poland, and gave its blessing and assistance to the formation of the Little Entente by Yugoslavia, Rumania, and Czechoslovakia. The tottering Weimar Republic thus found itself in a potential east–west vise similar to that which had preceded World War I.

DESIRE FOR AN AUSTRO-GERMAN UNION
Immediately after the collapse of Austria-Hungary and Germany, there was a strong movement for the union of the two defeated states.[1] Through the establishment of the independent states of Czechoslovakia, Hungary, and Yugoslavia, and through territorial cessions to Italy, Austria had been reduced to a tiny, economically weak state with some seven million inhabitants. Surrounded by hostile neighbors, a majority of Austrians thought the only chance for survival lay in union with Germany. After adopting a republican constitution in March 1919, the Austrian National Assembly promptly voted to integrate Austria into the new German Republic. However, the Allied powers, particularly France, opposed the extension of German influence into the upper Balkans. Hence they inserted clauses expressly prohibiting an Austro-German union in the Treaties of Versailles and of St. Germain (the

peace treaty with Austria). When, despite this prohibition, the Weimar constitution included a clause that "other territories may be taken into the *Reich*, if their people desire it through the right of self-determination," the Allies forced Germany to modify the clause and again recognize Austrian independence. The Austrians' desire for union did not wane immediately. In 1921, Tyrol and Salzburg voted to apply for membership in the German federal system. Once again the Allies interfered to prevent this move. It was only after the Austrian economy recovered gradually with the help of loans by the League of Nations that the pressure for union with Germany subsided.

During the early years of the Weimar Republic, however, the question of an Austro-German union was less important than two problems that dominated the foreign policy of Germany: one dealt with the attitude toward the Treaty of Versailles and the related question of reparations; the other concerned the direction of Germany's foreign orientation.

THE ATTITUDE TOWARD VERSAILLES
The conservative and nationalistic elements in the nation sought to pressure the government into avoiding compliance with the treaty, particularly with those stipulations dealing with reparations and disarmament. Where open defiance was not possible, they advocated clandestine circumvention. The more moderate and liberal groups, on the other hand, favored at least nominal compliance. Where this was not possible, as was true of the question of reparations, they hoped to convince the Allies through a demonstration of goodwill of the impossibility of Germany's fulfilling the demands. Through this attitude, they expected

to achieve Germany's readmission into the family of nations and the resumption of a strong voice in international affairs.

Germany's actual policy wavered between these extremes in the period 1919 to 1923. The moderates were not strong enough to pursue their preferred course without constant interference by the nationalists. Only the catastrophe of 1923—the Ruhr occupation and inflation—convinced enough political leaders of the folly of continued obstructionism and allowed the government at least temporarily to adopt an avowed policy of fulfilling the obligations incurred under the Treaty of Versailles.

THE ORIENTATION OF GERMANY'S FOREIGN POLICY The same divergence of political views affected the problem of Germany's foreign orientation. The conservatives and the army, like their predecessors in the nineteenth century, favored an eastern orientation, despite the fact that Russia was now Communist. Confident that friendship with Russia would not lead to a Bolshevization of Germany, they saw in an alliance with Russia the best means of regaining the lost territories in the east and of acquiring the strength needed to stand up against French demands in the west. It is symptomatic that during the Russo-Polish War of 1920, some conservative Free Corps units fought side by side with German Communists and the Red Army against the Polish defenders of Warsaw. Lenin and his successors also favored a *rapprochement* with Germany, which they thought would help sow disunity among the capitalist nations, and add ferment to the political turmoil within the Weimar Republic.

General Seeckt, the commander of the German *Reichswehr,* was a typical and highly influential proponent of the conservative point of view. He insisted that Germany "must carry on an active foreign policy," for without it, it would cease being a state. An active and purposeful foreign policy, in his view, required a *rapprochement,* if not a treaty, with Russia. Economic relations he considered useful, but more important were political and military links that would provide Germany with an immense "accretion in power." Seeckt considered himself to be a confirmed *Realpolitiker.* He scorned those who spoke of reviving Bismarck's formula of attempting friendship with both east and west. He insisted that politics be adapted to the needs of the moment and be based on the assumption "that every state is fundamentally egoistic in its policies." And France's policy he assessed as "a policy of annihilation, pure and simple." He thought that sooner or later England would woo Germany as a counterweight to France, and that England would be even more eager for such an alliance if Germany were strengthened through alignment with Russia.

The conservatives looked upon Poland as the core of the eastern question. "Poland's existence is intolerable and incompatible with Germany's vital interests," wrote Seeckt. "She must disappear." Russia and Germany, he concluded, had a strong common interest: the annihilation of Poland, which acted as France's buttress of the Versailles Treaty in the east. Hence he proclaimed the re-establishment of the 1914 borders with Russia as Germany's primary aim in foreign policy. To obtain it, he suggested that Germany

help arm Russia, thereby strengthening a potential ally and indirectly fortifying the German army itself. Seeckt's views exerted a strong influence on Germany's policies, not only in foreign affairs, but also inside Germany, where they became the basis for German secret rearmament.

The moderate politicians, on the other hand, were wary of an eastern orientation, particularly of a military consorting with Soviet Russia. Count Ulrich von Brockdorff-Rantzau (1869–1928), chief of the German delegation to Versailles and, after 1922, German ambassador in Moscow, warned that a policy "exclusively oriented to the east" would be not only premature but dangerous. He thought that Russia could not be trusted, that Germany should not get involved in a possible war over Poland, and that an alliance with Moscow would bring no economic gains, but would merely cement the Anglo-French Entente. Granting the die-hard enmity of France, Brockdorff-Rantzau saw the best course as one of friendship with England, which before long would need German assistance against French threats. To be sure, the moderates were no more ready than the conservatives to acquiesce in a permanent loss of the eastern territories, but they advocated a wait-and-see attitude, hoping for an eventual collapse of the new Polish regime that might permit a rectification of the borders.

By 1922, the conservative outlook had won temporary ascendancy. When the powers, including Russia and Germany, met at Genoa to discuss the problem of international financial obligations, and in particular the tsarist debts that the Communist regime refused to acknowledge, the two outcast nations effected a *rapprochement*. By the Treaty of Rapallo, a resort not far from Genoa where German and Russian delegates met secretly, Berlin and Moscow agreed to resume diplomatic relations. Furthermore, the two nations canceled all mutual claims for reparations and extended to each other the most-favored-nation clause in their commercial relations. Rapallo thus marked the beginning of Germany's *rapprochement* with Russia and an end to its postwar isolation. The treaty was hailed by the conservatives as a first step toward resuming an "active foreign policy" and bewailed by the liberals as an invitation to disaster. It was soon followed by secret arrangements for military cooperation to build up the Red Army and initiate the clandestine rearmament of Germany.

The Psychology and Culture of a Defeated Nation

Since the campaigns had been fought beyond the German borders and air raids on German cities had been rare, Germany emerged from the war with little physical destruction. Moreover, by 1923 no Allied troops occupied German soil, with the exception of the left bank of the Rhine and the Ruhr. Finally, those who had run the government during the crucial years of fighting—William II and the military—had been allowed to depart with unsullied hands, without signing the onerous armistice and the treaty of 1919. It was the civilian forces of liberal republicanism that had assumed the burden of guilt and odium that, in the German mind, was associated with the defeat and the "dictate of Versailles." As the course of the Weimar Republic showed, this was a serious

blunder by Allied diplomats and strategists, who should have insisted on surrender by William II and his staff, and on a brief military occupation of Germany, to convince the Germans that they had been defeated militarily, and that the war had been partially caused by the disastrous policies of their emperor.

Failure to convince the Germans of the incontrovertible fact of military defeat not only led to the insidious theory of the stab in the back but also helped produce a fatal cleavage in the psychological make-up of the young republic. The disillusionment of defeat, normally issuing in bitter resentment of the victorious enemy, was turned by the Germans into recriminations against their compatriots and particularly against the new system of government.

PESSIMISM AND ESCAPISM   As might be expected, the horrors of war and the ensuing political and financial chaos launched the Weimar Republic on a note of pessimism and disillusionment. Much of the literature of the 1920s captures this feeling of futility and general revulsion toward war. *All Quiet on the Western Front* and *The Road Back* by Erich Maria Remarque (1897–   ) were representative of this powerful trend of disenchantment and are perhaps the best known works of this trend.

Of course, disillusionment evoked varying reactions among the writers of the period. Some tried to isolate themselves from the stream of politics and turmoil and escape the uncertain temper of the times. This reinforced what some have called the ingrained indifference of German intellectuals toward politics, an attitude that may have contributed to the failure of the republic. Thus Germany's greatest poet, Rainer Maria Rilke, living mostly in voluntary exile, looked sadly upon the crass materialism of his homeland, and withdrew increasingly into the seclusion expressed by his esthetic and spiritual poetry. The young novelist Franz Werfel (1890–1945) turned to mysticism in some of his novels and dramas. Gerhart Hauptmann, who in his youth had thrown himself so passionately into the social questions of his time with his naturalistic dramas, now remained aloof from the sociopolitical dilemma of the day. Psychology and religious visions play a part in his superb short story, *The Heretic of Soana* (1918) and in the drama *The White Savior* (1919), while his novel *The Isle of the Great Mother* (1924) is a tongue-in-cheek analysis of the birth of religions. Even Thomas Mann was caught up in the pessimistic escapism of the Weimar era. He had established his fame before the war with his long novel *Buddenbrooks* and numerous short stories. During the war, he had sided with the conservatives. In his *The Magic Mountain* (1924), however, the hero Hans Castorp loses himself for seven timeless years at a tuberculosis sanatorium in Davos, where he had gone to visit a relative. In an atmosphere of decay and disorder, far removed from the turmoil of the "flat land," Castorp attempts to discover himself and the meaning of life. But the mood of pessimism in the end gives way to reaffirmation, indicative of Mann's own gradual acceptance of the Weimar Republic and democracy. A wiser Hans Castorp returns home to assume what he considers to be his responsibilities in life.

The pseudohistorian Oswald Speng-

ler (1880–1936) began on a similar tone of pessimism in *The Decline of the West* (completed in 1922), which brought him world-wide fame almost overnight. But to Thomas Mann's rationalism he opposed the antirational tradition of the neoromantics. His philosophy of history, describing the rise and fall of civilizations and predicting the decay and disintegration of the West, was based on the organic theory of the state so popular in the early nineteenth century. Once again the state, with its own destiny, its own instinct and feeling, was placed at the apex of all life. Spengler, like Mann, was disillusioned, but the remedy he suggested differed diametrically. Spengler complained that the Weimar Republic was not motivated by "power, honor, and glory," and followed no aims except those of selfish parties. "For five years," he wrote in 1924, "we have had no deeds, no decision, no thought." And in *The Decline of the West* he predicted that only a German Caesar could delay the decay of Europe by enthroning "life over reason," by channeling the animal-like war of races into its final stage in which one race dominates all others. Thus pessimism led Spengler to grasping the straw of authoritarian salvation.

Albert Schweitzer (1875–1965), the musicologist, organist, physician, theologian, and philosopher, attempted to analyze the dilemma of his time. He perceived the "great inward lack of confidence," poorly concealed behind a "self-confident exterior." Although Schweitzer was looking at Europe as a whole from his African mission, his admonition was particularly apt for Germany. "The acceptance of authoritarian truth," he warned in his autobiography *Out of My Life and Thought*

(1933), ". . . does not bring skepticism to an end; it merely covers it up."

LIBERALISM VERSUS CONSERVATISM
Two politically antagonistic streams of thought affected the literary trends of the period. On the one hand were those who fervently accepted the republic. As if infused with new vigor by the freer atmosphere of the period, literature flourished in the 1920s. Writers already important before World War I labored with new energy, and new faces appeared, making Weimar a rich period, particularly for the German novel. Liberal and rationalist in essence, these writers were generally violently antinationalistic and antimilitaristic. They exuded an almost revolutionary cosmopolitanism, and in politics varied from mild liberalism to confirmed socialism. Fritz von Unruh (1885–) with his antimilitary plays; Heinrich Mann (1871–1950) with his satirical novels against the old empire; Arnold Zweig (1887–1968) with his novels decrying the suppression of the individual by war and the impersonal state; Bertolt Brecht (1898–1956) with his experimental dramas against social inequities; Alfred Döblin (1878–1957), Hermann Hesse (1877–1962), and many others underlined their faith in the inherent dignity of the individual and saw in the overthrow of the empire the augury of a new era.

But opposed to this group were the more conservative, conventional writers. They detested the innovators, the coterie of those who experimented with psychological techniques and who championed liberal thought, rationalism, and social ideals. They hated them as passionately as they hated the political democracy of the Weimar Republic that seemingly had spawned them.

They considered these innovators subversive of Germany's true character, and labeled their writings "cultural bolshevism." Since many of the liberal and experimental writers were Jewish, the conservatives' hatred was marked by virulent anti-Semitism, which was also rampant in economic and professional circles.

Among the conservative writers was Stefan George (1868–1933) and his circle, who had gained fame before the war as the foremost exponents of German symbolism. Imbued with a conscious adoration of the elite, George despised the Weimar period, with its "decadent mass culture," and its debasing, democratic socialism. Like so many of his compatriots, George longed for the noble rebirth of the Reich under a new Siegfried whom the nation could follow into the dawn of a new glory.

Oswald Spengler, with his neoromanticism loosely clothed with scientific vocabulary, must be classed with this same group. Similarly, there were journalists and theoreticians, believing in the myth of an organic state and the ethnic legends of the past, who also despised democratic individualism. Railing at the rationalists, they became conscious forerunners of Hitler's ultimate "revolution to the Right." Most influential among them were Hans Grimm (1875–1959), whose *People without Living Space* (1926) bolstered the idea of a mystical relationship between ethnic cultures and the soil—an important doctrine of National Socialism—and Alfred Rosenberg (1893–1946), later Hitler's party philosopher whose books on racialism, written during the 1920s, all reveal the same contempt for the masses and advocate the myth of the racial elite.

THE DESIRE FOR EXPERIMENTATION

The Weimar period also experienced a great flourishing in many nonliterary fields. In science, philosophy, and some of the arts, Germany again achieved world fame. Since many of these scientists and philosophers ultimately emigrated from Hitler's Germany and settled in the United States, they are particularly well known to American readers: Albert Einstein (1879–1955) in physics; Wolfgang Köhler (1887–1967), one of the proponents of Gestalt psychology; the neo-Kantian Ernst Cassirer (1874–1945) in philosophy, and Martin Heidegger (1889–   ), who together with Karl Jaspers (1883–1969) helped found existentialism; Werner Sombart (1863–1941) the liberal economist, and numerous influential liberal historians, such as Friedrich Meinecke (1862–1954). In the arts, the Austrian-born Oskar Kokoschka (1886–   ) advanced the expressionist school, while Arnold Schönberg (1874–1951), also Austrian by birth, and Paul Hindemith (1895–1963) continued the musical revolution with experiments in atonal and twelve-tone compositions. Of greatest world-wide impact was the Bauhaus school of modern functionalism in architecture, launched in the 1920s by Walter Gropius (1883–1969), a development which revolutionized modern concepts of construction.

The Weimar period, in fact, scintillated with activity and experimentation. True to their democratic idealism, the national government, the states, and the municipalities demonstrated their solicitude for the masses by catering to their tastes for culture and amusement—regardless of the cost, which was usually borne by loans and deficit financing. Concert halls, theaters, public swimming pools, sports arenas

were built in many small as well as large communities. The motion-picture industry flourished and made its impact on Hollywood. Experiments in progressive education at the elementary level abounded. Innovations in stage productions were introduced. Publishers propagated culture for the masses in millions of inexpensive paper-backed books, printing works of the masters and new trash literature with equal gusto. As they did everywhere, the roaring twenties made their mark on the Weimar era. With fervor, the Germans fled from insecurity by abandoning themselves to the stupefaction of jazz music, dancing, cults, and fads.

THE YEARS OF STABILIZATION AND COOPERATION, 1924–1929

By the fall of 1923, Germany was approaching complete disintegration. Famine, unemployment, and runaway inflation had made a shambles of the nation's economy and the morale of its population. Passive resistance had failed, and Franco-Belgian troops remained in the Ruhr. Rightist putsches in Bavaria and Küstrin, leftist uprisings in Saxony and Hamburg, and separatist revolts in the Rhineland threatened to destroy the fragile structure of the Weimar Republic. And relations between Germany and the Allies, particularly with the French, were so bitter that open conflict seemed imminent.

At this point, a change of attitude by both the German and the Allied governments inaugurated a new era. The near-fatal experiences of the preceding years of shortsighted vengeance and obstructionism led the Allies to adopt a more moderate policy of co-

operation, and forced the Germans to seek internal stability and to resign themselves to accepting their international obligations. Conceived in late 1923, these new policies achieved the status of a credo in 1924 and in the succeeding years.

This era is often called "the period of fulfillment [of Versailles]" or "the period of the Locarno spirit." One might as well label it "the age of Chamberlain, Briand, and Stresemann," the three foreign ministers largely responsible for the tenor of the times. In England and France, initiation of the new policy coincided with a leftward shift in the government. In January 1924, the British Conservative party was succeeded by the first Labor government in English history, headed by Ramsay MacDonald, a stanch advocate of international cooperation. Although MacDonald's tenure of office was less than a year, the conciliatory Austen Chamberlain, foreign minister from 1924 to 1929, continued to guide England's foreign affairs in the new spirit. Similarly in France, the vindictive Poincaré was replaced by the more liberal Édouard Herriot, and then by the Socialist Aristide Briand, who remained in charge of French foreign affairs from 1925 to 1932.

Most responsible for the shift in German policy was Gustav Stresemann, the astute politician who as chancellor in the fall of 1923 initiated the measures that were to help German stabilization, and as foreign minister from 1923 to his death in 1929 worked for the reintegration of Germany into the family of nations. Stresemann, head of the mildly conservative German People's party, came to power with the aid of the Socialists and Democrats, those parties that, as was true in 1919,

were willing to cooperate with the Allies in order to save the German Republic. During Stresemann's long tenure as foreign minister, however, his political moves depended mostly on the sufferance of cabinets that, with few exceptions, moved more and more to the right of center. Many hailed Stresemann as the savior of the Weimar Republic, but more recently, as more archives have been made available, historians have seen in him one of the gravediggers of the republic. His political coloring was indeed mixed. Nationalism and internationalism, idealism and *Realpolitik,* conservatism and mild liberalism breathed within him side by side. With consummate skill, he showed the proper color to impress those with whom he had to deal.

In a Reichstag speech in April 1923, at the height of tension with France, he advertised his cosmopolitan idealism by calling for an economic union with France that foreshadowed the Schumann plan of 1951 (see page 353). He suggested that a joining of the French and German coal and iron-ore industries would in the long run be more important than squabbles over reparations, and would heal the wounds of war and cement a political *rapprochement* between the two states. On the other hand, he was an ardent nationalist, unwilling to cede an inch of German soil. He called for a "strong and justified national feeling." His policy of "fulfilling Versailles" was not meant to be a surrender to the West. By displaying willingness to cooperate and by stabilizing Germany internally, he sought to strengthen his nation sufficiently to resume the defense of its national interests. While flirting with the West, he secretly permitted the conservatives to strengthen Germany's economic, military, and political ties with Russia. Although he publicly reprimanded the ultraconservatives at home for advocating continued obstructionism, he freely supported internal conservatism. His conviction that political action must confine itself to the "realm of the achievable" made him shrink from embracing extremes. Therein lay his strength and his success.

Stabilization of the Economy

In September 1923, Chancellor Stresemann called off the futile passive resistance in the Ruhr in order to "preserve the state and its people." He proclaimed in the Reichstag that reconciliation with France was possible and that Germany should honor its reparations obligations, provided France did not demand territorial cessions along the Rhine. In October, the Reichstag voted him extraordinary emergency powers, for a maximum of six months, to deal with the financial, economic, and social chaos. His powers included the right to "deviate from the constitutional civil rights." Stresemann promptly declared a state of siege and used the *Reichswehr* to suppress the disorders in the various states and to reimpose the authority of the central government.[1]

The next step was aimed at halting the inflation. The financier Hjalmar Schacht (1877–   ) devised a new cur-

[1] His firm action against the Communists in Saxony, contrasted with the mild treatment of the monarchist and Hitlerite rising in Bavaria, led to protests by the Socialists and their resignation from the cabinet, causing the fall of Stresemann's government at the end of November 1923, after which he served only as foreign minister.

rency, the *Rentenmark,* backed theoretically by the real estate and industrial equipment of the entire nation, but in reality by foreign loans and renewed confidence in the future of the economy. The value of the new *Rentenmark* was pegged at 1,000,000,-000,000 to 1 in exchange for the old mark. The repercussions of inflation, deflation, and stabilization were drastic. The middle and lower classes lost their hard-earned savings, and the retired, the aged, widows, and disabled war veterans were deprived of their security. The reserves of labor unions were wiped out. These groups, normally the mainstay of a democracy, experienced profound disillusionment and loss of status that drove many to seek more radical solutions on the Left or the Right. Thus the foundation of the Weimar Republic was seriously undermined.

On the other hand, immense profits were made in the course of this financial maneuver. Government and industry were strengthened, since their debts were practically wiped out. Huge fortunes were made by speculators who bought up land, factories, and industrial equipment with inflated funds and had sufficient resources to retain them until after the stabilization of the new currency. Concentration of capital and industrial combines was thus favored and cartels grew more powerful, whereas the smaller entrepreneurs fell by the wayside. The small fortunate group thus strengthened and enriched boosted the power and resources of the conservative element. Many workers and many members of the lower-middle class, on the other hand, became impoverished and disillusioned. The results of the elections in the spring of 1924 showed the

repercussions of this "stabilization." The conservative parties—the German National People's party and the National Socialists—almost doubled their representation over that of 1922, rising from a combined 65 to 127 seats. The Communists increased from 16 to 62, while the moderate parties—Socialists, Centrists, Democrats, and the People's party—dropped from 344 to 238 (see Chart 2).

Stabilization of the economy also involved a readjustment of the reparations claims. Various international committees labored for half a year on new agreements that were finally accepted by Germany and the Allies in April 1924. Known as the Dawes Plan, the new reparations schedule remained vague about Germany's total obligation, but scaled down the annual payments to a more reasonable level. To place Germany back on its feet and enable it to meet its initial quotas, new loans to the amount of 200 million dollars were extended to Germany. The Reparations Commission was empowered to supervise German finances, in particular the operation of the Reichsbank and the state-owned railroads. Revenues from the railroads and from certain indirect taxes were pledged as security for the loans, the bulk of which came from America. It is curious in this respect that the United States was unwilling to reduce or cancel Allied debts, but was ready to lend money to Germany so that it could pay reparations to the other Allied nations, who in turn paid some of their debts to the United States. In view of the heavy American investment in Germany and the repercussions of the United States depression five years later, it has been said facetiously, though with some truth, that

German democracy was stabilized and later unstabilized by United States loans.

Thanks to Schacht's financial wizardry, the Dawes Plan, and foreign investments and loans, the German economy and finances became relatively stable during the half decade following the disaster of 1923. It has been estimated that between 1924 and 1929, Germany received foreign loans totaling 8 billion dollars, mostly in short-term commitments, whereas it paid out in reparations less than 2 billion. The difference of 6 billion, a huge sum in the 1920s, was used to rejuvenate industry, support public works and social services, extend unemployment insurance, and pay for subsidies to agriculture, particularly in the northeastern regions of Prussia.

Consequently, there was a considerable, if hollow, recovery of the economy. Cartels grew bigger and more powerful, wages rose, unions regained some strength, and heavy industry was able to divert funds and resources for secret rearmament. Cities built lavish opera houses and recreation parks, factories replaced old machinery and spent money unsparingly to develop new processes. Prosperity had seemingly reappeared, inviting many Germans to look upon these years as a period of affluence and stability.

But it was a hollow recovery, laced with political as well as economic dangers. Foreign supervision of large sectors of German finances, called for under the Dawes Plan, was resented by German nationalists as incompatible with the dignity of a sovereign state. Although acceptance of the plan was followed by complete French evacuation of the Ruhr, the conservatives decried the new reparations scheme as another step in the enslavement of their nation. Moreover, from an economic point of view, the Dawes Plan was woefully shortsighted. Unless Germany started to earn foreign credits by exporting more than it imported or through other means—tourism, shipping, and the like—it could never repay the enormous loans it was contracting. But Germany's balance of trade was unfavorable during most of the succeeding years. It was not only living on borrowed funds, but sinking ever more deeply into debt. "If ever a crisis hits us," Stresemann remarked prophetically in 1928, "and the Americans recall their short-term loans, we face bankruptcy."

The Era of International Goodwill

After Stresemann became foreign minister in late 1923, he devoted all his energies to finding a *modus vivendi* with the Allies,[1] despite the obstructionism of the conservative elements inside Germany. The first tangible result of this policy, after a year of difficult negotiations, were the five Locarno Treaties of October 1925. In the Treaty of Mutual Guaranty between Germany, Belgium, France, Great Britain, and Italy, the signatories guaranteed "the maintenance of the territorial *status quo*" and the "inviolability" of the borders between Germany, France, and Belgium. This agreement thus involved Germany's renewed recognition of the permanence of its western frontiers, as set by the Treaty of Versailles. The contracting parties furthermore undertook "in no case to resort to war against each other," unless such action were required by a mandate from the League of Nations. In four separate arbitration conventions with France,

Belgium, Poland, and Czechoslovakia, respectively, Germany subscribed to the peaceful settlement of all disputes, and declared that it would not attempt to change its eastern borders by unilateral force. The world hailed these treaties as an end to the years of distrust and the beginning of a period of international goodwill, the renowned "spirit of Locarno." Europe began to relax, and the three chief architects of the pacts, Stresemann, Briand, and Chamberlain, were awarded the Nobel Peace Prize.

Much has been written about the Locarno Treaties, in praise and in damnation. Many asserted that they were a logical first step in overcoming the age-old enmity between France and Germany, and that the ultimate failure was due to the economic collapse at the end of the decade rather than to any political flaws in them. The aura of idealistic optimism engendered by the pacts was such that Briand and Stresemann actually discussed such thorny issues as evacuation of the Rhineland, return of the Saar, termination of Germany's unilateral disarmament, and the retrocession of territories transferred to Belgium. But despite Locarno, France retained a strong residual fear of a German revival. As an added measure of insurance, it soon began construction of the Maginot Line in defense of its Rhineland border, and cemented closer relations with Poland and the Little Entente, particularly with Czechoslovakia.

Others were mainly critical of Locarno. Some Allied observers saw in it a German ploy for lulling France into lessened vigilance along the Rhine and for driving a subtle wedge into the Anglo-French alliance. Some called it "an ostrich policy" on the part of France, since the dangerous "powder keg" in the east—the question of Germany's frontier with Czechslovakia and Poland—remained. In recent decades, with the hindsight of experience in the Allied reaction to the rise of Hitler, some historians have seen in Locarno the inception of "appeasement."

More important here is the reaction inside Germany and the question of Stresemann's real intentions. German nationalists were horrified by the "sell-out" of Locarno. They accused Stresemann of signing the "enslaving" Treaty of Versailles a second time and treasonably abandoning Alsace-Lorraine by accepting the permanence of the Upper Rhine frontier. They also feared that his pro-western policy endangered their own eastern orientation.

Stresemann defended himself vigorously against these accusations. His speeches to the Reichstag and before conservative groups became so nationalistic that it is difficult to discern his true intentions. He may have been duping the West with his show of collaboration or else deceiving the conservatives at home with his patriotic boasting. A study of his private papers reveals that he was primarily an astute defender of Germany's national interests. He had "surrendered" to the Allies only what was at any rate lost—Alsace-Lorraine. All other German demands he held in abeyance. He boasted that he had rejected all notions of a nonaggression pact with Poland or Czechoslovakia, and that sooner or later the "impossible frontier lines in the east" would be corrected. "No German government," he claimed in a speech, "from the German nationalists to the Communists, would ever recognize this frontier." He did not even reject the

possibility of war under certain conditions. The recovery of German soil, including the Saar, union with Austria, rectification of all grievances imposed by Versailles—all these he felt could be achieved, but only at the rate of one step at a time. Insisting that the final advantage alone counted, he publicly implored the conservatives not to meddle in foreign affairs, no matter how much they disliked his initial steps. And as tangible proof of his good intentions toward the conservatives, he promptly negotiated a new treaty of friendship and neutrality with Russia that expanded Russo-German cooperation in trade and armaments.

As a result of Locarno, Germany's relations with the Allies improved immensely. In December 1925, Allied occupation troops evacuated Cologne and vicinity. In the following year, Germany was admitted to the League of Nations and given a seat on the Permanent Council. Stresemann hoped to use the League as a means for effecting gradual adjustments in the Treaty of Versailles. As a first step, in early 1927, Allied control over German armaments was discontinued. Thereafter the question of Germany's military status became enmeshed with the larger problems of world-wide disarmament discussed at numerous conferences under the auspices of the League of Nations. In 1928, Germany also became a signatory to the abortive Kellogg-Briand Pact for the renunciation of aggressive war, a further step in its re-entry as an equal partner into the family of nations.

Finally, in 1929, the reparations question was reopened and a new schedule of payments devised. Germany had been drifting deeper into debt, and many Germans were chafing under the Allied supervision of their finances. Even the United States, as chief creditor, was worried about the disturbing conditions in Germany's balance of payments. Hence when the Germans requested a re-examination of the reparations issue, the Allies proposed the Young Plan, which finally fixed the total sum to be paid by Germany over a period of fifty-nine years. Annual payments were considerably reduced below those stipulated by the Dawes Plan, and emergency clauses were included as safeguards against sudden financial fluctuations. In recognition of Germany's sovereign rights, foreign controls over its economy were abolished. Instead, a Bank for International Settlements was created in Basel to help arrange the yearly transfer of payments. Despite the better conditions offered by the Young Plan, the German nationalists campaigned vigorously against its acceptance, since the very payment of reparations involved tacit acceptance of the guilt clauses of Versailles. Still, the Young Plan was eventually accepted. Concomitantly, the Allies began the withdrawal of their last occupation troops from the Rhineland. With the Young Plan and the evacuation of the Rhineland, Stresemann had gained yet another step in his rehabilitation of Germany. He had accomplished much through peaceful means and perseverance. In October 1929, he died, some three weeks before the stock market crash in the United States, that radically undermined the recovery of Germany and eventually brought to the fore those forces determined to complete Stresemann's work through violence.

Resurgence of Political Conservatism

The years 1930–1933, between the Wall Street crash and Hitler's seizure of power, are commonly called the declining years of the Weimar Republic. True though this may be, one must not overlook that the so-called period of stability and cooperation, 1924–1929, saw a resurgence of political conservatism that foreshadowed the revolution of the National Socialists.

THE ELECTION OF HINDENBURG The death of President Ebert in early 1925 and the subsequent presidential election gave the conservatives an opportunity to test their strength. On the first ballot the votes were divided among seven major and several minor candidates, so that none received the required majority. Of the votes cast, 10.4 million were for the conservatives, 7.8 for the Socialists, 3.9 for the Center, 1.9 for the Communists, and a total of 2.9 for a number of other candidates, including Ludendorff.

To prepare for the second ballot, a month later, at which only a plurality was required for election, the parties formed voting blocs and launched joint electoral campaigns. The conservative *Reichsblock*—consisting of the DNVP, DVP, Bavarian People's party, Economic party, Bavarian Peasant League —chose as their new standard-bearer the seventy-eight-year-old, twice-retired General Hindenburg, largely because of his expected sentimental appeal to the nation at large. The tone of the electoral proclamation of the *Reichsblock* ominously foreshadowed the propaganda slogans of Hitler's Third Reich:

We deem it to be the irrefutable duty of all Germans . . . to labor with all force and devotion for our Hindenburg. Hindenburg was your *Führer* in glorious and difficult times; you obeyed him; you loved him! He never deserted you. Hence, fight for him now when, with the traditional loyalty of a leader, he wants to step again at the head of your columns, to serve his fatherland in peaceful reconstruction! Hence our motto: . . . Hindenburg, our savior from discord!

The Center, the SPD, and the DDP formed the *Volksblock* and jointly backed the former Catholic chancellor, Wilhelm Marx (1863–1946), a leader of the Center party. Their campaign slogan was "For the fatherland, for a popular government, for the Republic." The KPD, however, refused to join any voting bloc. Opposed on principle to the bourgeois Weimar Republic, they shortsightedly hoped to gain by undermining its structure.

On the second ballot, Hindenburg received 14.6 million votes, against 13.7 million for Marx and 1.9 million for the Communist Ernst Thälmann (1886–1944), and thus became the Weimar Republic's second president. In his inaugural address, the aged general promised to safeguard the laws and the constitution, to represent all Germans and not merely a particular party, region, or confession, and to act as the embodiment of the national will. Yet there was little doubt that Hindenburg's sympathies did not lie with the republic. He attempted to maintain official neutrality as demanded by his office, but did little to strengthen the republican forces. He cherished the memory of his army and of prewar Germany and hated all that was connected with the Treaty of Versailles.

Despite economic progress, there con-

tinued to be frequent cabinet crises during Hindenburg's regime, usually over sharp disagreements between conservatives and liberals. In 1925 the Prussian government, to the dismay of the Socialists, awarded a large financial indemnity to the Hohenzollerns, and returned to them many of their confiscated estates. When in the following year the central government proposed to compensate all former dynasties, the liberals forced the issue into a popular referendum. Since not enough votes were cast in favor of expropriation, the conservatives succeeded in passing a Reichstag bill granting compensation to all dispossessed princelings. Even the question of the German flag produced a cabinet crisis, at a time when the DVP, the party of Stresemann and Luther, was constantly growing more conservative. In 1926, DVP Chancellor Hans Luther (1879–1962) issued an order permitting the occasional use of the old black-white-red colors that had been the symbol of the empire. The Socialists and the Democrats, favoring the republican colors, black, red, and gold—the flag of 1848—protested vehemently and forced Luther's resignation.

GERMAN REARMAMENT   Another stronghold of antirepublicanism resided in the *Reichswehr* and the various paramilitary organizations, particularly the nationalistic *Stahlhelm* (literally, steel helmet). The German professional officers had never resigned themselves to the disarmament and arms limitations stipulated at Versailles. The weakness of the Weimar regime and its experience with putsches had forced the government to continue to rely on the army, and had made strange bedfellows of the liberal government and the conservative officer corps. The ministers were therefore forced to close their eyes to the activities of the military. Thus even a semistabilized republic could not solve the age-old problem of German politics: putting the military under effective civilian control. Although reduced in strength and power, the *Reichswehr* retained a surprising independence of action and planning.

As chief of the *Reichswehr* from 1920 to 1926, General Seeckt devised a vastly efficient, modern army in which relatively small size was compensated for by excellence of training and equipment. It was, in effect, a cadre army of actual or potential officers, capable of rapid expansion in times of emergency. The problem of manpower was partially solved through training in numerous paramilitary organizations. Above all, in order to produce modern equipment the military and industry cooperated to the benefit of both. Civil aviation was built up largely with a view toward its military potential. Synthetics, chemicals, transport, and shipbuilding were perfected, where possible with an eye to military applications, and certain industries actually experimented with modern weapons.

In part this rearmament—actual and potential—was secret and in part quite open. It was begun long before the famous *rapprochement* with Soviet Russia at Rapallo. The idea of German-Russian military collaboration against the West was shared by some Soviet leaders and nationalistic Germans as early as 1918. By 1921, Lenin had requested German assistance in reorganizing the Red Army, and Seeckt had eagerly complied. Thereafter the military of the two states worked in

close contact. German industrialists helped set up Russian war factories to produce experimental planes and tanks for both armies, and Russia's vast territory offered useful ground for the training of small German units in the use of special weapons. But the importance of this Russo-German co-operation should not be exaggerated. The Germans found it equally easy to set up branch factories in Holland, Denmark, Switzerland, and other neutral countries for the production of modern military equipment, particularly in the field of aviation.

The Allied Disarmament Commission in Berlin was, of course, not totally ignorant of these proceedings. But, short of complete military occupation of Germany, there was little the Allies could do to prevent them. Some British statesmen, in fact, were not averse to seeing a stronger Germany as a counterweight to France, whereas the French were thoroughly suspicious of German intentions. Inside Germany, the activities of the *Reichswehr* produced a political uneasiness. A few liberals and Socialists protested, but most remained silent for fear of being labeled traitors. The nationalists, of course, favored the development, and Stresemann, for diplomatic reasons, pretended ignorance.

In later years, much unwarranted defamation was directed against Germans because of this secret rearmament —primarily because of the subsequent militarism of Hitler. Yet it should be kept in mind that Versailles and the League of Nations had echoed Wilson's proposal for world-wide disarmament, but that in practical application only Germany had been disarmed. Only a highly idealistic German could be expected to remain content with such unilateral disarmament. To assert that all Germans who secretly or openly favored the rebuilding of an effective army were aggressive militarists is to let emotion override historical common sense. The damage to the republican structure was not perpetrated by the mere fact of secret rearmament, but by the failure to subordinate the military to the civilian government. The danger lay less in the desire of the military to strengthen Germany than in the fact that many of the officers and most of the members of the paramilitary organizations were opposed to the very republic itself. In a typical *Stahlhelm* proclamation of 1928, its members declared: "We detest the present form of government with all our heart . . . because it blocks all prospects for liberating the enslaved fatherland, for removing from the Germans the false stain of war guilt, for gaining the needed living space in the east, for rearming the German nation."

AGITATION AGAINST THE WEIMAR REPUBLIC In the elections of 1928, the conservative parties lost momentum, the Socialists gained, and for the first time since 1920, a Socialist, Hermann Müller, again became chancellor. Actually, the electoral losses merely led the antirepublican forces to increase their agitation. The presence in the cabinet of the "traitorous" Socialists who had signed Versailles made it all the easier for Hitler's growing National Socialist party to excoriate those in power. In 1928, Joseph Goebbels (1897–1945) called on his compatriots to "shed the red chains," and urged the overthrow of Stresemann. "As yet, the world bristles with arms, while Germany is disarmed down to the last leggings; as yet the Negroes are oc-

cupying the Rhine . . . but Stresemann remains."

The negotiations for the Young Plan in 1929 gave the nationalists a chance to flex their muscles. To prevent German acceptance of the new reparations schedule, Hugenberg's German National People's party, Hitler's National Socialists, and the *Stahlhelm* formed a "Reich committee for the Demands of the German People." This committee drafted a "Bill against the Enslavement of the German People," and obtained almost four million signatures to force its discussion by the Reichstag. The bill instructed the government to notify the Allies promptly that Germany rejected the guilt clause, that the occupied territories were to be vacated immediately and unconditionally, that the Germans refused all further financial obligations based in any way on the theory of war guilt, and that the German chancellor or any minister who signed an international agreement contrary to these instructions—that is, the Young Plan—would be guilty of high treason and punishable with imprisonment. Despite pressure from the extreme Right, the Reichstag defeated the proposed bill, 323 to 82, and adopted the Young Plan. In a subsequent popular referendum, the bill received 5.8 million votes, far short of the 51 percent required to pass it over the head of the Reichstag. Stresemann's successor rightly told the Reichstag that it was "sheer nonsense" to ask in a referendum whether the German people liked paying reparations. But he warned prophetically that the radical Right was proposing such cheap demagoguery less to free Germany from its foreign dilemma than to undermine the bourgeois republican government. Defeat in the referendum temporarily eclipsed the rising star of Hugenberg and Hitler, but, as became apparent in the following year, in no way destroyed it.

National Socialist Germany in Time of Peace, 1930–1937

THE COLLAPSE OF THE WEIMAR REPUBLIC

The period 1930–1933 saw the complete erosion of the republic's parliamentary structure and the gradual substitution of Hitler's dictatorship. Many volumes have been written attempting to diagnose the causes for the failure of Germany's republican experiment and for the rise of National Socialism. There is no need here to reiterate the well-known arguments. The preceding chapters on the Weimar Republic and on earlier periods described many weaknesses in the body politic of Germany as well as flaws in the international situation that eroded the young republic and paved the way for its totalitarian successor.

Yet a few words of caution against overly facile interpretations seem in order. Too many non-German analysts unconsciously adopt an inversion of Hitler's racialism. They attribute Germany's plunge into totalitarianism to the consequences of a supposed flaw in the German people. As Hitler saw in the *Volk* the driving power of spiritual and cultural superiority, so some writers have seen in the Germans an inherently cruel, militaristic attitude of which Hitler became the physical embodiment. Needless to say, such racialism is absurd. A second misinterpretation—equally misleading—rejects the theory of "racial guilt," but sees in Hitler and his disciples the incarnation of evil, which by deceit and revolution imposed itself on a naïve people.

Such black-and-white interpretations overlook the entire political, socioeconomic, and psychological frame that made National Socialism possible. They also disregard the aspirations of millions of people and distort the changeover to Hitler's dictatorship, which was pseudo legal rather than revolutionary. Interpretations of this type lead neither to a comprehension of the phenomenon of National Socialism with its appeal to the masses, nor to an understanding of the twentieth century itself, in which

extremist panaceas for crucial problems vie for allegiance. Rather, the rise of National Socialism must be viewed against the background of the general social erosion that gripped Europe in the decades after World War I. In almost all European states, economic dislocation, social tension, and class friction led certain groups to advocate the use of force for the solution of social, economic, and political problems. Fascist parties became important even in democratic France, Holland, and Belgium. Dictatorships were established in Austria, Italy, Spain, Portugal, and in ten eastern European countries from the Baltic states to Greece—with the exception of Czechoslovakia. Germany's resorting to dictatorship was therefore part of a general European phenomenon. That the German version involved such excesses of cruelty and barbarism raises a question that has provoked much speculation among analysts and journalists, but which in essence is unanswerable on the basis of our present methods of social and psychological research.

The Economic Crisis

Primary among the causes for the fall of the Weimar Republic was the economic crisis of the early 1930s. Even before the crash of the New York stock market in 1929, the world economy had been in imbalance. Higher and higher tariff walls—adopted as a source of additional government revenue, as a defense against depreciated foreign currencies, or simply as an expression of blatant nationalism—had hindered international trade. Agricultural overproduction and inflation, unbalanced budgets and uncollected debts had produced economic and financial dislocations in many nations. The boom and bust of 1929 finally ended the era of speculation. Repercussions of the collapse of Wall Street were soon felt all over Europe. By 1931, most nations were in full depression, with Germany and Austria suffering the most.

The sudden recall of short-term United States loans, coupled with a decline in stock values and a reduction of trade, rapidly swelled the German recession to disastrous proportions. Between 1929 and 1932, the German national income dropped by 20 percent. Unemployment, not severe during the pseudoprosperous years of 1925–1929, rose to 5 million in 1930 and exceeded 6 million by January 1932, or almost as many as the number of unemployed in all other European states combined. By the end of 1932, 43 percent of Germany's labor force was unemployed —as compared with 25 percent in the United States. While unemployment rose and bread lines lengthened, countless businesses went bankrupt. In the summer of 1931, even the Darmstädter Bank, one of Germany's largest, became insolvent, and the government was forced to close all banks and savings institutions for two days in a desperate effort to halt the financial catastrophe.

The depression was accompanied by grave psychological, social, and political repercussions. Business failures shook the self-reliance of the middle class. Unemployment and hunger increased class antagonism between rich and poor. And even among nations hatred between the "have" and the "have-not" states rose to a new pitch and became a dominant theme of international relations in the 1930s. Almost everywhere, people hoped to

escape from economic chaos by awarding more power to the central governments and by insisting that the state assume greater responsibility for the economic well-being of the nation. The remnants of nineteenth-century *laissez faire* gave way to increased state intervention, on the Continent as well as in the United States. And in many nations, the middle class and the proletariat were happy to escape from chaos by seeking their salvation in a dictatorship. The search for order was not limited to Germany.

Throughout 1931, Chancellor Heinrich Brüning (1885–1970) tried desperately to stem the economic and financial disaster. He hoped to balance the budget by reducing expenditures in all areas—lower salaries for government employees, lower pensions and welfare payments, less government housing, and other measures. Contrary to John Maynard Keynes's then current advocacy of pump priming, Brüning sought retrenchment everywhere. To put his unpopular—and unsuccessful—policy into effect, he was forced to resort constantly to Article 48 and rule by emergency decree (see page 200).

In the spring of 1931, Austria also neared economic collapse with the bankruptcy of the powerful Credit Anstalt, a bank that had dominated much of the Danubian trade. To help both nations and to improve trade, Berlin and Vienna negotiated the establishment of a Customs Union. The Little Entente—always fearful of Austrian resurgence—Italy, and France promptly protested against these negotiations. France even referred the matter to the World Court, which adjudged the proposed economic union contrary to the Treaty of Versailles. The German-Austrian Customs Union

had to be abandoned, furnishing further ammunition for the propaganda of the German nationalists, and Great Britain, although itself in financial straits, came to the rescue of the Credit Anstalt in order to avoid a complete collapse in Austria.

The depression also required reappraisal of the question of reparations and international debts. In the spring of 1931, President Hindenburg appealed to President Hoover for his intervention in favor of a temporary cessation of reparations demands. The United States finally felt forced to acknowledge a relationship between reparations and inter-Allied debts. Hoover proposed a one-year moratorium on all intergovernmental debts and interest payments, a suggestion greatly resented by France, which had not been so hard hit by the depression and feared the moratorium might lead to a permanent cancellation of reparations. As the crisis deepened and most countries abandoned the gold standard, frequent international conferences were held to debate the question of debts and reparations. The Young Committee, recalled for the purpose, announced that it seemed doubtful whether Germany would be in a position to resume payment of reparations upon expiration of the moratorium, and Chancellor Brüning finally proclaimed publicly that "continued political payments" were impossible. In the summer of 1932, a general conference met in Lausanne to work out a permanent solution. Significantly, England and France were represented by the same MacDonald and Herriot who had helped to create the spirit of Locarno. Some escape clauses notwithstanding, the Lausanne Conference amounted to an abandonment of all reparations

demands. The United States agreed to adjust but not to cancel the debts owed it—a useless gesture, for after 1934 all countries, except Finland, defaulted on their payments. For Germany, however, the decisions made at Lausanne represented another step in the unraveling of Versailles.

The Background of Hitler and His Movement

HIS EARLY CAREER Born in Austrian Braunau near the Bavarian border, Adolf Hitler was the third child of his father's third marriage. Intelligent but not well educated, Hitler aspired to become an artist in order to escape the narrower prospects offered by the career of a customs official, which his father had followed. In 1908, he moved to Vienna, where only frustration seemed to await him. He was not admitted to the School of Architecture because he had not graduated from an academic high school. Nor could he attend the Academy of Fine Arts, since he failed the requisite entrance tests. The examiners rejected the sample sketches he submitted—ironically on the required themes "Expulsion from Paradise" and "An Incident from the Deluge." During five years of poverty and occasional vagrancy, he earned his living by painting postcards, and devoted much time to haphazard reading. It was during these frustrating years in Vienna that he formed many of his ideas and prejudices. He came to hate the non-German peoples who crowded the polyglot capital of the Hapsburg empire. His German national feeling became intense. Liberalism, humanism, Christianity became hateful to him. He particularly despised Jews, Slavs, and intellectuals,

and disdained the masses with a scornful contempt he retained all his life.

In 1913 he moved to Munich, and in the following year his aimless life was given a new meaning through the outbreak of World War I. He volunteered for service with a Bavarian regiment and served as a messenger at the front. His sudden sense of belonging and achievement was shaken only by Germany's collapse in 1918. The end of the war found him in a military hospital, gassed and half-blind. Unable to conceive that Germany had lost the war fairly, he ardently embraced the idea of the stab in the back. After convalescence, he returned to Munich and decided to devote himself to politics.

Postwar Munich was filled with the tumultuous seesaw struggle between opposing ideologies. Hitler thrived in this hotbed of intrigues and street fighting. He was given a job by the *Reichswehr* to spy on various sprouting political fringe groups, among them the German Workers' party (founded in 1918 by Anton Drexler) with its mixed program of nationalism and socialism. Instead of spying on it, Hitler harangued the group on several occasions, then joined it and rapidly rose to a position of leadership. Henceforth, he became a full-time politician.

THE BEGINNINGS OF THE NSDAP In 1920, the German Workers' party adopted an official program of twenty-five points, largely elaborated by the militantly anticapitalistic economist Gottfried Feder (1883–1942). In it, nationalism, socialism, and racialism were mixed in forceful, albeit contradictory, terms. The twenty-five points—in some respects similar to Mussolini's program

of 1919—called for the union of all Germans, the return of Germany's colonies, the abrogation of the Versailles and St. Germain Treaties, and the equality of Germany with other nations. At home, the program purported to place the good of the community before that of the individual by threatening death to those who worked to the detriment of the public weal, by confiscating war profits, and by abolishing unearned incomes. The state, moreover, was to provide an adequate living for all citizens, nationalize the industrial trusts and share in the profits of big business, improve old-age pensions, aid small businesses, and institute agrarian reform. The state was to be purified by denying citizenship rights to Jews and expelling non-German immigrants. In public education, the program called for the teaching of "state ideals" and the improvement of the health of the youth. Nationalism was to be furthered by extirpating non-German—that is, Jewish and foreign—influences from the press, art, and literature, and by granting freedom of religion only when it did not "endanger the state or give offense to the moral and ethical feelings of the Germanic race." The program also called for abolition of the professional army in favor of a people's force.

Soon thereafter, the German Workers' party changed its name to the National Socialist German Workers' party (NSDAP), and began to extend its influence from Munich into other parts of Germany and into Austria. It acquired a party newspaper, the *Völkischer Beobachter* which, under the editorship of Alfred Rosenberg, propagated National Socialist ideas. In 1921, the growing NSDAP organized the SA

(*Sturmabteilung*, or storm troopers) under the command of the socialistic former army officer, Ernst Roehm (1887–1934). These brown-shirted storm troopers, fully armed like members of the Free Corps and the *Stahlhelm*, were used to guard party meetings, disrupt the work of other parties, and engage in the street fighting common to the period. Besides Hitler, Feder, Rosenberg, and Roehm, the party numbered among its early important members Gregor Strasser (1892–1934), Rudolf Hess (1894–   ) —soon Hitler's favorite adjutant—the colorful and venal ex-air force officer, Hermann Göring (1893–1946), the publicist Joseph Goebbels, and eventually the inscrutable Heinrich Himmler (1900–1945).

Methodically organized and fanatically devoted to its cause, the NSDAP grew substantially during its first three years. The economic and political dislocations of the early Weimar Republic, Mussolini's success in 1922, and tacit encouragement by *Reichswehr* officers and by the nationalistic Ludendorff persuaded Hitler to attempt the premature Beer Hall Putsch of 1923 (see page 208). Its disastrous outcome not merely landed Hitler in jail but convinced him that seizure of power by his party had to be carefully prepared and could probably be achieved only through pseudolegal means.

Outlawed after the putsch of 1923, the NSDAP was re-created in February 1925. In the same year, it added a second fighting arm, the black-uniformed SS (*Schutzstaffel*), composed of elite members with special duties. But during the ensuing years of apparent stabilization following the Pacts of Locarno, the party's growth was slow. At the end of 1928, it numbered only

some 60,000 members. Meanwhile its ideology was gradually being modified, and parts of the original program of twenty-five points were unofficially abandoned. Three books in particular helped change National Socialist dogma. In 1923 appeared *The Third Reich* by the journalist and literary historian Arthur Moeller van den Bruck (1876–1925). The author was not a member of the NSDAP, but exerted much influence in conservative circles. Moeller advocated "corporatism in state organization and economics," a system that would at first be revolutionary but would ultimately have a stabilizing and conservative effect. As an undaunted nationalist, he detested the international creed of the SPD and the KPD and insisted that Germany needed a "new Socialism" as the "foundation of Germany's Third Reich." Such a regime, he proclaimed, needed a leader who knew how to supplant international socialism by a new, nonliberal German type of socialism, which he labeled "National Socialism."

A few years later appeared Hitler's *Mein Kampf,* written during his imprisonment. With uncanny precision, Hitler depicted the future course of his movement, both in foreign affairs as well as in internal policies. Finally in 1930, Rosenberg's *The Myth of the Twentieth Century,* with its theories on the supremacy of the German race, was added to the party ideology. Meanwhile Hitler continued to deliver his inflammatory speeches in which he hammered again and again on the same few themes: denunciation of Versailles and the "November criminals" who had signed the armistice and created the Weimar Republic; condemnation of communism, socialism, free-masonry, and international Jewry; and a promise to redeem German honor and inaugurate for all Germans a glorious future. Although Hitler's speeches never deviated from these same themes, the basic party aims during the 1920s tended to lose the socialistic fervor of Gottfried Feder's original program and become more opportunistic.

After the stagnant period of the late 1920s, the NSDAP was infused with new vigor as a result of the economic crisis. By promising panaceas to everyone, Hitler suddenly attracted millions of discontents to his side. To the peasants, he offered higher agricultural prices; to labor, employment and higher wages; to the industrialists, safety from communism and unions; to the army and veterans, an expanded military machine; and to all German nationalists, the abrogation of Versailles and the establishment of a powerful *Grossdeutschland.* As membership and voter attraction increased, so did financial support of the party. Certain powerful industrial magnates of the Ruhr, such as Fritz Thyssen (1873–1951) and Emil Kirdorf, began to throw their financial support to the NSDAP. Banks and insurance companies contributed to party funds. Tired of the instability of the republican regime and fearful of a Communist coup, nationalistic conservatives saw in Hitler's movement a possible remedy. Hitler, for his part, abandoned even more the socialistic ideals of the party. He dismissed the anticapitalistic Gottfried Feder and took as his new economic adviser Walther Funk (1890–1960), whose conservative theories were more attuned to those of the Rhineland magnates, whom Hitler wished to attract to his movement.

The Political Disintegration of the Republic

When Hitler seized power in 1933, he did not have to overthrow the Weimar Republic. It had more or less ceased to exist. Never very stable during its brief life span, it had begun to disintegrate in the critical years of economic depression.

In March 1930, the Socialist Chancellor Müller resigned when the German People's party refused to remain in the government coalition. To raise additional funds for unemployment compensation, Müller had urged an increase in the contributions of both employers and employees. His plan was defeated by pressure from business and labor unions alike. When he requested permission from President Hindenburg to use the emergency powers of Article 48 to deal with the economic crisis and the growing disorders in the streets, he was also rebuffed. It seemed that Hindenburg would not entrust the powers of Article 48 to a Socialist. Hindenburg's court camarilla, primarily the influential intriguer General Kurt von Schleicher (1882–1934), was happy to use the occasion to topple the Socialists from power.

BRÜNING AND THE GROWING CRISIS   To replace Müller, Hindenburg selected the conservative Centrist leader Heinrich Brüning, a fiscal expert and at heart a monarchist who was only half-reconciled to the republican regime. Brüning formed a conservative cabinet that excluded the SPD, but he made it clear from the start that the new cabinet would not be bound to any coalition. Insisting that he ran the country for the benefit of the nation as a whole rather than for that of specific parties and interest groups, he resorted constantly to Article 48, with the wholehearted approval of President Hindenburg. Whatever he could not achieve through ordinary legislative process, he ordered by emergency decrees. Although isolated voices warned that excessive use of Article 48 would lead to dictatorship, those opposed to its use could not muster a majority in the Reichstag to overrule the chancellor. And there were many who no longer cared about democracy. An apt headline of 1930 noted: "The people long for guidance." The ensuing article stated: "It is no longer vital whether the government has a popular base or not. What matters is that it governs well."

During the summer of 1930, while the economic situation worsened, street battles between opposing paramilitary factions became the order of the day. Brown-shirts, red-shirts, green-shirts, and black-shirts terrorized the cities and fought each other in pitched battles. Hampered by continued obstructionism in the Reichstag by members of the DNVP, the NSDAP, the SPD, and the KPD who opposed his budget and his rule by Article 48, Brüning dissolved it and called for new elections. The republic's fifth national election, in September 1930, produced ominous results (see Chart 2). The moderate parties dropped in strength, with the SPD, the DVP and the DDP —now called the German State party —losing the most votes. The extremists on both sides showed huge gains. The Communists obtained 4.5 million votes, rising from 54 to 77 representatives in the Reichstag. The manifold right-wing splinter parties doubled their representation. The NSDAP—increasing its vote at the expense of the

DNVP, which declined by almost 50 percent—rose from the 800,000 votes of the last election to 6.4 million, thereby increasing its delegation in the Reichstag from 12 to 107.

The landslide victory of Hitler's movement boded ill for the future of the Republic. In a Reichstag speech, Gregor Strasser warned: "We favor democratic Weimar and its Constitution, so long as it suits us." The legislative process of the central government reached an impasse. Communists and National Socialists, both equally determined to topple the republic, shouted and fought during legislative sessions, proposed silly amendments, or staged walkouts—whatever might best disrupt the regular functioning of government. Yet there were many who failed to recognize the dangers. Even the Socialist prime minister of Prussia, Otto Braun (1872–1956), pretended that the electoral results of 1930 threatened "neither the Constitution, nor public safety, nor the course of foreign policy," and expressed confidence that a "coalition of all reasonable people" could be formed to guide Germany out of its quagmire. Two years later, this same Otto Braun was to be the victim of a nationalist *coup d'état* in Prussia.

Despite these difficulties, Brüning's government lasted for over two years. Relying on Article 48, and ruling with the confidence of Hindenburg rather than that of the nation, Brüning attempted to solve the economic chaos and at the same time placate enough factions to remain in power. Essentially a nationalist, he continually promised to "rebuild Germany in peaceful cooperation with all people." He frequently denounced Versailles, favored *Anschluss* (union) with Austria, and at the Geneva Disarmament Conference in 1932 insisted on "equal rights and equal security for all peoples"—meaning equality of armaments for Germany. He showed favors to the army, and proudly called his cabinet a "government of war veterans." He attempted to alleviate the economic distress by retrenching social services, aiding agriculture, and trying to balance the budget.

But none of Brüning's measures helped stem the tide of National Socialism. The NSDAP gradually gained control of several states. Although intent on assuming power by legal means, the party also made careful preparations for a coup if one seemed appropriate. Ordinances arranging for the institution of military government, for the ruthless suppression of all opposition, and for the summary application of the death penalty for political offenses were meticulously prepared by the NSDAP should a sudden collapse of the central government make revolution advisable.

In October 1931, the NSDAP gained added power by the formation of the so-called Harzburg Front. Through the intermediary of the financier Hjalmar Schacht, a working agreement was formed among Hitler's movement, Hugenberg's DNVP, certain Rhineland industrialists, and the *Stahlhelm*. In a public proclamation issued at Harzburg, the coalition derided the government's long-standing failure to suppress the "bloody terror of Marxism" and the "growing cultural bolshevism," and promised to heal the disunity in the nation and end the subservience to foreign powers. The group declared its readiness to "seize power," and warned that "in the coming disorder" it would "protect life and property of [only] those who openly side with us, but [would] not safeguard the present

regime." Not only was the Harzburg Front an open challenge to the Weimar Republic; it created discomfort within the ranks of the NSDAP. Although Wilhelm Frick (1877–1946) assured the members of his party that the "only aim of the coalition was to obtain power within the state," and that the NSDAP would see to it that it would lead the coalition, the more leftist members of the party objected to this "deal" with the ultrarightists and conservative industrialists. Hence the Harzburg Front increased the power of the party, but also contributed to its later split between the opportunists and those who took their "socialist" label more seriously.

In the midst of these political problems and the continuing economic crisis, new presidential elections were required upon the expiration of Hindenburg's term in 1932. It is symptomatic of the shift to the Right that Hindenburg, who in 1925 had been a candidate of the conservatives, became a candidate of the moderates and Socialists in 1932. Despite the senility of the eighty-four-year-old general, the Socialists rallied behind him as "a protective shield against the rise of Hitlerism." The aged Hindenburg himself felt uncomfortable in his new position. "Look at the situation into which Brüning has got me," he is supposed to have told his friend Franz von Papen (1879–1969). "Now I have been chosen by the Left, whereas the Right, my own people, have put up this lance-corporal."

On the first ballot, Hindenburg received 18.6 million votes against 11.3 for Hitler, 4.9 for the Communist Thälmann, and 2.5 for the *Stahlhelm* candidate. As in 1925, a second ballot was required. In the second election a month later, over a million fewer voters appeared at the polls—indicative perhaps of the feeling of futility among segments of the electorate. With the *Stahlhelm* deciding to throw its support to Hitler, the second ballot gave 19.3 million to Hindenburg, 13.4 to Hitler, and only 3.7 to Thälmann. The senile Hindenburg was thus elected for a second term.

THE MISCALCULATIONS OF PAPEN
Soon after the elections of 1932, Brüning, who had incurred the wrath of too many influential groups, was forced to resign. His proposal for a partial expropriation of the estates of East Prussian landlords for the purpose of settling peasants on unused Junker land had particularly infuriated Hindenburg and his circle of Junker supporters. Moreover, Brüning had incurred the deadly enmity of the NSDAP by outlawing the SA and SS in an attempt to quell the continued street fighting. Wilhelm Groener, the ever-optimistic minister of defense and of the interior, had hoped to absorb the paramilitary organizations of the NSDAP into a "gigantic sports club, supervised by the central government." But after Hindenburg's re-election and the continuation of street fighting, Brüning had decided on the sterner solution of a complete ban.

Since Brüning's cabinet had always existed at the sufferance of Hindenburg rather than through the support of a parliamentary majority, Hindenburg's displeasure was tantamount to Brüning's dismissal. On the advice of Schleicher and with the consent of the Harzburg Front, Hindenburg on June 1, 1932, appointed Franz von Papen as the new chancellor.

Papen, a friend of Schleicher's and Hindenburg's, and of many other aristocrats and nobles, was a self-con-

fident master of intrigue who believed he could forge a coalition of conservative Junkers, Rhineland industrialists, and army men that would keep Adolf Hitler out of power. Conservative and aristocratic, he disdained the rabble-rousing nature of National Socialism while admiring the nationalistic fervor of Hitler. But to get into office, Papen made a bargain with the NSDAP: he would lift the ban against the SA and SS in return for support from the National Socialists. Joseph Goebbels anticipated the consequences of such an agreement when he noted in his diary: "The *Reichstag* will be dissolved; all compulsory laws will be abrogated; we will get freedom to agitate and will deliver a masterpiece of propaganda."

Papen's cabinet was nicknamed a cabinet of "army officers and barons." It included Schleicher as minister of defense, four barons, and one count, among them Baron Konstantin von Neurath (1873–1956) for foreign affairs and Count Johann Schwerin von Krosigk (1887–1952) for finance, both of whom also served in Hitler's first cabinet. In foreign affairs, Papen's first half year in office was marked by a single success: the ending of the reparations obligations at the Lausanne Conference. Within Germany, his regime marked the further corrosion of the republican forms of government, since he continued the practice of governing by decree. Papen dissolved the Reichstag June 4. A week later, the ban against SA and SS was lifted, and street fighting resumed its usual violence. In Prussia, the National Socialists provoked increasing disorder on the floor of the diet. Pitched battles were fought between SA and Communists in the streets of Berlin. These

disorders in Prussia led Papen to take frankly dictatorial measures—much in the manner of Mussolini. He deposed the Socialist prime minister of Prussia, Otto Braun, on the charge that he was unable to maintain peace in his state, and placed Prussia under martial law. This unconstitutional move was designed to please the ultraconservatives. The Communists ordered a strike to protest against this outrage, but the Socialists and labor unions refused to cooperate with them, since they hated the KPD even more than they hated the Nazis.[1]

The new Reichstag elections took place on July 31, 1932. Once again Hitler's movement produced a landslide. His party polled 13.7 million votes and obtained 230 seats in the Reichstag, swallowing up most of the small right-wing splinter parties. Only the Center party and the Communists made slight gains, while all other groups declined (see Chart 2). As leader of the largest party, Hitler was clearly the man of the hour. The question no longer seemed to be whether he could come to power, but only how: whether legally or by *coup d'état*. Goebbels favored a pseudo-legal entry into the government, if necessary in coalition with the nationalistic DNVP, confident as he was that "seizure of power is fundamentally different from the ultimate aim" of the NSDAP. According to his later statement, Hitler opposed a *coup d'état*—perhaps in recollection of the Beer Hall Putsch—since he was afraid of the *Reichswehr*. Yet when Papen attempted to make a bargain with Hitler,

---

[1] The abbreviation "Nazi" was actually a term of contempt, used by Hitler's enemies, although foreigners gradually turned it into a general label for the movement.

the latter refused to join the government unless he were given full powers.

During the summer and fall of 1932, the Nazis straddled the issue. On the one hand, they acted as defenders of constitutionalism, deriding Papen for his dictatorial use of Article 48. On the other hand, they openly increased their terror. A famous incident revealed their real concept of the law. When five storm troopers broke into the house of a Communist worker and beat him to death in front of his mother, they were imprisoned by the government and condemned to death on the basis of a new law against political terrorism. Hitler at once sent a telegram to his imprisoned comrades: "Your freedom is a question of our honor!" And Rosenberg asked in the *Völkischer Beobachter* how one life, especially that of a Polish Communist, could possibly be worth the lives of five German veterans. "One soul does not equal another soul," he exclaimed, "one man not another. . . ."

At the same time, rifts seemed to appear within the NSDAP. Those Nazis who leaned toward Socialism became increasingly wary of Hitler's flirtation with big business. Gregor Strasser broke with Hitler, quit the party, and tried to induce others to follow him. Papen and Schleicher hoped to take advantage of Strasser's desertion to split the NSDAP. For this purpose, Schleicher negotiated with Strasser, and Papen once again dissolved the Reichstag and called for new elections, expecting the results would weaken Hitler's party. Another reason for dissolving the Reichstag was the chancellor's desire to anticipate a motion of censure by the conservatives, who disliked his economic measures. They had wanted to avail themselves

of a safety clause in Article 48 in order to countermand the president's emergency powers. The Nazis and the DNVP complained that Papen's dissolution of the Reichstag was illegal on the grounds that it prevented them from maintaining the supremacy of the Reichstag over the chancellor. Since the use of Article 48 had been made necessary to a great extent by the legislative obstructionism of the Nazis and the Communists, such an accusation seemed ironic.

In the November elections of 1932, Hitler lost 2 million votes and 34 seats in the Reichstag. The excessive Nazi terror had frightened some voters, and the split with the left wing of his party had disillusioned others. The SPD sustained further losses, while the DNVP and the KPD both showed some gains. But there was no sign that Germany was regaining political stability. None of the moderate parties showed any gains, and 1.4 million fewer Germans went to the polls.

THE SCHLEICHER INTERIM The elections were followed by a new government crisis. For the second time, Hindenburg offered the chancellorship to Hitler, but withdrew his offer when the latter demanded unlimited power. Hindenburg insisted that "his constitutional oath and his conscience" would not allow him to grant exclusive powers to Hitler, a step that would necessarily lead to "dictatorship by one party." Papen urged a change in the constitution that would permit the chancellor to govern without the Reichstag, but Hindenburg also rejected this proposal as unconstitutional. Finally Papen resigned and a new Cabinet was formed by Schleicher.

The new cabinet, which was to be

the Weimar Republic's twenty-first and last, existed for only two months. Schleicher, who until then had intrigued in the background, was now the standard-bearer of the camarilla. He had persuaded Hindenburg that he was capable of solving the crisis without forcing the president to break his constitutional oath. He felt confident that he could woo Strasser and the Nazi left wing into a coalition with the bourgeois and Socialist parties and thereby undermine Hitler's movement. Fearful that his beloved *Reichswehr* might be overshadowed by Hitler's personal army, he was now belatedly determined to stop the Nazi steamroller. But all his schemes failed. Hitler successfully wooed the masses, in and out of his party, so that Strasser was given no opportunity to split the NSDAP. Schleicher's government proved as unable to deal with the continuing economic crisis as its predecessors had been. December 1932 and January 1933 saw endless secret intriguing by Hitler, Papen, Schleicher, Hugenberg, Strasser, and Thyssen, each of whom was trying to dupe the others; above them stood the senile, uncomprehending Hindenburg, who was still important because his consent was needed for the appointment of a new chancellor.

In the end, Papen succeeded in toppling Schleicher by concluding a second bargain with Hitler. The latter agreed to abandon his demands for exclusive power and to form a coalition cabinet with Papen, Hugenberg, and other conservatives. Papen in turn undertook to persuade Hindenburg that such a combination would be acceptable. As a result, the President appointed Hitler as chancellor on January 30, 1933. When Hitler moved into the chancellery in Berlin, he is supposed to have remarked to Goebbels: "No one will ever get me out of here alive!"

THE ESTABLISHMENT OF HITLER'S DICTATORSHIP

In view of the later Nazi excesses— so clearly foreshadowed even before 1933 in their speeches, in their party newspaper, and in the actions of their storm troopers—many foreigners have wondered why the Germans allowed Hitler's rise to power. To explain these events, one must recall that Hitler was made chancellor not by the vote of a majority of the German people but by presidential fiat, and that he established his totalitarian dictatorship in installments. One must also keep in mind the conditions of the period: the economic chaos, the political vacillations of the government, the street fighting and the national frustration, as well as Hitler's reiterated pledges to find immediate remedies for all ills. Although a few cautious observers in 1933 warned that Hitler not only would annihilate the republic and all democratic elements, but would also pervert justice and freedom and degrade human values, there were millions who naïvely flocked to his ranks or tolerated his movement for lack of a better solution. Indeed, provided they closed an eye to this or that in the Nazi creed or behavior, most discontents could find much attraction in Hitler's promises. What scruples existed were easily effaced by the rationalization that the Nazi movement "after all, contained much good." Above all, the unemployed were promised reintegration into the nation's eco-

nomic life, and the bourgeois were guaranteed economic stability and safety from communism. Through remarkably skillful propaganda, the insecure masses were given a sense of belonging, a feeling of achievement in helping "to reconstruct the Reich." Moreover, many citizens abided by their ingrained respect for governmental authority which, by tradition, deserved obedience regardless of the citizen's personal feelings. Finally, the new regime provided enough scapegoats to allow the masses to sublimate their prejudices and tension. The Nazis' much-publicized intention of fighting the "black, red, and yellow internationals"—the Catholic Church, communism and socialism, and the Jews—attracted the anti-Catholics, the anti-Communists, and the anti-Semites.

The Creation of a One-Party State

Hitler's first cabinet was essentially based on the Harzburg Front. Three Nazis—Hitler, Göring, and Frick (Interior)—were flanked by nine independent conservatives and members of the DNVP and the *Stahlhelm.* Among them were Papen (vice-chancellor), Neurath (Foreign Affairs), Schwerin von Krosigk (Finance), Hugenberg (Economics and Agriculture), General Werner von Blomberg (1878–1946, Defense), and the head of the *Stahlhelm,* Franz Seldte (1882–1947, Labor). Hindenburg naïvely expected that the presence of so many non-Nazis in the cabinet would dam Hitler's drive toward dictatorship. But the gigantic torchlight victory parade, in which thousands of brown-shirted storm troopers marched past the chancellery on the evening of Hitler's appointment —the day Hitler called "the day of the national rising"—should have been an omen. And two days later, Hitler appealed to the German people: "Give us four years and then judge us!" Promising to end its "suffering from fourteen years of Marxism," he vowed to restore Germany's greatness.

As an initial step, Hitler dissolved the Reichstag and called for new elections in March, hoping to obtain the two-thirds majority required to alter the constitution. Intimidation of the electorate was expected to produce the desired result. Göring, who had become minister-president of Prussia, used the Prussian police and the SA to begin his "clean-up action." He boasted that he knew but two types of people: "those who work for the *Volk* and those who only destroy and annihilate." Urging the police not to hesitate to shoot down all enemies of the state, "regardless of the consequences," he loosed the Nazi terror into the streets and the homes of the nation.

On February 27, the Reichstag building went up in flames. Within hours, Göring and Goebbels denounced the fire as "a monstrous deed of Bolshevik terror." Recently some historians have tried to substantiate the accusation that members of the KPD actually started the fire, but most continue to believe that it was set by the Nazis themselves to provide a spectacular excuse for sharper repression of the opposition. Certainly the Nazis had stronger motives and had more to gain from the fire than the Communists.

In face of the "red threat," Hitler persuaded Hindenburg on the following day to issue "Ordinances for the Protection of the German State and Nation." "As defense against communistic acts of terror endangering the state," the ordinances set aside, without

time limit, most of the civil liberties guaranteed by the Weimar constitution, and converted the penalties for many crimes from imprisonment to death. Freedom of speech, press, and assembly; the secrecy of the postal service; habeas corpus; and the inviolability of home and property were all suspended. The powers of the central government were made clearly superior to those of the federal states. The Nazis promptly used the ordinances to close opposition newspapers, imprison opponents, and intimidate the population. "Enemies of the state," "traitors," "November criminals"—those who had helped establish the Weimar Republic in the November Revolution of 1918—were ruthlessly apprehended. As Goebbels noted gleefully in his diary: "Now Göring is cleaning up. What a delight! Now the red pestilence will be extirpated!"

Despite terror and intimidation, the elections of March 5, 1933, failed to give the National Socialists a majority (see Chart 2). In this last supposedly free election, with 88 percent of the eligible electorate participating, they received 44 percent of the votes or 17.3 million out of a total of 39.3 million. In coalition with the DNVP, which obtained 8 percent of the votes, the NSDAP could count on only a majority in the new Reichstag, far short of the 67 percent needed to change the constitution. The strength of the Center and the SPD parties had changed surprisingly little, and the KPD had dropped only slightly.

Actually, the electoral results were of little importance, since Hitler was busy undermining the remaining democratic institutions. During March, concentration camps were established; at first they were improvised in private homes, then they became specially prepared barbed-wire enclaves. The enemies of the regime began to disappear in the dead of the night. Interrogations, torture, or death awaited them. The concept of legality was giving way to that of the "national will" embodied in the Führer and his NSDAP. Three weeks after the elections, the Reichstag was deprived of all essential power. Through the Enabling Act of March 23 —officially labeled "Law for the Relief of the Distress of Nation and State"—Hitler's government was awarded the right to make laws and treaties without the approval of the Reichstag, even if they violated the Weimar constitution. The new law was to be valid for four years, unless Hitler's government should fall before expiration of this period.

The Enabling Act gave legal sanction to the establishment of Hitler's dictatorship. Of the delegates, 441, including all Centrists, voted for it, and only 94 Socialists (out of a total SPD delegation of 120) voted against it, warning that the act would destroy "legality, equality, and human values." The 81 Communists who had been elected to the Reichstag had been disqualified by a special law and hence could not vote on the issue. Since the 74 favorable votes of the Catholic Center—largely motivated by fear of Communism rather than by love of National Socialism—gave Hitler the required votes to pass the law, the Center was later accused of guilt by association with Nazism. After World War II, when Nazism was on trial, the German courts had to deal with this question and came to the conclusion that the Centrists had been unwise, perhaps even stupid, but not guilty.

During the next four months, Hitler

used the legislative powers awarded to him under the Enabling Act to transform Germany into a totalitarian state. The Socialist and Center parties were dissolved, the DNVP disbanded itself voluntarily, and the *Stahlhelm* was incorporated into the NSDAP. By a law of July 14, the NSDAP was made the sole legal party in Germany, and the attempt to organize new political groups was made a criminal offense. As Goebbels explained to the foreign press: "National Socialism requires all power and all responsibility." And he pointed out that "he who is convinced that his *Weltanschauung* [view of the world or philosophy of life] is correct . . . can suffer no competitor for power." To transform Germany from a federal into a unitary state, *Statthalter* (governors) were appointed by Hitler to supervise the administration of the various states. In addition, the Nazis divided all Germany into *Gaue* —an old Germanic word for "districts"—each of which was under the supervision of a specially appointed *Gauleiter* (district leader). Hitler was thus provided with two channels of authority over all German territory: the official government line through the *Statthalter* and the unofficial one through the party and the *Gauleiter*.

At the same time, the cabinet was rendered impotent when voting by ministers was abolished and the Führer was given all power of decision. A law for the "Rehabilitation of the Civil Service" also gave Hitler power to dismiss from government service all "non-Aryans"—that is, all Jews—all those who "show no aptitude," and "those who do not labor relentlessly for the national state." Strikes were forbidden in May, after which all labor unions were abolished, eventually to be replaced by an All-German Labor Front, including employers and employees, and closely supervised by the central government. Meanwhile, Goebbels began to infiltrate the fields of education, art, theater, newspapers, and literature, in order to eliminate from German culture all politically unreliable elements and impregnate it with National Socialist ideals.

Yet, despite Hitler's determination to eradicate voting, majority decisions, and any ideas of individual responsibility wherever pockets of democracy had left them, his political astuteness —like that of Mussolini and Stalin— required the retention of mock elections to demonstrate to the world the popular backing of his regime. Although the Reichstag had been disenfranchised through the abolition of all parties except the NSDAP, new elections were held in November 1933. The official party list of the NSDAP received 92.2 percent of the votes. Only 3.4 million Germans dared to brave reprisals by expressing their doubts about the regime and casting negative or invalid ballots. The new Nazi Reichstag was seldom called, since it had no legislative functions and served largely as a rostrum for Hitler's speeches.

The Elimination of Internal Opposition

The regular police forces, the SA, the SS, and the newly created Gestapo (secret state police) succeeded fairly rapidly in eliminating most overt signs of resistance. But before Hitler could claim to be a real Führer, he had to face the problem of disunion within his party and the related question of the obedience of the *Reichswehr*.

Once the Nazis had seized power, the rivalry between Roehm's SA, the "old fighters," and Himmler's SS, the black-shirted elite guard, had become more and more pronounced. Roehm and his brown-shirts represented the left wing of the party; they desired more of a social revolution, more of the spoils of victory, and incorporation of their units into the regular *Reichswehr,* a step that would give them more prestige and better weapons. Hitler, however, was losing his fondness for the plebeian SA that had helped him to power. To run the Reich he relied largely on the smaller, more tightly organized, and more fanatically devoted SS, and saw to it that its members were awarded choice posts in the government. Moreover, he hoped that by abasing the SA, he might gain the respect of the upper classes and the support of the *Reichswehr* officers, both of whom looked with fearful suspicion upon the inchoate mass of some three million brown-shirts.

In the early summer of 1934, Hitler decided to crush the independent power of the SA. To put its members off guard, they were sent on furlough, and Himmler spread among his most trusted SS officers the rumor that Roehm was plotting a conspiracy against the Führer. On June 30, the Nazis were ready for their St. Bartholomew Massacre. In a brief, savage week end, as the announcement later read, "Hitler acted as the Supreme Tribunal of the German people," and together with Göring, Himmler, and the SS "destroyed without mercy the undisciplined, the unsocial and sickly elements" within the NSDAP. Hitler personally went to Bad Wiessee near Munich to supervise the arrest of Roehm and other SA leaders. The arrested were taken to prison and promptly shot without legal procedures. Meanwhile, Göring and the SS similarly apprehended prominent SA leaders in Berlin and saw to their immediate execution. Accused of conspiring with Roehm, of being traitors or homosexuals, others were shot in homes and prisons throughout Germany upon advance orders of Hitler, Göring, Himmler, and Reinhard Heydrich (1904–1942), the head of the SS Security Division. General von Schleicher and his wife, Gregor Strasser, friends of Papen, prominent Catholics, suspected monarchists, personal enemies, and even victims of mistaken identity—all fell in this national blood bath. A few more fortunate suspects, such as Papen himself, were merely arrested, but not shot. The dead, by official count, numbered 74; the unofficial toll ran closer to 1000.

On the heels of this three-day purge, Hitler promulgated a law retroactively legalizing the killings of the preceding days as "emergency measures required for the suppression of treasonous attacks." And Göring elaborated the theory that no law could have been violated by the purge, since "law and the will of the Führer are one and the same," and Hitler had to save the nation. Meanwhile, Goebbels propagated the theme that Hitler had liberated the German people from the terror of Roehm's SA. In gratitude for the services of SS members in the purge, Hitler turned them into an independent organization within the party, subject only to himself and Himmler. In the end, Göring reassured the confused and terrified nation that

the *Führer* accomplished great deeds out of the greatness of his heart, the passion of his will, and the goodness of his soul. Faith in him is alone the basis of our life. He who dares touch that faith has

ceased to be a German and must be destroyed.

Two months later, the death of President Hindenburg provided Hitler with an opportunity to attack another problem: the relationship of the army to his movement. He still hoped eventually to subvert the traditional spirit of the army officers through universal military service that would swamp the professional soldiers with politically indoctrinated recruits. But considerations of foreign policy forced him to delay this step until March 1935. Since there could be no thought of an open confrontation with the well-armed military, Hitler meanwhile devised other means to bring them into tighter control.

A day before Hindenburg's death, Hitler promulgated a law combining the offices of president and chancellor, designed to come into effect with the death of Hindenburg. Through this measure, Hitler sought to obtain the post of commander in chief of the armed forces, traditionally lodged in the presidency. On the following day, barely hours after Hindenburg's death, the *Reichswehr* was required to take an oath of allegiance to Hitler as its new commander. Significantly, the wording of the oath was changed from the days of the Weimar Republic. For "faithful service to my people and my fatherland" were substituted the words "unquestioning obedience to the Commander in Chief of the *Wehrmacht*, the *Führer* of the German *Reich* and people, Adolf Hitler." Moreover, to stress the break with the past, Hitler changed the name of the German army from *Reichswehr* to *Wehrmacht*. Trained by tradition to live and die by their military oath, the officers and men of the *Wehrmacht* henceforth became obedient, albeit reluctant,

servants of the new regime. To get popular backing for this latest coup, Hitler ordered a plebiscite on the question of uniting the offices of president and chancellor. Only 5.1 million voted against it; 88.2 percent of the electorate approved the action.

THE NAZI STATE

From the beginning of their accession to power, Adolf Hitler and his associates, feeling responsible only "to the future of the German nation," started to construct the Third Reich, which, like the first German Empire, was to last a thousand years. Hitler felt convinced that destiny had chosen him to fulfill his task, which, according to Goebbels, was "the achievement of total revolution." The "National Socialist *Volksbewegung*" (popular movement) was to transform Germany in all aspects. Hitler asserted that he wanted to destroy all that was diseased (by which he meant the Weimar Republic), and then build up a new Germany. "Either Germany will become a world power," he had written in *Mein Kampf*, "or she will cease to exist." And so that Germany would win a possible future war and not again fall victim to a stab in the back as in 1918, he sought to construct the strongest possible home front by unifying the nation through total coordination and discipline.

Yet Nazi ideology and actions were more negative than positive. There was much the Nazis stood against, but little they stood for. National Socialism was anti-Communist, anti-Socialist, anti-Semitic, antiforeign, anti-internationalist, anti-Catholic, anti-Versailles, anti-Freemasonry, anti-League of Nations, and opposed to a plethora of

other groups, ideologies, and institutions. Its "positive" aims were few: the purification of the race and the building of a new Germany in which the totalitarian state would be supreme.

The State and the Judiciary

In political and other matters, the Nazis' aim was expressed by their favorite term *Gleichschaltung,* meaning literally "coordination" but in fact connoting "subordination." All thought and action were to be subordinated to the state, which, according to Frick, resided in the Führer (leader) and his followers (*Gefolgschaft*). Private life apart from the state was not to be tolerated, since it was deemed meaningless. "What benefits the state is right" became a favored motto. The individual German was left only with *duties* to the state. The state, on the other hand, had no duties to its citizens or to humanity at large, but only *rights* vis-à-vis other states. Hegel's ideas on the organic state were now distorted beyond recognition, and Rousseau's General Will became the will of the Führer. As Frick explained to a meeting of *Gauleiter,* "The *Volk* is a being, leading its own life and following its own laws . . . with its own historically formed blood community. Individualistic, liberal thinking must be overcome."

This all-powerful state, according to Hitler, knew no moral scruples and lived by a primordial instinct of survival. "The strongest has the right to enforce his will," he had announced in 1923; forever intoxicated with the thought of battle and might, five years later he added: "Man does not survive on humanitarian principles, but only through brutal struggle."

To control the German state, Hitler used his party and its numerous affiliates. Besides the SA and SS, there were the National Socialist Motorized Corps (NSKK), the Gestapo, the German Labor Front (DAF), the German Labor Service Battalions, the League of German Women (DFS), the Hitler Youth (HJ), the Union of German Girls (BDM), and dozens of other organizations—some uniformed, some provided only with distinctive insignias, but all hierarchically organized, thoroughly disciplined, and subject ultimately to the Führer. Keeping the masses organized made them easier to control, while at the same time it gave them a sense of purposeful participation.

The Nazis also hoped to turn Germany into a unified and unitary state, more susceptible to totalitarian control. In 1934 they abolished the remaining sovereign rights of the states as well as of the Reichsrat in which the states had been represented at the national level. *Gauleiter* and *Statthalter*—often one and the same person—retained sole rights of local control, theoretically, "in the name of the German people"; in fact, under the direction of the party and the central government. To symbolize the final achievement of German unification in 1934, young people were sent into the fields to collect all border posts marking the traditional limits between the German states, to bring them to the market places of towns and villages, and to burn them in a nation-wide bonfire of unity. To unite the people still more, the Nazis tried to mix the population by sending Germans from one region to work and settle in other parts of the Reich. Yet despite all these efforts, the traditional particularism did not die out. Even after

thirteen years of Hitlerism, the age-old antagonism between Bavarians and Prussians persisted.

Totalitarian control also required new concepts of law and legality. Law in all its aspects was deprived of its abstract or moral basis and became frankly political and opportunistic. Hans Frank (1900–1946), the Nazi Reich Commissioner for Justice, did his best to abolish "the old liberal idea of 'no penalty without a formal law.'" Nazi law, according to him, knew no equity or justice in the traditional sense, and people's actions were to be judged not on the basis of laws but rather on the basis of "the National Socialist *Weltanschauung*." In essence, the whole legal machinery was no longer to serve the individual, but solely the aims of the *Volksbewegung*. The protection of the law, according to Göring, was to be extended only to those who were true *Volksgenossen* (National Socialist-minded citizens). Since Hitler and his followers embodied the German people, those who disobeyed them were committing crimes against the German people and therefore deserved no protection of the law.

To implement these ideas, the judiciary was purged of all unreliable judges, and a special People's Court was set up in 1934 to judge cases of treason, which by definition could mean almost any political offense. The death penalty became common in the sentences passed by this court. Much of the law, however, was not administered through the courts; rather, it remained in the hands of the Gestapo, supervised first by Göring and later by Himmler. Proceedings here depended on the whims of the examiners and the importance of the case. Most

frequently, those arrested were "interrogated" and sent to a concentration camp for a few months or a few years as a salutary warning to like-minded discontents and as an intimidation to the people at large. But even during the early years, some were given a mock trial and promptly executed. Occasionally others died as a result of the "interrogation." As the regime grew to maturity, concentration camps multiplied, ultimately reaching perhaps as many as three hundred. Communists, Socialists, Jews, recalcitrant priests and ministers, defeatists, financial speculators, intellectuals—in fact, almost anybody who displeased someone in the hierarchy—were gradually herded into the ghastly compounds that were to become a black stigma on Western civilization.

Blood and Soil

With the aid of the party philosopher Rosenberg and the application of pseudo-scientific ideas, the Nazis developed racial theories that came to assume the place of a creed in their movement. Nationalistic to the point of absurdity, Rosenberg asserted that race was the primordial force in society, the basis of language and cultural traditions, of art, beauty, progress, and achievement. Among the races, the Nordic Aryans were not only the best, but were destined to rule the lower races—the Latins, the Slavs, the Semites, and the Negroes. In *Mein Kampf*, Hitler had stated: "All human culture and civilization depend on the Aryans." Without them "the earth would sink back under the dark veil of primitive times." But superior racial stock alone did not suffice to make a people great. Race, according to Rosen-

berg, stemmed from the soil. Blood and soil together produced the true folk soul (*Volksseele*) that alone could aspire to greatness. Hence it was not merely politically wrong, but "religiously" blasphemous to allow "German soil" to be contaminated by an alien race.

The fetish of race and racial purity, in which the extermination of the Jews was only incidental, became an end in itself in the Nazi ideology. The Nazis were imbued with an obsession against "racial impurity." "Racial mixing," Hitler wrote in *Mein Kampf,* "is the sole cause of the demise of all cultures." And he became fanatically convinced that the German *Volk* could be saved only by ensuring its "racial purity." As early as July 1933, the Nazis passed their first in a series of Eugenics Laws, designed to supervise the breeding of future generations. Strict medical examinations were required before marriage, especially for all members of the SS elite. A Hereditary Health Court was established, with powers to issue sterilization decrees for the mentally or physically diseased. Those of good Aryan stock were encouraged to keep up their health through physical exercise and to propagate, in and out of wedlock, so as to increase "the best of the race." State subsidies were provided for large families, and Hitler personally acted as godfather to the twelfth child of every married woman.

To unite the German race, to justify demands for more living space (*Lebensraum*), and to ensure that "250 million Germans will live on this continent in less than 100 years," the Nazis actively encouraged the return of Germans—or descendants of German families—living abroad. Various organizations were established to keep contact with these Germans living abroad (*Auslandsdeutsche*), especially in the United States and South America. Reduced fares were offered to entice them to come "home to the Reich."

Racial fanaticism, ingrained anti-Semitism, and the need for an effective scapegoat stimulated the Nazis' persecution of the Jews, whom Hitler called "the eternal parasites." In *Mein Kampf,* in a discussion of leadership and propaganda, Hitler asserted that "all truly great leaders" know that they must keep "the attention of the masses concentrated on a single enemy." If there are too many opponents, Hitler felt, the people become confused, and "may question whether indeed all others are in the wrong." He applied this dictum in his policy toward the Jews. In countless speeches, he and his party bigwigs drummed into their audience the idea that the Jews lurked behind all enemies: Jews had instigated the 1918 stab in the back; Jews had made the 1918 Revolution; Soviet Communism was run by Jews; democracy, majority rule, and liberalism were nefarious Jewish devices; Freemasons were Jews; the stock exchange was manipulated by Jews. The ubiquitous Jew was the cause of all Germany's ills.

The consequent persecution of the Jews, so well known to most readers, initially lacked any formal policy. An unofficial boycott of all Jewish businesses and professional services was inaugurated in April 1933; Jews were occasionally beaten up and imprisoned; and the emigration of Jews started. Meanwhile, the Nazis indoctrinated the nation with their racial theories. The doctrine of race was to supersede all religious considerations. Catholics and

Protestants were instructed to investigate their origins, for their religion and personal beliefs were no safeguard if their lineage revealed a single Jewish grandparent. Countless Germans suddenly discovered they were labeled Jews and hence inferior to their friends and colleagues.

Those Jews who were prominent in the professions, in the wholesale or the retail trades, in banking and certain industries, and therefore readily identifiable to the public, were the first to suffer. Businesses were wrecked, Jewish merchants were terrorized by storm troopers, and some Jews disappeared into concentration camps. The Jewish exodus from Germany increased, just as did the flight of Communists, Socialists, intellectuals, and sincere liberals. But emigration was soon made difficult. An emigration tax (*Reichsfluchtsteuer*) was imposed on all those who wanted to leave the country; at first it was only a small percentage of the emigrant's assets, but soon it was raised to a confiscatory 100 percent. Their inability to take along at least some savings discouraged many Jews from fleeing the country. Moreover, many Germans, ignorant of their Jewish ancestry until the advent of Hitler, had no wish to leave their homes, and remained in the hope that the Nazis' threats were mere propaganda.

But by 1935, discrimination and persecution were becoming systematized. Through the Nuremberg Laws and the Nationality Acts of September 1935, Jews—now legally defined as anyone with a single Jewish grandparent—were deprived of their citizenship and designated as "members but not citizens of the state." This automatically barred them from the civil service, the legal profession, the Labor Front, and all official organizations. Mixed marriages between Jews and non-Jews, or sexual relations between them, were prohibited by law. In the fall of 1938, anti-Jewish legislation and harassment went into high gear. Using as a pretext the murder of a secretary of the German Embassy in Paris by a young Jew, the Nazis unleashed ruthless attacks on the German Jews. Synagogues were burned; Jewish homes, apartments, and shops were destroyed; and a collective fine of 1 billion marks was imposed upon them. Thereafter more anti-Jewish legislation was issued almost weekly. Jews were barred from attending theaters, concerts, movies, or other public performances; they were forced to sell their real-estate and business holdings at ridiculous prices; they were not allowed to buy jewelry or gold; they could not walk on certain streets; they had to assume special Biblical names, such as "Israel" and "Sarah," entered in special identity papers that clearly marked them as Jews. Finally, they were forced to wear a large yellow star. Before the outbreak of World War II, some Jews were being restricted to ghettos and there were rumors in the Nazi hierarchy that the decision might ultimately be made to exterminate the Jews.

The New Religion

Hitler often used religious terminology in his pronouncements. However, what he called spirit and soul—words often found in his speeches—were not Christian concepts, but mystical embodiments of nationalism. When he invoked God—which he liked to do in his public addresses—he envisioned

some kind of Germanic god who could best be served by devotion to the German people. Despite his Catholic background, Hitler had no understanding of Christian ideals. Privately he insisted that "one is either a German or a Christian. One cannot be both." The Old and New Testaments and everything connected with Christian dogma were to him "all the same Jewish swindle." And he vowed: "In the end, I will eradicate Christianity in Germany, root and branch."

But in his early pronouncements of 1933, he promised, for obvious tactical reasons, not to meddle in religious affairs. He recognized the usefulness of seeking a temporary accommodation with the Catholic Church. And despite his personal conviction that "a German Church or German Christianity" was "sheer nonsense," he gave his consent to the attempt to create a Protestant Reich Church, which was to be coordinated with the state and act as a useful tool for the political orientation of the youth.

In July 1933, the German government concluded a Concordat with the Vatican. The Catholic Church hoped to obtain recognition of her traditional rights in the new Reich. In return for their assurance not to mix in politics, Hitler granted the Catholics freedom of religious activities. His main aim, of course, was to undermine the remaining strength of the Center party and of the Catholic unions, and to get valuable public recognition for his young regime. He had no intention of abiding by the agreements, for in the end the Catholics, too, were subjected to total integration.

Friction between the Nazis and the Catholic Church began in 1934. Catholic orders and schools were attacked, Catholic literature was censored, and church welfare agencies closed. Nazi interference and harassment finally led to an open break in 1937, when the pope publicly denounced Hitler's constant violation of the concordat and the heathenish deification of race and *Volk* practiced by the Nazi regime.

From then on, Catholicism was arraigned among the enemies of the people. Although some priests did not oppose Hitler, others were arrested and condemned on trumped-up charges, usually involving morals or devious financial dealings. A campaign of hatred and defamation against the church was launched in the National Socialist press. Churchmen in great numbers were herded into concentration camps. All possible means were used to deter the youth from attending religious services. In 1938, numerous Catholic churches suddenly burst into flames. On such occasions, the services of the local fire departments were usually unavailable or conveniently delayed, and the arsonists were never apprehended.

With the Protestant churches, Hitler faced a slightly different problem. Despite the outward union of the various Protestant sects in the so-called Evangelical Church in July 1933, the Protestants remained in fact disunited in dogma as well as in their attitude toward the new regime. On the one extreme, there were the "German Christians," wholly devoted to Hitlerism. They believed that God's law was being fulfilled in the Führer and the Nationalist Socialist state. Their motto was: "One *Volk!* One God! One *Reich!* One Church!" At the opposite pole were those led by Pastor Martin Niemöller (1892–   ) who opposed the Nazis's aims of converting their church into a political arm of the state. Be-

tween these two extremes, the bulk of the Protestants simply followed the Lutheran tradition of obedience to the constituted government, and tried to avoid becoming involved in the political struggle. Hitler hoped to use this division among the clergy to gain control of the entire church. In November 1933, he appointed a Protestant Reich bishop for the task of subordinating the church to the new regime. Clergy and dogma were to be gradually "Aryanized," that is, purified of all Hebrew-Christian influence. By 1935, religious *Gleichschaltung* had progressed to the point that Hitler created a Reich Ministry for Church Affairs with complete control over the Protestant churches. The minister, Hanns Kerrl (1887–1941), was given legal power to grant or withhold funds, confiscate church property, imprison ministers, and issue binding ordinances, all for the supposed purpose of "establishing order in the German Evangelical Church."

But a number of pastors refused to submit to the imposed ideology of the new Reich Church. Niemöller—although he had originally been a Nazi sympathizer—and like-minded ministers formed the Emergency League of Pastors in 1933, and in the following year established an independent church administration under the name of the German Confessional Church. The Confessionals refused to give the oath of allegiance to Hitler, required of all members of the Reich Church. They rejected the application of authoritarian principles within the church as well as the heathenish philosophy of the Nazis. By 1936, the fight between the regime and the Confessional Church was in high gear. Pastors were arrested in great numbers,

and their religious activities were curtailed wherever possible. In 1937, Niemöller disappeared into a concentration camp from which, with the exception of a short interval, he emerged only at the conclusion of World War II.

Persecution of ministers and the closing of churches reduced the activities of the Confessional Church, but it did not help Hanns Kerrl in building an effective, all-embracing Reich Church. This led Hitler gradually to abandon all expectation for using the church as a positive instrument of government and education. The regime turned to indoctrinating the youth and the masses with a new German creed, in which Hitler was the second Messiah. Children learned that "Jesus freed men from sin just as Hitler saved Germany from ruin"; that "Jesus worked for heaven, while Hitler works for the German earth." Faith in Hitler was given truly religious significance, and party rallies and pageants were turned into gigantic acts of devotion. Extremists even claimed that Christ had been a Nordic martyr, crucified by the Jews, an act now avenged by the Führer, whom these fanatics actually believed to be Christ in a second coming.

The *Führerprinzip*

Totalitarianism on the scale practiced by the Nazis required effective organization and unquestioned obedience within the hierarchical scale. Through their myriad organizations, the leaders of the party achieved hitherto inconceivable control over the life of the nation. National Socialism in fact represented the militarization of all life. The state demanded full obedience

and directed the individual in his work and leisure, his social, cultural, economic, and political activities. To establish lines of command, a pyramid of *Führer* was fashioned, from Adolf Hitler down to the lowest block warden, and at all levels of the ladder, obedience was stressed as a sacred duty.

While there was some semblance of collective leadership among the party bigwigs, Hitler stood far above the rest in the minds and affection of most Germans. He alone held in his hands all the vital powers. He was president —a title he never used—and chancellor; he was chief legislator, chief executive, and supreme judge—the division among the three branches having been abolished; he was head of the only legal political party and commander in chief of the armed forces. But more than all this, he was *der Führer,* the well-nigh infallible symbol of the race and the nation, the embodiment of the collective will. Some worshipers journeyed to Berchtesgaden to fill urns with earth on which the Führer might have stepped.

Hitler displayed tremendous self-assurance and an uncanny intuition— although some say that he actually suffered from a persecution complex and owed his success principally to good luck. Whatever his psychological aberrations, he was remarkably gifted for his chosen profession. He had stupendous oratorical gifts with which he swayed the multitudes and imbued in his audience the same fanatical devotion to his cause that he himself practiced. A vegetarian who loved Wagner's music but hated ordinary leisure and recreation, Hitler lived on a strange mixture of emotion and logic. He was no intellectual, in whatever sense the word is used. Success made him feel and act almost like a prophet, and one wonders whether his rage against those who disobeyed his will was not inspired by the conviction of his own infallibility.

Hitler believed that the end justified the means. He displayed no scruples, no political or moral principles. Only the ultimate goal counted, and could be attained through any opportune action. "I will do anything to facilitate the success of my policy," he announced, adding characteristically; "Why should I not make an agreement in good faith today and unhesitatingly break it tomorrow, if the future of the German people demands it?"

Among the echelon of secondary *Führer,* many occupied multiple posts, so that the ruling clique was surprisingly small. Göring, for example, headed the Reichstag, supervised the Four-Year Plan, commanded the air force, acted as minister of forestry and hunting, and later became a member of the cabinet council, besides discharging other tasks. Himmler ran the SS and the Gestapo, later commanded all military units inside Germany, and became Reich commissioner for "safeguarding German nationality." The party hierarchy consisted largely of lower-middle-class discontents who had used the party and the National Socialist revolution to emerge as *Bonzen* (which might be translated as "rowdy *nouveaux riches* with abusive political power"). But a surprising number were university graduates and former high school teachers. Although most of those in the party hierarchy were convinced and devoted Nazis, there were the inevitable opportunists who climbed on the band wagon.

Below the hierarchy lay the masses

who made the movement possible. Despite their lower-class origin, most of the minor leaders felt contempt for the people at large, in whose name they supposedly ruled. Obedience was all that mattered; mutual respect was of secondary importance. As Goebbels noted: "The strength of a political party does not depend on the mental prowess of its members, but rather on their disciplined obedience."

Propaganda and Education

To weld the nation into flag-waving frenzy, the Nazis employed terror, propaganda, and educational devices with consummate efficiency. Hitler had predicted in 1923: "We will unleash a storm! People shall not sleep; they shall know that a thunderstorm is brewing!" In *Mein Kampf,* he had outlined most of the methods later adopted by Goebbels in his position as minister for propaganda and for the enlightenment of the people. Hitler advised that "all propaganda . . . must be at the level of understanding of the least intelligent." The greater the lie, he thought, the more readily the masses will swallow it, especially if it is accompanied by judiciously applied terror and intimidation. The Führer himself gave the example by pronouncing everything with utter conviction, and labeling all whose views differed as either stupid or criminal.

Through the Reich Chamber of Culture (*Reichskulturkammer*), Goebbels supervised press, radio, and cinema, as well as literature, the theater, music, painting, and sculpture. Even architectural styles had to conform to the new ideal of regularity and massiveness. Writers and artists who did not wish to produce National Socialistic art either emigrated or grew silent. The Nazis even sought to purify the German language by eradicating foreign words where possible, and gradually developed their own vocabulary befitting the national struggle.

Above all, the educational system was revamped to fit the "new order." Special SS schools were created to foster a new elite. The staffs and students of existing universities and schools were purged of uncooperative elements. Textbooks were rewritten and new courses were added, such as geopolitics. Physical education was transformed into defense science. Instead of pitching balls, the young were taught to lob hand grenades; hide and seek games were turned into training in camouflage. And when not attending classes, young people were indoctrinated through various youth organizations.

In the educational process, Hitler was not interested in "improvement of the mind," but in developing "instinct, determination, and energy." Youth was to rediscover its "primitive nature." Frick insisted that the main purpose of schools was to produce students "whose thoughts and actions are dedicated to serving the nation and to self-sacrifice, if needed." With all means of communication controlled by the state, with the young indoctrinated to distrust, and if necessary to inform on their parents, young Germans were brought up to know little else but National Socialist morality and aims.

National Socialist Economics

Gleichschaltung was also the watchword for the national economy. But whereas most other Nazi accomplish-

ments were of dubious worth, their achievements in the area of economics were outstanding, even phenomenal. By using a mixture of state socialism and free enterprise, under strict government control, by ruthless economic planning, and by trampling on the rights of "all enemies of the state," the Nazis pulled Germany out of its economic slump. It was largely Hitler's success in providing a good measure of prosperity and stability that accounted for his popularity and persuaded so many to overlook the sinister aspects of his regime.

Industry and agriculture, labor and management, transport, trade, and communications—all were reorganized and supervised so as to strengthen the state. Using the German Labor Front as a gigantic superstructure, its administrator, Robert Ley (1890–1945), tried to weld labor and management into a community of interests. Within each industrial enterprise, the owner or manager (as *Betriebsführer* or leader of the establishment) was made responsible to the German people for his firm's contribution to the reconstruction of the Reich.

Under the direction of Schacht— made president of the Reichsbank in March 1933 and minister of economics in August 1934—and later of Göring, a Four-Year Plan was devised with the announced aim of helping the peasants and workers. The eradication of unemployment initially received priority in government planning, and was effected with astonishing success. Large-scale public works projects, such as the building of superhighways, huge sports arenas, monumental government edifices, and public housing, were inaugurated. Economic growth was stimulated, especially in heavy industry and the production of armaments.

Labor camps were set up and then converted into labor service battalions, to which all young men and women had to contribute a year of compulsory service. Jews, Communists, "undesirables," and many women were dismissed from their jobs, while more and more people were enrolled in full-time paramilitary or other party organizations. From 6 million unemployed in January 1933, the number dropped to 4 million by December of that year, to 2.6 million by December 1934, and to less than 1 million by the end of 1937. In 1938, when the huge fortifications were being constructed in the west, and rearmament was in full swing, there was a labor shortage.

Within the limits set by government requirements and the Four-Year Plan, the big industrialists enjoyed considerable power, prestige, and profits. During the early years of the regime those who had helped Hitler's rise had reason to feel satisfied with their decision. Although the government controlled prices and wages, and reduced profits to some extent by levying special taxes, the industrialists felt safe from the threat of general nationalization, were freed from labor troubles, and were guaranteed a booming market. The production of basic materials rose sharply. Between 1933 and 1938, hard-coal output increased from 110 to 186 million tons; soft coal, from 126 to 195 million tons; and raw steel from 7.6 to 22.7 million tons.

To bind the workers firmly to the regime and indoctrinate them with National Socialist ideology, the government asserted complete control over their economic existence. The state administered all welfare and social insurance plans as well as compulsory savings programs, set wages, supervised

working conditions, and had arbitrary power to assign workers to jobs. Even vacations were made compulsory. The government established a special agency, Strength through Joy (*Kraft durch Freude*), to organize and supervise the workers' leisure time. Film showings or theatrical productions, family camps in the mountains or vacations at the seashore, ocean cruises on government-owned Strength-through-Joy liners, all accompanied by free indoctrination, were made "compulsorily" available.

Hitler also sought to make Germany as self-sufficient as possible. Food imports were reduced so that more foreign credits could be diverted to the importation of basic raw materials—used at first for industrial expansion and later for strategic stockpiling. The invention and production of synthetics were pushed with deliberate speed, particularly in the fields of motor fuels, buna (a substitute for rubber), and artificial fibers. When the Second Four-Year Plan was inaugurated in 1936, Hitler stipulated as its primary purpose the achievement of economic autarky. In a secret memorandum, he expressed his conviction that Germany would soon be at war, and that economic mobilization, regardless of the cost, had to proceed hand in hand with the strengthening of the *Wehrmacht* and the building of German armaments, so as "to make Germany the first military power on earth." Production of food as well as of synthetics and basic machinery, rationing and allocation of quotas, regulation of imports and exports were now oriented to rendering Germany as independent as possible of shipments from abroad, in case war should entail another blockade. The Second Four-Year Plan thus inaugurated the period of "guns rather than butter." In a speech much ridiculed because of Göring's own obesity, he asked the nation: "Shall we import lard or metal ores? Let me tell you: preparedness makes us powerful. Butter merely makes us fat!" Although he was a nationalist, Schacht resented the increased political interference in economics involved in this plan. In November 1937, he resigned as minister of economics and was replaced by Funk.

But Schacht remained as president of the Reichsbank to continue his task of financing Hitler's ventures. As he had in 1923, he devised ingenious schemes that at first produced astonishing results. Germany became a closed economy. All exports and imports were handled by the government, all private fortunes abroad had to be placed at its disposal under penalty of death. Under this system, the government alone held foreign currencies and foreign credits, which it could allocate to strategic imports. Where possible, barter was used between Germany and foreign countries, since Germany was perennially short of gold and hard currencies. Heavy machinery, precision instruments, chemicals, transport equipment, and other manufactured goods were exchanged for food and needed raw materials. By being sealed off from the money markets of the world, the German mark could be kept at a fictitious level and thus ensure relative financial stability at home. The barter system and governmental control of all foreign trade also permitted Hitler to initiate economic warfare. By judiciously buying up major crops, often at prices above the world market —particularly in Greece, Yugoslavia, Rumania, and Bulgaria—Germany was able to apply increasing politico-economic pressure on the states of south-

eastern Europe, a pressure that helped expand German influence.

To obtain the required funds for internal spending, Schacht and the government resorted to various devices. Special contributions and even forced loans were frequently demanded. The property of Communists and Jews was gradually confiscated. Patriotic citizens were enjoined to surrender their gold rings and jewelry. Special extra postage stamps were sold to raise funds for social services. Yet in the long run, the expedient resorted to was to print more paper currency to cover the yearly deficit. Because prices and wages were fixed, the mark retained its apparent stability. But as government expenditures continued to increase, especially with the heavy armaments program after 1936, and as revenue remained more or less stationary, Schacht warned that it would be impossible to keep up the artificial value of the currency forever. In January 1939, he was dismissed from his post as president of the Reichsbank—although he continued to serve in the government as minister without portfolio until 1943. The printing of money continued, and with it the devaluation of the mark. By 1945, it had depreciated to about 1 percent of its 1933 value.

HITLER'S SUCCESS IN FOREIGN AFFAIRS

In *Mein Kampf,* Hitler defined the task of foreign policy as the "creation of a healthy, viable, and natural balance between the size and growth of a country's population on the one hand and the size and quality of its land on the other." As the particular goal of National Socialism, he stipulated the acquisition of territory as required by the German people. He predicted that such action would demand sacrifices in blood, since "only the might of a victorious sword" could solve the territorial question. He advised that Germany should seek land not in colonies, but "almost exclusively in Europe." "We shall take up where they [our forefathers] stopped six centuries ago," he wrote, "and look for land in the east. Land can be gained primarily in Russia and in the border states dominated by her."

His more immediate aims, proclaimed in almost every speech in the 1920s and reiterated after his assumption of power, were the abrogation of the Treaty of Versailles, the breaking of Germany's isolation, and its establishment as one of the dominant powers in the world.

To achieve his aims, Hitler conducted a highly successful, intensely active foreign policy. By keeping Germany constantly on the diplomatic offensive while lulling his opponents into a false sense of security, he succeeded beyond all expectations. Like a master tactician, he knew when it was opportune to shift from stern demands to holding out the olive branch. He frequently proclaimed his love of peace. He announced in 1933 that all outstanding questions could be settled "peacefully and by treaties." "No war," he intoned, "even if successful, is worth the sacrifices." His demands were clothed in reasonable principles. Germany deserved equality of rights with other nations, and the theory of self-determination for all peoples should be applied to solve disputed boundaries.

In the conduct of foreign affairs, most of which he directed personally, he was helped by his fanaticism and

his disregard for international morality. He was convinced that France would forever remain the deadly enemy of Germany, and constructed his policy accordingly. He felt equally certain that Russia, according to him dominated by Jews, would disintegrate, because the Jewish race was incapable of building a state. He could not conceive of alliances for the preservation of peace. "An alliance not aimed at war is senseless and without value," he wrote in *Mein Kampf*. "Alliances are only made for battle." In a sense, his pseudo Darwinism dominated his concept of international relations. Since all life was built on struggle, there was "really little difference between peace and war." Opportunism, guided by his intuition, dictated much of his action. "I am prepared to guarantee all frontiers and make non-aggression pacts and alliances with anybody," he once stated. "It would be stupid not to employ such measures merely because one might possibly one day have to break such solemn promises."

His success was, of course, also aided by the complicated international situation of the 1930s and the incredibly shortsighted selfishness of the nations. After the brief era of international cooperation from 1925 to 1930, during which statesmen had hoped to solve all problems at the conference table, the nations retreated to isolation and distrust. Each sought its own salvation, much to the benefit of the revisionist powers: Germany, Italy, and Japan.

Abrogation of Versailles

The first major breach of the Treaty of Versailles was made in October 1933, when Germany walked out of the sixty-nation disarmament conference in Ge-

neva and renounced its membership in the League of Nations. To be sure, the disarmament talks were not likely to produce tangible results, and the League had been discredited by its failure to prevent the Japanese conquest of Manchuria in 1931. But Germany's action signified that Hitler intended to rearm the nation. As an official excuse, Hitler complained that although in 1932 the Allies had agreed in principle to grant Germany equal rights, they were apparently no longer willing to abide by this agreement—because of his assumption of power. He called this a "discrimination dishonoring the German people," who no longer wished to remain a second-class nation. At the same time, the Führer stressed his "unshakable love of peace and his readiness to negotiate," and boasted that a plebiscite would prove the German people's "concept of honor." In November, the Germans were asked to vote on the question of withdrawal from the League. The referendum resulted in an affirmative vote of 95 percent.

In January 1935, according to the schedule contained in the Treaty of Versailles, a plebiscite was held in the Saar to determine whether its inhabitants wished to remain under the government of the League of Nations, join France, or return to German sovereignty. Voting was preceded by a violent campaign, in which the Nazis displayed to the world their virulence and fanaticism. Since most Saarlanders spoke German, and Germany appeared economically more prosperous than France, the outcome was a foregone conclusion. Yet the lopsided result of the plebiscite, supervised by the League, with 90 percent favoring Germany, surprised the world.

Jubilant over this success, Hitler as-

sured France that the German-French border was now settled, and that he renounced forever Germany's rights to Alsace-Lorraine, since he wished to spare Germany and Europe the bloody sacrifices of a war. He then launched his next step in the dismantling of Versailles. In March 1935, he publicly denounced the disarmament clauses of the treaty. A special law was promulgated, introducing universal military training and calling for an army of thirty-six divisions. At the same time, Hitler announced the official creation of a German air force. In reality, Hitler's announcements were merely a public avowal of an established fact. Secret rearmament had already brought the army to the proposed future strength; according to most estimates, the German air force at the time was as strong as England's.

The reaction of the powers to Hitler's unilateral destruction of Versailles revealed their disunity. They protested, but took no action. Italy, France, and England conferred at Stresa in Italy to discuss whether to seek safety in pacts with Germany or to take joint action against it. But this so-called Stresa Front produced no tangible results, and, in the end, each nation went its own way. France concluded an alliance with Russia, a step it had contemplated for some time in order to re-establish its traditional two-front pressure on Germany. France's answer to Hitler was to seek reinsurance rather than to deal with him. Italy, about to start its conquest of Abyssinia, preferred to remain completely neutral. England, however, decided to come to terms with Germany, at least in the area that concerned it most. In June, England concluded the Anglo-German naval agreement, allowing Germany to build up to 35 percent of Britain's tonnage. No limitations on submarines were included in the pact. England's accommodation with Germany boded ill for the peace of Europe. By sanctioning the construction of a German navy, no matter of what tonnage, it admitted that the Treaty of Versailles had in effect become invalid. Moreover, England took this step without consulting the other signatories to the Versailles Treaty, even though the pact was bound to worry Russia and France. The naval agreement abandoned the Baltic Sea to the German fleet, much to the dismay of the Soviet Union, and forced France to enter the naval race in order to keep up with Germany. Britain's action was also shortsighted in other respects. By allowing the re-creation of a strong German navy, the pact forced the Anglo-French fleets to concentrate more in the North Sea, thereby abandoning the Far East to Japan.

The disunity of the Allies and their preoccupation with the Ethiopian crisis emboldened Hitler to undertake the final scrapping of the Versailles Treaty in March 1936. Using as a pretext the need for securing Germany's border against the new Franco-Russian alliance, he repudiated the Locarno Pacts and sent his army to reoccupy the Rhineland, which, according to the Versailles Treaty, was to remain demilitarized. Again he held the sword in one hand, the olive branch in the other. While German troops marched toward the Rhine, Hitler harangued the world by radio, boasting of the strength of the German "defensive forces." At the same time, he offered to come to terms with the powers. If the world would not accept his action, which he said was designed

merely to gain equal rights for Germany, he proposed a demilitarized zone on *both* sides of the Franco-German border—a suggestion the French were bound to reject since it would require dismantling their Maginot Line. He also suggested a twenty-five-year nonaggression pact with France and Belgium, nonaggression pacts with the eastern states, and Germany's re-entry into the League of Nations.

Once again Hitler was successful. Britain, busy in the Mediterranean and increasingly pacifist in attitude, refused to consider countermeasures. Some Frenchmen desired action, but feared their army might be inadequate for the job of expelling the Germans from the Rhineland without full-scale mobilization, which might unleash a general war. According to testimony presented at the Nuremberg War Crimes Trials (see pages 316 ff), some German generals apparently felt that even a minor military demonstration by the French would have sent the German army in headlong retreat, since Hitler's army was as yet more bluff than reality. The question was finally turned over to the League of Nations, which found Germany guilty of violating the Treaties of Versailles and Locarno, but took no further action.

The End of German Isolation

While gradually dismantling the Versailles Treaty, Hitler was also busy strengthening Germany by expanding its influence abroad through various official and secret means. Besides economic penetration, the Nazis used what came to be known as fifth columns, local Nazi parties or organizations friendly to Germany. They received organizational help, financial support, and propaganda from Germany. Overseas, as, for example, in the United States, these pro-German associations never acquired much importance. In Europe, however, especially in the states bordering on Germany or in others with German-speaking minorities, local Nazi units became important instruments for spreading German influence. Austria, Czechoslovakia, Hungary, and Rumania were particularly affected by this internal subversion. Danzig, although officially remaining a free city under auspices of the League, was actually slowly taken over by local Nazis, and for all intents and purposes incorporated into the Nazi system long before the official annexation of 1939.

RELATIONS WITH POLAND AND RUSSIA
In order to concentrate on the opportune direction of the moment, Hitler found it advantageous to make temporary settlements in other areas. While working against the West on the abrogation of the Versailles Treaty, he found it expedient to avoid all tension in the east. In January 1934, he negotiated a ten-year nonaggression pact with Poland. The two nations, despite their previous distrust, agreed to maintain the existing borders and not to use force against each other under any circumstances. Since even the Weimar Republic had refused to accept the permanent loss of the eastern lands, it should have been obvious that Hitler's guarantee represented at the most a temporary expedient. Yet the Poles, wedged between Communist and Nazi states, accepted the pact at face value and relaxed their reliance on France. Hitler thus succeeded in undermining France's eastern security

system. When in September of the same year, the French tried to bolster their power by proposing to guarantee a mutual security pact among Germany, Russia, Poland, Czechoslovakia, Finland, and the three Baltic states, Hitler brushed them aside. Without equality in armaments, he argued, Germany could not afford to become involved in eastern conflicts.

German relations with Russia were similarly opportunistic. Despite Hitler's savage suppression of Communism and his stated intention of conquering Russian territories, commercial relations between the two nations continued to flourish as they had in the 1920s. For a while, even their military collaboration was retained. Hitler's stand was ambivalent. He pretended to be not anti-Russian but only anti-Communist. In 1936, he told the Reichstag: "I have never refused to collaborate with Russia for peace; I am only opposed to Bolshevik expansion." But a boastful anti-Communist stand was not meant solely for internal propaganda. He also hoped to attract to his campaign other nations, particularly England. He publicly requested others to help him "preserve European culture and civilization" and safeguard Europe from the "incursion of this destructive Asiatic ideology which topples all traditional values."

Worried by Japan's expansion in Manchuria and Germany's renascence, Russia joined the League of Nations in 1934 and became the most ardent advocate of collective security against the revisionist powers. In 1935, Communists everywhere were instructed by Moscow to abandon their traditional boycott of bourgeois politics and to cooperate with all anti-Fascist parties.

As a result, so-called popular front governments—comprising moderate parties, Socialists, and Communists—came to the fore in various countries with the aim of stemming the rising tide of Fascism and National Socialism.

ATTEMPTS AT UNION WITH AUSTRIA
In *Mein Kampf,* Hitler had stated that "related blood belongs in a common *Reich.*" One of his proposed tasks, therefore, was to unite Germany and Austria. During the early 1920s, the Austrian Socialists and liberals, mostly concentrated in Vienna, had also desired *Anschluss* with the Weimar Republic. The Austrian Catholics and the conservatives of the provinces had opposed it. But the question had remained academic, in view of the Allies' refusal to sanction such a union. During the late 1920s, Austria had become less and less stable. Economically it was always on the verge of bankruptcy. Street fighting was common. Three main groups, each with its own private army, vied for power: the Christian Socialists—growing daily more conservative; the Socialists; and the Nazis.

In 1932, the office of prime minister had been assumed by Engelbert Dollfuss (1892–1934), nominally a Christian Socialist. By this time, the Socialists of Vienna no longer desired union with Germany, whereas the Austrian Nazis and conservatives worked for it assiduously. An authoritarian at heart and an admirer of Mussolini, Dollfuss abrogated most constitutional freedoms in 1933 and ended parliamentarianism. To safeguard Austrian independence, he outlawed the Austrian Nazi party. Hitler retaliated by closing the flow of German tourists to Austria. By 1934, Dollfuss decided to establish a dictator-

ship, since he equally hated the Socialists on the one hand and the Austrian Nazis on the other. He outlawed all political parties except his own Fatherland Front, promulgated a semi-Fascistic constitution, and made an agreement with Mussolini designed to protect Austria's independence. A protest rising by the Socialists was quelled with much bloodshed.

Austria's turmoil and the fear that Dollfuss' independent dictatorship might be successful goaded Hitler into premature action. Encouraged by Berlin and more or less directed from Munich, the Austrian Nazis attempted a *coup d'état* in July 1934. They seized some government buildings and the radio station in Vienna and murdered Dollfuss, but failed to gain control of the government. Since Mussolini immediately sent troops to the Austrian border in order to help the Austrians against Germany, Hitler disavowed the entire affair and gave no further support to his fellow Nazis in Austria.

After the failure of this putsch, Dollfuss' successor, Kurt von Schuschnigg (1897–   ) pursued the same dictatorial policies. Like Germany, Austria began to rearm, and as a safeguard against German annexation, there was even talk of restoring the Hapsburgs. But Hitler had learned that he could not absorb Austria without first coming to terms with Italy; hence he decided on a temporary policy of conciliation. In 1935, he told the Reichstag: "Germany has no intention of interfering in Austrian affairs or of annexing Austria." What he wanted was merely "self-determination"—a principle Hitler could easily manipulate to Germany's advantage. In 1936, when he was eager to effect a *rapprochement*

with Italy, he even concluded a treaty with Austria recognizing its sovereignty and promising not to interfere in its internal affairs nor to help the Austrian Nazis, provided Austria would always act "in a manner behoving a German state." The latter clause affords an interesting insight into Hitler's definition of sovereignty. The treaty of 1936, at any rate, was designed by Hitler merely as a stopgap. Once Germany's friendship with Italy was cemented, Schuschnigg's position rapidly became hopeless. The Austrian Nazis grew in strength and prepared for the eventual *Anschluss*, which took place in 1938.

ITALO-GERMAN FRIENDSHIP The Austrian question and Mussolini's growing influence over the Balkans, an area on which Hitler had his own designs, made Italo-German cooperation more and more important for Germany. Ideologically, the two dictators shared many beliefs. Above all, both Italy and Germany were revisionist powers, dissatisfied with the results of World War I. But by 1933, Mussolini was an established dictator, whereas Hitler was still a parvenu. Mussolini represented an Allied country of the wartime coalition; his ambitions lay largely overseas and not in Europe. Hitler's demands for the union of all German-speaking peoples might be aimed at the South Tyrol, which Italy had absorbed as a result of World War I. Consequently, Mussolini sided with England and France during the early years of Hitler's regime. When Hitler visited Mussolini in June 1934, presumably to ascertain Italy's attitude toward Austria, no agreement between the two powers seemed possible. During the Vienna Putsch, Mussolini remained

anti-German, and in the following spring, when Germany announced its rearmament, he joined England and France in the anti-German Stresa Front.

The turning point came with the Abyssinian crisis in the fall of 1935. When Mussolini, after much hesitation and many negotiations, launched his invasion of Ethiopia in October, the League condemned Italy as an aggressor and imposed sanctions. But Germany, as a nonmember, continued its commercial support of Italy. Hitler made it clear to Mussolini that he could count on German benevolence during this crisis, and the Duce vowed that he would never forget that Germany did not join in the sanctions against Italy.

In 1936, Italo-German friendship ripened. The German-Austrian Treaty assuaged Mussolini's fears, and Hitler's official recognition of Italy's new empire in Ethiopia pleased his vanity. Above all, the outbreak of the Spanish Civil War helped to cement the friendship between the two countries. Italian ground troops and German technicians and pilots cooperated in Spain in support of Franco. Italian relations with England and France, already embittered by the sanctions provoked by the Abyssinian War, further deteriorated, since the Anglo-French favored nonintervention in Spain. Italy was thus thrown into the waiting arms of Germany. In October 1936, Italy's foreign minister visited Berlin to sign various cooperative agreements. Thus the beginnings of the Rome–Berlin axis were laid.

Further collaboration in Spain thenceforth drew the two dictators closer together. In September 1937, Mussolini visited Berlin, where he praised the renascence of Italy and Germany, and professed that they shared the same aims of national independence and greatness. Although Mussolini, temporarily satiated by the absorption of Abyssinia, still felt tempted, as he said, to jump to the "other side of the barricades" and side with England and France, continued friction in Spain brought him more and more firmly into the German camp.

While wooing Italy, Hitler succeeded in getting other friends. A likely partner was Japan, which had renounced the disarmament pacts and the naval limitations, had flouted the League of Nations, and was conducting an expansionist war in China. In November 1936, Tokyo and Berlin signed the Anti-Comintern Pact. Officially the two states agreed merely to "keep informed about the activities of the Communist International and to consult about necessary defensive measures." The pact also stated that the signatories would welcome other states whose "internal peace was threatened through the subversive activities of Communism." In reality, the pact was directed against Russia, located between the two revisionist powers.

A year later, in 1937, Italy agreed to become a signatory to the Anti-Comintern Pact. The revisionist powers were drawing closer together. Hitler could now declare: "Germany today stands no longer alone! First a European axis, now a great world-wide triangle!"

War and Axis Supremacy, 1938–1942

THE TURNING POINT

The 1930s witnessed many international crises: the rape of Manchuria and Abyssinia, the Civil War in Spain, and Hitler's scrapping of the Versailles Treaty. Confronted with these emergencies, the League of Nations proved ineffectual and collective security collapsed. Yet until 1937, a major conflict seemed evitable. The year 1938, however, marked a turning point: war was no longer avoidable. Japan's renewed invasion of China in 1937, followed in 1938 and 1939 by Germany's absorption of Austria and Czechoslovakia, Hungary's annexation of Ruthenia and parts of Slovakia, and Italy's seizure of Albania, marked the opening of the more active expansionist drive by the revisionist powers. Despite these nations' reiterations of their love of peace, the question was in reality no longer *whether* war would come, but *how soon*.

The war crimes trials at Nuremberg after World War II, with their public revelation of Hitler's aggressive plans, reinforced the conclusion that the Nazis were guilty of starting the war. The unbelievable horrors committed by the Germans in butchering millions in extermination camps buttressed this conviction. Although this judgment is unquestionably correct, it bolstered an unwarranted attitude of self-righteous innocence on the part of other nations and governments. One must not forget that the French occupation of the Ruhr, Japanese actions in Manchuria and China, and the Italian conquest of Ethiopia had demonstrated that the use of force remained an acceptable solution to international problems. Unquestionably, primary blame for the outbreak of war in the summer of 1939 must rest with Hitler. But British and French vacillation between fear of fascism and dread of communism, the indifference of the nations toward Japanese and Italian aggression, the readiness of the powers, particularly Russia, to make pacts with aggressors, made them also culpable to a certain degree.

That the years 1937–1938 were the

turning point is evident from the continuing internal political crisis in France, which made it incapable of resolute independent action, as well as from the fact that the idealistic and pacifistic Neville Chamberlain became prime minister of England. Inside Germany, the turning point there resulted from Hitler's personal conviction in late 1937 that the period of preparation had ended and the time of action was approaching. The Anti-Comintern triangle of Germany, Japan, and Italy gave him confidence of foreign support; above all, the progress of economic reconstruction and of rearmament made him feel better prepared to face a possible trial of arms.

The Progress of German Rearmament

Rearmament had started with Hitler's seizure of power, but had been given full priority only in the Second Four-Year Plan of 1936. In 1937 alone, Germany spent about 4.5 billion dollars on armaments, three times as much as the combined total for Britain and France. In February 1938, Hitler announced to the Reichstag that the German army—he liked to call it the *Friedensheer* (peace force)—was built. "A gigantic air force protects our homeland, a new sea power our shores," and he boasted of his accomplishments in increasing the industrial production requisite for executing such unparalleled rearmament. This speech was designed to impress his own people as well as to intimidate other powers, particularly Austria. Many observers thought he was bluffing, and most informed German officers believed Germany insufficiently prepared for any conflict. Hitler, of course, did not mean

that the task of rearming was completed and no further increase in armaments needed. The feverish build-up continued all through 1938. But his speech and actions revealed his conviction that the time for greater risks had come.

Despite frequent public protestations of his peaceful intentions, Hitler and his military planning staff had made preparations for war from the very beginning of his regime. By 1936, he was trying to convince his generals of the inevitability of war. In 1937, war plans became more specific. In June, Hitler ordered continuation of secret mobilization in case force were needed to crush Austria. The armed forces were ordered to be in position "suddenly to start a war and surprise the enemy."

In November 1937, Hitler held a secret conference with the leaders of the armed forces to inform them of his decisions regarding war. He argued that "the future of the German race of 85 million" rested exclusively on a solution of Germany's space requirements. Attainment of autarky in food, he asserted, was impossible on the basis of the arable land available in Germany, and reliance on world trade would place the Germans at the mercy of the British fleet. Hence, for the time being, Germany had to seek space on the Continent. "For Germany, the question is where can the greatest gains be made with the least risk." Since "history has proved that expansion always involves risks and requires the smashing of resistance," Hitler was convinced that "only force could solve the German question." He then laid out a timetable for this application of force. Under normal conditions, the action was to be launched at the latest in

the period 1943–1945, before the armaments race might give an advantage to the opponents. But if social unrest in France should suddenly paralyze the French army, or other unforeseen conditions arose, the German forces were to be prepared at any time to crush Czechoslovakia and Austria in a simultaneous, lightning blow. It is interesting that when Generals Werner von Blomberg and Werner von Fritsch (1880–1939) cautioned Hitler at this meeting that France and England might fight and that the Czech fortifications were formidable, Hitler brushed them aside with the assertion that France and England would not enter hostilities, that they had at any rate "written off" the Czechs and "become reconciled to the fact that this question would one day be cleaned up by Germany."

Hitler's Control over the Military

To be able to act ruthlessly and promptly in the crises he planned to unleash, Hitler decided to eliminate the hesitators in his entourage and to subordinate the *Wehrmacht* more completely to the party. "The tasks of the future," he explained to the Reichstag, "demand a closer bond between the political and military power of the Reich." Relations between the NSDAP and the army had remained cool, even after Hitler had become supreme commander in 1934. Jealousy and distrust among the SS, the SA, and *Wehrmacht* had continued. Universal military service and the expansion of the armed forces had helped swamp the lower ranks with properly indoctrinated recruits. But among the officers, various attitudes prevailed. A few were so grateful to Hitler for freeing the army

from the restrictions of the Versailles Treaty and helping to rebuild it to its former status that they became enthusiastic National Socialists. Many were simply opportunistic fence sitters who hoped to keep the army out of politics and, although not convinced of the blessings of the new regime, went along with it. Minister of Defense General Blomberg, a member of the original cabinet of 1933, belonged to this category. He was no convinced National Socialist; yet he played along with Hitler and supported him in his speeches, as when he pronounced in 1937 that "the *Wehrmacht* is the bearer and herald of the National Socialist *Weltanschauung*. Jointly with the NSDAP, with which it is indissolubly intertwined, the army forms the fundamental backbone of the *Reich*." Most of the tradition-bound higher-ranking officer corps, however, maintained a distinct aloofness toward the rabble-rousing Führer and his mob rule.

At the beginning of February 1938, Hitler suddenly purged the government and the High Command. Baron von Neurath, the nationalistic but moderate foreign minister who had learned his diplomatic formulas under the Weimar Republic, was replaced by the former champagne salesman Joachim von Ribbentrop (1893–1946). An obsequious admirer of Hitler, Ribbentrop had worked for eight years as the Führer's trusted diplomatic errand boy, and had performed rather tactless service as German ambassador to the Court of St. James's. The change from Neurath to Ribbentrop, in fact, signified Hitler's personal assumption of complete control over foreign affairs.

At the same time, sixteen generals and many other high-ranking officers were relieved of their positions of com-

mand. The Ministry of Defense was abolished and its head, General Blomberg, was dismissed. In its place a new High Command of the Army (OKW) was created, nominally in charge of the compliant General Wilhelm Keitel (1882–1946), but in fact under the personal supervision of Hitler. Moreover, General Fritsch was relieved as head of the army and replaced by General Walther von Brauchitsch (1881–1948), who was known to be more subservient and reckless than his predecessor. In this drastic reorganization of the upper echelon of the armed forces, Hitler not only gained added control but also tried to humiliate the officer caste in order to make its members more pliable. As commander in chief of the armed forces, he had the power simply to dismiss Blomberg and Fritsch. Instead, with the aid of Himmler's Gestapo, he disgraced the former by revealing that his wife was once a prostitute, and falsely accused the latter of being a homosexual.

EXPANSION IN TIME OF PEACE

H aving completed economic preparations and gained more direct control of the army, Hitler felt ready to strike his first expansionist blow. Despite the Austro-German Treaty of 1936, the Austrian Nazis had continued their agitation under orders from Berlin. Schuschnigg's dictatorial regime had grown increasingly feeble, since it lacked support both at home and abroad. Within Austria it faced the hostility of the Socialists and the Nazis. Moreover, it had been abandoned by Mussolini after his *rapprochement* with Hitler. Schuschnigg was finding it more and more difficult to cope with

Nazi provocations. Since the contemplated remedy of a Hapsburg restoration seemed impossible, the hapless Austrian chancellor looked abroad for French and Czechoslovakian support. Fearing that Austria's isolation might be broken, Hitler decided on immediate action.

Anschluss with Austria

On February 12, 1938, Schuschnigg visited Hitler at Berchtesgaden, the Führer's mountain retreat. Instead of discussing mutual problems, Hitler treated the Austrian with insolence and presented an ultimatum. Austria was to grant amnesty to all imprisoned National Socialists and permit them to join the only legal party, the Fatherland Front. The attorney Arthur Seyss-Inquart (1892–1946), one of the leaders of the Austrian Nazis since 1931, was to be made minister of the interior. Schuschnigg felt compelled to agree to these demands, hopefully telling Hitler that he expected the Nazis to respect the Austrian constitution.

A month of deceit followed. On February 16, Seyss-Inquart was appointed Austrian minister of the interior, and thereby given control over the police forces. On February 19, the Austrian Nazis were again given freedom of action. Supported by Berlin, they at once fomented disorders and riots throughout the tiny republic. Publicly, Hitler proclaimed once more he contemplated "no intervention in Austria." Secretly, he ordered his army to get ready to invade "in order to re-establish in Austria constitutional conditions and prevent further violence against her pro-German population." Mussolini agreed in advance not to interfere and to accept the Brenner

pass as the future common frontier between Italy and Germany. So confident was Hitler that France and England would abstain from action that he told the army to take no special security precautions on the German frontiers.

Unable to control the increasing violence, Schuschnigg made a belated attempt to rally the country behind him. He appealed to the workers, whom his dictatorship had estranged, and offered to take Socialists into his cabinet—a proposal that Hitler labeled a violation of the Berchtesgaden agreement. As a last resort, Schuschnigg called for a plebiscite on March 13, in which the people were to decide for or against "a free and German, independent and social, Christian and united Austria." Hitler feared that the outcome of this plebiscite might be unfavorable to his own plans. Göring at once notified Schuschnigg through Seyss-Inquart that the plebiscite violated the Berchtesgaden agreement, that Germany had lost confidence in the Austrian chancellor, and that he should resign immediately and turn his office over to Seyss-Inquart. Noncompliance within an hour would result in a military invasion of Austria.

To avoid bloodshed, Schuschnigg resigned on the evening of March 11. Seyss-Inquart became the new chancellor, and Göring dictated to him the text of a telegram he was to send at once to Berlin "requesting the German government to dispatch German troops as soon as possible" in order to help the new Austrian provisional government "restore law and order." At dawn on the following day, German troops crossed the frontier and rapidly occupied the whole country without encountering opposition. On March 13,

Seyss-Inquart passed a law abolishing Austrian sovereignty and making Austria an integral part of Germany. A day later, Hitler made his triumphal entry into Vienna. Thereafter the *Gleichschaltung* of Austria was accomplished with all speed. Members of the opposition were arrested; Schuschnigg himself disappeared into a concentration camp—from which he emerged only in 1945; and Jews were beaten. Nazi law, Nazi economics, Nazi education were introduced. Hitler proclaimed in Salzburg that he felt "convinced that he could rule Austria better than Schuschnigg or any one else." On April 10, the Austrians were asked in a plebiscite whether they approved of the merger with Germany. That 99.75 percent of the electorate gave their *ex post facto* approval of the *Anschluss* showed that Nazi intimidation was highly effective or that the Austrians expected miraculous economic benefits from union with Germany.

The seizure of Austria gave Germany an addition of seven million people and valuable raw materials, as well as greater influence over the Balkans and a common border with Fascist Italy. Moreover, it proved the effectiveness of Nazi methods—fomenting disorders in a neighboring country in order to have an excuse for sending in troops to re-establish order. The formula was to be used repeatedly until the outbreak of World War II.

The reaction of the powers to Hitler's coup was symptomatic. No more than whispered protests were heard from Paris and London. When interpellated in the House of Commons concerning Britain's inaction, Chamberlain replied that the government's only obligation toward Austria had been a commitment to consult with the

French and the Italians in the event of a threat to Austrian independence. He boasted that "we have fully discharged this pledge of consultation."

Annexation of the Sudetenland

Intent on retaining the initiative, Hitler eagerly rushed from crisis to crisis. Barely two weeks after the fall of Austria, he promised Konrad Henlein (1898–1945), the leader of the Nazis in Czechoslovakia, "to solve the Czech problem in the near future." The solution Hitler had in mind was the destruction of this relatively wealthy and rather heavily armed democracy that had shown surprising viability since its founding in 1918, despite the fact that it embraced countless mutually antagonistic minority groups. Under the guidance of President Eduard Beneš, Czechoslovakia had become an important link in the security systems of France and the Soviet Union and therefore presented an impediment to Hitler's projected eastward expansion.

Along the mountainous borders of western Bohemia lived some 3.5 million German-speaking Sudetens, who constituted a useful lever for Hitler's plan to annihilate the entire Czech state. By professing to protect kindred blood from alien oppression, he could advance his project under the banner of self-determination. As Seyss-Inquart had done in Austria, the Czech Konrad Henlein took his orders from Berlin. The success of the *Anschluss* made Henlein eager to try similar methods in the Sudetenland. At the end of March 1938, Henlein conferred in Berlin with Hitler and Ribbentrop. Jointly they elaborated the demands the Sudetens were to make on the Prague government. These included complete autonomy for the Sudetenland and a revision of Czechoslovakia's anti-German foreign policy. But Henlein was advised not to conclude agreements with the Czech government "which might leave the impression abroad that a solution is possible": no solution short of annexation was agreeable to Hitler.

THE FIRST CZECH CRISIS   Confident of Germany's support and secretly aided by the German ambassador in Prague, Henlein publicly presented his program to the Czech government. Its rejection by Beneš marked the opening of the first Czech crisis, April–May 1938. The Sudeten Germans provoked disorders, and England offered to mediate between Henlein and Beneš. Noting that Germany was concentrating troops on the Czech border, Beneš ordered partial mobilization. War or peace seemed to hang in the balance. By May, the crisis was at its height. England promised aid to France in case of "an unprovoked attack by Germany," but made it clear that it had no intention of undertaking "concerted military action in order to safeguard Czechoslovakia against a German attack." France and Russia, however, assured Beneš that they would fulfill their treaty obligations in case of aggression by Germany. Italy, although sympathetic to German aspirations, was still occupied in the Spanish Civil War.

These circumstances gave Hitler pause. Rather than take any military action that might provoke a war with the major powers, he preferred to wait for better political conditions. By June the crisis had abated. But the Führer had not abandoned his "unalterable decision to smash Czechoslovakia through a military action in the foreseeable future." He ordered the armed forces

to prepare not only for an invasion of Czechoslovakia, but also for a possible two-front war, involving France in the west. To protect the western frontier, and conceivably to lull France into a false sense of security through the misconception that Hitler's plans for expansion were solely aimed toward the east, he ordered the immediate construction of gigantic defense fortifications in front of France's Maginot Line. This so-called Siegfried Line was to protect Germany in the west while it was militarily involved in the east. At the same time, the army and air force were further increased in size.

Hitler's determined military build-up worried not only Paris, London, and Prague but also many high-ranking German officers. They insisted that Hitler was overplaying his hand and that Germany could not possibly win a general European war. They called it their duty to the German people to warn Hitler that a general war would not only undo his work but also spell ruin for Germany. As a last measure to save the army and Germany from certain destruction, some officers plotted to arrest Hitler if he unleashed a war over the Sudeten crisis. Since ultimately Hitler gained Czechoslovakia without hostilities, the conspiracy was abandoned.

During the summer, the crisis simmered. France continued to assure Beneš of its readiness to support him, but Chamberlain persisted in his ambivalent attitude; he refused "to indicate how and when Britain would act in circumstances which had not yet arrived." He urged Beneš to give in to Henlein to the maximum extent possible, and sent a mediator to Prague. But Henlein, on orders from Hitler, scuttled all attempts at compromise, while Goebbels launched his campaign to denounce Czech atrocities against the Sudetens.

THE SECOND CZECH CRISIS In May, Hitler had calculated that it would take until October 1 to complete all military preparations, including construction of the Siegfried Line. His timetable progressed on schedule, and he opened the second Czech crisis in mid-September. At the Nazi Party Congress at Nuremberg on September 12, Göring bragged of the Siegfried Line, of Germany's stockpile of raw materials, and of its invincible army, navy, and air force. Hitler then spoke of the riots in Sudetenland and upbraided Beneš. Sarcastically he exclaimed that "God did not create them [the Sudetens] to be surrendered by Versailles to a foreign power," and promised that "if these tortured souls cannot obtain rights and help themselves, they can obtain them from us!"

The crisis now flared up to new dimensions. The Sudeten riots became intensified to the point that Beneš declared martial law—thereby giving Hitler further excuse to rant about the oppression of German-speaking peoples. Konrad Henlein fled to Berlin, and called by radio on his fellow Sudetens to "march home to the Reich." He no longer demanded autonomy, but incorporation with Germany. German troops began to concentrate; France called up reservists.

At this point Chamberlain decided on personal intervention and visited Hitler at Berchtesgaden on September 15. After a lengthy discussion, in which Hitler alternated between threats and sweet reasonableness, Chamberlain agreed to discuss the question of self-determination for the Sudetens with

Prague and Paris. Presumably plebiscites were to be used to determine which areas contained 50 percent or more Germans, so that these regions could be ceded to Germany. With French approval, Chamberlain then pressured the reluctant Czech government to accept Hitler's demands, threatening to abandon Czechoslovakia to its fate if it did not comply. Meanwhile the German propaganda machine kept the crisis at a high pitch by constant, mostly inaccurate, reports about disorders and atrocities in Czechoslovakia.

On September 22, Chamberlain once again visited Hitler, this time at Bad Godesberg near Bonn. Although Chamberlain reported that he had been able to obtain Beneš's acceptance of Hitler's demands of September 12, the Führer now rejected the use of plebiscites. He insisted that time was of the essence to prevent further bloodshed in Sudetenland, and that "one way or another," the question had to be solved by October 1. He demanded immediate cession of all obviously German regions, with a possible later rectification of the new border after a subsequent plebiscite. He insisted that Czech property in the ceded areas be turned over to Germany without compensations, and that the territorial demands voiced by Poland and Hungary on Czechoslovakia be also satisfied as soon as possible. He curtly informed Chamberlain that German troops would act on October 1, unless a peaceful solution had been found before then.

Chamberlain's peace mission had failed, since the Czechs rejected these new demands of Hitler's. Instead, Beneš ordered mobilization, France called up some divisions, and even England readied its fleet. Russia again offered to aid Czechoslovakia in conjunction with France, but the West showed little eagerness to bring the Soviet Union into Central Europe. Moreover, Rumania and Poland refused to permit Russia, which lacked a common border with Czechoslovakia, either to fly over or march through their territory. Dread of Communism, it appeared, was as yet stronger than fear of expansionist Germany.

THE MUNICH AGREEMENT 'War was averted at the last moment when Mussolini, upon the urging of Chamberlain and Franklin Roosevelt, arranged an immediate conference to settle the Sudeten question. ' On September 29, Mussolini, Chamberlain, and French Premier Edouard Daladier met with Hitler in Munich, symbolically at the Brown House, the headquarters of the NSDAP. 'Hitler had refused to invite Beneš, and Chamberlain had not insisted, being more interested in safeguarding the peace than in saving Czechoslovakia. Beneš's presence at the vivisection of his country would be only a delaying hindrance. But failure to insist on Russian participation was most shortsighted of Britain and France. The Soviet Union was, after all, an ally of both France and Czechoslovakia, and the nation ultimately most threatened by Hitler's eastward expansion. As a result, Stalin inferred that the western powers were encouraging the Nazis' eastern designs so that they might accomplish their announced plans of exterminating Communism.

The Munich Agreement resulting from the conference awarded Hitler more or less what he had demanded at Bad Godesberg. Between October 1 and 10, the Czech forces were to evacuate the Sudetenland in advance of

occupation by the German army. An international commission was to fix the exact boundaries. Further arrangements were to be made to satisfy the territorial demands of Poland and Hungary. Britain and France guaranteed the new Czech frontiers, whereas Italy and Germany reserved such an undertaking until the Polish and Hungarian claims were settled. Finally, Chamberlain and Hitler signed an additional protocol of dubious value, in which they agreed jointly to work for peace and "never to go to war with one another again."

Munich delayed war momentarily, and throughout Europe there was untold relief. But Czechoslovakia had been dealt a mortal blow. Germany received about 10,000 square miles of strategic territory rich in minerals, with a population of approximately 3.5 million. Within a few weeks, Czechoslovakia had to cede the small territory of Teschen to Poland, and almost 5000 square miles and a million people to Hungary. Beneš resigned, and the truncated Czech state braced itself for the next onslaught. Hitler's prestige at home and abroad had been immensely elevated. The army officers who had _ted to overthrow Hitler began to _e more trust in his judgment; the _ller nations, especially in eastern _rope, started to wonder whether it might not be safer to come to terms with Hitler than to rely on their traditional, but evidently valueless, pacts with France.

Continued Prewar Expansion

Before Munich, Hitler had proclaimed that after the solution of the Czech question, "there were no further territorial problems for Germany in Eu-

rope." Optimistic observers therefore concluded that German demands had been satisfied by the Munich Agreement. But Hitler immediately prepared for the next step. As he admitted later, he had always considered the acquisition of the Sudetenland as only a "partial solution," since he required all of Czechoslovakia "as basis for the conquest of Poland."

Three weeks after Munich, he ordered the army to make plans for the seizure of Bohemia and Moravia. He cautioned the German press that endless invocations of peace might lead to softness among the Germans, and urged the journalists to help condition the people to demand force in the solution of future problems. To lull the suspicions of France, he concluded a pact with Paris that again stipulated the inviolability of the Franco-German border. But significantly, despite French requests, he refused to guarantee the new Czech borders, in accordance with the Munich Agreement.

During the winter of 1938–1939, the Nazis worked on undermining the truncated Czech state. To weaken the Prague government, they encouraged the independence movement of the Slovaks and the Ruthenians. They also exerted pressure on the new Czech president, Emil Hácha, to reshape his army and administration along lines suitable to Germany. Prague finally granted autonomy to the Slovaks and Ruthenians, but refused to award them complete independence. Hence Hitler again applied his trusted formula. Nazi agents encouraged disorders between Czechs and Slovaks, until, finally, on March 13, 1939, the leader of the Slovak independence movement rushed to Berlin to plead for Hitler's protection against Czech oppression. Hitler

promptly ordered President Hácha to Berlin and re-enacted the scene he had staged with Schuschnigg a year earlier. He bluntly told Hácha that he had decided to dispatch troops into Czechoslovakia on the following day in order to restore order to the state and incorporate it into Germany. If Hácha would order the Czech army not to resist, his people would be spared the horrors of a crushing defeat and would be rewarded with a "certain amount of national freedom" within the German Reich. If not, Czechoslovakia would be mercilessly crushed within two days, and "the world would not blink an eyelash." The frightened Hácha promptly telephoned Prague orders not to resist the German advance, and Hitler's troops occupied Bohemia and Moravia.

Two days later, on March 15, Hitler made his triumphal entrance into Prague. Bohemia-Moravia was made into a German dependency, Slovakia a German protectorate, and Ruthenia turned over to Hungary. The latter had just joined the Anti-Comintern Pact, and was rapidly becoming a convenient outpost for Hitler's growing influence in the Balkans.

England, France, Russia, and the United States all protested against Germany's destruction of Czechoslovakia, but the German government simply refused to receive such protests, since they "lacked all political, juridical, and moral grounds." Even the optimists now lost confidence in Hitler's assurances that he wanted merely to undo the injustice of Versailles and extend self-determination to all ethnic Germans. Despite Hitler's assertion in Prague that "Bohemia-Moravia have belonged to the *Lebensraum* of the German people for a thousand years,"

the Czechs were clearly not German-speaking peoples. If these disillusioned optimists had read *Mein Kampf,* they might have recognized Hitler's unlimited thirst for *Lebensraum.* "To demand restoration of the 1914 boundaries is political nonsense of criminal proportions," he had written, for he considered those frontiers neither logical nor appropriate from a military and geographical point of view.

Since success had been so easy, Germany now ordered the Lithuanians to cede the territory of Memel which they had received as a result of Versailles. Lithuania submitted to these demands at once, and Memel was incorporated into the Reich on March 21. At the same time, Hitler reiterated his demands on Poland that had been previously rejected by the Polish Foreign Office. He called for the incorporation of Danzig into the Reich and for the construction of an extraterritorial railroad and superhighway across the Polish Corridor to connect East Prussia with the rest of Germany. And while Hitler was thus preparing for the next and final crisis, Mussolini slipped across the Adriatic on April 7 to conquer and annex Albania.

The Prelude to War

Destruction of Czechoslovakia brought about a drastic change in British foreign policy. Two days after the fall of Prague, Chamberlain voiced his disappointment at Hitler's flagrant violation of promises given at Bad Godesberg and at Munich, and warned that Britain "favored peace, but valued freedom even more." On March 30, London proposed to Paris, Warsaw, and Moscow the formation of a coalition to resist all future German threats

against the independence of any state. France agreed at once. On the following day, England and France guaranteed Poland armed support "in the event of any action which clearly threatens Polish independence." A week later, this guarantee was converted into a mutual assistance pact. During the ensuing weeks, as the threat of war increased, the Anglo-French powers extended protective guarantees also to Rumania, Greece, and Turkey.

NEGOTIATIONS BETWEEN MOSCOW AND THE WEST But negotiations between the western powers and Russia—vastly more vital for the maintenance of peace —dragged on listlessly throughout the spring and early summer, until they were finally broken off on August 22. After Munich, Stalin had abandoned hope that collective security could ever be used effectively to contain Fascist aggression. The French ambassador in Moscow even warned that the Munich Agreement was bound to drive Russia into a *rapprochement* with Hitler, and that Stalin might attempt to divert Hitler's land hunger from the Ukraine by arranging for a partitioning of Poland between Russia and Germany. Stalin had become convinced that the western capitalists were afraid of a general war because they thought it might lead to revolutions and a strengthening of Communism. He believed they were happy to see the revisionist powers absorb the smaller states because they anticipated that the aggressors would ultimately hurl themselves against the Soviet Union. The appointment in May of the anti-western Vyacheslav Molotov as new commissar of foreign affairs clearly indicated this change in Russian policy.

Despite mutual suspicions, proposals and counterproposals shuttled back and forth between Moscow, London, and Paris. Russia showed hesitant readiness to negotiate a general mutual assistance pact with England, France, Poland, Rumania, and the three Baltic states. But hatred of Communism and fear of Russian imperialism, particularly on the part of the smaller eastern states, rendered conclusion of such a pact impossible. Questions of "indirect aggression" and of the stationing of the Red Army in case of a German attack presented the main stumbling blocks. In view of Hitler's proved method of preparing annexation through the fomenting of internal disorder in his victim and the use of fifth columns, Stalin demanded the right to dispatch troops to prevent Nazi subversion of the small countries. But Poland and Rumania, which had both gained land at the expense of Russia in 1918, refused to grant such permission. They even rejected the suggestion that in case of overt aggression by Germany, the Red Army should be allowed to traverse Polish or Rumanian territory, for they feared that once in the country, Soviet forces would remain in permanent occupation.

HITLER'S DEMANDS ON POLAND During these same months of fruitless negotiations between Russia and the West, Hitler made preparations "to solve the Polish problem." As usual, his official diplomatic offensive was accompanied by secret orders to the army to effect military preparedness. Since Germany now surrounded Poland on three sides, army and air force units were secretly deployed along a large perimeter, ready to accomplish the sudden and prompt destruction of the Polish army. Hitler's public demands

on Poland—annexation of Danzig with safeguards for Polish economic interests, and permission to build a German railroad and highway across the Corridor—sounded reasonable and negotiable. But his true intentions reached much further. "Danzig is not the real objective," he informed his generals and confidants in May. "Our aim is to round out our living space in the east and to solve our food problem."

In their negotiations with Warsaw, Hitler and Ribbentrop alternated between intimidation and promises of friendly collaboration. At one point Hitler tried to convince the Poles that Berlin and Warsaw should work together against the Soviet Union, since communism was their mutual enemy. On the other hand, Hitler denounced Germany's nonaggression pact with Poland on the pretext that Warsaw harbored aggressive intentions against Germany after the conclusion of the Anglo-French-Polish pact. For good measure, he also canceled the Anglo-German Naval Agreement of 1935, in order to intimidate his opponents. There followed the usual incidents in Danzig and the Corridor, which Goebbels' propaganda machine enlarged to frightening proportions so that Hitler could promise aid and protection to the ethnic Germans, "oppressed" by their Polish masters. Since Hitler wished to destroy Poland and not solve the disagreements, the several months of negotiations brought no results, and lasted only until his military and political preparations were completed.

In view of Britain's change of policy, it seemed likely that Germany's planned action against Poland would lead to a general European conflagration. Hence Hitler thought it expedient to secure the benevolent neutrality of as many countries as possible, so that the number of enemies he had to fight at the same time would be reduced. After conclusion of the Spanish Civil War, Spain at once joined the Anti-Comintern Pact and thereby signaled its continued friendship with Germany and Italy. During May, Hitler concluded nonaggression pacts with Estonia, Latvia, and Denmark. Sweden, Norway, and Finland rejected similar offers. On the other hand, friendly relations were established with Hungary, Yugoslavia, and Bulgaria. On May 22, Mussolini, although by no means militarily or economically prepared for war, agreed to convert the vague Rome-Berlin Axis into a tight alliance. The "Pact of Steel," as it was called, was not simply a defensive alliance, but actually obligated the signatories "to support the partner with all military forces," in case he became "embroiled in a war."

THE NAZI-SOVIET PACT   But Hitler realized that a two-front war, against Poland and Russia in the east, and England and France in the west, involved strategic risks that he preferred to avoid. If Russia could be kept out of the conflict—at least temporarily—Poland would remain isolated and could be crushed in a short time, after which German forces could turn west and either conquer France or conclude peace with the western powers. Consequently, Hitler decided on a *rapprochement* with Stalin. Preliminary negotiations began in May, and proceeded at first quite slowly. Understandably, Stalin and Hitler found it difficult to trust each other. But the Soviet dictator perceived the advantages of the situation: it offered easy territorial aggrandizement and at least

a temporary breathing spell for the Soviet Union. As time passed, Hitler grew more and more eager. A trade agreement was finally concluded as a prelude to further political negotiations. At last, after much German pressure, Ribbentrop was invited to Moscow and left Berlin immediately, endowed by Hitler with full powers of negotiation. On the same day—August 23—Ribbentrop, Molotov, and Stalin agreed on a pact of friendship and nonaggression. The pact itself, drawing together the two bitter ideological enemies, was remarkable enough. The secret protocol that accompanied it was even more ominous for the future.

In this protocol, Germany and Russia agreed on a "delimitation of their respective spheres of interest in eastern Europe." Finland, Estonia, Latvia, and Bessarabia were granted to the Soviet Union. Lithuania was reserved for Germany—although in a subsequent secret agreement of September 28, after the fall of Poland, Germany transferred this claim to Russia in return for a larger share of Poland. The protocol furthermore drew tentative borders for a division of Poland, "in case of territorial changes" in that country, and stipulated that all further Polish problems would be discussed by the two nations in a friendly and cooperative manner.

This cynical Nazi-Soviet Pact not only removed Hitler's last hesitation about attacking Poland, but had other far-reaching repercussions. It was obviously a temporary arrangement, for it contravened Hitler's long-planned eastward expansion by allowing Russia to move westward. For a short while, by giving it access to Russian food and raw materials, particularly petroleum,

it freed Germany from the fear of total wartime blockade. But these transitory advantages could not conceal the fact that Hitler had violated the spirit and letter of the Anti-Comintern Pact and had undermined the foundations of his anti-Communist ideology. Expediency had reached its high point. Rosenberg, the party philosopher, feared the consequences of Hitler's actions. "I have the feeling," he wrote in his diary two days after the signing of the pact, "that this Moscow Pact someday will backfire on National Socialism," for he felt that it negated the very essence of Hitler's movement. Less ardent Nazis saw even worse consequences for Germany and Europe. It is indeed ironic that Hitler, who always posed as the leading anti-Communist, granted Russia predominance over eastern Europe and awarded it the boundaries that Russia has since occupied and maintained.

Once Hitler was assured of Russian neutrality, only a few days of peace remained. Feverish diplomatic activity marked these last hectic days. Chamberlain, Daladier, Roosevelt, and even Mussolini tried to persuade Hitler to modify his stand. Mussolini made it plain that he would not join in a war in the foreseeable future unless Germany provided Italy with huge amounts of war matériel. Hitler hesitated for only a moment, hoping to get England to remain on the side lines. But Chamberlain re-emphasized Britain's guarantees to Poland in a new and stronger agreement, while at the same time offering to mediate between Warsaw and Berlin.

Despite the counsel of more cautious advisers, Hitler finally sent an ultimatum to Poland, and without waiting for a reply, issued his order of attack.

At dawn on September 1, 1939, German troops and air force went into action against Poland. Strict orders were given to provoke no hostilities on the French border, so that "the responsibility for opening of hostilities would be left up to England and France." After the German troops had begun their invasion of Poland, Italy once more tried to forestall war by calling for a conference. England and France mobilized, but informed Germany that negotiations could still save the peace if Hitler at once withdrew his invading forces from Polish soil. Since the troops continued to push on, and Hitler did not even bother to reply to the British demands for cessation of hostilities, England and France declared war on Germany on September 3.

THE PERIOD OF AXIS SUPREMACY, 1939-1942

In the gigantic war that followed, the Axis powers—consisting of Germany (with its annexed Austrian and Czech territories), later joined by Italy, Hungary, Rumania, Bulgaria, Finland, and Japan—enjoyed initial advantages that made them appear almost invincible. The Germans were better armed and far bolder in their employment of new tactics of surprise and mobility than the Allies, who at first relied on the old strategies that had won them World War I. Imbued with the revisionist myth of fighting for a new order, and streamlined in their command chain by dictatorial administration, the Axis powers at first also displayed far more unity of purpose and initiative than was possible in the loose coalition of the Allies.

Long-term strategic planning, ruthless diplomatic pressure, skillful use of fifth columns, thorough exploitation of conquered territories, and readiness to employ total war tactics made it easier for Hitler and his allies to win astounding success. As a result, the Nazi steamroller gained stupendous victories during the first three years of the war, until the tide gradually turned in the the winter of 1942-1943.

Initial Triumphs of German Arms

BLITZKRIEG IN POLAND   The German campaign against Poland, prepared meticulously down to the last required pontoon bridge, was a startling sample of *Blitzkrieg* (lightning warfare). The air force strafed and bombed military positions and civilian centers with ruthless precision; mechanized units of tanks and armored cars slashed through enemy lines to complete encircling movements. Within a few weeks, the Polish army of about 600,000 men was annihilated. After twenty-seven days, which included a prolonged and highly destructive siege of Warsaw, Poland lay prostrate and defeated.

During the last week of fighting, Russian armies crossed Poland's unguarded eastern border to seize their share of the spoils. Ribbentrop and Stalin then conferred again in Moscow to set a new Russo-German frontier across the heart of Poland. Each took approximately half the territory of Poland in this fourth partition, but Germany's western portion was more heavily populated. At the same time, Moscow and Berlin arranged for closer economic cooperation. Having pocketed without cost almost 80,000 square miles and 13 million new subjects, Russia then proceeded to seize the other awards made to Stalin in his pact with

Hitler. Within the next ten months, the Soviets acquired Lithuania, Latvia, Estonia, Bessarabia, and Bucovina, totaling another 92,000 square miles with about 9.5 million inhabitants. Only Finland resisted Russian demands but, after a short but hard-fought winter campaign, was finally obliged to cede to Russia some 16,000 square miles.

After the fall of Poland, Hitler addressed the Reichstag to boast of his accomplishment. Insolently mixing threats and enticements, he suggested to London and Paris that further bloodshed and destruction be avoided through prompt conclusion of peace and arrangements for general disarmament. Since Hitler showed no intention of restoring Poland, his peace offer was, of course, rejected.

Preparations were then made for the next campaigns. A special movie, "Blitzkrieg in Poland," showing the power of the German war machine and the horrors of modern warfare, was shown as widely as possible to bolster German morale and intimidate the nations of Europe. However, many German viewers, it appeared, were sickened by the cruelty in the film, and many a foreigner became more firm in his determination to resist Nazi aggression.

In the west, Anglo-French divisions behind the Maginot Line uneasily faced German troops in the Siegfried Line in the so-called *Sitzkrieg* (sitting war, as contrasted with the lighting war in Poland). Sporadic shelling was accompanied by propaganda leaflets and radio broadcasts sent across the trenches. Goebbels attempted to demoralize the French soldiers by reiterated insinuations that they were shedding their blood solely "for the benefit of the British capitalists."

Hitler's eagerness for action was not shared by many of his generals, who were not so convinced of the invincibility of their armies or the weakness of their opponents. They hesitated to launch a direct attack on France. In a memorable address to his staff, the Führer tried to demonstrate the advisability of speedy action in the west and the need for trust in his own infallible decisions: "I will attack and not capitulate. The fate of the *Reich* depends solely on me." And he assured them: "In all modesty I must speak of my own person as irreplaceable. Neither a military nor a civilian personality could replace me." And with similar modesty he continued: "I am convinced of the power of my brain and of my powers of decision."

But the Sitzkrieg continued throughout the winter, largely because of unfavorable weather. The only action of note occurred at sea, where German submarines sank Allied commercial and naval vessels, and where the German pocket battleship "Graf Spee" enjoyed her brief but memorable foray into the Atlantic, until she was overpowered by British pursuers and scuttled herself in the Bay of Montevideo.

SEIZURE OF DENMARK AND NORWAY
When the British decided to mine Norwegian coastal waters in order to halt the shipments of badly needed Swedish ores to Germany via the port of Narvik, Hitler suddenly shifted his attention to Scandinavia. Plans for German action had been previously elaborated, since the German air force and navy wanted to use Norway as a base of attack on England and on Allied shipping. On April 9, 1940, German troops suddenly occupied Denmark in a sweeping strike, and placed

the frightened little kingdom under military occupation for the duration of the war. On the same day, German naval and air-borne units seized strategic areas of Norway, aided in places by local fifth columnists. The Norwegian forces, supported by the British navy and a small Anglo-French expeditionary corps hastily dispatched to Norway, resisted fiercely for a few weeks. But by early May, the Germans had crushed most opposition, and Norway gradually disappeared into the German orbit, controlled by the German army, and governed by the pro-German Vidkun Quisling, as the head of a Nazi-dominated dictatorship.

Flushed by the brilliant success in Denmark and Norway, Hitler promptly ordered the attack on the west. Not squeamish about violating treaties and neutrality arrangements, he based his strategy on a modified Schlieffen plan. By speedily overrunning the three neutrals, Holland, Belgium, and Luxemburg, the German armies were to plunge into France from the north, and thus by-pass the Maginot defenses.

DEFEAT OF FRANCE   The attack was launched along the entire front on May 10. Once again surprise was achieved and maneuvers were executed with incredible speed. Highly mobile tank units, air-borne drops, bombing of cities, strafing of fleeing refugees, and occasional use of traitorous fifth columnists were all employed in efficient coordination. Within five days, air bombardment had reduced Rotterdam to a shambles, all strategic points had been occupied by German motorized units and paratroops, and Holland surrendered. Supported by British and French units, the Belgian army resisted for two weeks. But by driving straight to the Channel, the Germans

succeeded in cutting off the Allied armies in Belgium from their main forces in France. The story of their evacuation from Dunkirk across the Channel to England has been depicted frequently enough. By early June, four German armies were streaming into France, preceded by dive bombers and fighter planes that had complete command of the air. French equipment was largely outdated and inferior. Here and there, horse-drawn artillery tried valiantly to delay approaching *Panzer* columns. Refugees clogged the roads, disrupting communications and making French military movements difficult. Despite an occasional display of heroic bravery, most French units were pitifully demoralized and defeatism was rampant.

A month after the initial attack, the Germans had completely by-passed the Maginot Line and were within reach of both Paris and the Atlantic Ocean. On June 14, they seized Paris, after the French government had moved south. On June 16, the aged Marshal Henri Pétain became head of the French state, and with almost half of France under German control, he decided on the following day to request an armistice. The German armies continued their advance for another five days, until Hitler met the French envoys at Compiègne on June 22 to sign the terms of surrender. To satisfy his feelings of revenge, he insisted that the humiliating surrender of France be concluded in the same railroad carriage in which the Germans had accepted the 1918 armistice.

The successful campaign against the four western countries, which had lasted a mere forty-three days, was filled with drama, heroism, and treachery. Mussolini, in particular, showed the baseness of his bravado. He stood

on the side lines until certain that Hitler would be victorious in the west. Then on June 10, he declared war on France and Britain, and sent his troops over the poorly defended southern borders of France. An entirely different attitude was shown by the United States and England. Roosevelt urged the French to pursue the fight, even if the mainland of France had to be abandoned, and to continue the battle in North Africa. To aid in the struggle, he promised to dispatch war matériel. Churchill, who had become prime minister on May 10, begged France not to capitulate, and in a dramatic gesture offered to merge France and England in a Franco-British Union that would ultimately conquer the common enemy.

As a result of the armistice terms, France was temporarily divided into two sections. Northern France and the Atlantic seaboard were occupied by German armies and placed under military government. The remainder of France was allowed nominal sovereignty under Marshal Pétain who, with the aid of Pierre Laval, established a Fascist dictatorship that acted largely as a German puppet regime. Beyond the seas, however, in London and in most of the French dependencies, General Charles de Gaulle established a French National Committee to head the so-called Free French forces, which remained at war with Germany until the end.

Hitler's belief in his own infallibility now knew no bounds. In ten months of war he had conquered seven states. German domination extended from the Vistula to the Pyrenees, from the fjords of Norway to the Austrian Alps. But England remained undefeated, and in the east, Russia loomed as a question mark. Since his renewed peace offer

was bluntly rejected by Churchill, Hitler issued orders for the invasion of England. Unable to gather enough suitable ships to cross the Channel for an immediate landing, the Germans launched their air fleet against Britain and intensified their submarine blockade of the island. For three months, in the Battle of Britain, German bombers battered English coastal installations, inland military depots and factories, as well as the major cities—particularly London and Coventry—in order to reduce England's potential resistance to invasion and demoralize the population. Damage was tremendous, and the losses at sea caused by prowling submarines were frightening. Yet Britain remained defiant. Despite the German blockade, American supplies of war matériel and foodstuffs arrived in ever-greater quantities. The Royal Air Force retained command of the air space over the island, although Göring's *Luftwaffe* enjoyed numerical superiority. In fact, the RAF even launched retaliatory air raids on Berlin and some cities in the Ruhr, giving German civilians their first taste of war on the home front. In October 1940, the impossibility of defeating England by air became apparent even to Hitler, who officially postponed the invasion plans until spring, when for a brief period the heavy air raids on London and the countryside were resumed. Actually, Hitler's attention had been turned eastward to the Balkans and to Russia.

The Invasion of Russia

Some of Hitler's military advisers proposed that Germany could best undermine Britain's strength by expelling it from the Mediterranean and conquer-

ing its Near Eastern empire. Italy, in fact, pursued this idea, since Mussolini had always dreamed of converting the Mediterranean into an Italian sea. In September 1940, the Italians launched their invasion of Egypt, and in the following month attacked Greece. But, poorly equipped and ineffectively led, they were defeated in both areas, so that Hitler ultimately was forced to bail out his ally by sending troops to North Africa and Greece and by stationing air squadrons in Italy to reduce attacks by the British navy on the fast-dwindling Italian fleet. In Hitler's view, these were useless diversions. He rejected the thought of concentrating German efforts on the Mediterranean, being determined to conquer the Continent. This meant, in fact, conquering Russia.

There were many reasons why Hitler was adamant about his decision to destroy the Soviet Union. For one, he was convinced of the inevitability of ultimate conflict with Russia, and therefore wished to attack it as soon as possible, while Germany's military machine was at its most effective. Moreover, he did not trust Stalin and was fearful that Russia would attack Germany unexpectedly at a time of its own choosing. Hitler was also worried about Soviet expansion (which he himself had approved and facilitated), possibly because he came to realize that Stalin was almost as adept as he in absorbing neighboring states. There was friction over influence in the Balkans and in Finland, which German troops had gradually infiltrated under the guise of transit to northern Norway. Hitler also disliked being dependent on Russia for shipments of raw materials, and constantly accused the Russians of being in arrears in their deliveries. Most curious among

his reasons was his conviction that the best way to defeat England was to conquer Russia. "England's hope is Russia and America," he told his generals. Once Russia was defeated, he thought Japan would be the strongest power in East Asia and keep the United States so busy that it could no longer help England. Annihilation of Russia would thus deprive England of its main supply depot, the United States, and of its "continental dagger" against Germany. Except for his theories about Japan and the United States, Hitler's idea paralleled that of Napoleon, who, when his invasion plans of the island had to be abandoned, had also hoped to defeat England by attacking Russia.

POLITICAL AND MILITARY PREPARATIONS   Preparations for the invasion of Russia were begun in the summer of 1940, to be implemented in the following spring. Actually, several delays occurred. Meanwhile Russo-German relations cooled steadily. Russia resented Hitler's expanding influence in the Balkans, and refused to be pacified by Hitler's insinuation that it look for compensations in central or southern Asia—for example Iran and India.

In September 1940, Germany, Italy, and Japan signed the Tripartite Pact, in which the two European powers recognized Japan's right to establish "a new order in greater East Asia," while Japan agreed to respect Axis leadership in creating "a new order in Europe." The three powers, moreover, agreed "on mutual political, economic, and military assistance in case of an attack on one of the contracting parties by a power not presently engaged in the European war or the Sino-Japanese conflict." This alliance was obviously directed against the United States, but

could apply equally well to Russia.

Germany spent the winter and spring occupying the entire Balkan Peninsula, partly to help Mussolini and to expel the British who had landed in Greece, and partly to safeguard the right flank of the armies that were to be launched against Russia. Rumania, with its valuable oil fields, was taken in October 1940, after it had lost much territory to Russia, Hungary, and Bulgaria. Hungary joined the Axis alliance more or less voluntarily in the following month. In February 1941, Bulgaria was seized, followed two months later by Yugoslavia and Greece. Meanwhile an expeditionary force was dispatched to Africa, under Field Marshal Erwin Rommel (1891–1944), who helped the Italians launch another invasion of Egypt.

By June 1941, all the delaying tasks had been accomplished. With the Balkans secure, Hitler was ready to launch his gigantic attack against the Soviet Union. Like the *Grande Armée* of Napoleon, his forces included troops from client states—Italians, Rumanians, Hungarians, and Finns, later augmented by French, Spanish, and others. But significantly, he could not count on the assistance of Japan. Unwilling to become involved in a war in Siberia that would divert its forces from striking against Southeast Asia and the Pacific Islands, Japan had signed a nonaggression treaty with Moscow (April 1941).

INITIAL SUCCESSES On June 22, 1941, Hitler suddenly hurled over three million men against Russia on the entire front from the Baltic to the Black Sea. His pretext was that Russian troops had concentrated along the border with seemingly hostile intentions. The campaigns that ensued were of gigantic proportions, considering the vastness of the areas covered and the quantities of men and matériel involved. The Germans advanced in their usual lightning fashion, under an umbrella of thousands of planes, enveloping enemy units and strong points in huge pincer movements that netted them great numbers of prisoners. The tidal wave of German Panzers headed eastward so rapidly that most observers believed Russia would fall within a few weeks. During the first seven days, most of the buffer zone recently acquired by the Russians fell into German hands. By the middle of July, the Germans had seized Lithuania and Latvia, invaded the Ukraine, and on the central front, captured Smolensk, barely 250 miles west of Moscow. In September, German and Finnish forces laid siege to Leningrad, which, despite constant bombardment and near starvation, successfully withstood a siege of a year and a half. By October, almost the entire Ukraine, with its major cities Kiev and Kharkov, had been seized by the Germans, the Crimean peninsula was under invasion, and the battle for Moscow had begun. Vast tank battles rolled over the central Russian lands frozen by the early approach of winter, and at the end of November, the Germans reached the suburbs of Russia's capital and were almost within sight of the Kremlin towers. In five months, they had won innumerable battles, advanced some 600 miles, taken great numbers of prisoners, but, as they now were forced to realize, they had not defeated Russia.

The Russians had displayed unexpected tenacity and skill in defending their vast areas. They scorched the earth so as to leave no food for the advancing enemy; guerrilla fighters constantly interrupted German com-

munications; hit-and-run attacks undermined German morale and took a great toll among German soldiers behind the front lines. Moreover, Russia possessed more war matériel than suspected by Hitler, who had perhaps been misled by the poor showing of Russian arms in the Finnish War of 1939. And Stalin expected aid and supplies from abroad. On July 13, Moscow and London signed a mutual aid agreement. In the following month, British and Russian troops occupied Iran in order to establish a supply line for aid to Russia, and Roosevelt's adviser, Harry Hopkins, visited Moscow to discuss the shipment of American supplies.

THE FIRST REVERSES In the winter of 1941, the Germans suddenly suffered their first defeats. On December 6, the Russians launched a heavy counteroffensive that gained immediate success and pushed back the German lines before Moscow and in the northern Ukraine. Throughout the winter the Red Army retained the initiative until warm weather returned in the following May. Unaccustomed to being subjected to serious attack, and poorly protected against the Russian winter, the German troops quickly lost their morale. Hitler, who had spent most of the months of the campaign at army headquarters meddling in the tasks of his generals with the delight of a boy playing with tin soldiers, now ranted at his officers. His infallibility seemed at stake. He reshuffled important commands, personally assumed the title of Commander in Chief of the Army, and directed the defenses against the Russian attacks, disregarding his subordinates' advice to establish shorter lines of communication by a general withdrawal. Under Hitler's fanatic direc-

tion, the troops gave way only under severe pressure, and no rout developed. Yet the tremendous suffering of the troops boded ill for Germany's future unless Russia could be defeated before a second winter.

Within a few days of the beginning of the Soviet counteroffensive, two other events forecast a turning point in Germany's chances for victory. After Japan's assault on Pearl Harbor, Hitler gleefully seized the opportunity to declare war on the United States, despite the counsel of more sober-minded advisers. He completely underestimated the industrial and military potential of the United States. His reason for challenging it was certainly not based on any sense of obligation to stand by his ally Japan. Rather, he expected that open hostilities against the United States would allow German submarines to patrol its coasts and successfully intercept the American supply line to Britain and Russia—particularly since the United States Navy would be fully occupied in the Pacific war against Japan. Actually, Hitler's calculations were exaggerated but not completely erroneous. Allied shipping losses through German submarine attacks during 1942 became almost catastrophic. But in the final analysis, Hitler did not have quite enough submarines, and the United States succeeded in building ships much faster than German submarines could sink them, so that by the middle of 1943, the Battle of the Atlantic was to turn in favor of the Allies.

The second event foreshadowing a change occurred on December 11, 1941, when British and Commonwealth troops invaded Libya and successfully drove back Rommel's *Afrika Korps*. Militarily this British drive bore few long-term consequences, but it afforded

a great boost in morale to the British, for whom it represented the first outright victory over German troops.

Despite these temporary defeats, Germany resumed the offensive in the spring of 1942. Rommel in North Africa repulsed the British and burst into Egypt, as part of a vague plan to penetrate into the Middle East, where a link might be made with Japan in its drive through Southeast Asia and India.

In Russia, Hitler directed the summer offensive southward. Overly confident of his tactical knowledge and contemptuous of generals who warned against the risk, he divided his forces, sending one along the Black Sea toward the Caucasus, the other due east to Stalingrad on the Volga. For several months, the German steamroller again made fantastic gains. The southernmost spearheads came within 100 miles of the Caspian Sea, but in the end, the Germans succeeded neither in capturing the Caucasian oil fields nor in cutting Russia's major supply lines on the Volga. In the fall came the great turning point. The Germans had slowly fought their way into the center of Stalingrad, fiercely defended block by block by Soviet troops and partisans. Suddenly they found themselves threatened by strong Russian counteroffensives to the north and south of the city. Despite the threat of imminent encirclement, Hitler would not countenance a retreat. The Russians were allowed to close a tight ring around the 22 German divisions trapped in the city. After about 240,000 men were killed in the battle, in faithful obedience to Hitler's fanatic command to "stand and die," the remaining 90,000 troops, including 24 generals, capitulated at the beginning of February 1943.

Surprisingly, in addition to those used in the Battle of Stalingrad the Russians had enough men and supplies to mount a general winter offensive along the entire front. They forced the Germans to lift the siege of Leningrad, to withdraw along the central front, and to evacuate almost half of the Ukraine in the south. Only in March 1943 did the lines become temporarily stabilized. By then, it had become evident that the Russian winter offensive had once and for all broken the back of German power. Henceforth the initiative was to remain almost exclusively in Russian hands, and the Germans were to begin their two-year rear guard action that ended in the Battle of Berlin.

The fall of 1942 brought similar changes on the other fronts. In October, the British resumed their drive into Libya. A month later, a task force of American, British, and Free French troops landed in Morocco and Algeria. The Germans rushed reinforcements to Tunisia, but by May all North Africa had been conquered by the Allies. In their retreat, Germany and Italy sustained great losses in men, matériel, and shipping, and the Italian peninsula became exposed to possible Allied invasion. Germany's only success in these black months was the seizure of the rest of defenseless France in retaliation for the Allied conquest of Algeria and Morocco; but its aim of securing the remaining French fleet was frustrated when most of the ships were scuttled by their crews in the harbor of Toulon.

Even in the far-off Pacific, the fall of 1942 marked a turning point, in that the battles on and around the Solomon Islands signaled the end of Japanese victories and the beginning of the American offensive.

II

Retreat and Total Collapse,

1943–1945

RETREAT AND DEFEAT

The shift of power from Axis to Allies that occurred in 1943 was symbolized by the meeting of Roosevelt and Churchill in Casablanca in January of that year. Here the two western nations announced their determination to insist on the eventual unconditional surrender of the enemy powers. The two heads of state also discussed the strategy required to achieve this aim, and the Allied air staff adopted a policy of total air war against Germany, designed not only to destroy its military, industrial, and economic life, but also to undermine "the morale of the German people to the point where their capacity for armed resistance is fatally weakened."

To be sure, serious disagreements among the Allies in some cases delayed military action. Stalin continued to press for the immediate opening of a second front in western Europe so as to draw off German divisions from Russia. Repeated postponement of a second front made him increasingly suspicious of Allied intentions. Moreover, America, Britain, and China did not see eye to eye over the campaigns in southeast Asia and the treatment of India. Above all, Churchill wanted to invade fortress Europe through the Balkans, whereas the American military staff favored a direct cross-Channel invasion of the flat regions of northern France, where Allied armored divisions could operate more effectively under an air umbrella provided from nearby British airports. But these disagreements did not save Germany from an almost unbroken string of defeats.

The Reverses of 1943

In 1943, the Soviet Army launched its first summer offensive. Despite skillful defensive moves, the Germans were slowly driven back. By the end of the year, Hitler's armies had been pushed to the prewar border of Poland in the north, and retained only a precarious foothold in the western Ukraine and parts of the Crimea.

In the Mediterranean, the Allies crossed from Tunisia to conquer Sicily in a hard-fought, month-long battle. Faced with the prospect of invasion of their homeland, most Italians became disenchanted with their Duce. The Fascist Grand Council and the Italian king suddenly deposed Mussolini and had him arrested. The ambitious chief of staff, Marshal Pietro Badoglio, then dissolved the Fascist regime and secretly got in touch with the Allies to negotiate an armistice, even offering to let Italian troops aid the western powers against Germany. But negotiations between the emissaries of Badoglio and General Dwight Eisenhower were so protracted that the German army found time to consolidate its position throughout central and northern Italy. Consequently, when the armistice was finally agreed upon and Allied troops tried to take over Italy, they succeeded in seizing only the lower third of the peninsula before getting bogged down in front of the strong defenses that the Germans had rapidly thrown across Italy, halfway between Naples and Rome.

The fall of Mussolini thus represented a German loss but no clear-cut Allied victory. The liberated southern portion of Italy under Badoglio declared war on Hitler, and furnished the Anglo-Americans a firm foothold on the Continent from which to increase their bombing raids on the heart of Europe. But another year of costly fighting was to be required before central Italy could be conquered. The Germans meanwhile rescued Mussolini from prison and set him up as a puppet in charge of the so-called North Italian Republic, which furnished them some help against the Allies. Still, the loss of half of Italy as a cobelligerent and the need to concentrate more troops south of the Alps were serious blows to German morale and resources.

During 1943, the Germans faced other setbacks. Partisans in Yugoslavia and Greece, with the aid of air-dropped British and American supplies, were increasing their disruptive activities and pinning down dozens of German divisions that would otherwise have been used on the Russian front. The submarine campaign was rapidly failing as the Allies improved their convoy system, installed better radar devices, and increased their air patrols of the Atlantic shipping lanes. The air war was also changing in character. The Allies were building planes and training pilots at such a rate that they could afford to bomb German cities, industrial complexes, and transportation networks by day as well as by night, in raids frequently comprising 500 or 1000 bombers. Although the German air force and air defenses were still formidable and inflicted a heavy toll on the attackers, they could not save the German cities from ghastly destruction.

Russian Gains in 1944

In 1944, German defeats multiplied so rapidly that the final collapse became inevitable. Unquestionably, if Nazi propaganda had not misinformed the Germans and if Hitler's fanaticism had not inspired so many of them to fight to the bitter end, if fear of Russia and misgivings about Allied intentions in view of the much-publicized demand for unconditional surrender had not frightened many into blind resistance, the war would have ended in late summer of that year.

In the course of 1944, the Russians cleared their homeland of foreign

troops. Then in rapid succession, they seized over half of Poland, forced Finland out of the war, occupied Estonia, Latvia, Rumania, and Bulgaria, helped Tito's partisans liberate most of Yugoslavia, and invaded eastern Czechoslovakia and Hungary. In December, the Red armies stood along a line from Memel on the Baltic, past Warsaw and Budapest, to the Adriatic near Fiume, poised to invade Germany.

The Soviet advance and the German retreat entailed further frightful massacres in eastern Europe. When the Red Army approached the Vistula in August, the Poles of Warsaw rose in rebellion to hasten their liberation from the Germans. But since the Polish rebels were mostly bourgeois and anti-Communist, the nearby Russian armies refused to aid them. Anglo-American supplies were flown in all the way from Britain, but without ground support, the premature rebellion could not succeed. After a costly siege of two months, the Germans once again seized Warsaw and massacred the rebels, while the Russians, entrenched across the Vistula, were apparently content to see the Nazis wipe out the non-Communist Polish resistance movement. A similar event occurred at the same time in Slovakia, where non-Communist resistance fighters were wiped out by the Germans in a bloody two-month campaign, while the Red Army, only a few miles away, refused to aid their fellow Slavs.

Hungary, like Italy, was thrown into civil war as a result of the German retreat. When the Russians invaded the country, the Hungarian government attempted to conclude an armistice and withdraw from the fighting. But the Germans arrested the regent (Admiral Miklós Horthy) and set up

their own puppet government, while the invading Russians established their own pro-Communist regime. During the subsequent three-month siege of Budapest, Hungarians were thus forced to fight on both sides in support of their respective foreign masters.

The front in Italy changed relatively little during 1944. Heavy fighting south of Rome finally led to an Allied breakthrough in June and to the seizure of central Italy. But north of Florence the Germans had constructed a second defensive line that kept the Allies at bay for another eight months, until the total collapse of Germany in the spring of 1945.

The Second Front in the West

In the west, the Allied landing in Normandy on June 6, 1944, opened up the second front that the German military had always dreaded and that Stalin had requested for so long. In anticipation of such an assault, the Germans had fortified the entire coast line from Denmark to the Bay of Biscay and had stationed reserve divisions in strategic locations. But the Allies had made meticulous, long-term preparations. By this time they had gained unquestioned air superiority that permitted massive strategic bombing to disrupt the transportation system by which German supplies and reserves could reach the Normandy front. Actually, production of German airplanes, in factories placed underground or hidden in caves in the Bavarian Alps, was still increasing in 1944, despite constant Allied air assaults, but a growing shortage of both fuel and trained pilots was sapping the effectiveness of the once-formidable Luftwaffe.

The invasion was preceded by heavy

bombing and shelling of the coastal areas, and the landing of parachutists, who, together with French underground forces, cut communications between Normandy and the rest of the German-held territories. The landing operation itself was gigantic, involving thousands of ships, hundreds of thousands of vehicles, and millions of men, as well as almost unlimited supplies. Fuel was piped across the Channel in numerous pipe lines hastily laid under water from England to France. After establishing their beachhead, the Allies spent almost a month consolidating it and resisting tenacious counterattacks by the Germans. Field Marshal Rommel, who commanded the army group in northern France, warned Hitler in July that a disaster seemed imminent. In view of the Allies' domination of the sky and their logistical superiority, especially in artillery and armor, he saw no way of containing their armies and preventing them from overrunning all France. He complained that he was receiving practically no supplies and replacements: for 225 tanks lost, he had been sent 17 replacements, and 6000 men had replaced 97,000 casualties. He begged Hitler "to draw the proper conclusions without delay."

But as before, Hitler refused to countenance strategic withdrawals. He ordered the army to hold every inch of ground, no matter how hopeless. In mid-July, the Americans broke out of the beachhead, and Rommel's predictions came true. Within two months, the Allied armies, joined by new forces that landed in the south of France on August 15, occupied almost all France and Belgium. Paris fell on August 25, Brussels on September 4, and on September 11, American units

crossed the German border at two points. Hitler refused to see the inevitable and threw all blame on his generals, some of whom became implicated in the plot on his life, on July 20 (see pages 300 ff.). After Rommel was forced to commit suicide because of indirect involvement in the assassination attempt, the trusted Field Marshal Hans-Günther von Kluge (1882–1944) was given the hopeless task of stemming the Allied tide. In August, when his failure became apparent, he, too, was relieved of his command. In a final letter, Kluge implored Hitler not to rely on last-minute miracles, but to spare the German people continued suffering. "You have fought an honest and truly great battle," he flattered Hitler. "Now prove your greatness by putting an end to a hopeless struggle." After writing this letter, Kluge committed suicide. His successor, Field Marshal Walther Model (1891–1945), who could hardly do any better, committed suicide in 1945.

The Final Months

With invasion imminent from two sides, some Nazis now looked at the political rather than the military aspects of their desperate situation. They properly assessed the inherent incompatibility of the Russians and the western Allies, and hoped to find a way not merely of driving a wedge between them but of possibly enticing the Anglo-Americans to join a German crusade against Communist Russia. Some advocated that, for this purpose, the eastern front should be held at all costs, while only token resistance should be offered in the west. Some even reasoned that if occupation of German soil was inevitable, it would

be preferable to let in the western forces rather than the Red Army, which was clearly bent on avenging the horrors inflicted on Russia by the Nazis.

Hitler himself toyed with such ideas, but ultimately remained determined to fight on both fronts with equal vigor. In December 1944, he even ordered the famous counteroffensive in Belgium, designed to split the Allies by a quick thrust to the Channel between the American and British forces. But by January, this Battle of the Bulge, too, was lost, and the American armies were clawing their way through the Siegfried Line.

Thereafter, the final assault on Germany was started. In February, the Russians crossed the Oder River and raced to within thirty miles of Berlin, while the Americans conquered the left bank of the Rhine. In March, United States, British, and French forces crossed the Rhine and within five weeks occupied most of Germany west of the Elbe, while the Russians began their siege of Berlin. By late April, all resistance in Italy had ceased. Mussolini had been captured and hanged by Italian partisans. And German armies in most areas were preparing to capitulate. Only Hitler, in his Berlin bunker surrounded by a few faithful, was still speaking of ultimate victory until his suicide on April 30.

THE GERMAN HOME FRONT

The first two years of the war, until June 1941, were for most Germans a period of undiluted victories and delights. Hitler's easy triumphs, the perceptible growth of Greater Germany, and the unquestioned superiority of German arms swelled the breasts of all those who did not bother to analyze the likely consequences of ruthless application of might and violence. German casualties in the Polish and French campaigns were light; the occasional token air raids by the RAF barely interrupted the normal life of the cities; an acquaintance here or there might disappear, presumably into a concentration camp; a Jewish family next door might be deported; but relatively few Germans suffered. The exploitation of conquered lands permitted an increase in food rations and brought luxury items back on the market. The average German felt convinced that all was well with his world.

This mood changed with the invasion of Russia. Bewildered at first by the new twist in Goebbels' propaganda, which reconverted the Soviet Union into an archenemy, many Germans were soon shaken by the endless casualty reports from the Russian front. By 1942, morale in the fatherland began to sink. Shortages of food and consumer goods appeared; soldiers on leave from the eastern front reported the horrors of winter warfare on the frozen steppes; the destructive rain of explosives and fire bombs began to gut German cities and impress on their populations the reality of war.

Concomitant changes were felt in almost all areas of life, in and outside the Nazi spectrum. After 1941, the Nazi treatment of the Jews, of the conquered populations, and of their own German subjects became more and more ruthless and brutal, as if the leaders unconsciously sensed the impending doom. The more radical elements in the party came to the fore, and at the same time anti-Nazi resistance movements grew more active.

German Control
of Occupied Territories

The Nazis soon learned that it was easier to conquer Europe than to establish their so-called New Order. By the fall of 1941, they found themselves in direct or indirect control of the entire Continent, with the exception of Portugal, Spain, Switzerland, Sweden, the British Isles, and the unconquered portions of Russia. Their basic aims were simple: to exploit Europe economically for the benefit of Germany, and to maintain control over the subject and dependent populations. But no clear-cut and consistent policy was ever evolved on how to organize the Continent for such a purpose. Partly because of the military requirements of the war and the haphazard way in which territories were acquired, administrative measures remained opportunistic, confused, and sometimes contradictory. Plans for the New Order had to be adapted to geographic and economic conditions and take into consideration the presence or absence of strong political cohesion in the conquered lands.

The conquest of the more sparsely settled, vast regions of the east afforded the racists the opportunity to experiment with schemes for the New Order. Rosenberg, as minister for occupied eastern territories, favored colonization of the Baltic region. He collected families of Germans, Dutch, and kindred "superior racial stock" and settled them on farms in the northeast. He held visions of "purified" colonial enclaves, gradually spreading throughout much of European Russia, surrounded by the local slave populations who toiled for their German masters. Himmler on the other hand, who in 1943 became minister for the interior and commissioner for "safeguarding German nationality," thought of establishing in the heart of Europe a racially pure paradise. For this purpose he hoped to eliminate within Germany all "impure" elements, and repatriate all ethnic Germans—from the Baltic region, the lower Volga, Yugoslavia, and other areas—for settlement in and around Germany. A kernel of "ethnic purity" would thus arise in central Europe that could easily dominate the outlying areas of "racial inferiors." Caught between these contradictory schemes of Himmler's and Rosenberg's, some families were actually uprooted twice, being first sent out to colonize the Baltic, and then repatriated by Himmler's orders.

Arrangements for the political control of occupied Europe remained multifarious. Areas that had belonged to Bismarck's Reich, or that contained many ethnic Germans, were directly annexed to Greater Germany, and either converted into *Gaue* (districts) or appended to a neighboring German *Gau*. Among others, these included Austria, the Sudetenland, Memel, Danzig, West Prussia, Poznan, Alsace-Lorraine, and even Slovenia in northern Yugoslavia. Some territories became directly or indirectly subordinate, such as Bohemia-Moravia and Poland, which were administered almost exclusively by Germans. Norway and Holland were controlled by a German Reich commissioner with the aid of German army, SS, and police units, since the legal Norwegian and Dutch governments had fled to London and established official governments-in-exile. Denmark, on the other hand, whose king and his government had remained on Danish soil, was placed under mili-

tary occupation, although not, strictly speaking, under military government. The Balkan states, all occupied by German armies and controlled by puppet regimes, acted as nominal allies of Germany but actual administrative power resided in Berlin. The occupied portions of Russia, of course, remained a theater of war, where army and SS units clashed over policies and spheres of jurisdiction.

Where possible, the economic, political, and legal life of subject territories was "coordinated" along the lines adopted in Germany. Economic planning was applied to satisfy the requirements of total war, laws were redesigned to meet National Socialist ends, and anti-Jewish policies were enforced. Although countless German agencies and departments were involved in this gigantic task of exploitation and domination, overwhelming power resided in Heinrich Himmler, who not only commanded the SS and the Gestapo, but, as minister of the interior, also controlled the police.

The actual treatment of conquered populations varied from place to place —or one might say, from "race to race." The official hierarchy of "races" awarded preference to Nordic peoples. Latins were considered superior to Slavs, and the "sub-human" Jews were rated below all others. In Holland, Denmark, and Norway, the occupying soldiers generally treated the people with relative respect, even though the overbearing SS troops frequently acted as conquerors rather than "liberators." In France and Belgium, the Nazis' contempt for a "weaker race" mixed uneasily with the admiration felt by most officers for the cultural traditions of the Franco-Belgians. In the east, es-

pecially in Poland and Russia, the behavior of the SS army units (*Waffen* SS) and even of most regular troops ranged from mere contempt and exploitation to primitive barbarism. Polish and Russian prisoners and civilians, regardless of sex or age, were kicked, whipped, tortured, and exterminated at random. In one of Himmler's typical exhortations to his SS leaders in 1943, he warned that a show of sympathy for non-German peoples, particularly the Russians, was a crime against "our *Volk* and our blood. Whether the others live in prosperity or perish from hunger concerns me only in so far as we need them as slaves." And as a practical example, he added: "Whether during the construction of a tank trap 10,000 Russian women perish from exhaustion or not concerns me only if the tank trap should not get completed."

Besides violating all humanitarian considerations, the behavior of the German occupiers, particularly in the Ukraine, was also political folly. Many Ukrainians, at heart anti-Communist and proud of their former independence, might have welcomed the Germans as liberators from Soviet Russian domination. Instead, German atrocities quickly turned them into fierce anti-German guerrilla fighters. Instead of recognizing this tactical and political blunder, Hitler welcomed the guerrilla warfare: "It gives us the possibility of exterminating whoever opposes us," he bluntly told Rosenberg and other advisers.

German looting and arrogance naturally provoked the local populations, not only in the east but also in the west and north. Resistance groups were gradually forming everywhere, gather-

ing arms, establishing contact with the Allies, helping the escape of downed Allied flyers, and engaging in sabotage. Some of these groups were dominated by Communists, others by moderate or right-wing elements. In Yugoslavia, where partisan activity was the fiercest, internecine civil war between Communist and non-Communist guerrillas sapped much of the energy that might have been used against the Germans. But everywhere the resistance movements grew more powerful and active as German military power declined in 1943 and 1944. In many countries, such as, for example, France, Yugoslavia, and Greece, these nuclei of resistance formed the embryonic bases of the provisional governments that helped govern their countries after the withdrawal of the German occupation troops.

But Germany could never have dominated most of Europe if it had been faced by nothing but hostility and active resistance everywhere. In most countries, from Norway, Holland, and France to the Balkans, the Nazis found surprising numbers of sympathizers who were eager and proud to help establish the "new order," either because of ideological conviction or because of sheer opportunism. Nationals from all occupied nations volunteered to work in Germany, where economic conditions were presumably better than in their own defeated or occupied countries. Thousands of them voluntarily enlisted to fight against Russia side by side with the Nazi troops, apparently persuaded that Communism was a greater danger than Nazism. Such local support by the so-called collaborators enabled the Germans to control and exploit surprisingly large areas

with a relatively limited number of occupation troops.

Total War

The demands of total war, according to the Nazis, required total dictatorship. In April 1942, Hitler informed the Reichstag that everything—traditional rights, justice, and administration—had to be subordinated to the sole task of achieving victory! He requested the Reichstag to grant him legal power "to force everyone to fulfill his duty," using whatever penalties he saw fit, and leaving the definition of duty up to his conscience. Upon a motion by Göring praising "the wisdom, justice, goodness, greatness, and above all the genius of the Führer," the Reichstag approved Hitler's request by acclamation and granted him the right to act "without being bound by existing legislation."

Even more than before, every aspect of public and private life was now subject to arbitrary interference by the various agencies of the party. While Goebbels droned endlessly by radio and press that victory was in sight, terror and coercion increased in proportion to the real hopelessness of the situation. Special courts awarded death sentences on the slightest pretext and meticulously forwarded the bill for the cost of execution, including postage, to the nearest relative of the condemned. A typical example is that of a minor government clerk in Rostock, who in 1943, after the fall of Mussolini, said in a streetcar that what happened in Italy would happen in Germany, and that the Führer should resign, since victory was no longer possible. For this he was condemned to death on the

charge of undermining the National Socialist defense effort.

As the war continued beyond its expected duration, stockpiles of strategic raw materials became depleted and the problem of shortages arose. The Allied blockade permitted no imports, except from Sweden and Spain, and the conquered lands provided less than had been anticipated. Moreover, strategic bombing by the Allies took its toll of industrial complexes. In 1942, Albert Speer (1905–   ) was appointed minister for armaments and munitions and awarded far-reaching dictatorial powers over industry and transport. At the same time, Fritz Sauckel (1894–1946) was made commissioner general for manpower in all occupied territories. The shortage of labor in Germany had become so severe that even careful and often forced assignment to jobs could not fill the required needs. Hence the German government began to recruit workers in occupied countries. Initially, sufficient volunteers could be found, but gradually Sauckel resorted to conscript labor. As in everything else, racial bias affected the treatment of these foreign workers employed in German industry and agriculture. Those from the east, working mostly on farms, were usually treated as slaves. By 1945, five million foreigners had been forcibly assigned to labor in Germany.

Even these measures could not furnish sufficient manpower to meet the demands of industry and replace the mounting civilian and military casualties. In September 1944, Hitler and his deputy Martin Bormann (1900–1945?) created the *Volkssturm,* a people's militia based on the compulsory enrollment of all able German males aged sixteen to sixty, with the task of

"defending the homeland with all weapons and means, in as much as they appear suitable." With young boys and old men called into the fighting, with women and the handicapped manning the factories, with imported slaves working the fields, and daily air raids destroying the cities and burying their inhabitants under mountains of rubble, everyone was made to perform his duty in Hitler's total war.

Extermination of the Jews

The Nazi program for "racial purity" was instituted with the same gradualness as the abrogation of the Treaty of Versailles or the establishment of Hitler's dictatorship. If Hitler and his followers had attempted in 1933 to gas the 600,000 Jews of Germany, there is little question that a revolution would have toppled them from power. But by proceeding step by step, while securing their regime and indoctrinating the people in the morals of brutality, they could progress from discrimination to persecution, then to mass deportation, and finally to complete extermination without endangering their control of the government. The Nuremberg Racial Laws of 1935 and the pogrom of November 1938 were major turning points in the anti-Jewish program, but the decisive change came with the outbreak of World War II. Before 1939, the Jews of Germany— and eventually of Austria and Czechoslovakia—were subjected to discrimination, degradation, and persecution, and some died in concentration camps. After 1939, they were at first deported, and then massacred. It is a measure of the incredible brutalization of life and of the adaptability of man that, compared with the final bestial solution,

the excesses of the earlier period appear almost humane.

There were many reasons why the outbreak of war added such impetus to the campaigns against the Jews. In *Mein Kampf,* Hitler had predicted that war would result "in the extermination of the Jewish race in Europe." He repeated this prophecy in a Reichstag speech of January 1939. Military exigencies always permit greater latitude of ruthlessness. The fanatic Nazis, convinced that Bolshevism, capitalism, and democracy were all a cloak for international Jewry, believed they had to eradicate the Jewish enemy within before being able to defeat the same enemy abroad. They were also practical considerations. In wartime, relatively more secrecy could be used to shield the extermination proceedings from the scrutiny of public and foreign opinion. An even more important link between the war and the intensified anti-Jewish program were the German conquests in the east. So many more Jews lived in eastern Europe—Poland alone having over three million—that the seizure of Poland, White Russia, and the Ukraine greatly multiplied the number of Jews under Nazi control.

From the outbreak of war to the invasion of Russia, the policies more or less followed the directive given by Göring to Reinhard Heydrich: "to prepare a solution to the Jewish question, in the form of emigration or evacuation, which favorably fits existing conditions." As head of the Security Division of the SS, Heydrich was charged with implementing this directive. To "purify" central Europe, Jews from Austria, Bohemia, and parts of Germany were deported to Poland, where ghettos were established at Lodz, Warsaw, and other communities. Dur-

ing 1941, Jews from western countries and the Balkans were rounded up where possible, and shipped in sealed trains to the new Polish ghettos. To make use of this concentration of cheap manpower, forced labor was ordered for all Jews in Poland.

The invasion of Russia in 1941 and Rosenberg's dream of colonizing the east with ethnic Germans led to the final step in the program. The increasing desperate pace of the war and the growing power of the fanatics in the party led to more radical "solutions." If eastern Europe was to provide *Lebensraum* and not merely be a food basket for Germany, then the concentration of millions of Jews seemed contrary to Nazi aims. In the fall of 1941, the final mass deportation of German Jews to the east was begun. On the pretext that they were being resettled or "going on vacation," the Gestapo permitted the deportees to take along 50 kilos of luggage and 100 marks. The rest of their property was confiscated by the state. But most of them were no longer destined for eastern ghettos, but for the new extermination camps that were being constructed at Auschwitz, Belzec, Chelmno, Sobibor, Treblinka, and other places.

The "final solution to the Jewish problem" was discussed and elaborated at a meeting of party and state officials and SS leaders in January 1942. Careful organization and planning was needed "to comb through Europe from west to east" so as to apprehend all Jews, to make available the transportation required to ship them to the extermination camps, and to cover the cost of such a gigantic operation by using the labor of the condemned and by extracting whatever profit there

remained in their bodies—shoes and clothing, gold teeth and jewelry, and human hair for industrial purposes. On the basis of the "practical experiences" gathered in 1941, the conferees decided that the physically weak Jews should be exterminated forthwith, while those capable of heavy work should for the time being be used to build roads in the east. In the course of such work, it was assumed, "a great number would undoubtedly be lost through natural decrease." But, lest the survivors of these work teams form the germinal nucleus of a new Jewish renascence, these "would have to be treated accordingly," as soon as their work tasks were completed.

The nightmare now took on the most ghastly proportions. Unless hidden by friends or protected by local governments—as, for example, in the case of Denmark—Jews from all over occupied Europe were herded together, thrown into cattle trains, and gassed, shot, or beaten to death in the special extermination camps that rapidly increased in number in order to accommodate the constantly growing volume of the operation. Special task forces (*Einsatzkommandos*), consisting of between 500 and 1000 police and SS, roamed through Russian territory behind the invading troops to clean out Jews, gypsies, and Communist leaders, whom they either slaughtered on the spot or dispatched to death camps.

There is no need to shock the reader by a description of the horrors committed in these camps. The atrocities have received wide notoriety since the end of the war. Nor is it necessary to quibble over statistics concerning the number of victims—as if the inhumanity of the Nazis would have been less reprehensible if they had exterminated three million instead of five or six million persons.

The question of responsibility and of the abetting guilt of the Germans as a whole has been debated ever since 1945. Most Germans abide by the convenient claim that they knew nothing of the brutal excesses perpetrated by the Nazis. They insist that when they were occasionally informed about them during the last year of the war through Allied leaflets or radio broadcasts, they disregarded the reports as propaganda; and that only after the collapse in 1945 they became gradually, although hesitatingly, convinced of the truth of Allied accusations.

It is, of course, true that relatively few Germans were involved in the actual operation of the gas chambers. Wherever possible, the Nazis used prisoners and candidates for later extermination to perform the varied tasks required—sorting the clothes of the victims, cutting off their hair, dragging the bodies out of the gas chambers, pulling out gold teeth, digging the mass graves, and dumping in the bodies. Perhaps only a few thousand SS actually whipped the endless columns of naked Jews into the extermination chambers or pulled the triggers of the machine pistols on victims lined up before open graves. Yet hundreds of thousands of Germans were involved in, or were witnesses to, some part of this gigantic operation: doctors who performed medical experiments on prisoners, chauffeurs who drove the gassing trucks in which the victims were asphyxiated, engineers who ran the deportation trains, police and SS who guarded the camps, officials who visited the compounds, and soldiers near the front who saw the task forces in action. And these hundreds of thou-

sands must have spoken about what they knew to millions of friends and relatives.

It is also certain that most Germans during these years of terror saw Jews being dragged out of their houses and kicked by a booted SS into a waiting truck. Perhaps they looked away or hurried to their local beer cellar. When the same Jew was never again seen, he was presumably deemed to be living comfortably in a new Polish ghetto. And when news came of his death, as it often did, one felt sorry for a minute, and then ordered another beer. The general attitude was less one of ignorance than of numb and convenient indifference. As the student resistance leaders Hans and Sophie Scholl proclaimed in one of the leaflets distributed in the winter of 1942–1943, in which they pointed out that since the conquest of Poland the Nazis had murdered 300,000 Jews, "Everyone wants to absolve himself of share in the guilt, everyone does it, and then falls asleep with the clearest of consciences."

Anti-Nazi Resistance

After the collapse of Hitler's regime, a great many Germans claimed that they had been members of the anti-Nazi resistance, and protested that they should not have to suffer because of crimes committed by the terrorists whom they themselves had fought for years. These claims raised not only the problem of collective guilt but also the question of the numerical strength of the opposition to Hitler. Actually, no precise answers can be given to these questions. The nature of the Nazi regime required utmost secrecy in all underground opposi-

tional ventures. To escape detection by the Gestapo, the more effective resistance fighters were organized into small independent cells, working in ignorance of one another, so that the arrest of one member, who might reveal secrets under torture, would not result in the discovery of the entire organizational net. Moreover, the term "resistance" is subject to many different interpretations: silent, mitigating, and active—to mention three major types.

No doubt the vast majority of Germans belonged at one time or another to what might be called the "silent" resistance. These people felt—and sometimes showed—a lack of enthusiasm for the regime, or were disconcerted by some aspect of the Nazi program. This sort of mild disenchantment naturally grew stronger as victory turned into disaster, as food and supplies became scarce, and as German cities crumbled under incessant air bombardment. Needless to say, such behavior, which the Nazis on occasion punished with imprisonment or death, never presented a serious threat to Hitler's monopoly of power. Yet it infuriated Goebbels' vanity, for it seemed to prove a flaw in his program of total indoctrination.

The "mitigators" were those moderate sympathizers with National Socialism who disliked certain excesses of the regime, but remained at their posts and actively served Hitler with the expectation of being able to mitigate the more nefarious aspects of the system. Hjalmar Schacht, certain officials in the Foreign Office, and other civil servants and professionals might be placed in this category. By softening the execution of harsh decrees or resisting the total introduction of Nazi practices into their bureaus, they

claimed to have obstructed the regime. It is, of course, impossible to establish how far they were successful in their professed aims, or how much they deluded themselves. Nor can one really ascertain whether they were sheer opportunists who later convinced themselves and the world of their basically honorable intentions, or whether they deserve a measure of moral praise for doing their best under difficult circumstances to diminish the horrors of the regime. The fact that Schacht was acquitted by the tribunal at Nuremberg hardly proves that he was a "mitigator," since the indictments were for specific crimes against peace or against humanity.

THE ACTIVE RESISTANCE   The majority of those who participated in the active resistance labored to undermine the regime but did not actively attempt to overthrow it. There were various distinct groups, each engaging in minor acts of resistance. Some distributed anti-Nazi leaflets or listened to foreign broadcasts—acts punishable by death. Some helped Jews or political suspects to hide from the Gestapo or to escape abroad. Some engaged in economic sabotage. Others kept in contact with like-minded organizations abroad. Most of them were largely intent on preserving the ideals of their own fields of activity—religion, politics, the legal profession, academic life, and so on—from contamination by National Socialist ideology.

Their overriding interest in their own spheres of life, their different social backgrounds, and, above all their divergent hopes for the reconstruction of a Germany without Hitler prevented these groups from uniting during the entire peacetime period. Collaboration among them was effected only in the face of the disasters of the war. Although there were many such groups, a few deserve special attention.

Most of the Communist leaders fled from Germany in 1933 to escape imprisonment. They went to Russia, where they helped found the National Committee for a Free Germany. Except during the period of Nazi-Soviet collaboration, 1939–1941, they maintained contact with small Communist underground cells inside Germany, called the Red Chapel (*Die Rote Kapelle*). The Communist underground was particularly active in trying to sabotage factories, in slowing down production, or in attempting to weaken the war effort on the eastern front. A few of the Communists were convinced anti-Stalinists. Whether remaining in Germany or fleeing to France, England, or Mexico, they maintained their belief that a popular front, in which all antifascist groups would cooperate, might ultimately become the basis for the reconstruction of Germany.

The headquarters of the outlawed SPD moved to Prague in 1933, then to Paris in 1938, and finally to London in 1940. Until the outbreak of war, contact between Socialists in and out of Germany remained fairly close, and much illegal literature was smuggled into the Reich for clandestine distribution. The Socialists, however, were not united in their ultimate aims. The more radical wing resembled the USPD of 1919. They regarded the failure to adopt a thoroughly Marxist program after World War I as the cause for Hitler's rise to power and for the weakness of the Weimar Republic. Hence they believed that only an orthodox Marxist program could wean the workers away from National Socialism

and offer hope for the future success of a socialistic democracy.

The official program of the underground SPD, however, remained revisionist and thoroughly anti-Communist. It rejected the thought of a popular front for fear that the SPD might fall under the domination of the better financed, though smaller, Communist underground. The most active leader of the underground SPD, Wilhelm Leuschner (1888–1944), a former trade-unionist and minister in the Hessian government, worked closely with secret representatives of the non-Socialist Christian trade-unions. Convinced that the workers alone could never overthrow Hitler and establish a Socialist government, Leuschner hoped to attract the middle class with a program resembling that of the Labor party in England. As a supplier to the German navy, Leuschner had relative freedom to travel, which allowed him during the war years to become an important link among various anti-Nazi circles and one of the organizers of the attempt to overthrow Hitler in 1944.

The churches were also centers of resistance. A number of courageous clergymen publicly denounced the Nazis' pagan ideology and virulent racialism. The Catholic Church, as well as the Confessional Church of the Protestants and other Protestant sects, such as Jehovah's Witnesses, tried to use moral pressure and sometimes even chose martyrdom in order to resist the inroads of National Socialist *Gleichschaltung*. A considerable number of priests and ministers suffered for their convictions in concentration camps. But most of this resistance by ecclesiastics was defensive in that they wanted to preserve Christianity and Christian morality. Only a few members of the clergy actually joined plots to overthrow the regime.

Besides political and religious bodies, there were other, less well-defined groups who participated in occasional acts of resistance. A few university professors, especially during the earlier years of National Socialism, tried to uphold the traditional values of western civilization and publicly denounced the chauvinism of Hitler's movement. Student organizations printed and distributed clandestine leaflets calling on the Germans to rid themselves of the Nazi nightmare. Some lawyers, economists, philosophers, and writers—the so-called inner emigrants—did what they could to resist the destruction of their professions, and a few joined the active anti-Hitler fighters. But most of the intellectuals who had not fled abroad maintained a tenuous and compromising appearance of apolitical indifference.

Finally, a considerable number of army officers formed a part of the resistance. Their motives varied. Fear and jealousy of the Nazi paramilitary units, class hatred of aristocrats for the upstart Nazis, and above all, the danger that Hitler would ruin the *Wehrmacht* through his flamboyant diplomatic and military ventures drove many an officer into quiet opposition to Hitler. But very few of them dared to violate the sanctity of their oath to the Führer and to participate in the active resistance.

It is impossible to estimate the magnitude of this active resistance. The fact that so many non-Jews were executed by the Nazis or lingered in concentration camps, or that about a quarter of a million joined the Society of Victims of Fascism after the war

sheds little reliable light on the question. National Socialist justice and terror sent to the gallows countless people who were in no way members of the resistance. Telling a joke about Goebbels' clubfoot or Göring's obesity, hoarding an extra pound of lard, possessing foreign currency, or failing to salute the swastika during a parade of storm troopers—under the Nazi regime any of these insignificant acts might lead to a jail sentence or to death.

But even without the benefit of statistics, it appears that the size and effectiveness of this active resistance was not considerable. The ubiquity of police spies and informers, the octopus-like organization of party and state, and, above all, the cold-blooded brutality of Nazi coercion frightened all but the most resolute from expressing the slightest overt displeasure.

PLANNED COUPS AGAINST HITLER
There is no evidence of any serious, organized plot to overthrow the regime before 1938.[1] In this connection, it must be recalled that Hitler's assumption of power was pseudo-legal, and that his dictatorship was instituted by installments. Consequently, the opposition at first believed that Hitler's government might be terminated by similar pseudo-legal means. It is difficult to ascertain at what point the more active plotters concluded that only an armed coup could topple the entrenched Nazis.

Planning for a successful anti-Nazi coup involved three major problems, apart from the difficulty of avoiding detection by the Gestapo. For one, the conspirators required the collaboration of some armed organization in order to overthrow the regime and impose their rule on the country. A few

thought that disloyal Nazi units, perhaps under the ambitious Göring, might be used to topple Hitler. But realizing that such boring from within the party was not likely to eradicate the objectionable aspects of National Socialism, most of the plotters concluded that their only hope lay in enlisting the aid of the regular armed forces.

A second problem involved the type of government to be installed after the overthrow of Hitler. Assassination of the Führer and his immediate subordinates would produce a political vacuum that the plotters would have to fill promptly with an adequate substitute government. In view of the Weimar experience, many of the conspirators were apprehensive about the viability of a democracy. Their divergent backgrounds also made it difficult for them to reach a conclusion about the degree of nationalization to be instituted after the overthrow of Hitler.

The third problem was perhaps the most complicated: in order to please the masses, the plotters would have to guarantee the preservation of the gains made by Hitler without resorting to Nazi tactics. The longer the underground waited, the more Hitler's almost unbroken string of successes complicated this aspect of their task. On the home front, for example, the conspirators could hardly risk sending millions of workers back into unemployment after Hitler had found jobs for them. Similarly on the foreign scene, lest they be accused of being less patriotic than the Nazis, they felt they had to match Hitler's success in scrapping the Versailles Treaty and aggrandizing Germany.

Even by 1938, the various active resistance groups had not found a

common solution to these major problems. In that year, however, the unwelcome prospect of a war against Czechoslovakia stirred certain high-ranking army officers and civilian officials to adopt a plan for the removal of Hitler (see page 269). Among the officers, the most active was General Ludwig Beck (1880–1944), chief of the General Staff of the army until his resignation in August 1938. In addition, Field Marshal Erich von Witzleben (1881–1944), commander of the Military District of Berlin, General Franz Halder (1884–   ), Beck's successor as chief of the General Staff, and others formed part of the conspiracy. Among the civilians, who included diplomats, police officials, and members of the clergy, the driving force was Carl Goerdeler (1884–1945), the former mayor of Leipzig, who was to remain one of the most active members of the resistance until his imprisonment in 1944. During the Sudeten crisis of September 1938, the conspirators secretly urged the British government to take a firm, public stand against Hitler's demands on Czechoslovakia. If in the face of a determined Anglo-French stand, Hitler backed down, his regime would be seriously weakened by the resulting diplomatic defeat. If he attempted war, Goerdeler informed London, "the leaders of the army declared their readiness to countermand Hitler's policy by force of arms." The Munich Agreement vitiated all these plans. The conspirators were interested only in preventing a war for which they felt unprepared. They saw no reason to object to the peaceful absorption of the Sudetenland.

After the abandonment of the 1938 plot, the conspirators became less active for a number of years. Most army officers seemed bewitched by Hitler's stupendous success. Some of them feared the overextension of the theater of war and opposed the attacks on Scandinavia, France, and Russia. But Hitler's triumphal march through the west, the Balkans, and into the east made their caution seem hopelessly untenable. In the final analysis, they considered it treasonous to undermine the war effort while Hitler continued to be successful.

Hitler's victories also complicated the question of possible peace terms. Even during the early years of the war, Beck and Goerdeler made several contacts with the British government to discuss a possible settlement in case Hitler were overthrown. But no agreement was ever reached, for the British remained suspicious and the German demands were high—either because the members of the resistance were themselves supernationalists, or because they feared to lose face with the German people if they settled for less than Hitler had achieved. Even the peace note of May 1941, sent to England by Goerdeler, who was considered a moderate, contained far-reaching demands. While promising to restore the sovereignty of all neutral lands occupied during the war, the note demanded that Germany retain Austria, the Sudetenland, and Memel, regain its 1914 borders with Belgium, France, and Poland, and receive back its overseas colonies.

But a few convinced officers, such as General Beck, and a number of civilians, particularly Goerdeler, Leuschner, and Ulrich von Hassel (1881–1944), a member of the diplomatic corps, became increasingly disturbed by the immoral excesses of the regime in its foreign as well as domestic policies.

They came to fear military victory as much as defeat, since either would ruin Germany—the one by perpetuating National Socialism, the other by destroying the country. And they saw no solution. Goerdeler unceasingly tried to convince key generals of the need for prompt action against Hitler, but as long as they hesitated, nothing serious could be undertaken.

While waiting to find an opportunity for removing Hitler, various resistance groups began to coalesce into a more all-inclusive movement. Most influential of these groupings was the "Kreisau Circle," so named after the Silesian estate of Count Helmuth von Moltke (1907–1945). Starting in 1940, the young Moltke and his friend Count Peter Yorck von Wartenburg (1904–1944), both scions of famous Prussian noble families, gathered representatives from various opposition groups in order to debate solutions to the problem of Germany's postwar reconstruction. The Kreisau Circle represented many shades of sociopolitical opinion —Catholics and Protestants, trade-unionists and entrepreneurs, Socialists, liberals, and conservatives. Many members became key figures in the revolutionary plots of the later war years, and the deliberations of this group strongly influenced the program ultimately adopted by the plotters.

THE PLOT OF JULY 1944 Active resistance was infused with new vigor when Hitler's chain of victories suddenly broke before the gates of Moscow. In 1942, serious disaffection reappeared among certain army officers who recognized the hopelessness of the Russian campaign and the potential military strength of the United States. A new opposition cell was formed inside the Counter Intelligence Service by its chief, Admiral Wilhelm Canaris (1887–1945), while in Munich students organized a concerted campaign to distribute in many parts of Germany leaflets calling for the overthrow of Hitler.

In 1943, after the debacle of Stalingrad, a few officers were willing to risk their life and honor in an effort to oust Hitler. But apparently only one serious attempt was made, when the chief of staff of the Central Army Group in Russia (General Henning von Treschow, 1901–1944) smuggled a time bomb in the guise of two cognac bottles into Hitler's airplane. The timer failed to go off. Although a few more assassination plans were hatched, no more serious attempts were made in that year. The officer corps as a whole feared that a *coup d'état* might lead to a breakdown of the Russian front and a subsequent Soviet invasion of Germany. Moreover, the announced Allied insistence on unconditional surrender made them feel justified in continuing the war. Contacts of the underground with the American OSS in Switzerland failed to bring firm assurance that the overthrow of Hitler would permit Germany to expect more favorable armistice terms.

Spurred by the continuous military defeats and the example of the overthrow of Mussolini, the conspirators around Beck and Goerdeler finally completed their plans by the fall of 1943. They reached agreement on detailed plans for the reconstruction of Germany after the overthrow of Hitler. During the first days of disorder, a military government was to control Germany under a state of siege. Once order was established, a provisional government was to take over, with Beck as president, Goerdeler as chan-

cellor, and Leuschner as vice-chancellor. The state of Prussia—which had retained its huge size despite the *Gleichschaltung* of the Nazis—was to be cut up, and Germany was to be divided into new states (*Länder*), each with about three to five million inhabitants. The administration was to be liberal but not completely democratic. Elections for the lower house were to be indirect, and the upper house was to be based on estates rather than on geographic distribution. The program called for nationalization of certain industrial monopolies and for special privileges to trade-unions.

After reaching this agreement, the conspirators were ready. In the thirty-six-year-old Count Klaus Schenk von Stauffenberg (1907–1944), whose position in the General Staff allowed him access to Hitler, they found a devoted activist who quickly became the soul of the conspiracy. But the contemplated action required the cooperation of more than merely a few ardent anti-Nazis, and months passed before the conspirators could persuade enough officers to join in the plot. The bulk of the officers continued to hesitate. Fear of committing treason, hesitation about violating their oath to the Führer, the absence of a promise of better terms from the Allies—these and a variety of other reasons served to justify their reluctance.

In the end, only the hopeless situation resulting from the Allied landings in Normandy and the Russian advances in the east persuaded enough officers to support the plot. They hoped the overthrow of Hitler would at least permit them to make peace in the west and throw their total strength against the Red Army. In July 1944, Stauffenberg was given the signal that all was ready. Twice he delayed setting the bomb because Himmler and Göring were not present, and he hoped to kill them together with Hitler. On July 20, during a meeting at Hitler's headquarters in East Prussia, Stauffenberg placed his briefcase, containing a time bomb, against Hitler's conference table, and flew to Berlin, where Generals Beck and Witzleben were seizing key buildings and notifying certain army commanders that Hitler had been killed and that they had assumed command. Actually Hitler was only slightly wounded by the blast, which blew him out of the flimsy wooden structure where the temporary headquarters were located. Many army officers refused to act until convinced of Hitler's death. Their hesitation, together with Goebbels' prompt action in telephoning Hitler from Berlin and convincing loyal army and SS units that the Führer was alive, doomed the plot from its very beginning. The conspirators were rounded up, and Hitler assured the Germans by radio that he had escaped the plot of a few "criminal and stupid officers, who are now being mercilessly exterminated." Stauffenberg and those most immediately involved were shot on the same day. Beck, Rommel, and others committed suicide. The People's Court held mock trials for Witzleben, Wartenburg, Moltke, Leuschner, Hassel, Goerdeler, and many others before executing them. Some conspirators or suspects simply disappeared behind the bars of Gestapo prisons or concentration camps. The total number of executions has never been established.

The attempt of July 20, 1944, was the last—and one should add the only thoroughly planned—attempt of the underground to remove Hitler. The repressions following its failure wiped

out most of the leaders of the active resistance. With few exceptions, the army officers again cowered in awe before the Führer and stood by him to the bitter end of Germany's total destruction.

COLLAPSE

Germany could have been spared much of the devastation of its cities and hundreds of thousands of lives could have been spared by all belligerents if the war had been terminated in late 1944 or at least at the beginning of 1945. Had rational leaders governed Germany, they would have requested an armistice at the latest in January 1945, after the failure of the Battle of the Bulge and the collapse of the German central lines in the east. But Hitler's maniacal fanaticism prolonged the war for an agonizing four months.

The Suicidal Temper
of Final Resistance

In order to keep the Germans fighting, the Nazis used whatever means they could devise. Goebbels constantly assured them that victory was in sight and that secret weapons would soon be used to hurl the invaders back on all fronts. Himmler appealed to all German women to spur their men into giving their last to assure final victory. "We stand by the holy conviction," he stated in a proclamation, "that God has given to Germany in our Führer Adolf Hitler the one man who can ward off this danger [the Bolshevik seizure of Europe], and that in the end He will award victory to our brave and heroic people and thus to the true Europe."

In a final effort, the propaganda machine tried to scare into fighting those who could not be enticed voluntarily to give their lives in a hopeless struggle. News of the atrocities committed by the advancing Russians on the eastern front and of the American Morgenthau Plan (see page 309) helped the Nazis in this task. Hitler warned the Germans that "the enemy's ultimate aim is the eradication of the German people." And many became convinced that they might as well resist to the end in the hope that the final catastrophe could somehow be averted.

Where enticement or fear did not help, ruthless terror was applied. In February 1945, soldiers were informed that if they surrendered at the front, their kinsmen at home would be imprisoned or shot. Special court-martial tribunals were set up throughout Germany to see to it that "all Germans" —civilians as well as military—prove their "readiness to fight and their devotion unto death." Acting under martial law, these tribunals—composed of a judge, a member of the NSDAP, and an officer of the army, police, or SS— were empowered to pronounce only one of two sentences: death or exoneration. Moreover, some fanatics devised the plan of concentrating all Germans in a central territory of the Reich, which would be turned into an impregnable fortress. A mass exodus from the east had begun, as German civilians fled before the advancing Soviet armies. The Nazis now forced further evacuations from the east, a gigantic operation that complicated military operations and added to the dangerous dislocation of food supplies. Martin Bormann contemplated applying this same idea to the west of Germany, so that the advancing Allies

would find nothing but depopulated areas.

Even in early April, when American, British, and French troops were racing across Germany from the west, and the Russians stood within sight of Berlin, SS fanatics saw to it that every inch of ground was defended. Young boys and women were impressed into paramilitary formations to help defend towns by building tank barriers or sniping from rooftops. The SS issued an order prohibiting the surrender of a single house. If a white flag was hoisted in a house, SS detachments had permission promptly to shoot all male occupants.

During these months of carnage on the ground, made infinitely worse by incessant air bombardments, Hitler lived in the chancellery in Berlin, where he had returned in January, after the loss of the Battle of the Bulge, which he had personally directed from army headquarters. Daily injections of various concoctions were given him to calm his nerves, but his mood alternated between fits of rage and despondency. Air raids and later the bombardment by Russian artillery forced him to spend most of his time in an underground bunker, where he lost himself in a world of fantasies.

As late as April, he clung to his belief in ultimate victory, and distrusted the judgment of even his closest collaborators when they expressed fears about the imminence of defeat. Even after the Russians had entered the outskirts of Berlin, he predicted that the anti-German coalition would split, since the western powers would never permit the Communists to overrun Germany. Above all, he frequently spoke of his secret weapons that would still turn the tide. It is true that Germany had produced surprising new

weapons during the last year of the war. In June 1944, England was suddenly subjected to devastating attacks by V-1 robot bombs, fired with surprising accuracy from installations on the Continent. By the fall, a new model, the V-2, which traveled faster than the speed of sound, made its appearance and was directed against Antwerp and other coastal towns used by the Allied armies for shipment of supplies and reinforcements. But despite the heavy damage caused by these new devices, they could not slow down the Allied advance. Nor could the new turbojet fighter plane that the dwindling German air force suddenly launched against the slower, propeller-driven Allied machines prevent the destruction of German cities and transport networks. And the atomic bomb, on which the Germans were feverishly working at the same time as the Americans, was not completed before the total collapse.

Despite his hopes for a miraculous turn of fortune, Hitler issued a vicious decree in March, ordering the total destruction of everything within the territory of the Reich, "which somehow sooner or later could be used by the enemy in the continuation of his struggle." Included in his list were all military installations, transport and communications facilities, industrial complexes, supply depots "as well as objects of value." The *Gauleiter* were made responsible for the execution of this scorched-earth policy, which aimed at turning Germany into a barren desert. Actually, Minister Speer interceded and to a large extent countermanded Hitler's order, insisting that only bridges be destroyed to delay the advance of the enemy, but not the agricultural and industrial basis of the nation's future existence.

But Hitler's destructive order had not been motivated by military considerations. Rather, it resulted from his manic determination to destroy everything that did not live up to his conception of Germany's destiny. Increasing megalomania had seemingly convinced him of the truth of Nazi propaganda that the Führer was the embodiment of the German people. Since Hitler had no intention of surviving defeat, he saw no reason for the people to outlive the war. To him their defeat merely meant that, contrary to his expectations, the Germans were the weaker people: there was no sense in safeguarding the bases of existence of a people who did not merit survival.

The Last Days

During the last ten days of April, contact among Hitler, the Nazi leaders, and the commanders in the field became increasingly difficult. Berlin was surrounded by a tightening ring of Soviet armies, and the rest of Germany was split by the rapid American advance across the center toward Czechoslovakia. Grand Admiral Karl Doenitz (1891–   ), the commander in chief of the German navy, was given command over all armed forces in the north, while Field Marshal Albert Kesselring (1885–1960) was placed in charge of all armies in the south.

On April 20, Hitler's fifty-sixth birthday, the last conference of the major leaders took place in the Führer's bunker in Berlin. Thereafter they scattered, some of them to engage in last-minute maneuverings for personal power. Hitler himself decided to remain in Berlin, rather than flee to rela-

tive safety in the Bavarian Alps. With him stayed Goebbels, devoted to the Führer until the end, and Bormann, eager to inherit Hitler's power. Once away from Berlin, Göring acted as if he were the chief of state, claiming Hitler was a prisoner in Berlin. He established contacts with the Allies in the hope of extracting better terms for himself. Infuriated by such "treason," Hitler expelled him from all his posts and appointed a new commander of the air force. Meanwhile Himmler had also left Berlin, had started his own futile negotiations with the Allies, and had attempted to persuade Admiral Doenitz to make a joint bid for power. Oblivious of the agony of Germany, the leading Nazis were busy fighting over the cadaver of the regime.

On April 28, it became evident that all efforts to break the Russian siege of Berlin were hopeless. On the following day, in a final fit of respectability, Hitler married his mistress Eva Braun. After that he wrote two testaments. One dealt largely with personal matters, the other concerned the fate of Germany. In the latter, he reiterated the claim that neither he "nor anyone else in Germany wanted war in 1939," and that he had done everything possible to avoid a war that, in the final analysis, had been "instigated exclusively by those international statesmen who were either Jewish or worked for Jewish interests." After stressing his own devotion to peace and to the German people, Hitler expelled Göring and Himmler from the Nazi party and transferred all power to a new government in which Doenitz was to serve as chancellor, Bormann as head of the party, and Seyss-Inquart as foreign minister. At the end of the testament,

all Germans were enjoined to obey the new government unto death, and the leaders of the nation were commanded to observe the racial laws and put up "merciless resistance against international Jewry, the world poisoner of all people."

On April 30, Eva Braun took poison and Hitler shot himself. Despite his promise to Hitler to carry on the struggle, Goebbels on the following day poisoned his six children and then with his wife committed suicide. Bormann, the only other important witness to Hitler's death, tried to gain advantage from the confusion. Although he notified the surprised Doenitz of his appointment as successor to Hitler, he at first delayed the news of Hitler's death. On May 1, he finally informed Doenitz that the testament was in force and that Hitler had died on the preceding day, but urged the admiral to delay any action until he could join him. Bormann then left the bunker to make his way out of embattled Berlin, and disappeared. No certain proof of his death has ever been discovered.

In the afternoon of May 1, Doenitz announced over the German radio that Hitler had died and that he himself had assumed the arduous tasks of government. In view of the hopeless military situation—Berlin was lost, Hamburg had capitulated, the Italian front had collapsed, and over half of Germany was in enemy hands—Doenitz's only hope lay in concluding an immediate armistice with the Anglo-Americans, allowing him, if possible, to continue the war against the Russians. Disregarding Hitler's testamentary appointments, he chose his own, politically more moderate, provisional advisers and made arrangements to establish contact with Allied headquarters in the west. He was embarrassed in these actions by the increasing breakdown of communications, by the presence of Himmler, who persisted in hovering around the admiral despite his reiterated dismissal, and by the approaching columns of the Red Army.

On May 2, Doenitz moved his headquarters to Flensburg, near the Danish border in order to escape capture by the Russians. On the same day, all German forces in Italy surrendered unconditionally. Two days later, while negotiations proceeded with General Bernard Montgomery, a partial capitulation of the German armies in northern Germany, Holland, and Denmark was signed, all submarine warfare ceased, and German crews began to scuttle their U-boats in their home ports.

In accordance with inter-Allied agreements, the western powers refused to sign a unilateral surrender, and insisted on Germany's unconditional capitulation on all fronts. Finally, on May 7, Doenitz's plenipotentiaries signed the unconditional surrender terms with the western Allies at Reims, followed by similar agreements in Berlin with the Russians on May 8. The armistice came into force at one minute past midnight on May 9.

During the subsequent two weeks, American, British, French, and Russian forces quickly disarmed the German units and took over control of the entire country, while Doenitz, from his headquarters in Flensburg, attempted to supervise the dismantlement of the remaining German war machine and the dissolution of the Nazi regime.

Germany's Troubled Resurgence:
Occupation, 1945–1949

ALLIED OCCUPATION

With the German unconditional surrender that became effective on May 9, 1945, the task of governing Germany was assumed by the occupying powers: England, Russia, and the United States, soon joined by France. Retention of a German central government under Admiral Doenitz was merely a transitional measure to facilitate the transfer of authority into Allied hands and to implement the Allied decision that the Germans be forced to dissolve the Nazi regime themselves and to demobilize their own war machine. On May 23, the pretense of the Doenitz government was terminated. The admiral was imprisoned to await trial as a war criminal, and the last shreds of a central German administration vanished.

Allied Military Government now assumed powers far surpassing those of previous military occupiers. According to the Hague Convention of 1907 on general rules of warfare, the rights of an occupying army are strictly limited and its duties largely confined to the maintenance of law and order. The Allied war aims, however, included the total reorganization of Germany as well as the reorientation of German political thinking. The occupying forces therefore set out to destroy German militarism and war potential, to obliterate the Hitler regime in all its aspects, to house and feed the German population, and to rebuild the German political, economic, and social structure. Even if the Allies had been in complete harmony on all facets of this formidable program, its accomplishment would have represented an enormous challenge.

Fruits of Total War

In the summer of 1945, Germany lay in ruins. Dire misery prevailed. Bombs and artillery shells had reduced the major cities to grotesque heaps of rubble. Apartments and shops, office buildings and factories lay in shambles;

water and gas mains were ruptured, electric and telephone wires were cut in thousands of places. Hamburg, for example, was 52 percent destroyed, with some 1.5 billion cubic feet of debris covering large sections of the town. In Cologne, 75 percent of the dwellings were uninhabitable. Over 25 percent of all German housing lay in ruins, at a time when the vast influx of refugees and expellees greatly augmented the need for shelter.

Communication and transport were at a standstill, major roads were impassable, all railroad bridges across the Rhine, the Weser, and the Danube had been blown up or damaged, and over half the locomotives and freight cars had been destroyed. In western Germany alone, inland shipping was blocked by almost 4000 obstructions—dynamited bridges, sunken barges, or damaged locks. Wartime losses and Allied seizures had reduced the merchant marine from 4 million gross tons (1939) to a mere 100,000.

Agricultural production was dangerously lowered through loss of food-producing areas (seized by Poland), lack of fertilizer and farm equipment, and disruption of transport. Shortages of food, clothing, and fuel brought threats of epidemics and starvation. The confusion was aggravated by the ceaseless flow of refugees from the east and by the chaotic streams of displaced persons crossing Germany in all directions. The population of Germany, although reduced by war casualties and by the millions that were still prisoners of war, was in fact vastly increased: 6 to 7 million aliens had been brought to Germany as slave laborers or had fled to Germany for other reasons. In addition, there were the millions of Germans who had fled before the advancing Red Army and were seeking shelter and support, and the millions of others expelled from eastern countries who arrived in the following months.

At the same time, the economic life of the nation lay in ruins. The German mark was worthless; the nation's total assets had been reduced by over 40 percent through the loss of territories, Allied seizures, confiscation of foreign holdings, and war destruction. Local government administration and normal police activities, educational institutions, news media, and municipal services—all had practically ground to a halt.

Added to the material devastation was the psychological trauma. Until the very end, Goebbels' propaganda machine had assured the Germans of imminent victory. The sudden realization of national humiliation came as a shock, and readjustment to the new reality caused anxiety and bewilderment. The generation that had come of age after 1933, had fought in Hitler's *Wehrmacht,* or had worked on the home front as a matter of duty, was suddenly confronted with the assertion that the ideals of their youth were not the pronouncements of an infallible Führer but the ravings of a war criminal. What had been sacred truth for twelve years was now declared a demoniacal lie. Their accepted system of values was swept away by the bombs and the occupation armies. Sitting beside the rubble of their former dwellings, nibbling on a crust of bread, smoking a cigarette butt saved from the crushing heel of an Allied soldier, many Germans faced the agonizing need for re-evaluating their lives. With their illusions dashed, some fell into self-effacing humility before the con-

quering occupants, some bolstered their ego with haughty self-exculpation. The bulk of the population, overwhelmed by the sheer exigencies of keeping alive, sank into a temporary stupor.

The Aims of Allied Occupation

For the purpose of reshaping Germany, the occupying powers attempted to work out common aims and policies.

WARTIME PLANNING   The three principal Allied powers had discussed the projected treatment of Germany at numerous conferences between 1941 and 1945. In the Atlantic Charter (August 1941), Roosevelt and Churchill had denounced "territorial changes that do not accord with the freely expressed wishes of the peoples concerned." Yet it soon appeared that "the struggle for victory over Hitlerism" pledged by the Allies in the Declaration of the United Nations (January 1, 1942) required agreement not only on the political frame for postwar Germany but also on the question of Germany's frontiers. At two Moscow conferences in 1941, Stalin had suggested that after the war Austria and Czechoslovakia be restored, that East Prussia be turned over to Poland, the Ruhr detached from Germany, and that the Germans be forced to pay reparations. The western powers at the time considered such suggestions premature.

During 1942 and 1943, however, Churchill and Roosevelt became more interested in discussing postwar territorial settlements. The United States and Great Britain gradually accepted the suggestion of dividing Germany, either by encouraging separatist movements or by carving it up. They also lessened their opposition to ceding East Prussia to Poland, provided the local population be permitted to emigrate. But growing distrust between Stalin and the western powers prevented any agreement. Their delay in opening a second front in western Europe made Stalin increasingly suspicious of the Anglo-Americans, while rumors of separate Russo-German peace negotiations worried London and Washington. There was no consensus even on the terms of surrender. Stalin, who favored harsh but specifically stated conditions, objected to the stipulation of unconditional surrender announced at Casablanca (January 1943).

At the Quebec, Moscow, and Teheran Conferences of 1943, some decisions were reached. The surrender was to be signed by the Nazis themselves, so as to force the Germans to admit total defeat. The three Allies were to occupy Germany, assume political and economic power, and remove all Nazis from positions of influence. Thereafter the occupiers were to exercise minimum interference in local German government. Germany's political structure was to be decentralized, its arms factories were to be dismantled, its industry was to remain under permanent Allied inspection, and the Germans were to pay reparations. But no agreement on Germany's frontiers resulted.

On the one hand, the West shared Stalin's fear that Germany might recover rapidly after the war if it were not dismembered. Roosevelt was willing to see Germany divided into five states, whereas Churchill suggested that Prussia in the north remain more or less as it was and that the southern states be combined with Austria into a Danubian confederation. However,

Churchill and Roosevelt feared that the dismemberment of Germany would create a political vacuum in central Europe open to Soviet penetration. Hence they questioned the advisability of carving up Germany. For similar reasons, they sought ways to strengthen Poland as a possible buffer against Russian expansion. Since Poland was likely to lose territory in the east that Russia claimed and soon occupied, London and Washington came to favor Polish claims to East Prussia and to lands along Poland's western borders. As a possible boundary between Poland and Germany, the Big Three discussed the Oder-Neisse Line but reached no agreement.

At Quebec, in August 1944, Roosevelt and Churchill debated the assignment of occupation zones. They rejected plans for a combined western zone, which would have been politically and economically advantageous, although militarily and administratively more complicated. Instead, northern Germany was allotted to England, and the southern areas to the United States. At Quebec, the two heads of state also adopted the Morgenthau Plan, which had encountered much opposition in Roosevelt's cabinet and was to raise great controversy in the ensuing years. The Morgenthau Plan aimed at preventing "renewed rearmament by Germany" by closing down and dismantling the industries of the Ruhr and the Saar, and by having "some body under the world organization" ensure that these industries "were not started up again by some subterfuge." The dismantled machinery was to be used as reparations to restore the industries of countries devastated by the Germans. The proposed limitations on Germany's "metallurgical, chemical, and electrical industries" that could easily "be converted from peace to war," as well as suggestions for re-education, for political decentralization, and for the punishment of war criminals were later incorporated into the Potsdam Agreements. One statement, however—not contained in Morgenthau's original version, but somehow inserted in the communique signed by Churchill and Roosevelt— created discomfort in Allied ranks and provided useful ammunition for the Nazis' exhortation to their countrymen to fight to the bitter end. This was the phrase that the Allies were "looking forward to converting Germany into a country primarily agricultural and pastoral in its character."

At the Yalta Conference a few months later (February 1945), Stalin, Churchill, and Roosevelt reaffirmed their aims of destroying German militarism and Nazism and of bringing all war criminals to justice. Moreover it was decided that German reparations were to be extracted in three ways: (1) by removal of "equipment, machine-tools, ships, rolling stock, German investments abroad, shares of industrial, transport, and other enterprises in Germany," largely with the aim of destroying "the war potential of Germany"; (2) by "annual deliveries of goods from current production"; and (3) by Allied "use of German labor" for reconstruction of devastated areas in their own territories. An Allied Reparations Commission was to elaborate the details on the basis of a tentative total of 20 billion dollars, half of which was to go to the Soviet Union. At Yalta, the Big Three also decided that Germany was to be divided into four zones of occupation, with France receiving a portion of the regions pre-

viously assigned to the English and the Americans. Detailed zonal boundaries were to be fixed by a special commission. Germany as a whole was to be governed by a quadripartite Allied Control Council with headquarters in Berlin. Finally, Churchill and Roosevelt agreed that Poland should cede land to Russia in the east—along a border more or less following the Curzon Line proposed after World War I —and that in compensation, Poland should "receive substantial accessions of territory in the North and West" from Germany.

THE POTSDAM CONFERENCE Thus the general aims of the Allies had been outlined during the war and reaffirmed in the Berlin Declaration of June 5, 1945. In order to elaborate details and to discuss the continuation of the war against Japan, the Big Three held another summit conference at Potsdam near Berlin in July 1945. Of the wartime leaders who had participated in the previous meetings, only Stalin attended the session of two and a half weeks. After the Labor party victory in England, Clement Attlee replaced Churchill during the conference; President Harry S. Truman represented the United States.

The Potsdam Agreements, signed on August 2, 1945, were of decisive importance for the treatment of the German population and for the fate of Germany. Even though violated in many instances by one or another of the occupying powers, the Potsdam Decrees were regarded as the "Bible" of Allied Military Government for several years.

Like the Berlin Declaration, the Potsdam Agreements defined Germany's boundaries as those of Decem-

ber 31, 1937, before Hitler began his series of annexations. Within the frontiers of 1937, certain special, temporary arrangements were made (see Map 15). The coal-rich Saar was attached economically to France, and was to be treated differently from the remaining German territory, although its future political status was not stipulated. Furthermore, the Big Three "agreed in principle" to "ultimate transfer to the Soviet Union of the City of Königsberg and the area adjacent to it," and Truman and Churchill declared that their countries would support this cession "at the forthcoming peace settlement." It was also agreed that the territories to the east of the Oder and Neisse Rivers (with the exception of the Königsberg area) were to be separated from Germany and placed under temporary Polish administration, although it was stipulated that "the final delimitation of the western frontier of Poland should await the peace settlement." The area in question contained some 40,000 square miles (the former Prussian regions of East Prussia, eastern Pomerania, Silesia, and eastern Brandenburg), with a prewar population of about 9.5 million. Although this arrangement was provisional, the Potsdam Agreements exempted these lands from the jurisdiction of the Allied Control Authority (see page 313), and thus awarded Poland a free hand to treat them as it wished.

The remaining 138,000 square miles of Germany were divided into four zones of occupation, to be controlled by the four zone commanders, under the joint supervision of the Allied Control Authority. Soviet Russia was given some 43,000 square miles (all or part of the former regions of Pomerania, Mecklenburg, Brandenburg, Saxony,

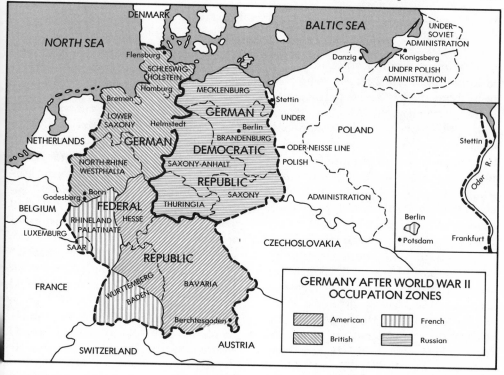

GERMANY AFTER WORLD WAR II
OCCUPATION ZONES

American   French

British   Russian

MAP 15

and Thuringia), with a population of about 20 million. The second largest zone, some 42,000 square miles with roughly 23 million inhabitants, was occupied by England. It included Schleswig-Holstein, Lower Saxony, the city-state of Hamburg, and a new German state called North Rhine–Westphalia, comprising Westphalia, the Ruhr, and the Lower Rhineland. The American Zone, some 36,000 square miles with 17 million people, consisted of Bavaria, Hesse, and parts of Württemberg-Baden. In addition, Britain ceded to the United States the occupation rights to the port of Bremen to provide the American forces with port facilities for supplying their troops. Finally, a small zone of 17,000 square miles with 6 million inhabitants (including the Palatinate and the Upper

Rhine Valley) was turned over to France. A special status was reserved for Berlin, which was to be divided into four sectors, each occupied by troops of one of the four powers, and administered jointly by an Inter-Allied Kommandatura. Separate bilateral arrangements, not contained in the Potsdam Agreements, were drawn up between the western occupants and Russia to permit free access by rail, canal, highway, and air between the western zones and Berlin.

The Potsdam Decrees contained directives designed "permanently to prevent the revival or reorganization of German militarism and Nazism." To this end, army, navy, air force, SS, SA, the Gestapo, the General Staff, military reserves, veterans' units, paramilitary outfits, and all Nazi organizations were

to be abolished, all Nazi institutions dissolved, and all Nazi laws abrogated in so far as they contained "discrimination on grounds of race, creed, or political opinion." Nazis "who had been more than nominal participants" in the movement were to be removed from public office. The German educational and judicial systems were to be reorganized, war criminals put on trial, and the German people as a whole made to recognize that "their own ruthless warfare . . . [had] made chaos and suffering inevitable."

The political reconstruction of Germany was to be based on maximum administrative decentralization, with strong emphasis on local self-government, on the elective principle at all levels of government, and on the strengthening of democratic political parties. Freedom of speech, press, and religion was to be guaranteed, as well as the free development of trade-unions, "subject to maintenance of military security"—a phrase easily susceptible of misuse. In order to maintain a semblance of German unity, German central administrative departments for finance, transport, communications, foreign trade, and industry were to be set up under the supervision of the Allied Control Council, but "for the time being, no central German Government [was to] be established."

To disarm Germany permanently and to furnish the basis for reparations, the Allies projected various economic measures, many of which resembled those submitted by Morgenthau in his secret "Program to Prevent Germany from Starting a World War III." Industries producing aircraft, arms, or ammunition, as well as others easily converted to war production, were to be entirely prohibited, with the fac-

tories destroyed or turned over to the Allies as reparations. The level of industrial production, particularly in metals, chemicals, and heavy machinery, was to be fixed by the Allied Control Authority in order to prevent German rearmament, meet the needs of the occupying forces, and assure that the German standard of living would not exceed "the average of the standards of living of European countries." Agriculture and "peaceful domestic industry" were to be favored, and German industrial complexes broken up in order to eliminate "the present excessive concentration of economic power." To ensure the pooling of resources from the four zones, Potsdam stipulated that "during the period of occupation, Germany shall be treated as a single economic unit," a stipulation largely ignored by the occupiers, particularly the Russians and French.

Arrangements for reparations followed more or less the basis established at Yalta. The bulk of the claims of the Soviet Union and Poland were to be satisfied by removals from the Soviet Zone and by seizure of German foreign assets in Bulgaria, Finland, Hungary, Rumania, and eastern Austria. In addition, Russia was to receive from the Western zones 25 percent of the German industrial equipment declared "unnecessary for the German peace economy," in return for a portion of which it was to deliver to the western zones "an equivalent value of food, coal, potash, zinc, timber, clay products, petroleum products, and such other commodities as may be agreed upon." This arrangement led to considerable disagreement between Russia and the western powers. The claims of the eighteen other Allies were to be met from the western zones or from other

German foreign assets. The practice whereby each occupying power dismantled its own zone evoked much suspicion and recrimination, even though in theory quadripartite inspection teams were to decide which factories to remove. Moreover, it was specified that all dismantling of industrial equipment was to be completed within two and a half years—a stipulation that the western Allies accused the Russians of violating in 1948.

At Potsdam, the Big Three also acknowledged the need for transferring to Germany "German populations, or elements thereof, remaining in Poland, Czechoslovakia, and Hungary." These transfers were to "be effected in an orderly and humane manner," and the expulsions then in progress were to be temporarily suspended until the Control Council could undertake a census of those who had already fled to Germany from the east, could settle "the question of the equitable distribution of these Germans among the several zones of occupation," and establish "the time and rate at which further transfers could be carried out." The Allies acquiesced in this mass deportation, since the Germans (in prewar times an estimated five million) living in Poland, Czechoslovakia, and to a lesser extent in Hungary, had given Hitler an excuse for his drive to the east. No mention was made, however, of transfers from other countries from which Germans were then being expelled or from which they were fleeing —the Baltic states, Yugoslavia, Rumania, Russia and the Polish-occupied lands beyond the Oder-Neisse line.

Finally, the Big Three set up a Council of Foreign Ministers, including representatives of Russia, Britain, France, America, and China. This council was authorized to draw up peace treaties with Germany's five European allies (Finland, Italy, Hungary, Bulgaria, and Rumania), and was charged with the "preparation of a peace settlement for Germany to be accepted by the Government of Germany when a government adequate for the purpose is established."

The Allied Control Authority in Action

Soon after the Potsdam Conference, the Allies set up the Allied Control Authority (ACA) in Berlin. The four zone commanders, constituting the Control Council, met periodically to decide on policy for Germany as a whole. Below the Control Council sat a permanent quadripartite Coordinating Committee to supervise the functioning of the quadripartite directorates. The twelve directorates (respectively in charge of transport, finance, reparations and restitutions, prisoners of war and displaced persons, manpower, internal affairs and communications, as well as military, naval, air, political, economic, and legal matters) acted like all-German ministries, but lacked executive powers, which were vested in the individual zone commanders. Each directorate, with its committees, subcommittees, and working teams composed of delegates from the four occupying powers, attempted to elaborate common solutions for the treatment of Germany.

The occupying powers sought to deal immediately with the task of demilitarization and denazification. It was easy to disarm the population and dismantle military installations. Eradicating "militarism" was infinitely more

complicated, and largely a matter of education and sociopolitical readjustments. The Control Council took the initiative by dissolving all military and paramilitary organizations and abolishing the state of Prussia on the grounds that "from early days . . . [it] has been a bearer of militarism and reaction in Germany." Equally difficult was the question of denazification.

DENAZIFICATION From the beginning, the Allies tried to distinguish between ferreting out and punishing those accused of specific crimes—a difficult though definable task—and eradicating Nazism—an immensely complicated and amorphous undertaking. During the early months of occupation, while the Control Council debated various drafts of anti-Nazi legislation, each zone commander initiated denazification proceedings in his zone according to the dictates of his own government.

The Russians and French generally favored summary removal of all Nazis from public positions, while the English and the Americans proceeded more slowly, attempting to observe legal formalities. In all zones, there were, of course, cases in which Nazis with technical skills were retained because of lack of non-Nazi replacements. Still, the early months of occupation were marked by a widespread removal of Nazis. Some were simply deprived of their jobs, while perhaps as many as one million (no detailed statistics are available for all zones) were herded into internment camps to await either trial or further disposition of their cases.

By early 1946, denazification proceedings had become more systematic. All Germans over eighteen years had to complete detailed questionnaires, so that intelligence personnel could distinguish among those Nazis criminally liable, those merely to be kept from positions of influence, and those to be completely exonerated. The United States favored turning over the denazification proceedings to the Germans themselves, on the theory that they should be forced to clean their own house. In each state (*Land*) in the American Zone, the Americans created German Ministries for Political Liberation, and forced the Germans to pass a "Law for Liberation from National Socialism and Militarism" (March 1946). By the end of 1946, 425 German denazification courts in the American Zone alone were combing through 11.5 million questionnaires and instituting proceedings as quickly as the dockets could be cleared for new cases. American authorities also turned over most internment camps to German control, retaining direct supervision only of those housing prisoners suspected of war crimes.

Detailed common policy for all of Germany was fixed by the Control Council in October 1946 in its directive on "The Arrest and Punishment of War Criminals, Nazis, and Militarists, and the Internment, Control, and Surveillance of Potentially Dangerous Germans." This directive delineated a clear distinction—already made in practice—between punishment of persons who had committed war crimes or crimes against humanity, and "internment of potentially dangerous persons who may be confined because their freedom would contribute a danger to the Allied Cause."

The Control Council directive defined five categories of Nazis: (1) *Major Offenders* were subject to penalties in-

cluding death or life imprisonment, confiscation of property, loss of pensions, ineligibility for public office, or other punishments that would permanently remove them from public life. (2) *Offenders*—activists, militarists, or profiteers—those who actively helped advance Nazi tyranny but did not commit specific crimes, could be sentenced to a maximum of ten years in prison. (3) *Lesser Offenders* were those activists who, because of youth or other extenuating circumstances, deserved leniency; they were to be placed on probation for two or three years, during which time they could not operate or control a business, could not teach, write, or preach, or otherwise engage in public activities. (4) *Followers,* nominal supporters of the regime, were to be placed under police surveillance, could not stand for election to public office, and were obliged to pay a special contribution for reparations. (5) *Exonerated Persons* were former members of Nazi organizations who had been either passively or actively resisting Nazi tyranny and had themselves suffered from Nazi harassment. No sanctions were to be applied against the members of this category.

This Control Council directive gave a semblance of uniformity to the denazification proceedings throughout Germany, although differences of implementation continued among the zones. But the directive could not solve some of the problems inherent in the denazification process. In certain occupations, for instance, the number of Nazis or Nazi followers was so great that the occupiers had to retain at least "temporarily" the services of known Nazis. Moreover, the policy of forcing the Germans to do most of the denazifying them-

selves raised problems. The occupiers frequently had to interfere in German proceedings when they suspected the decisions of the German courts had not been just. Such interference created resentment; and those Germans who collaborated with the occupation authorities by informing on former Nazis, testifying against them, or participating in denazification courts were sometimes subjected to social ostracism. The treatment of hundreds of thousands of interned Nazis also presented difficulties. Inevitably some of those interned were mistreated, their food rations were kept at the lowest possible minimum, and some died in the camps. Germans who resented the Allied occupation were thus furnished ample ammunition for later denouncing the "atrocities of the Allies" and for comparing the internment centers for Nazis with Himmler's concentration camps. Finally, the exceedingly slow pace of the denazification process was denounced by many Germans who preferred to make a break with the past and to concentrate on building a new and different Germany.

Unquestionably, injustice was done in some cases, and many who deserved censure escaped it. Yet in view of the immensity of the undertaking, which no conqueror had ever before attempted in such scope, the denazification proceedings were relatively successful in accomplishing the desired aims.

WAR CRIMES TRIALS Considerably easier to accomplish was the punishment of Nazis for specific crimes. As early as 1942, nine Allied governments had declared their intention of trying Germans for crimes committed in occupied countries, such as "mass expulsions, execution of hostages, and mas-

sacres." In the Moscow Declaration of October 1943, Russia, Great Britain, and the United States had agreed to let individual countries try Germans for crimes committed on their territories or against their nationals. But a joint Allied tribunal was to try major offenders whose crimes involved more than one country. Thereafter, representatives from France, Russia, the United States, and Great Britain worked on detailed agreements for an International Military Tribunal. The study group faced countless questions: whether to advocate summary justice or formal legal proceedings; whether to try only individuals or also entire organizations; and whether people could be declared guilty on the basis of their association with a group. Furthermore, many Nazi crimes were not covered by existing international law. Hence the committee had to decide whether it was legal—and indeed advisable—to create new law.

The International Military Tribunal was finally established in August 1945 and endowed with a charter of jurisdiction. The tribunal was to prosecute "war criminals whose offenses have no particular geographic location whether they be accused individually or in their capacity as members of organizations or groups or in both capacities."

Eventually twenty-two individuals and seven organizations were tried by this tribunal in Nuremberg, in proceedings lasting from November 1945 to October 1946. There were four kinds of indictments: conspiracy to prepare aggressive war; crimes against the peace, namely "waging of a war of aggression, or a war in violation of international treaties"; war crimes, that is, violations of the customs of war (murder, use of slave labor, killing of hostages, plunder of cities); and crimes against humanity (extermination, enslavement, deportation, persecution). Of the seven organizations indicted, three were found innocent: the Reich cabinet, the General Staff and High Command of the army, and the SA. The remaining four—the Leadership Corps of the NSDAP, the SS, the security force (SD), and the Gestapo—were found guilty, but the verdict stipulated that membership in these organizations did not automatically make an individual a criminal. When passing judgments, the lower courts were to consider extenuating circumstances or the accused's possible ignorance of the aims of the organization.

Of the twenty-two persons tried before the tribunal, three were acquitted: Schacht, Papen, and the propagandist Hans Fritsche (1900–   ). Of the remaining defendants, twelve were sentenced to death by hanging—including Göring (who committed suicide before his scheduled execution), Ribbentrop, Rosenberg, Seyss-Inquart, and Bormann (*in absentia*). Hess, Funk, and Grand Admiral Erich Raeder (1876–1960), the head of the navy before he was replaced by Doenitz in 1943, were sentenced to life imprisonment. The remaining four, including Doenitz, received sentences of ten to twenty years' imprisonment.

In addition to the International Military Tribunal, special military government courts within each zone prosecuted Nazis for atrocities, murder, mass deportation, and other crimes against humanity or infringements on international rules of warfare. Allied nations not participating in the occupation of Germany—such as Czechoslovakia and Yugoslavia—also held trials of extradited Germans for crimes com-

mitted against their own nationals in the course of the German occupation of their country. After 1949, the Germans themselves gradually assumed responsibility for trying wartime offenders and criminals of the Nazi regime. These investigations and trials dragged on for years, at times in a somewhat desultory fashion, until new vigor was infused into the proceedings in 1958 (see page 369).

PROBLEMS OF GOVERNING GERMANY The occupying powers faced many other tasks and problems. In the matter of permanent disarmament, for instance, it was relatively easy to prohibit the production of war matériel, but difficult to determine what factories could easily be reconverted to wartime production. For example, a plant that had manufactured periscopes for submarines could be used to produce mirrors or camera lenses; yet it might be easily reconverted to wartime use. A similar difficulty in delineating a clear dividing line between peaceful and military research faced the Allies in regard to surveillance of scientific activities.

Another problem of the ACA concerned agreement on a level at which to hold German industrial production. Since its industrial capacity had successfully supported Germany's war effort, and since many powerful industrialists in Germany had overtly or passively supported the Nazi movement, it seemed advisable to lower the German level of production and to break up the huge industrial cartels so that a few individuals could not wield disproportionate economic power. On the other hand, there were sound reasons for maintaining, if not raising, the level of German industry.

Over 10 million more people were now crowded into an area reduced by almost 25 percent. Since the lands provisionally ceded to Poland were largely agricultural, industrial output might have to be raised so that more exports could pay for increased imports of food. A high level of industrial production might also provide surpluses to be used for reparations in kind. Finally, some Allied advisers pointed to the interdependence of the European economy as a whole, and argued that the creation of an economic desert in Germany might ruin all chances for a rapid economic recovery in the surrounding European states.

In March 1946, the Control Council finally adopted the Level of Industry Plan for all of Germany. It contained blanket prohibitions for certain industries, such as those manufacturing aircraft, seagoing vessels, radio transmitting equipment, ball bearings, and many synthetics and machine tools. Production rates in most industries were strictly limited: steel was fixed at 7.5 million tons a year, basic chemicals were limited to 40 percent of the 1936 level, and a ceiling was placed on the manufacture of trucks, busses, and tractors. Actually most of these limitations were never enforced, for inter-Allied disagreements during the following years completely altered the attitude of most nations, particularly the United States, toward European and German economic reconstruction.

One of the busiest of the ACA directorates dealt with prisoners of war, displaced persons, and expellees. Displaced persons were non-Germans found in Germany at the end of the war; expellees were ethnic Germans expelled from Eastern Europe. Ini-

tially, the repatriation of German prisoners of war, particularly from British and American camps, had proceeded rapidly. Yet by December 1946, almost 4 million German prisoners had not yet returned to their homes. Over half a million remained in France, working on reconstruction projects, and over 3 million were presumably working in the Soviet Union or being detained in Russian compounds. It proved impossible for the directorate or the International Red Cross to obtain precise reports on the number remaining in Russia.

The problem of displaced persons proved equally complicated. During the first half year of occupation, more than 5 million were repatriated to their homelands. But more than a million remained in Germany, about 70 percent of these being unacceptable to their native country or unwilling to return for political or other reasons. These lived in special camps—most of them in the American and British zones—under supervision of Allied Military Government. In 1946, the United Nations Relief and Rehabilitation Agency assumed the care of these persons, many of whom remained in German compounds for years before finding homes in Australia, New Zealand, Argentina, the United States, or elsewhere.

The greatest task of the Prisoner of War and Displaced Persons Directorate was to supervise the assignment of expellees from the east to one of the four zones. According to quadripartite agreements, some 5 million Germans were to be admitted. These were assigned to numerous reception camps, and statistics were prepared to show how many trainloads could be received in each zone in a given month. But the preparations fell far short of the needs. Czechoslovakia, Hungary, and Poland expelled more people than had been stipulated. In addition, Poland drove out over a million Germans from the territories under its provisional administration, Rumania, Bulgaria, and Yugoslavia also contributed to the stream of expellees, and countless Germans fled on their own into occupied Germany. As a result, instead of the 5 million expected, almost 10 million expellees and refugees surged into Germany in the first two years of occupation. A large proportion of the expellees were women and old people, many unable to work. Until German authorities could take over the care of these millions, the occupation forces housed them in emergency compounds or even in abandoned Nazi concentration camps.

Differences in Zonal Administration

The Potsdam Agreements had stipulated that "so far as is practicable, there shall be uniformity of treatment of the German population throughout Germany." Yet the basic directives of the ACA received widely differing interpretation and implementation by the four zone commanders, each of whom was in fact supreme in his own domain. As a result, Germany was subjected to four different policies of administration. As United States Secretary of State James Byrnes complained (September 1946): "So far as many vital questions are concerned, the Control Council is neither governing Germany nor allowing Germany to govern itself." The divergent policies of the four Allies were particularly evi-

dent in their respective plans for the political reconstruction of Germany.

CENTRALISM VERSUS FEDERALISM As might be expected, France preferred to see Germany emerge as a loose confederation of states. Throughout the centuries, France had benefited from the disunity among the German states; the unification of Germany in 1870 had paved the way for the three invasions that France suffered at the hands of a united and centralized German state. Consequently the French proposed that the sixteen individual German states (*Länder*) be turned into quasi-sovereign units, exercising all powers not specifically reserved to the confederation. The federal legislature was to consist solely of an upper house representing the several states. The proposal envisioned a long delay before such a confederation would be created. Meanwhile Allied Military Government would exercise the necessary coordinating authority, except in purely technical fields, which could be entrusted sooner to German agencies. The administrative policy followed in the French Zone reflected these views. Establishment of political organs was largely limited to the states. All-zonal organizations were created only in technical areas where over-all coordination was essential, such as price control, post and telegraph, social insurance, and finance. The French thus hoped to make the states politically as self-sufficient as possible in order to obviate the need for a strong central government.

The Soviet proposal for reconstructing Germany was diametrically opposed to that of the French. Russia favored a highly centralized state, more

unitary than the Weimar Republic. Although the Russians did not wish to revive a strong Germany, their social theories required the creation of a strong central government. Through the aid of the Communist party, they hoped to direct the activities of this government in accordance with Russian interests. As early as September 1945, Soviet Military Government created German administrative agencies with jurisdiction over the entire Soviet Zone in such fields as industry, labor, education, agriculture, health, and justice. Initially only advisory in capacity, these central agencies were soon accorded substantial executive power. The state governments on the other hand, were never awarded much political power in the Soviet Zone.

The British Labor government, itself fairly centralized, also favored a unitary state, although one not so completely centralized as that supported by the Russians. The British allowed the states powers similar to those stipulated in the Weimar Constitution. Control over most fields, including economy, finance, and justice, was retained by Military Government, which acted as a sort of zonal government. As a result, the states in the British Zone exercised relatively unimportant functions until the beginning of 1947, when the economic merger of the British and American zones necessitated an adaptation of the political systems of the two zones to each other.

The United States hoped to turn Germany into a federal state. The three states of the American Zone were to receive legislative and executive powers similar to those exercised by the American states. To coordinate their activities, a zonal conference of

the minister-presidents of the states was organized in the fall of 1945, with regular meetings supervised by Military Government. The American Zone was thus decentralized in administrative functions, although it enjoyed a certain amount of coordination among the state governments.

THE BEGINNING OF POLITICAL PARTIES Similar divergences characterized the attitudes of the occupying authorities toward the formation of political parties. The Potsdam Agreements stipulated that "local self-government be restored throughout Germany . . . as rapidly as is consistent with military security," and that for this purpose "all democratic political parties with rights of assembly and of public discussion be allowed and encouraged throughout Germany."

But even before the Potsdam Conference, the Allies diverged in practice. When the western armies were streaming into Germany in April 1945, SHAEF (Supreme Headquarters Allied Expeditionary Forces) ordered its forces not to allow the Germans to publish political papers or engage in political activities. Although an occasional local military commander permitted former members of Weimar parties to hold meetings, as a result of the SHAEF order anti-Nazi underground forces could not form political groups and the formation of parties in the western zones had a late start.

The Russians, however, speedily pushed the formation of parties. On June 10, 1945, the Russian zone commander licensed four groups—the Communists (KPD), the Socialists (SPD), the Christian Democrats (CDU), and the Liberal Democrats (LDP). By late July, when the Allies were gathering at Potsdam, the four parties were fully operative on an all-zonal level, publishing their own papers (under Soviet censorship) and holding party meetings (under Soviet direction). From the beginning, therefore, the Russian occupation forces used centralized German political organs for influencing public opinion, under the guise of promoting cooperation among all "anti-Fascist parties."

The western powers proceeded more slowly with the reconstruction of German political life, and tried to introduce decentralized control at the grassroots level. The Americans were the first to authorize the formation of parties, at the county (*Kreis*) level in August 1945. All-zonal mergers of parties were allowed only in early 1946. Similarly, elections in the American Zone began with rural districts and small communities in January 1946, and ended with elections to the three state legislatures in December of that year. This slow pace, according to the American directive, was designed to promote the development of "genuine democratic institutions in Germany." American authorities carefully supervised the elections—regulating electoral codes, suffrage rules, and campaign procedures—and retained control over the licensing of parties until November 1948.

British authorities allowed the formation of parties immediately on an all-zonal level (September 1945). However, the first elections in the British Zone were held only in September 1946, and the British retained close control over all parties until 1950. The French, for their part, were extremely reluctant to permit the revival of po-

litical life in Germany. Initial permission for the reconstitution of parties was given in December 1945, but so many obstructions were placed in the way of politicians that parties began to form only in the spring of 1946, after local elections had already been held in the American Zone.

SOCIAL, ECONOMIC, AND EDUCATIONAL POLICIES   In almost all other facets of occupation policy, there was little uniformity among the four zones. Economic unity was not achieved. Surpluses from the Russian Zone were not made available to fill deficits in other zones. Industrial complexes with branch factories located in different zones could not function as units. Even the normal interzonal exchange of railroad freight cars was hampered by obstructionism, usually by Russian or French authorities; and the Allies could not agree on uniform rations throughout Germany.

The attitude toward labor unions furnished a typical example of the divergent policies of the western and the Russian authorities. The reconstruction of labor organizations in the western zones received the active support of American, British, and French unions. The occupation authorities favored free trade-unions, organized democratically and based on free election of union officials. At the same time they insisted that unions be politically neutral. By the end of 1946, unions in the American Zone were allowed to operate on the level of the states, but not at that time on a zonal basis. In the other western zones, they were kept even more decentralized.

The Russians, however, asserted that grass-roots control of unions might permit their infiltration by neo-Fascist elements. Hence they immediately set up hierarchically organized unions on an all-zonal basis, with control tightly lodged in a Russian-picked executive committee. Membership in unions was made more or less compulsory, and unions were turned into political pressure groups. The Russian authorities could thus use the unions as another instrument for governing their zone.

In the field of education, the Potsdam Agreements had stipulated that "Nazi and militarist doctrines" be eliminated from German education, and the "development of democratic ideas" encouraged. But the ACA could reach no agreement on the implementation of these principles. At the beginning of the occupation, all schools were closed. By the fall of 1945, elementary schools in all the zones began to reopen, despite shortages of buildings, acceptable textbooks, and non-Nazi teachers. All four occupation authorities helped train new teachers and produce textbooks free from Nazi indoctrination, and they sought to eliminate the social distinctions imbedded in the former German school system. But wide differences among the zones arose in the organization of school administration, the curriculums at the higher levels, the admission policies of universities, as well as the establishment of youth movements.

Most of these differences in occupation policies also characterized the quadripartite administration of Berlin. Although in theory common procedures were determined by the Allied Kommandatura for Berlin, in practice each occupation sector of the city was administered differently—a situation

full of complications, since it affected people living within the same city, sometimes only a few blocks apart.

BEGINNING OF RECOVERY AND THE COLD WAR

Starting in 1946, and especially in 1947, differences among the Allies coagulated into the cold war between Russia and the West. This tension gradually affected most facets of Allied occupation policy, and ultimately brought about the division of Germany into two separate states.

Rebuilding the Economic Life

During the first two years, primary efforts were devoted to satisfying the desperate need for food, shelter, and fuel. At the same time, considerable progress was made in clearing away the rubble—especially in the American and the British zones—and in restoring public utilities and transportation. By February 1946, for instance, almost 96 percent of the primary railroad lines in the American Zone were again usable. The British, meanwhile, concentrated on reactivating coal production. Special food rations were issued to miners, and by the spring of 1946, production of hard coal, almost at a standstill at war's end, stood at over 50 percent of capacity. But because a portion of this coal was allocated as part of reparations, shortages in Germany remained acute.

Some sectors of the German economy were in better condition than expected, and furnished a potential basis for German economic recovery. During the war, industrial capacity had been expanded, and Allied strategic bombing had hurt German production more by disrupting transport and keeping workers off their jobs than by obliterating plant facilities. Hence a relatively large number of plants, blast furnaces, and machine tools were either ready for operation in 1945, or reparable within a short time, provided sufficient transport, energy, manpower, and raw materials could be made available.

Still, this industrial recuperation was more potential than actual. Besides shortages of materials and manpower, there was financial instability and uncertainty about the future. In the western zones—especially in Berlin—the German middle class feared that the western powers might withdraw and abandon the Germans to Communist expropriation. Moreover, the German mark was being printed in reckless quantities, the price structure was erratic, and inflation was rampant. Three different price levels existed. Wages and rationed food were kept at a controlled level. A pound of bread at the official price cost the equivalent of 2 U.S. cents, and wages varied between 8 and 18 cents an hour. Prices on articles of current production were flexible. For instance, a cheap ashtray, made from scrap aluminum salvaged from a downed airplane, might sell for $1.50. On the black market, however, bread cost $4 a pound, a pack of cigarettes in Berlin up to $20, and two drinks and some poor food in an ordinary nightclub about $100. Without a stable price structure, it seemed impossible to initiate a sound revival of the economy.

Uncertainty in industry and commerce was also caused by the unclear policy concerning nationalization and decartelization. Starting in 1946, the Russians sponsored popular referen-

dums in some states for the approval of laws to expropriate "reactionary" concerns. In this manner, mines and other basic industries were gradually nationalized. During 1947 alone, some two thousand enterprises passed from private ownership into the possession of county or municipal governments, or of specially organized cooperatives. The authorities in the western zones, on the other hand, left all decisions about nationalization up to a future all-German government. Even this policy did not reassure the industrialists, since the major political parties, including at first the various Christian Democratic groups, advocated some form of nationalization in their party programs. Moreover, the French adamantly demanded international ownership and control of the coal and steel industries in the Ruhr as a vital requisite for ensuring European peace.

The policy on decartelization was equally nebulous. In accordance with the mandate of Potsdam, this problem was frequently discussed at the ACA, and in November 1945 the Control Council enacted a law for the decartelization of the huge I. G. Farben concern. But it proved impossible to formulate a general law on the permissible size of industrial or financial complexes and on interlocking management. In 1947 and 1948, British and American authorities issued laws in their zones for the control and decartelization of coal, steel, iron, chemical, and electric industries, as well as of financial institutions. Few concerns were actually affected, and most cartels were never split up. In fact, after 1950, large enterprises were recartelized and vast new concentrations were created.

The unsettled issues of reparations and restitution also delayed economic recovery. So long as it was not determined which factories were to be earmarked for reparations, industrialists were reluctant to repair war damage or improve production facilities. Moreover, even after the Allies officially announced the Level of Industry Plan, it was obvious that their decision was subject to revision, so that it remained difficult for Germans to make long-range economic forecasts.

The question of restitution was also clouded. Although it was fairly easy to identify and restore foreign goods seized by the Germans during the war, restitution within Germany was more complicated. Thousands of industrial and commercial concerns had been confiscated by the Nazis from Jews or from other "enemies of the state," or acquired in forced sales. After the collapse of the Nazi regime, their ownership remained in doubt. The Allies merely stressed the need for making equitable restitution, and it was a long time before the Germans, lacking a central government, evolved a consistent policy of restitution and compensation.

AMERICAN ASSISTANCE In order to prevent starvation and economic collapse as well as to rekindle the economy, the United States and England furnished large-scale aid to Germany. In the first three postwar years, before the initiation of the Marshall Plan, American grants and credits amounted to almost 1.2 billion dollars. At the same time, American military establishments contributed heavily to Germany's reconstruction, and private American citizens mounted a relief campaign of magnitude. To coordinate the multifarious efforts of private organizations, the United States govern-

ment in February 1946 recognized the Council of Relief Agencies Licensed for Operation in Germany (CRALOG), composed of eleven private agencies engaged in shipping food, clothing, and medical supplies to the American Zone. In 1946, also, the Cooperative for American Remittances to Europe (CARE) set up facilities for shipping relief parcels to individual German families in the American Zone, an arrangement soon extended to the other zones of occupation.

This public and private aid unquestionably helped tide the Germans over the first two harsh winters and alleviated some of the suffering. But the anomaly of the situation was soon recognized. The United States was extending grants and credits not only to Germany but to nineteen other European nations (a total of about 12.5 billion dollars between July 1945 and June 1948). As long as each European country was attempting to recuperate in economic isolation, waste and needless duplication in the aid program were inevitable. Moreover, it appeared shortsighted to keep the German level of production to a minimum when German productive capacity could be used to help rehabilitate the economy of Europe as a whole. Finally, the American government began to realize that it was shipping into Germany on an emergency basis some of the same materials that Russia was withdrawing from Germany under the guise of reparations. These considerations soon led to a fundamental reappraisal of American policy that resulted in the Marshall Plan for economic aid to Europe as well as in the establishment of Bizonia in Germany.

THE CREATION OF BIZONIA At the Paris meeting of the Council of For-

eign Ministers in July 1946, United States Secretary of State Byrnes declared: "We cannot continue to administer Germany in four airtight compartments, preventing . . . exchange between the four zones of goods, communications, and even ideas." Complaining that the existing arrangement produced "inflation and economic paralysis" and resulted in "increased costs to the occupying powers and unnecessary suffering to the German people," he proposed the immediate "establishment of central German administrative agencies necessary to secure economic unity in Germany." In order to assuage French apprehensions, he suggested that the coal-rich Saar might be retained for a time under separate French control in order to aid the economic reconstruction of France. If all the other powers were unwilling to accept the American proposal, Byrnes offered to merge the American Zone economically with the zone of any other nation, on the theory that economic unity of two zones would be better than none.

Byrnes's proposal was rejected by both Russia and France. Intent on first satisfying its reparations claims, Russia was unwilling to pool all Germany's resources. And France persisted in opposing the creation of any central German agencies, except in return for wide concessions—the separation from Germany of the Ruhr, the Rhineland, and the Saar. The French, who had not participated in the Potsdam Conference, did not feel bound by the agreements made there concerning German economic unity.

A few weeks later, the United States representative on the Control Council (General Joseph T. McNarney), repeated Byrnes's offer. The British promptly accepted, and they and the

Americans established five German agencies for the administration of economics, finance, transport, communications, and agriculture for both zones, under the supervision of joint English and American control boards. Exports and imports for the two zones were merged, and the cost of necessary imports was shared by the two Allied governments. In order to make all vital resources available to Bizonia, British authorities withdrew control of the iron and steel industries in their zone from ACA jurisdiction, a move that infuriated the Russian and French governments. The establishment of Bizonia, officially inaugurated on January 1, 1947, thus marked an important step in granting more self-administration to the Germans, and signaled a beginning of the division of Germany.

The creation of Bizonia was also accompanied by a change in the American attitude toward Germany. As Secretary Byrnes noted in a speech in Stuttgart in September 1946, the policy of distrust and nonfraternization had given way to friendship. He also urged that, if reparations continued to be taken from current German output, the levels of industrial production should immediately be raised. Finally, he suggested that an all-Germany currency reform was essential to place the German economy on a sound footing.

The establishment of Bizonia in effect foreshadowed the creation of a West German state closely tied to the economic life of the western nations. While in their zone the Russians continued dismantling factories during 1947 and even tore up railroad tracks for shipment to the Soviet Union, the English and Americans temporarily suspended dismantling operations and attempted to raise industrial produc-

tion so as to lessen the unfavorable balance in Germany's foreign trade. In August 1947, they officially revised the proposed level of industry, and permitted Germany to increase its steel production to 11.7 million tons a year. At the same time, free travel by Germans between the two zones was permitted, and, where possible, political, legal, and other matters were put on a common level.

Political Parties, Old and New

First on the scene was the German Communist party (KPD), formed with the active support of the Russian occupation authorities by *émigrés* returned from Russia. Initially there was a tendency also in the western zones to favor the KPD, since its members were known to be stanch anti-Nazis. Among the leaders of the party, officially founded in Berlin in June 1945, were Wilhelm Pieck (1876–1960) and Walter Ulbricht (1893–   ), both cofounders of the KPD in 1918 and members of the National Committee for a Free Germany formed in Moscow during World War II. The first program of the KPD was moderate. Hoping to attract liberals and democrats, the Communists announced that the Soviet system was not applicable to Germany, and that all anti-Nazi parties should cooperate in a joint program of denazification, economic and political reconstruction, freedom of religion, and cooperation with other nations. However, when left-wing leaders of the Social Democratic party (SPD)—Max Fechner (1892–   ) and Otto Grotewohl (1894–1964)—suggested cooperation between the SPD and KPD so as to eliminate the traditional cleavage among the workers, Ulbricht at first rejected the offer, feeling confident that the

KPD alone, with financial, political, and propaganda support from the Russians, could seize the leadership of political life in Germany.

Soon, however, the Communists realized that their only hope of extending their influence, particularly in the western zones, lay in a merger with the numerically stronger SPD. They exerted pressure on left-wing SPD leaders in Berlin and in the Russian Zone, and appealed to SPD and KPD members in the western zones to present joint candidates at the elections. Western Socialists generally rejected this appeal, unless the union of the parties would be effected on an all-German basis, to assure the SPD a majority and thus safeguard the united party from Russian control. But the Russian authorities opposed the suggested grassroots approach of the Socialists. They jailed some recalcitrant SPD leaders, and harassed the activities of the Socialist party in their zone until preparations were completed to effect a forced merger of the two parties. Without consulting the rank-and-file members, Pieck, Grotewohl, and other hand-picked KPD and SPD leaders voted a formal union of the two parties in April 1946. The resulting Socialist Unity party (SED) was not a real merger; rather, it submerged the Socialists under Communist domination in the Russian Zone.

Despite the sham existence of other political parties, the SED became a real state party. In the 1946 Russian Zone elections, it obtained a clear majority at the communal level, and received an average of 48.7 percent in district and state-wide balloting. By the use of voting lists, by putting up sham parties in order to draw away votes from opposition groups, by rationing newsprint and employing other devices, the SED gained control of all state governments and legislatures in the Russian Zone. In the western sectors of Berlin, however, where the Communists had initially filled all important posts in the city administration, the SED failed in its avowed purpose. In city elections in October 1946 only 20 percent of the votes went to the SED, as contrasted with 48.7 percent to the SPD.

In the three western zones the KPD initially posed as a democratic, anti-Nazi organization favoring cooperation with all liberal parties. Its platform called for wide-scale nationalization of industry and expropriation of large landholdings. In all three zones, the KPD emerged as the third largest party, although it polled only between 5 and 8 percent in the various elections between 1946 and 1948. In some states (Hesse and North Rhine–Westphalia). Communists obtained posts in state governments. The strength of the KPD in the western zones, however, was short-lived. After the creation of a West German state in 1948, the party abandoned its policy of cooperating with other groups, and adopted a more clearly Moscow-oriented direction. Its attraction for the voters fell rapidly. In 1953, it captured only 2.2 percent of the votes, and in 1956, the West German Constitutional Court declared the KPD to be "unconstitutional," and outlawed it.

Simultaneously with the Communists, Socialist leaders in the various zones re-established the German Social Democratic party. The veteran Socialist Kurt Schumacher (1895–1952), who had languished for ten years in a Nazi concentration camp, early assumed control over the party's reconstruction, and

became the official SPD chairman for all three western zones in May 1946. The party's platform, formed at Wenningen in October 1945, stipulated that all German Socialists should follow identical policies in order to preserve the unity of Germany, that cooperation with democratic parties should be encouraged, and that the Communists' offer to fuse the two workers' parties should be rejected. The Wenningen program was imbued with a strongly nationalistic fervor. Perhaps in bitter recollection of the 1920s, when the SPD had been accused of being traitorously un-German, Schumacher was determined to make his party the voice of German nationalism. It rejected the notion of collective war guilt for all Germans, and attacked the aims of the Morgenthau plan. Dismantling of industry was decried as economically unsound. The SPD demanded the rapid creation of a strongly centralized national government, in opposition to the federalism advocated by some of the other political parties. The state was to direct German reconstruction, control financial institutions, and nationalize basic industries. But the SPD platform rejected state ownership in favor of a system of cooperatives in which governments, local groups, and consumers participated.

The SPD grew rapidly during 1946 and emerged as the strongest or second strongest party in all the western states. It exerted much influence on the writing of many of their constitutions. In 1948–1949, it sent the largest number of delegates (although not a majority) to the Parliamentary Council charged with drafting a constitution for West Germany (the Basic Law of 1949). Although the SPD failed in its aim of maximizing the powers awarded

the proposed central government, it was able to force a compromise with the bourgeois parties on other points of disagreement; the role of the churches in education, the social duties of the state, and other contended points were left undefined in the final draft.

Although the SPD of 1945 was essentially a revival of the Socialist party of the Weimar Republic, Schumacher gave it a wider base of appeal than its predecessor had. Instead of concentrating on workers and intellectuals, the new party also attracted lower bourgeois and small peasants. By toning down its anticlericalism, the party could court religious-minded Socialists. And its nationalistic, antiforeign stand appealed to German patriots.

Another party, the strongest in the West, was the Christian Democratic Union (CDU). Officially founded as an all-German party at Bad Godesberg in December 1946, the CDU at first remained a loosely knit organization, held together by the conviction that only a religiously oriented middle-class party with a moderate platform might counteract the strength of the SPD and KPD. The diverse Christian Democratic groups were gradually molded into a real party only through the need for nation-wide electioneering for the 1949 elections, and the party held its first formal all-German convention only in October 1950.

The CDU is both a new party and a revival of the old Center party. Like the former Center, it adheres to the middle of the road, without appealing to a specific class or region, reconciling within its ranks various conflicting economic interests. Like the Weimar Center, the CDU can shift to the Left or the Right, and enter coalitions with conservative parties or with the Social-

ists. Among its first executive committee of thirty, eighteen had been members of the Center party before 1933. But the CDU is also essentially a new and different party. The influential Cologne group within the party, among whose leaders was Konrad Adenauer (1876–1967), considered the Catholic framework of the former Center too restrictive, and insisted that Protestants be included to give the party a broader base. The Berlin group, founded by members of the Kreisau Circle (see page 300) and other anti-Nazis who had been involved in the plot of July 20, 1944, and had learned the need for cooperation between diverse points of view in the underground, advocated a program of liberal social legislation. The CDU thus embraced Protestants and Catholics, conservatives and liberals, members of the former DNVP as well as former Socialists. Its original executive committee contained industrialists, civil servants, scientists, agriculturalists, workers, lawyers, educators, artisans, as well as a journalist and a housewife.

Despite this broad base, the Bavarians who had formed their own Christian-Social Union (CSU) on the basis of similar ideals refused to amalgamate their party with the CDU. Although from its inception, the CSU usually cooperated with the CDU in all national questions, it remains to this day a separate party.

The initial platform of the CDU was quite liberal. In 1945, it demanded the strictest anti-Nazi measures, the abolition of monopolistic capitalism, the nationalization of coal mines and energy resources, and confiscatory taxes on war profits. By 1946, its anti-Nazi fervor had slackened, and with the ascendancy of Konrad Adenauer, its liberalism paled. Still, the "CDU Eco-

nomic and Social Program" formulated at Ahlen in February 1947 was surprisingly liberal. It attacked "the unlimited domination of private capital," advocated decartelization of big industry and establishment of a planned cooperative economy, assuring "social justice." The program also called for "the right of codetermination" for workers by permitting labor representatives to participate in management councils. The Ahlen program was thus a frank attempt to bridge the cleavage between workers and capitalists and to attract labor votes, an attempt that proved successful even in the solid SPD territory of the Ruhr.

For a while the CDU seemed determined to implement its Ahlen platform. When Bizonia was created, CDU members called for agrarian and currency reform; for laws to equalize the burdens caused by war, reparations, and the need to care for refugees; and for a total reorganization of industry in accordance with the Ahlen proposal. Yet the cleavage between SPD and CDU remained severe. When the Bizonal Economic Council—consisting of 20 SPD, 20 CDU, 3 KPD, and 10 members of smaller bourgeois parties—elected its five directors in July 1947, the bourgeois majority showed its usual distrust of the Socialists by choosing a directorate composed exclusively of CDU members. The CDU thus assumed primary responsibility for planning the economic reconstruction of the western zones, just as in the following years, it was the dominant voice in the establishment of the West German state. Involvement in the leadership of the nation turned the CDU into the strongest political party in West Germany and rapidly gave its ideals an increasingly conservative coloring.

Besides the three major parties—CDU, SPD, and KPD (SED)—there were various smaller political organizations with moderate programs. In the British Zone, some former Centrists refused to join the CDU, and revived the old Center party, with a progressive program of socialization and federalism, combined with a strong stand against close collaboration with the west for fear of endangering German unity. The Center party distrusted the conservative wing of the CDU, and although working in coalition with the Christian Democrats in North Rhine–Westphalia, opposed Adenauer's party in the first *Bundestag*. It never acquired much national importance, gaining only 3.1 percent of the 1949 vote. Even its collaboration with the small Bavarian party (BP) did not prevent its decline. By 1953, it polled less than 1 percent in the national elections and sank to obscurity.

Of greater long-range consequence were the numerous semiconservative middle-class parties that in 1948 banded together in the three western zones to form the Free Democratic party (FDP). The FDP rapidly rose to national importance, and became the third largest party in 1949, with 11.9 percent of the votes. Composed mostly of businessmen, civil servants, and intellectuals, most of whom were members of the former Democratic and German People's parties, the FDP stood to the right of the CDU, advocating a nonsectarian program of free enterprise and individual freedom. It opposed all schemes for socialization or codetermination in industry. Like the SPD, it favored noninterference in religious matters, a strongly nationalistic program, and a more centralized government than that preferred by the CDU. Unlike the CDU, it opposed

closer ties with the West until German reunification was achieved. But on most other matters it could readily cooperate with the CDU, so that in 1949, it formed a coalition government with Adenauer, assuring the election of its chairman, Theodor Heuss (1884–1963) to the presidency of West Germany.

In addition there arose many small conservative parties, only a few of which reached national stature. Many championed particularistic rights, such as the South Schleswig Association and the Bavarian party. The program of the German party (DP), a conservative group, some of whose members favored restoration of the monarchy, was federalistic, antiunion, and in favor of a completely private economy. It opposed the denazification program, demanded better treatment of former army officers, and enjoyed a long-lasting although relatively unimportant political existence. Finally, there were various authoritarian or neo-Nazi organizations, which gathered in former members of the DNVP and NSDAP. Among these were the German Conservative party (DKP) and the short-lived German Rightist party (DRP). The most successful, the German Social Reich party (SRP) was, like the NSDAP, socialistic only in name. Founded in 1949, it enjoyed a moment of national importance, but was quickly swept aside by the growing democratic current, and dissolved by order of the Federal Constitutional Court in October 1952.

The East-West Split of Germany

BREAKDOWN OF QUADRIPARTITE GOVERNMENT None of the foreign ministers' conferences held during 1946 and 1947 produced a quadripartite solution to the German problem. The

four wartime Allies remained dead-locked over Russian reparations de-mands, German economic unity, and establishment of a German central gov-ernment. For the United States the issue involved primarily financial con-siderations. Since its external assets of about 2 billion dollars had been con-fiscated, Germany could not pay for vital imports unless it increased its exports to earn the necessary funds. But so long as Russia was claiming Germany's excess production as repa-rations while America was paying for Germany's imports, American taxpay-ers were in fact financing German reparations to other countries. At the London Conference in December 1947, Secretary of State George C. Marshall sharply criticized Soviet intransigence and accused the Russians of wanting to impose "conditions which would not only enslave the German people but would seriously retard the recovery of all Europe."

Consequently the West decided to act unilaterally. France, Britain, and the United States joined delegates from the Benelux countries (Holland, Bel-gium, and Luxemburg) in a series of conferences in London between Feb-ruary and June 1948 at which they reviewed the German problem. The Russians promptly protested against these meetings, accusing the West of violating occupation agreements. When the meetings continued and the West publicly placed all blame on the Soviet Union for preventing German eco-nomic and political unity, the Rus-sian delegates walked out of the Con-trol Council meetings in Berlin on March 20, 1948, dramatizing the end of the quadripartite administration of Germany.

Meanwhile the western powers pro-ceeded with the amalgamation of their zones. A German Bizonal Economic Administration, a German High Court, and the *Bank Deutscher Länder* (Bank of the German States) were established in February 1948. The six powers then decided at London to create Trizonia (effective June 1, 1948) by merging the French Zone with Bizonia, to allow the Germans to draft a provisional con-stitution for the three zones, and to establish a German federal government subject to only limited Allied super-vision as defined in a special Occupa-tion Statute. The conferees also agreed to make minor border adjustments in Germany's frontier with Belgium and Holland (involving some 52 square miles of territory), to set up an Inter-national Authority for the Ruhr, and to integrate Germany's economy into the European Recovery Plan.

The Russians, for their part, refused further invitations to merge their zone with those of the West and, in re-prisal, initiated their harassment of Allied access to Berlin. On April 1, they imposed restrictive inspections on Allied military and freight trains, and then began to hamper all rail and barge traffic. On June 12, they closed the Autobahn bridge over the Elbe, ostensibly for repairs, and arranged for a time-consuming detour by ferry. These and other Russian measures brought to light the precariousness of western access to Berlin and gave rise to the "Berlin question" that was to plague Germany and the world in the ensuing years.

By the middle of June, the crisis be-came acute. It was unleashed by Rus-sian reaction to western plans for a German currency reform. From the beginning of the occupation, the four Allies had issued special occupation

money, but excessive printing of currency by the Russians and low German productivity had devalued the occupation mark as well as Germany's own currency. To stabilize the financial structure, kindle economic growth, and undercut the flourishing black market, the western powers decided to issue a new currency. They offered to supply the new mark for distribution in the Russian Zone, but rejected Russia's demand for locating the printing presses in Leipzig (in the Soviet Zone), lest the Russians print money without western control and re-create the inflationary conditions of 1945. Although the real points of contention were more far reaching, the Russians chose this incident as a pretext for their blockade of Berlin.

On June 16, the Russians withdrew their representatives also from the quadripartite Kommandatura for Berlin. Two days later, the West officially announced its currency reform for Trizonia, with the stipulation that the new *Deutsche Mark*—to be exchanged at the official ratio of one *Deutsche Mark* for ten *Reichsmark* or occupation marks for all legally acquired funds— was not to be introduced into Berlin. On June 19, the Russians replied by stopping all passenger trains and automobiles between Trizonia and Berlin, and restricting the movement of freight on trains and barges. At a four-power conference in Berlin three days later, Russia announced that it would issue its own currency not only for its zone but also for *all* sectors of Berlin, and that this currency would not be subject to four-power control. The dispute thus involved the control of Berlin as much as it did the financial reconstruction of Germany: a Russian currency in West Berlin would integrate

this area economically into the Russian Zone. Although the West rejected their plan, the Russians proceeded to issue their own currency (later known as the *Ost Mark*) for their zone and presumably for *all* of Berlin. Thereupon, as a countermeasure, the west introduced the *Deutsche Mark* into the western sectors of Berlin on June 23, and the Russians retaliated with a full-fledged blockade of the city.

Allied and West German access to Berlin by road, rail, and canal was gradually sealed off; even delivery of electricity and food from East to West Berlin was stopped. The Russians at first gave "technical difficulties" as reasons for the severance of communications and access to Berlin, but soon admitted a relationship between the Berlin blockade and the currency reform. Actually, discussions between the western powers and the Soviet Union, which continued during the blockade at various ministerial levels, soon revealed that the issue was not merely the currency reform and Russia's hope of dislodging the other powers from Berlin, but also Russian intention of preventing the integration of West Germany into the economic net of western Europe.

In answer to the blockade, the West organized an airlift to Berlin, dubbed "Operation Vittles" by American airmen. From June 26, 1948 until the final lifting of the blockade on May 12, 1949, Allied planes from airports in Trizonia supplied the 2 million inhabitants of West Berlin with food, coal, and raw materials. In the fall, daily shipments rose to about 4000 tons a day; by April of the following year, the daily rate was 8000 tons. Meanwhile the dispute had been taken up by the U. N. Security Council, which

voted in October 1948 for immediate removal of all Berlin travel restrictions. But the Russians rejected the U.N. resolution. Only the West's proved ability to supply Berlin by air for indefinite periods ultimately led the Russians to lift the unsuccessful blockade, which had aroused German enmity toward the Russians and evoked gratitude and admiration toward the western powers.

THE CREATION OF TWO SEPARATE STATES   On July 1, 1948, the military governors of the three western zones met with the minister-presidents of the eleven western German states to discuss implementation of the London Agreements (see page 330). The Germans raised some objections regarding the proposed Constituent Assembly, the powers reserved to the Allies, as well as the intended limitations on the Ruhr industries. But on July 26, the German state governments accepted the London provisions in principle and called for a Parliamentary Council to convene in Bonn on September 1 in order to draft a provisional constitution. The drafting committee of 65 delegates, chosen by their respective state legislatures, consisted of 27 SPD, 19 CDU, 8 CSU, 5 FDP, 2 Center, 2 DP, and 2 KPD. Although the Socialists constituted the largest single party, the bourgeois parties, especially the CDU, CSU, and FDP, banded together and elected the CDU's Konrad Adenauer as president of the Parliamentary Council.

The labors of the drafting committee dragged on for eight months. The western military governors frequently interfered in its deliberations, either to break deadlocks or to guide the drafting along lines acceptable to the West. Interminable delays were caused by the general reluctance to accept the Ruhr Statute, as well as by disagreements, particularly between SPD and CDU/CSU council members, on the question of federal versus states rights. Moreover, despite the provisional character of the proposed constitution and the fact that membership in the new state was to be open to the Russian Zone, the representatives feared that setting up a West German government might split Germany permanently. This apprehension was particularly evident after February 1949, when the Russians offered to lift the siege of Berlin and rejoin the ACA in return for a four-power conference to discuss the entire German problem. The western powers had little faith that such a conference might succeed and rejected the proposal, but the Germans favored any step that might narrow the gulf between east and west.

Delays were also caused by disagreements among the three Allies over German economic rehabilitation, over the security measures to be imposed upon Germany, and over the constitutional framework for the proposed West German government. The three military governors debated for months on the formulation of the Occupation Statute to set limits to the sovereignty of the proposed German state and define the powers reserved for the occupation authorities. Eventually, the Allies adopted the Ruhr Statute setting up a Ruhr Authority, composed of Allied, Benelux, and German representatives, charged with supervising the decartelization of certain industries and with controlling the new, increased level of coal and steel production, set considerably higher than the French had hoped. During these negotiations, the Ameri

cans secretly promised Adenauer not to dismantle certain chemical and steel plants, in return for German agreement to join the international Ruhr Authority. When revealed, these promises infuriated the SPD because of the favoritism shown to big business, and disturbed the French because of the added power given Germany. Finally, in April 1949, Britain and France reluctantly accepted the United States proposal to permit German production of certain items prohibited by the Potsdam Agreements—such as oceangoing ships, ball bearings, and aluminum.

Cold-war strategy, which during the same period resulted in the formulation of the North Atlantic Defense Treaty (signed April 4, 1949), finally led the Allies to compose their disagreements on the Occupation Statute and to oblige the Germans to terminate their work of drafting the constitution. On May 8, 1949, the Parliamentary Council adopted its draft by a vote of 53 to 12. To emphasize its provisional character, which would at all times permit the admission of the Russian Zone, the document was called the Basic Law rather than a constitution. Four days later, the military governors recognized the Basic Law with the reservation that Berlin, although a state of West Germany, was not to be governed by the Bonn government nor to send voting delegates to its legislatures. The eleven states were then asked to ratify the Basic Law. Only the still particularistic Bavarian Landtag rejected it, and on May 23, the law was proclaimed in effect.

During the summer, the three Allies prepared to transfer power from Military Government to a new Allied High Commission, and the Germans held their first elections to the Bundestag, the newly created lower house of the West German legislature. The CDU/ CSU coalition obtained 7,359,100 votes (31 percent) and 139 seats. With 6,935,-000 votes, the SPD received 131 seats, while the FDP groups won 52. Eight other parties earned representation in the Bundestag: the Center with 10 seats, the KPD with 15, and various conservative parties with a combined total of 55. On September 12, Theodor Heuss of the FDP was elected first president of the Federal Republic of Germany, with its temporary capital established at Bonn. A few days later, Konrad Adenauer formed a coalition government of CDU, CSU, FDP, and the conservative DP, and was elected chancellor by an extraordinarily slim margin. Of the 402 deputies, only 202 cast their ballot for him.

The western Allies formally recognized the Federal Republic on September 21 and awarded it conditional sovereignty, subject to the limitations contained in the Occupation Statute. Two weeks later, the division of Germany became complete when the Russians turned their zone into the German Democratic Republic, under the presidency of Wilhelm Pieck and the premiership of the SED's Otto Grotewohl. Since that time Germany has been governed by two German administrations, each claiming to have the exclusive right to speak for the country as a whole.

Germany's Troubled Resurgence:

Division and the Resumption of

Sovereignty, 1949–1955

Most foreign observers, especially those in the Communist orbit, look upon the division of Germany as twofold—with the German Federal Republic in the west and the German Democratic Republic in the east. The West Germans, however, speak of a threefold division: West Germany (the Federal Republic), Middle Germany (the German Democratic Republic), and East Germany (the lands east of the Oder-Neisse under Polish and Soviet administration). In accordance with the Potsdam Agreements, they cling to the hope that the Oder-Neisse boundary is temporary.

The dividing lines between these two—or three—parts of Germany gradually hardened after 1949, largely as a result of the growing tensions of the cold war. The Poles and the Russians treated their occupied lands east of the Oder-Neisse as permanent acquisitions; the Soviet Union and the Western powers, each in their own way, courted their respective protégés by awarding them more and more attributes of sovereignty—an anomalous reversal from the days of 1945. In this process, the western Allies generally took the first steps, and their actions were reluctantly emulated by the Russians, who at heart felt more hesitant about granting freedom of action to the East Germans.

With the coming into being of an East and a West Germany, the political, social, economic, and cultural development of the two states became so divergent that they must be discussed as separate entities, even though, according to international law, there are not two German states.

THE EVOLUTION OF THE GERMAN FEDERAL REPUBLIC

The Basic Law and the Occupation Statute

The Basic Law for the Federal Republic of Germany, with its 146 articles, is designed, according to the preamble, to permit Germany "to pre-

serve its national and political unity and to serve world peace as an equal partner in a united Europe." Besides stressing European solidarity, the document underscores its "transitional" character, in view of the hope for the ultimate reunification of Germany. It emphasizes "the unity and freedom of Germany," and asserts that it speaks "on behalf of those Germans to whom participation was denied."

Opening with an extensive bill of rights, which stipulates that basic inalienable rights cannot be altered by constitutional amendments, the Basic Law defines the powers of the federal government versus those of the states, as well as the prerogatives of the various agencies of the central government. The legislature is bicameral, with most powers lodged in the lower house or *Bundestag,* elected every four years "in universal, free, equal, direct, and secret elections." The original number of 402 deputies was raised to 487 in 1953, in view of the considerable increase in population. West Berlin was permitted to send 8 (22 after 1953) nonvoting observers to the Bundestag, in order to underline Berlin's integration into West Germany without vitiating the separate occupation status of the city.

The upper house, the Bundesrat, representing the eleven states (reduced to nine in 1952 by amalgamation of three states into Baden-Württemberg, and increased to ten in 1957 with the admission of the Saar as a new state), enjoys the right to be kept informed "on the conduct of federal affairs," to veto certain legislation, and to ratify treaties, but in reality exerts relatively little influence. The federal president was given less authority than his counterpart had in the Weimar Republic. Elected by a federal convention (mem-

bers of the Bundestag and "an equal number of members elected by the popular representative bodies of the *Länder*") rather than by popular suffrage, he may serve a maximum of two consecutive five-year terms. He may grant pardons and must sign treaties and accredit ambassadors; he appoints the federal chancellor in accordance with the choice of the Bundestag, but on the whole his prerogatives are largely ceremonial. By reducing the powers of the president, the Basic Law increased those of the federal chancellor, whose tenure of office was made more strictly dependent on the consent of the Bundestag. But in order to prevent recurrence of the governmental instability typical of the Weimar Republic and to force the Bundestag to follow a constructive course, Article 67 stipulates that the Bundestag's vote of no confidence is not valid until a successor has been chosen and a new cabinet approved. In this way, government vacancies are made impossible and the chancellorship is rendered more stable.

A large section of the Basic Law is devoted to circumscribing the jurisdiction of the federal government. The areas of foreign affairs, citizenship, postal and railroad service, criminal police and customs, inland waterways, and financial matters (like currency), are reserved to the federal government. In certain fields, such as civil and criminal law, refugees and expellees, public welfare, war damage, and compensation, there is concurrent jurisdiction between federal and state governments. But in everything else, ultimate sovereignty is reserved to the states. Over the years, the question of states' versus federal rights has caused considerable acrimony in German politics, and de-

spite the CDU's vaunted devotion to federalism, the rights of the federal government have been gradually increased in various fields, including finance, communications, and education.

The Basic Law contains various innovations that reflect German feeling in the postwar period. The determination to prevent a revival of Nazism prompted Article 21, which stipulates that "parties, which according to their aims and behavior of their members seek to impair or abolish the free and democratic basic order or to jeopardize the existence of the Federal Republic of Germany, shall be unconstitutional." This article has been used to outlaw extremist groups. Similarly, Germany's new international or European orientation is strikingly underscored in Article 24 of the Basic Law, which specifies that "the Federation may, by legislation, transfer sovereign powers to international institutions," thus providing the government with authority to proceed boldly toward European integration.

The operation of the Basic Law was at first coupled with the limitations contained in the Occupation Statute. This document reserved for the Allied High Commission control over German disarmament and demilitarization, over the conduct of German foreign affairs, and over "the Ruhr, restitution, reparations, decartelization, . . . foreign interests in Germany and claims against Germany." The western Allies furthermore were allowed to station troops in Germany and to abrogate German legislation or countermand German action "if they consider that to do so is essential to security or to preserve democratic government in Germany."

The organization of federal ministries reflected some of Germany's postwar problems. Until the revision of the Occupation Statute in 1951, no Foreign Ministry was created. German foreign relations were handled by the Allies. In consonance with the new ideal of federalism and in an effort to avoid the pitfalls of Goebbels' Propaganda Ministry, no federal Ministry of Culture was established. Cultural and educational matters were left to the jurisdiction of the states. This decentralization led to great divergence among them, particularly in the educational system, and became an issue for considerable debate. Hence a cultural section was later set up in the federal Ministry of the Interior, and a permanent conference of the state ministers of culture was organized in order to coordinate educational matters throughout West Germany. On the other hand, several unusual federal ministries were created, in addition to the normal agencies found in most European countries. The Ministry for Expellee Affairs coordinated the equitable settlement of expelled persons in the various states; the Ministry of Housing dealt with reconstruction; the Ministry for All-German Affairs supervised relations between West Germany and East Germany, and kept alive the hope for eventual reunification; the Ministry for Economic Cooperation handled the Marshall Plan and later the numerous schemes for European economic integration.

The Political Life of the Young Republic

The early years after 1949 saw the development of a number of political trends that remained characteristic of West German politics. Unlike the situation that developed in the Weimar

Republic, extremist parties on the Right and the Left failed to gain momentum. None of them attracted many voters, some were declared unconstitutional, and those that survived remained at the fringe of the political spectrum. In contrast to the Weimar Republic, the proliferation of parties was steadily replaced by the growth of a few larger parties at the national level. This consolidation was furthered by a 1953 regulation stipulating that only parties obtaining at least 5 percent of all votes cast throughout West Germany, or three seats on the basis of direct suffrage in their constituencies, could gain representation in the Bundestag. In 1949, eleven parties earned seats in the Bundestag (counting the CDU/CSU as a single group). In the 1953 elections, only six parties won representation in Bonn. In 1957, the number shrank to four, and in 1961 to three. A further noteworthy difference from the Weimar days is that all parties operating at the national level are loyal to the democratic regime, so that political struggles are carried on within a framework freely accepted by all contenders.

Another trend was growing conservatism in the major parties, not only in the CDU and the FDP, but also in the SPD. Although the CDU's early platforms (see page 620) had stressed the need for socialization, its Düsseldorf program of 1949 rejected economic planning, nationalization, and controls over consumption. Instead, the party advocated a free market economy with reduced taxes on higher incomes and increased indirect levies. This shift in policy no doubt stemmed from various causes. The dismal example of economic planning in the Russian Zone served as a deterrent, while the sudden

economic and industrial growth in the west, sparked by the currency reform of 1948 and by foreign aid, seemed to obviate the need for nationalization as a means for ensuring recovery. Pressure of Protestant industrial circles within the CDU and the strong influence of the United States government, all favoring a free economy, also contributed to the shift. There was also the growing influence within the party of its two conservative leaders: Konrad Adenauer, who was made CDU chairman in 1950, and Ludwig Erhard (1897–   ), who became vice-chancellor and federal minister of economics in Adenauer's first cabinet.

Konrad Adenauer, a lawyer and former member of the Center party and of the Prussian upper house, had served as lord mayor of Cologne from 1917 to 1933. During the Weimar period, he had gained many influential friends in Rhineland industrial and financial circles, and through his second wife, the daughter of a German-American professor (Ferdinand Zinsser), he numbered important Americans among his relatives and friends. One of his sisters-in-law had married Lewis W. Douglas, United States ambassador to London (1947–1950), another had become the wife of John Jay McCloy, United States high commissioner to Germany (1949–1952). In 1933, Adenauer had been dismissed by the Nazis and part of his property was confiscated. He spent the twelve years of National Socialist rule in political retirement, and although not engaged in any active anti-Nazi movement, he was three times incarcerated for brief periods. After the war, the British reinstated him as mayor of Cologne, but his decision to give priority to rebuilding the Cologne town hall rather than to reconstructing

homes led to a dispute with British Military Government and his dismissal. Subsequently, he turned again to full-time politics and rapidly acquired paramount importance in the growing CDU.

Ludwig Erhard, who had been minister of economics in Bavaria and had lectured on economics at the University of Munich, brought to the CDU his stanch belief in free enterprise. He soon became the prophet of what he called Germany's "Social Market Economy," a system that stressed the free search for profits, combined with the employers' responsibility to the social security of the community. In a Social Market Economy, Erhard felt, there should be private initiative and free competition, but not unbridled *laissez faire*. While the federal government should interfere as little as possible in the nation's economic life, it should enforce the observance of social responsibility, particularly in areas of shortages, such as housing, and should intervene in times of crisis, such as unemployment or overconcentration of economic power. Similarly, the government should ensure the free interplay of economic forces by outlawing monopolistic cartels, except where needed for the rationalization of industry.

Erhard's economic theories found rapid acceptance in the CDU. At the party congress of 1950 held at Goslar, Erhard insisted that nationalization could never cement close bonds between workers and industry, whereas individual participation in industry through profit-sharing devices would best serve the economy. Hence the Ahlen program was abandoned and replaced by the Social Market Economy. In line with the new policy and under pressure from the United States

(as well as from Britain after Churchill replaced Attlee in October 1951), the CDU then initiated the removal of price restrictions and a new tax program that favored industrial investment.

The bitter electoral campaign of 1953 was partly fought on the issue of economic recovery, for which the CDU claimed full credit. The SPD accused the government of being the tool of big industry; the CDU charged that the Socialists were getting financial support from East Germany. The voters evidently liked "the republic of prosperity." The CDU/CSU coalition increased its electoral support from 31 to 45.2 percent, while the SPD percentage remained more or less unchanged. To assure himself not merely a majority but the two-thirds margin required for the passage of constitutional amendments in connection with rearmament (see page 351), Adenauer formed a coalition comprising all major parties (CDU, CSU, FDP, DP, and the new Refugee party, for a total of 333 seats) except the SPD (154 seats).

The SPD, for its part, also grew markedly more conservative and, like most European Socialist parties, gradually abandoned its doctrinaire Marxism during the 1950s. To be sure, it rejected Erhard's Social Market Economy as harmful to wage earners, fought the tax reductions on the grounds that there were no guarantees that the freed capital would be used for socially beneficial investments, and opposed the increase of indirect taxes that burdened primarily the lower-income groups. But despite these disagreements with the CDU on economic and social theories as well as on foreign policy, the Socialist program became more moderate. The SPD helped channel the demand

of the mammoth German Federation of Trade Unions (DGB), comprising some 40 percent of all trade-union members, toward seeking elaboration of the right of codetermination (see page 328) rather than nationalization. Its party chairman after 1952, Erich Ollenhauer (1901–1963), and Willy Brandt (1913–   ), the mayor of Berlin, its most influential leader after the late 1950s, were decidedly more concerned with immediate political, social, and economic gains than with the search for utopias. Moreover, the constant electoral success of the CDU (the party gained even more in the 1957 elections than it had in 1953) seemed to call for a revised program on the part of the SPD. In the new Socialist platform of 1959, total economic planning was no longer demanded. Instead, the Socialists called for "free competition as far as possible—economic planning as far as necessary," and advocated "the taming of the power of big business" without destroying private initiative.

Refugees and Expellees

Even after the initial postwar flood of refugees and expellees into West Germany had abated, the population of the western zones continued to grow at a rapid pace. Excesses of births over deaths amounted to a yearly average of almost 300,000. The influx of expellees from eastern Europe or from the territories beyond the Oder-Neisse, and of refugees from the Russian Zone, amounted to 900,000 in 1947 and 870,000 in 1948. Thereafter, expulsions from eastern Europe ceased, but the average number of refugees from the Russian Zone remained at over 300,000 a year. Between 1949, the year the

two German states were created, and 1961, when the Berlin Wall was built, about 2.8 million Germans fled from East Germany and an additional 700,000 moved their domiciles from East to West Germany without requesting refugee status.

As a result of this migration, one of every five inhabitants of West Germany was either a refugee or an expellee. These uprooted persons were primarily concentrated in Schleswig-Holstein, Lower Saxony, and Bavaria. In 1947, they were awarded the same legal rights as other West Germans. Yet the tasks of the German states, at first exclusively responsible for housing and feeding them, were immense. Initially it proved impossible to integrate them into Germany's shattered economy. In August 1949, a first step was taken at the national level to solve the problem of relief. The Immediate Aid Act provided for special taxes on real estate and other private holdings to finance aid for refugees and expellees, as well as indemnification for those native Germans who had suffered war damage. Proceeds from this tax paid for subsistence, housing, education, replacement of lost savings for old age, and compensation for bomb damage.

With the creation of the Federal Republic and the establishment of the Ministry for Expellee Affairs, the federal government assumed the coordination of the numerous state laws for the rehabilitation of refugees and expellees, and helped settle the newcomers with housing, jobs, farms, and credit. In May 1950, it helped found a special Expellee Bank to speed up their economic integration. Finally, the Bundestag passed a comprehensive Equalization of Burdens Law in 1952, imposing a special levy of 50 percent

(at the June 1948 value) on all real property in West Germany. Revenue from this tax, payable in quarterly installments over a period of thirty years, is accumulated in a federal Equalization of Burdens Fund, for the purpose of compensating expellees, refugees, and victims of air raids or of other war damage. Compensatory payments are made at a ratio of 5 to 10 percent for large losses, and up to 50 percent for small losses. Besides financing indemnities, the fund also pays for the retraining of expellees and refugees and for the establishment of new handicraft industries to employ the newcomers.

Despite such governmental solicitude, the plight of the refugees and expellees was at first bitter. As late as 1951 there were still some 2700 camps housing over 400,000 people. Even for those who had found housing and employment, integration into the social and political life was difficult. From the beginning, certain refugee groups had sought to form political parties of their own in order to further their demands for redress. But Military Government had refused to license such groups as political parties, ostensibly because their existence would render integration of the refugees and expellees more difficult. In reality it was also feared that such parties might be extremist in their views and fan irredentism for the lost eastern territories.

Nevertheless, the expellees founded numerous local associations, based on either the territory in which they were resettled (for example, *Land* Association of Expelled Germans in the Rhineland-Palatinate), or the region from which they had been expelled (such as the Union of Pomeranian Compatriots, Association of Carpathian Germans from Slovakia, and Union of Germans from Rumania). In August 1950, these associations held a joint rally in Stuttgart at which they signed "a solemn declaration to the German people and to the entire world" in the form of a "Charter of the German Expellees." They demanded a "reasonable repartition of the burdens of the last war" and "a sensible integration" of the expellees "into the life of the German people." But they also stressed their God-given right to live in their native land. Renouncing "all thought of revenge and retaliation," they proposed the establishment of a "free and united Europe" as one of the ways of regaining access to their lost homes.

In the same year, after licensing of new parties was no longer required, a special refugee party was formed in Schleswig-Holstein—the Block of Expellees and Victims of Injustice (BHE). Within six months, the BHE grew to be the second strongest party in Schleswig-Holstein, polling 23.4 percent of the vote in the *Landtag* (State legislature) elections. In January 1951, the BHE became a national party, with a platform for foreign affairs demanding restoration of the Saar and of the German territories in the east, as well as equal rights for Germany within the framework of a united Europe. In internal matters, the party opposed federalism, and stressed the need for an effective equalization of burdens and for compensation to expellees in the form of real-estate grants. Although the BHE counted among its members some extremists, its program on the whole was moderate and sufficiently vague to allow the party to enter a coalition government with the SPD in Hesse, while remaining a stanch opponent of the Socialists in Hanover. In 1952, the

BHE changed its party label to All-German Bloc (GB); in the federal elections of 1953 it polled 1.6 million votes and obtained 27 seats in the Bundestag. Such electoral success showed the potential political strength of the expellees.

Thereafter, the expellees continued to constitute a political and economic problem, but the GB failed to develop its potential. Although its party chairman (Waldemar Kraft) was given a post in Adenauer's cabinet after the 1953 elections, increasing prosperity, the gradual integration of the expellees into German life, and their tacit realization of the hopelessness of returning to their native lands sapped the strength of the GB. In 1957, it failed to poll sufficient votes in the federal elections to obtain representation in the Bundestag. Although it retained some importance in a few German states, even a political merger with the German party (DP) for the 1961 elections did not save it from political extinction at the national level.

Economic Rehabilitation

Foreign aid, the currency reform of 1948, the establishment of the Bonn government in 1949, growing financial and economic cooperation among the European nations, the managerial skill of German entrepreneurs, the hard work and cooperative attitude of German labor, and, above all, the new aura of hope and self-confidence pulled Germany out of the economic quagmire after 1950. West Germany's resurgence to third place among the industrial nations of the world by 1955, with a share of 7.1 percent of world trade, has often been labeled a "miracle."

The Federal Republic (with its 95,000 square miles as contrasted with the 181,000 square miles of the prewar Reich) had become a relatively small country with a vastly increased population. The influx of people had swelled the number of inhabitants by 25 percent and turned the Federal Republic into one of the world's most densely populated countries, with a density of over 500 people per square mile. Since the separated lands to the east had been areas producing a surplus of food, West Germany's food shortage was more acute than before the war. Hence Germany had to increase domestic food production and raise its industrial output so that a greater volume of exports would permit the importing of essential food and raw materials. On both counts, the West Germans proved eminently successful.

By 1955, agricultural output in the federal territory had been increased by 22 percent over prewar production. General industrial production was growing at three times the rate of some of Germany's neighbors. On the basis of 100 for 1948, the industrial index in 1955 stood at 297, as contrasted with 127 for France. With 49 percent of its national income derived from industry, Germany had become the most industrialized country in the world. In 1955 alone, it produced over 21 million tons of crude steel and built almost 1 million gross tons of merchant shipping, about half on consignment for other countries.

By 1955, West Germany was exporting 6.5 billion dollars worth of goods (motor vehicles, machinery, merchant vessels, precision instruments, electrical goods, chemicals, and the like), and had achieved a favorable balance of

trade (about 300 million dollars). Within the European Payments Union, a financial cooperative organization embracing most European non-Communist countries, it had become the chief creditor. The *Deutsche mark* had become one of the world's most stable currencies, with Germany's gold and foreign exchange reserves standing at close to 3 billion dollars by the end of 1955.

Internally, the price and wage structure had been kept remarkably non-inflationary. Unions cooperated with management, and strikes were rare. By the end of 1955, there was almost full employment, although some 10 percent of the expellees had not yet found adequate employment, largely because their skills were not in demand. A slight shortage of unskilled labor was even developing, and some Italian workers were being imported, the first of an ever-growing contingent of foreign laborers to find employment in the Federal Republic.

Despite this miraculous resurgence, which brought material comforts and self-satisfaction to the German middle class, vast problems remained to be solved. The housing shortage persisted. With 20 percent of housing in the Federal Republic destroyed by the war and an increase of 25 percent in the population, there was a shortage of about 5 million dwelling units. Although about 3.6 million units were built or rebuilt during the decade 1945–1955, the demand for adequate living space still far exceeded available housing. Moreover, it was doubtful whether the industrial boom could be sustained indefinitely, once the most urgent needs of reconstruction were met. The federal budget continued to be more or less balanced, although nearly half of all public expenditures was devoted to burdens arising from the war: relief for expellees and refugees, pensions, indemnification, and Allied occupation costs. The decision to force German rearmament and to oblige the Federal Republic to contribute more substantially to the defense of western Europe brought increased expenditures for which new sources of revenue had to be found.

CREATION OF THE GERMAN DEMOCRATIC REPUBLIC

Like the Federal Republic, the German Democratic Republic (DDR) was officially created in East Germany in the autumn of 1949. Immediately after the announcement of its establishment on October 7, West German Chancellor Adenauer declared it illegal on the grounds that it was not based on free elections; and on October 10, the Allied High Commission proclaimed that the DDR represented neither all of Germany nor East Germany. To this day, the western powers and the Bonn government have refused to recognize the *de jure* existence of the East German government. The West German press still calls East Germany "the Soviet Zone of Occupation" or "the so-called DDR." However, on a *de facto* basis, the governments of Bonn and of the DDR have continually been forced to deal with each other.

The Formation of the Government and Its Constitution

The Communist government of East Germany gradually evolved through a series of people's congresses by which

the Russians hoped to bring about the formation of a Communist-dominated all-German central government.

After the Russian-supported SED failed to obtain 50 percent of the vote in the state elections of October 1946, the Communists decided to suspend all further free elections and to consolidate their position by resorting to a system of bloc politics and people's congresses. They created an Anti-Fascist Democratic Bloc, comprising not only the SED as well as the LDP and CDU —both of which were allowed to retain a sham existence—but also two new political parties and numerous mass organizations, all indirectly controlled by the SED. By granting mock representation to diverse groups within the state, the Russians wished to create the illusion of mass support for their regime and to impede the formation of an organized opposition. The mass organizations that, subject to Communist approval, sent delegates to the Anti-Fascist Democratic Bloc, included the compulsory Free Trade Union Federation (FDGB), the Free German Youth (FDJ), the Democratic Women's League of Germany (DFD), the Cultural League (KB), and the League of Nazi Victims (VVN). For the same reason, the Communists created two new political parties in 1948. The National Democratic party of Germany (NDPD) was to attract conservatives, nationalistic middle-class elements, former army officers, and ex-Nazis. Leadership of the NDPD was strictly controlled by the Communists, and, as part of the bloc, this new party became a useful device for binding the middle class to the regime and rendering it politically innocuous. Similarly, the Democratic Peasant party of Germany (DBD), also under strict Communist

supervision, was set up to attract rural interests and wean them away from possible antigovernment activity.

The Anti-Fascist Democratic Bloc was then used to form the First People's Congress. In December 1947, the bloc parties and mass organizations delegated, without regular elections, representatives to a people's congress that in turn issued invitations to West German political parties. Although the western parties declined to send delegates, the congress alleged to speak for Germany as a whole, and demanded an immediate peace treaty together with an end to military occupation.

In March 1948, a Second People's Congress was convened through a similar device. This congress selected from its members a German People's Council of 400 delegates who were given advisory functions on governmental matters. The council then delegated a committee to draft a constitution for East Germany. The draft was published in October 1948 and submitted for popular discussion by means of press, radio, and political meetings. Again, it was the Communists' intention to demonstrate apparent popular approval for their work, and the German People's Council actually accepted some minor modifications in the draft. On March 19, 1949, the council finally approved the modified draft. National elections for a Third People's Congress were then held in May. The voters were presented with a single list of names of members of the bloc parties and the mass organizations, together called the "National Front." The list had been drawn up by the People's Council on the basis of the existing representative ratio of the various parties in the Second People's Congress. The ballot asked for ap-

proval of the official list and for a vote in favor of "German unity and a just peace," with voters given the choice of voting "yes" or "no" or invalidating their ballots. Of the total votes cast, 61.8 percent were affirmative but in East Berlin only 51.7 percent voted for this list.

On May 30, the Third People's Congress ratified the constitution, and elected a new People's Council of 330 delegates (70 additional delegates were to represent West Germany). But the Russians held up enactment of the constitution to await political developments in the west. After the western powers completed their establishment of the Federal Republic, the People's Council, on October 7, changed its name to "Provisional People's Chamber," by promulgating a special law without further reference to the electorate. At the same time, a provisional government of the DDR was appointed, a provisional upper house (*Länderkammer*) was formed, and the constitution was declared in force. All bodies were designated as "provisional" until confirmed by elections, eventually held in July 1950.

The first DDR constitution stressed the sovereignty of the people and was extremely democratic in appearance. But, like the Russian constitution, it did not provide for a clear separation of power among the three branches of government nor for judicial review. In theory, the legislature was bicameral, whereas in fact East Germany was a unitary state. The upper house, representing the states, initially endowed with even less power than the Bundesrat of West Germany, was shorn of all significance in 1952, and although the lower house or people's chamber (*Volkskammer*) dominates the states as well as the executive, in reality the party elite controls all facets of government.

Centralization was applied everywhere, with even East Berlin incorporated into the new state, whose capital is Pankow, a working-class suburb of Berlin. Finances and police, social insurance, justice, and even cultural matters are all directed by central agencies. Actually, the constitution was less important for the functioning of everyday government than were the special government decrees, some of which overtly contradicted the terms of the constitution. Significantly, the Russians did not impose an occupation statute, on the assumption that Communist control of the SED and the presence of Russian armed forces were sufficient to keep the new East German state in line with their policies.

The electoral system was also designed to keep the SED in power. Age requirements were low (eighteen for voting and twenty-one for eligibility for elected offices) in order to attract the pliable youth. National elections, held every four years, were retained as window dressing. The constitution stipulated "universal, equal, direct, and secret elections," but lacked the term "free," included in the Basic Law of the Federal Republic. For the 1950 elections to the lower house, the usual bloc list was compiled by the SED, but in view of the experience of 1949, the voters were no longer given the possibility of voting "no." The choice was between voting "yes" and casting an invalid ballot. Soon even secrecy of voting was abolished in many places. The new electoral code for the Trade Chambers stipulates: "Elections are secret. . . . Upon decision by the majority of those present, voting will be public." Under similar arrangements, most voting was soon made compulsory and public.

Economic Planning and Socialization

From their inception, the SED plans for the reconstruction of East Germany were based on the Soviet model, modified to meet German conditions. Proceeding from a Half Year Plan in 1948, followed by a Two-Year Plan for 1949–1950, the government inaugurated its first full-fledged Five-Year Plan in 1951. Directed primarily at doubling industrial production—particularly in fuel and energy, coal, iron, steel, chemicals, and machine tools—the plan called for increased "Socialist competition" and higher work norms. Although concerned largely with economic goals, the plan embraced all areas of public life, including transport, education, health and welfare, and even sports and culture. At the same time, socialization of industry and agriculture was intensified, particularly after 1952, so that by 1953 approximately 85 percent of the economy had been sequestered from private ownership. Rather than outright nationalization, however, a system of productive associations and semiprivate cooperatives was used in both agriculture and industry in order to permit a more gradual transition to socialism. Simultaneously the SED began its campaign to infiltrate and ultimately control all cultural and educational activities, its aim being to inculcate proletarian values in the coming generation. These efforts to dominate the youth soon led to a prolonged struggle with the German Protestant Church, which opposed the materialistic creed of the new regime.

Although the economic, social, and educational planning of the early years took East Germany far down the road toward socialism—and helped deepen the cleavage between East and West Germany—the SED and its Russian backers felt that progress was too slow. At a SED party conference in July 1952, it was decided to abandon the old "Anti-Fascist Democratic" order, which had been based on a compromise with the bourgeois. Instead, the party leaders called for the dictatorship of the proletariat and the accelerated implementation of true socialism. This decision created considerable unrest among large segments of the East German population, many of whom had already shown their unhappiness with economic restraints and lack of freedom by "voting with their feet," as the saying went—fleeing to West Germany.

On June 9, 1953, after barely eleven months, the "acceleration of socialism" was canceled. Faulty economic planning, inefficiency of the party bureaucracy, an impending economic crisis, the threatening restlessness of the population, as well as the general relaxation in the Socialist countries after the death of Stalin, forced Walter Ulbricht to adopt a "new course," which in some respects resembled Lenin's New Economic Policy of the 1920s. Without abandoning basic principles, the new course called for a temporary delay in the rapid sovietization of East Germany. It softened the demands of the Five-Year Plan; repudiated the call for the complete elimination of private enterprise; lowered the quotas of compulsory deliveries from farmers; promised an increase in food rations, consumer goods, and wages; announced a relaxation of travel restrictions to West Germany; and relented on some measures taken against religious institutions.

Even the announcement of the new course did not prevent the uprising of June 1953. On June 16, some workers in East Berlin went on strike to

demonstrate against an increase of 10 percent in their daily work norms. Although the government canceled the demanded increase at noon, the strikers, joined by other Berliners, marched downtown, demanding free elections, the resignation of the SED government, and assurances of better living conditions. The Vopos (people's police) did not interfere with the march of the rioters.

On June 17, the riots spread to the suburbs. Some 12,000 workers from outlying districts entered Berlin to march on the ministries. They burned SED party offices and propaganda bureaus and, without organization or planning, attempted to gain control of certain sectors of the city. Although some Vopos joined the marchers, most of the police tried to put down the revolt. Early that afternoon the Russian commandant placed the city under martial law, and two Russian divisions with supporting tanks entered Berlin. After a few brief clashes, in which German workers fought Russian armor with bricks and sticks, the revolt was put down. The news of the risings caused similar revolts in various East German cities, but despite some temporary successes, all were quickly suppressed by Russian troops. The revolts of June 17 became a symbol of heroism and may have made Ulbricht's government temporarily somewhat cautious but they hardly altered the basic course of East Germany's development.

The new course was retained in most essentials until 1955, when the post-Stalin era of uncertainty ended with Nikita Khrushchev's ascension to power. Thereafter the economic development of East Germany, as well as its foreign policy, was more and more clearly subordinated to the over-all needs of the Soviet bloc, regardless of ideological refinements.

Despite the planning and the hard work of the population, economic recovery in East Germany was slow until 1955. Food shortages continued and rubble cluttered the streets. The new currency, issued in 1948, rapidly sank to a ratio of 3 to 1, and then 4 to 1 to West Germany's *Deutsche Mark,* since productivity remained insufficient to cover the enormous demands made by Russia and the satellites, and at the same time allow exports to non-Communist nations. Moreover, the population was shrinking and the labor force was being constantly depleted, as skilled workers and professional people fled to West Germany.

East Germany's Foreign Policy

The roles played by East and West Germany in international affairs during the period 1949 to 1955 were, of course, largely determined by the respective occupying powers. But whereas the western Allies accorded the West Germans a modicum of self-determination after 1951, Moscow retained tight control of East Germany's policies.

The Pankow regime continued to claim that it spoke for all Germans, and persisted in its demands for unification on terms that would assure the continued power of the SED. At the same time it initiated a program of rearmament. By 1950, the 220,000 Vopos were armed with automatic weapons and were receiving military training. An additional 50,000 "emergency units" were supplied with howitzers, antiaircraft guns, and tanks.

The Russians forced the East Germans to settle the border dispute with Poland so as to reconcile internal dif-

ferences within the Communist camp. In June 1950, Walter Ulbricht, as deputy prime minister of East Germany, negotiated with Warsaw a bilateral accord, sanctioned by the Soviet Union, whereby the Oder-Neisse line was recognized as the permanent border between Germany and Poland. At the same time, Poland granted East Germany use of the harbor of Stettin, pending German reunification. Bonn immediately repudiated this agreement between Warsaw and Pankow, and London and Washington protested that the settlement of frontiers had to await a final peace treaty.

GERMANY IN THE INTERNATIONAL SCENE

Even after the Germans had been given control over most of their own internal affairs, the four occupying powers still faced the task of solving Germany's international problems: agreement on its permanent frontiers (the status of the Saar and of the lands beyond the Oder-Neisse); the question of reunification; the integration of Germany's economy with that of the rest of Europe; and the decision whether it should be permanently neutralized and disarmed, or permitted to join international power alignments. All these questions had to be solved before a peace treaty with a united Germany could be signed.

Allied Meetings and the German Peace Treaty

Immediately after the termination of the Berlin blockade in May 1949, the four powers held another foreign min-

isters' conference in Paris to discuss the German question. Again the meeting ended in a deadlock. After a considerable lull during 1950, when the eyes of the world were averted to the conflict in Korea, negotiations were resumed in the spring of 1951. But after 73 negotiating sessions in Paris, the deputy foreign ministers could report no progress. Thereafter, an almost constant stream of official and semi-official communiqués crossed back and forth between Washington, London, Paris, and Moscow without bringing the four any closer to agreement.

During the early years of occupation, the main East-West disagreements over Germany had been economic and financial. In the 1950s, however, after each of the two Germanies had been integrated into the economic orbit of its respective occupying powers, the German question turned more and more into a political problem. The West now sought to rearm West Germany and to bind it ever closer into the NATO alliance, while Russia was determined to frustrate the Allied plans, if necessary by turning Germany into a neutralized nation.

In November 1952, Chancellor Adenauer once again called on Russia to permit German reunification by allowing "free all-German elections . . . under international supervision." Such elections were to be followed by the formation of a "Constituent National Assembly, which in turn would have to install an all-German government." Such a government could then conclude a negotiated peace with the four powers. The western Big Three supported this stand. The sequence in this proposed maneuver was all-important. Free elections had to precede the formation of an all-German govern-

ment, for such elections were bound to produce a democratic, pro-western majority. The Russians, however, remained adamant in insisting on the reverse order: the four Allies were first to conclude peace with both German governments, a step the West rejected since it involved *de jure* recognition of Ulbricht's regime. Conclusion of peace was to be followed by the establishment of an all-German government by merging the governments of Bonn and Pankow, a proposal the West found unacceptable because it would have awarded the SED power out of proportion to its strength in a reunited Germany. As a third and last step, the Russians proposed the holding of elections.

Although under the Occupation Statute, negotiations of the German question with Russia were to be conducted by the western powers, the Bonn government frequently expressed its views on the issue. In June 1953, the Bundestag passed a resolution calling for elections, an all-German government, and a "freely negotiated peace treaty" in the sequence acceptable to the West, adding that the treaty should include the "settlement of all outstanding territorial questions" and should safeguard "freedom of action for an all-German parliament and an all-German government within the framework of the principles and the aims of the United Nations." By stressing "freedom of action," the West German legislature enunciated its opposition to the neutralization of Germany. In October of the same year, as the four powers once again prepared for a conference on Germany, Adenauer delivered a major foreign policy address to the Bundestag in which he defined the "central issues" for Germany as "restoration of its own independence,"

"reunification," and the "unification of free Europe and the integration of Germany into the European Community." He also hoped to forestall any possible inter-Allied bargain over the eastern border. "Following the numerous declarations by the *Bundestag* and the Federal Government," he announced, "the German people will never recognize the so-called Oder-Neisse frontier. But let me emphasize one thing here: the problem connected with the Oder-Neisse line shall never be settled by force but only by peaceful means."

Finally, in January 1954, a new Big Four conference was held in Berlin, the first full-fledged meeting of the foreign ministers in almost five years. The sessions alternated between the eastern and western sectors of the city, and lasted for almost four weeks. Russia was in the throes of the post-Stalin era, and the Korean War had been settled by an armistice; hence there was considerable hope that east-west differences over Germany could be bridged at the conference, despite the fact that Russia was still represented by the same V. M. Molotov who had proved intractable at previous meetings. Actually, the respective views announced in advance of the conference showed the divergence between the two positions: Russia sought to discuss global solutions to world problems, and for this purpose wanted Communist China to be represented; the West preferred to center the discussions on concluding an Austrian peace treaty and discussing means for reunifying Germany.

In the course of the Berlin conference, the west presented its joint program for Germany: general elections, followed by the formation of an all-German government, and the conclu-

sion of a peace treaty. The only disagreement among the three western powers, which they tried unsuccessfully to hide from Russia, concerned Germany's international role after the conclusion of peace. Great Britain wished to leave a united Germany free to rearm and free to join NATO if the German people wished it; the United States believed that a united and rearmed Germany should be more or less compelled to join NATO; France preferred that a united Germany remain demilitarized. Russia for its part was primarily interested in preventing West German rearmament. Besides the usual Russian demand for establishment of a unified government in advance of elections, Molotov specified that such elections be held without international supervision, that a united Germany not be allowed to join the contemplated European Defense Community, and that the peace treaty for Germany be drafted not merely by the Big Four but by all former Allied powers. In addition, the Russians demanded an end to the stationing of atomic weapons on German soil—a reference to American atomic artillery. They also called for an "immediate ban on militaristic and fascist organizations and expulsion of Hitler officials from the West German Government"—a proposal that the East Germans might have used to deny authority to any anti-Communist official of Bonn.

In the end, the long conference resulted in another deadlock. It proved impossible to negotiate a treaty for Austria and no agreement was reached on the German question. Consequently, the western Allies proceeded with their plans for initiating the rearmament of Germany and for granting it full sovereignty.

The Courtship
of the Federal Republic by the West

Unlike the Russians, who could dictate the political behavior of the East German regime through Communist party channels, the west found it more difficult to persuade the Federal Republic to adopt certain policies without infringing on the quasi-sovereign character of the Bonn government. Hence the years between 1949 and 1955 witnessed a long courtship of West Germany, full of gentle persuasion interspersed with more importunate pressure. The ultimate aim of the West was to assure the integration of a rearmed Germany into a western economic and military community, in return for the granting of full sovereignty to the Federal Republic.

An early step was taken in November 1949, when the Bonn government was allowed to participate in international organizations and to establish commercial and consular relations with other countries. The outbreak of the Korean War in June 1950 caused a redoubling of western efforts to erect an integrated European Defense Community with German participation, and to assure the pooling of western Europe's economic resources. As a first step, the Big Three issued a declaration in September, stating that they would consider an attack on the western zones or on West Berlin tantamount to an attack on themselves. This unilateral guarantee sought to prevent Germany from becoming another Korea, but it contained no stipulation that the Germans should themselves contribute to Europe's defense.

Chancellor Adenauer suggested as a preliminary measure that the Occupation Statute be replaced by negotiated agreements between Bonn and the

three western powers. But at first the Allies were willing merely to revise the Occupation Statute, the first major revision being granted in March 1951. The Federal Republic was allowed to establish a Foreign Office (Adenauer himself became the first foreign minister) and a full-fledged diplomatic service. At the same time, restrictions on German industrial production were again reduced in conjunction with the signing of the Schuman Plan (see page 353), and shortly thereafter England, France, and the United States passed legislation to terminate the state of war with Germany—despite the absence of a formal peace treaty.

In September 1951, the three Allies notified Bonn that they were willing to replace the Occupation Statute with Contractual Agreements, provided the Germans would contribute armed forces to a European Defense Community (EDC), consisting of French, Italian, Dutch, Belgian, Luxemburgian, and German units. Rearming Germany, of course, presented countless problems. The French objected to it unless the proposed German forces be strictly subordinated to a non-German command, and the British viewed it with certain apprehensions.

Even many Germans were confused by the prospect. For six years, the Germans had been told that militarism was bad, and that Germany should remain permanently disarmed. The youth, in particular, had begun to accept the new antimilitary creed. As a result, there was a considerable feeling in Germany against rearming and in favor of neutralism. The neutralists, some of whom adopted the slogan *"Ohne mich"* ("Count me out"), were motivated by various reasons. Many merely reacted to the horrors of war

and defeat, and resolved to keep Germany out of any future conflict. Some were nationalists who hoped to rid Germany of all outside interference and commitments by preaching a neutral course. Others were convinced that the Americans would inevitably withdraw to their own shores, and since they placed little confidence in Franco-British help, saw no reason for Germany alone to face the onslaught of Soviet Russia. Most of the neutralists, however, opposed rearmament simply because aligning the two Germanies with two opposing power blocs would tend to create a permanent division of Germany.

Although neutralist opinion was strong in the early 1950s, there were few organized groups to promote its tenets. The so-called Nauheim Circle favored neutrality as the only path to reunification, although some of its more nationalistic members demanded a neutral, independent, but remilitarized Germany, free to choose its own orientation in foreign affairs. Some leaders of the German Evangelical Church also advocated neutralism, presumably as the only way of reuniting the two separated branches of the German Protestant Church. Moreover, there were intellectual circles and democratic groups, such as those grouped around the magazine *Frankfurter Hefte,* which preached German neutrality as an essential preliminary step in the unification of Europe.

Despite this reluctance to rearm, shared to some extent by the SPD and the FDP, the western Allies negotiated with Bonn from November 1951 to May 1952 for the conclusion of Contractual Agreements. This "Convention on Relations between the Three Powers and the Federal Republic of Germany," signed on May 26, 1952, was

to replace the Occupation Statute, grant virtual sovereignty to West Germany, and arrange for a defensive alliance between Germany and the western powers. The Allies were to retain control over the question of unification, and would be allowed to station troops on German soil. In return, Germany would "participate in the European Defense Community in order to contribute to the common defense of the free world." On the following day, the EDC treaty was signed in Paris, providing for integrated forces of the six European countries in close cooperation with NATO.

The mere signing of the Contractual Agreements and of the EDC Treaty brought no solution to the question of German rearmament. Lengthy parliamentary debates followed in the Allied capitals and at Bonn. America and England finally ratified the Contractual Agreements in late 1953. But France continued to hesitate, and in the summer of 1954, the French National Assembly finally rejected the EDC Treaty, which was an integral part of the Contractual Agreements. Within Germany, ratification also presented problems. The Bundestag approved the Contractual Agreements and the EDC Treaty in March 1953 by a vote of 224 to 165, and the Bundesrat ratified both in May. But President Heuss could not sign the treaties, since the SPD brought a lawsuit before the newly created Federal Constitutional Court, claiming that the treaties were unconstitutional, since the Basic Law made no provision for rearmament. Because amendments to the Basic Law require a two-thirds vote in both houses, and Adenauer's coalition did not command such a majority, an impasse had seemingly been reached. The campaign for the September 1953 elections centered in

part on the issue of rearmament. The SPD insisted that arming West Germany and integrating it militarily into Western Europe would cause the permanent division of Germany. The CDU/CSU replied that only a strong Federal Republic, backed by the full weight of the western powers, could hope to gain the respect of Soviet Russia and successfully negotiate the reunification of Germany.

The September elections gave Adenauer the opportunity to form a new five-party coalition (see page 338) that assured him a two-thirds majority in both houses and thus sufficient votes to amend the Basic Law. Hence President Heuss signed the Contractual Agreements and the EDC Treaty in March 1954, even though the constitutional amendment permitting German rearmament was enacted only in 1956. Had France ratified EDC, West Germany would have assumed sovereignty in 1954.

After the failure of EDC, a new round of negotiations was started. The United States and other NATO powers urged France to find a solution for bringing the Federal Republic into the western defense network. In return for British guarantees to maintain troops on the Continent alongside those of France as a counterbalance to a rearmed Germany, France finally acquiesced. Details of new agreements were worked out at a London conference in October 1954 among representatives of the United States, Canada, Great Britain, France, Italy, West Germany, and the Benelux nations. These agreements were then included in the Paris Treaties, signed later in the same month by all NATO countries and by Chancellor Adenauer.

The Paris Treaties consisted of four main agreements. In the treaty of

sovereignty for Germany, the United States, Britain, and France stated their intention of terminating the occupation of West Germany, *except* for West Berlin. They retained the right to station forces of "effective strength" on German soil for the "defense of the free world," and the responsibility for governing Berlin, defending Germany, and negotiating the question of reunification. In return for Adenauer's reassurance not to use force to obtain unification or to change existing boundaries, the Big Three pledged to recognize the Bonn government as the "only German government freely and legitimately constituted and entitled to speak . . . for the German people in international affairs," and they reiterated their declaration that an attack on West Berlin would be considered as an attack on themselves.

The second Paris agreement admitted West Germany and Italy to the Western European Union (WEU), an extension of the 1948 Brussels Pact that had created a fifty-year defense alliance among France, England, and the Benelux countries. The seven-nation WEU was given power to limit German armaments and armaments production, and to supervise the creation of a German army of half a million men, a tactical air force, and a small navy. Chancellor Adenauer gave assurances that Germany would not engage in the production of atomic, biological, or chemical weapons, and would refrain from building specified articles of war (mines, tanks, strategic bombers, guided missiles, and large warships or submarines), *unless* NATO specifically requested Germany to produce such items, and the WEU Council approved such a request. In the third treaty, West Germany was admitted to membership in NATO, with the pro-vision that all of Germany's armed forces were to be integrated into WEU and NATO—a provision made to assuage the misgivings of France concerning German rearmament.

The last agreement reached in Paris attempted to solve the Saar question. In 1946, the French had begun to incorporate the rich Saar basin into the economic life of France, with the hope of ultimate political annexation. But the Saarlanders, who at first had seen advantages in a union with France, began to agitate for a return to Germany when the Federal Republic started its spiraling climb to prosperity. In 1951, the governments of Bonn and Paris agreed to postpone discussion of the Saar question until conclusion of a peace treaty; but in the following year, the Bundestag passed a resolution declaring that the Saar was German unless a plebiscite showed otherwise. The Paris Treaties of 1954 finally attempted a compromise by making the Saar independent, with economic ties with France but subject to international supervision by the WEU. This agreement, however, was subject to approval by the Saarlanders.

Thus the Paris Treaties paved the way for a return of sovereignty to a remilitarized West Germany. During the process of ratification, the treaties were heatedly debated in the various capitals. The German SPD, the Trade Union Federation, and many members of the FDP persisted in their opposition to rearmament until "all possibilities for negotiation on reunification have been exhausted." But in the end, the Bonn legislature as well as the other governments ratified the treaties. On May 5, 1955, ten years after the termination of World War II, the agreements were implemented, and West Germany attained its sovereignty.

In the same month, Russia and the west finally compromised on a state treaty for Austria containing a provision for its permanent neutrality.

Only the Saarlanders rejected the Paris agreements. After a heated election campaign, they voted in October 1955 overwhelmingly against international supervision, so that Bonn and Paris were forced to reopen negotiations. As one result of the increasingly friendly relations between the two countries, the Saar was incorporated into West Germany as a state in 1957, although it remained economically tied to France until 1959.

Consolidation of Western Europe

At the same time, West Germany was gradually being readmitted to the community of nations. In 1950, it became an associate member of the Council of Europe [1] and in 1951 obtained full membership. In the same year, West Germany joined various specialized agencies of the United Nations [2]—the World Health Organization, the International Labor Organization, and UNESCO—and became a signatory of GATT, the General Agreement on Tariffs and Trade. In 1952, it joined the World Bank and the International Monetary Fund.

But more decisive in the long run was the determination of the Adenauer government to effect a *rapprochement*

with France and to cement the unity of western Europe, in particular of the so-called Inner Six (France, Italy, Germany, and Benelux—the nucleus of the later Common Market). The European Coal and Steel Community, proposed by France's Foreign Minister Robert Schuman in 1950 and inaugurated in 1952, although perhaps the most spectacular and successful, was only one of the new organizations demonstrating the new "European" spirit that animated West Germany. By pooling the coal and steel resources of the six participating countries and placing them under a supranational High Authority, the Schuman Plan aimed not merely at preventing a possible future war between France and Germany and at speeding up European economic recovery; rather, the plan was part of a general movement in western Europe that sought to overcome the narrow horizons of petty nationalism and fuse the participating states into an economic, social, military, and ultimately, perhaps, even political unit.

This new "internationalism" or "Europeanism" marked a significant departure from the traditional German political thought of the last hundred years. The CDU became firmly committed to it, and with certain reservations, even the SPD and FDP supported it. It became a popular creed with the young and the intellectuals, and gradually became an accepted tenet of foreign policy. Even those who looked upon "Europeanism" with distrust did not, like their predecessors in the Weimar period, regard "internationalists" as unpatriotic. This transformation alone provides hopeful evidence that, with the creation of the Federal Republic, Germany entered a new era.

---

[1] An organization, created in 1949 with headquarters in Strassburg, dedicated to the achievement of greater cultural, economic, social, and political unity of Europe.

[2] Pending unification, Germany could not join the United Nations itself, unless Russia and the West were to admit both Germanies, a move that would imply *de jure* recognition of East Germany.

Germany under
Adenauer and Ulbricht

THE CONTINUED DIVISION OF GERMANY

International Conferences and German Foreign Policy

In reply to the integration of a re-militarized Germany into the western defense system, the Russians accelerated the militarization of East Germany. They officially ended the war between East Germany and the Communist Bloc (Russia, China, Albania, Bulgaria, Czechoslovakia, Poland, and Rumania), and included the DDR in the Warsaw Pact, Russia's newly created eastern defense system.

Simultaneously, however, the first "thaw" in the cold war appeared after Khrushchev, together with Nikolai Bulganin, assumed power in the Kremlin. Settlement of the war in Indo-China and agreement on an Austrian treaty again raised hopes that the German problem might be solved. In consequence, the Big Four (Eisenhower, Eden, Faure, and the team of Bulganin and Khrushchev) met in Geneva in July of 1955 at the first full-fledged summit meeting since Potsdam. But the friendly atmosphere in Geneva could not conceal the serious differences between East and West. Before 1955, the German problem had already been complicated; now the two Germanies were aligned with opposing power blocs, the problem seemed well-nigh insoluble unless East and West would agree to a military disengagement in Germany.

After the failure of the summit meeting, the Bonn government itself became active in the international field, although the western Allies were still legally responsible for negotiating German reunification. Chancellor Adenauer journeyed to Washington and London, exchanged several visits with France's prime minister, and then went to Moscow in September 1955. The Moscow discussions on German reunification proved fruitless, since Khrushchev simply advised Adenauer to negotiate directly with the Pankow government. But Adenauer's plea for the release of all German prisoners of war still detained in Russia evoked Bulganin's promise to repatriate some 10,000 Germans—although Bonn insisted that this number was far below the total still held by the Russians. At the same time,

Bonn and Moscow agreed to establish diplomatic relations.

Adenauer's trip to Moscow raised his popularity at home. The Russians actually released some prisoners—to both East and West Germany. The establishment of diplomatic relations with Soviet Russia pleased those Germans who believed that only direct negotiations with the Communists might achieve reunification and that only Moscow could redraw the Oder-Neisse boundary short of war. It also appealed to those who favored a pro-eastern orientation because of the enticing possibilities for trade in eastern Europe. In some western circles, however, Adenauer's action raised apprehensions that Germany might make a bargain with the Kremlin reminiscent of the Rapallo Treaty of 1922 or the Nazi-Soviet Pact of 1939. To reassure the west, Adenauer reaffirmed to the press that he would abide by the Paris Treaties and seek reunification only with western support. And the new foreign minister, Heinrich von Brentano (1904–1964), asserted: "The German people will not permit themselves to be pulled out of this [western] community, nor will they separate themselves voluntarily from it."

Yet Adenauer's Moscow trip involved an anomaly. By awarding diplomatic recognition to Bonn while at the same time granting sovereignty to East Germany, Russia bolstered its assertion that *two* separate Germanies existed legally, and that Germany could be unified only by merging the two governments. Adenauer, however, claimed to be speaking for *all* Germans, including those in East Germany, and persisted in denying recognition to the Pankow regime on the grounds that the Ulbricht government was a mere puppet of the Russian occupation forces. His state secretary, Walter Hallstein (1901–   ), initiated what came to be known as the Hallstein Doctrine, whereby Bonn refused to maintain diplomatic relations with all nations that recognized East Germany. Over the next eight years, thirteen communist nations (including Cuba in 1963) formally recognized the DDR; and in accordance with the Hallstein Doctrine, Bonn severed, or refused to establish, diplomatic relations with these states (with the exception of Russia). No other governments gave *de jure* recognition to East Germany, although many neutrals, such as Egypt, Finland, and India, established close, informal relations and carried on extensive trade with the Pankow regime.

The Hallstein Doctrine, designed to stress the theoretical indivisibility of Germany, rendered Bonn's eastern policy somewhat inflexible. This rigidity was supported by France, especially after the advent of Charles de Gaulle in 1958, but was often criticized by the SPD and FDP, and tacitly deplored by London and Washington. Actually, the Hallstein Doctrine was not consistently enforced by Bonn: the very recognition of the Soviet Union violated its principles. Moreover, it was a legal and political stand that carefully avoided trade restrictions or other economic measures. In spite of the public adamancy of Chancellor Adenauer against all dealings with Pankow and the Soviet satellites, there was in fact considerable contact. Extensive trade was also maintained with Yugoslavia, even after diplomatic relations were severed when Tito recognized Ulbricht's regime. Trade with Russia increased constantly. By 1958, the Krupp industrial complex was selling

30 million dollars worth of machinery annually to the Russians, prompting Khrushchev himself to toast the "continued health and prosperity of the firm" of Krupp. Between 1956 and 1958, when de-Stalinization effected a temporary relaxation of Russian control over the satellites, there was also a tentative *rapprochement* between Bonn and Warsaw. Polish–West German trade was increased, and some cabinet members and politicians, although not Adenauer, weighed the possibility of a political bargain with Warsaw. They thought that Poland might be persuaded to allow German reunification on western terms in return for West German recognition of the permanence of the Oder-Neisse line. Such a settlement with Bonn might have strengthened Poland's hand vis-à-vis the Kremlin and helped remove it from Russian influence. It was also in accord with the new United States policy of aiding the satellites, in particular Poland, in order to loosen Moscow's grip on eastern Europe.

In the long run, nothing came of this plan, largely because it proved impossible seriously to impair communist solidarity in eastern Europe and because the Polish government feared the resurgence of a united, militarized Germany on its western border even more than it resented the presence of Russian armies on its own soil. This became clear when, in 1958, Poland's foreign minister, Adam Rapacki, proposed his plan for a "nuclear-free zone" in Poland, Czechoslovakia, and the two Germanies that would eventually permit the withdrawal of foreign armed forces and the unification of a neutral Germany. Rapacki's plan, supported by Moscow, Prague, and Pankow, was largely aimed at disengaging West Germany from NATO. Bonn, Paris, London, and Washington for their part, found Rapacki's proposals unacceptable.

But West German discussions with Warsaw and Moscow foundered not only over the question of disengagement from NATO but also over the Oder-Neisse line. Most German politicians persisted in championing Germany's right to recover the frontiers of 1937. The Federal Ministry for All-German Affairs continues to disseminate the view that the lands beyond the Oder-Neisse form a historical, cultural, and economic part of Germany. Journals such as the *Zeitschrift für Ostforschung* (*Journal for Research on the East*) and research institutions supported by public funds, such as the Johann Gottfried Herder Institute in Marburg, produce a plethora of literature depicting Polish mismanagement of the Oder-Neisse territories and tacitly urging their return to German administration.

To be sure, the younger generation has generally shown little interest in the eastern lands. The expellee party eventually lost its political power and many irredentist organizations have been dissolved—although a few pressure groups, such as the *Bund Vertriebener Deutscher* (Union of Expelled Germans) still exist. Among the "Europeanists" there is hope that Germany's former *Drang nach Osten* can be permanently sublimated in a community of western Europe. Moreover, prosperity has taken the edge off irredentism, the voices of moderation are strong, and foreign pressure, especially by France, is seeking to discourage German hopes of regaining the lost lands.

Yet irredentism was being kept alive, almost artificially. Even in the 1961

federal elections, few German politicians and newspapers felt it wise to take a public stand favoring abandonment of the lands beyond the Oder-Neisse, not even to gain a bargaining point for reunification. Despite private indifference, the public position that the Oder-Neisse question was not negotiable was being stanchly maintained, and reluctance to abandon the eastern territories remained one of the stumbling blocks to reunification and to a peace settlement.

Thus neither the first "thaw" in the cold war—labeled "spirit of Geneva" in the American press—nor Bonn's own diplomatic efforts produced the slightest advance toward a solution to the German problem. Understandably, neither East nor West devoted its full energies to getting Germany reunified. But it is also questionable how ardently the West Germans themselves desire reunification. Probably half the people of West Germany have relatives or friends in East Germany. Many cherish traditional ties that bind them to the East German lands, in which some had economic interests they hope to recover. They also recognize that a united Germany, with some 77 million inhabitants, would at once rank next to Russia as the dominant power in Europe and would become the unquestioned leader of the Common Market or any other large European union that may be created. Yet among the population at large, there is in fact considerable apathy toward the question of reunification. The political opposition in Germany also questioned the sincerity of the Adenauer government and of the ruling circles, which publicly paid lip service to the demand for reunification but privately showed less eagerness to press for a solution to the problem. In a reunited Germany, the CDU would lose all hope of electoral parity with the SPD; the strength of the Roman Catholic Church would wane with the inclusion of primarily Protestant East Germany; conservatives and industralists would face the difficulties of amalgamating the socialized economy of the East with their own system of free enterprise; and wealthy West Germany would have to share its affluence to help build up the economically less advanced east.

Meanwhile, despite the Hallstein Doctrine and despite tacit misgivings, the Federal Ministry for All-German Affairs and many other public and private agencies attempted to increase contacts between the two Germanies, so that during their period of separation, the two states would not grow apart irremediably. Travel restrictions were almost completely lifted. In 1957 alone, some three million East Germans visited the Federal Republic, and millions of West Germans paid visits to the DDR. Trade was expanded. Trade fairs, church meetings, youth congresses, scientific exchanges, sport competitions, cultural exchanges, and numerous other arrangements permitted contact between Germans from both sides of the "iron curtain." There was cooperation in transport and communication, in public health problems, and in such legal matters as restitution for damage suffered under National Socialism or the clearing up of wills, stocks, and personal records. At the same time, federal committees in West Germany studied economic and social changes in East Germany to prepare for adjustments required in the event of reunification.

In 1958, however, East German authorities began to hamper travel be-

tween the two states. Gradually contact was choked off, and the differences between East and West began to grow at an accelerated pace.

The Berlin Crises

After countless exchanges of diplomatic notes between East and West and a series of reciprocal visits by the British, German, and French heads of state in 1958, Khrushchev suddenly revived tensions by opening the first of a series of Berlin crises. In November 1958, he proposed that West Berlin be turned into a demilitarized, free city, perhaps under U.N. supervision and guarantee, and that the occupying powers immediately conclude peace with both Germanies. The Russian leader intimated that unless the western powers agreed to his proposal within six months, he would sign a separate peace treaty with the DDR and relinquish to the East Germans all Russian responsibilities for western military communications with Berlin by rail, highway, and air. This Russian demand turned 1959 into a critical year of feverish diplomatic activity. Despite serious disagreement among the western powers on how best to counter Russia's threat, Bonn and the Big Three shared the apprehension that implementation of Khrushchev's proposal might result in the loss of Berlin for the West and the permanent splitting of Germany. If control of access routes to Berlin were turned over to Ulbricht, the West would be forced to deal with the DDR in an official capacity and thereby would extend recognition to the regime. In consequence, the West would no longer be able to deny the validity of Russia's claim that two Germanies existed, and

the western plan for reunification (see page 347) would have to be abandoned.

The year opened with threats and counterthreats, interspersed with Russian demands for a new summit meeting. After Chancellor Adenauer conferred with President Charles de Gaulle, and Prime Minister Harold Macmillan visited Bonn and Moscow, where Premier Khrushchev agreed to withdraw his six-month deadline, the powers arranged a foreign ministers' conference in Geneva. The ministers held thirty-one meetings during May and June. Although both sides ceded a few minor points, no solution was reached. The Russian threat to Berlin was not withdrawn but merely postponed, and to stress their determination Russian and East German authorities frequently harassed Allied traffic to Berlin.

Despite the patent incompatibility of the opposing views, a new thaw developed. Vice-President Richard Nixon went to Russia, and Premier Khrushchev visited the United States (September 1959) to discuss with President Eisenhower at Camp David ways of easing the cold war. While preparing for a new summit meeting, the four western Allies maneuvered to bridge their own differences. Eisenhower visited Bonn in August, and Adenauer journeyed to London in November and conferred with De Gaulle in Paris in early December.

The talks between Adenauer and De Gaulle opened an era of growing friendship between the two. Franco-German cooperation in the European Coal and Steel Community and in the Common Market (created in 1958), and perhaps a certain affinity between the two rigid and self-assured leaders, each of whom felt that he had personally

restored his country to greatness, led to an ever-closer *rapprochement* between them. There were, of course, points of difference between France and Germany. Starting in 1959, De Gaulle pressed for a separate atomic force for western Europe and a more independent policy for France, whereas Adenauer was less convinced of the desirability of an "atomic third force" and remained more devoted to the closest possible relations with England and America. Moreover, De Gaulle was not averse to accepting the Oder-Neisse line as permanent, whereas Adenauer rejected such a position. But in regard to the general approach to negotiations with Russia, Bonn and Paris were in agreement and differed from the Anglo-American position. Washington and London appeared willing to make minor concessions to the Russians in order to secure a temporary settlement of the Berlin issue. Adenauer and De Gaulle, however, preferred to see the *status quo* in Berlin rather than to make concessions to the Russians, and they opposed discussing Berlin as a separate issue from the rest of the German problem.

The Paris Conference, officially committed to the discussion of Berlin, Germany, and world disarmament, finally opened on May 16, 1960. But even before its opening, "the spirit of Camp David" had evaporated. By late April, the Geneva disarmament talks had been suspended, and Khrushchev had reiterated his warning that he would sign a separate peace with the DDR and force the western powers out of Berlin unless they agreed to his proposals. The U-2 incident—the downing of an American reconnaissance plane deep inside Russia—was used by the Soviet Union as a pretext for terminat-

ing the summit conference barely three hours after it had started.

In 1961, Khrushchev again intimated that he expected to settle the Berlin issue by the end of the year, presumably in order to put pressure on the newly installed administration of John F. Kennedy and to take advantage of discord among the Allies and within West Germany. Adenauer visited Paris, London, and Washington in the spring, but the Franco-German stand remained more rigid than that of Great Britain and the United States. Within Germany, the election campaign showed that many groups were growing weary of Adenauer's lack of success on Berlin and reunification. The SPD and the FDP called for a new approach to "the German problem," without proffering specific alternatives. The CDU, on the other hand, reiterated its "absolute rejection of any step that might lead to a neutralization of Germany," and warned that the negotiations on Berlin might be harmed if the FDP and the SPD injected foreign policy into the election campaign.

In June, President Kennedy met Premier Khrushchev in Vienna. The meeting produced no changes, since the Russians persisted in demanding that Berlin be turned into a "free city," and stressed their readiness to sign a separate peace and unleash a third Berlin crisis. New harassments of Allied traffic to Berlin followed, and the borders between East and West Germany were closed almost completely. Despite Khrushchev's call for "peaceful coexistence," the East Germans soon began to restrict access also between East and West Berlin. As if sensing that the DDR would soon be turned into a huge barbed wire encampment and sealed off like other Russian satellites,

over 30,000 East Germans and East Berliners used the last open escape route by fleeing to West Berlin in July, followed by 22,000 more in early August.

On August 13, 1961, Russia and the DDR suddenly announced the closure of the border between East and West Berlin, ostensibly to keep out West German saboteurs. A decree prohibited East Germans and East Berliners from entering West Berlin. East German army units and Vopos encircled the entire perimeter of West Berlin with barbed wire, which was replaced in the ensuing weeks by a wall of solid cement blocks, topped with broken glass and barbed wire.

Erection of the Berlin Wall was not merely a desperate measure to stop the flight of refugees, which was endangering East Germany's productive strength; it was also another attempt to weaken the resistance of West Berlin. The western powers did not try to prevent the construction of the wall. According to retired General Lucius Clay, the West is "responsible only for the independence, security, and well-being of West Berlin," whereas "East Berlin is a Soviet responsibility." But the West made plain its intention to remain in West Berlin and defend it. The wall, of course, caused much additional hardship to the people of Berlin, and imprisoned in East Germany all those who had hoped to flee to the West. But it failed to force the surrender of the city to East Germany.

Throughout 1962, the situation in Berlin remained unchanged. Occasional escapees tunneled or vaulted their way to freedom, and there were moments of tension when American and Russian tanks stood menacingly face to face at "Checkpoint Charlie," one of the few official crossing points between the

west and the east of the city. Communist Vopos and West Berlin police sometimes exchanged gunfire during the escape of a refugee. But both sides were clearly determined not to let the Berlin issue erupt into open conflict. Among the western powers there continued to be different views on the best procedure to follow. Adenauer once again journeyed to Washington in November, and further cemented relations with France by an official visit of state to Paris, followed by a return visit by De Gaulle and ultimately by the signing of a treaty of friendship and cooperation between France and Germany in January 1963. But despite the division of the western powers into a Franco-German and an Anglo-American camp, the four states presented a firm, united front to the Kremlin in regard to Berlin.

But East–West negotiations at various diplomatic levels produced no progress. In repeated public statements, Khrushchev called for a German settlement and made vague allusions to possible unilateral action. In his New Year's message for 1963, he again advocated a "normalization" of the status of Berlin, suggesting as a minimum that Allied forces in Berlin be placed under United Nations control. But even when he visited East Berlin in January 1963 to attend the party congress of the East German Communists, he refrained from setting new deadlines or voicing further precise demands for a change in the status of Berlin. Khrushchev's hesitation resulted not merely from his preoccupation with internal economic problems and the Sino-Russian dispute; he was also reluctant to award Walter Ulbricht full freedom of action that the German Communist might misuse to the embarrassment of the Russians.

THE GERMAN
DEMOCRATIC REPUBLIC

Under the strict tutelage of the Soviet Union, the East German Democratic Republic gradually emerged as a quasi-sovereign state in steps paralleling those taken by the west in regard to Bonn. In most cases, the Russians made their plans ahead of the western powers, but implemented them only in response to similar measures taken by the West. Moscow was more hesitant than the western powers to perpetuate the division of Germany, since the Communists had more to gain from converting Germany into a united but neutralized state, and thereby forcing Bonn's withdrawal from NATO.

Rearmament

As early as 1948, units of the people's police had been equipped with military weapons. A Vopo navy and air force had been created in 1950 and 1951, respectively, and the constitution had been amended in 1953 to permit rearmament. But the remilitarization of East Germany was publicly acknowledged only in 1955, when the DDR became an associate member of the Warsaw Pact. In the following year —officially in retaliation for the establishment of a West German army (*Bundeswehr*)—the East Germans established a Ministry of National Defense, under General Karl-Heinz Hoffman (1910–   )—a reliable party member and friend of Ulbricht's—and set up the NVA, the National People's Army. To staff the NVA, some Vopo units were converted into regular armed forces and equipped largely with Russian and Czech weapons.

During the subsequent years, the East German forces grew relatively slowly. By 1961, they had reached 110,000 men, including army, navy, and air force, although a new target of 170,000 men was set. Alone among the Warsaw Pact nations, the DDR instituted no official draft, and instead filled its military ranks with "volunteers," most of whom enlisted because of pressure or enticements exerted through various party and organizational channels. Leadership in the NVA was entrusted to those deemed politically reliable rather than to those with military experience; hence former *Wehrmacht* officers were gradually pushed aside in favor of younger and better indoctrinated men. The ideal of a nonpolitical army, preached by Bonn, was alien to Pankow. Typical of those in the upper echelons of the officer corps is the head of the air force, Lieutenant General Heinz Kessler (1920–   ), who had deserted to the Red Army on June 22, 1941, received his Communist apprenticeship in Moscow as a student in the anti-Fascist school and as a member of the Russian-sponsored National Committee for a Free Germany, and is a member of the SED Central Committee.

The relatively modest size of the National People's Army stems partly from Russian precautions not to let the Germans create a single large military force that might escape their political control. For this reason, the Russians preferred to see the militarization of numerous other organizations, each of which can be controlled through separate channels. Thus the Border Security Police (some 50,000 men), the Factory Guard Police (some 8000), the Security Alert Police (some 30,000), the Security Guard Police (some 5000), the Railroad Security Police (some 7000), the District Alert Police (some 5000), and the

Workers' Militia (some 350,000)—all of whom receive military training and considerable armaments—add almost half a million men to the pool of available forces. In addition, about 400,000 young men and women of the Association for Sports and Technical Crafts receive paramilitary training in parachute jumping, piloting, and marksmanship.

Together with its official permission to rearm, Russia reluctantly granted the Ulbricht regime other symbols of sovereign status. In September 1955, the DDR assumed control over its own frontiers, forcing the West Germans to deal increasingly with East German authorities, whose *de jure* existence the West still refuses to recognize. In 1957, Russia promised that the 400,000-man Red Army stationed on East German soil would refrain from interfering in the internal affairs of the DDR. In 1959, the Russians even ceased demanding reimbursement for the cost of the occupation troops, giving the DDR more nearly the illusion of being a bona fide ally of the Soviet Union.

Economic Progress

Economic progress at first remained slow. The balance of trade was still unfavorable, essential foods were in short supply, and the First Five-Year Plan fell short of its goals. By 1957, industrial output—initially severely handicapped by indiscriminate Russian dismantling and by poor planning—began to grow significantly, although the Second Five-Year Plan also fell behind schedule. Trade with the Russian bloc increased measurably, partly financed by extensive Russian credits. But despite increased industrial production, the economy as a whole suffered from the constant decline in population caused by the continued flights to West Germany. The DDR's population decreased from 20 million in 1948 to 17 million by 1960.

In the late 1950s, economic progress accelerated. In 1958, Ulbricht took a major step in his program of socialization, and at the same time attempted to assuage the discontent of the working population. Nationalization of small industry and the creation of state farms were now pushed vigorously, while food rationing was abolished and wages were increased. A concerted effort was made to raise the standard of living, although higher food prices partly wiped out the greater earning power of the workers. The drive for increased productivity was successful in industry at least. By 1959, the DDR had achieved a favorable balance of exports over imports and was increasing its trade not only with the Russian bloc and West Germany, but also with many nonaligned Near Eastern nations, such as Egypt and Iraq. Its recovery, in fact, placed East Germany in the industrial forefront of the Communist nations.

But the economic recovery was only one side of the coin, and was achieved under considerable strain. Ulbricht began to clamp down on travel to the West in order to slow down the exodus of refugees. He also resorted to a type of forced labor. After 1959, every child over eleven was forced to work one day a week on a farm or in a factory, and by 1960, all workers were assigned to jobs, regardless of personal preferences. Industrialization was stressed at the expense of consumer production, and agriculture was mismanaged and neglected. The forced collectivization in 1960 of all land remaining in private possession failed to increase the production of food. On the contrary,

by 1961 new food shortages forced the reintroduction of rationing of fats and even of potatoes in some regions. At the same time, industrial production slowed down. Despite East Germany's industrial prowess, Ulbricht found himself in ever-deeper economic trouble. United States agencies in West Berlin distributed free food parcels to East Germans, who, much to the embarrassment of the Communist regime, flocked there to supplement their meager diet. The Bonn government offered free shipments of food, and began to use economic pressure as a lever for negotiating political concessions. In late 1960, Bonn bargained successfully for an easing of travel restrictions for West Germans visiting Berlin or East Germany, in return for the renewal of trade agreements (11 percent of East Germany's foreign trade was with West Germany). In 1963, when East Germany was severely handicapped by a lack of foreign credits, Bonn offered Ulbricht a loan of $100 million, provided West Berliners were permitted to pass through the Berlin Wall to visit East Berlin. Under pressure from Russia, the Pankow government eventually rejected this offer.

Ulbricht's Dictatorship

Neither the failure to relieve shortages nor changes in the Communist party line in Moscow prevented Walter Ulbricht from gradually consolidating his grip on the DDR and from converting East Germany into a dictatorship. Among all the Stalinist satellite leaders, Ulbricht proved the most durable and agile, capable of shifting with every change of wind from Moscow, yet retaining a measure of independent power. To achieve unquestioned rule over East Germany and, he hopes,

ultimately over a united Germany, Ulbricht set out to suppress all opposition outside the SED, to eliminate rivals within his party, and to find a *modus vivendi* with Moscow.

Opposition at large that had not been channeled into innocuous pseudo parties centered around the Lutheran Church, led by Bishop Otto Dibelius (1880–1967), whose residence was in West Berlin but whose diocese included East Berlin and parts of the DDR. The struggle between the Lutheran Church and the SED continued all through the 1950s and early 1960s, with inconclusive results. As in the days of Hitler, the issue provoked a split in the church. Certain Lutheran leaders, most of whom belong to the Pastors' League (*Pfarrerbund*), accept a narrow interpretation of St. Paul's admonition that "the powers that be are ordained of God," and hence favor close cooperation between the Lutheran Church and the Communist regime. On the other hand, Dibelius and a majority of pastors and church members, chastened by the experience of National Socialism, assert that a totalitarian government cannot be permitted to rule Christian consciences.

In order to gain greater political power and capture the confidence of the workers, Ulbricht tried various approaches. The "soft line" adopted in 1956, when thousands of political prisoners were pardoned and more contact with West Germany was permitted, was abandoned in 1958. "De-Stalinization" was followed by a purge of unreliable SED leaders. Meanwhile, use of the "National Front" (see page 343) for elections continued to ensure a malleable legislature. The elections of 1957 gave the candidates of the official list a vote of 99.5 percent, and the shadow president, Wilhelm Pieck, was easily

re-elected to a third four-year term in the same year.

Yet in the face of new economic problems, Ulbricht required even more power and sought less cumbersome pretenses at playing democracy. His opportunity came with Pieck's death in 1960. Reminiscent of Hitler in 1934 at the death of Hindenburg, Ulbricht abolished the presidency and made himself chairman of a newly created Council of State. This council, whose twenty-three members were appointed for a term of four years by the SED—in reality by Ulbricht himself—was given power to promulgate legislation, sign international agreements, control foreign affairs, order elections, and even countermand existing legislation. At the same time, Ulbricht assumed the post of chairman of the new National Defense Council, with power over all land, sea, and air forces, while he retained his post as first party secretary of the SED. The fiction of a cabinet was retained, but Prime Minister Grotewohl, never very powerful, was in fact demoted to be a mere administrator. This new arrangement gave Ulbricht almost complete power over the state, under the guise of a collective party leadership. But when economic problems grew in 1962, responsibility for the failures was also placed more squarely at his feet. Arrests of discontents, stern reprisals, and dismissal of scapegoats only provoked further unrest.

Although the fate of the regime depends on the Soviet Union, the DDR at times took matters into its own hands. The Pankow regime repeatedly attempted bilateral negotiations with Bonn on questions of reunification, but Adenauer stanchly refused such overtures, although he increased commercial relations with Pankow. In answer, Ulbricht occasionally enacted his own reprisals, sometimes to the embarrassment of Russia. A favorite measure was interference with West German civilian traffic to West Berlin. The death strip of barbed wire and cleared fields, hermetically sealing off East Germany from the West, was another move revealing Ulbricht's desperation. And there is reason to believe that construction of the Berlin Wall initially was a measure conceived by Pankow and only reluctantly accepted by the Kremlin. At times, Ulbricht also seemed tempted to flirt with Communist China in an effort to bring pressure on Moscow for greater financial and political support. Despite his inherent distrust of Ulbricht, Khrushchev had no choice but to bolster the East German regime for fear of jeopardizing negotiations with the West. To raise the prestige of the Pankow government, he made frequent visits to East Berlin: 1955, 1957, 1959, 1960, 1963. At the SED Party Congress in January 1963, attended by Khrushchev, Vladislav Gomulka, and high-ranking delegates from all Communist countries, including Yugoslavia and China, the Russian leader again did his best to bolster Ulbricht's prestige, without, however, giving him greater freedom of action for solving the Berlin issue on his own terms.

THE FEDERAL REPUBLIC

West German Rearmament

The Paris Treaties called for a German army of 500,000 men, with a limited air force and navy. To create this army, the federal legislature

amended the Basic Law to permit rearmament (March 6, 1956), and appointed as Commander in Chief General Hans Speidel (1897–   ), a former chief of staff to Rommel. At that time, 10,000 men were transferred from the 20,000 man Federal Frontier Protection Service to form the nucleus of the federal defense force, and a law was passed permitting the recruitment of 150,000 volunteers. At the same time, Adenauer turned over the Ministry of Defense, which had been created in 1955, to Franz Joseph Strauss (1915–   ), a ranking member of the CSU and former lieutenant in World War II, who had first served in the Bavarian government and after 1953 held various posts in Adenauer's cabinet. Only 70,000 volunteers had enrolled by the end of 1956; hence the Bundestag enacted compulsory military service, effective January 1957, despite the protest of the SPD, which still feared a revival of militarism.

During 1957, the West German defense force continued its slow expansion. The federal government built airplanes for NATO, and the first three German divisions of light armor were transferred to NATO command. German military morale was given a considerable boost when General Speidel was appointed commander in chief of all NATO land forces in Europe.

But German rearmament faced serious problems. The Bundestag had to frame new codes of military conduct and justice that would place greater responsibility on the judgment of officers and enlisted men without undermining the traditional army hierarchy of command. In addition to assuring internal democratization of the armed forces, Bonn had to establish firm civilian control over the military. More-over, the military establishment required considerable financial expenditures. Many Germans were averse to seeing their funds diverted from buttressing economic growth to purchasing foreign weapons or financing an army. Also, the federal structure established by the Basic Law was not geared to large expenditures by the federal government, since it provided that the states retain the bulk of tax revenue (see page 368). These restrictions on Bonn's resources affected Germany's contributions toward NATO, as well as its ability to purchase British and American arms.

By 1958, the West German army had been expanded to seven divisions. As the Western European Union Council (see page 352) lifted its restrictions, the Germans increased the size of their naval vessels and air force. At the same time, Germany, Italy, and France decided to produce certain weapons jointly, such as tanks and fighter aircraft. With the French army deeply involved in the Algerian War and with De Gaulle withholding the bulk of his forces from NATO control, NATO planners began to rely increasingly on German contributions to western Europe's defense. As early as 1958, General Lauris Norstad, Supreme Allied Commander in Europe from 1956 to 1962, favored removing all remaining restrictions on German production and German use of conventional weapons. He also suggested that German artillery be equipped with nuclear warheads.

But the growth and equipment of the German army raised considerable debate. Minister Strauss urged that the federal defense force be awarded equal status with other western armies, even in its armaments. And there were some

in Germany who thought that Germans should not be mere foot soldiers in an alliance in which only Americans controlled the nuclear arms. Hence Strauss also felt that nuclear weapons in German hands would be justified, an assertion that raised a storm of protest in and out of Germany.

As the army grew, Strauss also insisted on the need for German training bases as well as depots of strategic stockpiles further removed from the "iron curtain" than the federal territory. In early 1960, he negotiated for German bases in Spain, a move perhaps militarily sound, but diplomatically tactless, since most WEU countries looked askance on the dictatorial regime of Generalissimo Franco. The resulting Allied protests revealed the ingrained apprehensions about a possible revival of German militarism, and Strauss abandoned his negotiations. But gradual military integration with the western powers continued.

In 1961, German troops were provided training bases in England and France, and the federal defense force was equipped with an increased number of short-range missiles. However, its growth continued to be hampered by financial problems. And so long as NATO leaders were undecided whether to press for large, conventional land forces, or ask for small, highly mobile, heavily armed units, the Germans felt little incentive to expand their land armies. By the beginning of 1963, the combined total for all three branches of the federal armed forces amounted to only 398,000 men, in spite of the fact the Paris Treaties had stipulated 500,000, and United States military planners in NATO were calling for a new goal of 700,000.

Continued Prosperity

West Germany's economic boom continued after 1955. The economy grew at a rate of over 7 percent annually, until it slowed down in 1961. Production of crude steel rose to over 34 million tons a year (1961). Unemployment disappeared completely, and by 1962 over half a million foreign workers, mostly from Italy, Spain, and Greece, were employed in the Federal Republic. The European Common Market proved eminently successful in further stimulating the growth of German trade and industry, although not until 1962 was a tentative solution found to the problem of reducing agricultural tariffs among the six members. France and Holland, in particular, favored freer trade in order to export their agricultural surpluses, while Germany and Italy, with high costs of agricultural production, preferred to keep high tariffs on farm produce.

Germany's high rate of industrial production further increased its favorable balance of trade. By 1962, German exports were valued at 13.7 billion dollars, and imports at 12.4 billion. Consequently, Germany's gold and foreign reserve holdings stood at 6.3 billion dollars at the beginning of 1963. The value of the German mark became so high that in 1961 Bonn gave in to pressure from the western powers to aid the general balance of payments problems by revaluing its currency upward by 5 percent. Germany also increased its share of carrying the financial burdens of the western world, although not to the degree hoped for by the Allies. In 1953, at the London Debt Conference, the Bonn government had already agreed to pay 3.2 billion dollars over a period of thirty-

five years for all prewar debts to the western powers. To help slow down the gold drain on the United States, Germany began in 1961 to repay its debts to the United States and Great Britain at an accelerated rate, and increased its foreign aid to underdeveloped countries to 1 billion dollars a year. Bonn also contributed to the Common Market Fund for aiding France's former overseas territories, joined the newly created Organization for Economic Cooperation and Development (OECD), and extended direct credits to nations in Africa and Asia.

Germany's industrial growth proceeded under the aegis of Ludwig Erhard's Social Market Economy. Economic controls were kept to a minimum, and social security programs vastly extended. But no measures were taken, as initially contemplated, to prevent the reconstitution of cartels. The decartelization of Krupp was constantly postponed, even though Chancellor Adenauer asserted in 1958 that "there is a great future danger that a handful of economic structures will control the German economy to such a degree that the government will be forced to take drastic steps against them." By 1962, the Krupp industries had become Europe's largest steel producer, with a yearly turnover of 1 billion dollars and branches operating on every continent of the world.

As part of its program supporting private enterprise, the Bonn government attempted to decrease the government's role in business by "privatizing" (denationalizing) parts of the huge industrial empire (worth almost 2 billion dollars) it had inherited from the Nazis. Grouped together in three large holding companies, the gov-

ernment's interests in steel, coal, aluminum, zinc, lead, oil, shipbuilding, automobile construction, and other enterprises made it in some fields the largest single producer in Germany (for example, it controlled 72 percent of the total aluminum output, 42 percent of automobile production). But almost ten years passed before an acceptable method was devised for selling government enterprises without upsetting the economy and without allowing private corporations to increase to monopolistic proportions by buying up the government's shares. Erhard's program of privatization encountered strong opposition. Although the SPD had abandoned its demands for nationalization, the Socialists saw no reason for the government's divesting itself of basic industries it already owned. Moreover, the federal minister of finance opposed the scheme assiduously, partly because the federal government would lose badly needed revenue, since the increased taxes paid by private business would largely accrue to the states rather than to the central government.

In late 1958, a compromise on privatization was achieved. By selling shares in government-owned concerns only to people of limited income, the CDU could claim to promote "people's capitalism." In March 1959, an initial bloc of 300,000 shares of the Preussag coal and oil combine, each with a nominal value of 100 marks, was offered to the public. Only Germans with an annual income of less than the equivalent of 4000 dollars were permitted to purchase the stocks, with a maximum of 5 shares per person. Sold at 145 marks each, the shares soared to 237 within five months, although they subsequently declined to a more real-

istic level. After this successful experiment, which according to some critics, encouraged stock market speculation among the normally staid German middle class, the government turned to denationalizing the highly profitable Volkswagen Works. Two years of litigation were required to determine whether this enterprise, originally founded by Goering and the Nazi Labor Front, legally belonged to the state of Lower Saxony, whose legislature opposed privatization, or to the federal government. Also to be determined was whether compensation should be made to those Germans who had paid the Nazis for a Volkswagen on the strength of Goering's promises but had never received one. The courts eventually decided that the federal government was the legal owner of the enterprise, and that those who had paid for a Volkswagen before World War II should be permitted to purchase one at a considerable discount. In March 1961, shares were finally sold to small investors with limitations similar to those applied to the Preussag shares.

In the early 1960s, the German economy faced new problems. Even with 34 percent of the gross national product devoted to taxes—probably the highest percentage in the world—the federal budget was no longer balanced in 1962, and a deficit of 750 million dollars was forecast for 1963. In addition to disbursements for social services, assistance to agriculture and industry, there were extraordinary expenditures for restitution—including 822 million dollars to Israel for Jewish claims against Germany—for refugees and expellees, subsidies to West Berlin, occupation costs, and pensions to veterans. Above all, there was the question of financing

the constantly rising defense budget, estimated at 4.6 billion dollars for 1963 (about 7 percent of the gross national product) out of a total federal budget of 15 billion dollars. In spite of the fact that West Germany is the richest country in western Europe, the federal government is constantly in financial straits because of the federalism embedded in the Basic Law. Its revenue is limited to customs duties, taxes on consumption (except beer), turnover taxes, and the special Equalization of Burdens Fund. The state governments, on the other hand, collect the profitable income and corporation taxes; the municipalities have their own local revenue. Since the receipts of the federal government do not suffice to pay for normal expenditures as well as for defense, annual agreements are negotiated between Bonn and the state governments concerning the share of state revenues to be turned over to the federal government. Since they involve the question of federal and states' rights, these negotiations engender constant political controversy.

The 1960s brought added economic problems. The trade-unions, which had scaled down their demands for years, now pressed for higher wages. A perceptible inflation set in, and economic growth slowed down. The gross national product, which stood at 67.7 billion dollars in 1960, was projected at about 100 billion dollars for 1970, indicating that the yearly rate of expansion had decreased to about 4 percent. At the same time, the growth of population was expected to slow down to an annual average of 0.8 percent, so that the Federal Republic was expected to reach about 57.6 million inhabitants by 1970.

Remnants of the Past

A 1959 cartoon in a Hamburg paper (*Die Welt*) depicted a set of volumes on German history on a shelf in a typical, comfortable German household. The collection showed a conspicuous gap for the years 1933 to 1945, the period of the Third Reich. The cartoon attacked the smug insouciance with which large segments of Germans view the Hitler years, an attitude greatly disturbing to many foreign observers and to some Germans as well. Prosperity and material comforts seem to have brought self-assurance, and a few billion marks of restitution have laid many troubled consciences to rest.

During the first decade after the war, the majority of the Germans buried the Hitler years in a deep silence. The history of 1933 to 1945 was not taught in the schools. Few Germans would have known how to teach it dispassionately, and few parents felt inclined to discuss it with their children. Those still believing in National Socialist dogma thought it unwise to admit the fact publicly. Those recognizing their folly hesitated to confess to their children that they had participated in it.

In the late 1950s, brushing the Nazi era under the carpet gave way to a serious campaign of instructing the youth in the history of the Third Reich. With official support from the federal Ministry of the Interior and the state Ministries of Culture, high school and university courses offered undiluted analyses of Nazi excesses. German films, books, radio, television, and editorials presented frank portrayals of the Nazi terror. The Germans were being asked to live with their past.

Even this concerted campaign hardly modified the attitude of the bulk of the population. The blame for whatever had happened and whatever new horrors were discovered in the course of continued war crimes trials was always placed on others. Convinced neo-Nazis clung to the conviction that Hitler himself did not know of the atrocities committed by a "few" demented underlings. This persistent self-exoneration by most Germans often led many observers to decry the "unreconstructed mentality" of the Germans and to assert that German democracy today is skin-deep and fragile and may all too easily give way to a revival of Nazism.

Although it is unquestionably true that Nazi prejudices and concepts persist in certain segments of German thought, it should also be realized that an entire population can hardly be expected to wear sackcloth indefinitely.

WAR CRIMES TRIALS AND DENAZIFICATION /After gaining sovereignty in 1955, the West Germans assumed complete control over all denazification measures and war crimes prosecutions, except where cases involved foreign nationals./ Since jurisdiction over anti-Nazi legislation, trials, and amnesties resided in the state governments, there were widespread differences in the zeal with which former Nazis were found and brought to trial. In 1958, a Central Office for Nazi Crimes was set up in Ludwigsburg, largely in answer to complaints by foreigners as well as by Germans that some state governments were lax in ferreting out war crimes suspects who were hiding behind pseudonyms or in the obscurity of German villages. The new agency gathered evi-

dence on Nazi criminals and coordinated the prosecution efforts of the various state governments. As a result, countless new clues were unearthed and many new suspects discovered. Supplied with documents by the Central Office, the local courts redoubled their efforts to try hundreds of concentration camp commandants, gas chamber operators, SS guards, and employers of slave labor. By 1962, the number of such trials had swollen to over 13,000, resulting in some 5000 convictions. The gruesome details revealed in these trials, which will continue until the statute of limitations becomes effective in 1979, were accurately reported in German newspapers and avidly read for their sensational value, just as the trial of Adolf Eichmann in 1961–1962 in Israel received ample coverage in the German press.

Denazification as such is today a matter of the past. In all the states of West Germany, Nazis who were removed from their jobs because of membership in certain Nazi organizations—except those in category "A," major offenders—became re-employable after January 1, 1960, in accordance with the Third Law on the Termination of Denazification. Many had found employment long before in industry and commerce. Even some members of the state and federal governments were former Nazi party members—a fact frequently denounced by their political opponents in West Germany and by the Communist press in the East. The official attitude on the employment of former Nazis was succinctly stated by Gerhard Schroeder (1911–   )—himself a nominal member of the NSDAP from 1933 to 1941—who served as federal minister of the interior before

becoming foreign minister in 1961. Schroeder asserted that "there will be no second denazification" and that he saw no reason for not allowing "reformed" Nazis to serve the government, provided they had discarded their Nazi sentiments.

NEO-NAZIS Despite denazification, war crimes trials, and "re-education," there were individuals and organized groups who continued to embrace aspects of Nazi ideology. The small but active "Ludendorff movement," organized around a right-wing circle that included the general's widow, Mathilde Ludendorff, trumpeted its virulently anti-Semitic and anti-Christian "pure German" program until it was legally banned in May 1961. Small, rightist student organizations, such as the *Bund Nationaler Studenten* (League of National Students) and the *Nationale Jugend Deutschland* (National Youth of Germany), worshiped Nazi symbols and uniforms as well as Hitler's *Mein Kampf* while awaiting the dawning of a Fourth Reich.

The *Deutsche Reichspartei* (DRP), successor to the outlawed Social Reich party, became a major rallying point for ex-Nazis and young people who felt drawn to ultranationalism. Like the NSDAP, the DRP derided "American and French concepts of democracy and economy," republicanism, freedom of the press, and big business. It opposed NATO, the presence of "foreign soldiers on German soil," and European integration, was stanchly anti-Semitic, and championed "the great German future." In December 1959, the DRP became involved in anti-Semitic vandalism when two members of its Cologne branch were arrested for desecrating Cologne's new synagogue by painting

swastikas and anti-Jewish slogans on its walls. For several weeks, a veritable rash of swastika-smearing and anti-Semitic incitements spread across Germany. Nazi symbols and slogans such as "Down with the Jews!" "Jews Get Out!" "Germany Awake!" and "Heil Hitler!" were daubed on Jewish homes, Catholic churches, and public buildings. A few of the apprehended vandals were members of student organizations typified by the *Bund Nationaler Studenten;* most were in their mid-twenties, and therefore had been about ten years old when Hitler died. Hence their anti-Semitism must have come from secondhand sources.

The anti-Semitic acts raised loud stirs of protest in Germany and in the forum of world opinion. Socialists and liberals held mass rallies; political and religious leaders, as well as journalists, denounced the incidents; Adenauer suggested that the hooligans receive a hiding on the spot, and his cabinet again considered promulgating special laws to deal with emergencies that might threaten the democratic order. Although these sporadic anti-Jewish outbreaks revealed a surprising residue of anti-Semitism in West Germany, which counts a Jewish population of only about thirty thousand, they shed little light on the remaining strength of Nazism: during the same months, similar swastika-daubings occured in Paris, London, New York, and other western cities.

Besides the DRP and the student organizations, there are other remnants of National Socialism and other neo-Nazi movements. The Association of the Victims of Denazification (VEB), with some 40,000 members, has been outlawed by the Ministry of the Interior on the national level, but is active in each state. Its aim is to obtain restitution and rehabilitation for those who suffered injustice from the denazification procedures, to expose atrocities committed during the period 1945 to 1947 by Allied and German guards in internment camps for Nazis, and to fight Communism with the skill and techniques acquired during their active participation in the National Socialist movement. Members of the VEB stress their political moderation, but their reverence for Hitler and his prophetic genius seems undiminished, and they assert that the horrors in the extermination camps were committed by a few criminals. A clique of unscrupulous Nazis, they believe, kept Hitler in the dark until almost the end of the war. Punishment, they insist, should have been reserved for those *few* who had actually committed atrocities, but not randomly inflicted on thousands of innocent party members "who had faithfully served an official political party which supported a state that was diplomatically recognized by all civilized nations of the world."

Some right-wing extremists, cognizant of the difficulty of reviving National Socialism, have seized upon the trend toward European integration as a vehicle for a new nationalistic supranationalism. The New European Movement (NEO), for example, established in Zurich in 1951 with strong German participation, would create a well-armed "Nation Europe" of some 300 million people, dominated by a racially oriented, dictatorially ruled Germany, and pitted in battle against "Bolshevist mongrels and capitalist Negroes"—its designation for east and west. Another group, the European Social Movement, also established in 1951, collaborated with neo-Fascists in various European

capitals, particularly with the Italian Movimento Soziale Italiano (MIS). Otto Strasser, whose brother was assassinated in the June purge of 1934, founded the Social Movement in 1956, followed in 1957 by the Social Organic Order Movement (SORBE), both dedicated to recasting Europe on an authoritarian basis under the rule of a racial elite.

Finally, in 1962, dissatisfaction with existing political parties produced the resurrection of another remnant of the past. In Kassel, a small group of conservatives re-established the DNVP, the Nationalist party of Hugenberg that had helped topple the Weimar regime and had pushed Hitler into power in 1933. Although the party's founders stressed their allegiance to the democratic system of Bonn and set as their aim the reunification of Germany through Russian-American cooperation, the choice of the party label "DNVP" evoked concern among some observers.

Chancellor Democracy

Despite these remnants of the past and despite the gloomy predictions of some observers who almost by habit refuse to concede that Germans can be "re-educated," democracy has taken firm roots in West Germany in the years elapsed since the fall of Hitler. Extremism remains discredited and, unlike the Weimar period, even the thorniest problems—reunification and acceptance of the Oder-Neisse line—rarely stir unreasonable political passions. At the local level, individual political action has again acquired meaning, and civil rights on the whole are respected.

But at the level of national politics and party life, and especially in the functioning of the legislature and of the executive, West German parliamentary democracy has developed its own peculiar characteristics. Just as Bismarck fashioned institutions and a political atmosphere suitable to his personal modes of action, so Konrad Adenauer in the course of his fourteen years in office molded the Bonn government to fit his own somewhat authoritarian temper. In this the chancellor was aided by the rather flabby submissiveness of most Bonn parliamentarians and politicians, and by the traditional party structure that reserves most power to a few professional leaders.

ELECTIONS The 1957 federal elections revealed popular satisfaction with Adenauer's regime, particularly with Germany's economic progress. The CDU/CSU group made considerable gains, obtaining 50.3 percent of the votes and 54.3 percent of the Bundestag seats (270). Although assured of a majority for the CDU/CSU, Adenauer formed a coalition cabinet with the DP (17 seats), so as to obtain a better voting margin over the SPD, which gained an additional 1.5 million votes over 1953 and received 169 seats in the Bundestag. The only other party earning representation in Bonn, the FDP with its 41 seats, stayed out of the government, although it frequently supported Adenauer's legislative program. After the new Bundestag convened, Adenauer was elected for his third term as chancellor by a vote of 274 to 193.

During the next few years, the trend toward a two-party system remained evident in the state elections. The CDU and SPD continued to grow at the expense of the smaller parties. By 1959 CDU/CSU held a total of 570 seats in all eleven state legislatures as against 564 for the SPD, out of a grand total

of 1345 seats. The Free Democrats (FDP) ran a poor third with 105 seats, with the remaining 106 shared by the other small parties. Despite the continued success of the CDU at the national level, the SPD added to its local strength. By 1959, it controlled five state governments (Hamburg, Lower Saxony, Bremen, Hesse, and West Berlin), and in subsequent Landtag elections in 1960 and 1962, it further increased its representation, particularly in North Rhine–Westphalia and Baden-Württemberg. In 1963, it scored a landslide victory of 62 percent in the West Berlin elections.

The CDU suffered its first major crisis in 1959. The electorate at large was grateful to their eighty-three-year-old chancellor, who was credited with gaining for West Germany the respect and prowess of a sovereign nation. But many felt that after ten years of rule, *der Alte* (the Old One) should gracefully retire to his rose garden on the banks of the Rhine and entrust the reins of government to a younger, more flexible candidate. Favored for such a post was Ludwig Erhard, popularly identified with Germany's prosperity. Moreover, Bonn parliamentarians and bureaucrats, and even members of the cabinet, chafed increasingly under the authoritarian and sometimes tactless manner in which the chancellor conducted the affairs of government. Adenauer handled foreign relations as though they were private matters, often refused to reveal negotiations to members of his own cabinet and party, frequently did not deign to answer criticism by the opposition, and did not permit cabinet members to make public statements without his approval.

Since Theodor Heuss's second term ended in July 1959 and he was not constitutionally re-eligible, some thought that Adenauer should be rewarded with the largely honorary post of president so that a new chancellor could be elected. In April, Adenauer agreed with the suggestion. He accepted his party's nomination as candidate for the presidency, and his election seemed assured. There remained the problem of finding a successor for the chancellorship from among the ranks of the CDU. The defects of "chancellor democracy" became at once apparent. Adenauer's one-man government had seemingly discouraged the development of suitable successors. Foreign Minister Brentano, sometimes considered the "heir apparent," was not favored by the leading circles in the CDU. Economics Minister Erhard seemed the more likely choice, although Adenauer distrusted his judgment in foreign affairs. But in June, while Erhard was on an official trip to Washington, Adenauer stunned Bonn by suddenly withdrawing his name as a presidential candidate. As official reason he indicated that the Berlin crisis, the Geneva Conference of Foreign Ministers, and other pressing foreign problems would make it unwise to change the leadership of the state. To his CDU colleagues he wrote: "I cannot, therefore, assume the responsibility of leaving my post during so critical a time."

It was symptomatic that the startled leaders of his own party grumblingly submitted to this decision. Although privately deploring their impotence, they continued to recognize the value of his leadership and his appeal with the voters at large. Consequently Adenauer remained chancellor. In July, the Electoral Assembly held its presidential election in Berlin—a symbolic gesture to underline the unity of West Berlin with West Germany. The CDU

candidate was Heinrich Luebke (1894–   ), a former member of the Center party who had served Adenauer as minister of food and agriculture. In opposition, the Socialists supported Carlo Schmid (1896–   ), a long-time leader of the SPD and vice-president of the Bundestag; the FDP put up its own candidate (Max Becker). As expected, Luebke was elected second president of the Federal Republic— although he obtained only six more votes than the minimum required on the second ballot.

The chancellor's about-face evoked considerable criticism in the press and grumbling among the deputies. Eugen Gerstenmaier (1906–   ), the CDU president of the Bundestag, urged his colleagues to cease being "yes men" and to assert their parliamentary privileges. But most CDU deputies stifled their displeasure in view of the 1961 elections and Adenauer's proved attraction with the voters.

The 1961 elections were fought under the shadow of the new crisis provoked by the erection of the Berlin Wall. Although the German and Refugee parties merged in a vain attempt to regain national stature, the electoral campaign was waged essentially by three parties. Adenauer vaunted his past achievements and his seeming indispensability. Having discarded most Marxist slogans in order to appeal to the middle class, the Socialists counted on the dynamic and popular Willy Brandt to sweep the electorate. Most remarkable was the active campaign of Erich Mende's FDP, which urged the voters to put an end to the "sole dominance of the CDU/CSU with its concomitant dangers of overweening pride and misuse of power." The FDP vowed not to enter a coalition with the SPD, which it accused

of desiring "the nationalization of man instead of the humanization of the state," and based its campaign on the theory that a two-party system was not proper "for German conditions in view of the ideological character of the two major parties." The FDP hoped to emulate the success of the Liberal party in England as a third force between Labor and Conservatives. It rejected the sectarian preferences of the CDU/CSU and the Socialist dogmas of the SPD, and called for a new approach to foreign problems; but it advanced few specific remedies in its own program. Above all, Erich Mende seemed bent on terminating Adenauer's rule.

The electoral results of September 1961 reflected the disenchantment of some of the voters. The CDU/CSU lost its majority, polling 45.3 percent and 242 seats (188 for CDU and 54 for CSU). The SPD rose to 36.3 percent and 190 seats, while the FDP, with 12.7 percent, obtained 67 seats. During seven weeks of negotiations for a new coalition, the FDP tried to implement its campaign promise of dislodging Adenauer immediately; but in the end, it had to accept the chancellor's statement that he would relinquish his post sometime before the 1965 elections, that he would seek new approaches to the question of reunification, and pursue a more forceful and independent course in foreign policy. After these backstage agreements, which provoked the resignation of Brentano, Adenauer formed his fourth coalition cabinet of 12 CDU, 3 CSU, and 5 FDP members. Thereafter he was elected to his fourth term as chancellor by the narrow margin of 258 to 239 (nays and abstentions). Twenty-six CDU members cast blank ballots to underline their disapproval of Adenauer's infatuation with power, and many delegates of

tentatiously refused to applaud when his re-election was announced. Thus Adenauer remained and "chancellor democracy" survived.

THE END OF THE ADENAUER ERA A freak scandal in late October 1962 provoked a political crisis that revealed the latent discontent with Adenauer's obstinate resistance to retirement. After the publication of a controversial article describing defects in the armed forces as revealed in NATO maneuvers, Rudolph Augstein (1923–   ), the publisher, and four staff members of the news magazine *Der Spiegel* were arrested in the middle of the night on charges of treason. Simultaneously, the writer of the article was apprehended in Spain and summarily returned to Germany. Political leaders, newspapers, and civic organizations decried the method of arrest, and expressed fear that the government was infringing on freedom of the press. *Der Spiegel*, it was noted, specialized in vitriolic attacks on the government; its publisher was a firm supporter of the FDP and a well-known foe of Defense Minister Strauss. The Free Democrats, long bitter about the minor role reserved for them by Adenauer in the coalition cabinet, seized the occasion to vent their discontent. Erich Mende threatened to withdraw his party from the government coalition immediately, on the grounds that the FDP minister of justice (Wolfgang Stammberger) had not been consulted before the arrests were made.

The *Spiegel* affair thus engendered a prolonged government crisis. Adenauer's bland disregard for due process of law when, before any trial had convicted the accused, he publicly accused *Der Spiegel's* publisher of making "money out of committing treason,"

infuriated many parliamentary delegates. Cries of "Gestapo!" were increasingly hurled at government officials. Growing suspicion was raised by the role of Minister Strauss, who initially asserted that he had nothing to do with the affair, but later admitted that he had personally telephoned Madrid to order the arrest of *Der Spiegel's* correspondent.

Strauss blandly contended that attacks on him merely aided the Communist cause by discrediting the German government and the German armed forces. When the Free Democrats clamored for Strauss's dismissal from the cabinet, Adenauer at first refused to drop him because he was a leader of the Christian Socialists and the chancellor feared losing the support of the 54 CSU Bundestag delegates. Erich Mende, however, sought to acquire new power and make his the pivotal party in German politics by forcing the CDU to form a new coalition with the Free Democrats, but without the Christian Socialists. Such a combination would command 255 votes as opposed to a total of 244 for the Socialist party (190) and the Christian Socialists (54). Hence the five FDP ministers resigned on November 19, hinting that the party would be willing to re-enter a coalition with the Christian Democrats "free from problems of personalities"—referring to their hope for Strauss's and Adenauer's retirement.

While the country at large took up the slogan "Franz Joseph and Konrad out," the chancellor found a way of disposing of Strauss without firing him. He persuaded all cabinet members to resign, so that he could form an entirely new cabinet—without Strauss. Although Strauss's position was strengthened on November 25 when his

Christian Socialists were victorious in the Bavarian diet elections, he finally agreed to stay out of the new cabinet, while permitting his party to join the government coalition.

But the crisis was not yet over. There remained the question of Adenauer's own retirement. The FDP and even some CDU members pressed the chancellor to set a terminal date for his tenure in office. Moreover, the chancellor now became determined to use the crisis in order to limit the power and "partisan tactics" of the FDP. In a sudden and unexpected move to destroy the Free Democrats, he opened coalition talks with his traditional opponents, the Socialists. As a primary condition, he asked for their agreement to amend the electoral law so as further to disenfranchise the smaller parties—in other words, the Free Democrats. Surprisingly, the SPD showed a willingness to enter a coalition, provided Adenauer would promise to step down in the foreseeable future, but they were unwilling to consent to changes in the electoral law.

Hence Adenauer reopened negotiations with the FDP and regretfully gave in to that party's demand for setting a date for his retirement. On December 7, he announced that he would step down in the fall of 1963. Four days later, the seven-week crisis ended with the formation of a new coalition cabinet, including 11 Christian Democrats, 4 Christian Socialists, and 5 Free Democrats. Erhard and Schroeder retained their posts, and a newcomer to Bonn, Kai-Uwe von Hassel (1913–   ) of the CDU, received the Ministry of Defense vacated by Strauss. But Adenauer's authoritarianism had not been chastened: instead of being personally told by the chancellor, some former cabinet ministers heard through the press or through secretaries that they were not being reappointed.

The prolonged crisis had proved the resilience of "chancellor democracy" and the boundless tenacity of *der Alte*. But there was widespread criticism of the chancellor in the press and in the Bundestag, although some representatives still hesitated to be iconoclasts. Adenauer's regime, at any rate, had suffered a serious loss of prestige, and the new cabinet was at best a shaky stopgap. The FDP distrusted the chancellor who had tried his best to ruin it through electoral reform and Adenauer looked askance at the FDP for its efforts to unseat him. Above all, Adenauer persistently refused to name an heir, perhaps in fear of becoming a lame-duck ruler. Ludwig Erhard was still a likely successor and was also acceptable to the FDP. But despite his occasional temptation to rebel, he was a spiritless rival who meekly suffered Adenauer's continued efforts to embarrass him. And there were other contenders, around whom political cliques were forming, sowing dissension among the CDU: Brentano, Schroeder, Hassel, and others. Finally in the late spring of 1963, the party leaders of the CDU, notwithstanding Adenauer's misgivings, agreed to name Erhard as chancellor-designate, and in October Adenauer turned over the reins of government to Erhard.

Konrad Adenauer unquestionably had performed an immense service to Germany by re-creating economic and political stability, bridging the enmity with France, and making West Germany one of the major powers in the world. But like Bismarck, he had clung to power beyond his appointed time.

The Post-Adenauer Years, 1963–1970

THE FEDERAL REPUBLIC

The Adenauer era (1949–1963) had been a period of construction and reconstruction. *Der Alte* had helped raise West Germany from ashes to prosperity and stability; he had engineered the integration of his state into Western Europe, and turned West Germany into a responsible member of the world community. By the early sixties, it was evident that the Federal Republic, which in 1949 had looked like a temporary creation, had become permanent. The Basic Law had outlasted the Weimar Constitution. It remains to be seen whether Adenauer's authoritarian view of chancellor democracy inflicted long term impairment on the body politic of the infant republic, or whether it was a necessary, temporary device during the period of German rehabilitation. Perhaps the chancellorship of Willy Brandt will provide an answer.

The Political Arena

The years after Adenauer's resignation in October 1963 saw a general increase in flexibility in foreign as well as domestic policies. Despite greater intra-party quarrels among political leaders, there occurred a pragmatic *rapprochement* in the platforms of the two major parties and a further movement toward the development of a two-party system. At the same time it became increasingly evident that extremist political views of the Right or the Left have little appeal to the bulk of the German electorate—perhaps even less so than in the United States where George Wallace polled 13.5% of the votes in the 1968 presidential campaign. The NDP and minor right-wing splinter parties together obtained barely five percent in the 1969 federal elections in West Germany (see p. 387). On the other hand, the sixties also found West Germany in occasional

economic problems and witnessed a growing disenchantment with the establishment among various groups of students, workers, and intellectuals.

THE ERHARD INTERLUDE October 1963 inaugurated a three-year rule by the sixty-six-year-old former minister of economics, Ludwig Erhard, who had been elected chancellor despite the political machinations of the eighty-seven-year-old Adenauer, who publicly called his successor unqualified for the top post in the federal government. Chancellor democracy continued under Erhard, but under the guidance of a less dynamic chancellor. The continuing coalition of CDU/CSU and FDP gave his government a strong majority in the Bundestag, 309 seats as against 190 for the SPD opposition (see Chart 3). Soon it became apparent, however, that Erhard's administration was hampered more by internal feuds, particularly with Adenauer and Strauss, than by opposition from the SPD. Ironically it may well be that Erhard was able to remain in power for three years because Article 67 of the Basic Law required a constructive vote of no confidence (see p. 335) and because the CDU/CSU had lost its majority position in the Bundestag in the 1961 elections and hence did not alone have enough votes to elect a new chancellor.

Erhard was generally supported by Gerhard Schroeder, who remained as minister of foreign affairs and who himself harbored ambitions for attaining the chancellorship. The two agreed on retaining most of the basic policies of the previous regime, while lessening Adenauer's heavy reliance on De Gaulle in order not to alienate Washington and London. Adequate cooperation existed also with the FDP chairman, Erich Mende, who served as vice-chancellor and minister for all-German affairs.

Konrad Adenauer, however, who retained his post as chairman of the CDU, continued to snap at Erhard from the side lines. Moreover, Franz Joseph Strauss, who had been dropped from the cabinet in 1962, made a rapid comeback in political influence and was overwhelmingly reelected chairman of the CSU in 1963. A strong Gaullist, Strauss repeatedly attacked Erhard's foreign policy and the administration's stand on the Nuclear Test Ban Treaty, for he believed with De Gaulle that Western Europe should develop its own nuclear defense, independent of the United States' protective shield.

In addition to attacks from members of his own coalition, Erhard confronted new domestic and foreign problems. The German economy, until then so buoyant, took a downturn with a marked decrease in productive growth and concomitant inflationary pressures (see p. 385). The farmers, normally stanch supporters of the CDU/CSU, were unhappy with a decrease in agricultural prices resulting from the lowering of tariffs within the Common Market. Since Erhard's popularity had been based largely on his reputed economic wizardry that had engendered the economic recovery of the 1950s, these setbacks proved particularly embarrassing to his regime.

Furthermore, Erhard had to face the first repercussions from the Russo-American *détente* which gained momentum after the Cuban missile crisis of 1962. He appeared perplexed as to how to deal with the changed international conditions. Nor was it easy for

Chart 3   COALITIONS AND OPPOSITION PARTIES IN THE BUNDESTAG

Years	Governing Coalition Parties	(seats)	Opposition Parties	(seats)	Total seats in Bundestag *
1949–	CDU/CSU	139	SPD	131	402
	FDP	52	BP	17	
	DP	17	KPD	15	
	Total	208	WAV	12	
			ZP	10	
			DRP	5	
			SSW	1	
			Total	191 + 3 independents	
1953–	CDU/CSU	243	SPD	151	487
	FDP	48	Total	151 + 3 independents	
	GB/BHE	27			
	DP	15			
	Total	333			
1957–	CDU/CSU	270	SPD	169	497
	DP	17	FDP	41	
	Total	287	Total	210	
1961–	CDU/CSU	242	SPD	190	499
	FDP	67			
	Total	309			
1965–	CDU/CSU	245	SPD	202	496
	FDP	49			
	Total	294			
1966 Dec.–	CDU/CSU	245	FDP	49	496
	SPD	202			
	Total	447			
1969	SPD	224	CDU/CSU	242	496
	FDP	30			
	Total	254			

* Not including the nonvoting members from West Berlin. Note that the total number of members has changed from election to election.

EXPLANATION OF PARTY SYMBOLS:

BP Bavarian Party—**CDU/CSU** Christian Democratic Union/Christian-Social Union—**DP** German Party—**DRP** German Rightist Party—**FDP** Free Democratic Party—**GB/BHE** Refugee Party—**KPD** Communist Party—**SPD** Social Democratic Party—**SSW** South Schleswig Voters' Association—**WAV** Economic Reconstruction Party—**ZP** Center Party

him to maneuver between De Gaulle and President Johnson. The former was at the time redoubling his stand against NATO and was further developing his own *force de frappe*. Johnson, on the other hand, was pressing for a multilateral atomic defense force (see p. 385).

Despite these difficulties, Erhard's CDU faced the 1965 federal elections with relative confidence, notwithstanding apparent increases in the strength of the opposition SPD. The Bundestag elections of September 1965 indeed resulted in a slight gain for the CDU/CSU combination, a somewhat larger gain for the SPD, and a loss for the FDP (see Chart 3). They also proved once again that the smaller splinter parties seemed to have no chance of gaining federal representation. Despite Erhard's respectable electoral success, more than a month of political maneuvering ensued during which Adenauer and Strauss attempted to oust Erhard even at the expense of forming a coalition with the SPD. In the end, Erhard was successful in forming another coalition with Mende's FDP. Again Schroeder retained the important Ministry of Foreign Affairs.

A year later, however, the Erhard interlude—and with it to some extent chancellor democracy—came to an end. During 1966, Land elections showed Erhard slipping in popularity, while the SPD gained further support. The latter's "chameleonlike" transformation, as Adenauer once characterized it, from "a Marxist-Leninist party into a bourgeois party," continually helped it acquire more confidence among the lower middle class. Moreover, the FDP's left wing was growing stronger, and many voters were demanding a more dynamic foreign and domestic policy. In October 1966, the FDP members of

Erhard's coalition cabinet resigned. They protested against a proposed increase in taxes to pay for American arms and favored a reduced budget. The resultant government crisis infused a new climate into West German political affairs by bringing the Social Democrats back into the government for the first time in over three decades.

THE GRAND COALITION AND THE SOCIALISTS   The collapse of the Erhard coalition produced a thirty-four-day crisis in the political arena of the Federal Republic. Willy Brandt considered forming a coalition with the FDP which would have given him the chancellorship, but he could not agree with Erich Mende on the same issue of fiscal policy that had broken up the Erhard coalition. Moreover, an SPD/FDP coalition would have assured Brandt of only 251 out of 496 votes in the Bundestag, a dangerously narrow margin. (One might note that two years later, when actually forming such a coalition, Brandt contented himself with an almost equally precarious majority of 254 out of 496. See Chart 3.) The SPD's party theoretician, Herbert Wehner (1906–   ), for his part, urged a coalition with the CDU, notwithstanding the distaste such an alignment would arouse among left-wing Socialists. Meanwhile, Franz Joseph Strauss was promoting the candidacy of Kurt Georg Kiesinger (1904–   ), a former member of the Bundestag and minister-president of the state of Baden-Württemberg. In the eyes of many, however, Kiesinger's earlier affiliation with the Nazi party made him a poor choice, despite his proven vote-getting ability and suave political demeanor.

In the end, a so-called grand coalition of CDU/CSU and SPD was

formed. The partners agreed not to belabor the issue of Kiesinger's Nazi past and concurred in his becoming the Federal Republic's third chancellor, with Willy Brandt as vice chancellor and minister of foreign affairs. Although the SPD was the smaller party, it obtained ten of the nineteen cabinet seats. Strauss returned to the government as minister of finance, Schroeder took over the Department of Defense, Wehner oversaw all-German affairs, and the Socialist Professor Karl Schiller (1911–   ) ran the Ministry of Economics in a manner that greatly helped increase popular trust in the Social Democratic Party.

The two years of the grand coalition saw a significant reappraisal of foreign policy, spearheaded largely by Willy Brandt (see p. 396). The national economy again turned upward, and the German mark resurged to its phenomenal strength. But the voting strength of the grand coalition was so overwhelming—447 as against 49 for the opposition FDP—that there was in fact no opposition in the Bundestag. Genuine leftists felt betrayed by Brandt's "sellout" to the middle class, while ultrarightists deplored the presence of the Socialists in the government. Those unhappy with the government's policies complained of being disenfranchised and formed the *Ausserparlamentarische Opposition* (opposition outside of the Bundestag). Waves of student riots were a part of this phenomenon. Hence, some political analysts concluded that the grand coalition was a bad omen for the survival of German democracy.

Yet, as the 1969 federal elections approached, political realignments began to take shape. The new FDP chairman, Walter Scheel (1919–   ), moved his party decidedly to the Left in hopes of recouping its waning popularity. The ensuing *rapprochement* between the FDP and the SPD became evident when the two parties cooperated during the summer of 1969 to elect Gustav Heinemann (1899–   ) as third president of the Federal Republic, the first Socialist to attain this post since the death of Friedrich Ebert in 1925. Kiesinger, on the other hand, adopted a more conservative stance, partly to garner votes from the highly nationalistic NDP which seemed to be gaining strength (see p. 383). Above all, the SPD, occupying vital posts in foreign affairs, economics, justice, all-German affairs, and transport, proved itself "capable of governing" and thus enhanced its electoral chances.

The election campaign of 1969 was spirited. It included such innovations as a joint, nationwide television appearance of the four party leaders, Kiesinger, Brandt, Strauss, and Scheel, during which they were interviewed by journalists. Vital economic and fiscal issues separated the contesting parties, including the question of upvaluing the mark, augmenting inheritance taxes, increasing labor participation in the management of industry, and arranging for distribution of capital gains among workers—all proposals favored by the SPD. The CDU, pointing to its twenty years of experience as the governing party and the engineer of German prosperity, naturally campaigned in a more conservative vein. "What we have, we know," was one of their slogans. For the first time in an electoral campaign, there was public debate on the question of official recognition of Ulbricht's German Democratic Republic, hitherto a taboo among politicians. The CDU generally persisted in its dis-

approval of extending official recognition to Ulbricht's regime on the grounds that it would permanently cement the division of Germany. The Socialists, for their part, sought a new approach. As foreign minister in the grand coalition, Willy Brandt had already initiated a new opening to the East. Hence, the Socialists' platform suggested that Bonn should "take cognizance of the political realities" and cease "to deny the existence of the other part of Germany." The FDP's Walter Scheel, finally, actually advocated the recognition of the German Democratic Republic as a sovereign state within some larger concept of a German nation.

The results of the September 1969 elections, in which eighty-seven percent of the qualified voters participated, may prove to be a turning point in the Republic's twenty-year history (see Chart 3). The Socialists polled slightly over a million fewer votes than the CDU/CSU, which still remained the largest party. But the FDP lost significantly and the right-wing NDP failed to gain representation in the Bundestag. In coalition with Scheel's FDP, Willy Brandt was made chancellor, and the Christian Democrats, for the first time in the history of the Federal Republic, found themselves occupying the benches of the opposition.

The jovial new chancellor and his ebullient foreign minister, Walter Scheel, together with Schiller as minister of economics and the rest of Brandt's eager team, promptly sought to set a more relaxed and less staid tone in Bonn. They immediately upvalued the mark and initiated diplomatic moves to test the feasibility of Brandt's *Ostpolitik* (see p. 396). The new government began a house cleaning in the ranks of the army and foreign service, and announced its intentions in regards to social, economic, and educational reforms. Because of its partnership with the FDP, however, it seems unlikely that the Brandt administration can sponsor the much-discussed electoral reforms to eliminate the smaller parties in favor of a two-party system, so as to obviate the need for coalition governments.

As of the beginning of 1970, it appears that Brandt's regime can contribute measurably to greater mobility in European international affairs. Yet, in view of its mildly conservative middle-class stand, it will probably not effect social and economic reforms that differ drastically from the policies of the CDU. Perhaps Germany, like England and America, is finding a path toward middle-of-the-road, capitalistic welfare democracy.

THE RIGHT AND THE LEFT During the early 1930s, the Weimar Republic had disintegrated under the onslaught of extremists from both sides of the political spectrum. During the 1950s, however, as we saw, parties with strong nationalistic or revanchist programs, or those advocating total social reform, had fared poorly. They had either died at the polls or had been outlawed. Despite prognostications by some foreign, in particular American, observers, as well as by some German writers, the 1960s proved equally unsuccessful for the parties of the extreme Left and Right.

Membership in the outlawed Communist party dropped sharply from some sixty thousand to an estimated seven thousand. A 1968 attempt to revive it in Frankfurt has borne little

fruit. Readily available comparisons between the Communist and non-Communist parts of Germany may account for the lack of appeal of outright Communist ideology.

The new Left, not Communist but vociferously anti-establishment, comprises students, workers, intellectuals, and some politico-religious groups. It is spearheaded by the *Sozialistischer Deutscher Studentenbund* (Association of German Socialist Students, or SDS), which split off from the SPD in 1960 when the latter became more bourgeois. It gained momentum during the days of the grand coalition, when it formed the backbone of the *Ausserparlamentarische Opposition*. Wary of manipulation by small interest groups, such as the Axel Springer Press (see p. 388), the new Left echoes Karl Jaspers' distaste for excessive concern with materialistic values and calls for more direct democracy and immediate university reforms. Its unyielding stand against vestiges of authoritarianism, American involvement in Vietnam, and police brutality led to a series of violent demonstrations and riots between 1967 and 1969.

On the Right, many small neo-Nazi groups were disbanded in the early 1960s, such as the "Ludendorff Movement" and the *Bund Nationaler Studenten*. On the other hand, new groups, some anti-Semitic, were constantly being formed but rarely survived long for lack of membership and funds. By the late 1960s, over one hundred miniscule rightist parties and groups were appealing to frustrated nationalists, but few attracted more than several dozen members.

In 1964, a new conservative party was formed at the national level in an effort to gather in one political movement the faltering smaller right-wing parties— DRP, BHE, DP, and others—so that conservatism could finally attain representation in the Bundestag. Originally, this new National Democratic Party (NDP) was led by a triumvirate. Then, in 1968, it passed under the control of a Prussian nobleman, Adolf von Thadden (1921–   ), whose choice of terms such as "treason" and "shame" during party rallies reminded some listeners of Hitler's rhetoric. The NDP found adherents primarily among the following groups: former refugees and expellees, disappointed nationalists among the lower middle class, and frustrated people in the twenty-five to thirty-five age group. Despite the creation of a rival conservative party, the National Political Work Group (ANP), the NDP succeeded particularly in middle-sized towns in attracting protest votes against the grand coalition.

The NDP's 1968 platform was vituperatively nationalistic but not truly neo-Nazi. Von Thadden called for American military and economic withdrawal from Europe, a German pullout from NATO, and an end of German subservience to foreign interests, including termination of reparations to Israel. He suggested that it was time to "fill in the graves" of the Nazi past, allowing Germans once again to be proud of being Germans. It was "treasonous," he argued, to accept the division of Germany as permanent. In connection with the future of Austria and the South Tyrol, he urged his followers to "honor the common blood heritage." Reminiscent of the Nazi slogan "Germany, awake!" von Thadden intoned: "We are the rallying point for a rebirth of the German nation."

Political leaders in Bonn were more worried with the possible blemish on

Germany's reputation abroad than with the actual menace of a chauvinistic revival embodied in the NDP. By 1968, NDP members had been elected to seats in the *Land* parliaments of six states. But electoral results showed that on a national scale von Thadden's rhetorical appeals found relatively little attraction. In the 1969 federal elections, the party gained only 4.3 percent of the popular vote, not enough to be granted representation in the Bundestag. So long as German prosperity continues, the NDP is not likely to gain truly significant influence.

Apprehension over student riots and open clashes between SDS and NDP, combined with a measure of pique against the vestigial occupation rights which gave America, Britain, and France authority to intercept mail and tap wires in the interest of safeguarding the Republic's democratic structure, rekindled interest in a ten-year controversy over a federal bill of emergency powers. Mindful of the abuse of Article 48 of the Weimar Constitution (see p. 200), the SPD in particular hesitated to grant excessive emergency powers to the government. Despite violent protests by the new Left, however, an Emergency Powers Law was enacted by a substantial majority of the Bundestag in the late spring of 1968. It authorized the use of the *Bundeswehr* when disorders threatened the "free democratic order of the Federation or of a Land," and established the framework for an emergency parliament in case the threat of attacks prevented the regular Bundestag from its normal functions. As a result of this legislation, the fate of German democracy was taken out of Allied hands, with only Berlin remaining the ward of the former occupying military powers.

THE BUNDESWEHR   By 1969, the *Bundeswehr* (Federal Defense Forces), including army, navy, and air force, still had only some 460,000 men, less than projected and called for by NATO, which retained supreme control over all German combat forces. Its growth was hampered by fiscal considerations, by a shortage of qualified officers and technicians, and by continued reluctance of the youth to serve in the military. Five percent of German draftees were conscientious objectors, a rate forty times higher than that in the United States. To discourage this antimilitary attitude, the 1969 Bundestag enacted a law requiring some other form of service by those pleading conscientious objection.

The *Bundeswehr* was further plagued by questions of civilian-military relations. In 1966, its commanding general resigned in protest when the Kiesinger government permitted unionization among the rank and file soldiers. At the same time, top ranking officers continued to call for less interference by civil servants in the military establishment. The question of *Innere Führung* (reliance on personal judgment) also remained crucial. It had been a basic issue at the Nuremberg War Crimes Trials and had been heatedly debated in the Bundestag when remilitarization was begun in 1956 (see p. 365). Many officers still feel that an efficient army can only be based on obedience, unclouded by the personal judgment of a subordinate. In 1969, however, the Brandt government demoted the commander in chief of the *Bundeswehr* because of his public criticism of the concept of *Innere Führung*.

Moreover, there were problems of armaments and military alignments. Strauss and Adenauer continued to

press for close military collaboration with France, even after De Gaulle had withdrawn his forces from the North Atlantic Alliance. Erhard and Schroeder, as well as the SPD, preferred to retain close military partnership with the United States, even though it was an expensive undertaking to purchase most weaponry from American manufacturers. Imported equipment could also cause embarrassment. The Germans produced the F–104 Starfighter under American license arrangements; yet, for whatever reason, over one hundred of these planes used by the German airforce had crashed by 1969.

Finally, the question of atomic armaments continued to be debated in wide circles. The Germans were willing to join the Multilateral Force (MLF) proposed by Presidents Kennedy and Johnson. This Polaris-equipped surface fleet, operating under NATO with an international crew, would have extended nuclear participation without nuclear proliferation and given the Germans some partial control over atomic weapons. The project, however, remained a dead letter, and Germany stayed out of the nuclear club. One of Willy Brandt's first acts as chancellor was to arrange for West Germany's adherence to the Nuclear Nonproliferation Treaty negotiated among the Soviet Union, the United States, and Great Britain.

Economic Cycles

West Germany's prosperity and economic prowess which undergirded its political stability generally continued its upward course during the 1960s. Still, weaknesses and problems were revealed that had not been apparent in the 1950s. A slackening of internal

consumer markets threatened to retard economic growth; cyclical labor shortages and an increased influx of foreign capital added to inflationary pressure; the imbalance in exports over imports grew despite stiffening Japanese competition in the world market. In short, the German economy showed unexpectedly that it, too, was vulnerable to recession.

All went reasonably well during the first half of the decade. Although the price index rose by fifteen percent from 1960 to 1965, labor was content since the average wage increased fifty-seven percent. Strikes remained rare and unemployment was practically unknown. One third of German women were employed, and 1.2 million foreign workers were imported for work in Germany. The national budget, however, rose sharply and showed a constant deficit, in part because of the high cost of social services.

Suddenly in 1966 a recession set in. Economic growth ceased and, with a decline in production, the Gross National Product actually decreased. Unemployment, a mere 0.4 percent in 1965, rose to 3.5 percent by early 1967, hundreds of thousands of workers were dismissed from their jobs, and prices rose 4.5 percent. These economic problems in part brought about the downfall of Erhard's cabinet and the formation of the grand coalition (see p. 380).

The imaginative minister of economics in the grand coalition, Karl Schiller, promptly applied Keynesian devices to stimulate the economy and produce what he termed "controlled growth." To effect this, the government was given greater power to regulate the economy. Labor-management cooperation was encouraged to rekindle productivity. Pressure on the German mark was slightly eased by stimulating

imports and discouraging foreign investments. To remedy problems in the coal industry, which was suffering from inefficient technology and the competition of oil and imports from the United States, the closing or merging of marginal coal mines was further encouraged. Between 1957 and 1967, 92 out of 162 coal mines had been closed. Now, coal output was reduced by thirty-one percent in a single year (1966–1967).

By 1968, Schiller's methods had proved successful. Inflation was reduced to one percent a year, productivity per man hour was up seven percent, and growth of the GNP resurged to 6.9 percent (and an estimated nine percent in 1969)—so that in the eight-year period from 1960 to 1968 the GNP almost doubled, from 72 billion dollars to 132 billion a year. By 1969, the German economy was again booming, a factor that undoubtedly affected the outcome of the federal elections in that year.

One of Willy Brandt's Socialist government's first steps was to tackle the currency crisis brought about in part by Germany's vast excess of exports over imports (25 billion dollars over 20.3 billion in 1968). With the British pound and the French franc once again devalued, the leading financial powers were putting increasing pressure on Germany to upvalue the mark, so that the flow of foreign capital into Germany would be slowed down while foreign imports into Germany would be encouraged. The grand coalition in its final days had allowed the German mark to float freely so that it could find its own level on the international monetary market. Shortly after his election as chancellor, Brandt delighted the financial world by officially upvaluing the mark—West Germany's second up-

valuation in the 1960s (see p. 366). At the same time, he assured the Germans that special support would be granted to agricultural and industrial interests that might be hurt by the revaluation.

Brandt's and Schiller's further tasks were outlined in various programs. Productivity per man-hour (an area in which Germany lagged behind France) was to be increased in order to alleviate the perennial labor shortage and permit higher wages without concomitant inflationary price rises. Internal consumption was to be stimulated so that, among others, the pressure to export surplus production would be reduced. Moreover, development aid to other countries might be expanded, although the Federal Republic already extended foreign aid to some ninety-four nations. Agriculture was to be modernized so as to compete more successfully with France within the framework of the Common Market. Finally, having abandoned all doctrinaire calls for the nationalization of industry, the new Socialist government announced its intention of extending the principle of codetermination from the coal and steel industries to other large industrial concerns (see p. 328). With over fifty percent of the Bundestag membership comprised of card-carrying union members, such legislation may indeed be passed during the Brandt regime and assure further cooperation between labor and management.

The Mood of the Young Republic

Despite political stability and the accent on youth—by 1969, thirty-six percent of the German population had been born after the termination of World War II and the average age of

(see p. 366)
(see p. 328)

the Bundestag deputies had dropped from fifty-four to forty-nine—the Germans were still haunted by the Nazi past. This fact could not be obscured by the people's materialistic and hedonistic preoccupations which sardonic observers likened to a series of "waves" engulfing the Germans. In some versions, these "waves" were called *Fresswelle, Autowelle, Wohnungswelle, Reisewelle, Edelfresswelle,* and *Sexwelle* (loosely translated, it means a mania first for basic food, then cars, then housing, travelling, gourmet food, and finally, sex). In fact, legal and moral dilemmas in regard to the Nazi era were constantly reopened through pressure from novelists and dramatists, as well as worry over Germany's reputation. The curiosity of a new generation, the qualms of concerned liberals, together with needling by propagandists from across Ulbricht's barbed border added to this uneasiness.

Official denazification had of course been terminated. Yet, as seen in political and literary debates, doubts persisted whether former Nazis—by party membership or by personal conviction —could ever be considered "rehabilitated" and trusted in public office.

More stormy were the arguments over continuation or cessation of the apprehension and prosecution of persons accused of crimes during the Nazi period. The much-publicized trial and execution of Adolf Eichmann (1906– 1962) in Israel, in 1962, who was convicted of organizing the transportation of Jews to extermination camps, seemed to infuse new vigor into the prosecution of suspected Nazi criminals, prior to the deadline when the statute of limitations would come into force in May 1965, twenty years after Germany's surrender. Yet, as 1965 approached, heated controversy resumed whether suspected perpetrators of crimes in the Hitler era, who had successfully remained in oblivion for two decades, should indeed remain unmolested. According to public opinion polls, a considerable majority of Germans opted against an extension of the statute of limitations. Nonetheless, despite vehement disagreement within the Bundestag and the cabinet, the statute was extended to the end of 1969 and prosecution of people newly indicted for Nazi crimes continued in a series of news-provoking trials.

As 1969 neared, the question of a further extension of the statute of limitations was reopened. The debate became particularly heated in view of the federal electoral campaign, the unfathomed potential of the NDP, and the usual weariness of possible repercussions of public opinion abroad. Aided by a verdict of the West German Supreme Court which upheld a differentiation between major and minor Nazi criminals—the latter were offenders who had acted *without base motives*— a compromise solution was enacted. The statute of limitations for *major* Nazi criminals was extended by a decade to December 31, 1979, but not for *minor* offenders, thus reducing possible future trials by an estimated twenty percent.

Despite the passing of a full generation, the Hitler era continued to evoke repercussions in many facets of German life. The question remained of how to acknowledge the past and how to build a new moral and cultural basis. Education was one area in which this problem had to be solved. Deeply impressed by the *Diary of Anne Frank,* the drama *The Deputy* (by Rolf Hochhuth), and by the revelations produced in continuing war crimes trials, the young became

more willing, even eager, to study the Hitler years than the older, more silent generation. An ever-increasing number of courses dealing with Nazi Germany was offered in German universities, more "civics" classes were introduced in the high schools, and contemporary history, formerly shunned, was added to the curriculum.

At the same time, the trend to liberalize and loosen the educational structure was accented. Instead of being locked into irrevocable tracks—one providing basic terminal education for the bulk of non-professional people, the other offering advanced high school training in preparation for study at the university or at technical schools—more children were given the opportunity for transfer into the advanced tracks as late as the ninth school year. Coupled with prosperity and increasing job-migration, encouraged by the labor shortage, this liberalization of the educational structure may contribute to greater class mobility. Although the individual *Länder* retained control over their educational systems in accordance with the Basic Law, the Permanent Conference of the Ministers for Cultural Affairs and Education (see p. 336) gradually attained more influence and strove to lessen the considerable diversity between the various systems.

It was more difficult to enact fundamental changes in Germany's overcrowded universities, where antiquated teaching methods still discouraged most students. To be sure, most student riots and demonstrations—such as those staged in 1967 in Berlin against a visit by the Shah of Iran, who was denounced as a symbol of paternalistic authoritarianism—contained political overtones. Yet, the riots also stemmed from frustration with an academic structure which still placed more emphasis on the venerability of professorial rank and on pedantic concern with minutiae than on social involvement and contemporary relevance. Student strikes for less autocratic teaching methods erupted even at some technical schools, normally attended by more conservative youths. During the days of the *Ausserparlamentarische Opposition,* the malaise of some university students expressed itself particularly in outbursts against the right-of-center Axel Springer publications, the largest newspaper publishing group in Europe. The patronizing tone of the Springer press, its defense of the *status quo* which "only fools or Utopians would throw . . . overboard," and its attacks on "any kind of political extremism" infuriated the students as much as its quasi-monopolistic control of large segments of the German press. Ninety-one percent of the youth magazines in West Germany, eighty-eight percent of Sunday papers, and eighty-one percent of newsstand papers, besides substantial portions of other journalistic areas, such as program magazines, were controlled by the Springer press.

During the 1960s, the West Germans became increasingly conscious of public opinion with the proliferation of opinion polls. Such polls revealed, for example, that the youth was becoming ever more European in outlook, and less nationalistic; that trust in America was decreasing, whereas reliance on friendship with France, and possibly Russia, was sharply increasing. They also showed considerable political apathy among the older generation. Continuing prosperity, assurance of status abroad, and, to a far lesser extent, the question of reunification, seemed to concern most West Germans

more than the complications of political maneuvers. Some observers concluded that the Federal Republic was indeed constructed on democratic forms, but that many of its citizens still thought it safer to let authority rather than individuals make decisions for the good of the state. The validity of such evaluations is hard to assess. The prominent novelists Günter Grass (1927–   ), Heinrich Böll (1917–   ), and Uwe Johnson (1934–   ), as well as the influential magazine *Der Spiegel* project a skeptical and critical but not pessimistic view of the democratic convictions of Germany.

THE GERMAN DEMOCRATIC REPUBLIC

In the late 1950s, during the era of de-Stalinization and the consequent turbulent readjustments in the Communist states of Eastern Europe, the future of Ulbricht's government seemed at times questionable. The erection of the Berlin Wall and of the death-strip between the two Germanies in 1961 appeared to betray desperation in East Germany's ruling circle. Yet, as it turned out, the construction of the unsightly wall, together with the end of the Cold War in the early 1960s, solidified the rule of the SED and assured more permanence to the German Democratic Republic.

The Economy

The Berlin wall had been erected largely to stem the exodus of skilled manpower from East Germany. Nonetheless, despite wall and barbed wire, another quarter of a million people fled to West Germany between 1961 and 1968, most of them via a third country. The loss was not compensated for by the migration of West Germans to the East or by an excess of births. For one reason or another, the population of the Democratic Republic did not grow. In 1949, 18.3 million people had inhabited the Soviet Zone of Occupation, including East Berlin. By the time the wall was erected in 1961, the population had shrunk to slightly over seventeen million, and in the ensuing seven years, it grew by only an estimated ten thousand. The Federal Republic, on the other hand, with forty-seven million people in 1949, increased to almost fifty-seven million by 1961, and then to over sixty million by 1968.

Despite East Germany's lack of growth in population, its economy made impressive strides. In heavy industry and the production of export items such as chemicals, machinery, and motor vehicles output spurted upward. The New Economic Planning System of 1963, which, despite central planning, allowed some consideration of a market-oriented economy, proved relatively effective. Within the Soviet bloc, East Germany acquired the highest standard of living and rose to second place behind Russia in industrial production. By 1969, in fact, it had become the twelfth greatest economic power in the world in terms of its Gross National Product. Agriculture, however, continued to present problems. Although collectivization was more or less completed, mechanization of farm implements remained slow and production failed to increase.

As in other Soviet bloc countries, the basic necessities of life—food, housing, basic clothing, and medicine—are cheap. Amenities, however, are rare and costly. The rulers have lately per-

mitted more resources to be devoted to the production of consumer goods in order to assuage discontent among the people, but, on the whole, the consumer's demands are still neglected. Unlike in West Germany, a considerable amount of war damage has not yet been repaired, while on the other hand entire new industrial centers with factories and workers' housing have been constructed.

Partly for political reasons, Ulbricht has established long-term economic contracts with the Soviet Union, with which the Democratic Republic exchanges about forty percent of its entire foreign trade. More than the rulers of the other satellite nations, Ulbricht would like to see even greater economic integration of the East bloc, so as to turn it into an Eastern common market. These close economic ties, in particular with the Soviet Union, however, do not leave East German exporters much leeway for finding possibly more profitable markets elsewhere.

The Political Climate

It is obvious by now that Walter Ulbricht's regime is not about to collapse, as some observers had expected in the 1950s. His hard-line, neo-Stalinist leadership, stressing strict Socialist discipline and loyalty to Moscow, may be frustrating to many East Germans, but the system has proved workable for the construction of an economically strong socialist state, albeit attained at the cost of great hardship and sacrifice on the part of the East German people. As in all dictatorships, the future of the system depends to a great extent upon the leader who will succeed Ulbricht (who attained the age of seventy-

six in 1969). Willy Stoph (1914–   ), who became chairman of the Council of Ministers upon the death of Otto Grotewohl in 1964, may not be the heir apparent. But no matter who ultimately assumes Ulbricht's role as first secretary of the Central Committee of the SED and president of the Council of State, it is likely that Stalinist controls will be further relaxed while Socialism will remain as a politico-economic guide and ideal.

Public recognition that the Democratic Republic is a Socialist rather than theoretically a Communist state is clearly enunciated in the new constitution which came into effect in the spring of 1968. The new constitution calls the DDR a "Socialist state of German nationality . . . under leadership of the working class." The existence of different classes is acknowledged in Article 2: "The firm alliance between the working class and the class of co-operative peasants, those belonging to the intelligentsia, and the other classes . . . forms the unchangeable basis for the Socialist structure of society." Unlike in the Soviet Union with its one-party system, the continuing existence of various parties and mass organizations was recognized in the constitution, although these parties remained lumped together in a National Front strictly controlled by the SED.

An unusual feature of this new constitution, which is presumably a long-term document, is its reference to the question of reunification with West Germany. Article 8 stipulates that "the national interests of the DDR call for the establishment and improvement of normal relations as well as collaboration between the two German states on a basis of equal rights," and calls for the reunification of the two Germanies on

a "foundation of democracy and Socialism."

An article in the new constitution guarantees freedom of press, radio, and TV, and officially the People's Chamber is the only legislative body in the DDR. Yet, the leaders of the SED and the Council of State exercise firm control over all public means of expression. Press, radio, and TV abound with stereotyped propaganda damning the "militaristic, revanchist, capitalistic, neo-Nazi" regime in Bonn and extolling the virtues of a Socialist society. Literature and the theater, subsidized by the state, flourish, provided they serve the propagation of Socialist realism and stress communal needs over individual subjectiveness. The essence of Brecht's dramas still exerts considerable influence on contemporary writings, although his plays are no longer frequently performed, perhaps because their semiromantic tinges reveal too much individualism. Despite insistence on conformity with officially proclaimed aesthetics, however, unconventional dramas and novels are still written, but, of course, they are then promptly outlawed because of their bourgeois subjectivism.

The older generation of East Germans apparently appreciates the relative security provided by Ulbricht's Socialism, but many grumble against the restrictive atmosphere of the regime and the inefficient bureaucratization that makes daily life an endless chain of paper applications and stamped permits. Significantly, the new constitution did not grant East Germans the right to strike or to emigrate, and travel abroad is still made difficult even for trusted citizens. A measure of some slight disenchantment may be detected in the fact that 99.95 percent of the votes cast in the 1963 elections were reported to favor

the official list of candidates of the National Front; whereas in 1968, the government admitted that 5.46 percent of those voting on ratification of the new constitution cast a negative ballot.

Greater possible disenchantment was noticeable among the youth, many of whom resented the introduction of military conscription in 1962. The younger generation, especially those living in East Berlin where the neon lights of West Berlin's carefree night life can be seen across the wall, deplore the drabness of Ulbricht's Germany. They are not anti-Socialist, but simply anti-establishment, in this case against Ulbricht's stultifying authoritarian bureaucracy. In 1968, the SED leadership was dismayed when some youths publicly protested against the suppression of Czechoslovakia's program of liberalization, an action in which East Germany played a major role. There was also concern that the young identified themselves increasingly with the new Left in West Germany. The DDR government sought to stem this youthful rebelliousness by imprisoning a few leaders of the movement. It also insisted on more obedience and military discipline in its gigantic youth organization, the Association for Sports and Technical Crafts, so that, true to their oath, its young members would become "courageous, disciplined soldiers of tomorrow, loyal to our socialist fatherland."

At the same time, education was stressed with the vigor typical of many Socialist countries. A large-scale state scholarship program subsidized all those youths who were deemed politically reliable, so that, in theory at least, all qualified children of workers could obtain an advanced education, a measure intended to lessen class distinctions. Technical education was stressed

more than the humanities and social sciences, areas that continued to be strongly colored by Marxist-Leninist indoctrination.

The SED's continuing effort to divert the people's allegiance away from religion—eighty-two percent of East Germany's population belongs nominally at least to the Evangelical faith—bore no striking results. As in many lands, the young showed less interest in organized religion, but the Lutheran Church, despite harassment by the regime, retained a considerable measure of power and influence.

Thus, after twenty years of separate existence, the Democratic Republic and the Federal Republic had each in its own way achieved stability and prosperity on the basis of widely divergent sociopolitical systems. Irrespective of international conditions, which of course affect the chances for reunification, the very stability of the two regimes makes a merger of the two Germanies less and less likely.

THE TWO GERMANIES IN WORLD AFFAIRS

The Berlin crises that had evoked frequent international tension subsided after the ouster of Khrushchev in 1964. Despite occasional minor tension over Berlin, friction between the two Germanies lessened considerably. Both governments were more concerned with carving out a niche for their own states on the international scene and with defining or redefining their relations with other powers in the wake of the diplomatic reshuffling that accompanied the demise of the Cold War and the end of bipolarity. Trade between East and West Germany increased and occasional, almost fraternal, discussions were held. Yet, the decade as a whole brought no significant progress in cooperation between Bonn and Pankow. On the contrary, each became more jealous of guarding its own sovereign status. Perhaps it is symptomatic that in 1964 the two found it possible to field a single "German" team for the Olympic games. By the 1968 games, however, when the International Olympic Committee insisted that a team could only use one national emblem, irreconcilable disputes over the flag under which the contestants would march made even such sportive cooperation impossible, and two separate teams were sent. It remains to be seen whether or not Willy Brandt's new *Ostpolitik* can radically alter relations between the two states.

Reunification and Berlin

"Freedom before unity" had been a CDU slogan during the Adenauer era, signifying that the Bonn government should remain firmly allied with the West and thus acquire a position of strength from which eventual reunification of the Germanies could be negotiated with the Soviet Union. This policy was based in part on the erroneous assumption that the DDR would prove to be more of a liability than an asset to the Kremlin rulers. By the early 1960s, the strategy, which had been supported by the Western Allies, had brought no progress toward unification; on the contrary, it had bolstered the ties between Moscow and Pankow. Still, Bonn's all-German policy under Erhard remained in essentially the same dead-locked position.

By the time the grand coalition took over in 1966, the East-West *détente* was threatening to isolate Bonn. Improved Russo-French and American-Soviet relations reawakened occasional old fears of encirclement. Moreover, it became clear that the *détente* did not depend on a solution of the German question. A relaxation of East-West tension had occurred without prior German reunification. In fact, preoccupied with Vietnam, the Sino-Soviet dispute, and the Arab-Israeli conflict, the powers showed less interest in the German problem. Hence, the Bonn government initiated a cautious reappraisal of its all-German policy, resulting in the conclusion that normalization of relations and *rapprochement* with Eastern Europe were prerequisites for reunification.

With the concurrence of Chancellor Kiesinger, Foreign Minister Willy Brandt gradually developed a new *Ostpolitik* that was at first cautiously and then enthusiastically supported by Washington. This new policy called for increased contacts and cooperation with individual East European states, an endeavor facilitated by the loosening of the Communist bloc. The result, it was hoped, would lead to improved relations with East Germany.

Actually, amity between the two Germanies was much of the time at a low ebb, notwithstanding low-level administrative contacts between the two governments in regard to trade, transport, and other joint concerns. Both sides bombarded one another with propaganda invectives launched across the barbed wire by radio, television, smuggled pamphlets, and secret agents. The special passes for West Berliners to visit relatives in East Berlin on particular holidays, which Ulbricht's government had granted three times between 1961 and 1965, were discontinued. Joint East-West church meetings were prohibited by Pankow and bishops from West Berlin were prevented from visiting their flock in the East. When Bonn suggested an exchange of speakers and other closer contacts with Pankow, the latter rejected such arrangements.

In all this, the fate of Berlin remained a major issue. The wall may have helped the DDR, but it did not ruin West Berlin as Ulbricht probably expected. After an initial exodus from West Berlin by people who saw no future in a walled city, the tide was reversed. With costly subsidies by the Bonn government, West Berlin's industry was expanded, new labor forces were attracted from West Germany, and tourism was encouraged to keep the former metropolis economically viable.

Occasionally, East German authorities in conjunction with Soviet troops harassed the access routes to Berlin to remind the West that the city was an enclave within the territory of the DDR. Such harassment occurred usually in response to symbolic gestures which the Bonn government made to underscore the close union between West Berlin and the Federal Republic. In 1963, for instance, Eugen Gerstenmaier, as president of the Bundestag, and Erich Mende, as vice chancellor, ceremoniously reinaugurated the south wing of the partially reconstructed Reichstag building in Berlin. Thereafter, the building was occasionally used for meetings of Bundestag committees. Pankow and Moscow looked upon such actions as provocative and illegal, insisting that Berlin, which still remained a responsibility of the Allied occupiers, had a separate political status from the Federal Republic. The East German government also protested loudly when the

West Germans used Berlin as the site for holding the Federal Assembly for the election of a new president in 1969. The Western Allies, too, were accused of violating the status of Berlin by permitting the manufacture of war materiel in the city, which was then shipped across East Germany for use by the *Bundeswehr.*

Cooperation between the two Germanies was also hamstrung by the unresolved status of the Oder-Neisse boundary. Erhard and Kiesinger retained Adenauer's insistence that Germany was divided into three and not two parts, and that the future of the "German lands" east of the Oder-Neisse remained unsettled. If possible, they hoped to use the border problem in an eventual bargain with Russia over the question of reunification. As foreign minister, Willy Brandt decided to break with this CDU position and to use the boundary question as an electoral issue in the 1969 federal election campaign. Sensing that a majority of West Germans had at any rate written off the eastern lands, Brandt publicly called for recognition of the Oder-Neisse line as the new Polish-German frontier, without waiting for the conclusion of an official peace treaty. If actually underwritten by the Bonn government, such recognition would add measurably to a further *détente* between Bonn, Pankow, Warsaw, and Moscow.

After Brandt became chancellor, he promptly announced his "wish for closer relations with East Germany," which significantly was no longer referred to as simply the "Soviet Zone of Occupation." Brandt called for an increase in trade, the extension of more credits, cultural exchanges, and an ease on travel restrictions. He made it clear that East German publications could circulate freely in West Germany and hoped for reciprocity on the part of the Ulbricht government. Seeking to open up new contacts at all levels, he initiated a public exchange of letters with Walter Ulbricht. The East German government replied favorably to all proposals, but insisted on prior full and official diplomatic recognition before undertaking any bilateral negotiations for closer contacts. Since Brandt hesitated to make this major concession, which would terminate Bonn's claim to represent "all" Germans, a solution to the reunification problem seems no nearer in early 1970 than it had been during the previous decade. Perhaps the best that can be hoped for during the foreseeable future is close collaboration in all possible areas between two separate but friendly political units within the vague framework of a nonpolitical German nation or within an extended European Community.

Relations with Other Nations

During the 1960s, the Democratic Republic became more and more firmly tied to Soviet policy. Walter Ulbricht ceased his vague flirtations with Communist China (see p. 364), a ploy that had been intended to bring some leverage to East German foreign policy. In fact, the Pankow government joined the Soviet Union in its campaign of denunciation of Mao Tse-tung. In 1964, Ulbricht and Khrushchev concluded a treaty of friendship, a boon to the Pankow government and somewhat of an echo of the Bonn-Paris pact of the preceding year. Still, Russia deferred signing a separate peace treaty with East Germany, a threat it had so frequently hurled at the Western powers during

times of Cold War crises. Such a separate peace, although invalid in the eyes of the West, might have further solidified the status of East Germany among the nations of the nonaligned world.

Using its industrial strength as a lever, the Pankow government sought to gain a preeminent position behind Russia among the states of the Warsaw Pact. Thus, East Germany was at the forefront of those urging military intervention against the liberalizing regime in Czechoslovakia in 1968. Most of the Warsaw Pact nations, however, which were reorienting their foreign policies and were trying to improve relations with the West, looked somewhat askance at the neo-Stalinist regime of Ulbricht and his seeming subservience to Moscow. Perhaps they were oblivious of the fact that some twenty Soviet divisions were still stationed on East German soil.

In the world beyond Europe, the Pankow government sought assiduously to expand its role. Since, among non-Communist nations, only Cambodia and the Republic of the Congo had exchanged official, full diplomatic relations with the DDR by 1970, the latter tried to woo African and Asian states through economic and cultural missions and the expansion of trade. East Germany's role thus acquired some significance abroad, particularly in the Arab world. On the whole, however, its choices in foreign affairs were highly restricted through its close association with the Soviet Union, infinitely more limited than the foreign policy of the Federal Republic.

The foreign policy of the Bonn government changed gradually over the decade, influenced by the growing Russo-American *détente,* by changes in French policy, and, of course, by the internal shift in power from the CDU to the grand coalition and then to the Socialist government of Willy Brandt.

Within the CDU, there was deep division over relations with France, a split which complicated Erhard's work as chancellor. The Gaullists within the CDU/CSU, in particular Adenauer, Strauss, and Gerstenmaier, advocated strict adherence to the Franco-German pact of friendship of 1963 (see p. 360). They supported close alignment with France rather than sole reliance on Washington for the defense of Western Europe. Erhard and Schroeder, on the other hand, preferred to keep the Adenauer-De Gaulle pact in mothballs. De Gaulle's unilateral actions in regard to NATO, his recognition of Communist China, his pro-Arab stance, and other steps made the chancellor reluctant to place too much reliance on Paris. While willing to cooperate with France, Erhard preferred closer partnership with Washington and London, particularly over such questions as the future of NATO, the MLF (see p. 385), and Britain's eventual entry into the Common Market.

The advent of the grand coalition gave further flexibility to Franco-German relations. Although opinion polls showed that among West Germans France had superseded the United States as a trusted friend, the new Bonn government felt at times uneasy over De Gaulle's increasing *rapprochement* with East European nations. After De Gaulle's resignation from the presidency in 1969, Bonn felt freer to pursue its own foreign policy within the framework of a less restrictive, though friendly relationship with France.

Bonn's relations with the United States also changed in the direction of somewhat greater independence. To be

sure, there was continuing cooperation between the two governments within NATO, as well as in economic and financial matters. Ironical as it seems in view of Germany's prostration in 1945, West German financial policy and investments in the United States helped shore up the sagging dollar in the 1950s. Yet, generally speaking, Washington's preoccupation with Vietnam and its tendency to deal bilaterally with the Soviet Union gave Bonn greater opportunity to develop its own new pattern of foreign relations.

Freed from the wardship of Paris and the tutelage of Washington, encouraged by the new post-Cold War climate, and, one might add, liberated from the rigidity of Adenauer's views, Bonn began a new *Ostpolitik*.

During the early 1960s, the opening to the East, supported vigorously by Foreign Minister Schroeder, consisted primarily of increased trade agreements with East bloc states. German trade missions were established in all East European countries except Chinese-dominated Albania and Czechoslovakia, which still harbored suspicions of possible German claims on the Sudetenland (see p. 268). Negotiations of these trade agreements were complicated not only by the absence of diplomatic relations, but also by the status of Berlin. The Communist states were reluctant to include trade items manufactured in West Berlin, a step that might imply, contrary to official Moscow policy, that that portion of the city was an integral part of West Germany. Agreements with Poland were, in addition, confounded by the absence of agreement on the Oder-Neisse frontier. Throughout, however, Bonn made it clear that trade missions did not signal diplomatic recognition and that the Hallstein doctrine of nonrecognition was still in force (see p. 355).

The real change in *Ostpolitik* came with the grand coalition, in December 1966. Chancellor Kiesinger launched the new policy with an official statement renouncing the 1938 Munich Agreement which, according to nationalistic Germans, was theoretically still in effect. Kiesinger sought not only to reassure the Czechs but also to indicate symbolically to East Europe at large that *Ostpolitik* was not a revival of the *Drang nach Osten*. In the following month, Vice-Chancellor Brandt told the Council of Europe: "For centuries, Germany formed a bridge between Western and Eastern Europe. We intend to rebuild that broken bridge." The Federal Republic, he implied, no longer wished to live on the fringes of the West, but sought a firm position between East and West. Hence, the Hallstein doctrine was scrapped and, to the dismay of Walter Ulbricht who feared a lessening of East German influence among the Warsaw Pact nations, the Bonn government established full diplomatic relations with Rumania in 1967 and Yugoslavia in 1968. At the SPD party conference of 1968, Brandt sought to reassure those foreign observers who suspected that the new *Ostpolitik* might signify a "new Rapallo" (see p. 215). According to him, it was not a question of an Eastern *or* a Western policy, since Bonn's *Ostpolitik* needed the backing of the West. Since Washington, too, was embarked on a search for improved relations with the East bloc, President Johnson endorsed the probing steps of the grand coalition.

Upon Brandt's assumption of the chancellorship, the pace of the new *Ostpolitik* was sharply intensified, with primary aim of attaining "closer rela-

tions with East Germany." The Bonn government promptly launched an exchange of letters with East European leaders, suggesting more economic, technical, and cultural exchanges; it offered to discuss the question of European security, including bilateral or multilateral renunciation of force and the possible conclusion of nonaggression pacts. New overtures were made particularly to Warsaw, Prague, and Moscow. A trade agreement was signed with Russia, incorporating the sale of large-scale pipe to the Soviet Union—an item hitherto blacklisted by NATO as being of strategic value. In return, Russia agreed to deliver Siberian gas to southern Germany. A group of German banks extended credit to the Kremlin to finance these transactions.

By the beginning of 1970, it seemed evident that Bonn had seized a measure of diplomatic initiative that was greater than anything experienced since the early days of the Adenauer era, whereas Pankow's stance remained rather rigidly fixed. Ulbricht's Stalinist traditionalism in favor of bloc action appeared to lose out in favor of the more flexible approach offered by Bonn, which was welcomed by the more independent-minded nations of Eastern Europe. The result is likely to further ease residual tensions in Central and Eastern Europe, but is not likely to lead to a solution of the German problem in the foreseeable future. After centuries of "German history," the questions of who belongs within the German state and who should lead it—in other terms, the questions of German unification and boundaries—are still not solved. In this sense, Germany's history is indeed a tragic one.

Glossary of German Terms

Abgeordnetenhaus House of Deputies: lower chamber of Prussian parliament (1850–1918).

Afrika Korps Africa corps: German expeditionary forces in North Africa in World War II.

Alle deutsche Blätter All-German Pamphlets: a publication of the All-German League during the time of William II.

An meine lieben Berliner "To my dear Berliners": an open letter from King Frederick William IV of Prussia (March, 1848).

Anschluss Union of Germany and Austria.

Auslandsdeutsche Germans living abroad.

Ausserparlamentarische Opposition Extraparliamentary opposition.

Bank Deutscher Länder Bank of the German states: West German central bank of issue, created 1948.

Betriebsführer Manager of an industrial enterprise.

Blitzkrieg Lightning warfare: highly coordinated air and mechanized ground attack, carried out with lightning speed.

Bonzen A derogative term, denoting newly enriched and abusively powerful Nazi officials.

Bund der Landwirte League of Landlords: a pressure group of mostly Prussian estate owners, founded in 1893.

Bund Nationaler Studenten League of National Students: a rightist student organization in West Germany after World War II.

Bund Vertriebener Deutscher Union of Expelled Germans.

Bundesrat Federal Council: upper chamber of North German Confederation (1867–1871) and of German Federal Republic (1949–).

Bundestag Federal Diet: lower chamber of German Federal Republic (1949–).

Bundeswehr Federal Defense Forces: the army of the German Federal Republic (1956–).

Burgfrieden Literally, "peace in the castle": tacit truce among political parties during the early months of World War I.

Der Alte "The old one": a designation frequently applied to Adenauer by both admirers and political opponents.

Der Spiegel The Mirror: influential contemporary weekly magazine in West Germany.

Deutsche Bank German Bank.

Deutsche Bauernbund League of German Peasants: an association of smaller peasant proprietors.

Deutsche Mark German Mark, currency used in West Germany (1948–).

Deutsche Reichspartei German Reich party (DRP): right-wing party in West Germany (1950s).

Die Welt The World: a Hamburg newspaper.

Diktat Literally, "dictation": a derogatory reference to the Versailles Treaty of 1919.

Drang nach Osten Drive to the East.

Einkreisungsangst Fear of encirclement.

Einsatzkommandos Special task forces: organized by Germans to clean Eastern Europe of "undesirables" during World War II.

Frankfurter Hefte Frankfort Booklets: West German magazine.

Freisinnige Partei Literally, "freethinking party," that is, Progressive Party.

Freisinnige Vereinigung Progressive Union.

Freisinnige Volkspartei Progressive People's Party.

Friedensheer Peace force or peace army: a term often used by Hitler for his army, prior to outbreak of World War II.

Führer Leader: favorite Nazi designation for Adolf Hitler.

Gau (pl., **Gaue**) Old Germanic term for a district: revived by Nazis to designate subdivisions of Germany under control of a party official.

Gauleiter Leader of a Gau: a Nazi official in charge of a district of Germany.

Gefolgschaft Body of followers: a Nazi term for the immediate entourage of Hitler himself or the subordinates of any important lesser Nazi leader.

Gleichschaltung Coordination: a Nazi term for subordinating all aspects of German public and private life to centralized control.

Grossdeutschland Great or Greater Germany, that is, Germany and Austria together.

Gründerzeit Period of the founders: the initial decades after 1871.

Hansa-Bund Hanse League: a bourgeois association for the defense of commercial and industrial interests, founded in 1909.

Heimatkunst Literally, "regional art": referring mostly to literature depicting regional, nonurban life.

Herrenhaus House of Lords: upper chamber of Prussian parliament (1850–1918).

Innere Führung Inner guidance: the concept that a soldier's conscience may force him to disobey the orders of a superior.

Kaiser Emperor.

Kampfpolitik Aggressive course in politics.

Kleindeutschland Germany without Austria.

Kolonialverein German Colonial Society: founded 1882.

Kraft durch Freude Literally, "strength through joy": a Nazi agency to organize the leisure time of Germans.

Kreuzzeitung The Cross Newspaper: a conservative Prussian newspaper.

Kulturkampf Literally, "battle of cultures": a term applied to Bismarck's struggle with the Catholic Church (1871–1878).

Land (pl., **Länder**) State.

Länderkammer Chamber of States: the upper chamber of the German Democratic Republic (1950–1952).

Landtag Diet.

Landwehr Home guard.

Lebensraum Living space.

Luftwaffe Airforce.

Mein Kampf *My Battle:* Hitler's book containing his plans for Germany.

Nationale Jugend Deutschland National Youth of Germany: neo-Nazi movement in West Germany (1950s).

Nationalverein National Association: a group active in 1860s to unify Germany, forerunner of National Liberal Party.

Neue Rheinische Zeitung New Rhenish Gazette: edited by Karl Marx.

Notgeld Emergency money: issued during the run-away inflation of 1923.

Ohne mich "Without me" or "count me out": a slogan of West Germans who objected to remilitarization in the 1950s.

Ost Mark East Mark: currency used in East Germany (1948–).

Ostpolitik Eastern policy: Germany's foreign policy toward Eastern Europe.

Pfarrerbund Pastors' League: Lutheran organization in German Democratic Republic.

Preussische Wochenblatt Prussian Weekly: a moderate Prussian publication.

Putsch Rebellion, uprising, or attempted *coup d'état.*

Realpolitik Practical, pragmatic politics, backed by strength.

Reich Empire: term used particularly as label for Holy Roman Empire (962–1806), German Empire (1871–1918), and Hitler's Third Reich (1933–1945).

Reichsblock Reich bloc: conservative coalition during 1925 presidential elections.

Reichsfeindlich Hostile to the Reich: Bismarck's label for some of his political opponents.

Reichsfluchtsteuer Literally, "tax on fleeing the Reich": a special Nazi levy on those who wanted to emigrate from Germany.

Reichskulturkammer Reich Chamber of Culture: the organ through which Goebbels controlled communications media and the arts in Nazi Germany.

Reichsland Imperial territory: term used to describe the special status of Alsace-Lorraine within the German Empire (1871–1911).

Reichsmarineamt Imperial Naval Office.

Reichsmark German currency (1924–1948).

Reichspartei Reich party, or Free Conservatives.

Reichsrat Council of the Reich: upper chamber of the German Empire (1871–1918) and of Weimar Republic (1919–1933).

Reichstag Diet of the Reich: lower chamber of German Empire (1871–1918) and of Weimar Republic (1919–1933), and pseudo-legislative body during Hitler period.

Reichswehr Defense Forces of the Reich: regular German Army (1919–1934).

Rentenmark Temporary German currency, backed by real estate, used 1923–1924 to stabilize German financial structure.

Rote Kapelle Red Chapel: Communist underground organization in Nazi Germany.

Schutzstaffel or **SS** Literally, "protective corps": Hitler's black-shirted elite paramilitary organization.

Sozialistischer Deutscher Studentenbund Association of German Socialist Students (SDS).

Sonderrechte Special rights: granted to Bavaria and Württemberg when German Empire was created in 1871.

Staatsministerium Ministry of State.

Staatsrat Council of State.

Stahlhelm Steel Helmet: name of paramilitary and political organization (1918–1935).

Statthalter Governor.

Sturmabteilung or **SA** Storm division or storm troopers, Hitler's brown-shirted private paramilitary organization.

Truppenamt Literally, "troop office": General Staff of German Army during Weimar Republic.

Umsturzparteien Revolutionary parties: Bismarck's term for political parties hostile to his regime, especially those of the Left.

Volk Folk: an ethnic concept of the German people.

Völkischer Beobachter People's Observer: Nazi party newspaper.

Volksbewegung Popular movement: Nazi term often used by Hitler to describe his National Socialist revolutionary movement.

Volksblock People's bloc: moderate coalition during 1925 presidential elections.

Volksgenossen Comrades belonging to the folk, favorite Nazi term for National Socialist-minded citizens.

Volkskammer People's Chamber: lower house of German Democratic Republic.

Volksseele Folk soul.

Volkssturm People's militia organized by Nazis toward end of World War II.

Waffen SS SS army units.

Wandervögel Literally, "Wandering Birds": conservative youth organization in pre-World War I Germany.

Wehrmacht Defense force: regular German army (1934–1945).

Weltanschauung World view: philosophy of life.

Weltpolitik World politics: a foreign policy involving Germany on a worldwide scale.

Weltreich Global empire.

Zollverein Customs union.

Bibliography

PERTINENT BOOKS COVERING MORE THAN ONE TIME PERIOD

Bithell, Jethro, *Modern German Literature 1880–1950* (reprint, 1969).

Chalmers, Douglas A., *The Social Democratic Party of Germany from Working Class Movement to Modern Political Party* (1964, o.p.).

Craig, Gordon A., *From Bismarck to Adenauer: Aspects of German Statecraft* (1958).

Craig, Gordon A., *The Politics of the Prussian Army: 1640–1945* (reprint, 1964).

Dehio, Ludwig, *Germany and World Politics in the Twentieth Century*, tr. by Dieter Pevsner (reprint, 1967).

Demeter, Karl, *The German Officer-Corps; In Society and State, 1650–1945*, tr. by Angus Malcolm (1965).

Elkins, T. H., *Germany: An Introductory Geography* (rev. ed., 1968).

Ernst, Fritz, *The Germans and Their Modern History*, tr. by Charles M. Prugh (1966). Lectures on German problems for the period 1911 to 1961.

Görlitz, Walter, *History of the German General Staff, 1657–1945*, tr. by Brian Battershaw (1953, o.p.)

Iggers, Georg C., *The German Conception of History: The National Tradition of Historical Thought from Herder to the Present* (1968)

Jacob, Herbert, *German Administration since Bismarck: Central Authority Versus Local Autonomy* (1963).

Laqueur, Walter, *Russia and Germany: A Century of Conflict* (1965).

Maehl, William H., *German Militarism and Socialism* (1968). A series of essays.

Muhlen, Norbert, *The Incredible Krupps: The Rise, Fall and Comeback of Germany's Industrial Family* (reprint, 1969).

Rose, Ernst A., *A History of German Literature* (1960).

Snyder, Louis L., ed., *Documents of German History* (1958).

1848–1871

Revolutions of 1848/1849

Bruun, Geoffrey, *Revolution and Reaction, 1848–1852* (1958). A general survey of the 1848 revolutions in Europe with documents.

Note: o.p. = out of print   n.d. = not dated

Engels, Friedrich, *The German Revolutions: The Peasant War in Germany and Germany: Revolution and Counter-Revolution* (1967).

Eyck, Frank, *The Frankfurt Parliament, 1848–1849* (1968).

Hamerow, Theodore S., *Restoration, Revolution, Reaction: Economics and Politics in Germany, 1815–1871* (1958).

Kranzberg, Melvin, ed., *1848: A Turning Point?* (1959). A collection of excerpts, dealing in part with Germany.

Namier, Lewis B., *1848: Revolution of the Intellectuals* (reprint, 1964).

Noyes, P. H., *Organization and Revolution: Working-Class Associations in the German Revolutions of 1848–1849* (1966).

Robertson, Priscilla, *Revolutions of 1848: A Social History* (1952).

Schwarzenberg, Adolph, *Prince Felix zu Schwarzenberg: Prime Minister of Austria, 1848–1852* (reprint, 1969).

Valentin, Veit, *1848: Chapters of German History*, transl. by E. T. Scheffauer (reprint, 1965). A condensed version of a large, two-volume work defending the liberal, middle class view.

Prussia and Social Questions

Anderson, E. N., *The Social and Political Conflict in Prussia, 1858–1864* (1954, o.p.).

Bismarck, Otto von, *The Memoirs, Being the Reflections and Reminiscences of Otto, Prince von Bismarck*, 2 Vols., tr. by A. J. Butler (1966).

Footman, David, *Ferdinand Lassalle, Romantic Revolutionary* (1947, o.p.).

Henderson, William O., *The State and the Industrial Revolution in Prussia, 1740–1870* (1958, o.p.).

Morgan, R. P., *The German Social Democrats and the First International, 1864–1872* (1965).

Reichard, Richard W., *Crippled from Birth: German Social Democracy, 1844–1870* (1969).

Rohr, Donald G., *The Origins of Social Liberalism in Germany* (1963).

The Unification of Germany

Bonnin, Georges, ed., *Bismarck and the Hohenzollern Candidature for the Spanish Throne: The Documents in the German Diplomatic Archives*, tr. by Isabella Massey (1957, o.p.).

Clark, Chester W., *Franz Joseph and Bismarck: The Diplomacy of Austria before the War of 1866* (reprint, 1968).

Darmstaedter, Friedrich, *Bismarck and the Creation of the Second Reich* (reprint, 1965).

Eyck, Erich, *Bismarck and the German Empire* (1964). A translated condensed version of an earlier three-volume work.

Friedjung, Heinrich, *The Struggle for Supremacy in Germany, 1859–1866*, tr. by Taylor and McElwee (reprint, 1966). An Austrian viewpoint of the unification question.

Hamerow, Theodore S., ed., *Otto von Bismarck: Reflections and Reminiscences* (1968). Excerpts from conflicting interpretations.

Henderson, William O., *The Zollverein* (1959, o.p.).

Howard, Michael, *The Franco-Prussian War; the German Invasion of France, 1870–1871* (1969).

Mosse, W. E., *The European Powers and the German Question, 1848–1871* (reprint, 1969).

Pflanze, Otto, *Bismarck and the Devel*

opment of Germany, Vol. I: *The Period of Unification, 1815–1871* (1963).

Pflanze, Otto, ed., *The Unification of Germany, 1848–1871* (1968). Excerpts from critical treatments.

Steefel, Lawrence D., *Bismarck, The Hohenzollern Candidacy and the Origins of the Franco-German War of 1870* (1962).

Sybel, Heinrich von, *The Founding of the German Empire by William I,* 7 Vols., tr. by Marshall L. Perrin (1968). The semi-official Prussian version of the period 1848 to 1870, written in the 1890s.

Windell, George G., *The Catholics and German Unity, 1866–1871* (1954). Mostly about the southern states and the creation of the Center Party.

1871–1890

Domestic Affairs

Barkeley, Richard, *The Empress Frederica, Daughter of Queen Victoria* (1956, o.p.).

Bramsted, Ernest, *Aristocracy and the Middle-Classes in Germany, Social Types in German Literature, 1830–1900* (rev. ed., 1964).

Bry, Gerhard, *Wages in Germany, 1871–1945* (1960, o.p.). General discussion of German Labor policies.

Gerschenkron, Alexander, *Bread and Democracy in Germany* (reprint, n.d.). On tariff policy, 1870–1914, originally published in 1943.

Hollyday, Frederic B. M., *Bismarck's Rival; A Political Biography of General and Admiral Albrecht Von Stosch* (1960).

Lidtke, Vernon L., *The Outlawed Party: Social Democracy in Germany, 1878–1890* (1966).

Medlicott, William N., *Bismarck and Modern Germany* (reprint, 1965). Brief biography.

Pflanze, Otto, *Bismarck and the Development of Germany* Vol. II: *Period of Consolidation, 1871–1890* (n.d.).

Richter, Werner, *Bismarck* (1965).

Simon, Walter Michael, *Germany in the Age of Bismarck* (1968). Mostly documents.

Stolper, Gustav, Häuser, Karl, and Borchardt, Knut, *The German Economy: 1870 to the Present,* tr. by Toni Stolper (1967).

Foreign Affairs

Brandenburg, Erich, *From Bismarck to the World War; A History of German Foreign Policy, 1870–1914,* tr. by Annie E. Adams (1927, o.p.).

Henderson, W. O., *Studies in German Colonial History* (1962, o.p.).

Kent, George O., *Arnim and Bismarck* (1968). Mostly on German relations with France and Italy.

Langer, William L., *European Alliances and Alignments, 1871–1890* (1931).

May, Arthur J., *The Hapsburg Monarchy, 1867–1914* (reprint, 1968).

Sontag, Raymond J., *Germany and England, Background of Conflict, 1848–1894* (reprint, 1969).

Taylor, A. J. P., *Bismarck: The Man and the Statesman* (1967).

Taylor, A. J., *The Struggle for Mastery in Europe, 1848–1918* (1954).

Townsend, Mary E., *The Rise and Fall of Germany's Colonial Empire, 1884–1918* (reprint, n.d.). Originally published in 1930.

1890–1914

Domestic Affairs

Balfour, Michael, *The Kaiser and His Times* (1965). A biographical study centering on William II's family.

Bruck, Werner Frederick, *A Social and Economic History of Germany from William the Second to Hitler, 1888–1938: A Comparative Study* (reprint, 1962).

Bülow, Bernhard, Prince von, *Memoirs of Prince von Bülow,* 4 Vols., tr. by F. A. Voigt (1931–1932).

Cecil, Lamar, *Albert Ballin: Business and Politics in Imperial Germany, 1888–1918* (1967).

Cowles, Virginia S., *The Kaiser* (1963).

Hammer, Simon C., *William the Second as Seen in Contemporary Documents and Judged on Evidence of His Own Speeches* (1917, o.p.).

Hohenlohe-Schillingsfuerst, Chlodwig K., *Memoirs of Prince Chlodwig of Hohenlohe-Schillingsfuerst,* 2 Vols., ed. by Friedrich Curtius (reprint, n.d.). Originally published in 1906.

Kitchen, Martin, *The German Officer Corps, 1890–1914* (1968).

Kürenberg, J. von, *The Kaiser: A Life of Wilhelm II, Last Emperor of Germany,* tr. by H. T. Russell and Herta Hagen (1954, o.p.).

Ludwig, Emil, *Wilhelm Hohenzollern, the Last of the Kaisers* (reprint, n.d.). A psychological interpretation, originally published in 1927.

Müller, Georg Alexander von, *The Kaiser and His Court; The Diaries, Note Books, and Letters of Admiral Georg Alexander von Müller, Chief of the Naval Cabinet, 1914–1918,* ed. by Walter Görlitz and tr. by Mervyn Savill (1964, o.p.).

Nichols, J. Alden, *Germany after Bismarck: The Caprivi Era, 1890–1894* (1958).

Rohl, John C., *Germany without Bismarck: The Crisis of Government in the Second Reich, 1890–1900* (1968).

Roth, Guenther, *The Social Democrats in Imperial Germany: A Study in Working-Class Isolation and National Integration* (1963).

Smith, Alson J., *A View of the Spree* (1962, o.p.). Dealing with intrigues at the court of William II.

Veblen, Thorstein, *Imperial Germany and the Industrial Revolution* (rev. ed., 1968).

William II, *My Early Life* (reprint, n.d.). William II's memoirs to 1888, dictated in retirement. Original translation published in 1926.

Foreign Affairs

Anderson, Pauline Relyea, *The Background of Anti-English Feeling in Germany, 1890–1902* (reprint, 1969).

Bernhardi, Friedrich von, *Germany and the Next War,* tr. by Allen H. Powles (1912, o.p.).

Carroll, E. Malcolm, *Germany and the Great Powers, 1866–1914; A Study in Public Opinion and Foreign Policy* (reprint, 1966, o.p.).

Gifford, Prosser, and Louis, William Roger, eds., *Britain and Germany in Africa: Imperial Rivalry and Colonial Rule* (1967).

Hammann, Otto, *The World Policy of Germany, 1890–1912,* tr. by Maude A. Huttman (1927, o.p.).

Levine, Isaac D., *The Kaiser's Letters to the Tsar, Copied from Government Archives in Petrograd,* ed. by Neil F. Grant (1921, o.p.). Covers 1894–1914.

Lichnowsky, Karl Max von, *Revela-*

tions of the Last German Ambassador in England; My Mission to London, 1912–1914 (1918, o.p.).

Murad, Anatol, *Franz Joseph I of Austria and His Empire* (1968).

Pribram, Alfred Franzis, *The Secret Treaties of Austria-Hungary, 1879–1914,* tr. by Myers and D'Arcy Paul (reprint, 1967).

Rich, Norman, *Friedrich von Holstein; Politics and Diplomacy in the Era of Bismarck and Wilhelm II,* 2 Vols. (1965).

Schmitt, Bernadotte E., *England and Germany, 1740–1914* (1967).

Von Holstein, F., *The Holstein Papers,* 4 Vols. (1955–1963). Memoirs, diaries, political observations, and correspondences.

Woodward, E. L., *Great Britain and the German Navy* (1935, o.p.).

The Coming of World War I

Bernstein, Herman, ed., *The Willy-Nicky Correspondence, Being The Secret and Intimate Telegrams Exchanged between the Kaiser and the Tsar* (1918, o.p.).

Fay, Sidney B., *Origins of the World War,* 2 Vols. (second ed., n.d.). The first of the revisionist histories concerning Germany's sole guilt for World War I, originally published in 1928.

Geiss, Imanuel, ed., *July 1914; The Outbreak of the First World War: Selected Documents,* tr. by H. M. Hughes and others (1968, o.p.).

Lafore, Laurence, *The Long Fuse: An Interpretation of the Origins of World War I* (1964).

Lee, Dwight E., *The Outbreak of the First World War: Who or What Was Responsible?* (rev. ed., 1963). Excerpts from conflicting interpretations.

Reiners, Ludwig, *The Lamps Went Out in Europe,* tr. by Richard and Clara Winston (reprint, n.d.). Deals with William II's reign, primarily during World War I; originally published in 1955.

Schmitt, Bernadotte E., *The Coming of the War, 1914,* 2 Vols. (reprint, 1958).

Seton-Watson, Robert William, *German, Slav, and Magyar; A Study in the Origins of the Great War* (reprint, 1968).

Thomson, George Malcolm, *The Twelve Days: 24 July to 4 August 1914* (1964, o.p.).

Tuchman, Barbara, *The Guns of August* (1962).

1914–1919

World War I

Bennett, Geoffrey, *The Battle of Jutland* (1964, o.p.).

Feldman, Gerald D., *Army, Industry, and Labor in Germany, 1914–1918* (1966).

Fischer, Fritz, *Germany's Aims in the First World War* (1967).

Gatzke, Hans W., *Germany's Drive to the West: A Study of Germany's Western War Aims during the First World War* (1950).

Goodspeed, D. J., *Ludendorff: Soldier: Dictator: Revolutionary* (1966, o.p.).

Haeussler, Helmut, *General William Groener and the Imperial German Army* (1962).

Mendelssohn-Bartholdy, Albrecht, *The War and German Society* (reprint, n.d.). Originally published in 1937.

Nelson, Harold I., *Land and Power: British and Allied Policy on Germany's Frontiers, 1916–1919* (1963).

Ritter, Gerhard, *The Schlieffen Plan: Critique of a Myth*, tr. by Andrew and Eva Wilson (reprint, 1968).

Rudin, Harry, *Armistice, 1918* (reprint, 1967).

Schorske, Carl E., *German Social Democracy, 1905–1917* (reprint, 1969).

Siney, Marion C., *The Allied Blockade of Germany, 1914–1916* (1957, o.p.).

Taylor, A. J. P., *An Illustrated History of the First World War* (1964, o.p.).

Thoumin, General Richard L., *The First World War*, ed. and tr. by Martin Kieffer (reprint, 1964).

Trumpener, Ulrich, *Germany and the Ottoman Empire, 1914–1918* (1968). Deals in part with the question of responsibility for World War I.

Wheeler-Bennett, Sir John W., *Brest-Litovsk: The Forgotten Peace, March 1918* (reprint, 1957).

1918–1919; The Eisner Regime and the Soviet Republic (1965).

Rosenberg, Arthur, *The Birth of the German Republic, 1871–1918*, tr. by I. F. D. Morrow (reprint, 1970).

Ryder, A. J., *The German Revolution of 1918; A Study of German Socialism in War and Revolt* (1967).

Scheidemann, Philipp, *The Making of New Germany; The Memoirs of Philipp Scheidemann*, tr. by J. E. Mitchell, 2 Vols. (1929, o.p.).

Waldman, Eric, *The Spartacist Uprising of 1919 and the Crisis of the German Socialist Movement: A Study of Political Theory and Party Practice* (1958).

Watt, Richard M., *The Kings Depart; The Tragedy of Germany: Versailles and the German Revolution* (1969). Deals with period from the armistice to the signing of the Versailles Treaty.

The Revolution of 1918

Berlau, A. J., *The German Social Democratic Party, 1914–1921* (1949, o.p.).

Coper, Rudolf, *Failure of a Revolution; Germany in 1918–1919* (1955, o.p.).

Crankshaw, Edward, *The Fall of the House of Hapsburg* (1963).

Lutz, Ralph H., *The Fall of the German Empire, 1914–1918; Documents of the German Revolution*, 2 Vols. (reprint, 1969).

Lutz, Ralph H., *The German Revolution, 1918–1919* (reprint, n.d.). Originally published in 1922.

Maximilian, *The Memoirs of Prince Max of Baden*, tr. by W. M. Calder and C. W. H. Sutton (1928, o.p.).

Mitchell, Allan, *Revolution in Bavaria,*

The Treaty of Versailles

Birdsall, Paul, *Versailles Twenty Years After* (reprint, 1962).

Craig, Gordon A., and Gilbert, Felix, eds., *The Diplomats 1919–1939* (reprint, n.d.). Originally published in 1953.

Lederer, Ivo J., ed., *The Versailles Settlement: Was It Foredoomed to Failure?* (1960). Excerpts from conflicting interpretations.

Luckau, A., *The German Delegation at the Paris Peace Conference* (reprint, n.d.). Originally published in 1941.

Mayer, Arno J., *Political Origins of the New Diplomacy, 1917–1918* (reprint, n.d.). Originally published in 1959.

Mayer, Arno J., *Politics and Diplomacy of Peacemaking; Containment and*

Counter Revolution at Versailles, 1918–1919 (1968).

Nicolson, Harold, *Peacemaking, 1919* (reprint, 1965).

Seymour, Charles, *Geography, Justice, and Politics at the Paris Peace Conference of 1919* (1951, o.p.).

Shotwell, James T., *At the Paris Peace Conference* (1937, o.p.).

1919–1933

General Histories of the Weimar Republic

Eyck, Erich, *A History of the Weimar Republic,* tr. by Harlan P. Hanson and Robert G. Waite, 2 Vols. (1962–1963).

Grunberger, Richard, *Germany, 1918–1945* (1964).

Halperin, Samuel, *Germany Tried Democracy; A Political History of the Reich from 1918–1933* (reprint, 1965).

Hunt, Richard N., ed., *The Creation of the Weimar Republic: Stillborn Democracy?* (1969). Excerpts from conflicting interpretations.

Nicholls, Anthony James, *Weimar and the Rise of Hitler* (1969). Very brief survey.

Rosenberg, Arthur, *A History of the German Republic,* tr. by Ian F. D. Morrow and L. Marie Sieveking (1936, o.p.). On early Weimar only.

Scheele, Godfrey, *The Weimar Republic; Overture to the Third Reich* (1946, o.p.).

Domestic Affairs

Anderson, Evelyn, *Hammer or Anvil: The Story of the German Working-Class Movement* (1945, o.p.). Deals especially with Weimar and Hitler periods.

Angress, Werner T., *Stillborn Revolution; The Communist Bid for Power in Germany, 1921–1923* (1963, o.p.).

Dorpalen, Andreas, *Hindenburg and the Weimar Republic* (1964).

Epstein, Klaus, *The Genesis of German Conservatism* (1966).

Epstein, Klaus, *Matthias Erzberger and the Dilemma of German Democracy* (reprint, n.d.). Originally published in 1959.

Hertzman, Lewis, *DNVP: The Right-Wing Opposition in the Weimar Republic, 1918–1924* (1963).

Hunt, Richard N., *German Social Democracy, 1918–1933* (1964, o.p.).

Kaufmann, Walter H., *Monarchism in the Weimar Republic* (1953, o.p.).

Freund, Gerald, *Unholy Alliance; Russian-German Relations from the Treaty of Brest-Litovsk to the Treaty of Berlin* (1957).

Hilger, Gustav, and Meyer, Alfred G., *The Incompatible Allies; A Memoir-History of German-Soviet Relations, 1918–1941* (1953, o.p.).

Jordan, W. M., *Great Britain, France and the German Problem, 1918–1939; A Study of Anglo-French Relations in the Making and Maintenance of the Versailles Settlement* (1943, o.p.).

Kimmich, Christoph M., *The Free City; Danzig and German Foreign Policy, 1919–1934* (1968).

Korbel, Josef, *Poland between East and West: Soviet and German Diplomacy toward Poland, 1919–1933* (1963).

Schmidt, Royal J., *Versailles and the Ruhr: Seedbed of World War II* (1968.)

Turner, Henry Ashby, Jr., *Stresemann and the Politics of the Weimar Republic* (1963).

Documents on German Foreign Policy, 1918–1945 (1948 ff.). Mostly captured German documents, published by the U.S. Department of State.

Weimar Culture

Bonn, Moritz, *Wandering Scholar* (1948, o.p.). On Weimar culture and thought.

Deak, Istvan, *Weimar Germany's Left-Wing Intellectuals; A Political History of the Weltbühne and Its Circle* (1968). Mostly on literature of the 1910s and 1920s and the non-Communist Left of Weimar.

Gay, Peter, *Weimar Culture: The Outsider as Insider* (1968). An essay on Weimar not tinted by the Hitlerian postlude.

Klemperer, Klemens von, *Germany's New Conservatism: Its History and Dilemma in the Twentieth Century* (1957). On Weimar's swing to the Right.

Lebovics, Herman, *Social Conservatism and the Middle Classes in Germany, 1914–1933* (1969).

Ringer, Fritz K., ed., *The German Inflation of 1923* (1969). A collection of documents and critical analyses.

Wheeler-Bennett, Sir John W., *Hindenburg: The Wooden Titan* (second ed., 1967).

Foreign Affairs

Bennett, Edward W., *Germany and the Diplomacy of the Financial Crisis, 1931* (1962).

Bretton, Henry L., *Stresemann and the Revision of Versailles* (1953).

Carr, Edward H., *German-Soviet Relations between the Two World Wars, 1919–1939* (1951).

Dyck, H. L., *Weimar Germany and Soviet Russia, 1926–1933; A Study in Diplomatic Instability* (1966).

Fischer, Ruth, *Stalin and German Communism; A Study in the Origins of the State Party* (1948, o.p.). Mostly on the 1920s.

Poor, Harold L., *Kurt Tucholsky and the Ordeal of Germany, 1914–1935* (1968). A biography of the writer whose aim was to criticize the weakness of Weimar.

Stern, Fritz, *Politics of Cultural Despair: A Study in the Rise of the Germanic Ideology* (reprint, 1965). On Lagarde, Langbehn, and Moeller van den Bruck as precursors of National Socialism.

Vermeil, Edmond, *Germany in the Twentieth Century: A Political and Cultural History of the Weimar Republic and the Third Reich* (1956, o.p.).

Rearmament under Weimar

Gatzke, Hans W., *Stresemann and the Rearmament of Germany* (1954).

Gordon, H. J., Jr., *The Reichswehr and the German Republic, 1919–1926* (1957, o.p.). Mostly on Seeckt.

Meier-Welcker, Hans, *Seeckt* (1967, o.p.).

Waite, Robert G. L., *Vanguard of Nazism: The Free Corps Movement in Postwar Germany, 1918–1923* (reprint, 1969).

Wheeler-Bennett, Sir John W., *The Nemesis of Power: The German Army in Politics, 1918–1945* (reprint of second edition, 1964).

The Demise of Weimar

Almond, Gabriel A., ed., *The Struggle for Democracy in Germany* (1949, o.p.). Essays, mostly dealing with Nazi period.

Brecht, Arnold, *Prelude to Silence— The End of the German Republic*

(reprint, 1968). On Weimar; political science analysis.

Clark, R. T., *The Fall of the German Republic* (reprint, n.d.). On last years of Weimar. Originally published in 1935.

Eschenburg, T., *et al.*, *The Road to Dictatorship: Germany, 1918–1933*, transl. by L. Wilson (1964, o.p.).

Kraus, Herbert, *The Crisis of German Democracy* (1933, o.p.).

Walkins, Frederick Mandell, *The Failure of Constitutional Emergency Powers under the German Republic* (1939, o.p.).

Conway, John, transl. and ed., *The Path to Dictatorship, 1918–1933. Ten Essays by German Scholars* (1966).

1933–1945

Background of National Socialism and Seizure of Power

Allen, William S., *The Nazi Seizure of Power: The Experience of a Single German Town, 1930–1935* (1965).

Butler, Rohan D'O., *The Roots of National Socialism, 1783–1933* (reprint, 1968). A rather biased view of German intellectual history from Herder to Hitler.

Heiden, Konrad, *Der Führer: Hitler's Rise to Power*, tr. by R. Manheim (reprint, 1969). Deals with the period up to 1934.

Hoover, Calvin E., *Germany Enters the Third Reich* (1933, o.p.).

Jenks, William, *Vienna and the Young Hitler* (1960, o.p.).

Mosse, George L., *The Crisis of German Ideology: Intellectual Origins of the Third Reich* (1964).

Orlow, Dietrich, *The History of the Nazi Party, 1919–1933* (1969).

Tobias, Fritz, *The Reichstag Fire* (1964, o.p.).

Wheaton, Eliot Barculo, *Prelude to Calamity: The Nazi Revolution 1933–1935; with a Background Survey of the Weimar Era* (1968).

The Nazi State

Broszat, Martin, *German National Socialism, 1919–1945*, tr. by K. Rosenbaum and I. P. Boehm (1966). A brief analysis of some theoretical aspects of National Socialism.

Buchheim, Hans, *Totalitarian Rule: Its Nature and Characteristics*, tr. by Ruth Hein (1968). Mostly on Germany and Russia.

Bullock, Alan, *Hitler, a Study in Tyranny* (rev. ed., 1963).

Burden, Hamilton T., *The Nuremberg Party Rallies: 1923–1939* (1967).

Ebenstein, William, *The German Record, a Political Portrait* (1945, o.p.).

Ebenstein, William, *The Nazi State* (1943, o.p.).

Jarman, T. L., *The Rise and Fall of Nazi Germany* (1956).

Kelley, Douglas M., *Twenty-two Cells in Nuremberg* (1947). A psychological study of Hitler based on interviews of Nazi leaders in Nuremberg prison.

Lichtenberger, Henri, *The Third Reich*, tr. and ed. by Koppel S. Pinson (1937, o.p.).

Meinecke, Friedrich, *The German Catastrophe*, tr. by S. B. Fay (reprint, 1963).

Morstein Marx, Fritz, *Government in the Third Reich* (1937, o.p.).

Neumann, Franz L., *Behemoth: The Structure and Practice of National Socialism, 1933–1944* (second ed., 1963).

Nolte, Ernst, *Three Faces of Fascism:*

Action Française, Italian Fascism, National Socialism, tr. by Leita Vennewitz (1965).

Reitlinger, Gerald, *The S.S.: Alibi of a Nation, 1922–1945* (reprint, 1968).

Shirer, William L., *Berlin Diary* (1943, o.p.).

Shirer, William L., *The Rise and Fall of the Third Reich: A History of Nazi Germany* (1960).

Snell, John L., ed., *The Nazi Revolution: Germany's Guilt or Germany's Fate?* (1959). Excerpts from conflicting interpretations.

Waite, Robert G. L., ed., *Hitler and Nazi Germany* (1965). Excerpts from conflicting interpretations.

Internal Affairs

Hale, Oron James, *The Captive Press in the Third Reich* (1964).

Hitler, Adolph, *Hitler's Secret Book,* tr. by Salvator Attanasio (1961, o.p.). Written in 1928, deals mostly with foreign policy.

Hitler, Adolph, *Mein Kampf,* tr. by R. Manne (n.d.). Originally written in two volumes between 1924 and 1926.

Hitler, Adolph, *Secret Conversations, 1941–1944,* tr. by Norman Cameron and R. H. Stevens (1953, o.p.).

Kracauer, Siegfried, *From Caligari to Hitler: A Psychological History of the German Film* (1947).

Lochner, Louis Paul, ed. and tr., *The Goebbels Diaries, 1942–1943* (1948, o.p.).

Manvell, Roger, and Fraenkel, H., *Dr. Goebbels, His Life and Death* (1960, o.p.).

Mayer, Milton, *They Thought They Were Free: The Germans, 1933–1945* (second ed., 1966).

Mosse, George L., ed., *Nazi Culture: Intellectual, Cultural, and Social Life in the Third Reich,* tr. by Salvator Attanasio and others (1966).

O'Neill, Robert J., *The German Army and the Nazi Party, 1933–1939* (1967).

Papen, Franz von, *Memoirs,* tr. by B. Connell (1952, o.p.).

Peterson, Edward Norman, *Hjalmar Schacht: For and Against Hitler* (1954).

Raeder, Erich, *My Life,* tr. by Henry W. Drexel (1960).

Schoenbaum, David, *Hitler's Social Revolution: Class and Status in Nazi Germany, 1933–1939* (1966).

Speer, Albert, *Memoirs* (1970).

Strasser, Otto, *Flight from Terror* (1943, o.p.).

Taylor, Telford, *Sword and Swastika: Generals and Nazis in Third Reich* (reprint, 1969).

Trevor-Roper, Hugh R., *Last Days of Hitler* (third ed., 1966).

Zeman, Z. A. B., *Nazi Propaganda* (1964).

Economics

DuBois, Josiah E., Jr., *The Devil's Chemists; 24 Conspirators of the International Farben Cartel Who Manufacture Wars* (1952, o.p.).

Guillebaud, C. S., *The Economic Recovery of Germany from 1933 to the Incorporation of Austria in March 1938* (1939, o.p.).

Homze, Edward L., *Foreign Labor in Nazi Germany* (1966).

Klein, Burton H., *Germany's Economic Preparations for War* (1959).

Lochner, Louis P., *Tycoons and Tyrant: German Industry from Hitler to Adenauer* (1954, o.p.).

Schacht, Hjalmar, *Confessions of "the Old Wizard,"* tr. by Diana Pyke (1956, o.p.).

Schweitzer, Arthur, *Big Business in the Third Reich* (1964).

Persecution

Barkai, Meyer, ed. and tr., *The Fighting Ghettos* (1962).

Boehm, Eric H., *We Survived; Fourteen Histories of the Hidden and Hunted of Nazi Germany* (1966, o.p.).

Conway, J. S., *The Nazi Persecution of the Churches, 1933–1945* (1969).

Crankshaw, Edward, *Gestapo, Instrument of Tyranny* (1956, o.p.).

Delarue, Jacques, *The Gestapo: A History of Horror*, tr. by Mervin Y. N. Savill (1964).

Hausner, Gideon, *Justice in Jerusalem* (reprint, 1968).

Hilberg, Raul, *The Destruction of the European Jews* (1961).

Kogon, Eugen, *The Theory and Practice of Hell*, tr. by Heinz Norden (n.d.). On Nazi persecutions and concentration camps. Originally published in 1950.

Krausnick, Helmut, *et al.*, *Anatomy of the SS State*, transl. by R. Barry and others (1968).

Levin, Nora, *The Holocaust; The Destruction of European Jewry, 1933–1945* (1968).

Lewy, Guenter, *The Catholic Church and Nazi Germany* (1964).

Phillips, Peter, *The Tragedy of Nazi Germany* (1969).

Reitlinger, Gerald, *The Final Solution* (rev. ed., 1961).

Ringelblum, Emmanuel, *Notes from the Warsaw Ghetto: The Journal of Emmanuel Ringelblum* (1958, o.p.).

Schechtmann, Joseph B., *European Population Transfers, 1939–1945* (1946, o.p.).

Foreign Affairs

Deakin, F. W., *The Brutal Friendship: Mussolini, Hitler, and the Fall of Italian Fascism* (1963).

Frye, Alton, *Nazi Germany and the American Hemisphere, 1931–1941* (1967).

Harper, Glenn T., *German Economic Policy in Spain during the Spanish Civil War, 1936–1939* (1967).

Iklé, Frank William, *German-Japanese Relations, 1936–1940* (1956, o.p.).

Kertesz, Stephen Denis, *Diplomacy in a Whirlpool; Hungary between Nazi Germany and Soviet Russia* (1958).

Lipski, Jósef, *Diplomat in Berlin, 1933–1939; Papers and Memoirs of Jósef Lipski, Ambassador of Poland*, ed. by Waclaw Jedrzejewicz (1968).

Luža, Radomír, *The Transfer of the Sudeten Germans; A Study of Czech-German Relations, 1933–1962* (1964).

Meskill, Johanna Menzel, *Hitler and Japan: The Hollow Alliance* (1966).

Presseissen, Ernst L., *Germany and Japan: A Study in Totalitarian Diplomacy, 1933–1941* (reprint, n.d.). Originally published in 1958.

Seabury, Paul, *The Wilhelmstrasse: A Study of German Diplomats under the Nazi Regime* (1954, o.p.).

Toynbee, Arnold, ed., *Survey of International Affairs: Hitler's Europe*, Vol. IV (1955, o.p.).

Trefousse, H. L., *Germany and American Neutrality, 1939–1941* (reprint, 1969).

Resistance

Deutsch, Harold C., *The Conspiracy against Hitler in the Twilight War* (1968).

Dulles, Allen W., *Germany's Underground* (1947, o.p.).

Edinger, Lewis J., *German Exile Politics; The Social Democratic Executive Committee in the Nazi Era* (1956, o.p.).

Fitzgibbon, Constantine, *20 July* (reprint, 1968).

Gallin, Mary Alice, *German Resistance to Hitler: Ethical and Religious Factors* (1961).

Gisevius, Hans Bernd, *To the Bitter End,* tr. by Richard and Clara Winston (1947, o.p.).

Hassell, Ulrich von, *The Von Hassell Diaries, 1938–1944; The Story of the Forces against Hitler inside Germany, as Recorded by Ambassador Ulrich von Hassell, a Leader of the Movement* (1947, o.p.).

Kramarz, Joachim, *Stauffenberg* (1967).

Leber, Annedore, ed., *Conscience in Revolt: Sixty-four Stories of Resistance in Germany, 1933–1945,* tr. by Rosemary O'Neill (1957, o.p.). Brief biographies of resistance leaders.

Manvell, Roger, and Fraenkel, Heinrich, *The Canaris Conspiracy: The Secret Resistance to Hitler in the German Army* (1969).

Manvell, Roger, and Fraenkel, Heinrich, *The Men Who Tried to Kill Hitler* (reprint, n.d.). Originally published in 1964.

Prittie, Terence, *Germans against Hitler* (1964, o.p.).

Ritter, Gerhard, *The German Resistance: Carl Goerdeler's Struggle against Tyranny,* tr. by R. T. Clark (1959, o.p.).

Rothfels, Hans, *The German Opposition to Hitler* (reprint, 1962).

Schlabrendorff, Fabian von, *Secret War against Hitler* (1965).

Schramm, Wilhelm von, *Conspiracy among Generals,* tr. and ed. by R. T. Clark (1956, o.p.).

Sykes, Christopher, *Tormented Loyalty; The Story of a German Aristocrat Who Defied Hitler* (1969).

Zeller, Eberhard, *The Flame of Freedom; The German Struggle against Hitler,* tr. by R. P. Heller and D. R. Masters (1969).

Approach of World War II

Eubank, Keith, *Munich* (reprint, 1965).

Kennan, George Frost, *From Prague after Munich; Diplomatic Papers, 1938–1940* (1968).

Klein, Burton H., *Germany's Economic Preparations for War* (1959). Tries to show that Nazi Germany was not economically prepared for a long war.

Lee, Dwight E., ed., *Munich: Blunder, Plot, or Tragic Necessity?* (1970). Excerpts from conflicting interpretations.

Loewenheim, Francis L., ed., *Peace or Appeasement; Hitler, Chamberlain, and the Munich Crisis* (1965). A collection of documents, excerpts from memoirs and critical analyses.

McSherry, James E., *Stalin, Hitler, and Europe,* Vol. I: *Origins of World War II, 1933–1939* (1968).

Mosley, Leonard, *On Borrowed Time; How World War II Began* (1969).

Renouvin, Pierre, *World War II and Its Origins; International Relations, 1929–1945,* tr. by R. I. Hall (1969).

Robertson, Esmond M., *Hitler's Pre-War Policy and Military Plans, 1933–1939* (reprint, 1967).

Shepherd, Gordon, *The Anschluss; The Rape of Austria* (1963, o.p.).

Taylor, A. J. P., *The Origins of the Second World War* (rev. ed., 1968).

Toscano, Mario, *The Origins of the Pact of Steel* (1968).

Weinberg, Gerhard L., *Germany and the Soviet Union, 1939–1941* (1954, o.p.).

Wheeler-Bennett, Sir John W., *Munich: Prologue to Tragedy* (reprint, 1964).

War—Military

Ansel, Walter, *Hitler Confronts England* (1960). Dealing with question of invading England, 1940.

Baldwin, Hanson, *Battles Lost and Won; Great Campaigns of World War II* (1966).

Baumbach, Werner, *The Life and Death of the Luftwaffe* (reprint, 1967).

Carver, Michael, *Tobruk* (1964).

Chuikov, Marshall Vasili I., *The Fall of Berlin* (1968).

Clark, Alan, *Barbarossa: The Russian-German Conflict, 1941–1945* (1965).

Gilbert, Felix, ed., *Hitler Directs His War: The Secret Records of His Daily Military Conferences* (1950, o.p.).

Heilbrunn, Otto, *Warfare in the Enemy's Rear* (1964).

Hibbert, Christopher, *The Battle of Arnhem* (1962, o.p.).

Hinsley, Francis H., *Hitler's Strategy* (1951, o.p.). A brief summary.

Irving, David, *The Destruction of Dresden* (1964).

Liddell Hart, Basil H., *The Other Side of the Hill; Germany's Generals, Their Rise and Fall, with Their Own Account of Military Events, 1939–1945* (1948, o.p.).

MacDonald, Charles B., *The Battle of the Huertgen Forest* (1963).

Manstein, Erich von, *Lost Victories*, ed. and tr. by Anthony G. Powell (1958, o.p.).

Seth, Ronald, *Stalingrad: Point of Re-turn; The Story of the Battle, August 1942–February 1943* (1959, o.p.).

Trevor-Roper, Hugh R., ed., *Blitzkrieg to Defeat: Hitler's War Directives, 1939–1945* (1964, o.p.).

Verrier, Anthony, *The Bomber Offensive* (1969).

Wheatley, Ronald, *Operation Sea Lion: German Plans for the Invasion of England, 1939–1942* (1958).

Wilmot, Chester, *The Struggle for Europe* (1952, o.p.).

War—Non-Military Aspects

Armstrong, Anne M., *Unconditional Surrender: The Impact of the Casablanca Policy upon World War II* (1961).

Burdick, Charles B., *Germany's Military Strategy and Spain in World War II* (1968).

Cole, J. A., *Lord Haw-Haw* (1965). On Nazi wartime propaganda.

Dallin, Alexander, *German Rule in Russia: 1941–1945; A Study of Occupation Policies* (1957, o.p.).

Irving, David, *The German Atomic Bomb* (1968).

Kamenetsky, Igor, *Secret Nazi Plans for Eastern Europe: A Study of Lebensraum Policies* (reprint, n.d.). Originally published in 1961.

Koehl, Robert L., *German Resettlement and Population Policy, 1939–1945: A History of the Reich Commission for the Strengthening of Germandom* (1957).

Launay, Jacques de, *Secret Diplomacy of World War II*, tr. by Edouard Nadier (1963, o.p.).

Leasor, James, *The Uninvited Envoy: The Mysterious Flight of Rudolf Hess* (1962, o.p.).

McGovern, James, *Crossbow and Over-*

cast (1964, o.p.). On German rocket programs.

Milward, Alan S., *The German Economy at War* (1965).

Orlow, Dietrich, *The Nazis in the Balkans: A Case Study of Totalitarian Politics* (1968).

Pirie, Anthony, *Operation Bernhard* (1962). On German financial warfare during World War II.

Prüller, Wilhelm, *Diary of a German Soldier*, ed. by H. C. R. Landon and S. Leitner (1963, o.p.).

Reitlinger, Gerald, *The House Built on Sand: The Conflicts of German Policy in Russia, 1939–1945* (1960, o.p.).

Stein, George H., *The Waffen SS: Hitler's Elite Guard at War, 1939–1945* (1966).

Trevor-Roper, H. R., *The Last Days of Hitler* (third ed., 1966).

Warlimont, Walter, *Inside Hitler's Headquarters, 1939–1945* (1964).

AFTER 1945

Allied Military Occupation

Balfour, Michael, and Mair, John, *Four-Power Control in Germany and Austria, 1945–1946* (1956).

Clay, Lucius D., *Decision in Germany* (1950, o.p.).

Davidson, Eugene, *The Death and Life of Germany; An Account of the American Occupation* (1959). Overview of 1945–1955 period.

Davis, Franklin M., Jr., *Come as a Conqueror: The United States Army's Occupation of Germany 1945–1949* (1967).

Friedmann, Wolfgang, *Allied Military Government in Germany* (1947, o.p.).

Gimbel, John, *The American Occupation of Germany: Politics and the Military, 1945–1949* (1968). Politics in U.S. Zone and at OMGUS.

Pollock, J. K., and Meisel, J. H., *Germany under Occupation; Illustrative Materials and Documents* (1947, o.p.).

Ruhm von Oppen, Beate, ed., *Documents on Germany under Occupation, 1945–1954* (1955).

U.S. Department of State, *Germany, 1947–1949; The Story in Documents* (1950, o.p.).

Willis, Roy F., *The French in Germany; 1945–1949* (1962).

Zink, Harold, *American Military Government in Germany* (1947, o.p.).

Zink, Harold, *The United States in Germany, 1944–1955* (1957, o.p.).

General Problems of the Occupation

Almond, Gabriel, ed., *The Struggle for Democracy in Germany* (1949, o.p.).

Brown, Lewis H., *A Report on Germany* (1947, o.p.).

Feis, Herbert, *Between War and Peace: The Potsdam Conference* (1960).

Jaksch, Wenzel, and Glaser, Kurt, eds. and trs., *Europe's Road to Potsdam* (1964).

Litchfield, Edward H., ed., *Governing Postwar Germany* (1953, o.p.).

Morgenthau, Henry, Jr., *Germany Is Our Problem* (1945, o.p.). Contains proposals for pastoralization of Germany.

Snell, John L., *Wartime Origins of the East-West Dilemma over Germany* (1959, o.p.).

Vernant, J., *The Refugee in the Postwar World* (1953, o.p.).

Denazification and War Crimes Trials

Davidson, Eugene, *The Trial of the Germans; An Account of the Twenty-*

Two Defendants before the International Military Tribunal at Nuremberg (1966, o.p.) Concerns the trial of war criminals.

Glueck, S., *The Nuremberg Trial and Aggressive War* (reprint, n.d.). Originally published in 1946.

Kormann, John G., *U.S. Denazification Policy in Germany, 1944–1950* (1952, o.p.). Published by the Office of the U.S. High Commissioner for Germany.

———, *Nazi Conspiracy and Aggression,* 10 Vols. (1947–1949). Part II of the Nuremberg records, consisting of translations of prosecution documents as well as some defense documents used at the Nuremberg trials.

———, *Trials of the Major War Criminals before the International Military Tribunal,* 42 Vols. (1947–1949). Part I of the Nuremberg records.

———, *Trials of War Criminals before the Nuremberg Military Tribunals under Control Council Law No. 10,* 15 Vols. (1951–1953). Part III of the Nuremberg records, consisting of excerpts of records and documents of trials after the major trials, e.g. Krupp, I. G. Farben, etc.

Heller, Deane and David, *The Berlin Wall* (1962, o.p.).

Her Majesty's Stationery Office, *Selected Documents on Germany and the Question of Berlin, 1944–1961* (1961).

Legien, Rudolf, *The Four Power Agreements on Berlin; Alternative Solutions to the Status Quo?,* tr. by Trevo Davies (1960, o.p.).

McDermott, Geoffrey, *Berlin: Success of a Mission?* (1963, o.p.).

Pounds, Norman J. G., *Divided Germany and Berlin* (1962).

Robson, Charles B., tr., *Berlin: Pivot of German Destiny* (1960).

Rodrigo, Robert, *Berlin Airlift* (1960, o.p.).

Smith, Jean Edward, *The Defense of Berlin* (1963). A series of essays on the Berlin and German problems from the 1941 conferences to 1962.

Speier, Hans, *Divided Berlin: The Anatomy of Soviet Political Blackmail* (1961, o.p.).

Stanger, Roland J., ed., *West Berlin: The Legal Context* (1966).

Windsor, Philip, *City on Leave; A History of Berlin, 1945–1962* (1963, o.p.). Mostly on diplomatic maneuvers concerning the fate of Berlin.

The Berlin Question

Butler, Ewan, *City Divided: Berlin 1955* (1955, o.p.).

Charles, Max, *Berlin Blockade* (1959, o.p.).

Davison, W. Phillips, *The Berlin Blockade; A Study in Cold War Politics* (1958).

Gablentz, O. M. von der, ed., *Documents on the Status of Berlin, 1944–1959* (1959, o.p.).

Gottlieb, Manuel, *The German Peace Settlement and the Berlin Crisis* (1960, o.p.).

West Germany in General

Balfour, Michael L. G., *West Germany* (1968). A survey to 1966.

Bar-Zohar, Michael, *The Avengers,* tr. by Len Ortzen (1969). On continuing efforts to apprehend suspected or known Nazi war criminals.

Chamberlin, William H., *The German Phoenix* (1963, o.p.). On West Germany's resurgence after World War II.

Conant, James B., *Germany and Freedom; A Personal Appraisal* (1958).

Mostly on Germany's educational system.

Edinger, Lewis J., *Kurt Schumacher: A Study in Personality and Political Behavior* (1965).

Erhard, Ludwig, *Prosperity through Competition,* tr. and ed. by E. T. Roberts and J. B. Wood (1958, o.p.).

Grosser, Alfred, *The Federal Republic of Germany: A Concise History,* tr. by Nelson Aldrich (1964, o.p.).

Jaspers, Karl, *The Future of Germany,* tr. and ed. by E. B. Ashton (1967).

Press and Information Office of the Federal German government, *Facts about Germany* (published periodically).

Reuss, Frederick G., *Fiscal Policy for Growth without Inflation: The German Experiment* (1963).

Roskamp, Karl W., *Capital Formation in West Germany* (1965).

Stahl, Walter, *The Politics of Postwar Germany* (1963, o.p.). Essays, mostly on Berlin and German crises, 1946–1949 and 1958–1961.

Tauber, Kurt P., *Beyond Eagle and Swastika; German Nationalism since 1945,* 2 Vols. (1967).

Wallich, H. C., *Mainsprings of the German Revival* (1955).

West German Government and Politics

Adenauer, Konrad, *Memoirs, 1945–1953,* tr. by Beate Ruhm von Oppen (1966).

Alexander, Edgar, *Adenauer and the New Germany, the Chancellor of the Vanquished,* tr. by Thomas E. Goldstein (1957).

Bunn, Ronald F., *German Politics and the Spiegel Affair; A Case Study of the Bonn System* (1968).

Childs, David, *From Schumacher to Brandt: The Story of German Socialism 1945–1965* (1966).

Golay, John Ford, *The Founding of the Federal Republic of Germany* (1958). Mostly on the Basic Law and its clauses, 1948–1949 period.

Grosser, Alfred, *The Colossus Again; Western Germany from Defeat to Rearmament,* tr. by Richard Rees (1955, o.p.).

Heidenheimer, Arnold J., *Adenauer and the CDU; The Rise of the Leader and the Integration of the Party* (1960, o.p.).

Heidenheimer, Arnold J., *The Governments of Germany* (second ed., 1966).

Hiscocks, Richard, *The Adenauer Era* (1966).

Lane, John C., and Pollock, James K., *Source Materials on the Government and Politics of Germany* (1964).

McInnis, Edgar, Hiscocks, Richard, and Spencer, Robert, *The Shaping of Postwar Germany* (1960, o.p.).

Merkl, Peter H., *The Origin of the West German Republic* (1965). Mostly on constitutional and political problems involved in the creation of the Basic Law.

Pinney, Edward L., *Federalism, Bureaucracy, and Party Politics in Western Germany; The Role of the Bundesrat* (1963). Analysis of conservatism, primarily of the Bundesrat, 1949–1960.

Plischke, Elmer, *Contemporary Government of Germany* (second ed., 1969). Survey of governmental institutions of East and West Germany, as well as Berlin.

Schoenbaum, David, *The Spiegel Affair* (1968, o.p.).

Weymar, Paul, *Adenauer, His Authorized Biography,* tr. by Peter de Mendelssohn (1957, o.p.).

West German Foreign Affairs

Bathurst, M. E., and Simpson, J. L., *Germany and the North Atlantic Community, a Legal Survey* (1956, o.p.).

Davison, W. Phillips, and Speier, Hans, eds., *West German Leadership and Foreign Policy* (1957, o.p.).

Deutsch, Karl W., and Edinger, Lewis J., *Germany Rejoins the Powers; Mass Opinion, Interest Groups, and Elites in Contemporary German Foreign Policy* (1959, o.p.). On foreign policy, 1949 to 1959, against the background of the German internal scene.

Dulles, Eleanor L., *One Germany or Two: The Struggle at the Heart of Europe* (1969).

Feld, Werner, *Reunification and West German-Soviet Relations; The Role of the Reunification Issue in the Foreign Policy of the Federal Republic of Germany, 1949–1957, with Special Attention to Policy toward the Soviet Union* (1963, o.p.).

Freund, Gerald, *Germany between Two Worlds* (1961, o.p.).

Freymond, Jacques, *The Saar Conflict, 1945–1955* (1960, o.p.).

Hartmann, F. H., *Germany between East and West: Reunification Problem* (n.d.).

Kaiser, Karl, *German Foreign Policy in Transition, Bonn between East and West* (1969). Analysis of new *Ostpolitik*, primarily under the Grand Coalition, 1966–1968.

Szaz, Zoltan Michael, *Germany's Eastern Frontiers; The Problem of the Oder-Neisse Line* (1960, o.p.).

United States Senate, Committee on Foreign Relations, *Documents on Germany, 1944–1961* (1961).

Willis, F. Roy, *France, Germany, and the New Europe, 1945–1967* (rev. ed., 1968).

Wolfe, James H., *Indivisible Germany; Illusion or Reality?* (1963).

East Germany

Brant, Stefan, *The East German Rising, 17th June 1953*, tr. by Charles Wheeler (1955, o.p.).

Childs, David, *East Germany* (1969). A general survey.

Dornberg, John, *The Other Germany* (1968). Concentrates on East Germany's economic resurgence between 1961 and 1968.

Friedrich, Carl J., *The Soviet Zone of Germany* (1956, o.p.).

Göttinger, Arbeitskreis, *Eastern Germany; A Handbook*, ed. by Goetlingen Research Committee (1960, o.p.).

Hangen, Welles, *The Muted Revolution; East Germany's Challenge to Russia and the West* (1966). A journalistic survey of East German internal and external affairs.

Nesselrode, Franz von, *Germany's Other Half; A Journalist's Appraisal of East Germany* (1963, o.p.).

Nettl, John P., *The Eastern Zone and Soviet Policy in Germany 1945–1950* (1951, o.p.).

Smith, Jean Edward, *Germany Beyond the Wall; People, Politics, and Prosperity* (1969).

Solberg, Richard W., *God and Caesar in East Germany; The Conflicts of the Church and State in East Germany since 1945* (1961, o.p.).

Stolper, Wolfgang, and Roskamp, Karl W., *The Structure of the East German Economy* (1960).

Index

To Louise

THE QUEST FOR UNITY: MODERN GERMANY, 1848–1970, John E. Rodes

Library of Congress Catalog Card Number: 70-135289

SBN: 03–085194–7   9-25-71

Printed in the United States of America

12345   090   987654321

FOR UNITY

MODERN GERMANY

1848-1970

John E. Rodes OCCIDENTAL COLLEGE

Holt, Rinehart and Winston, Inc.

THE QUES

NEW YORK · CHICAGO · SAN FRANCISCO
ATLANTA · DALLAS · MONTREAL
TORONTO · LONDON · SYDNEY

THE QUEST FOR UNITY
MODERN GERMANY
1848-1970